PEARSON
Literature

GRADE 6

PEARSON

HOBOKEN, NEW JERSEY • BOSTON, MASSACHUSETTS
CHANDLER, ARIZONA • GLENVIEW, ILLINOIS

PEARSON

ISBN-13:   978-0-13-331980-4
ISBN-10:   0-13-331980-6

4   16

PEARSON

Literature

GRADE 6

PEARSON

HOBOKEN, NEW JERSEY • BOSTON, MASSACHUSETTS
CHANDLER, ARIZONA • GLENVIEW, ILLINOIS

Contributing Authors

The contributing authors guided the direction and philosophy of Pearson Literature. *They helped to build the pedagogical integrity of the program by contributing content expertise, knowledge of learning standards, and support for the shifts in instruction that are necessary for college and career readiness. Their knowledge, combined with classroom and professional experience, ensures that* Pearson Literature *is relevant for both teachers and students.*

William G. Brozo, Ph.D., is a Professor of Literacy in the Graduate School of Education at George Mason University in Fairfax, Virginia. He earned his bachelor's degree from the University of North Carolina and his master's and doctorate from the University of South Carolina. He has taught reading and language arts in the Carolinas and is the author of numerous articles on literacy development for children and young adults. His books include *To Be a Boy, To Be a Reader: Engaging Teen and Preteen Boys in Active Literacy; Readers, Teachers, Learners: Expanding Literacy Across the Content Areas; Content Literacy for Today's Adolescents: Honoring Diversity and Building Competence; Supporting Content Area Literacy with Technology* (Pearson); and *Setting the Pace: A Speed, Comprehension, and Study Skills Program.* His newest book is *RTI and the Adolescent Reader: Responsive Literacy Instruction in Secondary Schools.* As an international consultant, Dr. Brozo has provided technical support to teachers from the Balkans to the Middle East, and he is currently a member of a European Union research grant team developing curriculum and providing adolescent literacy professional development for teachers across Europe.

Diane Fettrow spent the majority of her teaching career in Broward County, Florida, teaching high school English courses and serving as department chair. She also worked as an adjunct instructor at Broward College, Nova Southeastern University, and Florida Atlantic University. After she left the classroom, she served as Secondary Language Arts Curriculum Supervisor for several years, working with more than 50 of the district's high schools, centers, and charter schools. During her time as curriculum supervisor, she served on numerous local and state committees; she also served as Florida's K–12 ELA content representative to the PARCC Model Content Frameworks Rapid Response Feedback Group and the PARCC K–12 and Upper Education Engagement Group. Currently she presents workshops on the Common Core State Standards and is working with Pearson on aligning materials to the CCSS.

Kelly Gallagher is a full-time English teacher at Magnolia High School in Anaheim, California, where he has taught for twenty-seven years. He is the former co-director of the South Basin Writing Project at California State University, Long Beach, and the author of *Reading Reasons: Motivational Mini-Lessons for Middle and High School; Deeper Reading: Comprehending Challenging Texts, 4–12; Teaching Adolescent Writers;* and *Readicide: How Schools Are Killing Reading and What You Can Do About It.* He is also a principal author of *Prentice Hall Writing Coach* (Pearson, 2012). Kelly's latest book is *Write Like This* (Stenhouse). Follow Kelly on Twitter @KellyGToGo, and visit him at www.kellygallagher.org.

Elfrieda "Freddy' Hiebert, Ph.D., is President and CEO of TextProject, a nonprofit organization that provides resources to support higher reading levels. She is also a research associate at the University of California, Santa Cruz. Dr. Hiebert received her Ph.D. in Educational Psychology from the University of Wisconsin-Madison. She has worked in the field of early reading acquisition for 45 years, first as a teacher's aide and teacher of primary-level students in California and, subsequently, as a teacher educator and researcher at the universities of Kentucky, Colorado-Boulder, Michigan, and California-Berkeley. Her research addresses how fluency, vocabulary, and knowledge can be fostered through appropriate texts. Professor Hiebert's research has been published in numerous scholarly journals, and she has authored or edited nine books. Professor Hiebert's model of accessible texts for beginning and struggling readers—TExT—has been used to develop numerous reading programs that are widely used in schools. Dr. Hiebert is the 2008 recipient of the William S. Gray Citation of Merit, awarded by the International Reading Association; is a member of the Reading Hall of Fame; and has chaired a group of early childhood literacy experts who served in an advisory capacity to the CCSS writers.

 Donald J. Leu, Ph.D., is the John and Maria Neag Endowed Chair in Literacy and Technology and holds a joint appointment in Curriculum and Instruction and Educational Psychology in the Neag School of Education at the University of Connecticut. Don is an international authority on literacy education, especially the new skills and strategies required to read, write, and learn with Internet technologies and the best instructional practices that prepare students for these new literacies. He is a member of the Reading Hall of Fame, a Past President of the National Reading Conference, and a former member of the Board of Directors of the International Reading Association. Don is a Principal Investigator on a number of federal research grants, and his work has been funded by the U.S. Department of Education, the National Science Foundation, and the Bill and Melinda Gates Foundation, among others. He recently edited the *Handbook of Research on New Literacies* (Erlbaum, 2008).

 **Ernest Morrell, Ph.D.,** is a professor of English Education at Teachers College, Columbia University, and the president-elect of the National Council of Teachers of English (NCTE). He is also the Director of Teachers College's Harlem-based Institute for Urban and Minority Education (IUME). Dr. Morrell was an award-winning high school English teacher in California, and he now works with teachers and schools across the country to infuse multicultural literature, youth popular culture, and media production into standards-based literacy curricula and after-school programs. He is the author of nearly 100 articles and book chapters as well as five books, including *Critical Media Pedagogy: Achievement, Production, and Justice in City Schools* and *Linking Literacy and Popular Culture*. In his spare time he coaches youth sports and writes poems and plays.

 Karen Wixson, Ph.D., is Dean of the School of Education at the University of North Carolina, Greensboro. She has published widely in the areas of literacy curriculum, instruction, and assessment. Dr. Wixson has been an advisor to the National Research Council and helped develop the National Assessment of Educational Progress (NAEP) reading tests. She is a former member of the IRA Board of Directors and co-chair of the IRA Commission on RTI. Recently, Dr. Wixson served on the English Language Arts Work Team that was part of the Common Core State Standards Initiative.

 Grant Wiggins, Ed.D., is the President of Authentic Education in Hopewell, New Jersey. He earned his Ed.D. from Harvard University and his B.A. from St. John's College in Annapolis. Grant consults with schools, districts, and state education departments on a variety of reform matters; organizes conferences and workshops; and develops print materials and Web resources on curricular change. He is perhaps best known for being the co-author, with Jay McTighe, of *Understanding by Design* and *The Understanding by Design Handbook,* the award-winning and highly successful materials on curriculum published by ASCD.

INTRODUCTORY UNIT   Contents

INTRODUCTORY UNIT: STUDENT WORKSHOPS

UNIT 1 Is conflict always bad?

DIGITAL ASSETS KEY

These digital resources, as well as audio and the Online Writer's Notebook, can be found at **pearsonrealize.com**.

🖥 Interactive Whiteboard Activities

🌐 Virtual Tour

📋 Close Reading Notebook

▶️ Video

🔍 Close Reading Tool for Annotating Texts

Ⓖ Grammar Tutorials

📚 Online Text Set

■ **READ**

Text Analysis
Plot
Characterization
Conflict and Resolution
Theme
Comparing Foreshadowing and Flashback
Setting
Alliteration
Tone
Author's Purpose
Imagery

Comprehension
Make Predictions
Make Inferences
Draw Conclusions

Language Study
Latin suffix -ation
Latin prefix dis-
Latin prefix ex-
Latin prefix com-

Conventions
Common, Proper, and Possessive Nouns
Personal and Possessive Pronouns
Interrogative, Indefinite, Reflexive, and
   Intensive Pronouns
Pronoun Case

Language Study Workshop
Using a Dictionary and Thesaurus

■ **DISCUSS**

Comprehension and Collaboration
Interview

Responding to Text
Group Discussion
Class Discussion
Partner Discussion

Speaking and Listening Workshop
Following Oral Directions

■ **RESEARCH**

Research and Technology
Brochure
Compare-and-Contrast Chart

Investigate the Topic: The Gold Rush
Gold Rush Struggles
Striking It Rich
Gold Rush Housing
Labor During the Gold Rush
The Gold Rush and Food

■ **WRITE**

Writing to Sources
List of Reasons
Letter of Recommendation
Persuasive Speech
Description
Essay
Cause-and-Effect Essay
Short Story
Journal Entry
Informational Text
Editorial
Argument

Writing Process Workshop
Narration: Short Story
   Voice
   Conventions: Revising for Pronoun-Antecedent
   Agreement

UNIT VOCABULARY

Academic Vocabulary appears in *blue*.

Introducing the Big Question *argue, battle, challenge, compete, conclude, convince, defend, game, issue, lose, negotiate, resist, resolve, survival, win*

Stray *timidly, trudged, grudgingly, ignore, exhausted, starvation*

The Tail *vow, anxious, routine, gnawing, mauled, spasm*

Zlateh the Goat *bound, astray, exuded, splendor, trace, flickering*

The Circuit *accompanied, drone, instinctively, savoring, enroll*

Lob's Girl; Jeremiah's Song *decisively, resolutions, melancholy, diagnosis, anticipate, conclude, refer, reveal*

The King of Mazy May *endured, liable, summit, passage, contribute, alter*

To Klondyke We've Paid Our Fare *defiance, privation, invincible, reveal, purpose, challenge*

Gold Rush: The Journey by Land *similarities, process, indicated*

A Woman's View of the Gold Rush *associate, scouring, tongues, specific*

Chinese and African Americans in the Gold Rush *exodus, testify, ambassador, determine, acquired*

Birds Struggle to Recover from Egg Thefts of 1800s *conservatively, entrepreneurs, faltered, establish, opinion, support*

DIGITAL ASSETS KEY

These digital resources, as well as audio and the Online Writer's Notebook, can be found at **pearsonrealize.com**.

🖥 Interactive Whiteboard Activities

🌐 Virtual Tour

▤ Close Reading Notebook

▶ Video

🔍 Close Reading Tool for Annotating Texts

G Grammar Tutorials

📚 Online Text Set

■ **UNIT VOCABULARY**

Academic Vocabulary appears in *blue*.

Introducing the Big Question   *concept, distinguish, examine, guess, judge, knowledge, limit,*
measure, narrow, observe, purpose, question, refer, source, study

The Drive-In Movies   *prelude, pulsating, migrated, evident, winced, vigorously*

Names/Nombres   *mistook, pursue, transport, inevitably, chaotic, inscribed*

Langston Terrace   *applications, community, resident, choral, reunion, homey*

from **The Pigman & Me**   *exact, demented, observant, undulating, distorted, condemnation*

The Seven Wonders of the World; Art, Architecture, and Learning in Egypt   *archaeologists,*
architect, colossal

Jackie Robinson: Justice at Last   *integrate, prejudiced, superb, support, opinions, affect*

Memories of an All-American Girl   *exhilarating, immortality, inductions, visual, reflecting*

Preserving a Great American Symbol   *doomed, extinction, amendment, cite, achieve, argue*

The Southpaw   *former, unreasonable, anticipate, conclude*

Red Sox Get Ready to Celebrate 100 Years at Fenway   *inaugural, deficit, deft, cite, unique,*
position

Why We Love Baseball   *premise, ventured, diversion, sources, facts, research*

Ted Williams Baseball Card   *reveal, contrast*

PART 3
TEXT SET DEVELOPING INSIGHT

DETERMINATION

PART 4
DEMONSTRATING INDEPENDENCE

Independent Reading

ONLINE TEXT SET 📖

PERSONAL ESSAY
The Lady and the Spider
Robert Fulghum

SHORT STORY
Dragon, Dragon
John Gardner

POEM
Ankylosaurus
Jack Prelutsky

DIGITAL ASSETS KEY

These digital resources, as well as audio and the Online Writer's Notebook, can be found at **pearsonrealize.com**.

🖥 Interactive Whiteboard Activities

🌐 Virtual Tour

📋 Close Reading Notebook

▶ Video

🔍 Close Reading Tool for Annotating Texts

Ⓖ Grammar Tutorials

📖 Online Text Set

■ READ

Text Analysis
Rhythm and Rhyme
Figurative Language
Forms of Poetry
Sound Devices and Tone
Comparing Imagery
Simile
Direct Quotation
Foreshadowing
Symbols
Central Idea
Author's Purpose

Comprehension
Context Clues
Paraphrasing

Language Study
Latin root -mal-
Suffix -ant
Greek prefix auto-
Suffix -y

Conventions
Adjectives and Adverbs
Comparisons with Adjectives and Adverbs
Conjunctions and Interjections
Sentence Parts and Types

Language Study Workshop
Words with Multiple Meanings

■ DISCUSS

Presentation of Ideas
Dramatic Poetry Reading

Responding to Text
Group Discussion
Partner Discussion
Small Group Discussion

Speaking and Listening Workshop
Problem-and-Solution Proposal

■ RESEARCH

Research and Technology
Illustrated Booklet
Presentation of a Poem
Résumé

Investigate the Topic: Determination
Survival Skills
College Challenges
Expedition to the South Pole
Financial Skills
Determination and the Declaration of
    Independence
Learning to Communicate
Politics and Determination

■ WRITE

Writing to Sources
Letter to an Author
Poem
Prose Description
Essay
Expository Essay
Autobiographical Narrative
Diary Entry
Autobiographical Narrative
Comparison-and-Contrast Essay
Argumentative Essay

Writing Process Workshop
Argument: Argumentative Essay
    Word Choice
    Sentence Fluency: Combining Sentences
    Using Coordinating Conjunctions

UNIT VOCABULARY

Academic Vocabulary appears in *blue*.

Introducing the Big Question   *communicate, connection, correspond, dialogue, expression, gesture, language, message, nonverbal, quote, reveal, share, symbolize, verbal, visual*

Poetry Collection 1   *deem, ravenous, cavernous, beseech, dismal, sympathize*

Poetry Collection 2   *sour, lullaby, pleasant, receive*

Poetry Collection 3   *skimming, asphalt, fellow*

Poetry Collection 4   *hollowed, dispersed, sculpted, thorny, offense, whirs*

who knows if the moon's; Dust of Snow   *steeples, rued, achieve, communicate, observe, symbolize*

Simile: Willow and Ginkgo   *crude, stubby, thrives, reveal, communicate, establish*

Angela Duckworth and the Research on "Grit"   *rigorous, persevere, insurmountable, essential, study, research*

Race to the End of the Earth   *plateau, expedition, polar, assess, evidence, perspective*

The Sound of Summer Running   *seized, suspended, revelation, symbolize, influence*

***from* Letter on Thomas Jefferson**   *felicity, explicit, procure, clarifies, evaluate, contrasts*

Water   *imitate, persisted, barriers, purpose, support, sources*

Determination   *context, quotation, facts*

PART 3
TEXT SET DEVELOPING INSIGHT

MARK TWAIN

PART 4
DEMONSTRATING INDEPENDENCE

Independent Reading

ONLINE TEXT SET

DIGITAL ASSETS KEY

These digital resources, as well as audio and the Online Writer's Notebook, can be found at **pearsonrealize.com.**

🖥 Interactive Whiteboard Activities

🌐 Virtual Tour

📋 Close Reading Notebook

🎬 Video

🔍 Close Reading Tool for Annotating Texts

Ⓖ Grammar Tutorials

📚 Online Text Set

■ **READ**

Text Analysis
Dialogue in Drama
Stage Directions
Author's Purpose
Theme
Humor
Point of View
Plot
Tone

Comprehension
Summary
Compare and Contrast

Language Study
Greek root -eth
Prefix trans-

Conventions
Prepositions and Appositives
Participles and Gerunds

Language Study Workshop
Connotation and Denotation

■ **DISCUSS**

Comprehension and Collaboration
Group Discussion

Responding to Text
Partner Discussion
Panel Discussion
Group Discussion
Small Group Discussion

Speaking and Listening Workshop
Delivering a Persuasive Speech

■ **RESEARCH**

Research and Technology
Multimedia Presentation

Investigate the Topic: Mark Twain
The Palace of Westminster
Stage Fright
Twain, According to Others
Twain's First Riverboat Journey
Twain's Quotations
Real Twain Interviews

■ **WRITE**

Writing to Sources
Summary
Review
Essay
Comparison-and-Contrast Essay
How-To Essay
Argument
Narrative

Writing Process Workshop
Argument: Problem-and-Solution Essay
Ideas: Support Your Ideas
Conventions: Combining Sentences
for Variety

UNIT VOCABULARY

Academic Vocabulary appears in *blue*.

Introducing the Big Question *appearance, conscious, custom, diverse, expectations, ideals, individuality, personality, perspective, reaction, reflect, respond, similar, trend, unique*

The Phantom Tollbooth, Act I *ignorance, precautionary, unethical, ferocious, misapprehension, unabridged*

The Phantom Tollbooth, Act II *dissonance, deficiency, admonishing, iridescent, malicious, transfixed*

***from* You're a Good Man, Charlie Brown; Happiness is a Charming Charlie Brown at Orlando Rep** *objectionable, tentatively, civic, evoking, embody, abundantly, opinion, reflect, respond, specific*

The Prince and the Pauper; *from* The Prince and the Pauper *pauper, affliction, sauntered, respond, technique, similar*

Stage Fright *compulsion, awed, agonizing, opinion, purpose, common*

My Papa, Mark Twain *striking, incessantly, consequently, identify, credible, convincing*

Mark Twain's First "Vacation" *vigor, deliberate, distinctly, conflict, achieve*

According to Mark Twain *modify, quotation, establish*

An Encounter With An Interviewer *astonishing, rapture, notorious, pose, interviews, refer*

UNIT 5 How much do our communities shape us?

PART 3
TEXT SET DEVELOPING INSIGHT

PEOPLE AND ANIMALS

PART 4
DEMONSTRATING INDEPENDENCE

Independent Reading

ONLINE TEXT SET

AUTOBIOGRAPHY
The Market Square Dog
James Herriot

SHORT STORY
Aaron's Gift
Myron Levoy

REFLECTIVE ESSAY
Childhood and Poetry
Pablo Neruda

DIGITAL ASSETS KEY

These digital resources, as well as audio and the Online Writer's Notebook, can be found at **pearsonrealize.com**.

- Interactive Whiteboard Activities
- Virtual Tour
- Close Reading Notebook
- Video
- Close Reading Tool for Annotating Texts
- Grammar Tutorials
- Online Text Set

■ **READ**

Text Analysis
Fables and Folk Tales
Myths
Universal Theme
Personification
Comparing Elements of Fantasy
Text Features
Conflict and Resolution
Expository Writing
Author's Influences

Comprehension
Cause and Effect
Setting a Purpose
Purpose for Reading

Language Study
Suffix -ment
Latin root -mort-
Latin root -van-
Suffix -ary

Conventions
Subject Complements
Direct and Indirect Objects
Independent and Dependent Clauses
Simple, Compound, and Complex Sentences

Language Study Workshop
Idioms

■ **DISCUSS**

Presentation of Ideas
Oral Report

Comprehension and Collaboration
Dramatic Reading

Responding to Text
Partner Discussion
Panel Discussion
Class Discussion
Group Discussion

Speaking and Listening Workshop
Oral Response to Literature

■ **RESEARCH**

Research and Technology
Annotated Bibliography Entries
Written and Visual Report

Investigate the Topic: People and Animals
The Role of Myths
Scientific Method
Oxygen Masks
Humans and Animals
Oceanographers
Wild Turkeys

■ **WRITE**

Writing to Sources
Fable
Comparison-and-Contrast Essay
Plot Proposal
Invitation
Essay
Cause-and-Effect Essay
Explanation
Nonfiction Narrative
Argument
Informative Essay
Persuasive Letter
Persuasive Essay

Writing Process Workshop
Explanatory Text: Cause-and-Effect Essay
   Conventions: Using Commas, Parentheses, and Dashes
   Sentence Fluency: Revising Choppy Sentences

UNIT VOCABULARY

Academic Vocabulary appears in *blue*.

Introducing the Big Question *belief, common, community, connection, culture, family, generation, group, history, influence, involve, isolate, participation, support, values*

The Tiger Who Would Be King; The Ant and the Dove *prowled, inquired, repulse, monarch, startled, repaid*

Arachne *obscure, humble, mortal, indignantly, obstinacy, strive*

The Stone *feeble, vanished, plight, jubilation, rue, sown*

Why the Tortoise's Shell Is Not Smooth *cunning, famine, orator, custom, eloquent, compound*

Mowgli's Brothers; *from* **James and the Giant Peach** *quarry, fostering, monotonous, dispute, intently, colossal, conflict, convince, encounter, unique*

Prologue from **The Whale Rider** *yearning, teemed, apex, sensory, observe, reveal*

The Case of the Monkeys That Fell From the Trees *incidents, abruptly, distress, study, observation, investigate*

Rescuers to Carry Oxygen Masks for Pets *resuscitation, unsolicited, inhalation, support, quotation, authorities*

2012 Pet Ownership Statistics *generalization, explain, subject*

The Old Woman Who Lived With the Wolves *coaxed, traversed, mystified, sensory, indicate, resolve*

Satellites and Sea Lions *navigate, marine, meteorologists, collaboratively, interaction, credible*

Turkeys *dilution, demise, vigilance, crucial*

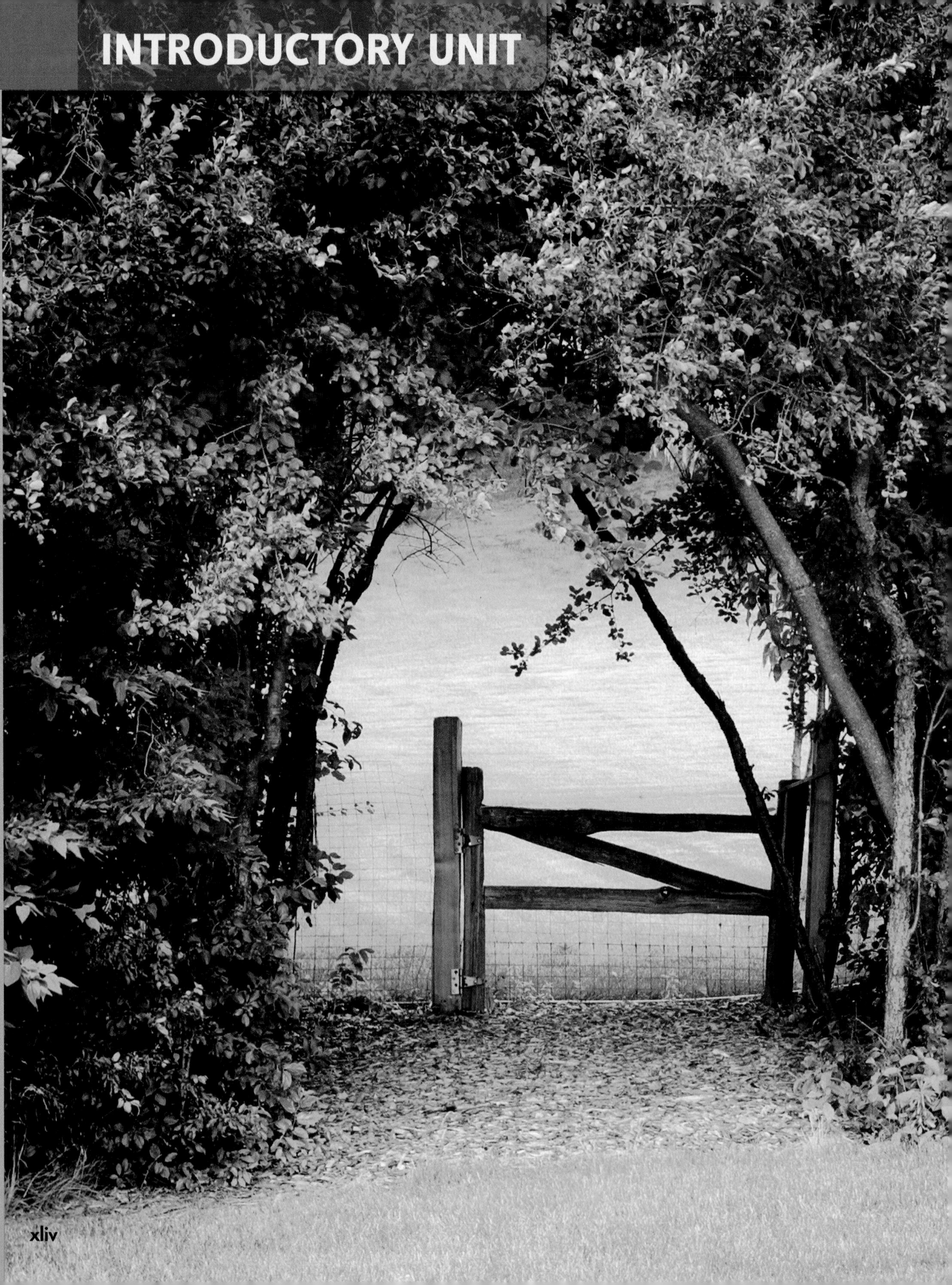

WORKSHOPS

- BUILDING ACADEMIC VOCABULARY

- WRITING AN OBJECTIVE SUMMARY

- COMPREHENDING COMPLEX TEXTS

- ANALYZING ARGUMENTS

- CONDUCTING RESEARCH

BUILDING ACADEMIC VOCABULARY

Academic vocabulary is the language you encounter in textbooks and on standardized tests and other assessments. Understanding these words and using them in your classroom discussions and writing will help you communicate your ideas clearly and effectively.

There are two basic types of academic vocabulary: general and domain-specific. **General academic vocabulary** includes words that are not specific to any single course of study. For example, the general academic vocabulary word *analyze* is used in language arts, math, social studies, art, and so on.

Domain-specific academic vocabulary includes words that are usually encountered in the study of a specific discipline. For example, the words *factor* and *remainder* are most often used in mathematics classrooms and texts.

General Academic Vocabulary

Word	Definition	Related Words	Word in Context
abandon (uh BAN duhn) *v.*	leave behind; give something up	abandoned abandoning	Maria decided to **abandon** the book after reading the first chapter.
accompany (uh KUM puh nee) *v.*	go along; travel with	accompanied accompanying	I will **accompany** Jake to school to get his backpack.
accurate (AK yuhr iht) *adj.*	free from error	accurately accuracy	Her research proved that her facts were **accurate**.
achieve (uh CHEEV) *v.*	bring to a successful end; gain	achieved achievement	Through hard work, I will **achieve** my goal of raising my English grade.
anticipate (an TIHS uh payt) *v.*	expect; foresee	anticipated anticipation	Greta can **anticipate** winning the spelling bee.
approach (uh PROHCH) *v.*	come near or nearer to	approached approaching	The school bus will **approach** the parking lot in 300 yards.
argue (AHR gyoo) *v.*	fight using words; debate	argument argumentative	During a debate, you must **argue** your point clearly.
assess (uh SEHS) *v.*	estimate the value of; evaluate	assessed assessment	The English test will **assess** our understanding of the poem.
authority (uh THAWR uh tee) *n.*	person with power or expertise; power to control	authorization authorize	The teacher has **authority** over her class.
challenge (CHAL uhnj) *n.*	act of calling into question; dare	challenge *v.* challenging	The character set a **challenge** for his opponent.
common (KOM uhn) *adj.*	ordinary or expected	commonness uncommon	It is **common** to have a conflict within a story's plot.

Word	Definition	Related Words	Word in Context
specific (spuh SIHF ihk) *adj.*	particular	specify specification	Give **specific** examples to support your ideas.
structure (STRUHK chuhr) *n.*	way in which parts are arranged to make a whole	structural structured	We studied the **structure** of the poem.
study (STUD ee) *n.*	research or investigation into a claim	studious	I cited a scientific **study** in my research report that supported my thesis.
study (STUD ee) *v.*	look into deeply	studied studying	The two friends in the story liked to **study** together for English class.
support (suh PAWRT) *v.*	stand behind or back up	supportive supporting	Details in your essay **support** your main idea.
suspend (suh SPEHND) *v.*	hang from something above; keep from falling; bring to a stop	suspenders suspense	In science lab, we have to **suspend** an object from a rope.
symbolize (SIHM buh lyz) *v.*	stand for	symbol symbolic	What might the flag **symbolize** in this story?
test (tehst) *n.*	method or process for proving or disproving a claim	testing tested	After the **test**, I knew my theory was correct.
unique (yoo NEEK) *adj.*	one of a kind	uniqueness	My favorite author has a truly **unique** writing style.
visual (VIHZH oo uhl) *adj.*	able to be seen or understood with the eyes	vision visually	The descriptive passage of the story gives a strong **visual** image of the scene.

Word	Definition	Related Words	Word in Context
communicate (kuh MYOO nuh kayt) *v.*	share thoughts or feelings, usually in words	communication communicative	Poets can **communicate** complex thoughts with very few words.
compile (kuhm PYL) *v.*	put together into one book or work	compiled compilation	The students will **compile** all their poems into one book.
concept (KON sehpt) *n.*	general idea or notion	conception conceptual	I was able to grasp the broad **concept** of the news article by skimming.
conclude (kuhn KLOOD) *v.*	bring to a close; end	conclusion concluded	The story will **conclude** when the main character has won the race.
confirm (kuhn FURM) *v.*	support or show to be correct	confirmation confirming	I need to **confirm** the facts for my research report.
conflict (KON flihkt) *n.*	fight, battle, or struggle	conflict *v.* conflicted	The **conflict** in the novel was resolved in the end.
consist (kuhn SIHST) *v.*	be made up of or composed of	consisted consistency	The test will **consist** of multiple-choice and short-answer questions.
context (KON tehkst) *n.*	set of circumstances or surrounding words that determine the meaning of a word or phrase	contextual	We defined the word in its **context** in the sentence.
contrast (KON trast) *v.*	show differences between or among	contrasted contrasting	When you **contrast** two characters, you find the differences between them.
convince (kuhn VIHNS) *v.*	persuade	convincing convinced	You don't need to **convince** me that Shakespeare was a brilliant writer!
coordinate (koh AWR dihn ayt) *v.*	show the proper order or relation of things	coordination coordinating	I had to **coordinate** my schedule to make time for homework.
correspond (KAWR uh SPOND) *v.*	agree with or be similar to	correspondence corresponding	My thoughts on the poem did not **correspond** to my partner's.
crucial (KROO shuhl) *adj.*	critical; extremely important	crucially	It is **crucial** that you do well on this test.
defend (dih FEHND) *v.*	guard from attack; protect	defense defending	The main character was able to **defend** himself against the bitter cold.
determine (dih TUR muhn) *v.*	settle; reach a conclusion	determined determination	The author's background can help you **determine** the author's purpose for writing.
display (dih SPLAY) *v.*	show or exhibit	displayed displaying	The characters **display** their traits through their words and actions.
distinguish (dih STIHNG gwihsh) *v.*	mark as different; set apart	distinguished distinguishing	It is important to notice traits that **distinguish** characters.
diverse (duh VURS) *adj.*	many and different; from different backgrounds	diversity diversify	There were **diverse** cultures represented in the article.
draft (draft) *n.*	rough or preliminary form of any writing	draft *v.* drafting	We had to hand in the first **draft** of our report.

Word	Definition	Related Words	Word in Context
encounter (ehn KOWN tuhr) v.	come upon or meet with, usually unexpectedly	encountered encountering	The main character will encounter many difficult situations.
establish (eh STAB lihsh) v.	bring into being; show to be true	established establishment	The author had to establish the reason the character in the book had lied.
evidence (EHV uh duhns) n.	proof in support of a claim or statement	evident evidently	The evidence she used in her essay supports her main idea.
examine (ehg ZAM uhn) v.	study in depth; look at closely	examination examined	To examine a character, look at what he says and also what is said about him.
fact (fakt) n.	idea or thought that is real or true	factual	Be sure something is a fact before you use it to support your argument.
indicate (IHN dih kayt) v.	be a sign of; show	indicative indication	You must indicate where you found your information.
influence (IHN floo uhns) v.	sway or affect in some other way	influential influenced	One author can often influence the work of another.
interpret (ihn TUR priht) v.	give or provide the meaning of; explain	interpreting interpretation	We were asked to interpret the poem.
investigate (ihn VEHS tuh gayt) v.	examine thoroughly, as an idea	investigation investigating	The characters went to investigate a mysterious disappearance.
involve (ihn VOLV) v.	include	involving involved	I want the plot of my short story to involve a space expedition.
isolate (Y suh layt) v.	set apart	isolated isolation	It is good to isolate each point when using point-by-point organization.
issue (IHSH oo) n.	point about which there is disagreement	issue v. reissue	We discussed the issue of revenge in class.
judge (juj) v.	form an opinion of or pass judgment on	judgment judgmental	In the story, the main character had to judge who was a true friend.
measure (MEHZH uhr) v.	place a value on	measurement measured	A writer tries to measure many different factors in his or her writing.
modify (MOD uh fy) v.	change the form or quality of	modified modification	We will modify our answers after we finish the book.
motive (MOH tihv) n.	something that causes a person to act a certain way	motivate motivation	Her motive for taking my book was that she had lost hers.
observe (uhb ZURV) v.	notice or see	observation observed	Observe the shape formed by the lines in this poem.
opinion (uh PIHN yuhn) n.	personal view or belief	opinionated	My opinion of the story is very different from that of my friend.
participation (pahr tihs uh PAY shuhn) n.	act of taking part in an event or activity	participate participant	The teacher appreciated the boy's participation in the group discussion of the novel.

Word	Definition	Related Words	Word in Context
perspective (puhr SPEHK tihv) n.	point of view		I chose to tell my story from the perspective of my family's dog.
pose (pohz) v.	display a specific attitude or stance	pose n. posture	He might pose as my friend to get my answers to the homework.
process (PROS ehs) n.	systematic series of actions or changes	process v. processor	Finishing the report was a process of writing and revising.
prove (proov) v.	establish the truth of, as in a claim or statement	proof disprove	I will prove my theory within my report.
purpose (PUR puhs) n.	what something is used for	purposeful purposeless	The author's purpose for writing became more clear as she read.
quote (kwoht) v.	refer to the words of a source	quotation quoted	Quote from a reputable author to add interest to an essay.
refer (rih FUR) v.	point back to, as an authority or expert	reference referral	When I write my final draft, I refer to my notes and my outline.
reflect (rih FLEHKT) v.	think about or consider	reflection reflecting	The character needed to reflect on what had happened before the conflict could be resolved.
research (REE suhrch) n.	investigation into a subject to find facts	research v. researching	The research supported her ideas.
resolve (rih ZOLV) v.	settle or bring to an end	resolution resolved	The characters decided to resolve their dispute and became friends.
respond (rih SPOND) v.	reply or answer	response responded	To respond to the essay question, I used evidence, examples, and my own thoughts.
reveal (rih VEEL) v.	show or uncover	revealing revealed	The detective would reveal the truth in the mystery story.
similar (SIHM uh luhr) adj.	alike	similarity similarly	The styles of the two poems are quite similar but the images are very different.
source (sawrs) n.	person or book that provides information	resource outsource	Check the source of that quotation to be sure it is trustworthy.

Ordinary Language: She told the story from an interesting angle.

Academic Language: She told the story from an interesting perspective.

Ordinary Language: The conflict in the story was brought to an end.

Academic Language: The conflict in the story was resolved.

Practice

Examples of various kinds of domain-specific academic vocabulary appear in the charts below. Some chart rows are not filled in. Look up the definitions of the remaining words, provide one or two related words, and use each word in context on a separate piece of paper.

Social Studies: Domain-Specific Academic Vocabulary

Word	Definition	Related Words	Word in Context
epic (EHP ihk) adj.	huge in size, duration, or importance; heroic	epical	*The Odyssey* tells of an epic journey made by Odysseus.
feudalism (FYOOD l ihz uhm) n.	social system in the Middle Ages based on land ownership by a privileged class	feudal	Feudalism gave power to lords, or men who owned land.
globalization (GLOH buh lih ZAY shuhn) n.	inclusion of all parts of the globe	globe global	Computers have made globalization possible.
interdependence (ihn tuhr dee PEHN duhns) n.	dependence on one another; mutual reliance	interdependent	Interdependence between the two countries keeps the peace.
mobility (moh BIHL uh tee) n.	ability of people to change location or position easily	mobile	Mobility increased with the invention of cars.
archaeologist (ahr kee OL uh jihst) n.			
civilization (sihv uh luh ZAY shuhn) n.			
irrigation (ihr uh GAY shuhn) n.			
monarchy (MON uhr kee) n.			
nomadic (noh MAD ihk) adj.			

Mathematics: Domain-Specific Academic Vocabulary

Word	Definition	Related Words	Word in Context
base (bays) n.	number that is raised to a power by an exponent	basic	In the number 3^2, the base is 3 and the exponent is 2.
circumference (suhr KUM fuhr uhns) n.	length of the boundary of a circle		We learned how to find the circumference of a circle.
degree (dih GREE) n.	unit of measure for temperature and angles		The teacher drew a 45-degree angle.
equilateral (ee kwih LAT uhr uhl) adj.	having sides of the same, or equal, length	equal	On the test, we were asked to draw an equilateral triangle.
prime factorization (prym fak tuhr uh ZAY shuhn) n.	process of breaking down a number into the prime numbers that divide it exactly	prime factor	We used prime factorization to find the factors of 39.
percent (puhr SEHNT) n.			
power (POW uhr) n.			
sample (SAM puhl) n.			
similarity (sihm uh LAR uh tee) n.			
simulation (sihm yuh LAY shuhn) n.			

Science: Domain-Specific Academic Vocabulary

Word	Definition	Related Words	Word in Context
atmosphere (AT muhs feer) n.	air or gaseous area around the earth or a planet	atmospheric	Earth's atmosphere is different from that of Mars.
atom (AT uhm) n.	smallest part of an element with all the element's properties	atomic	An atom is too small to see with the human eye.
cell (sehl) n.	basic unit of living organisms	cellular	A plant cell is very tiny.
decomposer (dee kuhm POH zuhr) n.	organism that feeds on and breaks down dead plant or animal matter	decompose decomposition	A decomposer is an important part of the food web.
prey (pray) n.	animal hunted for food	prey v. preying	The deer was the hungry lion's prey.

Science: Domain-Specific Academic Vocabulary (continued)

Word	Definition	Related Words	Word in Context
climate (KLY muht) n.			
crystal (KRIHS tuhl) n.			
fungus (FUNG guhs) n.			
gene (jeen) n.			
molecule (MOL uh kyool) n.			

Art: Domain-Specific Academic Vocabulary

Word	Definition	Related Words	Word in Context
diagonal (dy AG uh nuhl) adj.	on a slant	diagonally	The student used diagonal lines to draw a slanted roof.
horizontal (hawr uh ZONT l) adj.	side to side	horizontally	Use horizontal lines to draw the floor and ceiling of a room.
hue (hyoo) n.	color; form of a color		She used a purple hue in her painting.
tint (tihnt) n.	mixture of a hue plus white	tint v. tinting	The art teacher mixed white with red to create a pink tint.
vertical (VUR tih kuhl) adj.	straight up and down	vertically	The painter used vertical lines to paint the walls of a building.
color (KUHL uhr) n.			
curved (kurvd) adj.			
edge (ehj) n.			
line (lyn) n.			
shade (shayd) n.			

Technology: Domain-Specific Academic Vocabulary

Word	Definition	Related Words	Word in Context
desktop (DEHSK top) *adj.*	referring to a type of computer that fits on a desk but is not portable	laptop	The classroom had many **desktop** computers on long tables.
file (fyl) *n.*	organized collection of data in a single location	file *v.* filing	I saved my report in a **file** on my computer.
hardware (HAHRD wayr) *n.*	electronic devices that make up a computer	software	A computer monitor is an example of **hardware**.
icon (Y kon) *n.*	small picture that stands for a command or file	iconic	Click on the folder **icon** to open a new file.
monitor (MON ih tuhr) *n.*	device that displays images and text	monitor *v.* monitoring	A large **monitor** is handy for showing graphics and photos.
backspace (key) (BAK spays) *n.*			
delete (key) (dih LEET) *n.*			
enter (key) (EHN tuhr) *n.*			
escape (key) (ih SKAYP) *n.*			
online (ON LYN) *adj.*			

Increasing Your Word Knowledge

Increase your word knowledge and chances of success by taking an active role in developing your vocabulary. Here are some tips for you.

To own a word, follow these steps:

Steps to Follow	Model
1. Learn to identify the word and its basic meaning.	The word *examine* means "to look at closely."
2. Take note of the word's spelling.	*Examine* begins and ends with an *e*.
3. Practice pronouncing the word so that you can use it in conversation.	The *e* on the end of the word *examine* is silent. Its second syllable gets the most stress.
4. Visualize the word and illustrate its key meaning.	When I think of the word *examine*, I visualize a doctor checking a patient's health.
5. Learn the various forms of the word and its related words.	*Examination* and *exam* are forms of the word *examine*.
6. Compare the word with similar words.	*Examine, peruse,* and *study* are synonyms.
7. Contrast the word with similar words.	*Examine* suggests a more detailed study than *read* or *look at*.
8. Use the word in various contexts.	"I'd like to *examine* the footprints more closely." "I will *examine* the use of imagery in this poem."

Building Your Speaking Vocabulary

Language gives us the ability to express ourselves. The more words you know, the better able you will be to get your points across. There are two main aspects of language: reading and speaking. Using the steps above will help you acquire a rich vocabulary. Follow these steps to help you learn to use this rich vocabulary in discussions, speeches, and conversations.

Steps to Follow	Tip
1. Practice pronouncing the word.	Become familiar with pronunciation guides to allow you to sound out unfamiliar words. Listening to audio books as you read the text will help you learn pronunciations of words.
2. Learn word forms.	Dictionaries often list forms of words following the main word entry. Practice saying word families aloud: "generate," "generated," "generation," "regenerate," "generator."
3. Translate your thoughts.	Restate your own thoughts and ideas in a variety of ways, to inject formality or to change your tone, for example.
4. Hold discussions.	With a classmate, practice using academic vocabulary words in discussions about the text. Choose one term to practice at a time, and see how many statements you can create using that term.
5. Record yourself.	Analyze your word choices by listening to yourself objectively. Note places your word choice could be strengthened or changed.

Introductory Unit

WRITING AN OBJECTIVE SUMMARY

The ability to write objective summaries is key to success in college and in many careers. Writing an effective objective summary involves recording the key ideas of a text as well as demonstrating your understanding.

What Is an Objective Summary?

An effective objective summary is a short, accurate, and objective overview of a text. Following are key elements of an objective summary:

- A good summary focuses on a text's main points. It includes specific, relevant details that support the main point, but it leaves out unnecessary details.
- A summary should be a restatement of the text's main points, in the order in which they appear in the original text.
- A summary should accurately capture the essence of the longer text it is describing.

What to Avoid in an Objective Summary

- An objective summary is not a collection of sentences or paragraphs copied from the original source.
- It does not include every event, detail, or point in the original text.
- Finally, a good summary does not include evaluative comments, such as the reader's overall opinion of or reaction to the selection.
- An objective summary is not the reader's interpretation or critical analysis of the text.

Model Objective Summary

Review the elements of an effective objective summary called out in the sidenotes. Then, write an objective summary of a text you have read. Review your summary. Delete any unnecessary details or opinions.

Summary of "King Midas and the Golden Touch"

"King Midas and the Golden Touch" is a myth that tells the tale of a king who is granted a magical wish.

King Midas, the main character in this ~~popular~~ myth, loved gold. He would go into his dungeon to admire his shiny treasure. However, he did love one thing more than his gold—his daughter Aurelia.

Aurelia loved her father, and every day she would pick a bouquet of colorful, fragrant roses from his garden and bring them to him.

One day the king's guards found an old man asleep in the king's rose garden. Instead of punishing the man, the king invited him to dinner.

After the old man departed, King Midas went to the dungeon to admire his gold. All of a sudden, the glowing figure of a young man appeared. The apparition spoke to the shocked king and explained that he was the old man. To reward Midas for his kindness, the young stranger offered him one wish. King Midas wished that everything he touched would turn to gold.

The next day the king woke up and found that his wish had come true. His bedcovers were spun gold as were his clothes. ~~When he put his glasses on, they, too, turned to gold. That meant he couldn't see through them.~~ Midas rushed out to the garden and excitedly turned his roses into gold.

At breakfast, Aurelia was crying because her roses were made of gold. Midas convinced her to have breakfast with him. Midas lifted a spoonful of porridge to his mouth, but as soon as the porridge touched his lips it turned into a hard golden lump. When Aurelia noticed her father's concern, she went over to comfort him. To the king's horror, Aurelia became a lifeless golden statue at his touch.

As Midas cried, the mysterious stranger suddenly appeared. The stranger told him how to change things back to their original form.

King Midas brought Aurelia and the roses back to life. He did, however, keep one golden rose to remind himself of his experience with the golden touch. ~~Midas learned a good lesson.~~

A one-sentence synopsis highlighting the theme or central idea of the story can be an effective start to a summary.

An adjective describing the story indicates an opinion and should not be included in an objective summary.

Relating the development of the text in chronological order makes a summary easy to follow.

Unnecessary details should be eliminated.

This sentence should be paraphrased rather than copied exactly from the story.

The writer's opinions should not appear in an objective summary.

COMPREHENDING COMPLEX TEXTS

During the coming years in school, you will be required to read increasingly complex texts to prepare you for college and the workplace. A complex text is a text that contains challenging vocabulary; long, complex sentences; figurative language; multiple levels of meaning; or unfamiliar settings and situations. The selections in this textbook include a range of readings, from short stories to autobiographies, poetry, drama, myths, and even science and social studies texts. Some of these texts will fall within your comfort zone; others may be more challenging.

Strategy 1: **Multidraft Reading**

Good readers develop the habit of rereading texts in order to comprehend them completely. Just as an actor practices his lines over and over again in order to learn them, good readers return to texts to more fully enjoy and comprehend them. To fully understand a text, try this multidraft reading strategy:

1st Reading

The first time you read a text, read to gain its basic meaning. If you are reading a narrative text, look for story basics: who the story is about and what happens. If the text is nonfiction, look for main ideas. If you are reading poetry, read first to get an overall impression of the poem.

2nd Reading

During your second reading of a text, focus on ways in which the writer uses language and text structures. Think about why the author chose those words or organizational patterns. Then, examine the author's creative uses of language and the effects of that language. For example, has the author used rhyme, exaggeration, or words with multiple meanings?

3rd Reading

After your third reading, compare and contrast the text with others of its kind you have read. For example, if you have read another myth before, think of ways the myths are alike or different. Evaluate the text's overall effectiveness and its central idea or theme.

Independent Practice

As you read this short poem, practice the multidraft reading strategy by completing a chart like the one below.

"Storm" by H. D. (Hilda Doolittle)

You crash over the trees,

you crack the live branch—

the branch is white,

the green crushed,

each leaf is rent like split wood.

You burden the trees

with black drops,

you swirl and crash—

you have broken off a weighted leaf

in the wind,

it is hurled out,

whirls up and sinks,

a green stone.

Multidraft Reading Chart

	My Understanding
1st Reading Look for key ideas and details that unlock basic meaning.	
2nd Reading Read for deeper meanings. Look for ways in which the author used text structures and language to create effects.	
3rd Reading Read to integrate your knowledge and ideas. Connect the text to other texts and to your own experience.	

Introductory Unit

Strategy 2: **Close Read the Text**

Complex texts require close reading, a careful analysis of the words, phrases, and sentences. When you close read, use the following tips to comprehend the text:

Tips for Close Reading

1. **Break down long sentences into parts.** Look for the subject of the sentence and its verb. Then identify which parts of the sentence modify, or give more information about, its subject.

2. **Reread passages.** When reading complex texts, be sure to reread passages to confirm that you understand their meaning.

3. **Look for context clues,** such as the types listed below.

   a. Restatement of an idea. For example, in this sentence, "have everlasting life" restates the adjective *immortal*.

      Gilgamesh wanted to be **immortal**, or have everlasting life

   b. Definition of sophisticated words. In this sentence, the underlined information defines the word *empire*.

      An **empire** is a <u>large territory made up of many different places all under the control of a single ruler.</u>

   c. Examples of concepts and topics.

      Flowers <u>such as nasturtiums, daisies, and marigolds</u> grew along the side of the walk.

   d. Contrasts of ideas and topics. In the following sentence, the phrase "on the other hand" indicates a contrast. You can guess that *loquacious* means the opposite of "not talkative."

      President Coolidge was not talkative; President Clinton, <u>on the other hand,</u> was **loquacious.**

4. **Identify pronoun antecedents.** If long sentences contain pronouns, reread the text to make sure you know to what the pronouns refer. The pronoun *its* in the following sentence refers to Yellowstone National Park, not the U.S. government.

   Yellowstone National Park was set aside by the U.S. government for people to enjoy for **its** natural beauty.

5. **Look for conjunctions,** such as *and, or,* and *yet,* to understand relationships between ideas.

6. **Paraphrase,** or restate in your own words, passages of difficult text in order to check your understanding. Remember that a paraphrase is a word-for-word rephrasing of an original text; it is not a summary.

Close Reading Model

As you read this complex document, take note of the sidenotes that model ways to unlock meaning in the text.

from "How to Tell a Story" by Mark Twain

. . . The humorous story is American, the comic story is English, the witty story is French. The humorous story depends for its effect upon the manner of the telling; the comic story and the witty story upon the matter. . . .

The humorous story is strictly a work of art—high and delicate art—and only an artist can tell it; but no art is necessary in telling the comic and the witty story; anybody can do it. The art of telling a humorous story—understand, I mean by word of mouth, not print—was created in America, and has remained at home.

The humorous story is told gravely; the teller does his best to conceal the fact that he even dimly suspects that there is anything funny about it; but the teller of the comic story tells you beforehand that it is one of the funniest things he has ever heard, then tells it with eager delight, and is the first person to laugh when he gets through. And sometimes, if he has had good success, he is so glad and happy that he will repeat the "nub" of it and glance around from face to face, collecting applause, and then repeat it again. It is a pathetic thing to see.

Very often, of course, the rambling and disjointed humorous story finishes with a nub, point, snapper, or whatever you like to call it. Then the listener must be alert, for in many cases the teller will divert attention from that nub by dropping it in a carefully casual and indifferent way, with the pretence that he does not know it is a nub.

The word *but* signals a contrast in ideas.

The dashes indicate an interruption of thought. The main part of this sentence appears in yellow highlight. Less important information appears in green.

Context clues that appear in purple highlighting help you understand the meaning of the word *gravely*.

Additional examples and commentary help you get an idea of the meaning of *nub*.

Strategy 3: Ask Questions

Be an attentive reader by asking questions as you read. Throughout this textbook, we have provided questions for you following each selection. These questions are sorted into three basic categories that build in sophistication and lead you to a deeper understanding of the texts you read. Here is an example from this text:

Some questions are about **Key Ideas and Details** in the text. To answer these questions, you will need to locate and cite explicit information in the text or draw inferences from what you have read.

Some questions are about **Craft and Structure** in the text. To answer these questions, you will need to analyze how the author developed and structured the text. You will also look for ways in which the author artfully used language and how those word choices impacted the meaning and tone of the work.

Gluskabe and Old Man Winter

Close Reading Activities

Read

Comprehension: Key Ideas and Details

1. **Interpret:** In Scene I, what signs do you see that Gluskabe will successfully help the people?
2. **(a)** Find details in the stage directions that establish the seasons at various points in the play. **(b) Connect:** How are these details connected to the main conflict?

3. **(a) Distinguish:** How does the playwright characterize Old Man Winter? **(b) Infer:** What does this characterization suggest about the winter season?
4. **Summarize:** Write a brief objective summary of the drama. Cite story details in your writing.

Text Analysis: Craft and Structure

5. **(a)** What happens in each of the play's four scenes? **(b) Analyze:** Explain how the scenes form a plot with a conflict, rising action, climax, and resolution.
6. **(a) Infer:** Gluskabe speaks with Grandmother Woodchuck after Old Man Winter defeats him the first time. What

new information about Gluskabe do you learn from this conversation? **(b)** How does the dialogue move the story forward? Explain.
7. **(a)** What does the last stage direction describe? **(b) Analyze:** How is this stage direction essential to the play's plot?

Connections: Integration of Knowledge and Ideas

Discuss
Conduct a **small-group discussion** about the personification of winter and summer in the drama. Discuss why the Abenaki people might give human characteristics to these elements of nature.

Research
Briefly res...

Write
Many traditional tales helped people make sense of the world. Write an essay in which you describe how *Gluskabe and Old Man Winter* explains an aspect of nature. Cite details from the play to support your analysis.

Some questions are about the **Integration of Knowledge and Ideas** in the text. These questions ask you to evaluate a text in many different ways, such as comparing texts, analyzing arguments in the text, and using many other methods of thinking critically about a text's ideas.

As you read independently, ask similar types of questions to ensure that you fully enjoy and comprehend texts you read for school and for pleasure. We have provided sets of questions for you on the Independent Reading pages at the end of each unit.

Preparing to Read Complex Texts

Attentive Reading As you read on your own, ask yourself questions like these to enrich your reading experience.

When reading drama, ask yourself…

Comprehension: Key Ideas and Details

- Who is the main character? What struggles does this character face?
- What other characters are important? How do these characters relate to the main character?
- Where and when does the play take place? Do the time and place of the setting affect the characters? If so, how?
- Do the characters, settings, and events seem real? Why or why not?
- How does the play end? How does the ending make me feel?

Text Analysis: Craft and Structure

- Does the playwright include background information? If so, how does this help me understand what I am reading?
- How many acts are in this play? What happens in each act?
- Does the dialogue sound like real speech? Are there passages that seem especially real? Are there any that seem false?
- What do the stage directions tell me about the ways char...

Model

Following is an example of a complex text. The sidenotes show sample questions that an attentive reader might ask while reading.

from "Rendezvous with Despair" by Thomas E. Dewey

The President has said we have a rendezvous with destiny. We seem to be on our way toward a rendezvous with despair.

Fellow Republicans, as a party, let us turn away from that rendezvous and let us start going in the other direction and start now.

The one ultimate unforgivable crime is to despair of the republic. The one essential to the survival of the republic is to know it will survive and will survive into a future that is always larger, always better. In every era for a century and a half it has been doomed to death by gloomy young theorists and by tired and hopeless elders. And history laughs at them as each time the dynamic forces of a free republic led by free men have given the lie to the defeatists while the system of free economic enterprise has marched onward, sweeping the nation's increased population to full employment and ever higher living standards.

Key Ideas and Details Who is the we in these sentences? Who is the us in the next sentence?

Craft and Structure In what ways does Dewey use language creatively in this text?

Integration of Knowledge and Ideas Do you agree with Dewey's point of view? Why or why not?

Independent Practice

Write three to five questions you might ask yourself as you read this passage from a speech delivered by Herbert Hoover in 1935.

from "The Bill of Rights" by Herbert Hoover

Our Constitution is not alone the working plan of a great Federation of States under representative government. There is embedded in it also the vital principles of the American system of liberty . . . which not even the government may infringe and which we call the Bill of Rights. It does not require a lawyer to interpret those provisions. . . . Among others the freedom of worship, freedom of speech and of the press, the right of peaceable assembly, equality before the law, just trial for crime, freedom from unreasonable search, and security from being deprived of life, liberty, or property without due process of law, are the principles which distinguish our civilization. . . . Herein is the expression of the spirit of men who would be forever free.

ANALYZING ARGUMENTS

The ability to evaluate an argument, as well as to make one, is an important skill for success in college and in the workplace.

What Is an Argument?

When you think of the word *argument,* you might think of a disagreement between two people. This type of argument involves trading opinions and evidence in a conversation. A formal argument, however, presents one side of a controversial or debatable issue. A good argument is supported by reasoning and evidence.

Purposes of Argument

There are three main purposes for writing a formal argument:

- to change the reader's mind
- to convince the reader to accept what is written
- to motivate the reader to take action, based on what is written

Elements of Argument

Claim (assertion)—what the writer is trying to prove

Example: *Local governments should give vouchers (an allowance to be used for schooling) to parents who send their children to private schools.*

Grounds (evidence)—the support used to convince the reader

Example: *The parents pay taxes to support local schools. Children are required by law to attend school.*

Justification—the link between the grounds and the claim; why the grounds are credible

Example: *If the children don't attend a public school, they are not getting the benefit of the tax dollars their parents have paid. Local governments should support parents' choices of schools for their children by giving them vouchers.*

Evaluating Claims

When reading or listening to a formal argument, critically assess the claims that are made. Which claims are based on fact or can be proved true? Also, evaluate evidence that supports the claims. If there is little or no reasoning or evidence provided to support the claims, the argument may not be sound or valid.

Model Argument

Nelson Mandela's Address Upon His Release From Prison

…Today the majority of South Africans, black and white, recognize that apartheid has no future. It has to be ended by our own decisive mass action in order to build peace and security. The mass campaign of defiance and other actions of our organization and people can only culminate in the establishment of democracy. The destruction caused by apartheid on our sub-continent is incalculable. The fabric of family life of millions of my people has been shattered. . . . Our economy lies in ruins and our people are embroiled in political strife. . . .

The need to unite the people of our country is as important a task now as it always has been. No individual leader is able to take on this enormous task on his own. . . .

Our struggle has reached a decisive moment. We call on our people to seize this moment so that the process towards democracy is rapid and uninterrupted. We have waited too long for our freedom. We can no longer wait. Now is the time to intensify the struggle on all fronts. To relax our efforts now would be a mistake which generations to come will not be able to forgive. The sight of freedom looming on the horizon should encourage us to redouble our efforts.

…We call on the international community to continue the campaign to isolate the apartheid regime. To lift sanctions now would be to run the risk of aborting the process towards the complete eradication of apartheid.

Our march to freedom is irreversible. . . . Universal suffrage on a common voters' role in a united democratic and non-racial South Africa is the only way to peace and racial harmony.

In conclusion I wish to quote my own words during my trial in 1964. They are true today as they were then:

'I have fought against white domination and I have fought against black domination. I have cherished the ideal of a democratic and free society in which all persons live together in harmony and with equal opportunities. It is an ideal which I hope to live for and to achieve. But if needs be, it is an ideal for which I am prepared to die.'

Claim: All South Africans must work together to end apartheid.

Justification: Apartheid has caused problems for the people as well as the country.

Grounds: No one can do the job alone.

Grounds: Black South Africans have waited too long for their freedom.

An opposing argument would be to support apartheid. Mandela points out what would happen if the international community lifted sanctions.

Grounds: Universal suffrage is key to peace and racial harmony.

A strong conclusion does more than simply restate the claim.

THE ART OF ARGUMENT: RHETORICAL DEVICES AND PERSUASIVE TECHNIQUES

Rhetorical Devices

Rhetoric is the art of using language in order to make a point or to persuade listeners. Rhetorical devices such as the ones listed below are accepted elements of argument. Their use is regarded as a key part of an effective argument.

Rhetorical Devices	Examples
Repetition The repeated use of certain words, phrases, or sentences	**Vote** for me. **Vote** for honesty. **Vote** for progress.
Parallelism The repeated use of similar grammatical structures	<u>To teach</u> is <u>to inspire</u>. <u>To learn</u> is <u>to explore</u>.
Rhetorical Question A question that calls attention to an issue by implying an obvious answer	Aren't all people equal under the law?
Sound Devices The use of alliteration, assonance, rhyme, or rhythm	Waste not, want not.
Simile and Metaphor The comparison of two seemingly unlike things or the assertion that one thing *is* another	The trees surrounded the house <u>like guards on patrol</u>.

Persuasive Techniques

The persuasive techniques below are often found in informal persuasion.

Persuasive Techniques	Examples
Bandwagon Approach/Anti-Bandwagon Approach Appeals to a person's desire to belong/Encourages or celebrates individuality	You have to see that movie; everyone in our class has seen it. Use your best judgment; don't follow the crowd.
Emotional Appeal Capitalizes on people's fear, anger, or desire	Without a sprinkler system, this school building is a fire trap.
Endorsement/Testimony Employs a well-known person to promote a product or an idea	Meditation and positive thinking have helped me become president of this company.
Loaded Language Uses words that are charged with emotion	This medal recognizes the integrity of the brave people who defend our beloved country.
"Plain Folks" Appeal Shows a connection to everyday, ordinary people	I worry about rising gas prices just like you do.
Hyperbole Exaggerates to make a point	If I've heard that complaint once, I've heard it a thousand times.

Model Speech

The excerpted speech below includes examples of rhetorical devices and persuasive techniques.

from "Speech Celebrating George Washington's Birthday" by Jane Addams

… What is a great man who has made his mark upon history? Every time, if we think far enough, he is a man who has looked through the confusion of the moment and has seen the moral issue involved; he is a man who has refused to have his sense of justice distorted; he has listened to his conscience until conscience becomes a trumpet call to like-minded men, so that they gather about him and together, with mutual purpose and mutual aid, they make a new period in history. . . .

If we go back to George Washington, and ask what he would be doing were he bearing our burdens now, and facing our problems at this moment, we would, of course, have to study his life bit by bit; his life as a soldier, as a statesman, and as a simple Virginia planter.

First, as a soldier. What is it that we admire about the soldier? It certainly is not that he goes into battle; what we admire about the soldier is that he has the power of losing his own life for the life or a larger cause; that he holds his personal suffering of no account; that he flings down in the gage of battle his all, and says, "I will stand or fall with this cause." That, it seems to me, is the glorious thing we most admire, and if we are going to preserve that same spirit of the soldier, we will have to found a similar spirit in the civil life of the people, the same pride in civil warfare, the spirit of courage, and the spirit of self-surrender which lies back of this. . . .

This rhetorical question gives the reader a purpose for reading.

Repeated grammatical structures give the speech rhythm.

The metaphor comparing conscience to a trumpet call emphasizes the importance of the statement.

Sound devices, such as alliteration, emphasize a phrase.

The parallel grammatical structure provides a rhythm, and introduces the organization of the remainder of the speech.

Addams uses parallelism and repetition to emphasize her main points.

COMPOSING AN ARGUMENT

Choosing a Topic

You should choose a topic that matters to people—and to you. Once you have chosen a topic, you should check to make sure you can make an arguable claim. Ask yourself these questions:

1. What am I trying to prove? What ideas should I express?
2. Are there people who would disagree with my claim? What opinions might they have?
3. Do I have enough relevant evidence to support my claim?

If you are able to put into words what you want to prove and answered "yes" to questions 2 and 3, you have an arguable claim.

Introducing the Claim and Establishing Its Significance

Before you begin writing, think about your audience and how much you think they already know about your chosen topic. Then, provide only as much background information as necessary. Remember that you are not writing a summary of the issue—you are developing an argument. Once you have provided context for your argument, you should clearly state your claim, or thesis. A written argument's claim often, but not always, appears in the first paragraph.

Developing Your Claim with Reasoning and Evidence

Now that you have made your claim, you must support it with evidence, or grounds. A good argument should have at least three solid pieces of evidence to support the claim. Evidence can range from personal experience to researched data or expert opinion. Knowing your audience's knowledge level, concerns, values, and possible biases can help inform your decision on what kind of evidence will have the strongest impact. Make sure your evidence is up to date and comes from a credible source. Don't forget to credit your sources. You should also address the opposing counterclaim within the body of your argument. Consider points you have made or evidence you have provided that a person might challenge. Decide how best to respond to these counterclaims.

Writing a Concluding Statement or Section

Restate your claim in the conclusion of your argument, and synthesize, or pull together, the evidence you have provided. Make your conclusion strong enough to be memorable to the reader; leave him or her with something to think about.

Practice

Complete an outline like the one below to help you plan your own argument.

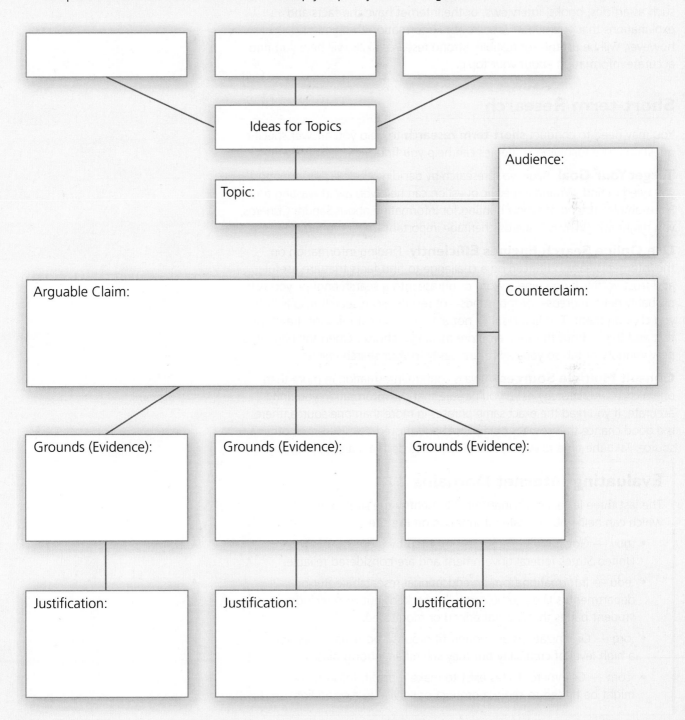

Ideas for Topics

Topic:

Audience:

Arguable Claim:

Counterclaim:

Grounds (Evidence):

Grounds (Evidence):

Grounds (Evidence):

Justification:

Justification:

Justification:

CONDUCTING RESEARCH

To gain more knowledge about a topic, you can conduct research. Sources such as articles, books, interviews, or the Internet have the facts and explanations that you need. Not all of the information that you find, however, will be useful—or reliable. Strong research skills will help you find accurate information about your topic.

Short-term Research

You may need to conduct **short-term research** to help you answer specific questions. The following strategies can help you find the best information.

Target Your Goal Begin your research by deciding the exact information you need to find. Writing a specific question can help you avoid wasting time. For example, instead of simply hunting for information about Sandra Cisneros, you might ask "Why is Cisneros's heritage important to her writing?"

Use Online Search Engines Efficiently Finding information on the Internet is easy, but it can be a challenge to find facts that are useful and trustworthy. If you type a word or phrase into a search engine, you will probably get hundreds—or thousands—of results. Scan search results before you click on them. The first result is not always the most relevant. Read the text and think about the source before making a choice. Open the page in a new window or tab so you can return easily to your search results.

Consult Multiple Sources Always confirm information in more than one source. This strategy helps you be sure that the information you find is accurate. If you read the exact same phrases in more than one source, there is a good chance that someone simply cut-and-pasted details from another source. Take the time to evaluate each source to decide if it is trustworthy.

Evaluating Internet Domains

The last three letters of an Internet URL identify the site's domain, which can help you evaluate information on the site.

- .gov — Government sites are sponsored by a branch of the United States federal government and are considered reliable.

- .edu — Information from an educational research center or department is likely to be carefully checked, but may include student pages that are not edited or monitored.

- .org — Organizations are nonprofit groups and usually maintain a high level of credibility but may still reflect strong biases.

- .com — Commercial sites exist to make a profit. Information might be biased to show a product or service in a good light.

Long-term Research

When you want to really explore a topic, **long-term research** allows you to carry out a detailed, comprehensive investigation. An organized research plan will help you gather and synthesize information from multiple sources.

As this flowchart shows, long-term research is a flexible process. Throughout your research, you might decide to refocus your topic, gather more information, or reflect on what you have learned.

The Research Process

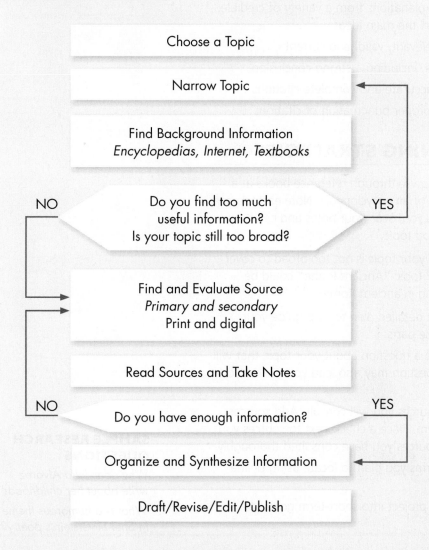

Refer to the Research Process Workshop (pp. lxxii–lxxvi) for more details about the steps in this flowchart.

RESEARCH PROCESS WORKSHOP

Research Writing: Research Paper

A **research paper** presents facts and information gathered from credible sources and includes a Works Cited list that credits each source. You might use elements of this form in reports, articles, or speeches.

Elements of a Research Paper

- a topic for inquiry that is narrow enough to cover thoroughly
- a strong introduction that clearly defines the topic
- facts, details, examples, and explanations from a variety of credible, authoritative sources to support the main ideas
- information that is accurate, relevant, valid, and current
- a clear method of organization, including a strong conclusion
- a Works Cited list containing accurate and complete citations
- error-free grammar, including proper punctuation of citations

PREWRITING/PLANNING STRATEGIES

Browse to choose a topic. Browse through reference books at a library, such as an atlas or a volume of an encyclopedia. Note each person, place, object, or event that interests you. Scan your notes and circle any words or phrases that suggest a good topic.

Narrow your topic. Make sure your topic is not too broad to cover effectively. For example, the general topic "Ancient Rome" could be narrowed down to a specific building in ancient Rome.

Create a research plan. Use a detailed plan to help guide your research. Your plan can include these parts:

- **Research Question** Compose a question about your topic that will help you stay on track. This question may also lead you to find your topic sentence.
- **Source List** Create a list of sources you will consult. Add sources to your list as you discover them. Place a check next to sources you have located, and underline sources you have consulted thoroughly.
- **Search Terms** Write down terms you plan to locate using online search engines.
- **Deadlines** Break a long-term project into short-term goals to prevent last-minute stress.

SAMPLE RESEARCH QUESTIONS

Why does Julia Alvarez write about her childhood?

What is a humorous theme in Shel Silverstein's poetry?

GATHERING DETAILS THROUGH RESEARCH

Use multiple sources. An effective research project combines information from multiple sources. It is important not to rely too heavily on a single source. The creativity and originality of your research depends on how you combine ideas from many places. Plan to include a variety of these resources:

- **Primary and Secondary Resources** Use both primary sources (firsthand or original accounts, such as interview transcripts and newspaper articles) and secondary sources (accounts that are not original, such as encyclopedia entries or an online library catalog) in your research.

- **Print and Digital Resources** The Internet allows fast access to data, but print resources are often edited more carefully. Plan to include both print and digital resources in order to guarantee that your work is accurate.

- **Media Resources** You can find valuable information in media resources such as documentaries, television programs, podcasts, and museum exhibitions. Public lectures by experts also offer an opportunity to hear an expert's thoughts on a topic.

- **Original Research** Depending on your topic, you may wish to conduct original research to include among your sources. For example, you might interview experts or eyewitnesses or conduct a survey to find out about beliefs in your community.

Take clear notes from a variety of sources. Use different strategies to take notes:

- Use index cards to create **note cards** and **source cards.** On each source card, record information about each source that you use—title, author, publication date and place, and page numbers. On each note card, record information to use in your report. Use quotation marks when you copy exact words, and indicate the page number on which the quotation appears.

- Photocopy articles and copyright pages; then, highlight relevant information. Remember to include the Web addresses of printouts from online sources.

- Print articles from the Internet or copy them directly into a "notes" folder.

You will use these notes to help you write original text.

Notecard

> **Education**
> Papp, p.5
>
> Only the upper classes could read.
>
> Most of the common people in Shakespeare's time could not read.

Source Card

> Papp, Joseph
> and Kirkland, Elizabeth
>
> **Shakespeare Alive!**
>
> New York: Bantam Books, 1988

DRAFTING STRATEGIES

Use an outline to organize information. Group your notes by categories that break your topic into subtopics. For example, if you are writing about the Colosseum, you might use these topics in your outline:

- architecture
- construction
- events held
- spectators

Use Roman numerals (I, II, III) to number the subtopics and letters (A, B, C) to show details and facts related to each subtopic, as in the outline shown on this page.

Match your draft to your outline. A solid, detailed outline will serve as a map, guiding you through the writing of your draft. The headings with Roman numerals indicate main sections of your report. You may need to write several paragraphs to cover each Roman numeral topic fully. Organize your paragraphs around the topics with capital letters.

Support main ideas with facts. Using your outline, write sentences to express each of your main ideas. Then, refer to your note cards and provide support for your main ideas with facts, details, examples, and explanations that you gathered through your research.

Cite sources. To avoid plagiarism—presenting another's work as your own without giving credit—you must include documentation every time you use another writer's ideas.

It is important to use ethical practices when conducting research.

Plan Your Citations Whether you are paraphrasing, summarizing, or using a direct quotation, you must give credit. As you draft, remember to use quotation marks around any words that you pick-up directly from a source. You should also give credit for ideas or facts that are unique to one source.

I. Introduction
II. Architecture of Colosseum
   A. measurements
   B. building material
III. Construction of Colosseum
   A. beginning date
   B. workers
IV. Conclusion

Citing Sources Tips:

- For *paraphrased information* or facts that are not common knowledge, insert parentheses for the author's last name and the page number(s) from which the information came:

  The Colosseum holds 50,000 spectators (Smith 87–88).

- For a *direct quotation,* use quotation marks. After the end quotation mark, insert in parentheses the author's last name and the page number(s) from which the quotation came: *"It is the Romans' greatest work of architecture." (Smith 87).*

REVISING STRATEGIES

Check for effective paragraph structure. In a research report, most body paragraphs should be built according to this plan:

- a **topic sentence (T)** stating the paragraph's main idea
- a **restatement (R)** or elaboration of the topic sentence
- strong **illustrations (I),** including facts, examples, or details about the main idea

Review your draft. Label each of your sentences **T, R,** or **I.** If a paragraph contains a group of I's, make sure that you have a strong **T** that they support. If you find a **T** by itself, add I's to support it.

Revise for unity. In writing that has **unity,** everything comes together to form a complete, self-contained whole. Use the following checklist to assess your report's unity.

Unity Checklist

✓ Every paragraph develops my thesis statement.

✓ All of my paragraphs contain topic sentences that support the thesis.

✓ I have eliminated any sentences that do not support my main idea.

Define technical terms and difficult words. While researching, you may have learned new words—either technical terms related to your topic or difficult words that were unfamiliar to you. Help your readers to understand and enjoy your report by adding context clues or definitions to make these words easier to understand.

Difficult: A popular show at the Roman Colosseum featured **gladiators.**

Defined: A popular show at the Roman Colosseum featured **gladiators,** trained fighters who often faced other men or even wild animals.

Create a works-cited list. A "Works Cited" page provides readers with full bibliographic information on each source you cite. The author and page number within your report will lead your reader to the specific source in your Works Cited page. Readers can use that information to read more about your topic. Review pp. lxxx–lxxxi to see the appropriate format for citing sources.

EDITING AND PROOFREADING

During editing you will focus on giving credit to the sources you used. You should also review your draft to correct errors in grammar, spelling, and punctuation. Demonstrate your keyboarding skills by typing your entire paper carefully and avoiding the introduction of errors.

Proofread for accuracy. Check the names of the authors you quote and the names of the books, articles, or other sources you used. Be sure that you have used quotation marks correctly, and that each open quotation mark has a corresponding closing quotation mark. Carefully reread your draft to find and correct errors in spelling, grammar, and punctuation.

Focus on citations. Cite the sources for quotations, factual information, and ideas that are not your own. Some word-processing programs have features that allow you to create footnotes and endnotes.

Create a reference list. Following the format your teacher prefers, create a Works Cited list of the information you used to write your research report. (For more information, see Citing Sources, pp. lxiv–lxv.)

Focus on format. Follow the report requirements by including an appropriate title page, pagination, spacing and margins, and citations. Make sure you have used the preferred system for crediting sources in your paper and for bibliographical sources at the end.

Publishing and Presenting

Consider one of these options for sharing your findings.

Give an oral report. Use your research report as the basis for an oral presentation on your topic. Keep your audience in mind and revise accordingly as you prepare your presentation.

Create a multimedia presentation. Computer software makes it easy to combine interesting videos, sound effects, music, and images in your presentation.

Identifying Missing Citations

These strategies can help you find facts and details that should be cited in your report.

- Look for facts that are not general knowledge. If a fact was unique to one source, it needs a citation.
- Read your report aloud. Listen for words or phrases that do not sound like your writing style. You might have picked them up from a source. If so, use your notes to find the source, place the words in quotation marks, and give credit.
- Review your notes. Look for ideas that you used in your report, but did not cite.

STUDENT MODEL: RESEARCH PAPER

This student includes information to support the topic of her research paper. Notice how she integrates facts and details into her argument. She also uses parentheses to give credit for ideas taken from resources. The Works Cited list at the end of the report gives more details about the reference sources she used during the research process.

Student Model: Elizabeth Cleary, Maplewood, NJ

Ice Ages

Ice ages occur every two hundred million years or so. An ice age is defined as a long period of cold where large amounts of water are trapped under ice. Although ice ages happened long ago, studying their causes and effects helps contemporary scientists understand geological conditions of the world today.

When an ice age does occur, ice covers much of the Earth. This ice forms when the climate changes. The polar regions become very cold and the temperatures drop everywhere else. The ice is trapped in enormous mountains of ice called *glaciers*. Glaciers can be as large as a continent in size. When the Earth's temperature warms up, the glaciers start to melt, forming rivers and lakes. Glaciers' tremendous weight and size can actually wear away mountains and valleys as the glaciers melt and move. The melting ice also raises ocean levels (*History of the Universe* Web site).

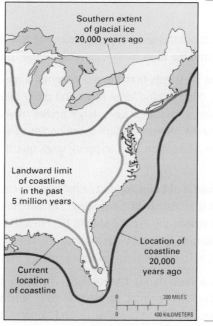

Effects of Ice Age on Eastern Coastline of United States

There are many different theories to explain why ice ages occur, but no one knows for sure. Many scientists agree that it is probably due to a combination of causes, including changes in the sun's intensity, the distance of the Earth from the sun, changes in ocean currents, the continental plates rubbing up against each other, and the varying amounts of carbon dioxide in the atmosphere (*PBS Nova* Web site).

The author defines her topic clearly in the highlighted sentence.

This map illustrates the writer's point that ice ages caused current conditions.

Here the author presents factual information related to the possible causes of ice ages.

During the last ice age, or the Wisconsin Ice Age, people lived on the Earth. These people saw ice and snow all the time. It was never warm enough for it to melt, so it piled up. In summertime, women fished in chilly streams. The men hunted year-round.

The skeleton of one person who lived and hunted during this time was found by some hikers in 1901 in the European Alps. He had been buried in the ice for nearly 5,000 years. Nicknamed the "Iceman," scientists believe that perhaps he was suddenly caught by a blizzard or that he possibly ran out of food, became weak, and died.

Scientists were able to learn a lot about this ancient period from the leather clothes and animal skins he was wearing and the tools he was carrying (Roberts, p. 38).

> Elizabeth clearly and accurately cites her sources to show where she obtained a set of specific details.

Ice ages also affect life today. The ice sheets that formed weighed a huge amount. When the ice retreated, it left behind large rocks and other debris which otherwise would not be there. Also, without ice ages, large bodies of water like the Great Lakes simply wouldn't exist. We depend on these bodies of water every day for fresh drinking water, recreation, and shipping large quantities of materials.

Scientists discovered ice ages because of Louis Agassiz, a nineteenth-century scientist who is sometimes called the "Father of Glaciology." In Switzerland, he saw boulders of granite far from where any granite should be. He also noticed scrapes and grooves, or striae. He theorized that glaciers had caused all of these geologic features (University of California Museum of Paleontology Web page).

> In each section, Elizabeth explores a different aspect of the ice ages. Here she is explaining scientific discovery.

Many animals that are extinct now lived during the Ice Age. The saber-toothed tiger and the mastodon, an elephant-like animal, formerly lived in North America. They became extinct because of climate change and hunting. Other animals became extinct as well because they could not adapt to the way the Earth was changing.

Baron Gerard de Geer, a Swedish geologist, did pioneering work which estimated the end of the last ice age. In a similar way to the way we count tree rings to estimate a tree's age, De Geer used layers of sediment left by glacier's summer melts to calculate the history of the Ice Age. He did much of his work in Sweden, but he also visited areas that had been affected by glaciers in New England (Department of Geosciences, University of Arizona Web page).

Thanks to scientists like De Geer and Agassiz, we know a great deal about that remote age when glaciers roamed the Earth. We can now estimate the history of ice ages and determine what features—valleys, inland seas, mountains, lakes, rocks—were caused, as you can see by the map displayed here of the Eastern United States. There is still a lot more to be discovered about the causes of ice ages, but one thing is clear: Glaciers had a powerful effect on the world as we know it today.

The author restates the main idea that she presented in the introduction and supported in the body of the paper.

Works Cited

"The Big Chill." *PBS Nova*. Web. 10 Nov. 2015.
   <http://www.pbs.org/wgbh/nova/ice/chill.html>.

Department of Geosciences, University of Arizona. Web. 10 Nov. 2015.
   <http://www.geoarizona.edu/Antevs/degeer.html>.

History of the Universe. Web. 11 Nov. 2015.
   <http://www.historyoftheuniverse.com/iceage.html>.

Roberts, David. "The Iceman." *National Geographic Magazine*,
   June 1993: 37–49. Print.

University of California Museum of Paleontology. Web. 11 Nov. 2015.
   <http://www.ucmp.berkeley.edu/history/agassiz.html>.

In her Works Cited list, Elizabeth provides information on all the sources she cites in her research paper.

Introductory Unit

CITING SOURCES AND PREPARING MANUSCRIPT

Proofreading and Preparing Manuscript

Before preparing a final copy, proofread your manuscript. The chart shows the standard symbols for marking corrections to be made.

Proofreading Symbols	
Insert	∧
delete	ℐ
close space	◠
new paragraph	¶
add comma	⌃
add period	⊙
transpose (switch)	∾
change to cap	a̲
change to lowercase	A̸

- Choose a standard, easy-to-read font.
- Type or print on one side of unlined 8 1/2" x 11" paper.
- Set the margins for the side, top, and bottom of your paper at approximately one inch. Most word-processing programs have a default setting that is appropriate.
- Double-space the document.
- Indent the first line of each paragraph.
- Number the pages in the upper right corner.

Follow your teacher's directions for formatting formal research papers. Most papers will have the following features:

- Title page
- Table of Contents or Outline
- Works-Cited List

Avoiding Plagiarism

Whether you are presenting a formal research paper or an opinion paper on a current event, you must be careful to give credit for any ideas or opinions that are not your own. Presenting someone else's ideas, research, or opinion as your own—even if you have phrased it in different words—is *plagiarism,* the equivalent of academic stealing, or fraud.

Do not use the ideas or research of others in place of your own. Read from several sources to draw your own conclusions and form your own opinions. Incorporate the ideas and research of others to support your points. Credit the source of the following types of support:

- Statistics
- Direct quotations
- Indirectly quoted statements of opinions
- Conclusions presented by an expert
- Facts available in only one or two sources

Crediting Sources

When you credit a source, you acknowledge where you found your information and you give your readers the details necessary for locating the source themselves. Within the body of the paper, you provide a short citation, a footnote number linked to a footnote, or an endnote number linked to an endnote reference. These brief references show the page numbers on which you found the information. Prepare a reference list at the end of the paper to provide full bibliographic information on your sources. These are two common types of reference lists:

- A bibliography provides a listing of all the resources you consulted during your research.
- A works-cited list indicates the works you have referenced in your paper.

The chart on the next page shows the Modern Language Association format for crediting sources. This is the most common format for papers written in the content areas in middle school and high school. Unless instructed otherwise by your teacher, use this format for crediting sources.

MLA Style for Listing Sources

Book with one author	Pyles, Thomas. *The Origins and Development of the English Language.* 2nd ed. New York: Harcourt, 1971. Print.
Book with two or three authors	McCrum, Robert, William Cran, and Robert MacNeil. *The Story of English.* New York: Penguin, 1987. Print.
Book with an editor	Truth, Sojourner. *Narrative of Sojourner Truth.* Ed. Margaret Washington. New York: Vintage, 1993. Print.
Book with more than three authors or editors	Donald, Robert B., et al. *Writing Clear Essays.* Upper Saddle River: Prentice, 1996. Print.
Single work in an anthology	Hawthorne, Nathaniel. "Young Goodman Brown." *Literature: An Introduction to Reading and Writing.* Ed. Edgar V. Roberts and H. E. Jacobs. Upper Saddle River: Prentice, 1998. 376–385. Print. [Indicate pages for the entire selection.]
Introduction to a work in a published edition	Washington, Margaret. Introduction. *Narrative of Sojourner Truth.* By Sojourner Truth. Ed. Washington. New York: Vintage, 1993. v–xi. Print.
Signed article from an encyclopedia	Askeland, Donald R. "Welding." *World Book Encyclopedia.* 1991 ed. Print.
Signed article in a weekly magazine	Wallace, Charles. "A Vodacious Deal." *Time* 14 Feb. 2000: 63. Print.
Signed article in a monthly magazine	Gustaitis, Joseph. "The Sticky History of Chewing Gum." *American History* Oct. 1998: 30–38. Print.
Newspaper	Thurow, Roger. "South Africans Who Fought for Sanctions Now Scrap for Investors." *Wall Street Journal* 11 Feb. 2000: A1+. Print. [For a multipage article that does not appear on consecutive pages, write only the first page number on which it appears, followed by the plus sign.]
Unsigned editorial or story	"Selective Silence." Editorial. *Wall Street Journal* 11 Feb. 2000: A14. Print. [If the editorial or story is signed, begin with the author's name.]
Signed pamphlet or brochure	[Treat the pamphlet as though it were a book.]
Work from a library subscription service	Ertman, Earl L. "Nefertiti's Eyes." *Archaeology* Mar.–Apr. 2008: 28–32. *Kids Search.* EBSCO. New York Public Library. Web. 18 June 2008 [Indicate the date you accessed the information.]
Filmstrips, slide programs, videocassettes, DVDs, and other audiovisual media	*The Diary of Anne Frank.* Dir. George Stevens. Perf. Millie Perkins, Shelley Winters, Joseph Schildkraut, Lou Jacobi, and Richard Beymer. 1959. Twentieth Century Fox, 2004. DVD.
CD-ROM (with multiple publishers)	Simms, James, ed. *Romeo and Juliet.* By William Shakespeare. Oxford: Attica Cybernetics; London: BBC Education; London: Harper, 1995. CD-ROM.
Radio or television program transcript	"Washington's Crossing of the Delaware." *Weekend Edition Sunday.* Natl. Public Radio. WNYC, New York. 23 Dec. 2003. Television transcript.
Internet Web page	"Fun Facts About Gum." NACGM site. 1999. National Association of Chewing Gum Manufacturers. Web. 19 Dec. 1999 [Indicate the date you accessed the information.]
Personal interview	Smith, Jane. Personal interview. 10 Feb. 2000.

All examples follow the style given in the *MLA Handbook for Writers of Research Papers,* seventh edition, by Joseph Gibaldi.

UNIT 1

THE BIG ? Is conflict always bad?

UNIT PATHWAY

PART 1
SETTING EXPECTATIONS

- INTRODUCING THE BIG QUESTION
- CLOSE READING WORKSHOP

PART 2
TEXT ANALYSIS
GUIDED EXPLORATION

CHARACTERS AND CONFLICT

PART 3
TEXT SET
DEVELOPING INSIGHT

THE GOLD RUSH

PART 4
DEMONSTRATING INDEPENDENCE

- INDEPENDENT READING
- ONLINE TEXT SET

CLOSE READING TOOL

Use this tool to practice the close reading strategies you learn.

STUDENT eTEXT

Bring learning to life with audio, video, and interactive tools.

ONLINE WRITER'S NOTEBOOK

Easily capture notes and complete assignments online.

Find all Digital Resources at **pearsonrealize.com**

THE BIG ?

Is conflict always bad?

A conflict is a struggle between opposing forces. There are many different types of conflict. One kind of conflict is an argument between people, such as who should get the last cookie. Another type is a battle between nations over freedom and liberty. When you compete against others in a sport or game, that is another kind of conflict. When you struggle over a decision, you are in conflict with yourself. There are many ways to resolve, or work out, conflicts of any kind. There are also many lessons to learn from these situations.

Exploring the Big Question

Collaboration: One-on-One Discussion Start thinking about the Big Question by identifying different types of conflict. Describe one specific example of each of the following types of conflict:

- a disagreement between friends over an issue
- a misunderstanding between two people
- a competition in sports or in a contest
- an individual's struggle to make a decision
- a battle against forces of nature
- a person's fight to overcome or accept a challenge

Share your examples with a partner. Discuss the cause of each conflict and how it was resolved. Listen attentively.

Connecting to the Literature Each reading in this unit will give you additional insight into the Big Question. After you read each text, pause to consider ways in which the characters handled conflict.

Vocabulary

Acquire and Use Academic Vocabulary The term "academic vocabulary" refers to words you typically encounter in scholarly and literary texts and in technical and business writing. Review the definitions of these academic vocabulary words.

argue (är´gyo͞o) *v.* fight using words; debate

challenge (chal´ənj) *v.* dare; *n.* a calling into question

conclude (kən klo͞od´) *v.* arrive at a judgment; end

convince (kən vins´) *v.* persuade

defend (dē fend´) *v.* guard from attack; protect

resolve (ri zälv´) *v.* settle; bring to an end

Gather Vocabulary Knowledge Additional vocabulary words are listed below. Categorize the words by deciding whether you know each one well, know it a little bit, or do not know it at all.

battle	issue	resist
compete	lose	survival
game	negotiate	win

Then, do the following:

1. Write the definitions of the words you know.

2. If you think you know a word's meaning, write it down. Consult a dictionary and revise your definition if necessary.

3. Using a print or an online dictionary, look up the meanings of words you do not know. Write down the meanings and study the pronunciations.

4. Use all of the words in two brief paragraphs. In the first paragraph, write about a conflict that had positive results. In the second, discuss a conflict that had negative results.

Close Reading Workshop

In this workshop you will learn an approach to reading that will deepen your understanding of literature and will help you better appreciate the author's craft. The workshop includes models for close reading, discussion, research, and writing activities. After you have reviewed the strategies and models, practice your skills with the Independent Practice selection.

CLOSE READING: SHORT STORY

In the beginning of this unit, you will focus on reading various short stories. Use these strategies as you read the texts.

Comprehension: Key Ideas and Details

- Read first to unlock basic meaning.
- Use context clues to define unfamiliar words. Consult a dictionary, if necessary.
- Identify unfamiliar details that you might need to clarify through research.
- Distinguish between what is stated directly and what must be inferred.

Ask yourself questions such as these:
- Who are the main characters?
- What is the setting?
- What is the main conflict?

Text Analysis: Craft and Structure

- Think about the genre of the work and how the author presents ideas.
- Take note of how the author uses dialogue to develop character.
- Determine how the narrator's point of view contributes to the story.

Ask yourself questions such as these:
- Why do the characters behave as they do? How do their actions advance the plot?
- How does the author's word choice affect the story's tone?

Connections: Integration of Knowledge and Ideas

- Look for relationships among key ideas. Identify causes and effects, and comparisons and contrasts.
- Look for important images and symbols and analyze their deeper meaning. Then, connect ideas to determine the theme.
- Compare and contrast this work with other works you have read.

Ask yourself questions such as these:
- How has this work increased my knowledge of a subject or author?
- What is surprising about the story's outcome?

Read

As you read this short story, take note of the annotations that model ways to closely read the text.

Reading Model

"The Old Grandfather and His Little Grandson" by Leo Tolstoy

The grandfather had become very old. His legs would not carry him, his eyes could not see, his ears could not hear, and he was toothless. When he ate, bits of food sometimes dropped out of his mouth. [1] His son and his son's wife no longer allowed him to eat with them at the table. He had to eat his meals in a corner near the stove. [2]

One day they gave him his food in a bowl. He tried to move the bowl closer; it fell to the floor and broke. [3] His daughter-in-law scolded him. She told him that he spoiled everything in the house and broke their dishes, and she said that from now on he would get his food in a wooden dish. The old man sighed and said nothing. [4]

A few days later, the old man's son and his wife were sitting in their hut, resting and watching their little boy playing on the floor. They saw him putting together something out of small pieces of wood. His father asked him, "What are you making, Misha?"

The little grandson said, "I'm making a wooden bucket. When you and Mamma get old, I'll feed you out of this wooden dish." [5]

The young peasant and his wife looked at each other, and tears filled their eyes. They were ashamed because they had treated the old grandfather so meanly, and from that day they again let the old man eat with them at the table and took better care of him. [6]

Craft and Structure
1 Short, simple words paint a clear picture of the frail and ailing grandfather.

Key Ideas and Details
2 The words "had to" suggest that the grandfather was given no choice; he was forced to eat in a corner.

Integration of Knowledge and Ideas
3 The broken bowl may be a symbol of the grandfather's broken body.

Key Ideas and Details
4 The grandfather's sigh indicates that he is used to being yelled at. His acceptance shows that he is meek and gentle.

Craft and Structure
5 Misha's innocent remark reveals the "lesson" he has learned from his parents. This passage marks the climax of the story.

Integration of Knowledge and Ideas
6 This change in the characters' behavior points to a theme: Treat others the way you wish to be treated.

Discuss

Sharing your own ideas and listening to the ideas of others can deepen your understanding of a text and help you look at a topic in a whole new way. As you participate in collaborative discussions, work to have a genuine exchange in which classmates build upon one another's ideas. Support your points with evidence and ask meaningful questions.

Discussion Model

Student 1: Tolstoy's description of the grandfather as nearly blind and deaf makes me feel sorry for him. But when I read the sentence, "When he ate, bits of food sometimes dropped out of his mouth," I thought that was a little gross.

Student 2: I agree. I still felt bad for the grandfather, but I also understood where the parents were coming from. Later in the story, when Misha made his parents feel ashamed, I felt kind of ashamed, too.

Student 3: Tolstoy found a good theme for the story. At times, everyone can be hurtful, but we also have the ability to change. This theme seems a lot like the Golden Rule, which says, "Treat others as you want to be treated." I wonder if Tolstoy wrote about the Golden Rule in his other stories and novels.

Research

Targeted research can clarify unfamiliar details and shed light on various aspects of a text. Consider questions that arise in your mind as you read, and use those questions as the basis for research.

Research Model

Question: *What did Tolstoy believe about how we should treat others?*

Key Words for Internet Search: Tolstoy and "Golden Rule"

Result: Journal abstract: Philosophy *Now*, Issue 54

What I Learned: According to scholars, Tolstoy favored "nonresistance to evil." This basically means that he vowed not to harm any human being, even if a person invaded his home and tried to rob him. Tolstoy's theory influenced nonviolent protestors of the twentieth century, including Mohandas Gandhi.

Write

Writing about a text will deepen your understanding of it and will also allow you to share your ideas more formally with others. The following model essay explores the moral tone and characterization of Tolstoy's story and cites evidence to support the main ideas.

Writing Model: Argument

Tolstoy and the Golden Rule

In "The Old Grandfather and His Little Grandson," Tolstoy uses characterizations of the grandfather, his son and daughter-in-law, and his grandson to argue that people should treat others the way they would like to be treated.

> Many effective essays begin with a thesis statement, or summary of the author's argument.

Tolstoy sketches his characters in just a few words. He tells the reader that the grandfather is "very old" and that "his legs would not carry him, his eyes could not see, his ears could not hear, and he was toothless." This description breaks the grandfather down into broken body parts, but it also creates sympathy for him.

> The writer supports claims with specific details from the story.

After the grandfather breaks a bowl, his daughter-in-law scolds him and tells him that he spoils "everything in the house," and he will have to eat from a wooden bowl from now on. The way the son and daughter-in-law treat the grandfather shows that they both lack sympathy. However, the reader can understand the couple's refusal to eat with someone who "drops bits of food" from his mouth.

> The writer cites a specific example to show how Tolstoy creates realistic situations that are complex.

The couple's son, Misha, reflects the idea that children learn the attitudes they observe in adults. Because Misha heard his parents telling his grandfather to eat out of a wooden dish, he assumes that is how to treat elderly people. The little boy's kindness shows when he thinks ahead, making a "wooden dish" for his parents to eat from when they are old. Misha's innocence and kindness make his parents feel ashamed of the way they have treated the grandfather. The couple—and the reader—realize they would not want to be treated that way when they are old and weak.

> By incorporating information from research, the writer makes a connection between Tolstoy's moral beliefs and the theme of the story.

Tolstoy held several moral beliefs that he often wrote about. He tried to avoid anger, show love for others through the "Golden Rule," and display nonviolent resistance to evil. The grandfather's response to the scolding from his daughter-in-law matches these beliefs: "The old man sighed and said nothing." The grandfather was being attacked, but he did not show anger. Instead, he nonviolently resisted his son's and daughter-in-law's cruel treatment.

As you read the story, apply the close reading strategies you have learned. You may need to read the story multiple times.

The Wounded Wolf

by Jean Craighead George

Meet the Author

Award-winning novelist, nonfiction writer, short-story writer, and memoirist **Jean Craighead George** (1919–2012) was born in Washington, D.C. A naturalist as much as an author, George wrote more than 100 books about the natural world, most of them for children. Her best-known works are *Julie of the Wolves* (1972) and *My Side of the Mountain* (1959).

CLOSE READING TOOL

Read and respond to this selection online using the **Close Reading Tool**.

A wounded wolf climbs Toklat Ridge,[1] a massive spine of rock and ice. As he limps, dawn strikes the ridge and lights it up with sparks and stars. Roko, the wounded wolf, blinks in the ice fire, then stops to rest and watch his pack run the thawing Arctic valley.

They plunge and turn. They fight the mighty caribou that struck young Roko with his hoof and wounded him. He jumped between the beast and Kiglo, leader of the Toklat pack. Young Roko spun and fell. Hooves, paws, and teeth roared over him. And then his pack and the beast were gone.

Gravely injured, Roko pulls himself toward the shelter rock. Weakness overcomes him. He stops. He and his pack are thin and hungry. This is the season of starvation. The winter's harvest has been taken. The produce of spring has not begun.

Young Roko glances down the valley. He droops his head and stiffens his tail to signal to his pack that he is badly hurt. Winds wail. A frigid blast picks up long shawls of snow and drapes them between young Roko and his pack. And so his message is not read.

A raven scouting Toklat Ridge sees Roko's signal. "Kong, kong, kong," he bells—death is coming to the ridge; there will be flesh and bone for all. His voice rolls out across the valley. It penetrates the rocky cracks where the Toklat ravens rest. One by one they hear and spread their wings. They beat their way to Toklat Ridge. They alight upon the snow and walk behind the wounded wolf.

"Kong," they toll[2] with keen excitement, for the raven clan is hungry, too. "Kong, kong"—there will be flesh and bone for all.

Roko snarls and hurries toward the shelter rock. A cloud of snow envelops him. He limps in blinding whiteness now.

A ghostly presence flits around. "Hahahahahahaha," the white fox states—death is coming to the Ridge. Roko smells the fox tagging at his heels.

The cloud whirls off. Two golden eyes look up at Roko. The snowy owl has heard the ravens and joined the deathwatch.

---

1. **Toklat Ridge** the top of a mountain located in Alaska's Denali National Park and Preserve.
2. **toll** (tōl) *v.* announce.

Roko limps along. The ravens walk. The white fox leaps. The snowy owl flies and hops along the rim of Toklat Ridge. Roko stops. Below the ledge out on the flats the musk-ox herd is circling. They form a ring and all face out, a fort of heads and horns and fur that sweeps down to their hooves. Their circle means to Roko that an enemy is present. He squints and smells the wind. It carries scents of thawing ice, broken grass—and earth. The grizzly bear is up! He has awakened from his winter's sleep. A craving need for flesh will drive him.

Roko sees the shelter rock. He strains to reach it. He stumbles. The ravens move in closer. The white fox boldly walks beside him. "Hahaha," he yaps. The snowy owl flies ahead, alights, and waits.

The grizzly hears the eager fox and rises on his flat hind feet. He twists his powerful neck and head. His great paws dangle at his chest. He sees the animal procession and hears the ravens' knell[3] of death. Dropping to all fours, he joins the march up Toklat Ridge.

Roko stops; his breath comes hard. A raven alights upon his back and picks the open wound. Roko snaps. The raven flies and circles back. The white fox nips at Roko's toes. The snowy owl inches closer. The grizzly bear, still dulled by sleep, stumbles onto Toklat Ridge.

Only yards from the shelter rock, Roko falls.

Instantly the ravens mob him. They scream and peck and stab at his eyes. The white fox leaps upon his wound. The snowy owl sits and waits.

Young Roko struggles to his feet. He bites the ravens. Snaps the fox. And lunges at the stoic[4] owl. He turns and warns the grizzly bear. Then he bursts into a run and falls against the shelter rock. The wounded wolf wedges down between the rock and barren ground. Now protected on three sides, he turns and faces all his foes.

The ravens step a few feet closer. The fox slides toward him on his belly. The snowy owl blinks and waits, and on the ridge rim roars the hungry grizzly bear.

Roko growls.

The sun comes up. Far across the Toklat Valley, Roko hears his pack's "hunt's end" song. The music wails and sobs, wilder than the bleating wind. The hunt song ends. Next comes the roll call. Each member of the Toklat pack barks to say that he is home and well.

---

3. knell (nel) *n.* mournful sound, like a slowly ringing bell—usually indicating a death.

4. stoic (stō ik) *adj.* calm and unaffected by hardship.

"Kiglo here," Roko hears his leader bark. There is a pause. It is young Roko's turn. He cannot lift his head to answer: the pack is silent. The leader starts the count once more. "Kiglo here."—a pause. Roko cannot answer.

The wounded wolf whimpers softly. A mindful raven hears. "Kong, kong, kong," he tolls—this is the end. His booming sounds across the valley. The wolf pack hears the raven's message that something is dying. They know it is Roko, who has not answered roll call.

The hours pass. The wind slams snow on Toklat Ridge. Massive clouds blot out the sun. In their gloom Roko sees the deathwatch move in closer. Suddenly he hears the musk-oxen thundering into their circle. The ice cracks as the grizzly leaves. The ravens burst into the air. The white fox runs. The snowy owl flaps to the top of the shelter rock. And Kiglo rounds the knoll.

In his mouth he carries meat. He drops it close to Roko's head and wags his tail excitedly. Roko licks Kiglo's chin to honor him. Then Kiglo puts his mouth around Roko's nose. This gesture says "I am your leader." And by mouthing Roko, he binds him and all the wolves together.

The wounded wolf wags his tail. Kiglo trots away.

Already Roko's wound feels better. He gulps the food and feels his strength return. He shatters bone, flesh, and gristle and shakes the scraps out on the snow. The hungry ravens swoop upon them. The white fox snatches up a bone. The snowy owl gulps down flesh and fur. And Roko wags his tail and watches.

For days Kiglo brings young Roko food. He **gnashes**, gorges, and shatters bits upon the snow.

A purple sandpiper winging north sees ravens, owl, and fox. And he drops in upon the feast. The long-tailed jaeger gull flies down and joins the crowd on Toklat Ridge. Roko wags his tail.

One dawn he moves his wounded leg. He stretches it and pulls himself into the sunlight. He walks—he romps. He runs in circles. He leaps and plays with chunks of ice. Suddenly he stops. The "hunt's end" song rings out. Next comes the roll call.

"Kiglo here."

"Roko here," he barks out strongly.

The pack is silent.

"Kiglo here," the leader repeats.

"Roko here."

Across the distance comes the sound of whoops and yips and barks and howls. They fill the dawn with celebration. And Roko prances down the Ridge.

Close Reading Activities

Read

Comprehension: **Key Ideas and Details**

1. (a) How was Roko injured? **(b) Analyze:** What actions does Roko take to save himself?

2. (a) How does Kiglo learn that Roko is hurt? **(b) Infer:** What does this evidence show about how wolves take care of pack members?

3. Summarize: Write a brief, objective summary of the story. Cite story details in your writing.

Text Analysis: **Craft and Structure**

4. (a) What are some specific words the author uses to describe Roko and his actions? **(b) Infer:** What information do these words suggest about Roko?

5. (a) Explain: What is the main conflict in the story? **(b) Interpret:** How is this conflict resolved?

6. (a) Describe: How does the author describe the setting? Cite specific details from the text. **(b) Apply:** How does the story's setting contribute to the conflict?

7. (a) List two examples that show how the wolves help each other in this story. **(b) Synthesize:** What insight can you gain from the wolves' behavior?

Connections: **Integration of Knowledge and Ideas**

Discuss

In a **small-group discussion,** share your ideas about where in the story the climax occurs. Use evidence from the text to support your main points.

Research

Jean Craighead George once spent a summer in Alaska, observing wolf packs and learning how they communicate. Briefly research the structure of wolf society, including: **(a)** pecking order; **(b)** the care and education of pups; **(c)** communication.

Take notes as you perform your research. Then, write an **explanation** of how George's depiction of wolf behavior in "The Wounded Wolf" compares with scientists' findings on this topic.

Write

Reread the story to identify ways in which Roko and the other animals behave like humans. Then, write a **comparison-and-contrast essay** in which you describe ways in which the animals are similar to humans and ways in which they are different. Cite details from the story to support your analysis.

> **Is conflict always bad?**
>
> Consider the conflicts between Roko and the forces of nature that oppose him. Would the story have had a happy ending if George had written it from another animal's point of view? Explain.

"If there is **no struggle**,
there is **no progress**."

—**Frederick Douglass**

CHARACTERS AND CONFLICT

As you read the stories in this section, explore ways in which the authors bring to life various characters who struggle to overcome conflicts. The quotation on the opposite page will help start your thinking about ways in which people triumph even in difficult situations.

◀ **CRITICAL VIEWING** What struggle might the person in this photograph be facing? Can dealing with struggles enhance a person's life? Explain.

READINGS IN PART 2

SHORT STORY
Stray
Cynthia Rylant (p. 20)

SHORT STORY
The Tail
Joyce Hansen (p. 30)

SHORT STORY
Zlateh the Goat
Isaac Bashevis Singer
(p. 46)

SHORT STORY
The Circuit
Francisco Jiménez (p. 60)

CLOSE READING TOOL

Use the **Close Reading Tool** to practice the strategies you learn in this unit.

Elements of a Short Story

A short story is a brief work of fiction that contains **plot, characters, setting,** and **theme.**

A **short story** is a brief fictional narrative that can usually be read in one sitting. Although it is short, it is a complete work featuring the same basic elements as longer works of fiction.

Plot is the sequence of events in a story. It consists of a series of scenes or episodes that are linked to each other. Early scenes advance the plot by bringing about later ones.

Conflict is a problem or struggle between opposing forces.

- An **internal conflict** takes place in the mind of a character. The character struggles to make a decision, take an action, or overcome an obstacle.
- An **external conflict** is a conflict in which a character struggles against an outside force, such as nature or another character.

Characters are the people or animals who take part in the action of a story. An author brings a character to life through **characterization**—the art of creating and developing a character.

- A **character's traits,** or qualities, help readers understand the character and his or her actions.
- A **character's motives** are the reasons for his or her actions.

Setting is the time and place of the story's action. Setting can create a specific atmosphere or **mood** in a story. It may even relate directly to the story's conflict.

Theme is the central insight expressed in a short story. It might be stated directly or hinted at through the words and actions of the characters.

Short stories are made up of several key elements.

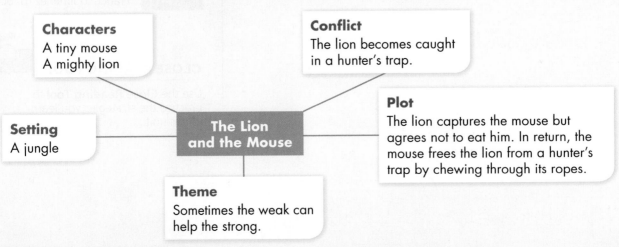

Characters
A tiny mouse
A mighty lion

Conflict
The lion becomes caught in a hunter's trap.

Plot
The lion captures the mouse but agrees not to eat him. In return, the mouse frees the lion from a hunter's trap by chewing through its ropes.

Setting
A jungle

The Lion and the Mouse

Theme
Sometimes the weak can help the strong.

Structure in Short Stories

A short story must grab a reader's attention right away. Because the work is brief, every part of the story must move the action forward. The **structure** of a short story is the way it is put together. A story's plot is structured in a way that helps the story progress. These elements make up the basic structure of a plot:

- **Exposition** is the story's setup. This part of the plot introduces the characters, setting, and basic situation. The story's conflict is usually introduced in the exposition.
- **Conflict** is the story's central problem. It might involve a struggle between characters, a struggle between a character and an outside force, or a struggle within the mind of a character.
- **Rising action** is made up of events and complications that increase the tension in the story. This tension builds to a climax.
- **Climax** is the high point of the story—its most intense, exciting, or important part. It is the point at which the story's outcome becomes clear.
- **Falling action** sets up the story's ending. It is the part of the story in which events are settled.
- **Resolution** is the final outcome of the story. Usually, a story's conflict is settled in the resolution. In some stories, however, the conflict is left unsettled.

In the best short stories, readers want to find out what will happen next and how the characters will respond or change.

As you read a short story, notice how particular words, sentences, and events fit into the structure and help you understand the setting, plot, and theme.

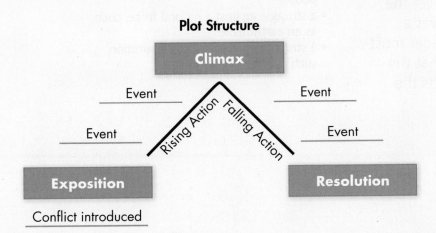

Plot Structure

Climax

Event

Rising Action   Falling Action

Event

Event

Event

Exposition

Resolution

Conflict introduced

Analyzing Structure, Conflict, and Characterization

Characters respond and change as a short story's plot unfolds.

The best short stories are **structured,** or put together, in ways that build readers' interest and move the action forward. In a good short story, each scene or episode has a purpose and contributes to the overall impact of the story. For example, the details in a specific scene can develop a key element, such as **setting.**

> ### Example: Scene Developing Setting
>
> The long, narrow hallway was completely deserted. I squinted in the dim light, struggling to see the door at the far end. The musty dampness sent a shiver through my body as I put one unsteady foot in front of the other.

In the example above, the words and sentences work together to develop the setting: a damp, dark, empty hallway. This scene also introduces another key story element. Notice that the narrator is *unsteady*. This detail indicates a possible **conflict,** or problem. Further details in the story will establish what specific conflict the narrator faces. Conflict moves a story forward because a reader must keep reading to find out what the problem is and how it affects the characters.

Types of Conflict As a short story progresses, scenes or events in the plot contribute to the conflict and its **resolution**—the way in which the conflict is settled. Conflicts may be *internal* or *external*. There are different types of external conflict, such as conflict with nature and conflict with society. Review the examples in the chart below. As you read a variety of short stories, you will find that some stories have several conflicts, which are usually related to each other.

> ### Types of Conflict
>
> **Internal Conflict:** a problem that takes place in a character's mind
> **Examples:**
> - a fight to overcome a feeling, like insecurity
> - a struggle to do the right thing
> - a struggle to choose between two courses of action
>
> **External Conflict:** a struggle against an outside force
> **Examples:**
> - a fight or argument between two people
> - a struggle against a natural force, such as an earthquake
> - a struggle against a social institution, such as a law or a tradition

Characterization A key part of the experience of reading a short story is getting to know the characters and finding out how they respond to the conflicts they face. Characterization is the method an author uses to develop characters and reveal their **traits,** or qualities.

There are two types of characterization. With **direct characterization,** the author makes statements that directly describe what the character is like.

Example: Direct Characterization
Mariah is the bravest girl in the sixth grade. She may be pale and tiny, but nothing scares her—not spiders, not huge barking dogs, not even mean old Mr. Jonas down the block.

With **indirect characterization,** the author reveals a character through that character's words and actions or through the words and actions of other characters.

Example: Indirect Characterization
I don't care what those young fools say; I will not leave this place. I have lived on this mountain since that roaring highway was a dirt road. My body may be bent, but I will stand firm.

Characters and Conflict As characters react to the conflicts in a story, their responses help advance the plot as well as fuel their own growth and development as characters. The example that follows describes a story about a young boy.

Notice how each of the boy's actions brings about a new development in the plot. In turn, each new development causes a change in the boy's actions or attitude.

Scene: A boy stays up late playing video games.

↓

Scene: The next morning, he remembers he has a math test. He fears he will do poorly because he did not study.

↓

Scene: The boy tells his mother he is sick so that she will let him stay home from school.

↓

Scene: The boy's mother says she is sorry he is sick, because the family will have to cancel a surprise trip to a theme park the next day.

↓

Scene: The boy tells his mother he feels better and wants to go to school after all.

Characters and Theme Often, the changes a character undergoes are clues to the story's theme, or the insight the story conveys. For instance, in the example above, the story's theme might be stated like this: *It is always best to tell the truth.* As you read, pay close attention to clues in dialogue or description that might provide a window into a story's theme.

Building Knowledge

Meet the Author

As a child, **Cynthia Rylant** (b. 1954) never imagined that she would become a writer. "I always felt my life was too limited," she says. At age twenty-four, however, she found that her life did in fact contain the seeds of many stories. Her first book, *When I Was Young in the Mountains,* describes her childhood in the hills of West Virginia. Rylant lived with her grandparents for four years in a tiny house without plumbing. The hardships she experienced are reflected in some of her stories. Since her first book, Rylant has written more than sixty children's books. Unlike many writers, she writes by hand, not on a computer.

Is conflict always bad?

Explore the Big Question as you read "Stray." Take notes on ways in which the story explores conflict in its plot.

CLOSE READING FOCUS

Key Ideas and Details: **Make Predictions**

A **prediction** is a developing idea about what will happen next in a story. You can use your prior knowledge to help you make predictions. To do this, make connections between information you already know and details in the story. For example, if you have ever moved to a new neighborhood, you know that making new friends can be challenging. If the story tells you that a character is shy and has moved to a new neighborhood, you can combine what you know with the information in the story to predict that the character may not make friends easily.

Craft and Structure: **Plot**

One key element of short stories is **plot**—the arrangement of events in a story. Plot includes the following elements:

- **Exposition:** introduction of setting, characters, and situation
- **Conflict:** the story's central problem
- **Rising Action:** events that increase tension
- **Climax:** high point of the story, when the story's outcome becomes clear and changes in the characters become apparent
- **Falling Action:** events that follow the climax
- **Resolution:** the final outcome

Vocabulary

Copy the following words from "Stray" in your notebook. Which of the words are adverbs? What suffix do they share?

timidly	grudgingly	exhausted
trudged	ignore	starvation

CLOSE READING MODEL

The passage below is from Cynthia Rylant's short story "Stray." The annotations to the right of the passage show ways in which you can use close reading skills to make predictions and analyze plot.

from **"Stray"**

In January, a puppy wandered onto the property [1] of Mr. Amos Lacey and his wife, Mamie, and their daughter, Doris. Icicles hung three feet or more from the eaves of the houses, snowdrifts swallowed up automobiles [1] and the birds were so fluffed up they looked comic.

The puppy had been abandoned, [1] and it made its way down the road toward the Laceys' small house, its ears tucked, its tail between its legs, shivering.

Doris, whose school had been called off because of the snow, was out shoveling the cinderblock front steps when she spotted the pup on the road. [2] She set down the shovel.

"Hey! Come on!" she called.

The puppy stopped in the road, wagging its tail timidly, trembling with shyness and cold.

Doris trudged through the yard, went up the shoveled drive and met the dog.

"Come on, Pooch."

"Where did *that* come from?" Mrs. Lacey asked as soon as Doris put the dog down in the kitchen. [3]

Mr. Lacey was at the table, cleaning his fingernails with his pocketknife. The snow was keeping him home from his job at the warehouse.

"I don't know where it came from," he said mildly, "but I know for sure where it's going." [4]

Plot

1 The opening paragraphs describe a family home during a heavy snowfall. They also describe an abandoned puppy. This exposition introduces the situation that will set the plot in motion.

Make Predictions

2 Doris spots the abandoned puppy "shivering" in the cold. Based on your prior knowledge, you may predict that she will want to take the puppy home.

Make Predictions

3 Mrs. Lacey's first reaction to the dog is cautious. Based on her words—referring to the puppy as "that"—you might predict that she will not allow the puppy in her home.

Plot

4 At this point, three characters—a daughter and her parents—have been introduced. Each reacts differently to the dog. Their reactions hint at conflicts that will appear as the plot develops.

Stray

Cynthia Rylant

In January, a puppy wandered onto the property of Mr. Amos Lacey and his wife, Mamie, and their daughter, Doris. Icicles hung three feet or more from the eaves of houses, snowdrifts swallowed up automobiles and the birds were so fluffed up they looked comic.

The puppy had been abandoned, and it made its way down the road toward the Laceys' small house, its ears tucked, its tail between its legs, shivering.

Doris, whose school had been called off because of the snow, was out shoveling the cinderblock front steps when she spotted the pup on the road. She set down the shovel.

"Hey! Come on!" she called.

The puppy stopped in the road, wagging its tail timidly, trembling with shyness and cold.

Doris trudged through the yard, went up the shoveled drive and met the dog.

"Come on, Pooch."

"Where did *that* come from?" Mrs. Lacey asked as soon as Doris put the dog down in the kitchen.

Mr. Lacey was at the table, cleaning his fingernails with his pocketknife. The snow was keeping him home from his job at the warehouse.

"I don't know where it came from," he said mildly, "but I know for sure where it's going."

Doris hugged the puppy hard against her. She said nothing.

Because the roads would be too bad for travel for many days, Mr. Lacey couldn't get out to take the puppy to the pound[1] in the city right away. He agreed to let it sleep in the basement while Mrs. Lacey grudgingly let Doris feed it table scraps. The woman was sensitive about throwing out food.

By the looks of it, Doris figured the puppy was about six months old, and on its way to being a big dog. She thought it might have some shepherd in it. •

Four days passed and the puppy did not complain. It never cried in the night or howled at the wind. It didn't tear up everything in the basement. It wouldn't even follow Doris up the basement steps unless it was invited.

It was a good dog.

Several times Doris had opened the door in the kitchen that led to the basement and the puppy had been there, all stretched out, on the top step. Doris knew it had wanted some company and that it had lain against the door,

____

1. **pound** (pound) *n.* animal shelter.

◄ **Vocabulary**
timidly (tim′ id lē) *adv.* in a way that shows fear or shyness

trudged (trudj′d) *v.* walked as if tired or with effort

grudgingly (gruj′ iŋ lē) *adv.* in an unwilling or resentful way

Make Predictions
Based on what you know about big dogs, do you predict that Mr. Lacey will change his mind?

Plot
What action up until this point in the story suggests a conflict? Explain.

Comprehension
How do Doris's parents feel about the puppy?

Critical Viewing ▲
Why might a girl like Doris become attached to a dog like this one?

Vocabulary ▶
ignore (ig nôr′) v.
pay no attention to

**Spiral Review
CHARACTER**
What do Doris's failed efforts to avoid crying tell you about her character?

listening to the talk in the kitchen, smelling the food, being a part of things. It always wagged its tail, eyes all sleepy, when she found it there.

Even after a week had gone by, Doris didn't name the dog. She knew her parents wouldn't let her keep it, that her father made so little money any pets were out of the question, and that the pup would definitely go to the pound when the weather cleared.

Still, she tried talking to them about the dog at dinner one night.

"She's a good dog, isn't she?" Doris said, hoping one of them would agree with her.

Her parents glanced at each other and went on eating.

"She's not much trouble," Doris added. "I like her." She smiled at them, but they continued to ignore her.

"I figure she's real smart," Doris said to her mother. "I could teach her things."

Mrs. Lacey just shook her head and stuffed a forkful of sweet potato in her mouth. Doris fell silent, praying the weather would never clear.

But on Saturday, nine days after the dog had arrived, the sun was shining and the roads were plowed. Mr. Lacey opened up the trunk of his car and came into the house.

Doris was sitting alone in the living room, hugging a pillow and rocking back and forth on the edge of a chair. She was trying not to cry but she was not strong enough. Her face was wet and red, her eyes full of distress.

Mrs. Lacey looked into the room from the doorway.

"Mama," Doris said in a small voice. "Please."

Mrs. Lacey shook her head.

"You know we can't afford a dog, Doris. You try to act more grown-up about this."

Doris pressed her face into the pillow.

Outside, she heard the trunk of the car slam shut, one of the doors open and close, the old engine cough and choke and finally start up.

"Daddy," she whispered. "Please."

She heard the car travel down the road, and, though it was early afternoon, she could do nothing but go to her bed. She cried herself to sleep, and her dreams were full of searching and searching for things lost. ●

It was nearly night when she finally woke up. Lying there, like stone, still exhausted, she wondered if she would ever in her life have anything. She stared at the wall for a while.

But she started feeling hungry, and she knew she'd have to make herself get out of bed and eat some dinner. She wanted not to go into the kitchen, past the basement door. She wanted not to face her parents.

But she rose up heavily.

Her parents were sitting at the table, dinner over, drinking coffee. They looked at her when she came in, but she kept her head down. No one spoke.

Doris made herself a glass of powdered milk and drank it all down. Then she picked up a cold biscuit and started out of the room.

"You'd better feed that mutt before it dies of starvation," Mr. Lacey said.

Doris turned around.

"What?"

"I said, you'd better feed your dog. I figure it's looking for you."

Doris put her hand to her mouth.

"You didn't take her?" she asked.

"Oh, I took her all right," her father

"Mama," Doris said in a small voice. "Please."

◄ **Vocabulary**
exhausted (eg zôst′ əd) *adj.* very tired

starvation (stär vā′ shən) *n.* state of extreme hunger

Comprehension
Why does Doris not want to get out of bed to eat?

Plot
What is surprising about the resolution of the conflict?

answered. "Worst looking place I've ever seen. Ten dogs to a cage. Smell was enough to knock you down. And they give an animal six days to live. Then they kill it with some kind of a shot."

Doris stared at her father.

"I wouldn't leave an *ant* in that place," he said. "So I brought the dog back."

Mrs. Lacey was smiling at him and shaking her head as if she would never, ever, understand him.

Mr. Lacey sipped his coffee.

"Well," he said, "are you going to feed it or not?"

Language Study

Vocabulary The words below appear in "Stray." Rewrite each sentence using one of the words. Your sentence should express a meaning similar to that of the original sentence.

timidly   trudged   grudgingly   ignore   exhausted

1. The boys pay no attention to the *No Swimming* sign.
2. Kay forces herself to congratulate the winner.
3. Juan blushes as he greets the new teacher.
4. Lucy was very tired after playing soccer for two hours.
5. Betty walked to school with slow, heavy steps.

WORD STUDY

The **Latin suffix -ation** changes a verb to a noun. It means "the condition or process of." In this story, Doris's dad says Doris should feed the dog or it will die of **starvation**, the condition of being starved.

Word Study

Part A Explain how the **Latin suffix -ation** contributes to the meaning of *alteration* and *realization*. Consult a dictionary if necessary.

Part B Use the context of the sentence and your knowledge of the suffix *-ation* to help you answer each question.

1. When might you ask for a friend's *recommendation*?
2. Why is *experimentation* important in science?

Literary Analysis

Key Ideas and Details

1. (a) What does Doris do when her father first tells her that she cannot keep the dog? **(b) Analyze:** Why does Doris react in this way?

2. Make Predictions The example in the chart on the right shows how you can use prior knowledge and details from the story to make a prediction. Use a similar chart to show how you make the following predictions. **(a)** What will Doris's parents say about the puppy? **(b)** What will her father do when the weather clears?

3. Make Predictions What characteristics, or personality traits, does Doris notice in the dog? How does the description of these traits help you predict the story's resolution?

Prior Knowledge
Puppies are cute.
(a)
(b)
Details From Story
The puppy is abandoned.
(a)
(b)
Prediction
Doris will want to keep it.
(a)
(b)

Craft and Structure

4. Plot (a) What is the main conflict in this story? **(b)** At what point in the story is the conflict evident? Cite details to support your response.

5. Plot What is the climax, or high point, in the story? Explain your answer.

6. Plot In what way is the snowstorm important to the plot and the resolution of the story?

Integration of Knowledge and Ideas

7. (a) Paraphrase: In the text, find Mr. Lacey's description of the pound and then restate it in your own words. **(b) Analyze:** Why does Mr. Lacey change his mind about keeping the dog?

8. (a) Make a Judgment: Do you think that Doris should have made a stronger case for keeping the dog? Why or why not? **(b) Speculate:** What could Doris do in the future to show her father that he was right about keeping the dog?

9. **Is conflict always bad?** Did any of the characters grow or change in a positive way as a result of the conflict in this story? Support your answer with specific details from the text.

ACADEMIC VOCABULARY

As you write and speak about "Stray," use the words related to conflict that you explored on page 3 of this text.

Conventions: Common, Proper, and Possessive Nouns

A **common noun** names any one of a group of people, places, or things. A **proper noun** names a particular person, place, or thing. A **possessive noun** shows belonging and is signaled by an apostrophe.

Common nouns are not capitalized unless they are at the beginning of a sentence or in a title. **Proper nouns** are always capitalized. **Possessive nouns** that are *singular* end in an apostrophe followed by the letter s ('s). **Possessive nouns** that are *plural* usually end in the letter s followed by an apostrophe (s').

Common Nouns	Proper Nouns	Possessive Nouns
Commuters drive **cars** to the **city** and park them on the **street**.	**Ms. Ryan** drove the **Cadillac** to **Miami** and parked it on **Market Street**.	The Cadillac is not **Ms. Ryan's**; it is her **parents'** car.

Practice A
Identify the noun(s) in each sentence and indicate whether they are *common, proper,* or *possessive*.

1. The stray puppy's sad face was pitiful to see.
2. Mr. Lacey planned to take the puppy to the pound.
3. Doris was upset by Mama's words.
4. The pound was a dismal place.

Reading Application In "Stray," find three common nouns, three proper nouns, and one possessive noun.

Practice B
Identify the proper noun in each sentence. Then, rewrite the sentence using the possessive form of that noun, without changing the sentence's meaning.

1. Doris lived in a small house.
2. The love of the Laceys for each other was clear to see.
3. The puppy belonged to Doris.
4. The opinion held by Mr. Lacey changed.

Writing Application In "Stray," find three sentences with proper nouns. Rewrite the sentences using common nouns. Each sentence you choose should have a different proper noun.

Writing to Sources

Explanatory Text Write a **list of reasons** Doris could give to her parents explaining why she should be allowed to keep the puppy.

- Reread the story, writing down specific details that show why the puppy would make a good pet.
- State your claim in a brief introduction. Then, list the reasons that support your claim.
- Use formal language to ensure that your ideas will be considered seriously. Write in complete sentences and do not use slang.
- With a small group of classmates, take turns reading your lists aloud. Ask your group to give feedback on whether or not you were successful in supporting your reasons with evidence from the story.

Grammar Application Correctly capitalize and punctuate the proper and possessive nouns in your list.

Research and Technology

Build and Present Knowledge With a group, create a **brochure** about puppy care that Doris could use to help her raise her dog. First, make a list of questions about the topic. Then, search the Internet to find answers.

- Use key words like these to search the Internet: *feeding a new puppy, training a puppy, puppy care, puppy health.*
- Include the following sections in your brochure: "Feeding Your Puppy," "Puppy Training Tips," "Happy, Healthy Puppies." Add other sections if you have ideas and find useful information.
- Assign everyone in your group a specific job, such as writing a section, revising and editing a section, or drawing illustrations.
- Make copies of your brochure to share with your classmates.

Meet the Author

Joyce Hansen (b. 1942) was born and raised in New York City and went to college there. She then spent twenty-two years teaching in the city's public schools. Her first three novels—*The Gift-Giver, Yellow Bird and Me,* and *Home Boy*—are all set in New York and focus on the lives of young people. Hansen, now a full-time writer, believes that writing for young people carries "a special responsibility." Four of her historical novels have earned the Coretta Scott King Honor Book Award.

Is conflict always bad?

Explore the Big Question as you read "The Tail." Take notes on ways in which the story explores the nature of conflict.

CLOSE READING FOCUS

Key Ideas and Details: **Make Inferences**

When you **make inferences**, you make logical assumptions about something that is not stated directly in the text. To make inferences, use details that the writer provides.

Example: Arnie *ran* to the mailbox to see if the package from his aunt had *finally* arrived.

• You can infer from the word *finally* that Arnie has been waiting to get the package.

• You can infer from *ran* that he is eager to get the package.

Craft and Structure: **Characterization**

Characterization is the way writers develop characters and reveal their traits, or qualities.

• With **direct characterization**, a writer makes straightforward statements about a character. For example, "Ron is honest."

• With **indirect characterization**, a writer presents a character's thoughts, words, and actions and reveal what others say and think about the character.

Once you analyze the qualities of a story's main characters, think about ways in which those qualities affect the plot of the story and its outcome. For example, a character's stubbornness may cause him to come into conflict with others in a story.

Vocabulary

You will encounter the following words in "The Tail." In your notebook, list the words in the order of how well you know them, writing the most familiar word first. As you read, record the definitions next to each word.

vow	routine	mauled
anxious	gnawing	spasm

CLOSE READING MODEL

The passage below is from Joyce Hansen's short story "The Tail."
The annotations to the right of the passage show ways in which
you can use close reading skills to make inferences and analyze
characterization.

from **"The Tail"**

Junior turned to me and raised his right hand.
"This is a vow of obedience." He looked up at the
ceiling. "I promise to do whatever Tasha says." [1]

"What do you know about vows?" I asked.

"I saw it on television. A man—"

"Shut up, Junior. I don't feel like hearing about
some television show. It's too early in the
morning." [2]

I went into the kitchen to start cleaning, when the
downstairs bell rang. "Answer the intercom, Junior.
If it's Naomi, tell her to wait for me on the stoop," [3]
I called out. I knew that it was Naomi, ready to
start our big, fun summer. After a few minutes the
bell rang again.

"Junior!" I yelled. "Answer the intercom."

The bell rang again and I ran into the living
room. Junior was sitting on the couch, looking at
cartoons. "What's wrong with you? Why won't
you answer the bell?"

He looked at me as if I were crazy. "You told me to
shut up. I told you I'd do everything you say." [4]

Make Inferences

1 A vow is a solemn promise. This
detail might lead you to infer that
Junior is very serious about obeying
Tasha.

Characterization

2 The narrator interrupts Junior
and speaks rudely to him. These
examples of indirect characterization
show that Tasha is impatient and not
interested in what Junior has to say.

Make Inferences

3 The text mentions *the downstairs
bell, the intercom,* and *the stoop.*
Based on these details, you might
infer that the characters live in an
apartment building.

Characterization

4 His words and actions show that
Junior is clever and full of mischief.
He might not have been serious
about obeying Tasha after all.

The TAIL
Joyce Hansen

It began as the worst summer of my life.

The evening before the first day of summer vacation, my mother broke the bad news to me. I was in the kitchen washing dishes and dreaming about the wonderful things my friends and I would be doing for two whole months— practicing for the annual double-dutch[1] contest, which we would definitely win; going to the roller skating rink, the swimming pool, the beach; and sleeping as late in the morning as I wanted to.

Critical Viewing ▲
What can you infer about the relationship between these two characters? Explain.

---

1. **double-dutch** a jump-rope game in which two ropes are used at the same time.

"Tasha," my ma broke into my happy thoughts, "your father and I decided that you're old enough now to take on certain responsibilities."

My heart came to a sudden halt. "Responsibilities?"

"Yes. You do know what that word means, don't you?"

I nodded, watching her dice an onion into small, perfect pieces.

"You're thirteen going on fourteen and your father and I decided that you're old enough to watch Junior this summer, because I'm going to start working again."

"Oh, no!" I broke the dish with a crash. "Not that, Mama." Junior is my seven-year-old brother and has been following me like a tail ever since he learned how to walk. And to make matters worse, there are no kids Junior's age on our block. Everyone is either older or younger than he is.

I'd rather be in school than minding Junior all day. I could've cried.

"Natasha! There won't be a dish left in this house. You're not going to spend all summer ripping and roaring. You'll baby-sit Junior."

"But, Ma," I said, "it'll be miserable. That's not fair. All summer with Junior. I won't be able to play with my friends."

She wiped her hands on her apron. "Life ain't always fair."

I knew she'd say that.

"You'll still be able to play with your friends," she continued, "but Junior comes first. He is your responsibility. We're a family and we all have to help out." •

Mama went to work that next morning. Junior and I both stood by the door as she gave her last-minute instructions. Junior held her hand and stared up at her with an innocent look in his bright brown eyes, which everyone thought were so cute. Dimples decorated his round cheeks as he smiled and nodded at me every time Ma gave me an order. I knew he was just waiting for her to leave so he could torment me.

"Tasha, I'm depending on you. Don't leave the block."

"Yes, Ma."

"No company."

"Not even Naomi? She's my best friend."

Make Inferences
Based on her words and actions, how does Tasha feel about baby-sitting her brother?

Comprehension
Why is Tasha unhappy with her mother's request?

Characterization
In this dialogue, does the author use direct or indirect characterization to develop Tasha's personality? Explain.

"No company when your father and I are not home."

"Yes, Ma."

"Don't let Junior hike in the park."

"Yes, Ma."

"Make yourself and Junior a sandwich for lunch."

"Yes, Ma."

"I'll be calling you at twelve, so you'd better be in here fixing lunch. I don't want you all eating junk food all day long."

"Yes, Ma."

"Don't ignore Junior."

"Yes, Ma."

"Clean the breakfast dishes."

"Yes, Ma."

"Don't open the door to strangers."

"Yes, Ma."

Characterization
Based on this dialogue, how would you describe Tasha's mother? Explain.

Then she turned to Junior. "Now you, young man. You are to listen to your sister."

"Yes, Mommy," he sang out.

"Don't give her a hard time. Show me what a big boy you can be."

"Mommy, I'll do whatever Tasha say."

She kissed us both good-bye and left. I wanted to cry. A whole summer with Junior.

Junior turned to me and raised his right hand. "This is a **vow** of obedience." He looked up at the ceiling. "I promise to do whatever Tasha says."

Vocabulary ▶
vow (vou) *n.*
promise or pledge

"What do you know about vows?" I asked.

"I saw it on television. A man—"

"Shut up, Junior. I don't feel like hearing about some television show. It's too early in the morning."

I went into the kitchen to start cleaning, when the downstairs bell rang. "Answer the intercom,[2] Junior. If it's Naomi, tell her to wait for me on the stoop," I called out. I knew that it was Naomi, ready to start our big, fun summer. After a few minutes the bell rang again.

"Junior!" I yelled. "Answer the intercom."

The bell rang again and I ran into the living room. Junior was sitting on the couch, looking at cartoons. "What's wrong with you? Why won't you answer the bell?"

---

2. **intercom** *n.* a communication system used in apartment buildings.

He looked at me as if I were crazy. "You told me to shut up. I told you I'd do everything you say."

I pulled my hair. "See, you're bugging me already. Do something to help around here."

I pressed the intercom on the wall. "That you, Naomi?"

"Yeah."

"I'll be down in a minute. Wait for me out front."

"Okay."

I quickly washed the dishes. I couldn't believe how messed up my plans were. Suddenly there was a loud blast from the living room. I was so startled that I dropped a plate and it smashed to smithereens. Ma will kill me, I thought as I ran to the living room. It sounded like whole pieces of furniture were being sucked into the vacuum cleaner.

"Junior," I screamed over the racket, "you have it on too high."

He couldn't even hear me. I turned it off myself.

"What's wrong?"

"Ma vacuumed the living room last night. It doesn't need cleaning."

"You told me to do something to help," he whined.

I finished the dishes in a hurry so that I could leave the apartment before Junior bugged out again. ●

I was so anxious to get outside that we ran down the four flights of stairs instead of waiting for the elevator. Junior clutched some comic books and his checkers game. He put his Mets baseball cap on backward as usual. Naomi sat on the stoop and Junior plopped right next to her like they were the best of friends.

"Hi, cutey." She smiled at him, turning his cap to the front of his head the way it was supposed to be.

"What are we going to do today, Naomi?" he asked.

Make Inferences
Why do you think Tasha pulls her hair?

◄ **Vocabulary**
anxious (aŋkˊshəs) *adj.* eager

Comprehension
What does Junior do to irritate Tasha?

"Junior, you're not going to be in our faces all day," I snapped at him.

"Mama said you have to watch me. So I have to be in your face."

"You're baby-sitting, Tasha?" Naomi asked.

"Yeah." I told her the whole story.

"Aw, that's not so bad. At least you don't have to stay in the house. Junior will be good. Right, cutey?"

He grinned as she pinched his cheeks.

"See, you think he's cute because you don't have no pesty little brother or sister to watch," I grumbled.

"You ready for double-dutch practice?" she asked. "Yvonne and Keisha are going to meet us in the playground."

"Mama said we have to stay on the block," Junior answered before I could even open my mouth.

"No one's talking to you, Junior." I pulled Naomi up off the stoop. "I promised my mother we'd stay on the block, but the playground is just across the street. I can see the block from there."

"It's still not the block," Junior mumbled as we raced across the street.

We always went over to the playground to jump rope. The playground was just by the entrance to the park. There was a lot of space for us to do our fancy steps. The park was like a big green mountain in the middle of Broadway.

I'd figure out a way to keep Junior from telling that we really didn't stay on the block. "Hey, Tasha, can I go inside the park and look for caves?" People said that if you went deep inside the park, there were caves that had been used centuries ago when Native Americans still lived in northern Manhattan.

"No, Ma said no hiking in the park."

"She said no leaving the block, too, and you left the block."

"Look how close we are to the block. I mean, we can even see it. You could get lost inside the park."

"I'm going to tell Ma you didn't stay on the block."

Characterization
What character trait does Tasha show by deciding to go to the playground?

"Okay, me and Naomi will hike with you up to the Cloisters later." That's a museum that sits at the top of the park, overlooking the Hudson River. "Now read your comic books."

"Will you play checkers with me too?"

"You know I hate checkers. Leave me alone." I spotted Keisha and Yvonne walking into the playground. All of us wore shorts and sneakers.

Junior tagged behind me and Naomi as we went to meet them. "Remember you're supposed to be watching me," he said.

"How could I forget."

The playground was crowded. Swings were all taken and the older boys played stickball. Some little kids played in the sandboxes.

Keisha and Yvonne turned and Naomi and I jumped together, practicing a new **routine**. We were so good that some of the boys in the stickball game watched us. A few elderly people stopped to look at us too. We had an audience, so I really showed off—spinning and doing a lot of fancy footwork.

Suddenly Junior jumped in the ropes with us and people laughed and clapped.

Make Inferences
What are Tasha's feelings as the girls begin to jump?

◀ **Vocabulary**
routine (rōō tēn´) *n.* usual way in which something is done

Comprehension
What does Junior threaten to tell his mother?

◀ **Critical Viewing**
Why might Tasha want to spend her summer in a park like this one?

Safety Connection

Pet Precautions Americans love their pets and often think of their dogs and cats as members of their families. However, not all animals are safe to approach. If you confront a stray dog, consider it dangerous until you know better. Follow these safety guidelines:

- Approach the dog slowly and gently and keep your face away from its face.
- If a dog is chasing you, stop running because it encourages the animal to chase you.
- Do not touch a dog that is growling, showing its teeth, or barking excitedly.
- Do not look an aggressive dog in the eye. Instead, back away slowly.

Connect to the Literature

Why might Tasha forget these rules as she searches for Junior?

"Junior!" I screamed. "Get out of here!"

"Remember, your job is to watch me." He grinned. My foot slipped and all three of us got tangled in the ropes and fell.

"Your feet are too big!" Junior yelled.

Everybody roared. I was too embarrassed. I tried to grab him, but he got away from me. "Get lost," I hollered after him as he ran toward the swings.

I tried to forget how stupid I must've looked and went back to the ropes. I don't know how long we'd been jumping when suddenly a little kid ran by us yelling, "There's a wild dog loose up there!" He pointed to the steps that led deep inside the park.

People had been saying for years that a pack of abandoned dogs who'd turned wild lived in the park, but no one ever really saw them.

We forgot about the kid and kept jumping. Then one of the boys our age who'd been playing stickball came over to us. "We're getting out of here," he said. "A big yellow dog with red eyes just bit a kid."

I took the rope from Yvonne. It was time for me and Naomi to turn. "That's ridiculous. Who ever heard of a yellow dog with red eyes?"

Naomi stopped turning. "Dogs look all kind of ways. Especially wild dogs. I'm leaving."

"Me too," Yvonne said.

Keisha was already gone. No one was in the swings or the sandboxes. I didn't even see the old men who usually sat on the benches. "Guess we'd better get out of here too," I said. Then I realized that I didn't see Junior anywhere.

"Junior!" I shouted.

"Maybe he went home," Naomi said.

We dashed across the street. Our block was empty. Yvonne ran ahead of us and didn't stop until she reached her stoop. When I got to my stoop I expected to see Junior there, but no Junior.

"Maybe he went upstairs," Naomi said.

"I have the key. He can't get in the house."

"Maybe he went to the candy store?"

"He doesn't have any money, I don't think. But let's look."

We ran around the corner to the candy store, but no Junior.

As we walked back to the block, I remembered something.

"Oh, no, Naomi, I told him to get lost. And that's just what he did."

"He's probably hiding from us somewhere. You know how he likes to tease." She looked around as we walked up our block. "He might be hiding and watching us right now looking for him." She peeped behind parked cars, in doorways, and even opened the lid of a trash can.

"Junior," I called. "Junior!"

No answer. Only the sounds of birds and cars, sirens and a distant radio. I looked at the empty stoop where Junior should have been sitting. A part of me was gone and I had to find it. And another part of me would be gone if my mother found out I'd lost Junior.

I ran back toward the playground and Naomi followed me. "He's got to be somewhere right around here," she panted.

I ran past the playground and into the park. "Tasha, you're not going in there, are you? The dog."

I didn't answer her and began climbing the stone steps that wound around and through the park. Naomi's eyes stretched all over her face and she grabbed my arm. "It's dangerous up here!"

I turned around. "If you're scared, don't come. Junior's my only baby brother. Dear God," I said out loud, "please let me find him. I will play any kind of game he wants. I'll never yell at him again. I promise never to be mean to him again in my life!"

Naomi breathed heavily behind me. "I don't think Junior would go this far by himself."

I stopped and caught my breath. The trees were thick and the city street sounds were far away now.

"I know Junior. He's somewhere up here making believe he's the king of this mountain. Hey, Junior," I called, "I was just kidding. Don't get lost." We heard a rustling in the

Spiral Review
THEME What is one theme about brothers and sisters that might apply to the story so far?

Make Inferences
How does Tasha feel about Junior's disappearance? How can you tell?

Comprehension
Why is Tasha suddenly worried about Junior?

> "Oh, no, Naomi, I told him to get lost. And that's just what he did."

Vocabulary ▶
gnawing (nô´ iŋ) v.
biting and cutting
with the teeth

bushes and grabbed each other. "Probably just a bird," I
said, trying to sound brave.

As we climbed some more, I tried not to imagine a huge
yellow dog with red eyes gnawing at my heels.

The steps turned a corner and ended. Naomi screamed
and pointed up ahead. "What's that?"

I saw a big brown and gray monstrous thing with
tentacles reaching toward the sky, jutting out of the curve
in the path. I screamed and almost ran.

"What is that, Naomi?"

"I don't know."

"This is a park in the middle of Manhattan. It can't be
a bear or anything." I screamed to the top of my lungs,
"Junior!" Some birds flew out of a tree, but the thing
never moved.

All Naomi could say was, "Dogs, Tasha."

I found a stick. "I'm going up. You wait here. If you hear
growling and screaming, run and get some help." I couldn't
believe how brave I was. Anyway, that thing, whatever it
was, couldn't hurt me any more than my mother would if I
didn't find Junior.

"You sure, Tasha?"

"No sense in both of us being mauled," I said.

Vocabulary ▶
mauled (môld) v.
badly injured by
being attacked

I tipped lightly up the steps, holding the stick like a club.
When I was a few feet away from the thing, I crumpled to
the ground and laughed so hard that Naomi ran to me.
"Naomi, look at what scared us."

She laughed too. "A dead tree trunk."

Make Inferences
What can you infer
from Tasha's reaction
to discovering Junior's
comic book?

We both laughed until we cried. Then I saw one of
Junior's comic books near a bush. I picked it up and
started to cry. "See, he was here. And that animal probably
tore him to pieces." Naomi patted my shaking shoulders.

Suddenly, there was an unbelievable growl. My legs
turned to air as I flew down the steps. Naomi was ahead of
me. Her two braids stuck out like propellers. My feet didn't
even touch the ground. We screamed all the way down the
steps. I tripped on the last step and was sprawled out on
the ground. Two women passing by bent over me. "Child,
are you hurt?" one of them asked.

Then I heard a familiar laugh above me and looked up
into Junior's dimpled face. He laughed so hard, he held

his stomach with one hand. His checkers game was in the other. A little tan, mangy[3] dog stood next to him, wagging its tail.

I got up slowly. "Junior, I'm going to choke you."

He doubled over with squeals and chuckles. I wiped my filthy shorts with one hand and stretched out the other to snatch Junior's neck. The stupid little dog had the nerve to growl.

"Me and Thunder hid in the bushes. We followed you." He continued laughing. Then he turned to the dog. "Thunder, didn't Tasha look funny holding that stick like she was going to beat up the tree trunk?"

I put my hands around Junior's neck. "This is the end of the tail," I said.

Junior grinned. "You promised. 'I'll play any game he wants. I'll never yell at him again. I promise never to be mean to him again in my life.' "

Naomi giggled. "That's what you said, Tasha." The mutt barked at me. Guess he called himself Junior's protector. I took my hands off Junior's neck.

Then Naomi had a laughing spasm. She pointed at the dog. "Is that what everyone was running from?"

"This is my trusted guard. People say he's wild. He just wants a friend."

"Thunder looks like he's already got a lot of friends living inside his fur," I said. We walked back to the block with the dog trotting right by Junior's side.

I checked my watch when we got to my building. "It's ten to twelve. I have to make lunch for Junior," I told Naomi. "But I'll be back out later."

The dog whined after Junior as we entered the building. "I'll be back soon, Thunder," he said, "after I beat my sister in five games of checkers."

Now he was going to blackmail me.

I heard Naomi giggling as Junior and I walked into the building. The phone rang just as we entered the apartment. I knew it was Ma.

> ## "Me and Thunder hid in the bushes. We followed you."

◀ **Vocabulary**
spasm (spaz´ əm) *n.* sudden short burst of energy or activity

Comprehension
Where were Junior and the dog?

---

3. mangy (mān´ jē) *adj.* shabby and dirty.

"Everything okay, Tasha? Nothing happened?"

"No, Ma, everything is fine. Nothing happened at all."

Well, the summer didn't turn out to be so terrible after all. My parents got Thunder cleaned up and let Junior keep him for a pet. Me and my friends practiced for the double-dutch contest right in front of my building, so I didn't have to leave the block. After lunch when it was too hot to jump rope, I'd play a game of checkers with Junior or read him a story. He wasn't as pesty as he used to be, because now he had Thunder. We won the double-dutch contest. And Junior never told my parents that I'd lost him. I found out that you never miss a tail until you almost lose it.

Language Study

Vocabulary The words below appear in "The Tail." The questions that follow use the words in context. Answer each question. Then explain your anwer.

anxious   routine   gnawing   mauled   spasm

1. Would having a back *spasm* be pleasant?

2. Would a dog enjoy *gnawing* on a bone?

3. Should lion tamers be afraid of getting *mauled*?

4. Are you *anxious* to go to the school fair?

5. Do you know what to expect when you follow a daily *routine*?

Word Study

Part A Explain how the **Latin prefix *dis-*** contributes to the meanings of the words *disinfect* and *dissatisfied.* Consult a dictionary if necessary.

Part B Use your knowledge of the Latin prefix *dis-* to answer each question.

1. Do you usually invite people you *dislike* to a party?

2. How would it feel to *dislocate* your shoulder?

WORD STUDY

The **Latin prefix *dis-*** often changes a word's meaning to its opposite. For example, *vow* and *avow* mean "to declare" or "admit something openly." In this short story, Tasha wants to *disavow*, or deny, responsibility for her brother.

Close Reading Activities

Literary Analysis

Key Ideas and Details

1. **Make Inferences** Using a chart like the one on the right, list the details from the story that helped you to make an inference about Tasha. One example is provided. Give at least two more examples.

2. **(a)** What information are Tasha and her friends given about a danger in the park? **(b) Draw Conclusions:** Why does this information suddenly cause Tasha great worry?

3. **(a) Interpret:** What does Tasha mean when she says, "I found out that you never miss a tail until you almost lose it"?
(b) Analyze: How does Tasha's statement show a change in her attitude? Cite textual details to support your response.

Craft and Structure

4. **Characterization** List two examples of direct characterization from the story. Cite the author's exact words from the text.

5. **Characterization (a)** In the text, find two descriptions of Tasha's actions or thoughts. What character traits, or qualities, are revealed in these examples of indirect characterization?
(b) How has Tasha changed by the story's resolution? What details in the text support your answer?

Integration of Knowledge and Ideas

6. **Evaluate:** Tasha learns some important lessons from her experience. What lesson do you think is most important? Support your ideas with details from the text.

7. At the end of the story, readers learn that Junior never told his parents that Tasha lost him. **Hypothesize:** Why do you think he kept this information to himself? Support your answer with details from the story.

8. **Is conflict always bad?** Junior makes a vow to always listen to Tasha. **(a)** How does his vow lead to conflict?
(b) What positive things can Tasha learn from the conflict?
(c) What does this story suggest about how conflict is often caused by misunderstandings and miscommunication?

Details

Tasha tells Naomi, "If you're scared, don't come. Junior's my only baby brother."

↓

Inferences

Tasha is worried and is determined to find Junior, with or without Naomi's help.

ACADEMIC VOCABULARY

As you write and speak about "The Tail," use the words related to conflict that you explored on page 3 of this text.

Conventions: Personal and Possessive Pronouns

A **pronoun** is a word that takes the place of a noun or another pronoun.

A **personal pronoun** refers to a specific noun or another pronoun elsewhere in the text. A **possessive pronoun** shows ownership.

Personal Pronouns	Possessive Pronouns
I, me, you, he, him, she, her, it, we, us, they, them	my, mine, your, yours, his, her, hers, its, our, ours, their, theirs

Practice A

Copy these sentences, choosing the correct pronoun for each.

1. "Fourteen is old enough to watch (you/ your) brother," Ma told Tasha.
2. (She/ Hers) wanted to jump rope with Naomi.
3. Junior liked to tease (him/ his) sister.
4. The stray dog wagged (it/ its) tail when (it/ its) saw Junior.
5. The girls were relieved when (they/ theirs) found Junior.

Reading Application Scan "The Tail" to find two personal pronouns and two possessive pronouns.

Practice B

Copy each sentence, adding the missing pronoun. Then, tell whether it is a personal or a possessive pronoun.

1. Tasha promised _____ mother to watch Junior carefully.
2. Junior vowed always to listen to _____ sister.
3. Naomi was afraid of the dog, but _____ kept searching for Junior.
4. "At least _____ don't have to stay in the house," Naomi said to Tasha.
5. Ma turned to Tasha and Junior, kissed _____ both goodbye, and left.

Writing Application Write two sentences that include both personal and possessive pronouns. (Example: *He was nervous about speaking in front of his classmates.*)

Writing to Sources

Explanatory Text Tasha's experiences with Junior could help her find a job as a baby sitter. Suppose that Tasha were to apply for a steady baby-sitting job. Write a **letter of recommendation** for her in which you list her qualifications for the job. Address your audience and purpose by following these steps:

- Take notes on the qualities and skills that baby-sitters should have.
- Draft your letter, describing ways in which Tasha is suitable for the job.
- Provide examples of Tasha's previous experiences in baby-sitting her brother.
- Check the organization of your letter to be sure it is clear.
- Revise your word choice, where necessary, to ensure its tone is formal and objective.

Grammar Application Review your letter to be sure you have used personal and possessive pronouns correctly.

Research and Technology

Presentation of Ideas In "The Tail," children play games in a city park. Make a **compare-and-contrast chart** about games that children can play outdoors. Conduct research to learn about Tasha's favorite activity, jumping rope. In addition, research one or two other outdoor games. In your chart, categorize the games based on level of difficulty, age-appropriateness, and number of players.

Follow these steps to complete the assignment:

- Take logical and complete notes on your research findings.
- Keep track of all similarities and differences.
- Be sure to note all of your source materials, or the resources you have consulted.
- Use headings to make your chart as clear as possible.
- Present your findings to your classmates in a brief oral report.

Meet the Author

Isaac Bashevis Singer (1904–1991) lived in the United States for half his life, but he never forgot the Polish villages of his youth. Prejudice against Jews led Singer to leave Poland for New York in 1935. After World War II devastated the Jewish villages of Eastern Europe, Singer kept writing about the world he remembered. He wrote in his native Yiddish, translating many stories into English. He said, "I always knew that a writer has to write in his own language or not at all." In 1978 Singer won the Nobel Prize in Literature.

? Is conflict always bad?

Explore the Big Question as you read "Zlateh the Goat." Take notes on the different conflicts the main character faces.

CLOSE READING FOCUS

Key Ideas and Details: **Make Inferences**

An **inference** is a logical assumption you develop about information that is not directly stated. To make an inference, combine text clues with your prior knowledge, or what you already know. For example, from the sentence, "Tina smiled when she saw the snow," you might infer that Tina is happy. This inference is based on your prior knowledge that people smile when they are happy. Because Tina is smiling at the snow, you can infer that the snow is the reason she is happy.

Craft and Structure: **Conflict and Resolution**

A **conflict** is a struggle between opposing forces. In a short story, the conflict drives the action. Events in the story contribute to the conflict and to the **resolution**—the way the conflict is settled. A conflict can be *external* or *internal*.

- **External conflict:** a character struggles against an outside force, such as another person or an element of nature.
- **Internal conflict:** a character struggles to make a choice, take an action, or overcome a feeling.

A story may have several conflicts, which may be related. As you read, think about the types of conflict that characters face and how the characters change through their experiences.

Vocabulary

You will encounter the following words in "Zlateh the Goat." Which two words have multiple meanings? List each word and its different definitions.

bound	astray	exuded
splendor	trace	flickering

CLOSE READING MODEL

The passage below is from Isaac Bashevis Singer's short story "Zlateh the Goat." The annotations to the right of the passage show ways in which you can use close reading skills to make inferences and analyze conflict and resolution.

from **"Zlateh the Goat"**

The snow grew thicker, falling to the ground in large, whirling flakes. Beneath it Aaron's boots touched the softness of a plowed field. He realized that he was no longer on the road. He had gone astray. He could no longer figure out which was east or west, which way was the village, the town. [1] The wind whistled, howled, whirled the snow about in eddies. It looked as if white imps were playing tag on the fields. A white dust rose above the ground. [2] Zlateh stopped. She could walk no longer. Stubbornly she anchored her cleft hooves in the earth and bleated as if pleading to be taken home. Icicles hung from her white beard, and her horns were glazed with frost.

Aaron did not want to admit the danger, but he knew just the same that if they did not find shelter they would freeze to death. [3] This was no ordinary storm. It was a mighty blizzard. The snow had reached his knees. His hands were numb, and he could no longer feel his toes. He choked when he breathed. His nose felt like wood, and he rubbed it with snow. Zlateh's bleating began to sound like crying.

Conflict and Resolution

1 These sentences introduce an external conflict: Aaron is lost during a terrible snowstorm.

Make Inferences

2 Singer's vivid description of the setting—the whistling and howling wind and the whirling snow—can help you infer that Aaron and Zlateh are in grave danger.

Conflict and Resolution

3 In addition to his external conflict with the storm, Aaron also experiences an internal conflict. He does not want to admit his fear, but he knows he must find shelter. His internal struggle suggests that he must overcome his fear to survive the storm.

Zlateh the Goat

Isaac Bashevis Singer

Conflict and Resolution
What conflict is resolved by Reuven's decision to sell Zlateh?

At Hanukkah[1] time the road from the village to the town is usually covered with snow, but this year the winter had been a mild one. Hanukkah had almost come, yet little snow had fallen. The sun shone most of the time. The peasants complained that because of the dry weather there would be a poor harvest of winter grain. New grass sprouted, and the peasants sent their cattle out to pasture.

For Reuven the furrier it was a bad year, and after long hesitation he decided to sell Zlateh the goat. She was old and gave little milk. Feivel the town butcher had offered eight gulden[2] for her. Such a sum would buy Hanukkah candles, potatoes and oil for pancakes, gifts for the children, and other holiday necessaries for the house. Reuven told his oldest boy Aaron to take the goat to town.

---

1. **Hanukkah** (khä′ nʊ kä) Jewish festival celebrated for eight days in early winter. Hanukkah is also called the "festival of lights" because a candle is lit on each of the eight days.
2. **gulden** (gʊl′ dən) *n.* unit of money.

Illustrations copyright © 1966 by Maurice Sendak, copyright renewed 1994 by Maurice Sendak.
Printed with permission from HarperCollins Publishers.

◄ **Critical Viewing**
What do you think life is like in a village like the one in this picture?

Aaron understood what taking the goat to Feivel meant, but had to obey his father. Leah, his mother, wiped the tears from her eyes when she heard the news. Aaron's younger sisters, Anna and Miriam, cried loudly. Aaron put on his quilted jacket and a cap with earmuffs, bound a rope around Zlateh's neck, and took along two slices of bread with cheese to eat on the road. Aaron was supposed

◄ **Vocabulary**
bound (boʊnd)
v. tied

Comprehension
Why is Aaron taking the goat to Feivel?

to deliver the goat by evening, spend the night at the butcher's, and return the next day with the money.

While the family said goodbye to the goat, and Aaron placed the rope around her neck, Zlateh stood as patiently and good-naturedly as ever. She licked Reuven's hand. She shook her small white beard. Zlateh trusted human beings. She knew that they always fed her and never did her any harm.

When Aaron brought her out on the road to town, she seemed somewhat astonished. She'd never been led in that direction before. She looked back at him questioningly, as if to say, "Where are you taking me?" But after a while she seemed to come to the conclusion that a goat shouldn't ask questions. Still, the road was different. They passed new fields, pastures, and huts with thatched roofs. Here and there a dog barked and came running after them, but Aaron chased it away with his stick.

The sun was shining when Aaron left the village. Suddenly the weather changed. A large black cloud with a bluish center appeared in the east and spread itself rapidly over the sky. A cold wind blew in with it. The crows flew low, croaking. At first it looked as if it would rain, but instead it began to hail as in summer. It was early in the day, but it became dark as dusk. After a while the hail turned to snow.

In his twelve years Aaron had seen all kinds of weather, but he had never experienced a snow like this one. It was so dense it shut out the light of the day. In a short time their path was completely covered. The wind became as cold as ice. The road to town was narrow and winding. Aaron no longer knew where he was. He could not see through the snow. The cold soon penetrated his quilted jacket.

At first Zlateh didn't seem to mind the change in weather. She, too, was twelve years old and knew what winter meant. But when her legs sank deeper and deeper into the snow, she began to turn her head and look at Aaron in wonderment. Her mild eyes seemed to ask, "Why are we out in such a storm?" Aaron hoped that a peasant would come along with his cart, but no one passed by.

The snow grew thicker, falling to the ground in large, whirling flakes. Beneath it Aaron's boots touched the softness of a plowed field. He realized that he was no longer on the road. He had gone **astray**. He could no longer figure out which was east or west, which way was the village, the town. The wind whistled, howled, whirled the snow about in eddies.[3] It looked as if white imps were playing tag on the fields. A white dust rose above the ground. Zlateh stopped. She could walk no longer. Stubbornly she anchored her cleft hooves in the earth and bleated as if pleading to be taken home. Icicles hung from her white beard, and her horns were glazed with frost.

Aaron did not want to admit the danger, but he knew just the same that if they did not find shelter they would freeze to death. This was no ordinary storm. It was a mighty blizzard. The snow had reached his knees. His hands were numb, and he could no longer feel his toes. He choked when he breathed. His nose felt like wood, and he rubbed it with snow. Zlateh's bleating began to sound like crying. Those humans in whom

Illustrations copyright © 1966 by Maurice Sendak, copyright renewed 1994 by Maurice Sendak. Printed with permission from HarperCollins Publishers.

◄ **Vocabulary**
astray (ə strā´)
adv. away from the correct path

Comprehension
What surprises Zlateh when she and Aaron reach the road?

---

3. eddies (ed´ ēz) *n.* currents of air moving in circular motions like little whirlwinds.

she had so much confidence had dragged her into a trap. Aaron began to pray to God for himself and for the innocent animal.

Suddenly he made out the shape of a hill. He wondered what it could be. Who had piled snow into such a huge heap? He moved toward it, dragging Zlateh after him. When he came near it, he realized that it was a large haystack which the snow had blanketed.

Aaron realized immediately that they were saved. With great effort he dug his way through the snow. He was a village boy and knew what to do. When he reached the hay, he hollowed out a nest for himself and the goat. No matter how cold it may be outside, in the hay it is always warm. And hay was food for Zlateh. The moment she smelled it she became contented and began to eat. Outside, the snow continued to fall. It quickly covered the passageway Aaron had dug. But a boy and an animal need to breathe, and there was hardly any air in their hideout. Aaron bored a kind of a window through the hay and snow and carefully kept the passage clear.

Zlateh, having eaten her fill, sat down on her hind legs and seemed to have regained her confidence in man. Aaron ate his two slices of bread and cheese, but after the difficult journey he was still hungry. He looked at Zlateh and noticed her udders were full. He lay down next to her, placing himself so that when he milked her he could squirt the milk into his mouth. It was rich and sweet. Zlateh was not accustomed to being milked that way, but she did not resist. On the contrary, she seemed eager to reward Aaron for bringing her to a shelter whose very walls, floor, and ceiling were made of food. •

Through the window Aaron could catch a glimpse of the chaos outside. The wind carried before it whole drifts of snow. It was completely dark, and he did not know whether night had already come or whether it was the darkness of the storm. Thank God that in the hay it was not cold. The dried hay, grass, and field flowers exuded the warmth of the summer sun. Zlateh ate frequently; she

Conflict and Resolution
How has the discovery of the haystack temporarily resolved Aaron's problem?

Vocabulary ▶
exuded (eg zyōōd´ əd)
v. gave off; oozed

nibbled from above, below, from the left and right. Her body gave forth an animal warmth, and Aaron cuddled up to her. He had always loved Zlateh, but now she was like a sister. He was alone, cut off from his family, and wanted to talk. He began to talk to Zlateh. "Zlateh, what do you think about what has happened to us?" he asked.

"Maaaa," Zlateh answered.

"If we hadn't found this stack of hay, we would both be frozen stiff by now," Aaron said.

"Maaaa," was the goat's reply.

"If the snow keeps on falling like this, we may have to stay here for days," Aaron explained.

"Maaaa," Zlateh bleated.

"What does 'maaaa' mean?" Aaron asked. "You'd better speak up clearly."

"Maaaa, maaaa," Zlateh tried.

"Well, let it be 'maaaa' then," Aaron said patiently. "You can't speak, but I know you understand. I need you and you need me. Isn't that right?"

"Maaaa."

Aaron became sleepy. He made a pillow out of some hay, leaned his head on it, and dozed off. Zlateh, too, fell asleep.

When Aaron opened his eyes, he didn't know whether it was morning or night. The snow had blocked up his window. He tried

Illustrations copyright © 1966 by Maurice Sendak, copyright renewed 1994 by Maurice Sendak. Printed with permission from HarperCollins Publishers.

▲ **Critical Viewing**
Why does Aaron look sad here?

Comprehension
What shelter do Aaron and Zlateh find?

Conflict and Resolution
In what way are Aaron and Zlateh still in danger from the storm?

to clear it, but when he had bored through to the length of his arm, he still hadn't reached the outside. Luckily he had his stick with him and was able to break through to the open air. It was still dark outside. The snow continued to fall and the wind wailed, first with one voice and then with many. Sometimes it had the sound of devilish laughter. Zlateh, too, awoke, and when Aaron greeted her, she answered, "Maaaa." Yes, Zlateh's language consisted of only one word, but it meant many things. Now she was saying, "We must accept all that God gives us—heat, cold, hunger, satisfaction, light, and darkness."

Aaron had awakened hungry. He had eaten up his food, but Zlateh had plenty of milk.

For three days Aaron and Zlateh stayed in the haystack. Aaron had always loved Zlateh, but in these three days he loved her more and more. She fed him with her milk and helped him keep warm. She comforted him with her patience. He told her many stories, and she always cocked her ears and listened. When he patted her, she licked his hand and his face. Then she said, "Maaaa," and he knew it meant, I love you, too.

Make Inferences
Using your own experience, what inference can you make about how Aaron feels, based on the details in this passage?

The snow fell for three days, though after the first day it was not as thick and the wind quieted down. Sometimes Aaron felt that there could never have been a summer, that the snow had always fallen, ever since he could remember. He, Aaron, never had a father or mother or sisters. He was a snow child, born of the snow, and so was Zlateh. It was so quiet in the hay that his ears rang in the stillness. Aaron and Zlateh slept all night and a good part of the day. As for Aaron's dreams, they were all about warm weather. He dreamed of green fields, trees covered with blossoms, clear brooks, and singing birds. By the third night the snow had stopped, but Aaron did not dare to find his way home in the darkness. The sky became clear and the moon shone, casting silvery nets on the snow. Aaron dug his way out and looked at the world. It was all white, quiet, dreaming dreams of heavenly splendor. The stars were large and close. The moon swam in the sky as in a sea.

Vocabulary ▶
splendor (splen´dər)
n. gorgeous appearance; magnificence

On the morning of the fourth day Aaron heard the ringing of sleigh bells. The haystack was not far from the road. The peasant who drove the sleigh pointed out the way to him—not to the town and Feivel the butcher, but home to the village. Aaron had decided in the haystack that he would never part with Zlateh.

Aaron's family and their neighbors had searched for the boy and the goat but had found no trace of them during the storm. They feared they were lost. Aaron's mother and sisters cried for him; his father remained silent and gloomy. Suddenly one of the neighbors came running to their house with the news that Aaron and Zlateh were coming up the road. •

There was great joy in the family. Aaron told them how he had found the stack of hay and how Zlateh had fed him with her milk. Aaron's sisters kissed and hugged Zlateh and gave her a special treat of chopped carrots and potato peels, which Zlateh gobbled up hungrily.

Nobody ever again thought of selling Zlateh, and now that the cold weather had finally set in, the villagers needed the services of Reuven the furrier once more. When Hanukkah came, Aaron's mother was able to fry pancakes every evening, and Zlateh got her portion, too. Even though Zlateh had her own pen, she often came to the kitchen, knocking on the door with her horns to indicate that she was ready to visit, and she was always admitted. In the evening Aaron, Miriam, and Anna played dreidel.[4] Zlateh sat near the stove watching the children and the flickering of the Hanukkah candles.

Once in a while Aaron would ask her, "Zlateh, do you remember the three days we spent together?"

And Zlateh would scratch her neck with a horn, shake her white bearded head, and come out with the single sound which expressed all her thoughts, and all her love.

◀ **Vocabulary**
trace (trās) *n.* mark left behind by something

◀ **Vocabulary**
flickering (flik´ər iŋ) *v.* burning unsteadily

Conflict and Resolution
How is the family's conflict over selling Zlateh resolved?

---

4. **dreidel** (drā´ dəl) *n.* small top with Hebrew letters on each of four sides, spun in a game played by children.

Illustrations copyright © 1966 by Maurice Sendak,
copyright renewed 1994 by Maurice Sendak.
Printed with permission from HarperCollins Publishers.

Language Study

Vocabulary The words below appear in "Zlateh the Goat."
Answer each question that follows, using a word from the list.

| bound | astray | splendor | trace | flickering |

1. Which word could describe footprints left in the snow?

2. How else could you say that you tied two things together?

3. How can you describe losing your way?

4. How might you describe the light from a star?

5. Which word can apply to a place of great beauty?

WORD STUDY

The **Latin prefix ex-**
means "out," "from," or
"beyond."

In this story, dried hay,
grass, and flowers
exuded the sun's
warmth, or sent out the
warmth of the sun.

Word Study

Part A Explain how the **Latin prefix ex-** contributes to the meanings
of the words *exceed* and *expand*. Consult a dictionary if necessary.

Part B Use context and what you know about the Latin prefix *ex-*
to explain your answer to each question.

1. What happens when you *exhale* a lot of air?

2. Would you vote to *extend* a school holiday?

Close Reading Activities

Literary Analysis

Key Ideas and Details

1. **Make Inferences** Aaron's mother and sisters cry over selling Zlateh. What inference can you make about their feelings for the goat?

2. **(a)** What happens to Aaron and Zlateh on the way to town? **(b) Deduce:** Why is their situation dangerous? Cite details from the text to support your responses.

3. **Make Inferences** What evidence in the story supports the inference that Aaron is quick-thinking and brave?

Craft and Structure

4. **Conflict and Resolution** In a chart like the one on the right, record each of the following **conflicts**, tell whether it is internal or external, and explain how it was resolved.

   (a) Reuven needs the money he could get for Zlateh, but he loves Zlateh.

   (b) Aaron and Zlateh need food and shelter but are caught in a blizzard.

5. **Conflict and Resolution** Explain how the resolution of the first conflict is connected to the second conflict. Support your response with textual evidence.

Integration of Knowledge and Ideas

6. **(a) Draw Conclusions:** Why does Reuven never again think of selling Zlateh after Aaron and the goat return home? **(b) Apply:** What is the story's message about friendship and trust?

7. **(a) Generalize:** What message does the story convey about animals and their relationships with people? **(b) Support:** What evidence from the story supports this message?

Conflict
What Kind?
Resolution

8. **Is conflict always bad? (a)** What does Aaron learn about himself during his struggle to survive the snowstorm? **(b)** What does he learn about Zlateh during this time? **(c)** What lessons does this story suggest about overcoming challenges and dangerous situations?

ACADEMIC VOCABULARY

As you write and speak about "Zlateh the Goat," use the words related to conflict that you explored on page 3 of this text.

Conventions: Interrogative, Indefinite, Reflexive, and Intensive Pronouns

A **pronoun** is a word that takes the place of a noun or another pronoun.

Interrogative pronouns are used in questions.

Indefinite pronouns refer to one or more unspecified people or things.

Reflexive pronouns are formed by adding *-self* or *-selves* to a pronoun, as in *herself* and *ourselves*. They point to the person or thing receiving the action when that person or thing is the same as the one performing the action.

Intensive pronouns add emphasis to another noun or pronoun in the sentence. Like reflexive pronouns, they are formed by adding *-self* or *-selves* to a pronoun. However, they are not essential to the meaning of the sentence. They are usually found very close to the noun or pronoun they emphasize.

Interrogative Pronouns	Indefinite Pronouns	Reflexive Pronouns	Intensive Pronouns
Who would like an apple?	*Some* of my friends live in Cleveland.	Jeremy gave *himself* a haircut.	Ana *herself* raised the flag.
Which of these hats is yours?	Please serve *all* of the cookies.	I don't want to make *myself* feel bad.	In a democracy, the people *themselves* rule.

Practice A
Identify the pronoun in each sentence as *interrogative* or *indefinite*.

1. What is the name of Aaron's father?
2. To whom might Aaron sell the goat?
3. Everyone feels sad about selling Zlateh.
4. Who shows Aaron the way home?
5. All of the family members are glad.

Reading Application In "Zlateh the Goat," find two interrogative pronouns and two indefinite pronouns.

Practice B
Identify the pronoun in each sentence as *reflexive* or *intensive*.

1. Aaron himself had a decision to make.
2. Zlateh helped herself to more hay.
3. The neighbors themselves searched for Aaron and Zlateh.
4. Aaron's mother cooked the Hanukkah meal by herself.

Writing Application Write two sentences about the story that include reflexive pronouns and intensive pronouns.

Writing to Sources

Argument Write and present a short **persuasive speech** that Aaron might give to urge his father to keep Zlateh. Address your audience and purpose by following these steps:

- State your position clearly and present at least two reasons that support it.
- Consider Aaron's father's concerns and the counterarguments he might make.
- Conclude your speech by summarizing your position. Avoid using the same words that you used to state your position.
- Rehearse your speech. Consider practicing in front of a mirror or another person. If possible, record your practice.
- Revise your speech to remove less-persuasive details. Then, practice your revised speech once again before presenting it.

Grammar Application Read over your speech and be sure you have used all intensive pronouns correctly.

Research and Technology

Presentation of Ideas Make and present a **compare-and-contrast chart.** Compare and contrast your hometown to a *shtetl*, a Jewish village in Eastern Europe before World War II, like the one in which Aaron and his family live. Follow these steps to complete the assignment:

- Use key words to search online databases for information.
- Organize the information according to categories such as population, resources, way of life, and so on.
- Fill in the chart with information for each category. Include visuals to clarify the information you find.
- Analyze the information and write a summary of your findings.
- Present your findings to the class. Invite comments and feedback when you finish.

Meet the Author

Francisco Jiménez (hē mä′ nəz) (b. 1943) was born in Mexico and came to the United States with his family when he was four years old. The family settled in California and became migrant workers. Jiménez could not go to school before the harvest ended, but he studied in the fields and read whenever he had the chance. He once said, "I came to realize that learning and knowledge were the only stable things in my life." In high school, his excellent grades won him three college scholarships. He went on to become an outstanding teacher and award-winning writer.

Is conflict always bad?

Explore the Big Question as you read "The Circuit." Take notes on ways in which the story explores ideas about conflict.

CLOSE READING FOCUS

Key Ideas and Details: Draw Conclusions

A **conclusion** is a decision or an opinion you reach based on details in a literary work. To draw conclusions, ask questions as you read, such as *Why is this character alone so often?* Then, look for story details that help you answer the question. For example, the character may like to show off in front of others. You might then draw the conclusion that the character is unpopular because people dislike those who constantly point out their superiority.

Craft and Structure: Theme

The **theme**, or central idea of a story, is a thought or an insight about life that the story conveys. Although the theme of a work is sometimes directly stated, more often it is hinted at or suggested. To figure out a theme that is *indirectly* conveyed, consider the following:

• the outcome of the conflict and the effect on characters
• knowledge or insights that characters gain in the course of the story
• the story's title

Together, these details can help you understand the story's theme.

Vocabulary

The following words are critical to understanding "The Circuit." Copy these words into your notebook. Challenge yourself to identify one related word for each listed word. For example, you might write *accompany* next to *accompanied*.

accompanied	drone	instinctively
savoring	enroll	

CLOSE READING MODEL

The passage below is from Francisco Jiménez's short story "The Circuit." The annotations to the right of the passage show ways in which you can use close reading skills to draw conclusions and analyze theme.

from "The Circuit"

At sunset we drove into a labor camp near Fresno. Since Papá did not speak English, Mamá asked the camp foreman if he needed any more workers. "We don't need no more," said the foreman, scratching his head. "Check with Sullivan down the road. [1] Can't miss him. He lives in a big white house with a fence around it."

When we got there, Mamá walked up to the house. She went through a white gate, past a row of rose bushes, up the stairs to the front door. She rang the doorbell. The porch light went on and a tall husky man came out. They exchanged a few words. After the man went in, Mamá clasped her hands and hurried back to the car. "We have work! Mr. Sullivan said we can stay there the whole season," [2] she said, gasping and pointing to an old garage near the stables.

The garage was worn out by the years. It had no windows. The walls, eaten by termites, strained to support the roof full of holes. The dirt floor, populated by earthworms, looked like a gray road map. [3]

That night, by the light of a kerosene lamp, we unpacked and cleaned our new home. [4]

Theme

1 These sentences show challenges that the narrator and his migrant family face when they travel to find work in labor camps. These details suggest that the story will deal with themes of hardship and survival.

Theme

2 Mamá's actions show her determination. Her excitement over the job offer conveys her sense of relief—her family is employed and housed for a whole season. Details such as these emphasize the ongoing cycle of working and moving.

Draw Conclusions

3 The family will live in a garage that is filled with termites and earthworms. You may conclude that migrant workers' comfort and health was not a big concern for their employers.

Draw Conclusions

4 The family works to settle their "new home." You might conclude that they want to create a sense of permanence and belonging, even though they move often.

The CIRCUIT

Francisco Jiménez

It was that time of year again. Ito, the strawberry sharecropper,[1] did not smile. It was natural. The peak of the strawberry season was over and the last few days the workers, most of them braceros,[2] were not picking as many boxes as they had during the months of June and July.

---

1. **sharecropper** (shər´ kräp´ ər) *n.* one who works for a share of a crop; tenant farmer.
2. **braceros** (brä ser´ os) *n.* migrant Mexican farm laborers who harvest crops.

◀ **Critical Viewing**
Do you think the type of work this man is doing is easy or difficult? Why?

As the last days of August disappeared, so did the number of *braceros*. Sunday, only one—the best picker—came to work. I liked him. Sometimes we talked during our half-hour lunch break. That is how I found out he was from Jalisco, the same state in Mexico my family was from. That Sunday was the last time I saw him.

When the sun had tired and sunk behind the mountains, Ito signaled us that it was time to go home. "*Ya esora*,"[3] he yelled in his broken Spanish. Those were the words I waited for twelve hours a day, every day, seven days a week, week after week. And the thought of not hearing them again saddened me.

As we drove home Papá did not say a word. With both hands on the wheel, he stared at the dirt road. My older brother, Roberto, was also silent. He leaned his head back and closed his eyes. Once in a while he cleared from his throat the dust that blew in from outside.

Yes, it was that time of year. When I opened the front door to the shack, I stopped. Everything we owned was neatly packed in cardboard boxes. Suddenly I felt even more the weight of hours, days, weeks, and months of work. I sat down on a box. The thought of having to move to Fresno[4] and knowing what was in store for me there brought tears to my eyes.

That night I could not sleep. I lay in bed thinking about how much I hated this move.

A little before five o'clock in the morning, Papá woke everyone up. A few minutes later, the yelling and screaming of my little brothers and sisters, for whom the move was a great adventure, broke the silence of dawn. Shortly, the barking of the dogs accompanied them.

While we packed the breakfast dishes, Papá went outside to start the "Carcanchita."[5] That was the name Papá gave his old '38 black Plymouth. He bought it in a used-car lot in Santa Rosa in the winter of 1949. Papá was very proud of his little jalopy. He had a right to be

Theme
What clues do this event and the narrator's actions give you about the story's theme?

Vocabulary ▶
accompanied (ə kum´ pə nēd) *v.* went along with; joined

---

3. *Ya esora* (yä es ô rä) Spanish for "It's time" (*Ya es hora*).
4. **Fresno** (frez´ nō) *n.* city in central California.
5. **Carcanchita** (kär kän chē´ tä) affectionate name for the car.

proud of it. He spent a lot of time looking at other cars before buying this one. When he finally chose the "Carcanchita," he checked it thoroughly before driving it out of the car lot. He examined every inch of the car. He listened to the motor, tilting his head from side to side like a parrot, trying to detect any noises that spelled car trouble. After being satisfied with the looks and sounds of the car, Papá then insisted on knowing who the original owner was. He never did find out from the car salesman, but he bought the car anyway. Papá figured the original owner must have been an important man because behind the rear seat of the car he found a blue necktie.

Papá parked the car out in front and left the motor running. "*Listo*,"[6] he yelled. Without saying a word, Roberto and I began to carry the boxes out to the car. Roberto carried the two big boxes and I carried the two smaller ones. Papá then threw the mattress on top of the car roof and tied it with ropes to the front and rear bumpers.

Everything was packed except Mamá's pot. It was an old large galvanized[7] pot she had picked up at an army surplus store in Santa María the year I was born. The pot had many dents and nicks, and the more dents and nicks it acquired the more Mamá liked it. "*Mi olla*,"[8] she used to say proudly.

I held the front door open as Mamá carefully carried out her pot by both handles, making sure not to spill

The grinder (La molendera), 1926, Diego Rivera, Museo Nacional de Arte Moderno, Instituto Nacional de Bellas Artes, Mexico City, D.F., Mexico. ©Banco de Mexico Diego Rivera & Frida Kahlo Museums Trust. Av. Cinco de Mayo No. 2, Col. Centro, Del. Cuauhtemoc 06059, Mexico, D.F. Reproduction authorized by the Instituto Nacional de Bellas Artes y Literatura.

▲ **Critical Viewing**
What are three words that describe the woman in this painting?

Draw Conclusions
What do the details so far tell you about the family's attitude toward moving again?

Comprehension
Why is Papá proud of "Carcanchita"?

---

6. *Listo* (lēs´ tō) Spanish for "Ready."
7. **galvanized** (gal´ və nīzd) *adj.* coated with zinc to prevent rusting.
8. *Mi olla* (mē ō´ yä) Spanish for "My pot."

Geography Connection

Agricultural Seasons

With sunny weather and a favorable climate, California produces more crops than any other state. At every point in the year, there is a different crop ready to be harvested in some part of the state. Migrant workers, such as Panchito's family, migrate from place to place to harvest the available crop. Grapes are picked in the summer and fall in the lush valleys of central and northern California. Peak strawberry season hits the southern coastal regions in the spring. Cotton is harvested in the dry valleys of central and southern California during the winter.

Connect to the Literature

Identify two ways the agricultural seasons affect the characters in this story.

the cooked beans. When she got to the car, Papá reached out to help her with it. Roberto opened the rear car door and Papá gently placed it on the floor behind the front seat. All of us then climbed in. Papá sighed, wiped the sweat off his forehead with his sleeve, and said wearily: "*Es todo.*"[9]

As we drove away, I felt a lump in my throat. I turned around and looked at our little shack for the last time.

At sunset we drove into a labor camp near Fresno. Since Papá did not speak English, Mamá asked the camp foreman if he needed any more workers. "We don't need no more," said the foreman, scratching his head. "Check with Sullivan down the road. Can't miss him. He lives in a big white house with a fence around it."

When we got there, Mamá walked up to the house. She went through a white gate, past a row of rose bushes, up the stairs to the front door. She rang the doorbell. The porch light went on and a tall husky man came out. They exchanged a few words. After the man went in, Mamá clasped her hands and hurried back to the car. "We have work! Mr. Sullivan said we can stay there the whole season," she said, gasping and pointing to an old garage near the stables.

The garage was worn out by the years. It had no windows. The walls, eaten by termites, strained to support the roof full of holes. The dirt floor, populated by earthworms, looked like a gray road map.

That night, by the light of a kerosene lamp, we unpacked and cleaned our new home. Roberto swept away the loose dirt, leaving the hard ground. Papá plugged the holes in the walls with old newspapers and tin can tops.

---

9. Es todo (es tō′ thō) Spanish for "That's everything."

Mamá fed my little brothers and sisters. Papá and Roberto then brought in the mattress and placed it on the far corner of the garage. "Mamá, you and the little ones sleep on the mattress. Roberto, Panchito, and I will sleep outside under the trees," Papá said.

Early next morning Mr. Sullivan showed us where his crop was, and after breakfast, Papá, Roberto, and I headed for the vineyard to pick.

Around nine o'clock the temperature had risen to almost one hundred degrees. I was completely soaked in sweat and my mouth felt as if I had been chewing on a handkerchief. I walked over to the end of the row, picked up the jug of water we had brought, and began drinking. "Don't drink too much; you'll get sick," Roberto shouted. No sooner had he said that than I felt sick to my stomach. I dropped to my knees and let the jug roll off my hands. I remained motionless with my eyes glued on the hot sandy ground. All I could hear was the **drone** of insects. Slowly I began to recover. I poured water over my face and neck and watched the dirty water run down my arms to the ground.

I still felt a little dizzy when we took a break to eat lunch. It was past two o'clock and we sat underneath a large walnut tree that was on the side of the road. While we ate, Papá jotted down the number of boxes we had picked. Roberto drew designs on the ground with a stick. Suddenly I noticed Papá's face turn pale as he looked down the road. "Here comes the school bus," he whispered loudly in alarm. **Instinctively**, Roberto and I ran and hid in the vineyards. We did not want to get in trouble for not going to school. The neatly dressed boys about my age got off. They carried books under their arms. After they crossed the street, the bus drove away. Roberto and I came out from hiding and joined Papá. "*Tienen que tener cuidado*,"[10] he warned us.

After lunch we went back to work. The sun kept beating down. The buzzing insects, the wet sweat, and the hot dry dust made the afternoon seem to last forever. Finally the mountains around the valley reached out and swallowed the sun. Within an hour it was too dark to continue

---

10. *Tienen que tener cuidado* (tē en´ en kä ten er´ kwē thä´ thō) Spanish for "You have to be careful."

◀ **Vocabulary**
drone (drōn) *n.* continuous humming sound

instinctively (in stiŋk´ tiv lē) *adv.* done automatically, without thinking

Comprehension
What makes work in the vineyard hard for Panchito?

picking. The vines blanketed the grapes, making it difficult to see the bunches. "*Vámonos*,"[11] said Papá, signaling to us that it was time to quit work. Papá then took out a pencil and began to figure out how much we had earned our first day. He wrote down numbers, crossed some out, wrote down some more. "*Quince*,"[12] he murmured.

When we arrived home, we took a cold shower underneath a waterhose. We then sat down to eat dinner around some wooden crates that served as a table. Mamá had cooked a special meal for us. We had rice and tortillas with "*carne con chile*,"[13] my favorite dish.

The next morning I could hardly move. My body ached all over. I felt little control over my arms and legs. This feeling went on every morning for days until my muscles finally got used to the work.

It was Monday, the first week of November. The grape season was over and I could now go to school. I woke up early that morning and lay in bed, looking at the stars and **savoring** the thought of not going to work and of starting sixth grade for the first time that year. Since I could not sleep, I decided to get up and join Papá and Roberto at breakfast. I sat at the table across from Roberto, but I kept my head down. I did not want to look up and face him. I knew he was sad. He was not going to school today. He was not going tomorrow, or next week, or next month. He would not go until the cotton season was over, and that was sometime in February. I rubbed my hands together and watched the dry, acid stained skin fall to the floor in little rolls.

When Papá and Roberto left for work, I felt relief. I walked to the top of a small grade next to the shack and watched the "Carcanchita" disappear in the distance in a cloud of dust.

Two hours later, around eight o'clock, I stood by the side of the road waiting for school bus number twenty. When it arrived I climbed in. Everyone was busy either talking or yelling. I sat in an empty seat in the back.

When the bus stopped in front of the school, I felt very nervous. I looked out the bus window and saw boys

Vocabulary ▶
savoring (sā´ vər iŋ)
v. enjoying; tasting with delight

Theme
How does the sentence that begins "He would not go" suggest that the family's life follows a cycle? How might this cycle relate to the story's theme?

---

11. *Vámonos* (vä´ mō nōs) Spanish for "Let's go."
12. *Quince* (kēn´ sā) Spanish for "Fifteen."
13. "*carne con chile*" (kär´ nā kən chil´ ā) dish of ground meat, hot peppers, beans, and tomatoes.

and girls carrying books under their arms. I put my hands in my pant pockets and walked to the principal's office. When I entered I heard a woman's voice say: "May I help you?" I was startled. I had not heard English for months. For a few seconds I remained speechless. I looked at the lady who waited for my answer. My first instinct was to answer her in Spanish, but I held back. Finally, after struggling for English words, I managed to tell her that I wanted to **enroll** in the sixth grade. After answering many questions, I was led to the classroom.

◀ **Vocabulary**
enroll (en rōl′) v.
place oneself on a
register or list

Mr. Lema, the sixth-grade teacher, greeted me and assigned me a desk. He then introduced me to the class. I was so nervous and scared at that moment when everyone's eyes were on me that I wished I were with Papá and Roberto picking cotton. After taking roll, Mr. Lema gave the class the assignment for the first hour. "The first thing we have to do this morning is finish reading the story we began yesterday," he said enthusiastically. He walked up to me, handed me an English book, and asked me to read. "We are on page 125," he said politely. When I heard this, I felt my blood rush to my head; I felt dizzy. "Would you like to read?" he asked hesitantly. I opened the book to page 125. My mouth was dry. My eyes began to water. I could not begin. "You can read later," Mr. Lema said understandingly. ●

For the rest of the reading period I kept getting angrier and angrier at myself. I should have read, I thought to myself.

During recess I went into the restroom and opened my English book to page 125. I began to read in a low voice, pretending I was in class. There were many words I did not know. I closed the book and headed back to the classroom.

Mr. Lema was sitting at his desk correcting papers. When I entered he looked up at me and smiled. I felt better. I walked up to him and asked if he could help me with the new words. "Gladly," he said.

Draw Conclusions
What do the details in this paragraph lead you to conclude about Mr. Lema's character?

Comprehension
Why is Roberto unable to go back to school?

The rest of the month I spent my lunch hours working on English with Mr. Lema, my best friend at school.

One Friday during lunch hour Mr. Lema asked me to take a walk with him to the music room. "Do you like music?" he asked me as we entered the building.

"Yes, I like *corridos*,"[14] I answered. He then picked up a trumpet, blew on it and handed it to me. The sound gave me goose bumps. I knew that sound. I had heard it in many corridos. "How would you like to learn how to play it?" he asked. He must have read my face because before I could answer, he added: "I'll teach you how to play it during our lunch hours."

That day I could hardly wait to get home to tell Papá and Mamá the great news. As I got off the bus, my little brothers and sisters ran up to meet me. They were yelling and screaming. I thought they were happy to see me, but when I opened the door to our shack, I saw that everything we owned was neatly packed in cardboard boxes.

Spiral Review
RESOLUTION What do the cardboard boxes signify to the narrator? How do they signal the story's resolution?

---

14. *corridos* (kō rēˊ thōs) *n.* ballads.

Language Study

Vocabulary The words below appear in "The Circuit." Match each numbered description with a word from the list.

    drone   **instinctively**   **savoring**   **enroll**

1. eating a delicious meal
2. how mother animals protect their young
3. the sound of bees buzzing
4. sign up for guitar lessons

WORD STUDY

The **Latin prefix com-** means "with," "together," or "next to." In this story, the narrator says that the barking of dogs **accompanied**, or mixed together with, his brothers' and sisters' yelling.

Word Study

Part A Explain how the **Latin prefix com-** contributes to the meanings of *commission* and *compression*. Use a dictionary if necessary.

Part B Use what you know about the Latin prefix *com-* to answer each question. Then, explain your responses.

1. If you are alone, do you have *company*?
2. Would you eat a *combination* of ice cream and vinegar?

Close Reading Activities

Literary Analysis

Key Ideas and Details

1. **Draw Conclusions** Complete a chart like the one on the right to draw conclusions about the story.

2. **(a)** What does Panchito do on his school lunch hours? **(b) Infer:** Why does Panchito call Mr. Lema his "best friend at school"? **(c) Interpret:** Based on the information in the story, how would you describe Panchito's personality?

3. **(a)** What is the best thing that happens to Panchito on the last day of school? **(b) Infer:** What is the worst thing?

Craft and Structure

4. **Theme (a)** What theme, or insight about life, does the story illustrate? **(b)** What details or events support the theme?

5. **Theme (a)** What is the meaning of "circuit," as used in the story's title? **(b)** How does the title relate to the story's theme?

6. **(a)** How well does the author develop Panchito's character? **(b) Analyze:** What specific details help readers understand Panchito?

Integration of Knowledge and Ideas

7. **(a) Draw Conclusions:** In what ways does Mr. Lema show understanding toward Panchito's situation? **(b)** Does Panchito grow or change as a result of Mr. Lema's help? Support your conclusion with evidence from the text.

8. **(a) Summarize:** Summarize the challenges Panchito's family face as they move from place to place. **(b) Assess:** How have Panchito and Roberto's lives been affected by being part of a migrant family? Cite textual details to support your answer.

Question	Text Details that Answer Question	Conclusion
Why does Panchito work so much?		
Why does Panchito not read aloud on the first day of school?		
Why are the family's belongings packed in boxes?		

9. **Is conflict always bad?** With a small group, discuss the following questions: **(a)** What might be done to ease the conflicts of families like Panchito's? **(b)** Examine the theme. Will Panchito grow stronger as a result of the conflicts he faces? Explain. **(c)** What ongoing conflicts does this story suggest about child migrant workers?

ACADEMIC VOCABULARY

As you write and speak about "The Circuit," use the words related to conflict that you explored on page 3 of this text.

Conventions: **Pronoun Case**

> The **pronoun case** is the form a pronoun takes to show whether it is being used as a subject, an object, or a possessive.

There are three pronoun cases:

- The **nominative case** is used to name the subject of a verb or in the predicate after a linking verb.
- The **objective case** is used to name the object of a verb or a preposition.
- The **possessive case** is used to show ownership.

Pronoun Cases	Examples
Nominative Case I, you, he, she, it, we, you, they	Subject of a verb: **They** wanted to stay in school.
	Predicate pronoun: The foreman is **he**.
Objective Case me, you, him, her, it, us, you, them	Direct object: Roberto took the pot and gave **it** to them.
	Indirect object: Please give **me** the book.
	Object of a preposition: The man gave the papers to **her**.
Possessive Case my, your, his, her, its, our, their, mine, yours, hers, ours, theirs	I reminded Papá to drive **his** car.

Practice A

Find the pronoun in each sentence and identify its case.

1. "Look at our boxes," Mamá said.
2. Panchito waited for Mr. Lema to walk with him.
3. You are a fine trumpet player.
4. Panchito made his way to the back of the bus.

Reading Application In "The Circuit," find one nominative pronoun, one objective pronoun, and one possessive pronoun.

Practice B

Replace each boldface noun with the appropriate pronoun. Identify the pronoun's case.

1. **Mamá** had cooked a special meal for us.
2. I let the **jug** roll off my hands.
3. Mr. Lema introduced me to the **students**.
4. Everything was packed except for **Mamá's** pot.

Writing Application Write three sentences about "The Circuit." Use one of the three pronoun cases in each sentence.

Writing to Sources

Explanatory Text Write a **description** of a character from "The Circuit."

- Identify details from the story that describe the character's appearance, actions, and personality.
- List details about the character's thoughts and words, and about other characters' reactions to the character you are describing.
- Make a cluster map of words, such as *smart, brave, mean,* or *fun-loving,* that capture the character's personality.
- Using words from your cluster map, write a description that identifies the controlling impression you want to convey.
- Include vivid details to help readers "see" the character.

Grammar Application Identify the pronouns in your description, and make sure they are written in the correct case.

Speaking and Listening

Comprehension and Collaboration With a partner, prepare and role-play an **interview** between a reporter and a migrant worker. The migrant worker may be Panchito or another character in "The Circuit."

Follow these steps to complete the assignment:

- Decide who will play each part.
- Reread the story to gather information.
- Prepare a list of relevant questions for the reporter to ask in the interview.
- Categorize the questions under headings such as Experience, Advice, and Lessons Learned.
- Develop the migrant worker's responses, with elaboration based on details from the story. Write down ideas you develop that you want to use in your interview.
- Rehearse with your partner, and then conduct your interview in front of the class.

Is conflict always bad?

Explore the Big Question as you read these stories. Take notes on the conflicts in each story. Then compare and contrast what the two stories suggest about the impact of conflict.

READING TO COMPARE FORESHADOWING AND FLASHBACK

Authors Joan Aiken and Walter Dean Myers use foreshadowing and flashback to add interest to their plots. As you read, notice how the authors hint about events that will happen in the future. Also consider how each story moves between past and present. When you finish reading, compare how the two authors use the techniques of foreshadowing and flashback.

"Lob's Girl"

Joan Aiken (1924–2004)
By the time she was a teenager, British author Joan Aiken was a published writer. Aiken's father was poet Conrad Aiken, and her brother and sister were both professional writers. Fans of all ages enjoy Aiken's unusual tales. Aiken once said, "Stories are like butterflies, which come fluttering out of nowhere, touch down for a brief instant, may be captured, may not, and then vanish into nowhere again."

"Jeremiah's Song"

Walter Dean Myers (b. 1937)
By the age of five, Walter Dean Myers was reading daily newspapers. Despite this impressive start with words, Myers did not think writing would be his career. However, in his twenties, he won a writing contest and had been writing ever since—mostly about his heritage and growing up in Harlem, a part of New York City.

Comparing Foreshadowing and Flashback

To develop exciting stories, writers use a range of **plot techniques** and literary devices to tell the events in a story.

- **Foreshadowing** is the author's use of clues to hint at what might happen later in a story. For example, the description of a dark cloud in a story might foreshadow something bad that is about to happen. Foreshadowing helps build suspense, the quality that keeps you wondering what will happen next.

- A **flashback** is a scene that interrupts a story to describe an earlier event. Writers use flashback to show something about a character's past. For example, a flashback about a happy childhood journey might explain why an adult character loves to travel.

Plot Devices and Plot Structure Some plots move from the beginning to the end with no interruption. A diagram of such a plot would look like an orderly timeline. Devices such as flashback change a plot's structure by changing the sequence of events.

Flashback takes readers on a short trip to the past. Foreshadowing does not move the plot to the future, but it moves the reader's attention to possible future events. Foreshadowing also adds to a sense of completeness in a plot. First readers recognize a hint, then they read about the event itself. Both devices can make the structure of a plot more interesting and more complex.

Compare the use of foreshadowing and flashback in "Lob's Girl" and "Jeremiah's Song" by using a chart such as the one shown.

	"Lob's Girl"	**"Jeremiah's Song"**
Foreshadowing		
Flashback		

Lob's Girl

Joan Aiken

Some people choose their dogs, and some dogs choose their people. The Pengelly family had no say in the choosing of Lob; he came to them in the second way, and very **decisively**.

It began on the beach, the summer when Sandy was five, Don, her older brother, twelve, and the twins were three. Sandy was really Alexandra, because her grandmother had a beautiful picture of a queen in a diamond tiara and high collar of pearls. It hung by Granny Pearce's kitchen sink and was as familiar as the doormat. When Sandy was born everyone agreed that she was the living spit of the picture, and so she was called Alexandra and Sandy for short.

On this summer day she was lying peacefully reading a comic and not keeping an eye on the twins, who didn't need it because they were occupied in seeing which of them could wrap the most seaweed around the other one's legs. Father—Bert Pengelly—and Don were up on the Hard painting the bottom boards of the boat in which Father went fishing for pilchards. And Mother—Jean Pengelly— was getting ahead with making the Christmas puddings because she never felt easy in her mind if they weren't made and safely put away by the end of August. As usual, each member of the family was happily getting on with his or her own affairs. Little did they guess how soon this state of things would be changed by the large new member who was going to erupt into their midst.

Sandy rolled onto her back to make sure that the twins were not climbing on slippery rocks or getting cut off by the tide. At the same moment a large body struck her forcibly in the midriff and she was covered by flying sand. Instinctively she shut her eyes and felt the sand being wiped off her face by something that seemed like a warm, rough, damp flannel. She opened her eyes and looked. It was a tongue. Its owner was a large and bouncy young Alsatian, or German shepherd, with topaz eyes, black-tipped prick ears, a thick, soft coat, and a bushy black-tipped tail.

"*Lob!*" shouted a man farther up the beach. "Lob, come here!"

But Lob, as if trying to atone[1] for the surprise he had given her, went on licking the sand off Sandy's face,

◀ Vocabulary
decisively (dē sī′siv lē′) *adv.* with determination

Foreshadowing and Flashback
Based on this hint that begins "Little did they guess," what do you think is going to happen in the story?

Comprehension
How does Sandy meet Lob?

---

1. atone (ə tōn′) *v.* make up for a wrong.

wagging his tail so hard while he kept on knocking up more clouds of sand. His owner, a gray-haired man with a limp, walked over as quickly as he could and seized him by the collar.

"I hope he didn't give you a fright?" the man said to Sandy. "He meant it in play—he's only young."

"Oh, no, I think he's *beautiful*." said Sandy truly. She picked up a bit of driftwood and threw it. Lob, whisking easily out of his master's grip, was after it like a sand-colored bullet. He came back with the stick, beaming, and gave it to Sandy. At the same time he gave himself, though no one else was aware of this at the time. But with Sandy, too, it was love at first sight, and when, after a lot more stick-throwing, she and the twins joined Father and Don to go home for tea, they cast many a backward glance at Lob being led firmly away by his master.

"I wish we could play with him every day." Tess sighed.

"Why can't we?" said Tim.

Sandy explained. "Because Mr. Dodsworth, who owns him, is from Liverpool, and he is only staying at the Fisherman's Arms till Saturday."

"Is Liverpool a long way off?"

"Right at the other end of England from Cornwall, I'm afraid."

It was a Cornish fishing village where the Pengelly family lived, with rocks and cliffs and a strip of beach and a little round harbor, and palm trees growing in the gardens of the little whitewashed stone houses. The village was approached by a narrow, steep, twisting hill-road, and guarded by a notice that said LOW GEAR FOR 1 ½ MILES, DANGEROUS TO CYCLISTS.

The Pengelly children went home to scones with Cornish cream and jam, thinking they had seen the last of Lob. But they were much mistaken. The whole family was

Foreshadowing and Flashback
What might this description of the road foreshadow?

Critical Viewing ▶
What details in this image are like the village described in the story?

playing cards by the fire in the front room after supper when there was a loud thump and a crash of china in the kitchen.

"My Christmas puddings!" exclaimed Jean, and ran out.

"Did you put TNT in them, then?" her husband said.

But it was Lob, who, finding the front door shut, had gone around to the back and bounced in through the open kitchen window, where the puddings were cooling on the sill. Luckily only the smallest was knocked down and broken.

Lob stood on his hind legs and plastered Sandy's face with licks. Then he did the same for the twins, who shrieked with joy.

"Where does this friend of yours come from?" inquired Mr. Pengelly.

"He's staying at the Fisherman's Arms—I mean his owner is."

"Then he must go back there. Find a bit of string, Sandy, to tie to his collar."

"I wonder how he found his way here," Mrs. Pengelly said, when the reluctant Lob had been led whining away and Sandy had explained about their afternoon's game on the beach. "Fisherman's Arms is right around the other side of the harbor."

Lob's owner scolded him and thanked Mr. Pengelly for bringing him back. Jean Pengelly warned the children that they had better not encourage Lob any more if they met him on the beach, or it would only lead to more trouble. So they dutifully took no notice of him the next day until he spoiled their good resolutions by dashing up to them with joyful barks, wagging his tail so hard that he winded Tess and knocked Tim's legs from under him.

They had a happy day, playing on the sand.

The next day was Saturday. Sandy had found out that Mr. Dodsworth was to catch the half-past-nine train. She went out secretly, down to the station, nodded to Mr. Hoskins, the stationmaster, who wouldn't dream of charging any local for a platform ticket, and climbed up on the footbridge that led over the tracks. She didn't want to be seen, but she did want to see. She saw Mr. Dodsworth get on the train, accompanied by an unhappy-looking Lob with

"I wish we could play with him every day."

◀ Vocabulary
resolutions
(rez´ ə lōō´ shənz) n.
intentions; things
decided

Comprehension
What causes the crash in the Pengellys' kitchen?

drooping ears and tail. Then she saw the train slide away out of sight around the next headland, with a **melancholy** wail that sounded like Lob's last good-bye.

Sandy wished she hadn't had the idea of coming to the station. She walked home miserably, with her shoulders hunched and her hands in her pockets. For the rest of the day she was so cross and unlike herself that Tess and Tim were quite surprised, and her mother gave her a dose of senna.

A week passed. Then, one evening, Mrs. Pengelly and the younger children were in the front room playing snakes and ladders. Mr. Pengelly and Don had gone fishing on the evening tide. If your father is a fisherman, he will never be home at the same time from one week to the next.

Suddenly, history repeating itself, there was a crash from the kitchen. Jean Pengelly leaped up, crying, "My blackberry jelly!" She and the children had spent the morning picking and the afternoon boiling fruit.

But Sandy was ahead of her mother. With flushed cheeks and eyes like stars she had darted into the kitchen, where she and Lob were hugging one another in a frenzy of joy.

About a yard of his tongue was out, and he was licking every part of her that he could reach.

"Good heavens!" exclaimed Jean. "How in the world did *he* get here?"

"He must have walked," said Sandy. "Look at his feet."

They were worn, dusty, and tarry. One had a cut on the pad.

"They ought to be bathed," said Jean Pengelly. "Sandy, run a bowl of warm water while I get disinfectant."

"What'll we do about him, Mother?" said Sandy anxiously.

Mrs. Pengelly looked at her daughter's pleading eyes and sighed.

"He must go back to his owner, of course," she said, making her voice firm. "Your dad can get the address from the Fisherman's tomorrow, and phone him or send a telegram. In the meantime he'd better have a long drink and a good meal."

Lob was very grateful for the drink and the meal, and made no objection to having his feet washed. Then he flopped down on the hearthrug and slept in front of the fire they had lit because it was a cold, wet evening, with his head on Sandy's feet. He was a very tired dog. He had walked all the way from Liverpool to Cornwall, which is more than four hundred miles.

The next day Mr. Pengelly phoned Lob's owner, and the following morning Mr. Dodsworth arrived off the night train, decidedly put out, to take his pet home. That parting was worse than the first. Lob whined, Don walked out of the house, the twins burst out crying, and Sandy crept up to her bedroom afterward and lay with her face pressed into the quilt, feeling as if she were bruised all over.

Jean Pengelly took them all into Plymouth to see the circus on the next day and the twins cheered up a little, but even the hour's ride in the train each way and the Liberty horses and performing seals could not cure Sandy's sore heart.

She need not have bothered, though. In ten days' time Lob was back—limping this time, with a torn ear and a patch missing out of his furry coat, as if he had met and tangled with an enemy or two in the course of his four-hundred-mile walk.

Bert Pengelly rang up Liverpool again. Mr. Dodsworth, when he answered, sounded weary. He said, "That dog has already cost me two days that I can't spare away from my work—plus endless time in police stations and drafting newspaper advertisements. I'm too old for these ups and downs. I think we'd better face the fact, Mr. Pengelly, that it's your family he wants to stay with—that is, if you want to have him."

Bert Pengelly gulped. He was not a rich man; and Lob was a pedigreed dog. He said cautiously, "How much would you be asking for him?"

"Good heavens, man, I'm not suggesting I'd sell him to you. You must have him as a gift. Think of the train fares I'll be saving. You'll be doing me a good turn."

Comprehension
Why does Mr. Dodsworth give Lob to the Pengelly family?

"Is he a big eater?" Bert asked doubtfully.

By this time the children, breathless in the background listening to one side of this conversation, had realized what was in the wind and were dancing up and down with their hands clasped beseechingly.

"Oh, not for his size," Lob's owner assured Bert. "Two or three pounds of meat a day and some vegetables and gravy and biscuits—he does very well on that."

Alexandra's father looked over the telephone at his daughter's swimming eyes and trembling lips. He reached a decision. "Well, then, Mr. Dodsworth," he said briskly, "we'll accept your offer and thank you very much. The children will be overjoyed and you can be sure Lob has come to a good home. They'll look after him and see he gets enough exercise. But I can tell you," he ended firmly, "if he wants to settle in with us he'll have to learn to eat a lot of fish."

So that was how Lob came to live with the Pengelly family. Everybody loved him and he loved them all. But there was never any question who came first with him. He was Sandy's dog. He slept by her bed and followed her everywhere he was allowed.

Nine years went by, and each summer Mr. Dodsworth came back to stay at the Fisherman's Arms and call on his erstwhile dog. Lob always met him with recognition and dignified pleasure, accompanied him for a walk or two—but showed no signs of wishing to return to Liverpool. His place, he intimated,[2] was definitely with the Pengellys.

In the course of nine years Lob changed less than Sandy. As she went into her teens he became a little slower, a little stiffer, there was a touch of gray on his nose, but he was still a handsome dog. He and Sandy still loved one another devotedly.

One evening in October all the summer visitors had left, and the little fishing town looked empty and secretive. It was a wet, windy dusk. When the children came home from school—even the twins were at high school now, and Don was a full-fledged fisherman—Jean Pengelly said, "Sandy, your Aunt Rebecca says she's lonesome because Uncle Will Hoskins has gone out trawling, and she wants one of you to go and spend the evening with her. You go, dear; you can take your homework with you."

---

2. **intimated** (in´ tə māt´ əd) v. hinted; made known indirectly.

Sandy looked far from enthusiastic.

"Can I take Lob with me?"

"You know Aunt Becky doesn't really like dogs—Oh, very well." Mrs. Pengelly sighed. "I suppose she'll have to put up with him as well as you."

Reluctantly Sandy tidied herself, took her schoolbag, put on the damp raincoat she had just taken off, fastened Lob's lead to his collar, and set off to walk through the dusk to Aunt Becky's cottage, which was five minutes' climb up the steep hill.

The wind was howling through the shrouds of boats drawn up on the Hard.

"Put some cheerful music on, do," said Jean Pengelly to the nearest twin. "Anything to drown that wretched sound while I make your dad's supper." So Don, who had just come in, put on some rock music, loud. Which was why the Pengellys did not hear the truck hurtle down the hill and crash against the post office wall a few minutes later.

Dr. Travers was driving through Cornwall with his wife, taking a late holiday before patients began coming down with winter colds and flu. He saw the sign that said STEEP HILL. LOW GEAR FOR 1 ½ MILES. Dutifully he changed into second gear.

"We must be nearly there," said his wife, looking out of her window. "I noticed a sign on the coast road that said the Fisherman's Arms was two miles. What a narrow, dangerous hill! But the cottages are very pretty—Oh, Frank, stop, *stop*! There's a child, I'm sure it's a child—by the wall over there!"

Dr. Travers jammed on his brakes and brought the car to a stop. A little stream ran down by the road in a shallow stone culvert, and half in the water lay something that

Foreshadowing and Flashback
What do you think the descriptions in these paragraphs foreshadow?

Critical Viewing ▲
What elements of danger do you see in this picture?

Comprehension
Where are Sandy and Lob going?

looked, in the dusk, like a pile of clothes—or was it the body of the child? Mrs. Travers was out of the car in a flash, but her husband was quicker.

"Don't touch her, Emily!" he said sharply. "She's been hit. Can't be more than a few minutes. Remember that truck that overtook us half a mile back, speeding like the devil? Here, quick, go into that cottage and phone for an ambulance. The girl's in a bad way. I'll stay here and do what I can to stop the bleeding. Don't waste a minute."

Doctors are expert at stopping dangerous bleeding, for they know the right places to press. This Dr. Travers was able to do, but he didn't dare do more; the girl was lying in a queerly crumpled heap, and he guessed she had a number of bones broken and that it would be highly dangerous to move her. He watched her with great concentration, wondering where the truck had got to and what other damage it had done.

Mrs. Travers was very quick. She had seen plenty of accident cases and knew the importance of speed. The first cottage she tried had a phone; in four minutes she was back, and in six an ambulance was wailing down the hill.

Its attendants lifted the child onto a stretcher as carefully as if she were made of fine thistledown. The ambulance sped off to Plymouth—for the local cottage hospital did not take serious accident cases—and Dr. Travers went down to the police station to report what he had done.

He found that the police already knew about the speeding truck—which had suffered from loss of brakes and ended up with its radiator halfway through the post-office wall. The driver was concussed and shocked, but the police thought he was the only person injured—until Dr. Travers told his tale.

At half-past nine that night Aunt Rebecca Hoskins was sitting by her fire thinking aggrieved[3] thoughts about the inconsiderateness of nieces who were asked to supper and never turned up, when she was startled by a neighbor, who burst in, exclaiming, "Have you heard about Sandy Pengelly, then, Mrs. Hoskins? Terrible thing, poor little soul, and they don't know if she's likely to live. Police have got the truck driver that hit her—ah, it didn't ought to be allowed,

Foreshadowing and Flashback
What hints does this paragraph contain about possible events to come?

---

3. **aggrieved** (ə grēvd′) *adj.* offended; wronged.

speeding through the place like that at umpty miles an hour, they ought to jail him for life—not that that'd be any comfort for poor Bert and Jean."

Horrified, Aunt Rebecca put on a coat and went down to her brother's house. She found the family with white shocked faces; Bert and Jean were about to drive off to the hospital where Sandy had been taken, and the twins were crying bitterly. Lob was nowhere to be seen. But Aunt Rebecca was not interested in dogs; she did not inquire about him.

"Thank the Lord you've come, Beck," said her brother. "Will you stay the night with Don and the twins? Don's out looking for Lob and heaven knows when we'll be back; we may get a bed with Jean's mother in Plymouth."

"Oh, if only I'd never invited the poor child," wailed Mrs. Hoskins. But Bert and Jean hardly heard her.

That night seemed to last forever. The twins cried themselves to sleep. Don came home very late and grim-faced. Bert and Jean sat in a waiting room of the Western Counties Hospital, but Sandy was unconscious, they were told, and she remained so. All that could be done for her was done. She was given transfusions to replace all the blood she had lost. The broken bones were set and put in slings and cradles.

"Is she a healthy girl? Has she a good constitution?" the emergency doctor asked.

"Aye, doctor, she is that," Bert said hoarsely. The lump in Jean's throat prevented her from answering; she merely nodded.

"Then she ought to have a chance. But I won't conceal from you that her condition is very serious, unless she shows signs of coming out from this coma."

But as hour succeeded hour, Sandy showed no signs of recovering consciousness. Her parents sat in the waiting room with haggard faces; sometimes one of them would go to telephone the family at home, or to try to get a little sleep at the home of Granny Pearce, not far away.

At noon next day Dr. and Mrs. Travers went to the Pengelly cottage to inquire how Sandy was doing, but the report was gloomy: "Still in a very serious condition."

Foreshadowing and Flashback
What clues in these paragraphs suggest that Lob may not be safe?

"She's been hit. Can't be more than a few minutes."

Comprehension
How does Sandy's family react to her condition?

Foreshadowing and Flashback

What do you learn about Sandy from the flashback in this paragraph?

The twins were miserably unhappy. They forgot that they had sometimes called their elder sister bossy and only remembered how often she had shared her pocket money with them, how she read to them and took them for picnics and helped with their homework. Now there was no Sandy, no Mother and Dad, Don went around with a gray, shuttered face, and worse still, there was no Lob.

The Western Counties Hospital is a large one, with dozens of different departments and five or six connected buildings, each with three or four entrances. By that afternoon it became noticeable that a dog seemed to have taken up position outside the hospital, with the fixed intention of getting in. Patiently he would try first one entrance and then another, all the way around, and then begin again. Sometimes he would get a little way inside, following a visitor, but animals were, of course, forbidden, and he was always kindly but firmly turned out again. Sometimes the guard at the main entrance gave him a pat or offered him a bit of sandwich—he looked so wet and beseeching and desperate. But he never ate the sandwich. No one seemed to own him or to know where he came from; Plymouth is a large city and he might have belonged to anybody.

At tea time Granny Pearce came through the pouring rain to bring a flask of hot tea with brandy in it to her daughter and son-in-law. Just as she reached the main entrance the guard was gently but forcibly shoving out a large, agitated, soaking-wet Alsatian dog.

"No, old fellow, you can *not* come in. Hospitals are for people, not for dogs."

"Why, bless me," exclaimed old Mrs. Pearce. "That's Lob! Here, Lob, Lobby boy!"

Lob ran to her, whining. Mrs. Pearce walked up to the desk.

"I'm sorry, madam, you can't bring that dog in here," the guard said.

Mrs. Pearce was a very determined old lady. She looked the porter in the eye.

"Now, see here, young man. That dog has walked twenty miles from St. Killan to get to my granddaughter. Heaven knows how he knew she was here, but it's plain he knows. And he ought to have his rights! He ought to get to see her!

Foreshadowing and Flashback

What do you think is foreshadowed when Granny Pearce recognizes the dog?

Do you know," she went on, bristling, "that dog has walked the length of England—*twice*—to be with that girl? And you think you can keep him out with your fiddling rules and regulations?"

"I'll have to ask the medical officer," the guard said weakly.

"You do that, young man." Granny Pearce sat down in a determined manner, shutting her umbrella, and Lob sat patiently dripping at her feet. Every now and then he shook his head, as if to dislodge something heavy that was tied around his neck.

Presently a tired, thin, intelligent-looking man in a white coat came downstairs, with an impressive, silver-haired man in a dark suit, and there was a low-voiced discussion. Granny Pearce eyed them, biding her time.

"Frankly. . . not much to lose," said the older man. The man in the white coat approached Granny Pearce.

"It's strictly against every rule, but as it's such a serious case we are making an exception," he said to her quietly. "But only *outside* her bedroom door—and only for a moment or two."

Without a word, Granny Pearce rose and stumped upstairs. Lob followed close to her skirts, as if he knew his hope lay with her.

They waited in the green-floored corridor outside Sandy's room. The door was half shut. Bert and Jean were inside. Everything was terribly quiet. A nurse came out. The white-coated man asked her something and she shook her head. She had left the door ajar and through it could now be seen a high, narrow bed with a lot of gadgets around it. Sandy lay there, very flat under the covers, very still. Her head was turned away. All Lob's attention was riveted on the bed. He strained toward it, but Granny Pearce clasped his collar firmly.

"I've done a lot for you, my boy, now you behave yourself," she whispered grimly. Lob let out a faint whine, anxious and pleading.

Comprehension
How does Lob get into the hospital to see Sandy?

Critical Viewing ▲
What details of this final image reinforce the relationship between Sandy and Lob?

At the sound of that whine Sandy stirred just a little. She sighed and moved her head the least fraction. Lob whined again. And then Sandy turned her head right over. Her eyes opened, looking at the door.

"Lob?" she murmured—no more than a breath of sound. "Lobby, boy?"

The doctor by Granny Pearce drew a quick, sharp breath. Sandy moved her left arm—the one that was not broken— from below the covers and let her hand dangle down, feeling, as she always did in the mornings, for Lob's furry head. The doctor nodded slowly.

"All right," he whispered. "Let him go to the bedside. But keep a hold of him."

Granny Pearce and Lob moved to the bedside. Now she could see Bert and Jean, white-faced and shocked, on the far side of the bed. But she didn't look at them. She looked at the smile on her granddaughter's face as the groping fingers found Lob's wet ears and gently pulled them. "Good boy," whispered Sandy, and fell asleep again.

Granny Pearce led Lob out into the passage again. There she let go of him and he ran off swiftly down the stairs. She would have followed him, but Bert and Jean had come out into the passage, and she spoke to Bert fiercely.

"I don't know why you were so foolish as not to bring the dog before! Leaving him to find the way here himself—"

"But, Mother!" said Jean Pengelly. "That can't have been Lob. What a chance to take! Suppose Sandy hadn't—" She stopped, with her handkerchief pressed to her mouth.

"Not Lob? I've known that dog nine years! I suppose I ought to know my own granddaughter's dog?"

"Listen, Mother," said Bert. "Lob was killed by the same truck that hit Sandy. Don found him—when he went to look for Sandy's schoolbag. He was—he was dead. Ribs all smashed. No question of that. Don told me on the phone—he and Will Hoskins rowed a half mile out to sea and sank the dog with a lump of concrete tied to his collar. Poor old boy. Still—he was getting on. Couldn't have lasted forever."

"*Sank him at sea?* Then what—?"

Slowly old Mrs. Pearce, and then the other two, turned to look at the trail of dripping-wet footprints that led down the hospital stairs.

In the Pengellys' garden they have a stone, under the palm tree. It says: "Lob. Sandy's dog. Buried at sea."

Foreshadowing and Flashback
Why does the author include this flashback to an earlier event?

Spiral Review
THEME Does this story convey the theme *love conquers all*? Explain.

Critical Thinking

1. **Key Ideas and Details (a)** How do Sandy and her family first meet Lob? **(b) Infer:** Why does Lob travel more than 400 miles to the Pengellys' house? **(c) Analyze:** How does Sandy feel about Lob? Support your answer.

2. **Key Ideas and Details** How do you think Mr. Dodsworth feels about giving the dog away? Support your answer with details from the story.

3. **Key Ideas and Details (a)** What happens when Sandy goes to visit her aunt? **(b)** How does Lob help Sandy at the hospital? **(c) Infer:** What does Lob's mysterious return suggest about his bond with Sandy?

4. **Craft and Structure (a) Analyze:** Why do you think the author chose to end the story in such an unusual way? **(b) Take a Position:** How important is the relationship between people and animals? Explain.

5. **Integration of Knowledge and Ideas (a) Speculate:** What conflicting feelings might the Pengellys experience because of what happened to Sandy and to Lob? **(b) Interpret:** What does the stone in the garden suggest about how they handle those feelings? *[Connect to the Big Question: Is conflict always bad?]*

Foreshadowing and Flashback
What clues here hint at a relationship developing between Macon and Grandpa Jeremiah?

grown. When Grandpa got sick he used to come around and help out with things around the house that was too hard for me to do. I mean, I could have done all the chores, but it would just take me longer.

When the work for the day was finished and the sows fed, Grandpa would kind of ease into one of his stories and Macon, he would sit and listen to them and be real interested. I didn't mind listening to the stories when Grandpa told them to Macon because he would be telling them in the middle of the afternoon and they would be past my mind by the time I had to go to bed.

Macon had an old guitar he used to mess with, too. He wasn't too bad on it, and sometimes Grandpa would tell him to play us a tune. He could play something he called "the Delta Blues" real good, but when Sister Todd or somebody from the church come around he'd play "Precious Lord" or "Just a Closer Walk With Thee."

Grandpa Jeremiah had been feeling poorly from that stroke, and one of his legs got a little drag to it. Just about the time Ellie come from school the next summer he was

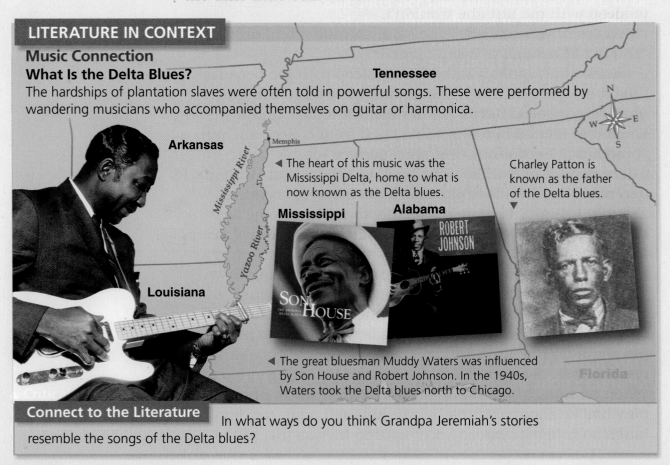

LITERATURE IN CONTEXT

Music Connection
What Is the Delta Blues?

The hardships of plantation slaves were often told in powerful songs. These were performed by wandering musicians who accompanied themselves on guitar or harmonica.

Tennessee

Arkansas

Memphis

Mississippi River

◄ The heart of this music was the Mississippi Delta, home to what is now known as the Delta blues.

Charley Patton is known as the father of the Delta blues. ▼

Louisiana

Yazoo River

Mississippi

Alabama

ROBERT JOHNSON

SON HOUSE

◄ The great bluesman Muddy Waters was influenced by Son House and Robert Johnson. In the 1940s, Waters took the Delta blues north to Chicago.

Florida

Connect to the Literature

In what ways do you think Grandpa Jeremiah's stories resemble the songs of the Delta blues?

real sick. He was breathing loud so you could hear it even in the next room and he would stay in bed a lot even when there was something that needed doing or fixing.

"I don't think he's going to make it much longer," Dr. Crawford said. "The only thing I can do is to give him something for the pain."

"Are you sure of your diagnosis?" Ellie asked. She was sitting around the table with Sister Todd, Deacon Turner, and his little skinny yellow wife.

◀ **Vocabulary**
diagnosis (dī əg nō´ sis) *n.* identification of a medical condition

Dr. Crawford looked at Ellie like he was surprised to hear her talking. "Yes, I'm sure," he said. "He had tests a few weeks ago and his condition was bad then."

"How much time he got?" Sister Todd asked.

"Maybe a week or two at best," Dr. Crawford said.

Spiral Review
THEME How does the doctor's diagnosis affect the family?

When he said that, Deacon Turner's wife started crying and goin' on and I give her a hard look but she just went on. I was the one who loved Grandpa Jeremiah the most and she didn't hardly even know him so I didn't see why she was crying.

Everybody started tiptoeing around the house after that. They would go in and ask Grandpa Jeremiah if he was comfortable and stuff like that or take him some food or a cold glass of lemonade. Sister Todd come over and stayed with us. Mostly what she did is make supper and do a lot of praying, which was good because I figured that maybe God would do something to make Grandpa Jeremiah well. When she wasn't doing that she was piecing on a fancy quilt she was making for some white people in Wilmington.

Ellie, she went around asking everybody how they felt about Dr. Crawford and then she went into town and asked about the tests and things. Sister Jenkins asked her if she thought she knowed more than Dr. Crawford, and Ellie rolled her eyes at her, but Sister Jenkins was reading out her Bible and didn't make no notice of it.

Then Macon come over.

He had been away on what he called "a little piece of a job" and hadn't heard how bad off Grandpa Jeremiah was. When he come over he talked to Ellie and she told him what was going on and then he got him a soft drink from the refrigerator and sat out on the porch and before you know it he was crying.

You could look at his face and tell the difference between him sweating and the tears. The sweat was close against his skin and shiny and the tears come down fatter and more sparkly.

Comprehension
How does Macon help Grandpa Jeremiah?

Critical Viewing ▲
Does this scene
seem similar to the
story's setting? Explain.

**Foreshadowing
and Flashback**

What does this
description of Grandpa
Jeremiah suggest about
events to come?

Macon sat on the porch, without saying a word, until the sun went down and the crickets started chirping and carrying on. Then he went in to where Grandpa Jeremiah was and stayed in there for a long time.

Sister Todd was saying that Grandpa Jeremiah needed his rest and Ellie went in to see what Macon was doing. Then she come out real mad.

"He got Grandpa telling those old stories again," Ellie said. "I told him Grandpa needed his rest and for him not to be staying all night."

He did leave soon, but bright and early the next morning Macon was back again. This time he brought his guitar with him and he went on in to Grandpa Jeremiah's room. I went in, too.

Grandpa Jeremiah's room smelled terrible. It was all closed up so no drafts could get on him and the whole room was smelled down with disinfect[1] and medicine. Grandpa Jeremiah lay propped up on the bed and he was so gray he looked scary. His hair wasn't combed down and his head on the pillow with his white hair sticking out was enough to send me flying if Macon hadn't been there. He was skinny, too. He looked like his skin got loose on his bones, and when he lifted his arms, it hung down like he was just wearing it instead of it being a part of him.

Macon sat slant-shouldered with his guitar across his lap. He was messin' with the guitar, not making any music, but just going over the strings as Grandpa talked.

"Old Carrie went around out back to where they kept the pigs penned up and she felt a cold wind across her face. . . ." Grandpa Jeremiah was telling the story about how a old woman out-tricked the Devil and got her son back. I had heard the story before, and I knew it was pretty scary. "When she felt the cold breeze she didn't blink nary an eye, but looked straight ahead. . . ."

---

1. disinfect (dis´ in fect´) *n.* dialect, or regional language, for disinfectant, a substance that kills germs.

All the time Grandpa Jeremiah was talking I could see Macon fingering his guitar. I tried to imagine what it would be like if he was actually plucking the strings. I tried to fix my mind on that because I didn't like the way the story went with the old woman wrestling with the Devil.

We sat there for nearly all the afternoon until Ellie and Sister Todd come in and said that supper was ready. Me and Macon went out and ate some collard greens, ham hocks, and rice. Then Macon he went back in and listened to some more of Grandpa's stories until it was time for him to go home. I wasn't about to go in there and listen to no stories at night.

Dr. Crawford come around a few days later and said that Grandpa Jeremiah was doing a little better.

"You think the Good Lord gonna pull him through?" Sister Todd asked.

"I don't tell the Good Lord what He should or should not be doing," Dr. Crawford said, looking over at Sister Todd and at Ellie. "I just said that *my* patient seems to be doing okay for his condition."

"He been telling Macon all his stories," I said.

"Macon doesn't seem to understand that Grandpa Jeremiah needs his strength," Ellie said. "Now that he's improving, we don't want him to have a setback."

"No use in stopping him from telling his stories," Dr. Crawford said. "If it makes him feel good it's as good as any medicine I can give him."

I saw that this didn't set with Ellie, and when Dr. Crawford had left I asked her why.

"Dr. Crawford means well," she said, "but we have to get away from the kind of life that keeps us in the past."

She didn't say why we should be trying to get away from the stories and I really didn't care too much. All I knew was that when Macon was sitting in the room with Grandpa Jeremiah I wasn't nearly as scared as I used to be when it was just me and Ellie listening. I told that to Macon.

"You getting to be a big man, that's all," he said.

That was true. Me and Macon was getting to be good friends, too. I didn't even mind so much when he started being friends with Ellie later. It seemed kind of natural, almost like Macon was supposed to be there with us instead of just visiting.

Grandpa wasn't getting no better, but he wasn't getting no worse, either.

Foreshadowing and Flashback
What does Macon's behavior suggest about what he might do later?

Comprehension
How does Macon react to Grandpa Jeremiah's illness?

Foreshadowing and Flashback
What details in this passage hint that something pleasant may lie ahead?

"You liking Macon now?" I asked Ellie when we got to the middle of July. She was dishing out a plate of smothered chops for him and I hadn't even heard him ask for anything to eat.

"Macon's funny," Ellie said, not answering my question. "He's in there listening to all of those old stories like he's really interested in them. It's almost as if he and Grandpa Jeremiah are talking about something more than the stories, a secret language."

I didn't think I was supposed to say anything about that to Macon, but once, when Ellie, Sister Todd, and Macon were out on the porch shelling butter beans after Grandpa got tired and was resting, I went into his room and told him what Ellie had said.

"She said that?" Grandpa Jeremiah's face was skinny and old looking but his eyes looked like a baby's, they was so bright.

"Right there in the kitchen is where she said it," I said. "And I don't know what it mean but I was wondering about it."

"I didn't think she had any feeling for them stories," Grandpa Jeremiah said. "If she think we talking secrets, maybe she don't."

"I think she getting a feeling for Macon," I said,

"That's okay, too," Grandpa Jeremiah said. "They both young."

"Yeah, but them stories you be telling, Grandpa, they about old people who lived a long time ago," I said.

"Well, those the folks you got to know about," Grandpa Jeremiah said. "You think on what those folks been through, and what they was feeling, and you add it up with what you been through and what you been feeling, then you got you something."

"What you got Grandpa?"

"You got you a bridge," Grandpa said. "And a meaning. Then when things get so hard you about to break, you can sneak across that bridge and see some folks who went before you and see how they didn't break. Some got bent and some got twisted and a few fell along the way, but they didn't break."

"Am I going to break, Grandpa?"

"You? As strong as you is?" Grandpa Jeremiah pushed himself up on his elbow and give me a look. "No way you going to break, boy. You gonna be strong as they come.

Foreshadowing and Flashback
In what way are Grandpa Jeremiah's stories like flashbacks?

One day you gonna tell all them stories I told you to your young'uns and they'll be as strong as you."

"Suppose I ain't got no stories, can I make some up?"

"Sure you can, boy. You make 'em up and twist 'em around. Don't make no mind. Long as you got 'em."

"Is that what Macon is doing?" I asked. "Making up stories to play on his guitar?"

"He'll do with 'em what he see fit, I suppose," Grandpa Jeremiah said. "Can't ask more than that from a man."

It rained the first three days of August. It wasn't a hard rain but it rained anyway. The mailman said it was good for the crops over East but I didn't care about that so I didn't pay him no mind. What I did mind was when it rain like that the field mice come in and get in things like the flour bin and I always got the blame for leaving it open.

When the rain stopped I was pretty glad. Macon come over and sat with Grandpa and had something to eat with us. Sister Todd come over, too.

"How Grandpa doing?" Sister Todd asked. "They been asking about him in the church."

"He's doing all right," Ellie said.

"He's kind of quiet today," Macon said. "He was just talking about how the hogs needed breeding."

"He must have run out of stories to tell," Sister Todd said. "He'll be repeating on himself like my father used to do. That's the way I *hear* old folks get."

Everybody laughed at that because Sister Todd was pretty old, too. Maybe we was all happy because the sun was out after so much rain. When Sister Todd went in to take Grandpa Jeremiah a plate of potato salad with no mayonnaise like he liked it, she told him about how people was asking for him and he told her to tell them he was doing okay and to remember him in their prayers.

Sister Todd came over the next afternoon, too, with some rhubarb pie with cheese on it, which is my favorite pie. When she took a piece into Grandpa Jeremiah's room she come right out again and told Ellie to go fetch the Bible.

It was a hot day when they had the funeral. Mostly everybody was there. The church was hot as anything, even though they had the window open. Some yellowjacks flew in and buzzed around Sister Todd's niece and then around Deacon Turner's wife and settled right on her hat and stayed there until we all stood and sang "Soon-a Will Be Done."

Foreshadowing and Flashback
What event may be foreshadowed in Macon's description? Explain.

Comprehension
How do Ellie's feelings for Macon change?

At the graveyard Macon played "Precious Lord" and I cried hard even though I told myself that I wasn't going to cry the way Ellie and Sister Todd was, but it was such a sad thing when we left and Grandpa Jeremiah was still out to the grave that I couldn't help it.

During the funeral and all, Macon kind of told everybody where to go and where to sit and which of the three cars to ride in. After it was over he come by the house and sat on the front porch and played on his guitar. Ellie was standing leaning against the rail and she was crying but it wasn't a hard crying. It was a soft crying, the kind that last inside of you for a long time.

Macon was playing a tune I hadn't heard before. I thought it might have been what he was working at when Grandpa Jeremiah was telling him those stories and I watched his fingers but I couldn't tell if it was or not. It wasn't nothing special, that tune Macon was playing, maybe halfway between them Delta blues he would do when Sister Todd wasn't around and something you would play at church. It was something different and something the same at the same time. I watched his fingers go over that guitar and figured I could learn that tune one day if I had a mind to.

Foreshadowing and Flashback
What event might this last sentence foreshadow?

Critical Thinking

1. **Key Ideas and Details** **(a)** What is Ellie's relationship to the narrator? **(b) Interpret:** Describe the narrator's feelings toward Ellie. Support your response with textual evidence.

2. **Key Ideas and Details** **(a)** Why does Ellie not want Macon around Grandpa Jeremiah's house at first? **(b) Draw Conclusions:** How does the narrator feel toward Macon? Cite details to support your response.

3. **Key Ideas and Details** **(a) Interpret:** What are Grandpa Jeremiah's "songs"? **(b) Take a Position:** Do you think songs and stories such as those Grandpa tells are important to future generations? Explain.

4. **Integration of Knowledge and Ideas** **(a)** How do Ellie and Macon feel about Grandpa? **(b) Draw Conclusions:** Why do they have a conflict over how best to care for him? *[Connect to the Big Question: Is conflict always bad?]*

Comparing Foreshadowing and Flashback

1. **Key Ideas and Details** Create a chart for each story. **(a)** In the left two columns, list clues in the story and the events they foreshadow. **(b)** In the right two columns, list flashbacks and tell what you learn from each one.

Foreshadowing		Flashback	
Clues ———————→ Event		Detail ———————→ Reveals	

2. **Craft and Structure** Based on your charts, which writer makes more use of these plot devices? Explain.

 Timed Writing

Explanatory Text: Essay

Compare and contrast the authors' use of foreshadowing and flashback in "Lob's Girl" and "Jeremiah's Song." In an essay, discuss the effects of these plot devices. **(30 minutes)**

5-Minute Planner

1. Read the prompt carefully and completely.

2. Review your charts for examples of foreshadowing and flashback in the stories.

3. Organize your thoughts by asking the following questions:

   • Which story has more suspense, based on the use of foreshadowing?

   • Which story's structure includes more flashbacks?

   • What is the effect of the combination of foreshadowing and flashback on each story?

4. Select an organizational strategy that will suit your essay, such as block format or point-by-point organization.

5. Reread the prompt, and then draft your essay.

USE ACADEMIC VOCABULARY

As you write, use academic language, including the following words or their related forms:

anticipate

conclude

refer

reveal

For more information about academic vocabulary, see pages xlvi–l.

Using a Dictionary and Thesaurus

A **dictionary** provides the meaning, pronunciation, and part of speech of words in the English language. It also gives a word's **etymology,** or origins. A word's etymology explains how words change, how they are borrowed from other languages, and how new words are invented, or "coined." Notice what this dictionary entry reveals about the word *athlete*.

> **athlete** (ath′ lēt′) *n.* [L *athleta* < Gr athlētēs, contestant in the games] a person trained in exercises, games, or contests requiring such qualities as physical strength, skills, and speed.

A **thesaurus** provides synonyms, or words with similar meanings, for many words in the English language. A thesaurus can help you find a word that means exactly what you want to say. The thesaurus entry shown gives several synonyms for *athlete*. Notice how each word has a slightly different meaning.

> **athlete** *n.* acrobat, gymnast, player, contestant, champion, sportsman, contender, challenger.

Follow these steps to use a thesaurus effectively:

- Identify a word in your writing that could be more precise.
- Read through the words that your thesaurus lists as synonyms.
- Choose the word that best expresses your intended meaning.
- Use a dictionary to make sure you are using the word correctly.

Where to Find a Dictionary and Thesaurus You can find these resources in book form at your school or library. You can also find them in electronic form on the Internet. Ask your teacher to recommend the best online word-study resources.

Practice A Find these words in a dictionary. Show how each one breaks into syllables and which syllable is stressed. Then, write each word's definition. Finally, use each word in a sentence that shows its meaning.

1. estimate   **2.** intuition   **3.** temporary   **4.** distinguish

Practice B Find each word in a thesaurus. Select two synonyms for the word. Explain how the meaning of each synonym is different from the meaning of the original word. Then, use each synonym in a sentence that shows its exact meaning. Remember to use a dictionary to check the meanings of your synonyms.

1. laugh (verb)   **2.** large (adjective)   **3.** story (noun)

Activity Create a quick-reference thesaurus of some commonly used words. Make notecards like the one shown for the words *strong, happy,* and *smart*. Share your words with classmates, collecting more synonyms. Then, with a partner, discuss the shades of meaning that each word conveys. You can use quick-reference cards like these to help you find precise words when you write.

Word:
Part of Speech:
Definition:
Synonym 1:
Synonym 1 Definition:
Synonym 2:
Synonym 2 Definition:

Comprehension and Collaboration

With a small group, take turns suggesting synonyms for the following words. Use a dictionary and a thesaurus to check your answers and to find additional synonyms.

- **look** (verb)
- **speak** (verb)
- **nervous** (adjective)

Speaking and Listening

Following Oral Directions

To understand and carry out **multistep oral directions**, or spoken directions with several steps, listen carefully to the speaker. Then, write down or restate the directions in the correct sequence. The following strategies will help you demonstrate effective listening skills.

Learn the Skills

Follow these guidelines to understand and apply oral directions.

Focus your attention. As you listen to directions, pay close attention to the speaker. Try to avoid or ignore distractions and focus on what is being said.

Notice action words and time-order words. Listen for the key action word in each step. These words tell you what to do. In the following directions for a fire drill, the action words are underlined:

- **Example:** First, <u>close</u> the doors and windows. Then, <u>walk</u> to the nearest exit. When you are outside, <u>stand</u> with your class while the teacher counts the people in the group.

Most directions are stated in chronological order, or the sequence in which they are meant to occur. For this reason, they usually include time-order words, such as *first, then, next,* and *last.*

Ask questions. Do not assume that the speaker will give you all the information you need. Instead, identify any information you think is missing or unclear and ask questions. You may need the speaker to be more precise in his or her description or to give you details that will clarify your understanding.

Paraphrase the directions. Clarify your understanding by paraphrasing the directions, or restating them in your own words. Ask the person giving the directions to clear up any misunderstandings.

Use action and time-order words. In your paraphrase, use action words to restate the action in each step. Use time-order words at the beginning of each step to restate multistep directions.

> ### Checklist
>
> #### Listen Carefully
> ☑ Focus on the speaker. Listen for main ideas.
> ☑ Notice the action word in each step.
> ☑ Notice time-order words.
> ☑ Ask questions.
>
> #### Restate Carefully
> ☑ Repeat the directions in your own words.
> ☑ Use action and time-order words.

Practice the Skills

Presentation of Knowledge and Ideas Use what you have learned in the workshop to perform the following activity.

ACTIVITY: Giving and Following Oral Directions

Work with a partner to take turns giving and following oral directions.

- Choose a multistep task that you can complete in your classroom, such as addressing an envelope, formatting a document, or taking and editing a photograph.
- Break the task into time-ordered steps, including transition words that show sequence.
- Deliver the directions clearly, without rushing.
- Clarify your directions by answering any questions your partner may have.
- When it is your turn to follow directions, listen carefully. Then, restate the directions, using each step in the checklist on the left page.
- Ask your partner any questions you have about the directions.
- Finally, carry out your partner's instructions and complete the task.

Use a guide for following directions like the one shown to take notes on your partner's presentation.

Guide for Following Oral Directions

Steps	Areas of Confusion
Record each step in chronological order. Write the action verb first.	Which steps are confusing? Do any terms need to be defined?
Step 1: _____	
Step 2: _____	**Summarize**
Step 3: _____	My restatement, or paraphrase, of the directions:
Step 4: _____	Does my restatement of the directions match those intended by my partner?
Step 5: _____	Can I successfully carry out these
Step 6: _____	directions?

Comprehension and Collaboration With your classmates, discuss which steps made following oral directions easy and which steps made following oral directions difficult.

Write a Narrative

Short Story

Defining the Form **Short stories** are brief works of fiction meant to entertain, to explore ideas, or to tell truths about life. They often feature a conflict, or a problem, faced by one or more characters. You might use elements of a short story in letters, scripts, and screenplays.

Assignment Write a short story about a person who faces a difficult challenge. Your short story should feature these elements:

✓ one or more *well-developed characters*

✓ an *interesting conflict* or problem

✓ a *plot* that moves toward a resolution of the conflict

✓ a clear and accurate *point of view,* or perspective

✓ concrete and *sensory details* that establish the *setting*

✓ *dialogue,* or conversations between characters

✓ error-free grammar, including the use of *correct pronoun-antecedent agreement*

To preview the criteria on which your short story may be judged, see the rubric on page 109.

FOCUS ON RESEARCH

As you prepare to write a short story, you might conduct research to

• find accurate details about the place your story is set.

• locate facts about life during another time period if your story takes place in the past.

• learn about an activity your characters perform or a sport they play.

Be sure to use reliable sources of information for your research. Double-check the accuracy of dates, statistics, and other data by confirming the information in two or more sources.

READING-WRITING CONNECTION

To get a feel for short stories, read "Stray" by Cynthia Rylant on page 20.

Prewriting/Planning Strategies

Freewrite. Set a timer and freewrite for five minutes. Start with an image—a person in a boat in the middle of the ocean—or a feeling: curiosity, fear, or loneliness. During freewriting, focus more on the flow of ideas than on spelling or grammar. After five minutes, review your freewriting. Circle ideas to use in your story.

Review art and photos. Look at several pieces of fine art or photography in your textbooks or other sources. For each, imagine a story based on what the image suggests. Choose one of these ideas as the basis of your story.

Identify the conflict. Once you have a general idea of the story you will tell, get a better idea of its conflict—the struggle between two opposing forces. To develop the conflict, ask yourself these questions:

- What does my main character want?
- Who or what is getting in the way?
- What will the character do to overcome this obstacle?

Create your main character. Fill in a web like the one shown to help you get to know your main character.

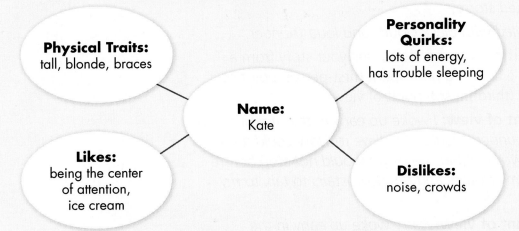

Physical Traits:
tall, blonde, braces

Personality Quirks:
lots of energy,
has trouble sleeping

Name:
Kate

Likes:
being the center
of attention,
ice cream

Dislikes:
noise, crowds

Give your story a title. With a clear idea of your topic and your main character, list possible titles for your story. Scan your list and choose the title that best captures the essence of what your story will convey.

Drafting Strategies

Develop your plot. Use a plot diagram like the one shown to organize the sequence of events in your short story. Make sure the events follow a sequence that unfolds naturally and logically. Plot often follows this pattern:

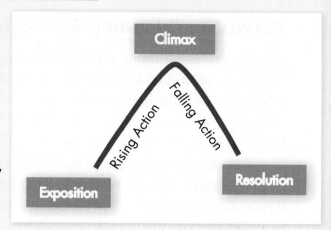

- **Exposition** introduces the characters and situation, including the conflict.
- The **conflict** develops during the **rising action,** which leads to the climax of the story.
- The **climax** is the point of greatest tension in the story.
- In the **falling action,** events and emotions wind down.
- In the **resolution,** the conflict is resolved and loose ends are tied up. The conclusion of your story should logically follow the events in the plot.

Use sensory details. As you draft your story, make your characters and setting come to life by including **sensory details**—language that describes how things look, sound, feel, taste, and smell. Having descriptive details will help you to develop a setting that the reader can visualize.

Dull: The sky *looked stormy.*

Vivid: The sky *boiled with black clouds and loud thunder.*

Write from a specific point of view. Tell your story from a single point of view, either as a participant (first-person point of view) or an observer (third-person point of view).

First-person point of view: *I woke up early in the morning to the sound of thunder. I couldn't believe it! How could it rain on my big day? I worried that the storm would not stop before noon. I pulled on my clothes and ran downstairs to talk to my mom.*

Third-person point of view: *Harry woke up early in the morning to the sound of thunder. He couldn't believe it! How could it rain on his big day? Harry's face revealed signs of worry and frustration. After dressing, he ran downstairs to talk to his mom.*

Voice

Voice is the personality behind a piece of writing. When voice comes through in an essay or a story, readers can almost hear someone speaking. Voice reveals the speaker's personality and attitude toward the world.

Finding a Fictional Voice When you write an essay, the voice you use should be a reflection of you. It should allow your personality and your ideas to shine through. When you write a short story, however, the narrator is not necessarily you.

If you write your story from a first-person point of view, the narrator is a character in the story. This character's way of speaking and attitude toward the other characters must reflect his or her personality.

If you write your story from a third-person point of view, the narrator is outside the story. You must imagine the character of that narrator.

Consider the following points as you develop your narrator's voice:

Characteristics	What the narrator is like will shape the way he or she tells the story.	**Consider these questions:** • How old is the narrator? • Is the narrator male or female?
Attitude	The narrator's attitude toward the different characters and their conflict will affect how he or she tells the story.	**Consider this question:** • Is the narrator sympathetic toward the main character? Why or why not?
Tone	Tone is the author's attitude toward his or her audience and subject. If your story is funny, you might want your narrator to convey a humorous tone.	**Consider these questions:** • What word describes the tone of your story? • How can your narrator convey that tone?
Word Choice	The narrator's words can reflect his or her traits. For example, a teen is likely to speak differently than an adult.	**Consider this question:** • What words or phrases would someone with the characteristics of the narrator use?

Evaluating Your Narrative Voice After you have drafted your story, read it aloud. Does the narrator sound right to you? Does his or her voice come across the way you want it to? If not, revise your word choice and sentence structures to better reflect your narrator's voice.

Revising Strategies

Create logical connections between events. Use a bead chart to make sure that events in your plot are logically connected.

- Underline the major events in your story.

- Summarize each event in a "bead" on a chart like the one shown.

- Show the connections between events by writing a word or phrase in the connector string. Make sure that these ideas have been developed in your story.

- If most of your connectors say *next*, review your story. If you cannot think of a good connection between events, delete or reshape one of the events.

- Transitional words, phrases, and clauses, such as *meanwhile, back in town, while Mike waited,* can help you show a shift in time or setting.

- Consider using literary devices such as suspense, foreshadowing, or flashback to add variety to your "string" of events.

Troy starts wondering where Leonard is. — he's curious, annoyed — **Troy yells to Leonard to stop searching.** — next — **Troy goes into woods to look for Leonard.** — **Troy doesn't hear any response from Leonard.** — he starts to worry

Evaluate point of view. Check that the point of view in your story remains the same throughout the story. For example, if the story begins with the point of view of a young boy named Daniel, it should not end with the point of view of Daniel's mother.

Use dialogue to give characters a voice. Review your draft for places to bring your story to life with dialogue. Keep in mind that realistic characters may use slang and interrupt each other.

Vary your sentences and word choices. Revise your story to include a variety of words and sentence lengths. Be sure to use a thesaurus to make descriptions more vivid and to choose precise words. Look for a balance of short and long sentences. Providing a variety of sentences will improve your story's flow.

Revising for Pronoun-Antecedent Agreement

A **pronoun** takes the place of a noun or another pronoun. The word that the pronoun refers to is called the **antecedent**.

Agreement in Number A pronoun and its antecedent must agree in number. Use a singular pronoun with a singular antecedent. Use a plural pronoun with a plural antecedent.

Singular Pronoun and Antecedent
<u>California</u> is a popular vacation spot because ***it*** has many beautiful beaches.

Plural Pronoun and Antecedent
My **parents** said that ***they*** would attend my play.

Agreement in Person and Gender A pronoun and its antecedent must agree in person and gender.

Third-Person Male Pronoun and Antecedent
<u>Juan</u> was late, but ***he*** had the books.

Third-Person Female Pronoun and Antecedent
<u>Shandra</u> said ***she*** wanted to borrow a book.

Clear Antecedent Every pronoun must have a clear antecedent. Problems may arise if a pronoun has more than one possible antecedent.

Unclear: <u>Patel</u> told <u>George</u> that ***he*** was late.

Clear: Patel told George that George was late.

Fixing Errors To find and fix errors related to pronoun use, follow these steps:

1. Identify each pronoun/antecedent pair that you used.
  - Make sure pronouns and their antecedents agree in number.
  - Make sure pronouns and their antecedents agree in person and gender.
  - Make sure pronouns refer to clear antecedents.

2. Follow the rules of agreement to fix any errors.

Grammar in Your Writing
Reread your short story. Look for pronouns and their antecedents. Then, use the rules above to make corrections.

Math Mackerel

I sat staring blankly at the sheet of notebook paper in front of me. My teacher had just finished explaining how to divide fractions. I didn't understand it at all. I hated math, and now in sixth grade, math was much harder.

"I wish someone could help me understand math." I whispered.

Suddenly, a fish appeared out of thin air. I stared at him. He was standing on his tail with a flowing red cape and on his chest he had a yellow emblem with the red letters "MM."

"W-who are you?" I stammered.

"I am Math Mackerel. I thought I heard someone asking for help with math," the fish stated proudly.

"Oh, that was me," I said.

"I'll see you at recess." Math Mackerel said as he disappeared with a swish of his tail and a flick of fins.

My teacher called out, "Time to put your math in your notebooks." I realized I hadn't written down a single problem on my paper.

"Drat!" I thought and put away my paper.

Outside, I sat in a secluded spot behind a bush and waited. Suddenly, Math Mackerel appeared.

"Greetings," said Math Mackerel happily. "I am here to help you with math."

"Are you going to give me all the knowledge I need?" I asked curiously.

"I could do that, but that would be cheating," scoffed Math Mackerel. He whipped out a deck of cards. I raised my eyebrows at him. I couldn't see how a deck of cards could help me with math.

"Do you know how to play Go Fish?" asked Math Mackerel.

"Yes, but how is . . ." I tried to ask.

"Good, I'll go first." And he began to deal the cards with his fins.

Twenty minutes later, we were still playing a hearty game of Go Fish.

"Got any nines?" I asked, peering over my cards.

"Yes, what is one and seven ninths divided by two thirds?" he asked.

"Two and two thirds," I answered.

"Good job!" Math Mackerel said as he slammed his nines on the ground. Suddenly I heard my teacher's whistle. It was time to go inside.

"I will see you tomorrow," Math Mackerel called as he disappeared.

Math Mackerel and I played Go Fish for three weeks, and I got better and better at math. Then one day, my teacher announced a math test to review what we had learned. Suddenly, all my confidence evaporated. Playing with Math Mackerel was something I could handle easily, but a test was a different matter.

At recess, Math Mackerel was already waiting for me.

"Time to continue yesterday's game," Math Mackerel said happily.

"There is going to be a math test on Friday! You have to be there!" I gasped.

"Just remember Go Fish, and you'll be fine." And he disappeared, as his cape swirled around him.

All week, I dreaded Friday. I gulped as the teacher passed out the papers. I worked through the problems and found them easy as I thought about Go Fish. My teacher returned the tests on Monday. I picked mine up and saw an A!

Karina introduces the conflict in the first paragraph of her story.

Karina chooses to write her story from the first-person point of view.

Karina creates dialogue between two central characters.

Here, Karina moves the plot forward to its climax.

Karina includes an exciting climax and ends with the resolution.

Editing and Proofreading

Revise to correct errors in grammar, spelling, and punctuation.

Focus on spelling. **Homophones** are words that sound the same and have similar spellings but have very different meanings. A spell checker will not find an error if a word is spelled correctly but is the wrong word choice; therefore, proofread carefully. Here are just a few examples of easily confused words: *our/are, than/then, know/now, lose/loose, accept/except, it's/its.*

Publishing and Presenting

Consider one of the following ways to share your writing:

Submit your story. Submit your story to your school's literary magazine, a national magazine, or an e-zine, or enter a contest that publishes student writing. Ask your teacher for suggestions.

Give a reading. Get together with a group of classmates and present a literary reading for an audience at your school.

Reflecting on Your Writing

Writer's Journal Jot down your answer to this question:

The next time you write a story, what do you think you might do differently as a result of this writing experience?

Rubric for Self-Assessment

Find evidence in your writing to address each category. Then use the rating scale to grade your work.

Spiral Review
Earlier in this unit, you learned about **personal and possessive pronouns** (p. 42) and **pronoun case** (p. 70). As you review your short story, be sure you have used pronouns correctly.

Rubric for Self-Assessment

Criteria	Rating Scale			
	not very .... *very*			
Purpose/Focus Clearly presents a narrative that develops real experiences and events	1	2	3	4
Organization Organizes events clearly and logically; presents a strong conclusion that follows from and reflects on events in the narrative	1	2	3	4
Development of Ideas/Elaboration Establishes a clear context and point of view; effectively uses narrative techniques, such as dialogue, pacing, and description	1	2	3	4
Language Uses precise words, descriptive details, and sensory language to convey experiences and events	1	2	3	4
Conventions Uses proper grammar, including correct use of pronouns and antecedents	1	2	3	4

SELECTED RESPONSE

I. Reading Literature

Directions: *Read the excerpt from "Becky and the Wheels-and-Brake Boys" by James Berry. Then, answer each question that follows.*

I found myself in the center of town, going through the busy Saturday crowd. I hoped Mum wouldn't be too cross. I went into the fire station. With lots of luck I came face to face with a round-faced man in uniform. He talked to me. "Little miss, can I help you?"

I told him I'd like to talk to the head man. He took me into the office and gave me a chair. I sat down. I opened out my brown paper parcel. I showed him my dad's sun helmet. I told him I thought it would make a good fireman's hat. I wanted to sell the helmet for some money toward a bike, I told him.

The fireman laughed a lot. I began to laugh, too. The fireman put me in a car and drove me back home.

Mum's eyes popped to see me bringing home the fireman. The round-faced fireman laughed at my adventure. Mum laughed, too, which was really good. The fireman gave Mum my dad's hat back. Then—mystery, mystery—Mum sent me outside while they talked.

My mum was only a little cross with me. Then—mystery and more mystery—my mum took me with the fireman in his car to his house.

The fireman brought out what? A bicycle! A beautiful, shining bicycle! His nephew's bike. His nephew had been taken away, all the way to America. The bike had been left with the fireman-uncle for him to sell it. And the good, kind fireman-uncle decided we could have the bike—on small payments. My mum looked uncertain. But in a big, big way, the fireman knew it was all right. And Mum smiled a little. My mum had good sense to know it was all right. My mum took the bike from the fireman Mr. Dean.

And guess what? Seeing my bike much, much newer than his, my cousin Ben's eyes <u>popped</u> with envy. But he took on the big job. He taught me to ride. Then he taught Shirnette.

1. **Part A** Which answer choice best summarizes the **plot** of this passage?

   A. Becky should save her money and buy a bike.
   B. Becky finds a way, with a stranger's help, to get a bike.
   C. Becky's family does not have enough money to buy a bike.
   D. Becky cannot have a bike.

   Part B Which phrase from the passage best presents the plot's **resolution**?

   A. "I wanted to sell the helmet"
   B. "The fireman gave Mum my Dad's hat back."
   C. "And the good, kind fireman-uncle decided we could have the bike"
   D. "The round-faced fireman laughed"

2. **Part A** Which phrase from the story shows **direct characterization** of the fireman?

   A. "...I came face to face with a round-faced man in uniform."
   B. "The fireman brought out what? A bicycle."
   C. "The fireman gave Mum my dad's hat back."
   D. "And the good, kind fireman-uncle decided we could have the bike..."

   Part B Which example of **indirect characterization** tells readers that the fireman is very kind?

   A. "He talked to me. 'Little miss, can I help you?'"
   B. "But...the fireman knew it was all right."
   C. "The fireman laughed a lot."
   D. "...I came face to face with a round-faced man in uniform."

3. What is the **internal conflict** felt by Becky's mother?

   A. She wants Becky to have a bike but is worried they cannot afford it.
   B. She does not like bicycles.
   C. She does not want Becky to talk to strangers but wants her to be friendly.
   D. She does not trust the fireman but has no other choice.

4. Which statement best captures the **theme** of the story?

   A. You should not want something too much—you might not be able to get it.
   B. If you cannot get something yourself, it's probably not worth it.
   C. Parents should get you what you want.
   D. If you really want something, you need to work with others to get it.

5. Which of the following statements best describes Becky?

   A. She has not earned her mother's trust.
   B. She is filled with pride by her new bike.
   C. She is willing to take a chance to get what she wants.
   D. She only wants what she cannot have.

6. Which phrase is closest in meaning to the underlined word *popped*?

   A. filled with tears
   B. looked angry
   C. narrowed suspiciously
   D. opened wide

⏱ Timed Writing

7. Write an original narrative that provides an alternative ending to the passage. Include both **direct characterization** and **indirect characterization**.

GO ON ➡

II. Reading Informational Text

Directions: *Read the passage. Then, answer each question that follows.*

Paper or Plastic?

After unloading your cart of groceries at the supermarket, you are faced with an important question: paper bags or plastic bags? How will you answer?

Paper comes from trees. The process of turning wood into paper uses great amounts of energy. Recycling paper requires the use of many different chemicals and a lot of energy. Even though paper is recyclable, it still fills half of all landfill space. Paper biodegrades more easily than plastic, but it is still a process that takes years.

Plastics come from the waste products of oil refining. Plastic bags require less energy to produce than do paper bags. They can also be recycled for uses such as relining wastebaskets. In landfills, plastic bags take up less room. However, plastic bags are often carelessly thrown away, harming marine life and causing clogs in sewers.

Conclusion Both paper bags and plastic bags use precious natural resources, but both can be recycled. So, what's the best choice? Neither one, we think. Our bag of choice? A reusable cotton bag.

Quick Facts: Why we should switch to reusable shopping bags
In one year, the average American uses about 350 plastic bags.
In one year, 14 million trees are cut down to make 10 billion paper bags.
Reusable bags are stronger and can be used for most shopping trips.

1. **Part A** The "Paper" and "Plastic" sections of the article answer these questions: *Where does it come from?* and *How much energy is used in making it?* What third question is answered by both sections?

   A. Can it be recycled?
   B. Will it harm the environment?
   C. Which is stronger?
   D. How much landfill space is used?

   Part B Which detail from the article best supports the answer to Part A?

   A. "Both paper bags and plastic bags use precious natural resources."
   B. "Plastic bags require less energy to produce than do paper bags."
   C. "They can also be recycled for uses such as relining wastebaskets."
   D. "In landfills, plastic bags take up less room."

III. Writing and Language Conventions

Directions: *Read the passage. Then, answer each question that follows.*

(1) Suddenly, Poppa stopped the car. (2) He wanted to show us something. (3) In my minds eye, I tried to picture what it might be. (4) Outside, the air was cool and damp. (5) I breathed in the rich, spicy odor of pine. (6) We hiked along, our feet padding on the soft, moist ground. (7) Poppa told us to follow them closely. (8) Beauty surrounded us completely. (9) Then I heard water splashing onto water. (10) A small sign pointed north to angel falls. (11) What would we see around the next turn? (12) Suddenly, there it was: a long white strip of water rushing over a tall cliff and plunging into a blue pool below.

1. What **personal pronoun** is used in sentence 2?
   A. He
   B. wanted
   C. show
   D. something

2. Which revision to sentence 10 uses correct capitalization of **proper nouns?**
   A. A small sign pointed North to Angel Falls.
   B. A small sign pointed north to Angel falls.
   C. A small sign pointed North to angel falls.
   D. A small sign pointed north to Angel Falls.

3. Which revision to sentence 7 uses correct **pronoun-antecedent agreement**?
   A. Poppa told we to follow them closely.
   B. Poppa told us to follow her closely.
   C. Poppa told us to follow him closely.
   D. Poppa told us to follow their closely.

4. Which sentence contains an example of an **interrogative pronoun**?
   A. sentence 1
   B. sentence 4
   C. sentence 8
   D. sentence 11

5. In sentence 3, what is the correct way to rewrite the **possessive noun** in the phrase "minds eye"?
   A. minds' eye
   B. mind's eye
   C. minds's eye
   D. mindes' eye

(STOP)

CONSTRUCTED RESPONSE

Directions: *Follow the instructions to complete the tasks below as required by your teacher.*

As you work on each task, incorporate both general academic vocabulary and literary terms you learned in Parts 1 and 2.

Writing

TASK 1 Literature

Analyze the Development of Plot

Write an essay in which you analyze the plot in a story from Part 2.

- State which story you will write about and briefly describe the basic plot.
- Explain the conflict or problem that starts the story moving. Identify the conflict as either internal or external.
- Then, describe how the plot unfolds in a series of scenes. Explain which scenes make up the exposition, the rising action, the climax, and the falling action.
- Describe how each scene adds information that finally leads to the story's resolution.

TASK 2 Literature

Describe Characters

Write an essay in which you describe a character from a story in Part 2.

- Identify the story and character you will discuss.
- Describe your chosen character. Include details about his or her looks, age, thoughts, feelings, and actions.
- Explain how the character responds to the events of the story. Describe what those responses tell you about the character.

- Discuss how the character changes from the beginning to the end of the story.
- Check to be sure you have used personal and possessive pronouns correctly.

TASK 3 Literature

Determine the Theme

Write an essay in which you explain the theme of a story from Part 2.

Part 1

- Tell which story you will discuss in your essay and write a brief summary of the text.
- Determine the theme of the story. Then, choose three key details from the story that convey the theme. Consider plot events, characters' actions and reactions, and characters' feelings.

Part 2

- Write an essay in which you describe what the characters learn about themselves or the world around them. Be sure to consider how the characters change by the end of the story.
- Organize your ideas logically, using transitional words and phrases. Pay close attention to your use of common, proper, and possessive nouns.

Speaking and Listening

Describe a Story's Episodes

Prepare a visual presentation of the main episodes, or scenes, from a story in Part 2.

- Break your chosen story into its major scenes. Identify how each scene fits into the parts of a story—exposition, rising action, climax, falling action, and resolution.
- Choose a graphic, such as a plot diagram, sequence-of-events chart, or storyboard, to visually present the episodes in order.
- As you present information to the class, describe how the story's plot unfolds and how the characters respond as the story moves toward its resolution.
- Practice your presentation in front of a mirror to make sure that you speak clearly and use appropriate eye contact.

Determine the Theme

Lead a small-group discussion about the theme of a story from Part 2.

- Prepare for the discussion by choosing a story and writing a paragraph about it. State the story's theme and note three details that contribute to the theme.
- Write down at least three questions you have about the story and its theme.
- Gather with your group and read the paragraph you wrote about the story. Invite the group to respond to your ideas.
- If you find the discussion slowing down, ask one of the questions you wrote down earlier.
- As a group, arrive at an agreement about the story's theme.

Research

Is conflict always bad?

In this unit, you have read literature about different types of conflicts. Now you will conduct a short research project on a conflict that has resulted in a positive change. Use both the literature you have read and your research to help think about and write about this unit's Big Question. Use the following research guidelines:

- Focus your research on one conflict. Try to determine benefits that have resulted from the conflict.
- Gather relevant information from at least two reliable print or digital sources.
- Take notes as you research the conflict and its benefits.
- Cite your sources.

When you have completed your research, write a brief essay in response to the Big Question. Discuss how your initial ideas about conflict have either changed or been reinforced. Support your response with an example from the literature you read and an example from your research.

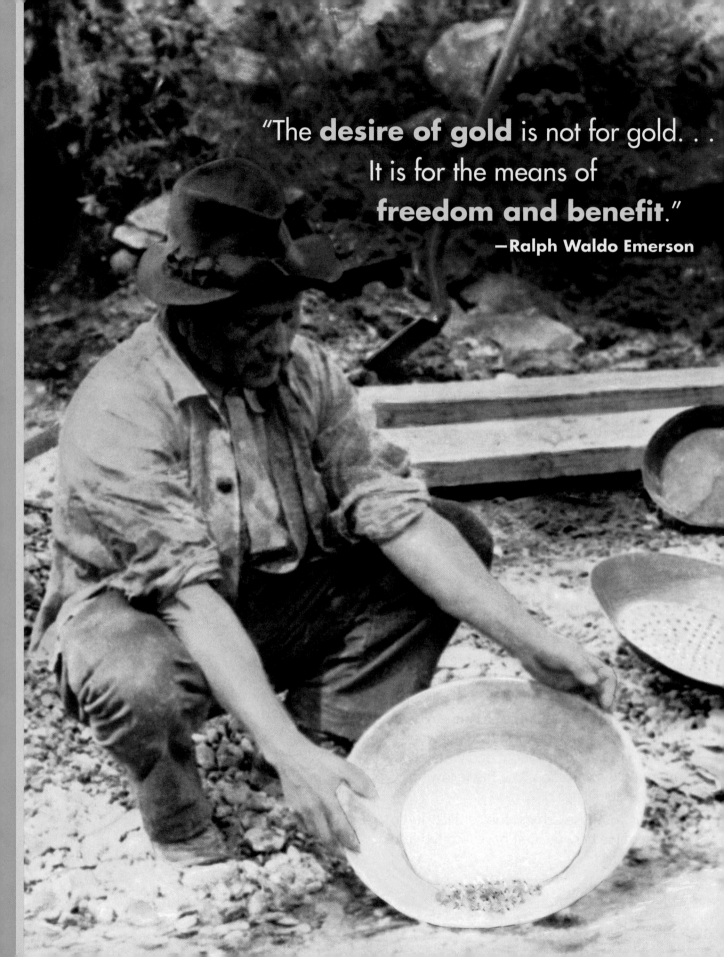

"The **desire of gold** is not for gold. . . It is for the means of **freedom and benefit**."

—Ralph Waldo Emerson

THE GOLD RUSH

The selections in this unit all deal with the Big Question: **Is conflict always bad?** Conflict can take place on a range of scales, from individual battles of will to life-and-death situations brought on by hardship and severe climate conditions. The selections that follow explore the challenges faced by those who sought their fortunes in the unsettled American West and Yukon Territory during the gold rushes. As you read the selections, take note of the various conflicts and their consequences—both good and bad.

◄ **CRITICAL VIEWING** Based on this photograph, what might have been some of the challenges faced by miners who panned for gold in the 1850s?

CLOSE READING TOOL

Use the **Close Reading Tool** to practice the strategies you learn in this unit.

READINGS IN PART 3

ANCHOR TEXT

SHORT STORY
The King of Mazy May
Jack London (p. 118)

SONG
To Klondyke We've Paid Our Fare
H. J. Dunham (p. 132)

ANNOTATED MAP
Gold Rush: The Journey by Land
from The Sacramento Bee (p. 136)

LETTER
A Woman's View of the Gold Rush
Mary B. Ballou (p. 138)

WEB ARTICLE
Chinese and African Americans in the Gold Rush
Johns Hopkins University (p. 144)

NEWS ARTICLE
Birds Struggle to Recover from Egg Thefts of 1800s
Edie Lau (p. 148)

The King of Mazy May

Jack London

Walt Masters is not a very large boy, but there is manliness in his make-up, and he himself, although he does not know a great deal that most boys know, knows much that other boys do not know. He has never seen a train of cars nor an elevator in his life, and for that matter he has never once looked upon a cornfield, a plow, a cow, or even a chicken. He has never had a pair of shoes on his feet, nor gone to a picnic or a party, nor talked to a girl. But he has seen the sun at midnight, watched the ice jams on one of the mightiest of rivers, and played beneath the northern lights,[1] the one white child in thousands of square miles of frozen wilderness.

Walt has walked all the fourteen years of his life in suntanned, moose-hide moccasins, and he can go to the Indian camps and "talk big" with the men, and trade calico and beads with them for their precious furs. He can make bread without baking powder, yeast, or hops, shoot a moose at three hundred yards, and drive the wild wolf dogs fifty miles a day on the packed trail.

Last of all, he has a good heart, and is not afraid of the darkness and loneliness, of man or beast or thing. His father is a good man, strong and brave, and Walt is growing up like him.

Walt was born a thousand miles or so down the Yukon,[2] in a trading post below the Ramparts. After his mother died, his father and he came up on the river, step by step, from camp to camp, till now they are settled down on the Mazy May Creek in the Klondike country. Last year they and several others had spent much toil and time on the Mazy

---

1. **northern lights** glowing bands or streamers of light, sometimes appearing in the night sky of the Northern Hemisphere.
2. **Yukon** (yoō′ kän) river flowing through the Yukon Territory of northwest Canada.

May, and **endured** great hardships; the creek, in turn, was just beginning to show up its richness and to reward them for their heavy labor. But with the news of their discoveries, strange men began to come and go through the short days and long nights, and many unjust things they did to the men who had worked so long upon the creek.

Si Hartman had gone away on a moose hunt, to return and find new stakes driven and his claim jumped.[3] George Lukens and his brother had lost their claims in a like manner, having delayed too long on the way to Dawson to record them. In short, it was the old story, and quite a number of the earnest, industrious prospectors had suffered similar losses.

But Walt Masters's father had recorded his claim at the start, so Walt had nothing to fear now that his father had gone on a short trip up the White River prospecting for quartz. Walt was well able to stay by himself in the cabin, cook his three meals a day, and look after things. Not only did he look after his father's claim, but he had agreed to keep an eye on the adjoining one of Loren Hall, who had started for Dawson to record it.

Loren Hall was an old man, and he had no dogs, so he had to travel very slowly. After he had been gone some time, word came up the river that he had broken through the ice at Rosebud Creek and frozen his feet so badly that he would not be able to travel for a couple of weeks. Then Walt Masters received the news that old Loren was nearly all right again, and about to move on afoot for Dawson as fast as a weakened man could.

Walt was worried, however; the claim was **liable** to be jumped at any moment because of this delay, and a fresh stampede had started in on the Mazy May. He did not like the looks of the newcomers, and one day, when five of them came by with crack dog teams and the lightest of camping outfits, he could see that they were prepared to make speed, and resolved to keep an eye on them. So he locked up the cabin and followed them, being at the same time careful to remain hidden.

He had not watched them long before he was sure that

---

3. claim jumped A claim is a piece of land marked by a miner with stakes to show where the borders are. A claim that is jumped is stolen by someone else.

they were professional stampeders, bent on jumping all the claims in sight. Walt crept along the snow at the rim of the creek and saw them change many stakes, destroy old ones, and set up new ones.

In the afternoon, with Walt always trailing on their heels, they came back down the creek, unharnessed their dogs, and went into camp within two claims of his cabin. When he saw them make preparations to cook, he hurried home to get something to eat himself, and then hurried back. He crept so close that he could hear them talking quite plainly, and by pushing the underbrush aside he could catch occasional glimpses of them. They had finished eating and were smoking around the fire.

"The creek is all right, boys," a large, black-bearded man, evidently the leader, said, "and I think the best thing we can do is to pull out tonight. The dogs can follow the trail; besides, it's going to be moonlight. What say you?"

"But it's going to be beastly cold," objected one of the party. "It's forty below zero now."

"An' sure, can't ye keep warm by jumpin' off the sleds an' runnin' after the dogs?" cried an Irishman. "An' who wouldn't? The creek's as rich as a United States mint! Faith, it's an ilegant chanst to be gettin' a run fer yer money! An' if ye don't run, it's mebbe you'll not get the money at all, at all."

"That's it," said the leader. "If we can get to Dawson and record, we're rich men; and there's no telling who's been sneaking along in our tracks, watching us, and perhaps now off to give the alarm. The thing for us to do is to rest the dogs a bit, and then hit the trail as hard as we can. What do you say?"

Evidently the men had agreed with their leader, for Walt Masters could hear nothing but the rattle of the tin dishes which were being washed. Peering out cautiously, he could see the leader studying a piece of paper. Walt knew what it was at a glance—a list of all the unrecorded claims on Mazy May. Any man could get these lists by applying to the gold commissioner at Dawson.

"Thirty-two," the leader said, lifting his face to the men. "Thirty-two isn't recorded, and this is thirty-three. Come on; let's take a look at it. I saw somebody had been working on it when we came up this morning."

Three of the men went with him, leaving one to remain in camp. Walt crept carefully after them till they came to Loren Hall's shaft. One of the men went down and built a fire on the bottom to thaw out the frozen gravel, while the others built another fire on the dump and melted water in a couple of gold pans. This they poured into a piece of canvas stretched between two logs, used by Loren Hall in which to wash his gold.

In a short time a couple of buckets of dirt were sent up by the man in the shaft, and Walt could see the others grouped anxiously about their leader as he proceeded to wash it. When this was finished, they stared at the broad streak of black sand and yellow gold grains on the bottom of the pan, and one of them called excitedly for the man who had remained in camp to come. Loren Hall had struck it rich and his claim was not yet recorded. It was plain that they were going to jump it.

Walt lay in the snow, thinking rapidly. He was only a boy, but in the face of the threatened injustice to old lame Loren Hall he felt that he must do something. He waited and watched, with his mind made up, till he saw the men begin to square up new stakes. Then he crawled away till out of hearing, and broke into a run for the camp of the stampeders. Walt's father had taken their own dogs with him prospecting, and the boy knew how impossible it was for him to undertake the seventy miles to Dawson without the aid of dogs.

Gaining the camp, he picked out, with an experienced eye, the easiest running sled and started to harness up the stampeders' dogs. There were three teams of six each, and from these he chose ten of the best. Realizing how necessary it was to have a good head dog, he strove to discover a leader amongst them; but he had little time in which to do it, for he could hear the voices of the returning men. By the time the team was in shape and everything ready, the claim-jumpers came into sight in an open place not more than a hundred yards from the trail, which ran down the bed of the creek. They cried out to Walt, but instead of giving heed to them he grabbed up one of their fur sleeping robes, which lay loosely in the snow, and leaped upon the sled.

"Mush! Hi! Mush on!" he cried to the animals, snapping the keen-lashed whip among them.

The dogs sprang against the yoke straps, and the sled jerked under way so suddenly as to almost throw him off. Then it curved into the creek, poising perilously on the runner. He was almost breathless with suspense, when it finally righted with a bound and sprang ahead again. The creek bank was high and he could not see the men, although he could hear their cries and knew they were running to cut him off. He did not dare to think what would happen if they caught him; he just clung to the sled, his heart beating wildly, and watched the snow rim of the bank above him.

Suddenly, over this snow rim came the flying body of the Irishman, who had leaped straight for the sled in a desperate attempt to capture it; but he was an instant too late. Striking on the very rear of it, he was thrown from his feet, backward, into the snow. Yet, with the quickness of a cat, he had clutched the end of the sled with one hand, turned over, and was dragging behind on his breast, swearing at the boy and threatening all kinds of terrible things if he did not stop the dogs; but Walt cracked him sharply across the knuckles with the butt of the dog whip till he let go.

It was eight miles from Walt's claim to the Yukon—eight very crooked miles, for the creek wound back and forth like a snake, "tying knots in itself," as George Lukens said. And because it was so crooked the dogs could not get up their best speed, while the sled ground heavily on its side against the curves, now to the right, now to the left.

Travelers who had come up and down the Mazy May on foot, with packs on their backs, had declined to go round all the bends, and instead had made shortcuts across the narrow necks of creek bottom. Two of his pursuers had gone back to harness the remaining dogs, but the others took advantage of these shortcuts, running on foot, and before he knew it they had almost overtaken him.

"Halt!" they cried after him. "Stop, or we'll shoot!"

But Walt only yelled the harder at the dogs, and dashed around the bend with a couple of revolver bullets singing after him. At the next bend they had drawn up closer still, and the bullets struck uncomfortably near him but at this point the Mazy May straightened out and ran for half a mile as the crow flies. Here the dogs stretched out in their long wolf swing, and the stampeders, quickly winded, slowed down and waited for their own sled to come up.

Looking over his shoulder, Walt reasoned that they had not given up the chase for good, and that they would soon be after him again. So he wrapped the fur robe about him to shut out the stinging air, and lay flat on the empty sled, encouraging the dogs, as he well knew how.

At last, twisting abruptly between two river islands, he came upon the mighty Yukon sweeping grandly to the north. He could not see from bank to bank, and in the quick-falling twilight it loomed a great white sea of frozen stillness. There was not a sound, save the breathing of the dogs, and the churn of the steel-shod sled.

No snow had fallen for several weeks, and the traffic had packed the main river trail till it was hard and glassy as glare

ice. Over this the sled flew along, and the dogs kept the trail fairly well, although Walt quickly discovered that he had made a mistake in choosing the leader. As they were driven in single file, without reins, he had to guide them by his voice, and it was evident the head dog had never learned the meaning of "gee" and "haw." He hugged the inside of the curves too closely, often forcing his comrades behind him into the soft snow, while several times he thus capsized the sled.

There was no wind, but the speed at which he traveled created a bitter blast, and with the thermometer down to forty below, this bit through fur and flesh to the very bones. Aware that if he remained constantly upon the sled he would freeze to death, and knowing the practice of Arctic travelers, Walt shortened up one of the lashing thongs, and whenever he felt chilled, seized hold of it, jumped off, and ran behind till warmth was restored. Then he would climb on and rest till the process had to be repeated.

Looking back he could see the sled of his pursuers, drawn by eight dogs, rising and falling over the ice hummocks like a boat in a seaway. The Irishman and the black-bearded leader were with it, taking turns in running and riding.

Night fell, and in the blackness of the first hour or so Walt toiled desperately with his dogs. On account of the poor lead dog, they were continually floundering off the beaten track into the soft snow, and the sled was as often riding on its side or top as it was in the proper way. This work and strain tried his strength sorely. Had he not been in such haste he could have avoided much of it, but he feared the stampeders would creep up in the darkness and overtake him. However, he could hear them yelling to their dogs, and knew from the sounds they were coming up very slowly.

When the moon rose he was off Sixty Mile, and Dawson was only fifty miles away. He was almost exhausted, and breathed a sigh of relief as he climbed on the sled again. Looking back, he saw his enemies had crawled up within four hundred yards. At this space they remained, a black speck of motion on the white river breast. Strive as they would, they could not shorten this distance, and strive as he would, he could not increase it.

Walt had now discovered the proper lead dog, and he knew he could easily run away from them if he could only change the bad leader for the good one. But this was impossible, for a moment's delay, at the speed they were running, would bring the men behind upon him.

When he was off the mouth of Rosebud Creek, just as he was topping a rise, the report of a gun and the ping of a bullet on the ice beside him told him that they were this time shooting at him with a rifle. And from then on, as he cleared the summit of each ice jam, he stretched flat on the leaping sled till the rifle shot from the rear warned him that he was safe till the next ice jam was reached.

Now it is very hard to lie on a moving sled, jumping and plunging and yawing[4] like a boat before the wind, and to shoot through the deceiving moonlight at an object four hundred yards away on another moving sled performing equally wild antics. So it is not to be wondered at that the black-bearded leader did not hit him.

After several hours of this, during which, perhaps, a score of bullets had struck about him, their ammunition began to give out and their fire slackened. They took greater care, and only whipped a shot at him at the most favorable opportunities. He was also leaving them behind, the distance slowly increasing to six hundred yards.

Lifting clear on the crest of a great jam off Indian River, Walt Masters met with his first accident. A bullet sang past his ears, and struck the bad lead dog.

The poor brute plunged in a heap, with the rest of the team on top of him.

Like a flash Walt was by the leader. Cutting the traces with his hunting knife, he dragged the dying animal to one side and straightened out the team.

He glanced back. The other sled was coming up like an express train. With half the dogs still over their traces, he cried "Mush on!" and leaped upon the sled just as the pursuers dashed abreast[5] of him.

The Irishman was preparing to spring for him—they were so sure they had him that they did not shoot—when Walt turned fiercely upon them with his whip.

He struck at their faces, and men must save their faces with their hands. So there was no shooting just then. Before

---

4. **yawing** (yô´ iŋ) adj. swinging from side to side.
5. **abreast** (ə brest´) adv. alongside.

they could recover from the hot rain of blows, Walt reached out from his sled, catching their wheel dog by the forelegs in midspring, and throwing him heavily. This snarled the team, capsizing the sled and tangling his enemies up beautifully.

Away Walt flew, the runners of his sled fairly screaming as they bounded over the frozen surface. And what had seemed an accident proved to be a blessing in disguise. The proper lead dog was now to the fore, and he stretched low and whined with joy as he jerked his comrades along.

By the time he reached Ainslie's Creek, seventeen miles from Dawson, Walt had left his pursuers, a tiny speck, far behind. At Monte Cristo Island he could no longer see them. And at Swede Creek, just as daylight was silvering the pines, he ran plump into the camp of old Loren Hall.

Almost as quick as it takes to tell it, Loren had his sleeping furs rolled up, and had joined Walt on the sled. They permitted the dogs to travel more slowly, as there was no sign of the chase in the rear, and just as they pulled up at the gold commissioner's office in Dawson, Walt, who had kept his eyes open to the last, fell asleep.

And because of what Walt Masters did on this night, the men of the Yukon have become proud of him, and speak of him now as the King of Mazy May.

ABOUT THE AUTHOR

Jack London (1876–1916)

Jack London lived an adventurous life. Before the age of 20, this Californian had worked in a factory, traveled as a hobo, captained a boat, and searched for gold. Though he dropped out of college, he taught himself by reading at public libraries and giving himself daily writing assignments. London's love of reading and his own adventures inspired him to write.

In 1897, London went to northwestern Canada, where gold had just been discovered. He did not find any gold, but he did have adventures on the way to Dawson, a town in the Yukon Territory. Once, for instance, he made a boat from trees and ran the dangerous White Horse rapids on the Yukon River. London wrote more than fifty books, including *The Call of the Wild* and *White Fang*.

Close Reading Activities

READ

Comprehension

Reread all or part of the text to help you answer the following questions.

1. What special skills does Walt possess?

2. Where does Walt live?

3. What events take place after Walt begins the trip to Dawson?

4. Why do the men of the Yukon call Walt the "King of Mazy May"?

Language Study

Selection Vocabulary The following phrases appear in "The King of Mazy May." Define each boldfaced word, and use all three words in a brief story of your own.

- …they and several others had spent much toil and time on the Mazy May, and **endured** great hardships…

- …the claim was **liable** to be jumped at any moment because of this delay…

- …as he cleared the **summit** of each ice jam, he stretched flat on the leaping sled…

Diction and Style Study the sentence below. Then, answer the questions.

> Away Walt flew, the runners of his sled fairly screaming as they bounded over the frozen surface.

1. **(a)** What do you notice about the word order in the phrase "Away Walt flew"? **(b)** What effect does the word order create?

2. **(a)** How is the sled described? **(b)** What effect is created through this use of description?

Research: Clarify Details This story may include references to life in the Yukon that are unfamiliar to you. Choose at least one detail and briefly research it. Explain how the information clarifies an aspect of the story.

Summarize Write an objective summary of the story. Remember that an objective summary is free from opinion and evaluation.

Conventions Read this passage from the story. Identify the common, proper, and possessive nouns. Then, explain how you identified the possessive noun.

> But Walt Masters's father had recorded his claim at the start, so Walt had nothing to fear now that his father had gone on a short trip up the White River prospecting for quartz…. Not only did he look after his father's claim, but he had agreed to keep an eye on the adjoining one of Loren Hall, who had started for Dawson to record it.

Academic Vocabulary

The following words appear in the instructions and questions on the facing page.

passage   contribute   alter

Categorize the words by deciding whether you know each one well, know it a little bit, or do not know it at all. Then, use a print or online dictionary to look up the definitions of the words you are unsure of or do not know at all.

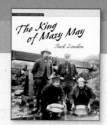

Literary Analysis

Reread the identified passages. Then, respond to the questions that follow:

> **Focus Passage 1** *(p. 123)*
>
> Suddenly, over this snow rim … till he let go.

> **Focus Passage 2** *(pp. 126–127)*
>
> He struck at their faces … tangling his enemies up beautifully.

Key Ideas and Details

1. Infer Which character seems to be winning the struggle in this **passage**? Cite details to support your answer.

Craft and Structure

2. (a) Interpret: What effect do word choices such as "suddenly," "clutched," and "threatening" create? **(b) Evaluate:** Would the passage be as suspenseful if London had chosen more neutral words? Explain.

3. Analyze: Examine London's sentence length and structures. What effect do these elements create?

Integration of Knowledge and Ideas

4. (a) Analyze: In what way has the author made the Irishman unsympathetic? **(b) Evaluate:** Does the character of the Irishman make you "root" harder for Walt? Explain.

Key Ideas and Details

1. (a) What are the two main events in this passage? **(b)** What does Walt do to keep the men from shooting at him?

Craft and Structure

2. (a) Analyze: What descriptive details express the main events of the passage? **(b) Interpret:** What images do these descriptions bring to mind?

3. Evaluate: How does this paragraph **contribute** to the plot of the story?

4. (a) Analyze: How would you describe the narrator's tone? **(b)** What clues point to the idea that the narrator admires Walt?

Integration of Knowledge and Ideas

5. Draw Conclusions: How does this passage illustrate the relationship between the humans and the dogs?

Setting

The **setting** of a literary work is the time and place of the action. The setting can **alter** the tone or mood of a story. Reread the story, and take notes on ways in which the author uses setting.

1. What story details bring to life its setting?

2. The Gold Rush In what way do the events of the Gold Rush affect the story's action and characters?

DISCUSS

From Text to Topic **Group Discussion**

Discuss the following passage with a group of classmates. Take notes during the discussion. Contribute your own ideas, and support them with examples from the text.

Walt Masters is not a very large boy, but there is manliness in his make-up, and he himself, although he does not know a great deal that most boys know, knows much that other boys do not know. He has never seen a train of cars nor an elevator in his life, and for that matter he has never once looked upon a cornfield, a plow, a cow, or even a chicken. He has never had a pair of shoes on his feet, nor gone to a picnic or a party, nor talked to a girl. But he has seen the sun at midnight, watched the ice jams on one of the mightiest of rivers, and played beneath the northern lights, the one white child in thousands of square miles of frozen wilderness.

QUESTIONS FOR DISCUSSION

1. How does the author compare Walt's experiences with those of other boys?

2. What do the details in this passage tell you about the narrator's attitude toward Walt?

3. In what way is Walt well suited to the challenges of his environment and circumstance?

WRITE

Writing to Sources **Informative Text**

Assignment
Write a **cause-and-effect essay** in which you analyze the main events of the story. Identify the causes and effects of these events or actions.

Prewriting and Planning Reread the story, looking for details, definitions, and examples that describe causes and effects of important events. Record your notes in a web diagram.

Drafting Choose a way to organize your essay. For example, if a number of unrelated events leads to a single result, focus one paragraph on each cause. If one cause leads to several effects, focus one paragraph on each effect. In your draft, cite specific examples and show clear relationships between your points.

Revising Reread your essay, making sure you have clearly explained links between ideas. Add transitional words and phrases where needed.

Editing and Proofreading Make sure your transitions clearly explain the relationships between events. In addition, make sure the verb tenses correctly reflect the order of the causes and effects.

CONVENTIONS

A **verb tense** tells whether the time of an action or a condition is in the past, present, or future. Clearly explain the timeline of events and relationships by using verb tenses to show sequence.

RESEARCH

Research **Investigate the Topic**

Gold Rush Struggles "The King of Mazy May" reveals some of the hardships gold prospectors faced in the Yukon, such as frigid temperatures and hard physical labor. Jack London had some personal experience with these hardships when he worked as a gold prospector, and he included details from his own experiences in this story.

Assignment

Conduct research to learn more about living conditions for gold prospectors in Canada in the 1890s. Consult books such as memoirs to learn about the prospectors' personal experiences. Take clear notes and carefully identify your sources so that you can easily access the information later. Share your findings in an **informal speech or presentation** for the class.

PREPARATION FOR ESSAY
You may use the knowledge you gain during this research assignment to support your claims in an essay you will write at the end of this section.

Gather Sources Find reliable print and electronic sources. Primary sources, such as letters, journals, or memoirs, provide firsthand accounts of experiences. These types of sources illustrate events in people's daily lives. You should also consult secondary sources, such as history books or encyclopedias. Look for sources that feature expert authors and up-to-date information.

Take Notes Take notes on each source, either electronically or on note cards. Use an organized note-taking strategy.

- Label each note card with its source information and main idea.
- Include important notes or quotations that support the main idea. Use quotation marks to indicate direct quotes.
- Create a timeline or web diagram to organize your main ideas.

Synthesize Multiple Sources Gather data from your sources and organize them into a presentation. Use information you learned from your research to draw conclusions about struggles during the Gold Rush. Use your notes to write an outline for your presentation. See the Citing Sources pages in the Introductory Unit of this textbook for help in creating a Works Cited list.

Organize and Present Ideas Review your outline and practice delivering your presentation. Be ready to answer questions from your audience.

TO KLONDYKE WE'VE PAID OUR FARE

WRITTEN AND COMPOSED

BY H.J. DUNHAM

We're a band of Argonauts[1] bold,
With a feverish fancy for gold.
We're ready and rough, and "out for the stuff,"
Tho the weather up north is cold.
We've carefully counted the cost,
Defiance we bid to Jack-Frost.
We're fill'd to the brim with courage and vim,
No tales of **privation** our vision can dim,
our vision of treasure untold.
We'll work the rich earth, for all it is worth,
And each with a fortune will feather his berth.[2]

defiance ▶
(de fī´əns) *n.* open resistance to authority

privation ▶
(prī vā´ shən) *n.* lack of necessities

---

1. **Argonauts** (är´gə nôts´) sailors on the *Argo*, the ship in the Greek myth of Jason and the Golden Fleece; adventurers.
2. **feather his berth** stuff his mattress; in this case, a figure of speech: he will be rich enough to stuff his mattress with money.

Refrain

To Klondyke we've paid our fare, our golden slippers we
soon will wear,
We'll live on pig and polar bear, and gather the nuggets we
know are there.

"We're a strictly respectable crowd,
No political pluggers allowed,
We've a preacher or two, to keep it in view,
That sobriety all have vowed.
We've maidens aged and young,
And Chinamen fresh from Hong Kong.
While a jolly street faker, a fat undertaker,
A lively grass widow, a dude and a quaker,[3]
have join'd our **invincible** throng,
We're not all alike, but we're bound for Klondyke,
And each is determin'd to make a big strike."

◄ **invincible**
(in vin´sə bəl) *adj.*
incapable of being
harmed or defeated

Repeat Refrain

If you're tired of tedious delay,
In the dawn of prosperity's day,
We'll give you a chance, your wealth to enhance,
In a venture that's sure to pay.
Our band-wagon's waiting below,
To carry us straight to Juneau[4],
So get into line, and in with us climb,
Put on your best clothes, get a shave and a shine,
Put a lunch in your pocket and go!
And when you return, your friends will all learn,
That you've come from the Klondyke with "money to burn."

Repeat Refrain

---

3. **grass widow** a woman who is separated from her husband; **dude** a city-dweller whose fancy
clothes make him stand out from other adventurers; **quaker** member of a Christian group that
opposes war.
4. **Juneau** (jü´nō) capital city of Alaska.

Close Reading Activities

READ

Comprehension

Reread all or part of the text to help you answer the following questions.

1. What is the song about?

2. When set to music, would this song be happy or sad? How do you know?

3. What does the song tell you about the Klondike Gold Rush?

Research: Clarify Details Choose one unfamiliar detail and briefly research it. Then, explain how the information you learned from research sheds light on an aspect of the song.

Summarize Write an objective summary of the song. Do not include opinions.

Language Study

Selection Vocabulary The following phrases appear in "To Klondyke We've Paid Our Fare." Define each boldfaced word, and then write a sentence for each word.

- **Defiance** we bid to Jack-Frost
- No tales of **privation** our vision can dim
- have join'd our **invincible** throng

Literary Analysis

Reread the identified passage. Then, respond to the questions that follow:

> **Focus Passage** (p. 133)
> We're a strictly respectable crowd, ... make a big strike.

Key Ideas and Details

1. **(a) Interpret:** What is the main idea of this verse? **(b) Analyze:** What specific words **reveal** the main idea?

2. **Draw Conclusions:** What does the listing of people indicate about the society the settlers will form?

Craft and Structure

3. Read the verse aloud to notice its rhythm and rhyme. **Evaluate:** Does the song have a regular pattern of sounds when read aloud? Explain.

Integration of Knowledge and Ideas

4. **(a) Interpret:** What might be the **purpose** of a song like this one? **(b)** What does the song **challenge** the listener to do?

Alliteration

Alliteration is the repetition of initial consonant sounds, such as the *b* sound in *big blue ball*. Reread the song, and note ways in which the author uses alliteration.

1. **(a)** Point out two examples of alliteration in the song. **(b) Analyze:** What effect does the alliteration create?

2. **The Gold Rush** Does this song effectively capture the spirit of the Gold Rush? Why or why not?

DISCUSS • RESEARCH • WRITE

From Text to Topic **Group Discussion**

Discuss the following passage with classmates. Contribute your own ideas, and support them with examples from the text.

> **Refrain:** To Klondyke we've paid our fare, our golden slippers we soon will wear,
> We'll live on pig and polar bear, and gather the nuggets we know are there.

Research **Investigate the Topic**

Striking It Rich The Klondike Gold Rush of 1898 was one of the last gold rushes, following the major rushes in California and Australia that had occurred fifty years earlier.

Assignment

Conduct research to find out information about the Klondike Gold Rush. Consult online and print sources such as encyclopedias, Klondike National Park's Web site, or news articles from the 1890s. Take clear notes, and carefully identify your sources so that you can easily access the information later. Capture your findings in a detailed **outline.**

Writing to Sources **Narrative**

"To Klondyke We've Paid Our Fare" captures the spirit of adventure that characterized the Gold Rush. The promise of riches and a new start made many people journey west.

Assignment

Write a **short story** from the point of view of someone who has heard this song and joins the Klondike Gold Rush. Follow these steps as you draft your story:

- Introduce your character and establish the setting.
- Create a smooth progression of events that build on one another.
- Use information from your research, where appropriate.
- Provide a logical, satisfying conclusion to your story.

QUESTIONS FOR DISCUSSION

1. How would you describe the mood of the song's refrain?
2. Why might a song like this have been popular with Gold Rush settlers?

PREPARATION FOR ESSAY

You may use the knowledge you gain during this research assignment to support your claims in an essay you will write at the end of this section.

ACADEMIC VOCABULARY

Academic terms appear in blue on these pages. If these words are not familiar to you, use a dictionary to find their definitions. Then, use them as you speak and write about the text.

Gold Rush: The Journey by Land

from The Sacramento Bee

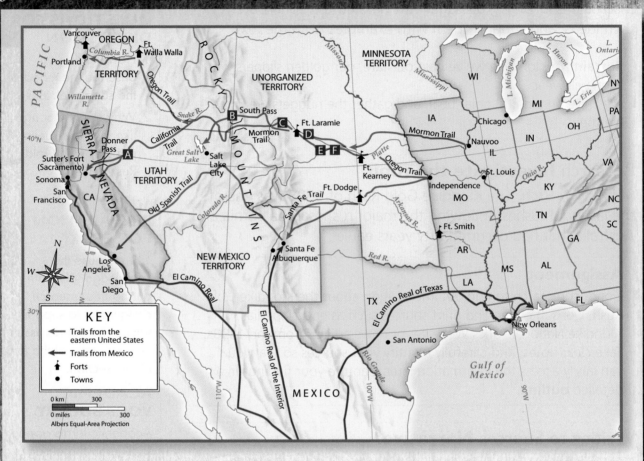

The Routes Taken

A The Humboldt Basin

The dreaded 40-mile stretch of Humboldt Basin promised severe heat, sand deep enough to trap oxen, and no food or water.

B The Continental Divide

Rivers to the east flowed toward the Atlantic. Rivers to the west flowed toward the Pacific.

C Independence Rock

This rock was marked on by hundreds of pioneers who passed it.

D Fort Laramie

More than 39,000 people were recorded passing through Fort Laramie in the first six months of 1849.

E The Platte River

The rains of 1849 made the overland journey difficult.

F Chimney Rock

This 500-foot column marks 550 miles from Independence, Missouri.

READ • DISCUSS • WRITE

Comprehension

Study the map and answer the following questions.

1. What tools help you read and analyze the map?

2. **(a)** What two major trails did people take on the journey?
   (b) Choose a trail and identify two sites that travelers on the trail might pass along the way.

Critical Analysis

Key Ideas and Details

1. **(a) Interpret:** What are the main end points for each of the trails? **(b) Infer:** Why did people want to travel to these places?

2. **Compare and Contrast:** What are some **similarities** and differences between the routes?

Craft and Structure

3. **Draw Conclusions:** Why did the mapmaker choose to call attention to the sites labeled with letters?

Integration of Knowledge and Ideas

4. **Interpret:** What does this map tell you about the hardships people encountered during the Gold Rush?

From Text to Topic **Class Discussion**

Discuss the map with classmates. Use the following discussion questions to focus your conversation.

1. What might have motivated people to endure hardships to travel such great distances?

2. How does the **process** of traveling across the country in the 1850s differ from the way we travel today?

3. How might the Gold Rush have changed the population of the western United States?

Writing to Sources **Narrative**

Write a brief **journal entry** from the point of view of a traveler on the Oregon or Mormon Trail. Briefly research one of the sites **indicated** on the map. Then write about your character's experiences there.

ACADEMIC VOCABULARY

Academic terms appear in blue on these pages. If these words are not familiar to you, use a dictionary to find their definitions. Then, use them as you speak and write about the text.

A Woman's View of the Gold Rush

Mary B. Ballou

October 30, 1852

My Dear Selden:

We are about as usual in health. Well I suppose you would like to know what I am doing in this gold region. Well I will try to tell you what my work is here in this muddy Place. All the kitchen that I have is four posts stuck down into the ground and covered over the top with factory cloth no floor but the ground. This is a Boarding House kitchen....

   Now I will try to tell you what my work is in this Boarding House. Well somtimes[1] I am washing and Ironing somtimes I am making mince pie and Apple pie and squash pies. Somtimes frying mince turnovers and Donuts. I make Buiscuit and now and then Indian jonny cake[2] and then again I am making minute puding filled with rasons and Indian Bake pudings and then again a nice Plum Puding and then again I am Stuffing a Ham of pork that cost forty cents a pound.... Three times a day I set my Table which is about thirty feet in length and do all the little fixings about it such as filling pepper boxes and vinegar cruits and mustard pots and Butter cups. Somtimes I am feeding my chickens and then again I am scareing the Hogs out of my kitchen and Driving the mules out of my Dining room. You can see by the description of that I have given you of my kitchen that anything can walk into the kitchen that chooses to walk in and there being no door to shut from the kitchen into the Dining room ... Hogs and mules can walk in any time day or night if they choose to do so. Somtimes I am up all times a night scaring the Hogs and mules out of the House. Last night there a large rat came down pounce down onto our bed in the night. Sometimes I take my fan and try to fan myself but I work so hard that my Arms pain me so severely that I kneed some

---

1. Misspellings in this selection reflect Mary Ballou's original letter.
2. **jonny cake** (jän´ ē kāk´) *n.* a thin, flat corn bread baked on a griddle.

one to fan me so I do not find much comfort anywhere. I made a Bluberry puding to day for Dinner. Somtimes I am making soups and cramberry tarts and Baking chicken that cost four Dollars a head and cooking Eggs at three Dollars a Dozen. Somtimes boiling cabbage and Turnips and frying fritters and Broiling stake and cooking codfish and potatoes. I often cook nice Salmon trout that weigh from ten to twenty pound apiece. Somtimes I am taking care of Babies and nursing at the rate of Fifty Dollars a week but I would not advise any Lady to come out here and suffer the toil and fatigue that I have suffered for the sake of a little gold neither do I advise any one to come. Clarks Simmon wife says if she was safe in the States she would not care if she had not one cent. She came in here last night and said, "Oh dear I am so homesick that I must die," and then again my other **associate** came in with tears in her eyes and said that she had cried all day. She said if she had as good a home as I had got she would not stay twenty five minutes in California....

associate ▶
(ə sō′ shē
it) *n.* friend
or partner

Now I will tell you a little more about my cooking. Somtimes I am cooking rabbits and Birds that are called quails here and I cook squrrels. Occasionly I run in and have a chat with Jane and Mrs. Durphy and I often have a hearty cry. No one but my maker knows my feelings. And then I run into my little cellar which is about four feet square as I have no other place to run that is cool....

The wind Blows verry hard here to day. I have three lights Burning and the wind blows so hard that it almost puts my lights out while I am trying to write. If you could but step in and see the inconvience that I have for writing you would not wonder that I cannot write any better you would wonder that I could write at all. Notwithstanding all the dificulty in writing I improve every leishure moment. It is quite cool here my fingers are so cold that I can hardly hold my pen. Well it is ten o'clock at night while I am writing....

There I hear the Hogs in my kitchen turning the Pots and kettles upside down so I must drop my pen and run and drive them out. So you [see] this is the way that I have to write—jump up every five minutes for somthing and then again I washed out about a Dollars worth of gold dust the fourth of July in the cradle so you see that I am doing a little mining in this gold region but I think it harder to rock the cradle to wash out gold than it is to rock the cradle for the Babies in the States....

I am making Flags with all the rest of the various kinds of work that I am doing and then again I am **scouring** candle sticks and washing the floor and making soft soap. The People tell me that it is the first Soft Soap they knew made in California. Somtimes I am making mattresses and sheets. I have no windows in my room. All the light that I have shines through canvas that covers the House and my eyes are so dim that I can hardly see to make a mark so I think you will excuse me for not writing any better. I have three Lights burning now but I am so tired and Blind that I can scearcely see and here I am among the French and Duch and Scoth and Jews and Italions and Sweeds and Chineese and Indians and all manner of **tongues** and nations but I am treated with due respect by them all....

◄ **scouring**
(skour´ iŋ) *v.* cleaning or polishing by vigorous rubbing

◄ **tongues**
(tuŋs) *n.* languages or dialects

I must close soon for I am so tired and almost sick. Oh my Dear Selden I am so Home sick.... I worry a great deal about my Dear children. It seems as though my heart would break when I realise how far I am from my Dear Loved ones. This from your affectionate mother,

Mary B. Ballou

Close Reading Activities

READ

Comprehension

Reread all or part of the text to help you answer the following questions.

1. What is Mary Ballou's job in the gold region? List three of her daily chores.

2. (a) To whom does Ballou write? **(b)** What information does this detail provide?

Research: Clarify Details Choose one unfamiliar detail from the text and briefly research it. Then, explain how your research clarifies an aspect of the letter.

Summarize Write an objective summary of the letter to confirm your comprehension.

Language Study

Selection Vocabulary The following phrases appear in the selection. Define each boldfaced word. Then, identify another meaning for the word.

- … my other **associate** came in with tears in her eyes…
- … I am **scouring** candle sticks…
- … all manner of **tongues** and nations…

Literary Analysis

Reread the identified passage. Then, respond to the questions that follow:

> **Focus Passage** *(p. 141)*
>
> I am making Flags with all the rest… I am treated with due respect by them all.

Cite details from the text to support your response.

Craft and Structure

2. Infer: What can you infer about Mary Ballou from her writing style? Cite details to support your response.

Integration of Knowledge and Ideas

3. Draw Conclusions: Why do you think the settlers treat one another with "respect"? Support your response with details.

Key Ideas and Details

1. (a) How does Ballou describe her environment? **(b) Analyze:** How does Ballou's environment affect her mood?

Tone

Tone, the attitude a writer displays toward his or her subject, is created through word choice.

1. The Gold Rush Find at least two details in the first paragraph of the letter that create a disapproving tone about Ballou's home environment.

2. Re-read the final paragraph of the letter. What tone is revealed by the writer's word choice? Support your response with details from the text.

DISCUSS • RESEARCH • WRITE

From Text to Topic **Partner Discussion**

Discuss the following passage with a partner. Take notes during the discussion. Contribute your own ideas, and support them with examples from the text.

> Somtimes I am taking care of Babies and nursing at the rate of Fifty Dollars a week but I would not advise any Lady to come out here and suffer the toil and fatigue that I have suffered for the sake of a little gold neither do I advise any one to come. Clarks Simmon wife says if she was safe in the States she would not care if she had not one cent.

Research **Investigate the Topic**

Gold Rush Housing Mary Ballou runs a boarding house in California during the Gold Rush. When miners came to California for gold, they found that housing conditions were usually poor.

Assignment

Conduct research to find information about housing during the Gold Rush. Consult the Internet or other reliable sources. Take clear notes, and carefully identify your sources so that you can easily access the information later. Share your findings in a brief **descriptive essay.**

Writing to Sources **Informative Text**

"A Woman's View of the Gold Rush" is an account of one woman's experience in California. Use information from Mary Ballou's letter to write about daily life for women during the Gold Rush.

Assignment

Write an **informational text** in which you explain living conditions and daily life for women during the Gold Rush. Follow these steps:

- Introduce the topic.
- Explain women's duties and jobs during the Gold Rush.
- Use specific information from the text to make generalizations.
- Write a conclusion in which you summarize your ideas.

QUESTIONS FOR DISCUSSION

1. Has Mary Ballou been successful in California? Cite **specific** details to support your answer.

2. California was a state in 1852. Explain the meaning of the comment by Simmon's wife about being "safe in the States."

PREPARATION FOR ESSAY

You may use the knowledge you gain during this research assignment to support your claims in an essay you will write at the end of this section.

ACADEMIC VOCABULARY

Academic terms appear in blue on these pages. If these words are not familiar to you, use a dictionary to find their definitions.

Gold Miners in Auburn, California

Chinese and African Americans in the Gold Rush

Johns Hopkins University

exodus ▶
(eks´ ə dəs) *n.*
departure of
a large group
of people

People from around the globe rushed to California in 1848. They came from China, Mexico, South America, Sweden, Ireland, Germany, and other lands. What caused this mad dash? Gold—and the promise of a better life. Free African Americans also joined the **exodus** west, hoping to find not only gold but greater freedom.

When news of the gold rush reached China, in 1848, thousands of Chinese headed to California. They wanted to escape the civil war, floods, droughts, and typhoons they faced back home. They thought they would get rich in "Gold Mountain," as California was known. Before the gold rush, only a few Chinese people lived in California, but by 1852, over twenty thousand Chinese immigrants had settled there.

The Chinese immigrants hoped for jobs and riches, but they faced many problems. They worked long hours for low pay. Some white miners thought the Chinese should be sent back to China. The Chinese miners (along with Mexican American miners) had to pay a special tax. Some places wouldn't hire Chinese workers or threw them out. They were not allowed to **testify** in court. But the Chinese stayed, and started organizations and unions. They also started newspapers and public schools.

Many African Americans came to California as well. They hoped to find freedom and good jobs. Most were free men and women from eastern cities. Some free African Americans had fled the east to escape the Fugitive Slave Law. This law punished anyone who helped runaway slaves. Even free men and women were afraid that a slave catcher would claim they were runaways and sell them south. Some free blacks came to California after reading success stories in Frederick Douglass'[1] newspaper, *North Star*. Others came as slaves and bought their freedom with gold they panned[2] from streams or dug out of mines. In the first three years of the gold rush, over a thousand African Americans came to California. About half of the three hundred and fifty African Americans in Sacramento, California, were free. Some miners formed all-black settlements such as Negro Bar and Negro Slide. Like other minorities in California, African Americans could not vote, testify in court, or attend public schools. In spite of this, they worked hard. They used their gold to free their families, start churches, schools, libraries and newspapers, and work for greater legal rights.

Mifflin Gibbs came to California in 1850 to work as a carpenter. After white carpenters refused to work with him because of his race, he started a business shining shoes and boots. A few years later, he and Peter Lester, another African American, opened a store. They worked hard and became rich. They later moved to Canada because California law did not protect their rights. Gibbs returned to the United States, became a lawyer, and was appointed an **ambassador**. Both men worked in the antislavery movement and to protect the rights of African Americans.

---

1. **Frederick Douglass** Escaped slave and noted scholar and speaker who lived during the nineteenth century. Douglass was a leader in the antislavery movement.
2. **gold they panned** Gold prospectors filled pans with river mud and then systematically shook and rinsed the mud several times. Since gold is heavier than dirt and water, gold particles sank to the bottom of the pan as the dirt washed away.

◀ **testify**
(tes´ tə fī) *v.* make a statement of fact or belief under oath; bear witness

◀ **ambassador**
(am bas´ ə dər) *n.* special representative, often one nation's official representative in another nation

Close Reading Activities

READ

Comprehension

Answer the following questions.

1. **(a)** Why did Chinese immigrants come to California? **(b)** What benefits did African Americans hope to find there?

2. What obstacles did minorities face during the Gold Rush?

3. What did African Americans and Chinese immigrants do in response to these obstacles?

Research: Clarify Details This informative text may include references that are unfamiliar to you. Choose at least one unfamiliar detail, and briefly research it. Then, explain how the information you learned from research sheds light on an aspect of the text.

Summarize Write an objective summary of the text. Remember that an objective summary is free from opinion and evaluation.

Language Study

Selection Vocabulary Define each boldfaced word, and use the word in a sentence of your own.

• Free African Americans also joined the **exodus** west, …

• They were not allowed to **testify** in court.

• Gibbs … became a lawyer, and was appointed an **ambassador**.

Literary Analysis

Reread the identified passage. Then, respond to the questions that follow.

> **Focus Passage** (p. 145)
> The Chinese immigrants … public schools.

Key Ideas and Details

1. **(a) Explain:** What is the main idea of the passage? **(b)** What details support your response?

Craft and Structure

2. **Analyze:** How and when does the mood, or overall feeling, of the passage change? Support your response with textual evidence.

Integration of Knowledge and Ideas

3. **Infer:** Why do you think some white miners wanted the Chinese immigrants to be sent home?

Author's Purpose

An **author's purpose** is his or her reason for writing about a subject. A reader can **determine** an author's purpose by analyzing word choice and tone.

1. Re-read the first paragraph. **(a)** What type of details does the author provide? **(b)** What purpose do these details serve?

2. **The Gold Rush (a)** What information is provided in the final paragraph? **(b)** Why might the author have chosen to end the text with this information?

DISCUSS • RESEARCH • WRITE

From Text to Topic **Group Discussion**

Discuss the following passage with a group of classmates. Take notes during the discussion. Contribute your own ideas, and support them with examples from the text.

> Many African Americans came to California as well. They hoped to find freedom and good jobs. Most were free men and women from eastern cities. Some free African Americans had fled the east to escape the Fugitive Slave Law.

Research **Investigate the Topic**

Labor During the Gold Rush Mining and panning were the two main ways that people **acquired** gold during the Gold Rush. This labor was time-consuming and often difficult and dangerous.

Assignment

Conduct research to learn more about the process of mining or panning for gold. Consult print and online sources such as encyclopedias. Also search for primary sources such as letters, journals, and memoirs. Present your findings in an **annotated poster**.

Writing to Sources **Argument**

"Chinese and African Americans in the Gold Rush" describes obstacles faced by two groups of workers during the Gold Rush. While some people mistreated these workers, many others believed that mistreatment of the workers was unfair and should be changed.

Assignment

Write an **editorial** from the point of view of a resident of Sacramento, California, in 1849. Present the argument that Chinese and African American workers are being treated badly. Follow these steps:

- Clearly state your position on the issue.
- Use facts and details from the text or from outside research to support your position and claims.
- Clarify the relationships among ideas with transitional words and phrases.

QUESTIONS FOR DISCUSSION

1. How did slavery affect the Gold Rush?
2. What issues motivated African American workers to travel west?

PREPARATION FOR ESSAY

You may use the knowledge you gain during this research assignment to support your claims in an essay you will write at the end of this section.

ACADEMIC VOCABULARY

Academic terms appear in blue on these pages. If these words are not familiar to you, use a dictionary to find their definitions.

Birds Struggle to Recover from Egg Thefts of 1800s

By Edie Lau
Bee Staff Writer

This time of year, sea birds that look somewhat like penguins are busy breeding on the Farallon Islands. Within a month after mating, these birds—called common murres—will lay speckled eggs, one per couple. The eggs are a gorgeous mixture of hues, and big.

The eggs also are said to taste good.

People who poured into Northern California for the Gold Rush ate millions of murre eggs that were collected from the Farallons, pointy rocks that jut from the ocean 27 miles west of San Francisco. The newcomers' hunger nearly wiped out the islands' most populous bird.

One-and-a-half centuries later, the Farallons' common murre colony is still trying to recover.

"It's growing, but it's not growing as fast as it could be," said William Sydeman, director of marine studies at the Point Reyes Bird Observatory. "If we get an oil spill at the wrong place at the wrong time, we could lose easily 50 percent. There's no cushion."

Murres (pronounced merz) once again are the most plentiful bird on the islands, breeding adults numbering about 80,000. But that's not many compared with their numbers before the Gold Rush. Biologists **conservatively** estimate that 500,000 adult murres—and possibly many more—raised chicks on the islands.

The Farallon Islands and surrounding ocean make a rich marine environment. The islands are known as the largest sea bird rookery[1] in the continental United States. The Farallons are alive and noisy with seagulls, puffins, auklets and cormorants, to name a few; the air is thick with the pungent scent of their guano. Sea lions and seals lounge on ledges or cavort in coves.

The Farallons' abundant wildlife impressed Yankee seamen and Russian explorers in the early 19th century. They hunted the seals for their pelts, meat and blubber. The Russians also enthusiastically collected sea bird eggs—for which they and Scandinavian peoples had developed a taste long before—according to Peter White of Martinez, an amateur naturalist and author of "The Farallon Islands: Sentinels of the Golden Gate."

Mining the National Archives in Washington, D.C., the California State Library in Sacramento and the public library in San Francisco, White found many colorful accounts of the commercial egging spurred by the Gold Rush.

One of the first to profit from the Farallon egg trade reportedly was a pharmacist from Maine known as "Doc" Robinson. Shortly after he arrived in San Francisco in 1849, Robinson

◀ **conservatively**
(kən sər´ və tiv lē)
adv. moderately or cautiously; safely

People who poured into Northern California for the Gold Rush ate millions of murre eggs . . .

and a companion sailed to the islands. By selling the eggs he gathered there, Robinson earned enough money to open a drug store.

Two years later, another group of **entrepreneurs** established a business known as the Pacific Egg Co. or the Farallone Egg Co. The company constructed buildings, roads and landing facilities on the island. During the months of May, June and July, as many as 30 laborers gathered eggs.

◀ **entrepreneurs**
(än´ trə prə nərz´)
n. people who organize and manage a business

---

1. **rookery** (rook´ ər ē) *n.* a breeding place or colony of birds or animals, such as penguins or seals.

In search of fresh eggs—not those with a visibly developing chick embryo—the gatherers, when they arrived for the season, would smash eggs that had already been laid, Sydeman said. That forced the birds to lay a second egg. Normally, murre couples produce a single chick in a year.

Eggers were rough men in a rough environment, according to witnesses' descriptions. Earnest Peixotto, a San Francisco artist who sketched the egg gatherers at work, wrote, "It made one shudder to see (the men)…scramble down the slippery cliffs, with boiling surf straight below, steadying themselves with one hand while with the other, they reached for the eggs."

While there were many bird eggs to choose from, murre eggs apparently were particularly desirable for their taste and ease of harvest, said Harry R. Carter, a sea bird biologist at the U.S. Geological Survey's Western Ecological Research Center in Dixon.

"They nested on the surface, so you could just walk along

The Farallon Islands

and pick them up," Carter said. "Other birds nested in holes on the ground."

In its infancy, California had no poultry industry, which further boosted the value of murre eggs. Carter cited one account of eggs sold away from market for as much as $6 to $9 a dozen. In San Francisco, prices began at $1.50 a dozen; by 1896, they had dropped to 12 cents a dozen.

The eggs were used predominantly by restaurants and bakeries in San Francisco, but Carter surmises that miners carried the nuggets of protein inland. "I imagine that these eggs were…transported wherever they could get to before they got bad," Carter said. "I imagine they went up to Sacramento, at least."

The egging company was ousted from the islands in 1881 by the federal government, which operated a lighthouse on the Farallons and challenged the company's presence from the start. Lighthouse keepers continued the practice of egg gathering until late 1896, when ornithologists[2] at the California Academy of Sciences successfully pressured the federal government to ban egging once and for all.

In the years since, the Farallons' breeding murre colony has swelled and shrunk. Chronic coastal oil pollution depressed the population's

In the years since, the Farallons' breeding murre colony has swelled and shrunk.

growth for much of this century, Sydeman said.

By the early 1980s, murre numbers rose to about 100,000. But the population **faltered** less than a decade later, this time because the birds were drowning in gill nets.[3] Now those fishing nets, for the most part, are not allowed where murres dive for food.

Around the world, common murres are, in fact, common, Sydeman said, with a global population of about 20 million. But Sydeman thinks the Farallon murres will never regain their pre-Gold Rush abundance. The environment has probably changed too much.

copyright © The Sacramento Bee

◄ **faltered**
(fôl′ tərd) *v.* lost strength; weakened

---

2. **ornithologists** (ôr′ nə thäl′ ə jists) people who study the branch of zoology dealing with birds.
3. **gill nets** *n.* nets set upright in the water to catch fish by entangling their gills.

Close Reading Activities

READ

Comprehension

Reread all or part of the text to help you answer the following questions.

1. Why were Californians interested in common murre eggs?

2. Name three reasons the common murre population in the Farallon Islands has decreased.

Research: Clarify Details Choose at least one unfamiliar detail from the text, and briefly research it. Then, explain how the information you learned from research sheds light on an aspect of the article.

Summarize Write an objective summary of the text to clarify your understanding.

Language Study

Selection Vocabulary Define each boldfaced word, and use the word in a sentence of your own.

• Biologists **conservatively** estimate that 500,000 adult murres...

• Two years later, another group of **entrepreneurs** established a business...

• But the population **faltered** less than a decade later, ...

Literary Analysis

Reread the identified passage. Then, respond to the questions that follow:

> **Focus Passage** (p. 150)
>
> In search of fresh eggs … reached for the eggs."

Key Ideas and Details

1. **(a)** What did the gatherers do when they arrived for the season? **(b) Analyze Causes and Effects:** How did their actions change the birds' behavior?

2. **Analyze:** In what kind of environment did the eggers work?

Craft and Structure

3. **(a)** List the verbs the writer uses to describe the eggers' actions.
   (b) Interpret: How do these verbs **establish** the eggers' characters?

Integration of Knowledge and Ideas

4. What is the writer's attitude toward the eggers? Use details from the text to support your response.

Imagery

Imagery is descriptive language that appeals to the five senses. Reread the article, and note the author's use of imagery.

1. **(a)** Find two examples of imagery in the text. **(b) Interpret:** To what senses do those images appeal?

2. **(a)** Find imagery that describes the Farallon Islands. **(b) Interpret:** What mood does the imagery develop?

DISCUSS • RESEARCH • WRITE

From Text to Topic **Group Discussion**

Discuss the following passage with a group of classmates. Take notes during the discussion. Contribute your own ideas, and support them with examples from the text.

> The Farallon Islands and surrounding ocean make a rich marine environment. The islands are known as the largest sea bird rookery in the continental United States. The Farallons are alive and noisy with seagulls, puffins, auklets and cormorants, to name a few; the air is thick with the pungent scent of their guano. Sea lions and seals lounge on ledges or cavort in coves.
>
> The Farallons' abundant wildlife impressed Yankee seamen and Russian explorers in the early nineteenth century. They hunted the seals for their pelts, meat and blubber.

Research **Investigate the Topic**

The Gold Rush and Food When people rushed to California, they had to adjust to unfamiliar plants and foods.

Assignment

Conduct research to find the types of food miners and their families ate during the Gold Rush. Consult the Internet and other sources. Take clear notes, and carefully identify your sources so that you can easily access the information later. Share your findings by creating a **menu** that lists popular food items.

Writing to Sources **Argument**

In the late 1800s, the federal government banned egging in California. While some people pushed for the ban, others disagreed with the decision.

Assignment

Write an **argument** in which you agree or disagree with the egging ban in California. Follow these steps:

- Introduce a problem or issue, and explain both sides.
- Clearly state your **opinion**.
- Cite evidence from the article to **support** your position.

QUESTIONS FOR DISCUSSION

1. How do the words the writer uses to describe the Farallon Islands suggest her attitude toward the subject?

2. Contrast the ways the islands' wildlife impresses the writer and the explorers.

PREPARATION FOR ESSAY

You may use the knowledge you gain during this research assignment to support your claims in an essay you will write at the end of this section.

ACADEMIC VOCABULARY

Academic terms appear in blue on these pages. If these words are not familiar to you, use a dictionary to find their definitions.

Speaking and Listening: **Group Discussion**

The Gold Rush and Conflict The texts in this section vary in genre, length, style, and perspective. However, all of the texts focus on an aspect or outcome of the Gold Rush. The effects of the Gold Rush on the environment, population, civil rights, and popular culture are fundamentally related to the Big Question addressed in this unit: **Is conflict always bad?**

▲ Refer to the selections you read in Part 3 as you complete the activities on this assessment.

Assignment

Conduct discussions. With a small group of classmates, conduct a discussion about issues of the Gold Rush and conflict. Refer to the texts in this section, other texts you have read, and your personal experience and knowledge to support your ideas. Begin your discussion by addressing the following questions:

- Why do significant international events, such as the Gold Rush, sometimes cause conflict?

- Was the outcome of the Gold Rush positive or negative? Why?

- How did the Gold Rush affect the following: U.S. population, the environment, and the treatment of minorities?

Summarize and present your ideas. After you have fully explored the topic, summarize your discussion and present your ideas to the class as a whole.

Criteria for Success

✓ **Organizes the group effectively**
Appoint a group leader and a timekeeper. The group leader should present the discussion questions. The timekeeper should make sure the discussion takes no longer than 20 minutes.

✓ **Maintains focus of discussion**
As a group, stay on topic and avoid straying into other subject areas.

✓ **Involves all participants equally and fully**
No one person should monopolize the conversation. Rather, everyone should take turns speaking and contributing ideas.

✓ **Follows the rules for collegial discussion**
As each group member speaks, others should listen carefully. Build on one another's ideas and support viewpoints and opinions with sound reasoning and evidence. Express disagreement respectfully.

USE NEW VOCABULARY

As you speak and share ideas, work to use the vocabulary words you have learned in this unit. The more you use new words, the more you will "own" them.

Writing: **Narrative**

The Gold Rush and Conflict Conflict characterizes the stories
we read and many of the historical events we study. Just as we face
conflict in our daily lives, those who participated in the Gold Rush
also dealt with conflict.

Assignment

Write a **short story** in which you include real events, places, or
people in a made-up narrative about the Gold Rush. This form of
writing is known as historical fiction. Your story should develop
conflicts between characters or highlight conflicts that result from
historical events or situations.

Criteria for Success

Purpose/Focus
✓ **Connects specific incidents with larger ideas**
Make clear connections between your characters and plot and
the texts you have read in this section.

✓ **Clearly conveys the significance of the story**
Provide a conclusion in which the conflict is resolved in a satisfying
and logical manner.

Organization
✓ **Sequences events logically**
Structure your narrative so that individual events build on one
another to create a coherent whole.

Development of Ideas/Elaboration
✓ **Supports insights**
Draw on your knowledge of the historical time period as you
develop your setting, conflict, and characters.

✓ **Uses narrative techniques effectively**
Consider using dialogue to help readers "hear" characters speak.

Language
✓ **Uses description effectively**
Use sensory details that bring to life settings and characters.

Conventions
✓ **Does not have errors**
Correct errors in grammar, spelling, and punctuation.

**INCORPORATE
RESEARCH**

As you plan your story,
refer to the notes you
took as you researched
the Gold Rush. Use what
you have learned about
that historic time period
as you develop your
story's characters and
settings.

Writing to Sources: Argument

The Gold Rush and Conflict The related readings in this section present a range of ideas about the Gold Rush and conflict. They raise questions, such as the following:

- How did individuals deal with the Gold Rush?
- What were the effects of the Gold Rush on minorities?
- How did people resolve conflicts during the Gold Rush?

Focus on the question that interests you the most, and then complete the following assignment.

INCORPORATE RESEARCH

Refer to the notes you took as you researched various aspects of the Gold Rush. Cite relevant details from your research in your argument.

> **Assignment**
>
> Write an **argumentative essay** in which you state and defend a claim about the effects of the Gold Rush on individuals, groups, or on the environment. Build evidence for your claim by analyzing the conflicts presented in two or more texts from this section. Clearly present, develop, and support your ideas with examples and details from the texts.

Prewriting and Planning

Choose texts. Review the texts in the section, and choose at least two to cite in your essay. Select at least two that will provide strong material to support your argument.

Gather details and craft a working thesis, or claim. Use a chart like the one shown to develop your claim.

Focus Question: Was conflict during the Gold Rush always negative?

Text	Passage	Notes
"The King of Mazy May"	"He did not like the looks of the newcomers, and one day, when five of them came by with crack dog teams and the lightest of camping outfits, he could see that they were prepared to make speed, and resolved to keep an eye on them."	narrator indicates that the Gold Rush has created conflict—in this case, suspicion—between the main characters
"Chinese and African Americans in the Gold Rush"	"They used their gold to free their families, start churches, schools, libraries and newspapers, and work for greater legal rights."	positive outcomes of hardship during the Gold Rush

Example Claim: Even though there were conflicts during the Gold Rush, the conflicts had many positive outcomes, such as making people stronger as individuals and more unified as groups.

Prepare counterarguments. Note a possible objection to each point that supports your claim. Plan to include the strongest of these counterclaims in your essay: Be sure to introduce and supply evidence to disprove it.

Drafting

Structure your ideas and evidence. Create an informal outline or list of ideas you want to present. Decide where you will include evidence and which evidence you will use to support each point.

Address counterclaims. Strong argumentation takes differing ideas into account and addresses them directly. As you order your ideas, explain opposing opinions or differing interpretations. Then, write a reasoned, well-supported response to those counterclaims.

Frame and connect ideas. Write an introduction that will grab the reader's attention. Consider beginning with a compelling quotation or a detail. Then, write a strong conclusion that ends your essay with a clear statement. Use words, phrases, and clauses to link the major sections of your essay and clarify the relationships between your claims and reasons, evidence, and counterclaims.

Revising and Editing

Review content. Make sure that your claim is clearly stated and that you have supported it with convincing evidence from the texts. Underline main ideas in your paper and confirm that each one is supported. Add more proof as needed.

Review style. Revise to cut wordy language. Adapt your language, as needed, to achieve a formal, objective tone. Then, proofread to eliminate errors in spelling and grammar.

CITE RESEARCH CORRECTLY

Review your argument, and note the details that came from an outside source. Cite your source material for each detail. Refer to the Research Workshop in the front of this book for citation guidelines.

Self-Evaluation Rubric

Use the following criteria to evaluate the effectiveness of your essay.

Criteria	Rating Scale			
Purpose/Focus Introduces a precise claim and supports the argument with clear reasons and evidence	*not very .... very*			
	1	2	3	4
Organization Establishes a logical organization; uses words, phrases, and clauses to clarify the relationships among ideas	1	2	3	4
Development of Ideas/Elaboration Develops the claim and counterclaims fairly, supplying evidence for each; provides a concluding statement that follows from the argument presented	1	2	3	4
Language Establishes and maintains a formal style and an objective tone	1	2	3	4
Conventions Uses correct conventions of grammar, spelling, and punctuation	1	2	3	4

Independent Reading

Titles for Extended Reading

In this unit, you have read texts in a variety of genres. Continue to read on your own. Select works that you enjoy, but challenge yourself to explore new authors and works of increasing depth and complexity. These titles will help you get started.

INFORMATIONAL TEXT

All Creatures Great and Small
by James Herriot

James Herriot describes his first years as a veterinarian in this collection of **narrative nonfiction.** His tales of helping animals in the English countryside have delighted readers for over twenty-five years.

Discoveries: Trouble Ahead

The **essays** in this collection cover topics that range from ancient Greece to baseball. Each essay features a conflict that the participants turn into an advantage.

Cathedral: The Story of Its Construction
by David Macaulay   EXEMPLAR TEXT

In this illustrated **informational text**, David Macaulay uses detailed pen-and-ink drawings to show how a magnificent cathedral would have been built in the year 1252.

LITERATURE

The Sherlock Holmes Mysteries
by Sir Arthur Conan Doyle
Signet, 1985

Sherlock Holmes is considered one of the greatest fictional detectives of all time. In this **short story** collection, the brilliant Holmes solves baffling crimes with the help of his partner, Dr. Watson.

An Island Like You: Stories of the Barrio
by Judith Ortiz Cofer
Orchard Books, 1995

In this collection of **short stories**, teenagers deal with conflicts between their American culture and their parents' Puerto Rican heritage.

My Side of the Mountain
by Jean Craighead George
Scholastic Book Services, 1988

In this gripping adventure **novel**, Sam Gribley leaves his comfortable home in New York City, bound for the Catskill Mountains. Read how he bravely endures a harsh year in the wilderness.

The Book of Questions
by Pablo Neruda   EXEMPLAR TEXT

Pablo Neruda wrote this collection of **poems** near the end of his life. Each poem is a thought-provoking question, or series of questions, about nature, life, or death.

ONLINE TEXT SET

SHORT STORY
Eleven Sandra Cisneros

BIOGRAPHY
A Backwoods Boy Russell Freedman

LETTER
Letter to Scottie F. Scott Fitzgerald

Preparing to Read Complex Texts

Attentive Reading As you read on your own, ask yourself questions like these to enrich your reading experience.

When reading narratives, ask yourself…

Comprehension: **Key Ideas and Details**

- Can I clearly picture the time and place of the action? Which details help me do so?
- Can I picture the characters clearly? Why or why not?
- Do the characters behave like real people? Why or why not?
- Which characters do I like and which do I dislike? Why?
- Do I understand why the characters act as they do? Why or why not?
- What does the story mean to me? Does it express a meaning or an insight I find important and true?

Text Analysis: **Craft and Structure**

- Does the story grab my attention immediately? Why or why not?
- Do I want to keep reading? Why or why not?
- Can I follow the sequence of events in the story? Am I confused at any point? If so, what information would make the sequence clearer?
- Do the characters change as the story progresses? If so, do the changes seem believable?
- Are there any passages that I find especially moving, interesting, or well written? If so, why?

Connections: **Integration of Knowledge and Ideas**

- How is this story similar to and different from other stories I have read?
- How do my feelings toward the characters affect my experience of reading the story?
- Did the story teach me something new or cause me to look at something in a new way? If so, what did I learn?
- Would I recommend this story to others? Why or why not?
- Would I like to read other works by this author? Why or why not?

101010
10100110101
0011

What is important to know?

UNIT PATHWAY

PART 1
SETTING EXPECTATIONS

- INTRODUCING THE BIG QUESTION
- CLOSE READING WORKSHOP

PART 2
TEXT ANALYSIS
GUIDED EXPLORATION

LIFE STORIES

PART 3
TEXT SET
DEVELOPING INSIGHT

BASEBALL

PART 4
DEMONSTRATING INDEPENDENCE

- INDEPENDENT READING
- ONLINE TEXT SET

CLOSE READING TOOL

Use this tool to practice the close reading strategies you learn.

STUDENT eTEXT

Bring learning to life with audio, video, and interactive tools.

ONLINE WRITER'S NOTEBOOK

Easily capture notes and complete assignments online.

Find all Digital Resources at **pearsonrealize.com.**

Introducing the Big Question

What is important to know?

Knowledge does not come only from books and the Internet. It also comes from participating in life. You gain knowledge from your daily experience—when you observe what happens around you and when you examine the ideas and events that spark your curiosity. On the one hand, there is no limit to what you can know. Yet, on the other hand, you cannot know everything.

With all the information that is available to you, it is helpful to decide what you think is most important to know.

Exploring the Big Question

Collaboration: One-on-One Discussion Start thinking about the Big Question by exploring what you already know and what you would like to learn. Begin by making a list. Give at least two examples of things that you think are important to know in each of these situations:

- Getting along with family members
- Doing well in school
- Making new friends
- Learning about the world around you
- Facing challenges

Share your examples with a partner. Discuss why you believe the examples on your list are important. Work together to decide which information seems important. Use the vocabulary words in your discussion.

Connecting to the Literature Each reading in this unit will give you additional insight into the Big Question. After you read each text, pause to consider the ways that we gain and use knowledge about ourselves and the world.

Vocabulary

Acquire and Use Academic Vocabulary The term "academic vocabulary" refers to words you typically encounter in scholarly and literary texts and in technical and business writing. Review the definitions of these academic vocabulary words.

concept (kän´ sept´) *n.* general idea or notion

distinguish (di stiŋ´ gwish) *v.* mark as different; set apart

examine (eg zam´ ən) *v.* study or look at closely

judge (juj) *v.* form an opinion about; decide on

measure (mezh´ ər) *v.* find the value of

observe (əb zurv´) *v.* see or notice

purpose (pur´ pəs) *n.* use; function

question (kwes´ chən) *v.* doubt; wonder about

refer (ri fur´) *v.* turn to for information such as to a book or an expert

source (sôrs) *n.* something that gives information, such as a book, Web site, or person

study (stud´ ē) *v.* look into deeply; examine

Gather Vocabulary Knowledge Additional vocabulary words are listed below. Categorize the words by deciding whether you know each one well, know it a little bit, or do not know it at all.

guess	limit
knowledge	narrow

Then, do the following:

1. Write the definitions of the words you know.
2. Consult a dictionary to confirm the meanings of the words you know. Revise your definitions if necessary.
3. Next, use a print or an online dictionary to look up the meanings of the words you do not know. Then, write the meanings.
4. Use all of the words in a brief paragraph about knowledge.

Close Reading Workshop

In this workshop you will learn an approach to reading that will deepen your understanding of literature and will help you better appreciate author's craft. The workshop includes models for the close reading, discussion, research, and writing activities. After you have reviewed the strategies and models, practice your skills with the Independent Practice selection.

CLOSE READING: NONFICTION

In the beginning of this unit you will focus on reading various types of nonfiction. Use these strategies as you read the texts.

Comprehension: Key Ideas and Details

- Read first to unlock basic meaning.
- Use context clues to help you determine the meanings of unfamiliar words. Consult a dictionary, if necessary.
- Identify unfamiliar details that you can clarify through research.
- Distinguish between what is stated directly and what must be inferred.

Ask yourself questions such as these:
- Who or what is the subject?
- When and where do the events take place?
- What are the main ideas in the text?

Text Analysis: Craft and Structure

- Think about the genre of the work and how the author presents facts and details.
- Analyze the author's word choice, writing style, and tone.
- Determine the author's point of view. Notice how this perspective affects what the author says.

Ask yourself questions such as these:
- What do I learn from the quotations and *anecdotes*—stories that make a point—that the author includes?
- How does the author's word choice help convey his or her point of view?
- What is the author's attitude toward his or her subject?

Connections: Integration of Knowledge and Ideas

- Look for relationships among key ideas. Identify causes and effects, and comparisons and contrasts.
- Look for clues that help you identify the purpose of the text.

Ask yourself questions such as these:
- How has this work increased my knowledge of a subject or author?
- Why is it worthwhile to learn about this subject?

Read

As you read this selection from a biography, take note of the annotations that model ways to closely read the text.

Reading Model

from **"Rambling 'Round"** [1] by Elizabeth Partridge

"I hate a song that makes you think that you're not any good. I hate a song that makes you think you are just born to lose. I am out to fight those kind of songs to my very last breath of air and my last drop of blood." [2]

Woody Guthrie could never cure himself of wandering off. One minute he'd be there, the next he'd be gone, vanishing without a word to anyone, abandoning those he loved best. He'd throw on a few extra shirts, one on top of the other, sling his guitar over his shoulder, and hit the road. He'd stick out his thumb and hitchhike, swing onto moving freight trains, and hunker down with other traveling men [3] in flophouses, hobo jungles, and Hoovervilles across Depression America. [4]

He moved restlessly from state to state, soaking up songs: work songs, mountain and cowboy songs, sea chanteys, songs from the southern chain gangs. He added them to the dozens he already knew from his childhood until he was bursting with American folk songs. Playing the guitar and singing, he started making up new ones: hardbitten, rough-edged songs that told it like it was, full of anger and hardship and hope and love.

Woody said the best songs came to him when he was walking down a road. He always had fifteen or twenty songs running around in his mind, [5] just waiting to be put together. Sometimes he knew the words, but not the melody. Usually he'd borrow a tune that was already well known—the simpler the better. As he walked along, he tried to catch a good, easy song [5] that people could sing the first time they heard it, remember, and sing again later.

Key Ideas and Details

1 The title suggests that this work will be about a person on the move. The repeated *r* sounds give the title a musical quality.

Craft and Structure

2 The author introduces her subject with the words of Woody Guthrie himself. Well-chosen quotations are an important feature of biographies.

Craft and Structure

3 The author uses long sentences that contain many clauses. Her sentences seem to "ramble" around just like Guthrie.

Key Ideas and Details

4 Through research you can learn that *flophouses* and *Hoovervilles* were temporary houses for poor people during the Great Depression of the 1930s.

Integration of Knowledge and Ideas

5 These details reinforce the main idea that Guthrie was a "rambler." The author's word choice and tone throughout the passage suggest that she wants readers to learn about and like Guthrie.

Discuss

Sharing your own ideas and listening to the ideas of others can deepen your understanding of a text and help you look at a topic in a whole new way. As you participate in collaborative discussions, work to have a genuine exchange in which classmates build upon one another's ideas. Support your points with evidence and ask meaningful questions.

Discussion Model

Student 1: I think the quote from Woody Guthrie is really interesting. Usually, I think of songs as entertainment, but for him, they meant a lot more. It seems like he learned as many songs as he could during his travels.

Student 2: And Guthrie spent a lot of time with people who had lost everything in hard times. Maybe he understood how important music was to the people he met. There wasn't much to be happy about during the Great Depression.

Student 3: That's a good point. He wanted his songs to make people feel good about themselves and their lives. I wonder what his songs say and what they sound like.

Research

Targeted research can clarify unfamiliar details and shed light on various aspects of a text. Consider questions that arise in your mind as you read, and use those questions as the basis for research.

Research Model

Questions: *What songs did Woody Guthrie write? How did his songs influence other musicians?*

Key Words for Internet Search: Woody Guthrie + music

Result: WoodyGuthrie.org, The Guardian (U.K.)

What I Learned: Woody Guthrie was an important writer of folk and children's songs, including "This Land Is Your Land" and "So Long It's Been Good to Know You." His music inspired many modern songwriters, including Bob Dylan and Bruce Springsteen.

Write

Writing about a text will deepen your understanding of it and will also allow you to share your ideas more formally with others. The following model essay evaluates the author's biographical essay about Woody Guthrie and cites evidence to support the main ideas.

Writing Model: Informative Text

An Introduction to Woody Guthrie

In "Rambling 'Round," Elizabeth Partridge introduces readers to Woody Guthrie, a free-spirited man who traveled across America writing songs inspired by the people he met. The author's engaging portrait of Guthrie makes readers want to learn more about the man and his music.

> In the first paragraph, the writer clearly states the purpose of the essay.

Partridge begins the biography with a quotation from Guthrie, allowing readers to hear his "voice." "I hate a song that makes you think you are just born to lose," he says. "I am out to fight those kind of songs to my very last breath of air and my last drop of blood." In other words, songs were more to Guthrie than just words and a melody. Instead, Guthrie saw his music as a way to give people hope.

> The writer includes direct quotations from the text and analyzes what they mean.

Guthrie lived and wrote during a period of great hardship. In the 1930s, the Great Depression caused many banks to fail and factories to close, leaving people without jobs or money. The "flophouses, hobo jungles, and Hoovervilles" in which Guthrie spent time were temporary shelters for people who were looking for ways to make a living.

However, even though Guthrie lived during hard times, Partridge portrays him as easygoing. She uses short clauses, strung together into long, descriptive sentences that paint a clear picture of the songwriter: "He'd stick out his thumb and hitchhike, swing onto moving freight trains, and hunker down with other traveling men." Partridge also gives readers a clear sense of Guthrie's "ramblin'." She uses phrases such as "hit the road," "hunker down," "restlessly," and "running around" to describe his actions. Partridge rounds out her portrayal of Guthrie by showing that even though he acted carefree, he told the truth in his music: Even if it is sometimes "rough-edged" and "hard-bitten," life is still full of "hope and love."

> Examples from the text support the writer's claims about the author's style.

"Rambling 'Round" should encourage readers to find recordings of Guthrie's music and listen to songs like "This Land Is Your Land" and "So Long (Been Good to Know You)." Guthrie died in 1967, but his influence upon songwriters lives on. Today, musicians such as Bob Dylan and Bruce Springsteen keep Guthrie's legacy alive in their own music.

> Details and facts obtained through research support the writer's evaluation of the text and provide a useful reference for the reader.

As you read the following selection, apply the close reading strategies you have learned. You may need to read the selection multiple times.

from *Zlata's Diary*
by Zlata Filipović

Meet the Author

When she was a girl, **Zlata Filipović** (b. 1980) kept a diary in which she wrote about life in the war-torn city of Sarajevo, which was under attack between 1992 and 1996. Her diary has been translated into over 30 languages and is read around the world.

CLOSE READING TOOL

Read and respond to this selection online using the **Close Reading Tool.**

Monday, March 30, 1992

Hey, Diary! You know what I think? Since Anne Frank[1] called her diary Kitty, maybe I could give you a name too. What about:
ASFALTINA PIDZAMETA
SEFIKA HIKMETA
SEVALA MIMMY
or something else???
I'm thinking, thinking . . .
I've decided! I'm going to call you
MIMMY
All right, then, let's start.

Dear Mimmy,
It's almost half-term. We're all studying for our tests. Tomorrow we're supposed to go to a classical music concert at the Skenderija Hall. Our teacher says we shouldn't go because there will be 10,000 people, pardon me, children, there, and somebody might take us as hostages or plant a bomb in the concert hall. Mommy says I shouldn't go. So I won't.

Hey! You know who won the Yugovision Song Contest?! EXTRA NENA!!!???

I'm afraid to say this next thing. Melica says she heard at the hairdresser's that on Saturday, April 4, 1992, there's going to be BOOM—BOOM, BANG—BANG, CRASH Sarajevo. Translation: they're going to bomb Sarajevo.

Love,
Zlata

---

1. Anne Frank In 1942, 13-year-old Anne Frank began a diary that she kept for the two years she and her family and some others hid from the Nazis in an attic in Amsterdam. Anne died in a concentration camp in 1945. Her father published parts of the diary in 1947, and it has since become a classic.

Sunday, April 12, 1992

Dear Mimmy,
The new sections of town—Dobrinja, Mojmilo, Vojnicko polje—
are being badly shelled. Everything is being destroyed, burned,
the people are in shelters. Here in the middle of town, where we
live, it's different. It's quiet.

People go out. It was a nice warm spring day today. We went out
too. Vaso Miskin Street was full of people, children. It looked like
a peace march. People came out to be together, they don't want
war. They want to live and enjoy themselves the way they used
to. That's only natural, isn't it? Who likes or wants war, when
it's the worst thing in the world?

I keep thinking about the march I joined today. It's bigger and
stronger than war. That's why it will win. The people must be
the ones to win, not the war, because war has nothing to do with
humanity. War is something inhuman.

Zlata

Tuesday, April 14, 1992

Dear Mimmy,
People are leaving Sarajevo. The airport, train and bus stations
are packed. I saw sad pictures on TV of people parting. Families,
friends separating. Some are leaving, others staying. It's so sad.
Why? These people and children aren't guilty of anything. Keka
and Braco[2] came early this morning. They're in the kitchen with
Mommy and Daddy, whispering. Keka and Mommy are crying. I
don't think they know what to do—whether to stay or to go. Neither
way is good.

Zlata

---

2. **Keka and Braco** nicknames of a husband and wife who are friends of Zlata's parents.

Dear Mimmy,

Today was truly, absolutely the worst day ever in Sarajevo. The shooting started around noon. Mommy and I moved into the hall. Daddy was in his office, under our apartment, at the time. We told him on the intercom to run quickly to the downstairs lobby where we'd meet him. We brought Cicko[3] with us. The gunfire was getting worse, and we couldn't get over the wall to the Bobars',[4] so we ran down to our own cellar.

The cellar is ugly, dark, smelly. Mommy, who's terrified of mice, had two fears to cope with. The three of us were in the same corner as the other day. We listened to the pounding shells, the shooting, the thundering noise overhead. We even heard planes. At one moment I realized that this awful cellar was the only place that could save our lives. Suddenly, it started to look almost warm and nice. It was the only way we could defend ourselves against all this terrible shooting. We heard glass shattering in our street. Horrible. I put my fingers in my ears to block out the terrible sounds. I was worried about Cicko. We had left him behind in the lobby. Would he catch cold there? Would something hit him? I was terribly hungry and thirsty. We had left our half-cooked lunch in the kitchen.

When the shooting died down a bit, Daddy ran over to our apartment and brought us back some sandwiches. He said he could smell something burning and that the phones weren't working. He brought our TV set down to the cellar. That's when we learned that the main post office (near us) was on fire and that they had kidnapped our President. At around 8:00 we went back up to our apartment. Almost every window in our street was broken. Ours were all right, thank God. I saw the post office in flames. A terrible sight. The fire-fighters battled with the raging fire. Daddy took a few photos of the post office being devoured by the flames. He said they wouldn't come out because I had been fiddling with something on the camera. I was sorry. The whole apartment smelled of the burning fire. God, and I used to pass by there every day. It had just been done up. It was huge and beautiful, and now it was being swallowed up by the flames. It was disappearing. That's what this neighborhood of mine looks like, my Mimmy.

---

3. **Cicko** (chēk´ ō) Zlata's canary.
4. **Bobars'** (Bō´ bĕrs) next-door neighbors.

I wonder what it's like in other parts of town? I heard on the radio that it was awful around the Eternal Flame.[5] The place is knee-deep in glass. We're worried about Grandma and Granddad. They live there. Tomorrow, if we can go out, we'll see how they are. A terrible day. This has been the worst, most awful day in my eleven-year-old life. I hope it will be the only one. Mommy and Daddy are very edgy. I have to go to bed.

Ciao![6]
Zlata

Tuesday, May 5, 1992

Dear Mimmy,
The shooting seems to be dying down. I guess they've caused enough misery, although I don't know why. It has something to do with politics. I just hope the "kids" come to some agreement. Oh, if only they would, so we could live and breathe as human beings again. The things that have happened here these past few days are terrible. I want it to stop forever. PEACE! PEACE!

I didn't tell you, Mimmy, that we've rearranged things in the apartment. My room and Mommy and Daddy's are too dangerous to be in. They face the hills, which is where they're shooting from. If only you knew how scared I am to go near the windows and into those rooms. So, we turned a safe corner of the sitting room into a "bedroom." We sleep on mattresses on the floor. It's strange and awful. But, it's safer that way. We've turned everything around for safety. We put Cicko in the kitchen. He's safe there, although once the shooting starts there's nowhere safe except the cellar. I suppose all this will stop and we'll all go back to our usual places.

Ciao!
Zlata

---

5. **Eternal Flame** Sarajevo landmark that honors those who died resisting the Nazi occupation during World War II.
6. **Ciao!** (chou) *interj.* hello or goodbye.

Thursday, May 7, 1992

Dear Mimmy,

I was almost positive the war would stop, but today . . . Today a shell fell on the park in front of my house, the park where I used to play and sit with my girlfriends. A lot of people were hurt. From what I hear Jaca, Jaca's mother, Selma, Nina, our neighbor Dado and who knows how many other people who happened to be there were wounded. Dado, Jaca and her mother have come home from the hospital, Selma lost a kidney but I don't know how she is, because she's still in the hospital. AND NINA IS DEAD. A piece of shrapnel lodged in her brain and she died. She was such a sweet, nice little girl. We went to kindergarten together, and we used to play together in the park. Is it possible I'll never see Nina again? Nina, an innocent eleven-year-old little girl—the victim of a stupid war. I feel sad. I cry and wonder why? She didn't do anything. A disgusting war has destroyed a young child's life. Nina. I'll always remember you as a wonderful little girl.

Love, Mimmy,
Zlata

Monday, June 29, 1992

Dear Mimmy,
BOREDOM!!! SHOOTING!!! SHELLING!!! PEOPLE BEING KILLED!!! DESPAIR!!! HUNGER!!! MISERY!!! FEAR!!!

That's my life! The life of an innocent eleven-year-old schoolgirl!! A schoolgirl without a school, without the fun and excitement of school. A child without games, without friends, without the sun, without birds, without nature, without fruit, without chocolate or sweets, with just a little powdered milk. In short, a child without a childhood. A wartime child. I now realize that I am really living through a war, I am witnessing an ugly, disgusting war. I and thousands of other children in this town that is being destroyed, that is crying, weeping, seeking help, but getting none. God, will this ever stop, will I ever be a schoolgirl again, will I ever enjoy my childhood again? I once heard that childhood is the most wonderful time of your life. And it is. I loved it, and now an ugly war is taking it all away from me. Why? I feel sad. I feel like crying. I am crying.

Your Zlata

Thursday, October 29, 1992

Dear Mimmy,
Mommy and Auntie Ivanka (from her office) have received grants
to specialize in Holland. They have letters of guarantee,[7] and
there's even one for me. But Mommy can't decide. If she accepts,
she leaves behind Daddy, her parents, her brother. I think it's
a hard decision to make. One minute I think—no, I'm against
it. But then I remember the war, winter, hunger, my stolen
childhood and I feel like going. Then I think of Daddy, Grandma
and Granddad, and I don't want to go. It's hard to know what to
do. I'm really on edge, Mimmy, I can't write anymore.

Your Zlata

Monday, November 2, 1992

Dear Mimmy,
Mommy thought it over, talked to Daddy, Grandma and
Granddad, and to me, and she's decided to go. The reason for
her decision is—ME. What's happening in Sarajevo is already too
much for me, and the coming winter will make it even harder.
All right. But . . . well, I suppose it's better for me to go. I really
can't stand it here anymore. I talked to Auntie Ivanka today and
she told me that this war is hardest on the children, and that
the children should be got out of the city. Daddy will manage,
maybe he'll even get to come with us.

Ciao!
Zlata

---

7. **letters of guarantee** letters from people or companies promising to help individuals who
   wanted to leave the country during the war.

Thursday, December 3, 1992

Dear Mimmy,

Today is my birthday. My first wartime birthday. Twelve years old. Congratulations. Happy birthday to me!

The day started off with kisses and congratulations. First Mommy and Daddy, then everyone else. Mommy and Daddy gave me three Chinese vanity cases—with flowers on them!

As usual there was no electricity. Auntie Melica came with her family (Kenan, Naida, Nihad) and gave me a book. And Braco Lajtner came, of course. The whole neighborhood got together in the evening. I got chocolate, vitamins, a heart-shaped soap (small, orange), a key chain with a picture of Maja and Bojana, a pendant made of a stone from Cyprus, a ring (silver) and earrings (bingo!).

The table was nicely laid, with little rolls, fish and rice salad, cream cheese (with Feta), canned corned beef, a pie, and, of course—a birthday cake. Not how it used to be, but there's a war on. Luckily there was no shooting, so we could celebrate.

It was nice, but something was missing. It's called peace!

Your Zlata

Tuesday, July 27, 1993

Dear Mimmy,

Journalists, reporters, TV and radio crews from all over the world (even Japan). They're interested in you, Mimmy, and ask me about you, but also about me. It's exciting. Nice. Unusual for a wartime child.

My days have changed a little. They're more interesting now. It takes my mind off things. When I go to bed at night I think about the day behind me. Nice, as though it weren't wartime, and with such thoughts I happily fall asleep.

But in the morning, when the wheels of the water carts wake me up, I realize that there's a war on, that mine is a wartime life. SHOOTING, NO ELECTRICITY, NO WATER, NO GAS, NO FOOD. Almost no life.

Zlata

Thursday, October 7, 1993

Dear Mimmy,

Things are the way they used to be, lately. There's no shooting (thank God), I go to school, read, play the piano . . .

Winter is approaching, but we have nothing to heat with.

I look at the calendar and it seems as though this year of 1993 will again be marked by war. God, we've lost two years listening to gunfire, battling with electricity, water, food, and waiting for peace.

I look at Mommy and Daddy. In two years they've aged ten. And me? I haven't aged, but I've grown, although I honestly don't know how. I don't eat fruit or vegetables, I don't drink juices, I don't eat meat . . . I am a child of rice, peas and spaghetti. There I am talking about food again. I often catch myself dreaming about chicken, a good cutlet, pizza, lasagna . . . Oh, enough of that.

Zlata

Tuesday, October 12, 1993

Dear Mimmy,
I don't remember whether I told you that last summer I sent a letter through school to a pen-pal in America. It was a letter for an American girl or boy.

Today I got an answer. A boy wrote to me. His name is Brandon, he's twelve like me, and lives in Harrisburg, Pennsylvania. It really made me happy.

I don't know who invented the mail and letters, but thank you whoever you are. I now have a friend in America, and Brandon has a friend in Sarajevo. This is my first letter from across the Atlantic. And in it is a reply envelope, and a lovely pencil.

A Canadian TV crew and journalist from *The Sunday Times* (Janine) came to our gym class today. They brought me two chocolate bars. What a treat. It's been a long time since I've had sweets.

Love,
Zlata

December 1993

Dear Mimmy,
PARIS. There's electricity, there's water, there's gas. There's, there's . . . life, Mimmy. Yes, life; bright lights, traffic, people, food . . . Don't think I've gone nuts, Mimmy. Hey, listen to me, Paris!? No, I'm not crazy, I'm not kidding, it really is Paris and (can you believe it?) me in it. Me, my Mommy and my Daddy. At last. You're 100% sure I'm crazy, but I'm serious, I'm telling you, dear Mimmy, that I have arrived in Paris. I've come to be with you. You're mine again now and together we're moving into the light. The darkness has played out its part. The darkness is behind us; now we're bathed in light lit by good people. Remember that—good people. Bulb by bulb, not candles, but bulb by bulb, and me bathing in the lights of Paris. Yes, Paris. Incredible. You don't understand. You know, I don't think I understand either. I feel as though I must be crazy, dreaming, as though it's a fairy tale, but it's all TRUE.

Close Reading Activities

Read

Comprehension: Key Ideas and Details

1. Infer: Why does Zlata decide to give her diary a name?

2. (a) What hardships do Zlata and her family endure during the war? **(b) Analyze:** Why did Zlata still have mixed feelings about leaving Sarajevo?

3. (a) Describe Zlata's birthday party. **(b) Connect:** Based on earlier diary entries, what gift does she most want?

4. Summarize: Write a brief, objective summary of the diary. Cite story details.

Text Analysis: Craft and Structure

5. Zlata describes the horrors of war from a specific point of view. How might her perspective differ from that of her parents?

6. (a) Analyze: Why is the fact that this is a diary important to consider? **(b) Explain:** How would your understanding of the text change if *Zlata's Diary* was a fictional story?

7. (a) What is Zlata's purpose for starting a diary? **(b) Analyze:** How does this purpose change over time?

8. (a) Describe the *tone*—the writer's attitude—of the last entry. **(b) Analyze:** What words and phrases create this tone?

Connections: Integration of Knowledge and Ideas

Discuss

Conduct a **small-group discussion** about the themes that develop over the course of *Zlata's Diary.* Why do you think she does not talk about the causes of the war or about the politics of either side?

Research

The events in *Zlata's Diary* happen in a particular time and place. Briefly research the following:

a. Sarajevo

b. The civil war in the former Yugoslavia

c. Similar texts, such as *The Diary of a Young Girl* by Anne Frank

Take notes as you perform your research. Then, write a brief **explanation** of why information about historical events and setting helps you understand Zlata's experiences.

Write

Zlata describes a peace march as being "bigger and stronger than war." Write an **essay** in which you analyze her statement. What does Zlata mean? How is the theme of peace emphasized throughout the diary? Cite details to support your analysis.

? What is important to know?

Zlata's Diary is read all over the world. What does Zlata write about in her diary that is important to know? Explain your answer.

"**Everyone** is necessarily
the **hero** of his own life story."

—John Barth

LIFE STORIES

In this section, authors share their own memories of personal struggles and unique achievements. Consider the quotation on the opposite page, and think about the ways a person can triumph from both mistakes and accomplishments, no matter how big or small.

◀ **CRITICAL VIEWING** How does this photograph represent the idea of looking both forward and back over one's life and experiences?

READINGS IN PART 2

CLOSE READING TOOL

Use the **Close Reading Tool** to practice the strategies you learn in this unit.

Focus on Craft and Structure

Elements of Nonfiction

Nonfiction writing tells about **real people, places, objects,** or **events.**

Nonfiction writing is about real life. Some forms of nonfiction, such as histories, have been around since ancient times. Others, such as blogs and Web pages, came into being more recently. Nonfiction writing changes with people and technology. It is a large, ever-developing category of literature. Still, all forms of nonfiction have certain basic elements.

- They are written for one or more **purposes,** or reasons.
- They express the writer's unique **point of view,** or perspective, about a subject.
- They use words and phrases that project a certain **tone,** or attitude.
- They **develop or explain ideas** in a logical, organized way.

Informative Texts Many nonfiction texts—like this textbook—are informative. Their main purpose is to inform, or give information to the reader. Newspaper reports, encyclopedia articles, and science books are examples of informative texts.

Narrative Nonfiction Narrative nonfiction tells the story of real people, places, things, and events. These texts usually aim to entertain *and* inform the reader. They might tell the story of a single person's life or the story of an entire group of people. They might describe a dramatic, real-life event.

Literary Nonfiction Authors of literary nonfiction use elements of literature, such as language, in creative ways. They choose words that stir up feelings in the reader. These writers may also use the kinds of comparisons you might find in a poem, or they may include vivid details to make their writing rich and interesting.

The best nonfiction writing opens new windows on the world for the reader. It says, "This is what I see, from the place where I happen to be."

Nonfiction texts . . .	This element of nonfiction is called . . .
Are written from the unique perspective of the author.	Point of View
Are written for one or more reasons.	Author's Purpose
Use specific words to convey specific meanings.	Word Choice
Use vivid details that appeal to the five senses: sight, sound, touch, taste, and smell.	Imagery
Organize ideas in ways that are easy for readers to follow.	Organization

Forms of Nonfiction

There are many forms of nonfiction.

An **autobiography** is a story about the writer's own life, told by the writer. Autobiographies take many different forms.

- A **memoir** describes one or more meaningful events, and may express strong feelings.
- A **diary** is a personal record of events and experiences. Most diaries are updated regularly.
- An **autobiographical sketch** is a brief description of the high points of a person's life.

An **essay** is a short work about a single subject. Essays are written for many purposes.

- A **persuasive essay, or argument,** is meant to convince readers to adopt a particular point of view or take a certain action.
- A **narrative essay** tells the story of an event that happened in real life, often one that the writer witnessed, or saw.
- An **expository essay** presents facts, ideas, and explanations.
- A **reflective essay** presents the writer's thoughts and beliefs about a subject or an event.

A **speech** is an oral, or spoken, presentation of a speaker's ideas and beliefs.

- **Persuasive speeches** urge listeners to adopt certain beliefs or take certain actions.
- An **address** is a formal speech to a specific group of people. It may offer deep thoughts on an important occasion.
- A **talk** is an informal presentation in which the speaker shares his or her knowledge on a subject.

Other Forms of Nonfiction

Advertisement	Letter	Editorial	Functional Text
• Written for a target audience who might be interested in a product or service • Often includes visuals • Aims to persuade	• Addressed to a specific individual or group • May be personal or formal • Aims to share thoughts, describe events, or request action or information	• States the writer's position on an issue • Featured in newspapers or magazines • Aims to persuade	• Presents facts in an easy-to-read form • Examples include schedules, menus, charts • Aims to inform

Determining Author's Purpose, Point of View, and Development of Ideas

A nonfiction text is written for specific **purposes**. Its **key ideas** convey the author's unique **point of view**.

Author's Purpose An author's purpose is his or her main reason for writing. Nonfiction texts are often written to **inform, persuade, entertain, describe,** or **express feelings.** In many cases, an author has more than one reason for writing. For example, an author might write an essay about the impacts of an oil spill to describe and to persuade.

Point of View Every writer views his or her subject through a certain lens, or **point of view,** that is shaped by the writer's values and beliefs.

Example: Graduation Speech
Today we celebrate your goals and accomplishments. We also celebrate your past and future failures—and the lessons that you have learned and will learn from them.

Point of View
The author respects the students, values the marking of occasions, and views life as a learning process.

Word Choice Looking closely at an author's word choice can help you understand his or her point of view. Authors choose specific words and phrases to stir up positive or negative feelings, or **connotations.**

Idea: "Love your neighbor"	Author's Point of View
Positive Connotation: We all know the **timeless truth** "Love your neighbor."	The author values the saying.
Negative Connotation: We have all heard the **tired cliché** "Love your neighbor."	The author finds the saying meaningless.

Tone Tone is the feeling or attitude that you can "hear" in the lines of a work. Tone can usually be summed up in a single word. The tone of the first sentence in the chart shown above might be described as approving. The tone of the second sentence might be described as critical.

Key Idea All nonfiction texts center on one or more **key ideas.** A key idea is the central idea a writer wishes to convey. Key ideas are usually linked to an author's purpose and the type of text he or she is writing.

- In a persuasive speech meant to convince listeners to vote, the key idea might be: Voting is an important right and responsibility for Americans.
- In an essay meant to reflect on sports in society, the key idea might be: Athletes should be role models.

Key ideas are sometimes stated directly; other times, they are *implied,* or suggested. To understand implied ideas, examine all the parts and details of the text to see what they have in common. Look for the key idea of each paragraph and see how it relates to the overall key idea of the text.

Developing and Supporting the Key Idea Whether stated or unstated, a key idea must be developed and supported. Writers use different types of details to elaborate a key idea. The following chart provides examples of various kinds of support that may be used to devlop a key idea.

Type of Support	Example
Anecdotes: brief stories used to make a point	"When I was a boy," Uncle Ramos began . . .
Facts: pieces of data that can be proven	4,000 tons of cans have been recycled.
Figurative language: colorful comparisons	Rivers are the bloodstreams of the world.
Examples: specific cases that illustrate ideas	Boots are "in." Cowboy boots are the most popular.
Quotations: the exact words of a key person	"I have a dream," said Dr. Martin Luther King, Jr.

Writers arrange supporting details in logical, artful ways.

- Writers may introduce the key idea with an anecdote or example at the beginning of a work.
- Writers develop the key idea with blocks of supporting ideas. They group related **sentences** into **paragraphs** and may divide long works into **chapters** or **sections.**
- Writers give their piece an **overall structure.** If the work tells a story, for example, a writer may arrange the events in time order.

Building Knowledge

Meet the Author

As a child, Gary Soto (b. 1952) loved the bustle and energy of his Fresno, California, neighborhood. When Soto was six years old, however, a government program changed his neighborhood by replacing many run-down buildings with new ones. "It didn't work in our area," Soto says. "The houses were bulldozed, and in their place grew weeds." As he grew older, Soto continued to feel a sense of loss over his old neighborhood. Writing helped him get his feelings down on paper, where he could see and think about them.

What is important to know?

Explore the Big Question as you read "The Drive-In Movies." Take notes on what the narrator learns through his experiences.

CLOSE READING FOCUS

Key Ideas and Details: **Make Predictions**

When you **make predictions,** you develop ideas about what is most likely to happen next. Base your predictions on details in the text and on your own experience. Keep track of your predictions by writing them down. Then, read ahead to check each prediction. When you find details that show your original prediction may be wrong, revise your prediction. Use these new details to correct and change your ideas.

Craft and Structure: **Narrator and Point of View**

The **narrator** is the voice that tells a true or imagined story. **Point of view** is the perspective from which the story is told. The narrator's point of view affects the kinds of details that are revealed to the reader.

- **First-person point of view:** The narrator takes part in the action of the story and refers to himself or herself as "I." Readers know only what the narrator sees, thinks, and feels.
- **Third-person point of view:** The narrator does not take part in the action. As an outside observer, a third-person narrator can share information that the characters do not know.

Most true stories about a writer's life are told from the first person point of view.

Vocabulary

Write these words from "The Drive-In Movies" in your notebook. Which words are past-tense verbs? How do you know?

prelude	pulsating	migrated
evident	winced	vigorously

CLOSE READING MODEL

The passage below is from Gary Soto's autobiographical narrative "The Drive-In Movies." The annotations to the right of the passage show ways in which you can use close reading skills to make predictions and analyze narrator and point of view.

from **"The Drive-In Movies"**

For our family, moviegoing was rare. But if our mom, tired from a week of candling eggs, woke up happy on a Saturday morning, there was a chance we might later scramble to our blue Chevy and beat nightfall to the Starlight Drive-In. [1] My brother and sister knew this. I knew this. So on Saturday we tried to be good. [2] We sat in the cool shadows of the TV with the volume low and watched cartoons, a prelude of what was to come.

One Saturday I decided to be extra good. [3] When she came out of the bedroom tying her robe, she yawned a hat-sized yawn and blinked red eyes at the weak brew of coffee I had fixed for her. I made her toast with strawberry jam spread to all the corners and set the three boxes of cereal in front of her. If she didn't care to eat cereal, she could always look at the back of the boxes as she drank her coffee.

I went outside. The lawn was tall but too wet with dew to mow. I picked up a trowel and began to weed the flower bed. [4]

Make Predictions

1 Based on the title and these sentences, you might predict that this selection will describe a family's "rare" trip to the drive-in movies.

Narrator and Point of View

2 The first-person pronouns *I* and *we* indicate that this narrative is told from the first-person point of view.

Narrator and Point of View

3 Soto shares his decision to be extra good. As a first-person narrator, he can share his own thoughts and feelings, but not the thoughts of his mother or any other character.

Make Predictions

4 Soto has been working hard to be "extra good." At this point you might make a prediction about whether or not his efforts will earn him a trip to the movies.

The DRIVE-IN MOVIES

Gary Soto

Narrator and Point of View
What clues here indicate the narrator is telling the story from the first-person point of view?

Vocabulary ▶
prelude (prā′ lo͞od′) *n.* introduction to a main event

For our family, moviegoing was rare. But if our mom, tired from a week of candling eggs,[1] woke up happy on a Saturday morning, there was a chance we might later scramble to our blue Chevy and beat nightfall to the Starlight Drive-In. My brother and sister knew this. I knew this. So on Saturday we tried to be good. We sat in the cool shadows of the TV with the volume low and watched cartoons, a **prelude** of what was to come.

---

1. **candling eggs** examining uncooked eggs for freshness by placing them in front of a burning candle.

One Saturday I decided to be extra good. When she came out of the bedroom tying her robe, she yawned a hat-sized yawn and blinked red eyes at the weak brew of coffee I had fixed for her. I made her toast with strawberry jam spread to all the corners and set the three boxes of cereal in front of her. If she didn't care to eat cereal, she could always look at the back of the boxes as she drank her coffee.

I went outside. The lawn was tall but too wet with dew to mow. I picked up a trowel[2] and began to weed the flower bed. The weeds were really bermuda grass, long stringers that ran finger-deep in the ground. I got to work quickly and in no time crescents of earth began rising under my fingernails. I was sweaty hot. My knees hurt from kneeling, and my brain was dull from making the trowel go up and down, dribbling crumbs of earth. I dug for half an hour, then stopped to play with the neighbor's dog and pop ticks from his poor snout.

---

2. **trowel** (trou´ əl) *n.* a small hand tool used by gardeners to weed or dig.

▼ **Critical Viewing**
How might seeing a movie at a drive-in like this one differ from seeing it in a regular theater?

Comprehension
Why is the narrator being extra good?

Vocabulary ▶
pulsating (pul´ sāt´ iŋ)
adj. beating or throbbing in a steady rhythm

migrated (mī´ grāt əd)
v. moved from one place to another

Spiral Review
CENTRAL IDEA How do these vivid details contribute to the author's central idea?

I then mowed the lawn, which was still beaded with dew and noisy with bees hovering over clover. This job was less dull because as I pushed the mower over the shaggy lawn, I could see it looked tidier. My brother and sister watched from the window. Their faces were fat with cereal, a third helping. I made a face at them when they asked how come I was working. Rick pointed to part of the lawn. "You missed some over there." I ignored him and kept my attention on the windmill of grassy blades. ●

While I was emptying the catcher, a bee stung the bottom of my foot. I danced on one leg and was ready to cry when Mother showed her face at the window. I sat down on the grass and examined my foot: the stinger was **pulsating.** I pulled it out quickly, ran water over the sting and packed it with mud, Grandmother's remedy.

Hobbling, I returned to the flower bed where I pulled more stringers and again played with the dog. More ticks had **migrated** to his snout. I swept the front steps, took out the garbage, cleaned the lint filter to the dryer (easy), plucked hair from the industrial wash basin in the garage (also easy), hosed off the patio, smashed three snails sucking paint from the house (disgusting but fun), tied a bundle of newspapers, put away toys, and, finally, seeing that almost everything was done and the sun was not too high, started waxing the car.

My brother joined me with an old gym sock, and our sister watched us while sucking on a cherry Kool-Aid ice cube. The liquid wax drooled onto the sock, and we began to swirl the white slop on the chrome. My arms ached from

buffing, which though less boring than weeding, was harder. But the beauty was evident. The shine, hurting our eyes and glinting like an armful of dimes, brought Mother out. She looked around the yard and said, "Pretty good." She winced at the grille and returned inside the house.

We began to wax the paint. My brother applied the liquid and I followed him rubbing hard in wide circles as we moved around the car. I began to hurry because my arms were hurting and my stung foot looked like a water balloon. We were working around the trunk when Rick pounded on the bottle of wax. He squeezed the bottle and it sneezed a few more white drops.

We looked at each other. "There's some on the sock," I said. "Let's keep going." ●

We polished and buffed, sweat weeping on our brows. We got scared when we noticed that the gym sock was now blue. The paint was coming off. Our sister fit ice cubes into our mouths and we worked harder, more intently, more dedicated to the car and our mother. We ran the sock over the chrome, trying to pick up extra wax. But there wasn't enough to cover the entire car. Only half got waxed, but we thought it was better than nothing and went inside for lunch. After lunch, we returned outside with tasty sandwiches.

Rick and I nearly jumped. The waxed side of the car was foggy white. We took a rag and began to polish vigorously and nearly in tears, but the fog wouldn't come off. I blamed Rick and he blamed me. Debra stood at the window, not wanting to get involved. Now, not only would we not go to the movies, but Mom would surely snap a branch from the plum tree and chase us around the yard.

Mom came out and looked at us with hands on her aproned hips. Finally, she said, "You boys worked so hard." She turned on the garden hose and washed the car. That night we did go to the drive-in. The first feature was about nothing, and the second feature, starring Jerry Lewis, was *Cinderfella*. I tried to stay awake. I kept a wad of homemade popcorn in my cheek and laughed when Jerry Lewis fit golf tees in his nose. I rubbed my watery eyes. I laughed and looked at my mom. I promised myself I would remember that scene with the golf tees and promised myself not to work so hard the coming Saturday. Twenty minutes into the movie, I fell asleep with one hand in the popcorn.

Make Predictions
How does this outcome fit with your prediction about how the narrator would feel after his day of work?

Language Study

Vocabulary The following words appear in "The Drive-In Movies." For each item, choose a synonym, or word with a similar meaning, from the vocabulary list.

pulsating	migrated	evident	winced	vigorously

1. clear, obvious, ?
2. shrank back, cringed, ?
3. throbbing, beating, ?
4. actively, energetically, ?
5. traveled, roamed, ?

WORD STUDY

The **Latin prefix pre-** means "before" or "in advance."

In this story, the narrator and his siblings begin Saturday mornings by watching television. This activity is a **prelude** to all the activities that they will do later on. It happens *before* the other activities.

Word Study

Part A Explain how the **Latin prefix pre-** contributes to the meaning of *precaution, predict,* and *preheat*. Consult a dictionary if necessary.

Part B Use sentence context and what you know about the Latin prefix *pre-* to explain your responses to the following questions.

1. How might a movie's *preview* help people decide whether or not to see that movie?
2. Does the *preface* appear at the end of a book?

Close Reading Activities

Literary Analysis

Key Ideas and Details

1. **(a) Make Predictions** Did you predict that Soto's mother would take the family to the drive-in movies? **(b)** On what details did you base your prediction?

2. **Make Predictions** As you read, did you change any of your predictions? Explain.

Craft and Structure

3. **Narrator and Point of View** Make a chart like the one on the right to note how the author develops point of view in the narrative. Include at least three examples.

4. **Narrator and Point of View** What details about the events described in the narrative would you expect to find if the narrator were Soto's mother?

Integration of Knowledge and Ideas

5. **(a)** How does Soto persuade his mother to take the family to the drive-in movies? **(b) Draw Conclusions:** Why do you think Soto's mother does not get angry with the children for making a mess with the car wax?

6. **(a)** What two things does Soto promise himself to remember? **(b) Assess:** Do you think he still has fond memories of that day and night? Explain.

7. **Make a Judgment:** Do you think children should have to do chores before their parents allow them to do something enjoyable? Why or why not? With a partner, discuss and support your responses.

8. **What is important to know?** With a small group, discuss the following questions. **(a)** As a child, what did Soto know and consider important about his family's Saturday activities? **(b)** As an adult, what does Soto know and consider important about his childhood Saturdays?

Event
The narrator is stung by a bee.

Details Provided by Narrator
The narrator wants to cry but takes the stinger out and packs the wound with mud.

ACADEMIC VOCABULARY

As you write and speak about "The Drive-In Movies," use the words related to gaining knowledge that you explored on page 163 of this text.

Conventions: **Principal Parts of Verbs**

Every verb has four main forms, or **principal parts**. These parts are used to form verb tenses that show time.

Regular verbs form their past tense and past participles by adding -ed or –d.

Irregular verbs, such as *rise* and *be*, form their past tense and past participles in different ways.

	Present	Present Participle	Past	Past Participle
Regular	talk(s)	(am, is, are) talking	talked	(has, have) talked
	serve(s)	(am, is, are) serving	served	(has, have) served
Irregular	be (am, is, are)	(am, is, are) being	was, were	(has, have) been
	has, have	(am, is, are) having	had	(has, have) had
	rise(s)	(am, is, are) rising	rose	(has, have) risen

Practice A
Identify the verb or verbs in each sentence. For each verb, indicate which of the four principal parts is used.

1. Soto's mother worked hard.
2. Soto falls asleep in the middle of the movie.
3. Soto is trying to be extra good.
4. His mother has taken them to the movies before.

Speaking Application Describe "The Drive-In Movies" to a partner. In your discussion, use at least three of the four principal parts of verbs.

Practice B
Rewrite each sentence, replacing the italicized verb with the principal part indicated in parentheses.

1. One Saturday, Gary *makes* breakfast for his mom. (past tense)
2. Gary *kneels* as he weeds the lawn. (present participle)
3. The boys *waxed* the car. (past participle)
4. On Saturday night, they *went* to the drive-in. (present tense)

Writing Application Find two sentences in "The Drive-In Movies" that use verbs in the past tense. Rewrite the sentences to use the past participle forms.

Writing to Sources

Narrative Text "The Drive-In Movies" is filled with details about events in author Gary Soto's early life. Write an **autobiographical narrative** about an interesting experience in your life. In your narrative, compare and contrast your experience to the one Soto describes.

- Think of important or humorous events in your life and jot them down.
- Narrow your topic and choose one experience.
- List the details of where, when, and with whom the experience took place. Number the events in the order in which they happened.
- Note ways in which your experience is similar to and different from Soto's experience. You might compare characters, settings, final outcomes, or lessons learned. Review "The Drive-In Movies" to find details to use in your comparisons.
- Use your notes and numbered list to write your narrative.

Grammar Application Use appropriate principal parts or the verbs you write in your narrative. Look for ways in which you can vary your use of principal parts.

Speaking and Listening

Comprehension and Collaboration With a partner, write a **conversation** that Gary Soto and his mother might have had the morning after their trip to the drive-in. Then, act out the conversation for the class or a small group.

Follow these steps to complete the assignment:

- Review the selection, jotting down details about each character that will help you invent interesting dialogue.
- Ask your partner questions and make observations, keeping each character's traits, goals, and feelings in mind.
- Practice using eye contact when listening and speaking.
- Finally, when you act out your conversation, use expressive tones of voice and gestures to engage your audience.

Building Knowledge

Meet the Author

Although **Julia Alvarez** (b. 1950) was born in New York City, her family soon returned to their original home, the Dominican Republic. After Julia's father worked to overthrow the dictator there, he and his family fled the country. Julia was ten years old when they arrived in the United States again. From the moment she landed in New York City, she felt she had to "translate her experience into English." Today, she says, "I write to find out what I'm thinking."

What is important to know?

Explore the Big Question as you read "Names/Nombres." Take notes on ways in which the story explores the importance of personal identity.

CLOSE READING FOCUS

Key Ideas and Details: **Fact and Opinion**

To evaluate the author's claims or ideas in a work of nonfiction, you must understand the difference between **fact** and **opinion.** A fact, unlike an opinion, can be proved. An opinion expresses a judgment that can be supported but not proved. You can check facts by using resources such as the following:

- dictionaries
- encyclopedias
- reliable Web sites

Craft and Structure: **Tone**

The **tone** of a literary work is the writer's attitude toward his or her audience and subject. The tone can often be described in one word, such as *playful, serious,* or *humorous.* Factors that contribute to tone include word choice, sentence structure, and sentence length. Notice how word choice creates a friendly tone in this example:

If you plan ahead, I promise you, you'll have the best party ever!

As you read, look for details that convey a certain tone.

Vocabulary

You will encounter the following words in "Names/Nombres." Write the words in your notebook, and rate them from the one you know most best (6) to the one you know least (1). As you read, look for the words and their definitions.

mistook	transport	chaotic
pursue	inevitably	inscribed

CLOSE READING MODEL

The passage below is from Julia Alvarez's personal narrative "Names/Nombres." The annotations to the right of the passage show ways in which you can use close reading skills to distinguish fact and opinion and to analyze tone.

from "Names/Nombres"

My little sister, Ana, had the easiest time of all. [1] She was plain *Anne*—that is, only her name was plain, for she turned out to be the pale, blond "American beauty" in the family. . . . [2]

Later, during her college years in the late '60s, there was a push to pronounce Third World names correctly. I remember calling her long distance at her group house and a roommate answering.

"Can I speak to Ana?" I asked, pronouncing her name the American way.

"Ana?" The man's voice hesitated. "Oh! You must mean *Ah-nah*!" [3]

Our first few years in the States, though, ethnicity was not yet "in." Those were the blond, blue-eyed, bobby sock years of junior high and high school before the '60s ushered in peasant blouses, hoop earrings, serapes. [4] My initial desire to be known by my correct Dominican name faded. I just wanted to be Judy and merge with the Sallys and Janes in my class.

Fact and Opinion

1 Alvarez states a personal feeling about her sister. It is an opinion because it cannot be proved. Ana might have a different opinion from Alvarez's.

Tone

2 In the phrases "plain Anne" and "that is, only her name was plain," Alvarez's word choice creates a humorous and friendly tone.

Tone

3 Alvarez uses a casual, humorous tone to share a funny story about mispronouncing her sister's name.

Fact and Opinion

4 You could consult print or online resources to confirm these facts about U.S. clothing fads of the 1950s and '60s.

Names/Nombres

Julia Alvarez

Fact and Opinion
What fact does the narrator state in the first paragraph?

When we arrived in New York City, our names changed almost immediately. At Immigration,[1] the officer asked my father, *Mister Elbures,* if he had anything to declare. My father shook his head, "No," and we were waved through. I was too afraid we wouldn't be let in if I corrected the man's pronunciation, but I said our name to myself, opening my mouth wide for the organ blast of the *a,* trilling my tongue for the drum-roll of the *r, All-vah-rrr-es!* How could anyone get *Elbures* out of that orchestra of sound?

At the hotel my mother was *Missus Alburest,* and I was little girl, as in, "Hey, *little girl,* stop riding the elevator up and down. It's *not* a toy."

---

1. **Immigration** government agency that processes people who have recently moved to the United States.

When we moved into our new apartment building, the super[2] called my father *Mister Alberase*, and the neighbors who became mother's friends pronounced her name *Jew-lee-ah* instead of *Hoo-lee-ah*. I, her namesake, was known as *Hoo-lee-tah* at home. But at school, I was *Judy* or *Judith*, and once an English teacher **mistook** me for *Juliet*.

It took awhile to get used to my new names. I wondered if I shouldn't correct my teachers and new friends. But my mother argued that it didn't matter. "You know what your friend Shakespeare said, *'A rose by any other name would smell as sweet.'*" My father had gotten into the habit of calling any famous author "my friend" because I had begun to write poems and stories in English class.

By the time I was in high school, I was a popular kid, and it showed in my name. Friends called me *Jules* or *Hey Jude*, and once a group of troublemaking friends my mother forbade me to hang out with called me *Alcatraz*. I was *Hoo-lee-tah* only to Mami and Papi and uncles and aunts who came over to eat *sancocho* on Sunday afternoons—old world folk whom I would just as soon go back to where they came from and leave me to **pursue** whatever mischief I wanted to in America.

JUDY ALCATRAZ: the name on the Wanted Poster would read. Who would ever trace her to me? •

My older sister had the hardest time getting an American name for herself because *Mauricia* did not translate into English. Ironically, although she had the most foreign-sounding name, she and I were the Americans in the family. We had been born in New York City when our parents had first tried immigration and then gone back "home," too homesick to

---

2. **super** *n.* superintendent; person who manages an apartment building.

PART 2 • Names/Nombres **197**

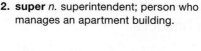

◄ **Vocabulary**
mistook (mis tŏŏk´) *v.* identified incorrectly; misunderstood

pursue (pər sōō´) *v.* be involved in; follow

Tone
What attitude does the author have toward her different names?

Fact and Opinion
What opinion does the narrator give in this paragraph?

Comprehension
What does Julia experience when she arrives in New York City?

▶ **Critical Viewing**
Does this picture accurately reflect Mami's feelings about baby Mauricia's name? Why or why not?

stay. My mother often told the story of how she had almost changed my sister's name in the hospital.

After the delivery, Mami and some other new mothers were cooing over their new baby sons and daughters and exchanging names and weights and delivery stories. My mother was embarrassed among the Sallys and Janes and Georges and Johns to reveal the rich, noisy name of *Mauricia*, so when her turn came to brag, she gave her baby's name as *Maureen*.

"Why'd ya give her an Irish name with so many pretty Spanish names to choose from?" one of the women asked.

My mother blushed and admitted her baby's real name to the group. Her mother-in-law had recently died, she apologized, and her husband had insisted that the first daughter be named after his mother, *Mauran*. My mother thought it the ugliest name she had ever heard, and she talked my father into what she believed was an improvement, a combination of *Mauran* and her own mother's name, *Felicia*.

"Her name is *Mao-ree-shee-ah*," my mother said to the group of women.

"Why that's a beautiful name," the new mothers cried. "*Moor-ee-sha, Moor-ee-sha*," they cooed into the pink blanket. *Moor-ee-sha* it was when we returned to the States eleven years later. Sometimes, American tongues found even that mispronunciation tough to say and called her *Maria* or *Marsha* or *Maudy* from her nickname *Maury*. I pitied her. What an awful name to have to **transport** across borders!

Vocabulary ▶
transport (trans pôrt´)
v. carry from one place to another

My little sister, Ana, had the easiest time of all. She was plain *Anne*—that is, only her name was plain, for she turned out to be the pale, blond "American beauty" in the family. The only Hispanic thing about her was the affectionate nicknames her boyfriends sometimes gave her. *Anita*, or as one goofy guy used to sing to her to the tune of the banana advertisement, *Anita Banana*.[3]

Later, during her college years in the late '60s, there was a push to pronounce Third World names correctly. I remember calling her long distance at her group house and a roommate answering.

"Can I speak to Ana?" I asked, pronouncing her name the American way.

"Ana?" The man's voice hesitated. "Oh! you must mean *Ah-nah*!"

Our first few years in the States, though, ethnicity was not yet "in." Those were the blond, blue-eyed, bobby sock years of junior high and high school before the '60s ushered in peasant blouses, hoop earrings, serapes.[4] My initial desire to be known by my correct Dominican name faded. I just wanted to be Judy and merge with the Sallys and Janes in my class. But **inevitably**, my accent and coloring gave me away. "So where are you from, Judy?"

"New York," I told my classmates. After all, I had been born blocks away at Columbia Presbyterian Hospital.

"I mean, *originally*."

"From the Caribbean," I answered vaguely, for if I specified, no one was quite sure on what continent our island was located.

"Really? I've been to Bermuda. We went last April for spring vacation. I got the worst sunburn! So, are you from Portoriko?"

"No," I sighed. "From the Dominican Republic."

"Where's that?"

"South of Bermuda."

> "Her name is Mao-ree-shee-ah," my mother said to the group of women.

◄ **Vocabulary**
inevitably
(in ev´ i tə blē) *adv.*
unavoidably

Fact and Opinion
How could you check the fact that the narrator was born in Columbia Presbyterian Hospital?

Comprehension
What other names was Julia known by when she came to the United States?

---

3. ***Anita Banana*** play on the name *Chiquita Banana*, a character in a company's ad.
4. **serapes** (sə rä´ pēz) *n.* colorful shawls worn in Latin America.

They were just being curious, I knew, but I burned with shame whenever they singled me out as a "foreigner," a rare, exotic friend.

"Say your name in Spanish, oh please say it!" I had made mouths drop one day by rattling off my full name, which according to Dominican custom, included my middle names, Mother's and Father's surnames for four generations back.

"Julia Altagracia María Teresa Álvarez Tavares Perello Espaillat Julia Pérez Rochet González," I pronounced it slowly, a name as **chaotic** with sounds as a Middle Eastern bazaar[5] or market day in a South American village. •

My Dominican heritage was never more apparent than when my extended family attended school occasions. For my graduation, they all came, the whole lot of aunts and uncles and the many little cousins who snuck in without tickets. They sat in the first row in order to better understand the Americans' fast-spoken English. But how

Vocabulary ▶
chaotic (kā ät´ ik) *adj.* completely confused

Spiral Review
CENTRAL IDEA Explain why Alvarez's Spanish name is an important detail in this essay.

5. **bazaar** (bə zär´) *n.* marketplace, frequently outdoors.

could they listen when they were constantly speaking among themselves in florid-sounding phrases, rococo[6] consonants, rich, rhyming vowels?

Introducing them to my friends was a further trial to me. These relatives had such complicated names and there were so many of them, and their relationships to myself were so convoluted. There was my Tía Josefina, who was not really an aunt but a much older cousin. And her daughter, Aida Margarita, who was adopted, *una hija de crianza*. My uncle of affection, Tío José, brought my *madrina* Tía Amelia and her *comadre* Tía Pilar. My friends rarely had more than a "Mom and Dad" to introduce.

After the commencement ceremony my family waited outside in the parking lot while my friends and I signed yearbooks with nicknames which recalled our high school good times: "Beans" and "Pepperoni" and "Alcatraz." We hugged and cried and promised to keep in touch.

---

6. **rococo** (rə kō′ kō) *adj.* fancy style of art of the early eighteenth century.

"Say your name in Spanish, oh please say it!"

Vocabulary ▶
inscribed (in skrībd')
adj. written on

Sometimes, if our goodbyes went on too long, I heard my father's voice calling out across the parking lot, "*Hoo-lee-tah! Vámonos!*"

Back home, my *tíos* and *tías* and *primas*, Mami and Papi, and *mis hermanas* had a party for me with *sancocho* and a storebought *pudín*, inscribed with *Happy Graduation, Julie.* There were many gifts—that was a plus to a large family! I got several wallets and a suitcase with my initials and a graduation charm from my godmother and money from my uncles. The biggest gift was a portable typewriter from my parents for writing my stories and poems.

Someday, the family predicted, my name would be well-known throughout the United States. I laughed to myself, wondering which one I would go by.

Language Study

Vocabulary Each statement below includes one of the following words from "Names/Nombres." Explain why you think each statement is true or false.

mistook   **pursue**   **transport**   **inevitably**   **chaotic**

1. A *chaotic* place is calm and relaxing.
2. If you do not study for a test, you will *inevitably* pass.
3. A net is a useful tool if you want to *transport* water.
4. A hospital is a good place to *pursue* a medical career.
5. If someone *mistook* you for your identical twin, you would be surprised.

WORD STUDY
The **Latin root -*scrib*-** or -*scrip*- means "to write."
In this story, the narrator's family buys a special cake for her graduation party. The cake is **inscribed** with writing that says "Happy Graduation."

Word Study

Part A Explain how the **Latin root -*scrib*-** or -*scrip*- contributes to the meanings of *prescription, scribe,* and *manuscript.* Consult a dictionary if necessary.

Part B Use context and what you know about the Latin root -*scrib*- or -*scrip*- to explain your answers.

1. How is the *script* of a play helpful to an actor?
2. Why might you get in trouble for *scribbling* in a book?

Close Reading Activities

Literary Analysis

Key Ideas and Details: Fact and Opinion

1. (a) How does Julia's family say her name? **(b) Analyze Cause and Effect** Explain why some English speakers mispronounce her name.

2. Fact and Opinion How might you verify where the Dominican Republic is located?

3. Fact and Opinion Alvarez relates the story of her sister's name by saying, "My mother thought it the ugliest name she had ever heard." Is her mother stating a fact or an opinion? Explain.

Craft and Structure: Tone

4. Tone "Names/Nombres" is written in an informal, or friendly, tone. In a chart like the one on the right, rewrite the two sentences in a more serious, or formal, tone.

5. Tone Tell which of the following sentences from "Names/Nombres" has a humorous tone, and which has a serious tone. Explain your answers. **(a)** *They were just being curious, I knew, but I burned with shame whenever they singled me out as a "foreigner," a rare exotic friend.* **(b)** *There were many gifts— that was a plus to a large family!*

Integration of Knowledge and Ideas

6. (a) How does Julia respond when her classmates ask her where she comes from? **(b) Draw Conclusions:** Why does she respond as she does? **(c) Evaluate:** Would you make the same decision in the same situation? Why or why not?

7. (a) Explain how the title captures the focus, or main topic, of Alvarez's narrative. **(b) Analyze:** How do Alvarez's feelings about the topic change over time? **(c) Synthesize:** What do names represent for Alvarez and others?

8. **What is important to know?** With a small group, discuss the following questions: **(a)** What do you think Alvarez learned about language differences from her experience as a young bilingual speaker? **(b)** Would it have been valuable for her to correct people who mispronounced her name? Explain your answer.

Informal Tone

"Later, during her college years in the late '60s, there was a push to pronounce Third World names correctly."

"Our first few years in the States, though, ethnicity was not yet 'in'."

Formal Tone

ACADEMIC VOCABULARY

As you write and speak about "Names/Nombres," use the words related to gaining knowledge that you explored on page 163 of this text.

Conventions: **Action and Linking Verbs**

A **verb** expresses an action or a state of being. Every complete sentence includes at least one verb.

An **action verb** such as *jump* or *dance* expresses an action of a person or thing. Some verbs, such as *guess, believe,* and *wish,* express mental actions rather than physical actions.

A **linking verb** such as *am, is,* or *were* connects a noun or pronoun to a word that identifies, renames, or describes it. Other common linking verbs include *seem, feel, look,* and *become.*

Action Verbs	Linking Verbs
Jacob *jumped* over the rocks.	Katie *is* an artist.
(The action is *jumping*.)	(*Is* links *Katie* to *artist. Artist* renames *Katie.*)
Tamara *guessed* the answer.	The blanket *feels* soft.
(The action is *guessing*.)	(*Feels* links *blanket* to *soft. Soft* describes the *blanket*.)

Practice A

Identify the verbs in these sentences and indicate whether they are action verbs or linking verbs.

1. Julia's mother was upset.
2. The whole family celebrated Julia's graduation.
3. The family moved from the Dominican Republic.
4. Julia made many friends at school.
5. Julia's long name seemed odd to her friends.

Reading Application In "Names/ Nombres," find one sentence that includes both an action verb and a linking verb.

Practice B

Rewrite each sentence so that it contains both an action verb and a linking verb.

1. Julia's family lived in an apartment building.
2. Of the three sisters, Ana fit in most easily.
3. Many people pronounced Mauricia's name incorrectly.
4. Julia's relatives celebrated her graduation.

Writing Application Write a short paragraph about "Names/Nombres." Use at least three action verbs and two linking verbs.

Writing to Sources

Narrative Text "Names/Nombres" relates a **personal anecdote**, a brief true story about a personal experience. Write a personal anecdote about a happy experience you had growing up.

- Brainstorm a list of interesting experiences you have had.
- Choose the experience you will most enjoy writing about.
- Review "Names/ Nombres" to see how a writer uses vivid details to convey an experience. Then, use descriptive and sensory language that captures what you saw, heard, and felt.
- Include brief descriptions of the setting in which the experience took place, and of other people who took part in the experience.
- Write down your reactions to the experience.
- Use your notes to write your personal narrative.

Grammar Application Use both action verbs and linking verbs in your anecdote.

Speaking and Listening

Comprehension and Collaboration A **monologue** is a speech in which someone expresses his or her thoughts. Write and deliver a monologue that presents the thoughts of young Julia Alvarez as she hears someone mispronounce her name for the first time. Deliver your monologue to a partner.

Follow these steps to complete the assignment:

- Jot down words and phrases that express the feelings you think Alvarez experienced.
- Describe why you, in the character of Alvarez, would feel that way.
- Use vocabulary that reflects Alvarez's personality. Review the selection to find words and phrases that Alvarez typically uses.
- Be sure to consistently use first-person pronouns such as *I, my, me, we,* and *us.*

Building Knowledge

Meet the Author

Young **Eloise Greenfield** (b. 1929) loved reading, but she did not enjoy writing. One day, though, she sat down and began to write. Since then, she has published more than thirty books. She once said, "I love words . . . sometimes they make me laugh. Other times, I feel a kind of pain in struggling to find the right ones. But I keep struggling because I want to do my best, and because I want children to have the best."

❓ What is important to know?

Explore the Big Question as you read "Langston Terrace." Take notes on ways in which the story explores the importance of knowing about place, culture, and history.

CLOSE READING FOCUS

Key Ideas and Details: **Main Idea**

The **main idea** is the most important point in a literary work. Sometimes the main idea is stated directly. At other times, you must infer, or figure out, the main idea by identifying key details in the text.

- Key details often reveal what a work is about.
- They are sometimes repeated throughout a work.
- They are related to other details in a work.
- Together, the key details support the main idea.

Craft and Structure: **Author's Influences**

An **author's influences** are the factors that affect his or her writing. These influences may include historical factors, such as world events that happened during the author's lifetime. For example, the gold rush of 1849 might have influenced the ideas of an author who grew up in California in the 1850s. Authors are also influenced by cultural factors such as the way they live and the issues they think are important. As you read, look for details that indicate the author's influences.

Vocabulary

You will encounter the following words in "Langston Terrace." Identify the ones that relate to the idea of people living together. Jot down the words in your notebook and find their definitions as you read.

applications	resident	reunion
community	choral	homey

CLOSE READING MODEL

The passage below is from Eloise Greenfield's memoir "Langston Terrace." The annotations to the right of the passage show ways in which you can use close reading skills to find the main idea and analyze the author's influences.

from "Langston Terrace"

I fell in love with Langston Terrace the very first time I saw it. **1** Our family had been living in two rooms of a three-story house when Mama and Daddy saw the newspaper article telling of the plans to build it. **2** It was going to be a low-rent housing project in northeast Washington, and it would be named in honor of John Mercer Langston, the famous black lawyer, educator, and congressman. **3**

So many people needed housing and wanted to live there, many more than there would be room for. They were all filling out applications, hoping to be one of the 274 families chosen. My parents filled one out, too.

I didn't want to move. I knew our house was crowded—there were eleven of us, six adults and five children—but I didn't want to leave my friends, and I didn't want to go to a strange place and be the new person in a neighborhood and a school where most of the other children already knew each other. I was eight years old, and I had been to three schools. We had moved five times since we'd been in Washington, each time trying to get more space and a better place to live. But rent was high so we'd always lived in a house with relatives and friends, and shared the rent. **4**

Main Idea

1 Greenfield states a main idea in this topic sentence: she "fell in love with Langston Terrace" the first time she saw it.

Author's Influences

2 Here Greenfield describes her family's living situation. An author's early life and experiences can strongly influence his or her writing.

Author's Influences

3 Greenfield explains that the housing project was named after a famous African American. You may infer that this detail influenced her feelings about Langston Terrace.

Main Idea

4 Greenfield states key details about her family, friends, and school to support the main idea that she did not want to move.

Langston Terrace
Eloise Greenfield

Builders in the City, 1993, Jacob Lawrence, The Jacob and Gwendolyn Lawrence Foundation/© Artists Rights Society (ARS), New York

▲ **Critical Viewing**
What do you think
these men are building?
Why do you think so?

Vocabulary ▶
applications (ap´ li kā´
shənz) *n.* forms filled
out to make a request

I fell in love with Langston Terrace the very first time I saw it. Our family had been living in two rooms of a three-story house when Mama and Daddy saw the newspaper article telling of the plans to build it. It was going to be a low-rent housing project in northeast Washington, and it would be named in honor of John Mercer Langston, the famous black lawyer, educator, and congressman.

So many people needed housing and wanted to live there, many more than there would be room for. They were all filling out **applications**, hoping to be one of the 274 families chosen. My parents filled out one, too.

I didn't want to move. I knew our house was crowded—there were eleven of us, six adults and five children—but I didn't want to leave my friends, and I didn't want to go to a strange place and be the new person in a neighborhood and a school where most of the other children already knew each other. I was eight years old, and I had been to three schools. We had moved five times since we'd been in Washington, each time trying to get more space and a better place to live. But rent was high so we'd always lived in a house with relatives and friends, and shared the rent. •

One of the people in our big household was Lillie, Daddy's cousin and Mama's best friend. She and her husband also applied for a place in the new project, and during the months that it was being built, Lillie and Mama would sometimes walk fifteen blocks just to stand and watch the workmen digging holes and laying bricks. They'd just stand there watching and wishing. And at home, that was all they could talk about. "When we get our new place . . ." "If we get our new place . . ."

Lillie got her good news first. I can still see her and Mama standing at the bottom of the hall steps, hugging and laughing and crying, happy for Lillie, then sitting on the steps, worrying and wishing again for Mama.

Finally, one evening, a woman came to the house with our good news, and Mama and Daddy went over and picked out the house they wanted. We moved on my ninth birthday. Wilbur, Gerald, and I went to school that morning from one house, and when Daddy came to pick us up, he took us home to another one. All the furniture had been moved while we were in school. •

Langston Terrace was a lovely birthday present. It was built on a hill, a group of tan brick houses and apartments with a playground as its center. The red mud surrounding the concrete walks had not yet been covered with black soil and grass seed, and the holes that would soon be homes for young trees were filled with rainwater. But it still looked beautiful to me.

We had a whole house all to ourselves. Upstairs and downstairs. Two bedrooms, and the living room would be my bedroom at night. Best of all, I wasn't the only new

Main Idea
What key details so far support the main idea that Langston Terrace is a good place to live?

person. Everybody was new to this new little community, and by the time school opened in the fall, we had gotten used to each other and had made friends with other children in the neighborhood, too. •

I guess most of the parents thought of the new place as an in-between place. They were glad to be there, but their dream was to save enough money to pay for a house that would be their own. Saving was hard, though, and slow, because each time somebody in a family got a raise on the job, it had to be reported to the manager of the project so that the rent could be raised, too. Most people stayed years longer than they had planned to, but they didn't let that stop them from enjoying life.

They formed a resident council to look into any neighborhood problems that might come up. They started a choral group and presented music and poetry programs on Sunday evenings in the social room or on the playground. On weekends, they played horseshoes and softball and other games. They had a reading club that met once a week at the Langston branch of the public library, after it opened in the basement of one of the apartment buildings.

Students with Books, 1966, Jacob Lawrence, The Jacob and Gwendolyn Lawrence Foundation/© Artists Rights Society (ARS), New York

Street Scene (Boy with Kite), 1962, Jacob Lawrence, The Jacob and Gwendolyn Lawrence Foundation/© Artists Rights Society (ARS), New York.

◄ **Critical Viewing**
What details in this painting would appeal to children? Why?

The library was very close to my house. I could leave by my back door and be there in two minutes. The playground was right in front of my house, and after my sister Vedie was born and we moved a few doors down to a three-bedroom house, I could just look out of my bedroom window to see if any of my friends were out playing.

There were so many games to play and things to do. We played hide-and-seek at the lamppost, paddle tennis and shuffleboard, dodge ball and jacks. We danced in fireplug showers, jumped rope to rhymes, played "Bouncy, Bouncy, Bally," swinging one leg over a bouncing ball, played baseball on a nearby field, had parties in the social room and bus trips to the beach. In the playroom, we played Ping-Pong and pool, learned to sew and embroider and crochet.

For us, Langston Terrace wasn't an in-between place. It was a growing-up place, a good growing-up place. Neighbors who cared, family and friends, and a lot of fun. Life was good. Not perfect, but good. We knew about problems, heard about them, saw them, lived through some hard ones ourselves, but our community wrapped itself around us, put itself between us and the hard knocks, to cushion the blows. ●

It's been many years since I moved away, but every once in a long while I go back, just to look at things and

Spiral Review
DEVELOPMENT OF IDEAS How important are memories to the author?

Author's Influences
How do the author's childhood experiences influence her attitude about the importance of family and friends?

remember. The large stone animals that decorated the playground are still there. A walrus, a hippo, a frog, and two horses. They've started to crack now, but I remember when they first came to live with us. They were friends, to climb on or to lean against, or to gather around in the evening. You could sit on the frog's head and look way out over the city at the tall trees and rooftops.

Nowadays, whenever I run into old friends, mostly at a funeral, or maybe a wedding, after we've talked about how we've been and what we've been doing, and how old our children are, we always end up talking about our childtime in our old neighborhood. And somebody will say, "One of these days we ought to have a Langston **reunion**." That's what we always called it, just "Langston," without the "Terrace." I guess because it sounded more **homey**. And that's what Langston was. It was home.

Vocabulary ▶
reunion (rē yōōn´ yən) *n.* a gathering of people who have been separated

homey (hōm´ ē) *adj.* comfortable; having a feeling of home

Language Study

Vocabulary The following words appear in "Langston Terrace." Answer each question with either *yes* or *no*. Then explain your answer.

| applications | community | choral | reunion | homey |

1. If someone wants a job, should he or she fill out an *application*?
2. Can a *community* help someone in need?
3. To see an old friend, should you go to a *reunion*?
4. If you hate to sing, should you join a *choral* group?
5. Does your school feel *homey*?

Word Study

Part A Explain how the **Latin suffix -ent** contributes to the meanings of the words *persistent*, *different*, and *evident*. Consult a dictionary if necessary.

Part B Use the context of the sentence and what you know about the suffix -*ent* to explain your answers to these questions.

1. Are you *patient* when you cannot wait for something?
2. If you really want something, should you be *insistent*?

WORD STUDY

The **Latin suffix -ent** can form an adjective or a noun. As a word part, it means "has," "shows," or "does."

In this story, the narrator is a **resident** of Langston Terrace, which means she has a residence, or home, there.

Close Reading Activities

Literary Analysis

Key Ideas and Details

1. **(a)** Why does Greenfield's family move many times before moving to Langston Terrace? **(b) Compare and Contrast:** How is the family's new home similar to the old home? How is it different?

2. **(a)** What is significant about the day Greenfield's family moves to Langston Terrace? **(b) Draw Conclusions:** How does Greenfield feel on that day?

3. **Main Idea** Greenfield's thoughts and feelings about Langston Terrace make up the main body of this essay. List four key details in the essay that show Greenfield's thoughts and feelings.

4. **Main Idea** In your own words, state the main idea of this essay.

Craft and Structure

5. **Author's Influences** In a chart like the one on the right, list cultural and historical factors that may have influenced Greenfield's writing of "Langston Terrace."

6. **Author's Influences** Which factors on your completed chart do you think influenced the author's writing the most? Explain.

Time and Place	Cultural Background	World Events

Integration of Knowledge and Ideas

7. **(a)** Why do some of the parents think of Langston Terrace as an "in-between place"? **(b) Speculate:** How might Greenfield's essay have been different if Langston Terrace had been an "in-between" place for her?

8. **(a)** As an adult, how does Greenfield feel about Langston Terrace? **(b) Speculate:** Why might former residents of Langston Terrace want to have a reunion? Explain.

9. **THE BIG ?** **What is important to know? (a)** What made Langston Terrace feel like home to Greenfield and her family? **(b)** Why is it important for a community to make newcomers feel comfortable?

ACADEMIC VOCABULARY

As you write and speak about "Langston Terrace," use the words related to gaining knowledge that you explored on page 163 of this text.

Conventions: **Simple Verb Tenses**

> A **verb** expresses an action or a state of being. A **verb tense** shows the time of the action or the state of being expressed by the verb.

There are three simple tenses.

Present tense indicates an action or a condition in the present. It may also indicate an action or a condition that occurs regularly.

Past tense tells that an action took place in the past.

Future tense tells that an action will take place in the future.

Tenses	Regular Verb: *cheer*	Irregular Verb: *have*
Present	I cheer	She has
Past	I cheered	She had
Future	I will cheer	She will have

Practice A
Identify the verb in each sentence and indicate its tense.

1. Eloise loved her new home.
2. Many people want a house on Langston Terrace.
3. Eloise will become a famous writer some day.
4. Eloise's mother walked to the building.
5. Eloise remembers Langston Terrace.

Reading Application Reread the first two paragraphs of "Langston Terrace." Select four verbs and identify the tense of each.

Practice B
Change the tense of each of the following sentences to the tense listed in parentheses.

1. Eloise will have vivid memories of her home. (past)
2. Some people thought of Langston Terrace as an in-between place. (present)
3. Eloise's parents filled out an application. (future)
4. Many people needed low-cost housing. (present)

Writing Application Choose two pictures in "Langston Terrace." Write a few sentences to describe each picture in the present tense. Then, convert the sentences to the future tense.

Writing to Sources

Narrative Write a **journal entry** as Eloise Greenfield.

- Review the essay to choose an event that especially interests you.
- Jot down notes about Greenfield's reaction to the event.
- Write an entry from Greenfield's point of view. Use descriptions to make the entry vivid.
- Adjust the pacing throughout your entry. Pacing is like rhythm. You can speed up the action or slow it down, depending on the effect you want. Pacing can help you build anticipation or draw attention to an important event or detail.
- Remember to include the thoughts, feelings, and reactions you think Greenfield might have.
- Consider using dialogue to show what you or others said during the event.

Grammar Application Check your writing to make sure that you have used verb tenses correctly.

Research and Technology

Build and Present Knowledge In a small group, use Internet or library resources to prepare an **informative presentation** on the importance of community.

Follow these steps to complete the assignment:

- Narrow your focus to two or three ways in which community is important.
- Research your topic using a variety of resource materials, including reputable online sources.
- Use details in "Langston Terrace" as a resource for information.
- Prepare a poster that highlights the most important facts about your topic. Use art or photographs to engage viewers.
- Present your findings to the class. Have each group member discuss a different aspect of your topic.

Meet the Author

As a teenager, **Paul Zindel** (1936–2003) lived for a while on Staten Island, New York, with his mother and sister. Before he wrote his famous novel *The Pigman*, Zindel taught high school science while writing in his spare time. After the success of *The Pigman*, he started writing full time. "I felt I could do more for teenagers by writing for them," he once said. Zindel discovered that most young adult books did not relate to the teenagers he knew. He made a list of pointers and then wrote another novel, following his own advice.

? What is important to know?

Explore the Big Question as you read the excerpt from *The Pigman & Me*. Take notes on ways in which the selection explores the importance of knowing the rules.

CLOSE READING FOCUS

Key Ideas and Details: **Main Idea**

The **main idea** is the most important point in a literary work. Individual paragraphs or sections may also have a central idea that supports the main idea of the work. To determine the main idea, distinguish between important and unimportant details. Important, or key, details support or tell more about the main idea.

- Ask yourself questions such as these about details in a literary work: *Why did the author include this detail? Does this detail help readers understand the main idea of the work?*
- Keep in mind that not all details support the main idea.

Craft and Structure: **Mood**

Mood is the overall feeling a literary work produces in a reader. For example, the mood of a work may be happy, scary, or hopeful. To create a particular mood, writers carefully choose words and create word pictures that appeal to the reader's senses.

Some literary works convey a single mood. In other works, the mood changes within the selection.

Vocabulary

You will encounter the following words in the excerpt from *The Pigman & Me*. Write the words in your notebook. Choose one and write its related forms in other parts of speech. For example, if you choose an adjective, write a related word in noun and verb form.

exact	observant	distorted
demented	undulating	condemnation

CLOSE READING MODEL

The passage below is from Paul Zindel's memoir *The Pigman & Me*. The annotations to the right of the passage show ways in which you can use close reading skills to find the main idea and analyze mood.

from *The Pigman & Me*

There, across the street in a field behind Ronkewitz's Candy Store, was a crowd of about 300 kids standing around like a big, undulating horseshoe, with John Quinn standing at the center bend glaring at me. **1**

"You could run," Jennifer suggested, tossing her hair all to the left side of her face. She looked much more than pretty now. She looked loyal to the bone.

"No," I said. I just walked forward toward my fate, with the blood in my temples pounding so hard I thought I was going to pass out. **2** Moose and Leon and Mike and Conehead and Little Frankfurter were sprinkled out in front of me, goading me forward. I didn't even hear what they said. I saw only their faces distorted in ecstasy and expectation. They looked like the mob I had seen in a sixteenth-century etching where folks in London had bought tickets to watch bulldogs attacking water buffalo. **3**

John stood with his black eye, and his fists up.

I stopped a few feet from him and put my fists up. A lot of kids in the crowd started to shout, "Kill him, Johnny!" but I may have imagined that part. **4**

Main Idea

1 Based on the details "about 300 kids" and "glaring at me," you can determine the main idea of this passage: the narrator, young Paul Zindel, feels alone and threatened.

Mood

2 Zindel's blood is pounding and he almost passes out. He describes himself as walking toward his "fate." These details create a mood of fearful acceptance.

Main Idea

3 Zindel compares the other boys to a "mob," and imagines himself as a buffalo being attacked by bulldogs. These details support the idea that he feels alone, different, and picked on.

Mood

4 Paul hears—or thinks he hears—the crowd shouting, "Kill him, Johnny!" His confusion between what is real and imagined intensifies the fearful mood.

from
The Pigman & Me

Paul Zindel

▲ **Critical Viewing**
What are some conflicts among students that might occur in a scene like this one?

When trouble came to me, it didn't involve anybody I thought it would. It involved the nice, normal, smart boy by the name of John Quinn. Life does that to us a lot. Just when we think something awful's going to happen one way, it throws you a curve and the something awful happens another way. This happened on the first Friday, during gym period, when we were allowed to play games in the school yard. A boy by the name of Richard Cahill, who lived near an old linoleum factory, asked me if I'd like to play paddle ball with him, and I said, "Yes." Some of the kids played softball, some played warball, and there were a few other games where you could sign out equipment and do what you wanted. What I didn't know was that you were allowed to sign out the paddles for only fifteen minutes per period so more kids could get a chance to use them. I just didn't happen to know that little rule, and Richard Cahill didn't think to tell me about it. Richard was getting a drink from the water fountain when John Quinn came up to me and told me I had to give him my paddle.

"No," I said, being a little paranoid about being the new kid and thinking everyone was going to try to take advantage of me.

"Look, you *have* to give it to me," John Quinn insisted.

That was when I did something berserk. I was so wound up and frightened that I didn't think, and I struck out at him with my right fist. I had forgotten I was holding the paddle, and it smacked into his face, giving him an instant black eye. John was shocked. I was shocked. Richard Cahill came running back and he was shocked.

"What's going on here?" Mr. Trellis, the gym teacher, growled.

"He hit me with the paddle," John moaned, holding his eye. He was red as a beet, as Little Frankfurter, Conehead, Moose, and lots of the others gathered around.

"He tried to take the paddle away from me!" I complained.

"His time was up," John said.

Mr. Trellis set me wise to the rules as he took John over to a supply locker and pulled out a first-aid kit.

"I'm sorry," I said, over and over again.

Then the bell rang, and all John Quinn whispered to me was that he was going to get even. He didn't say it like a nasty rotten kid, just more like an all-American boy who knew he'd have to regain his dignity about having to walk around school with a black eye. Before the end of school, Jennifer came running up to me in the halls and told me John Quinn had announced to everyone he was going to exact revenge on me after school on Monday. That was the note of disaster my first week at school ended on, and I was terrified because I didn't know how to fight. I had never even been in a fight. What had happened was all an accident. It really was. •

Main Idea
What details support the main idea that Paul did not expect or intend to injure John?

◀ **Vocabulary**
exact (eg zakt´) *v.* demand with force or authority

Comprehension
What misunderstanding takes place in the school yard?

Main Idea

Is the detail about "the twins, being such copy-cats" important to the main idea of the paragraph? Explain.

When Nonno Frankie arrived on Saturday morning, he found me sitting in the apple tree alone. Mom had told him it was O.K. to walk around the whole yard now, as long as he didn't do any diggings or mutilations other than weed-pulling on her side. I was expecting him to notice right off the bat that I was white with fear, but instead he stood looking at the carvings Jennifer and I had made in the trunk of the tree. I thought he was just intensely curious about what "ESCAPE! PAUL & JENNIFER!" meant. Of course, the twins, being such copycats, had already added their names so the full carving away of the bark now read, "ESCAPE! PAUL & JENNIFER! & NICKY & JOEY!" And the letters circled halfway around the tree.

"You're killing it," Nonno Frankie said sadly.

"What?" I jumped down to his side.

"The tree will die if you cut any more."

I thought he was kidding, because all we had done was carve off the outer pieces of bark. We hadn't carved deep into the tree, not into the *heart* of the tree. The tree was too important to us. It was the most crucial place to me and Jennifer, and the last thing we'd want to do was hurt it.

"The heart of a tree isn't deep inside of it. Its heart and blood are on the *outside*, just under the bark," Nonno Frankie explained. "That's the living part of a tree. If you carve in a circle all around the trunk, it's like slitting its throat. The water and juices and life of the tree can't move up from the roots!" I knew about the living layer of a tree, but I didn't know exposing it would kill the whole tree. I just never thought about it, or I figured trees patched themselves up.

"Now it can feed itself from only half its trunk," Nonno Frankie explained. "You must not cut any more."

"I won't," I promised. Then I felt worse than ever. Not only was I scheduled to get beat up by John Quinn after school on Monday, I was also a near tree-killer. Nonno Frankie finally looked closely at me.

"Your first week at school wasn't all juicy meatballs?" he asked.

That was all he had to say, and I spilled out each and every horrifying detail. Nonno Frankie let me babble on and on. He looked as if he understood exactly how I felt and wasn't going to call me stupid or demented or a big yellow coward. When I didn't have another word left in me, I just shut up and stared down at the ground.

"Stab nail at ill Italian bats!" Nonno Frankie finally said.

"What?"

He repeated the weird sentence and asked me what was special about it. I guessed, "It reads the same backward as forward?"

"Right! Ho! Ho! Ho! See, you learn! You remember things I teach you. So today I will teach you how to fight, and you will smack this John Quinn around like floured pizza dough."

"But I can't fight."

"I'll show you Sicilian combat tactics."

"Like what?"

"Everything about Italian fighting. It has to do with your mind and body. Things you have to know so you don't have to be afraid of bullies. Street smarts my father taught me. Like 'Never miss a good chance to shut up!'"

VAROOOOOOOOOOM!

A plane took off over our heads. We walked out beyond the yard to the great field overlooking the airport.

Nonno Frankie suddenly let out a yell. "Aaeeeeeyaaaayeeeeeh!" It was so blood-curdlingly weird, I decided to wait until he felt like explaining it.

"Aaeeeeeyaaaayeeeeeh!" he bellowed again. "It's good to be able to yell like Tarzan!" he said. "This confuses your enemy, and you can also yell it if you have to retreat. You run away roaring and everyone thinks you at least have guts! It confuses everybody!"

"Is that all I need to know?" I asked, now more afraid than ever of facing John Quinn in front of all the kids.

"No. Tonight I will cut your hair."

"Cut it?"

"Yes. It's too long!"

"It is?"

"Ah," Nonno Frankie said, "you'd be surprised how many kids lose fights because of their hair. Alexander the Great always ordered his entire army to shave their heads. Long hair makes it easy for an enemy to grab it and cut off your head."

◀ Vocabulary
demented (dē ment´ əd) *adj.*
insane; mad

"Aaeeeeeyaaaayeeeeeh!" he bellowed again. "It's good to be able to yell like Tarzan!"

Comprehension
What advice does Paul get from Nonno Frankie?

Main Idea
What details support the main idea that Nonno Frankie is an unusual character?

Mood
How does the author create a humorous mood?

Vocabulary ▶
observant (əb zurv´ ənt) *adj.* quick to notice; alert

"John Quinn just wants to beat me up!"

"You can never be too sure. This boy might have the spirit of Genghis Khan!"

"Who was Genghis Khan?"

"Who? He once killed two million enemies in one hour. Some of them he killed with yo-yos."

"Yo-yos?"

"See, these are the things you need to know. The yo-yo was first invented as a weapon. Of course, they were as heavy as steel pipes and had long rope cords, but they were still yo-yos!"

"I didn't know that," I admitted.

"That's why I'm telling you. You should always ask about the rules when you go to a new place."

"I didn't think there'd be a time limit on handball paddles."

"That's why you must ask."

"I can't ask everything," I complained.

"Then you *read*. You need to know all the rules wherever you go. Did you know it's illegal to hunt camels in Arizona?"

"No."

"See? These are little facts you pick up from books and teachers and parents as you grow older. Some facts and rules come in handy, some don't. You've got to be observant. Did you know that Mickey Mouse has only *four* fingers on each hand?"

"No."

"All you have to do is look. And rules change! You've got to remember that. In ancient Rome, my ancestors worshipped a god who ruled over mildew. Nobody does anymore, but it's an interesting thing to know. You have to be connected to the past and present and future. At NBC, when they put in a new cookie-cutting machine, I had to have an open mind. I had to prepare and draw upon everything I knew so that I didn't get hurt."

Nonno Frankie must have seen my mouth was open so wide a baseball could have flown into my throat and choked me to death. He stopped at the highest point in the rise of land above the airport. "I can see you want some meat and potatoes. You want to know exactly how to beat this vicious John Quinn."

"He's not vicious."

"Make believe he is. It'll give you more energy for the fight. When he comes at you, don't underestimate the power of negative thinking! You must have only positive thoughts in your heart that you're going to cripple this monster. Stick a piece of garlic in your pocket for good luck. A woman my mother knew in Palermo did this, and she was able to fight off a dozen three-foot-tall muscular Greeks who landed and tried to eat her. You think this is not true, but half her town saw it. The Greeks all had rough skin and wore backpacks and one-piece clothes. You have to go with what you feel in your heart. One of my teachers in Sicily believed the Portuguese man-of-war jellyfish originally came from England. He felt that in his heart, and he eventually proved it. He later went on to be awarded a government grant to study tourist swooning sickness in Florence."

"But how do I hold my hands to fight? How do I hold my fists?" I wanted to know.

"Like *this*!" Nonno Frankie demonstrated, taking a boxing stance with his left foot and fist forward.

"And then I just swing my right fist forward as hard as I can?"

"No. First you curse him."

"*Curse* him?"

"Yes, you curse this John Quinn. You tell him, 'May your left ear wither and fall into your right pocket!' And you tell him he looks like a fugitive from a brain gang! And tell him he has a face like a mattress! And that an espresso coffee cup would fit on his head like a sombrero. And then you just give him the big Sicilian surprise!"

"What?"

"You *kick* him in the shins!" •

By the time Monday morning came, I was a nervous wreck. Nonno Frankie had gone back to New York the night before, but had left me a special bowl of pasta and steamed octopus that he said I should eat for breakfast so I'd have "gusto" for combat. I had asked him not to discuss my upcoming bout with my mother or sister, and Betty didn't say anything so I assumed she hadn't heard about it.

Jennifer had offered to get one of her older brothers to protect me, and, if I wanted, she was willing to tell Miss

Main Idea
What is the main idea of this paragraph?

Spiral Review
FIGURATIVE LANGUAGE Identify the similes in this paragraph. How do they contribute to the intended effect?

Comprehension
Why does Nonno Frankie insist that Paul always know the rules?

Mood
How does the author create a different mood in this passage?

Vocabulary ▶
undulating (un´ jə lā tiŋ) *adj.* moving in waves, like a snake

distorted (di stôrt´ əd) *adj.* twisted out of normal shape

Haines so she could stop anything from happening. I told her, "No." I thought there was a chance John Quinn would have even forgotten the whole incident and wouldn't make good on his revenge threat. Nevertheless, my mind was numb with fear all day at school. In every class I went to, it seemed there were a dozen different kids coming over to me and telling me they heard John Quinn was going to beat me up after school.

At 3 p.m. sharp, the bell rang.

All the kids started to leave school.

I dawdled.

I cleaned my desk and took time packing up my books. Jennifer was at my side as we left the main exit of the building. There, across the street in a field behind Ronkewitz's Candy Store, was a crowd of about 300 kids standing around like a big, **undulating** horseshoe, with John Quinn standing at the center bend glaring at me.

"You could run," Jennifer suggested, tossing her hair all to the left side of her face. She looked much more than pretty now. She looked loyal to the bone.

"No," I said. I just walked forward toward my fate, with the blood in my temples pounding so hard I thought I was going to pass out. Moose and Leon and Mike and Conehead and Little Frankfurter were sprinkled out in front of me, goading me forward. I didn't even hear what they said. I saw only their faces **distorted** in ecstasy and expectation. They looked like the mob I had seen in a sixteenth-century etching where folks in London had bought tickets to watch bulldogs attacking water buffalo.

John stood with his black eye, and his fists up.

I stopped a few feet from him and put my fists up. A lot of kids in the crowd started to shout, "Kill him, Johnny!" but I may have imagined that part.

John came closer. He started to dance on his feet like all father-trained fighters do. I danced, too, as best I could. The crowd began to scream for blood. Jennifer kept shouting, "Hey, there's no need to fight! You don't have to fight, guys!"

But John came in for the kill. He was close enough now so any punch he threw could hit me. All I thought of was Nonno Frankie, but I couldn't remember half of what he told me and I didn't think any of it would work anyway.

"*Aaeeeeeyaaaaayeeeeeh!*" I suddenly screamed at John. He stopped in his tracks and the crowd froze in amazed silence. Instantly, I brought back my right foot, and shot it forward to kick John in his left shin. The crowd was shocked, and booed me with mass condemnation for my Sicilian fighting technique. I missed John's shin, and kicked vainly again. He threw a punch at me. It barely touched me, but I was so busy kicking, I tripped myself and fell down. The crowd cheered. I realized everyone including John thought his punch had floored me. I decided to go along with it. I groveled in the dirt for a few moments, and then stood up slowly holding my head as though I'd received a death blow. John put his fists down. He was satisfied justice had been done and his black eye had been avenged. He turned to leave, but Moose wasn't happy.

"Hey, ya didn't punch him enough," Moose complained to John.

"It's over," John said, like the decent kid he was.

"No, it's not," Moose yelled, and the crowd began to call for more blood. Now it was Moose coming toward me, and I figured I was dead meat. He came closer and closer. Jennifer shouted for him to stop and threatened to pull his eyeballs out, but he kept coming. And that was when something amazing happened. I was aware of a figure taller than me, running, charging. The figure had long blond hair, and it struck Moose from behind. I could see it was a girl and she had her hands right around Moose's neck,

▲ **Critical Viewing**
How are these boys similar to John and Paul?

◀ **Vocabulary**
condemnation
(kän´ dem nā´ shən)
n. expression of strong disapproval

Comprehension
How has Paul been feeling about this fight?

Mood

A fight scene would normally be scary. What details make the mood of this scene humorous?

Main Idea

What is the main idea of this final paragraph?

choking him. When she let him go, she threw him about ten feet, accidentally tearing off a religious medal from around his neck. Everyone stopped dead in their tracks, and I could see my savior was my sister.

"If any of you tries to hurt my brother again, I'll rip your guts out," she announced.

Moose was not happy. Conehead and Little Frankfurter were not happy. But the crowd broke up fast and everyone headed home. I guess that was the first day everybody learned that if nothing else, the Zindel kids stick together. As for Nonno Frankie's Sicilian fighting technique, I came to realize he was ahead of his time. In fact, these days it's called karate.

Language Study

Vocabulary The following words appear in *The Pigman & Me*. Write sentences that correctly use each word pair below.

   exact   demented   observant   undulating   condemnation

1. exact (as a verb); payment

2. undulating; necklace

3. demented; idea

4. observant; spy

5. condemnation; thieves

Word Study

WORD STUDY

The **Latin root -tort-** means "twist out of shape." In this story, the author describes his classmates' faces as **distorted**, or twisted out of normal shape.

Part A Explain how the **Latin root -tort-** contributes to the meanings of *retort*, *contort* and *torturous*. Consult a dictionary if necessary.

Part B Use the context of each sentence and what you know about the root -tort- to explain your answers to the following questions.

1. What can a *contortionist* do?

2. Can you watch television if the screen has a *distortion*?

Close Reading Activities

Literary Analysis

Key Ideas and Details

1. **Main Idea (a)** What is the main idea of this selection?
(b) What are two important details in the selection that support this main idea?

2. **Main Idea** What is one unimportant detail that does not support the main idea? Explain your choice.

Craft and Structure

3. **Mood (a)** What is one **mood**, or overall feeling, that the author creates in this selection? **(b)** What details create that mood?

4. **Mood (a)** Complete a chart like the one on the right to analyze a passage that has a different mood. **(b)** What effect does the change in mood have on readers?

Integration of Knowledge and Ideas

5. **(a)** Identify two pieces of advice that Nonno Frankie gives Paul.
(b) Analyze: Does Frankie's advice apply to more than the fight itself? Explain.

6. **(a)** What does Paul do after he falls down during the fight?
(b) Infer: Why does he do this? **(c) Criticize:** Is his strategy a good one? Explain your answer and support it with details from the selection.

7. **(a) Compare and Contrast:** Explain the difference between John's attitude and the attitude of the other students after Paul falls down. **(b) Analyze:** What problems does the attitude of the other students create for John and Paul?

8. **What is important to know? (a)** How does a lack of knowledge cause trouble for Paul? **(b) Draw Conclusions:** Was Nonno Frankie's advice helpful to Paul in his fight with John Quinn? Use specific details to support your answer. **(c) Speculate:** Will any of Nonno Frankie's advice be helpful to Paul in the future? Explain.

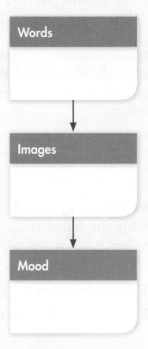

Words

Images

Mood

ACADEMIC VOCABULARY

As you write and speak about the excerpt from *The Pigman & Me*, use the words related to gaining knowledge that you explored on page 163 of this text.

Conventions: **Perfect Tenses of Verbs**

The **perfect tense** of a verb combines a form of *have* with the past participle of the verb.

from
The Pigman & Me
Paul Zindel

- The **present perfect** tense shows an action that began in the past and continues in the present.
- The **past perfect** tense shows a past action or condition that ended before another past action began.
- The **future perfect** tense shows a future action or condition that will have ended before another begins.

Present Perfect	Past Perfect	Future Perfect
have, has + past participle	*had* + past participle	*will have* + past participle
They *have voted* in this city for seventeen years.	They *had voted* by the time we arrived.	The council *will have voted* by summer.

Practice A

Identify the tense in each sentence. Indicate whether it is present perfect, past perfect, or future perfect.

1. Paul had never fought properly before.
2. Nanno Frankie will have returned home by then.
3. Paul has never been so afraid.
4. The other kids have treated Paul badly.

Reading Application Find three sentences in the past perfect tense in the selection. Rewrite each sentence in either the present perfect or the future perfect tense. You may have to change other verbs in the sentence or add words to the sentence.

Practice B

Rewrite each sentence using the tense indicated in parentheses.

1. Paul had listened carefully to Nonno Frankie. (present perfect)
2. Paul has recovered from his fear. (future perfect)
3. Before long, Paul and John will have become friends. (past perfect)
4. A huge crowd of students had appeared. (present perfect)
5. Paul will have learned an important lesson. (past perfect)

Writing Application Write three sentences describing a future day in Paul's life. In each sentence, use one of the perfect tenses.

Writing to Sources

Explanatory Text Write a **problem-and-solution essay** based on the excerpt from *The Pigman & Me*. Your essay should help a newcomer adjust to a new school.

- State a problem that newcomers might face. Review *The Pigman & Me* for possible ideas.
- Provide a step-by-step solution to the problem. Clearly explain the rules a newcomer should know.
- Explain why your solution will help solve the problem.
- Support each step of your suggested solution with concrete details, examples, and anecdotes, including ones from *The Pigman & Me*.

Grammar Application Check your writing to be sure that you have used perfect tenses correctly.

Speaking and Listening

Comprehension and Collaboration In a small group, hold an **informal discussion** based on the excerpt from *The Pigman & Me*. Discuss how students should act in order to make friends at a new school. Identify the social rules that students should know and follow. Include details from the selection and from your prior knowledge to make suggestions. You may also include things that student should *not* do.

Follow these steps to complete the assignment:

- Allow each person in the group an opportunity to offer opinions about the topic.
- Support opinions with facts and examples.
- Use good listening skills when others are talking.
- Jot down notes to remember important ideas and details. Your notes do not have to be a complete record of the discussion.
- At the end of the discussion, reflect on the group's responses and paraphrase the group's ideas.
- Share your paraphrase with the rest of the class.

ANALYZING EXPOSITORY TEXTS

Reading Skill: Use Text Aids and Features

Many writers of expository texts use **text aids and features** to organize details and highlight important information, including central ideas. Identifying text features as you read can help you locate specific information and understand key ideas. Text aids and features can also help you see the relationships among ideas in a text. As you read expository texts, identify the items listed in the chart below, and use them to guide your reading.

Text Aids	
Title	Identifies the subject of a chapter or complete work
Main heading	Identifies the general topic of a section
Subheading	Identifies a specific topic within the section's main topic
Highlighted vocabulary	Introduces and defines key terms
Text Features	
Maps, graphs, and charts	Provide visual and statistical information that supports the topic
Photographs, drawings, and diagrams with captions	Illustrate information in the text and provide additional details

Content-Area Vocabulary

These words appear in the selections that follow. You may also encounter them in other content-area texts.

- **archaeologists** (är′kē äl′ə jists) *n.* people who study human history by analyzing ancient objects and remains
- **architect** (är′ kə tekt) *n.* person who designs buildings
- **colossal** (kə läs′əl) *adj.* extremely large

The Seven Wonders of the World

from *Infoplease*®

Since ancient times, numerous "seven wonders" lists have been created. The content of these lists tends to vary and none is definitive. The seven wonders that are most widely agreed upon as being in the original list are the Seven Wonders of the Ancient World, which was compiled by ancient Greek historians and is thus confined to the most magnificent structures known to the ancient Greek world. Of all the Ancient Wonders, the pyramids alone survive.

The Pyramids of Egypt are three pyramids at Giza, outside modern Cairo. The largest pyramid, built by Khufu (Cheops), a king of the fourth dynasty, had an original estimated height of 482 feet (now approximately 450 feet). The base has sides 755 feet long. It contains 2,300,000 blocks; the average weight of each is 2.5 tons. The estimated date of completion is 2680 B.C.

The Hanging Gardens of Babylon were supposedly built by Nebuchadnezzar around 600 B.C. to please his queen, Amuhia. They are also associated with the mythical Assyrian queen Semiramis. Archaeologists surmise that the gardens were laid out atop a vaulted building, with provisions for raising water. The terraces were said to rise from 75 to 300 feet.

The Statue of Zeus (Jupiter) at Olympia was made of gold and ivory by the Greek sculptor Phidias (5th century B.C.). Reputed to be 40 feet high, the statue has been lost without a trace, except for reproductions on coins.

The Temple of Artemis (Diana) at Ephesus was begun about 350 B.C., in honor of a non-Hellenic goddess who later became identified with the Greek goddess of the same name. The temple, with Ionic columns 60 feet high, was destroyed by invading Goths in A.D. 262.

The Mausoleum at Halicarnassus was erected by Queen Artemisia in memory of her husband, King Mausolus of Caria in Asia Minor, who died in 353 B.C. Some remains of the structure are in the British Museum. This shrine is the source of the modern word mausoleum.

The Colossus at Rhodes was a bronze statue of Helios (Apollo), about 105 feet high. The work of the sculptor Chares, who reputedly labored for 12 years before completing it in 280 B.C., it was destroyed during an earthquake in 224 B.C.

The Pharos (Lighthouse) of Alexandria was built by Sostratus of Cnidus during the 3rd century B.C. on the island of Pharos off the coast of Egypt. It was destroyed by an earthquake in the 13th century.

(Some lists include the Walls of Babylon in place of the second or seventh wonder.)

See also <u>The Seven Wonders of the Modern World</u>.

Section 5

Art, Architecture, and Learning in Egypt

from *Prentice Hall Ancient Civilizations*

Homes for the Dead

One of the most important types of Egyptian buildings were temples. Most were built of mud or from stone that was quarried, or mined, far away, and then transported over long distances. The Egyptians created temples for their gods and tombs for their pharaohs.

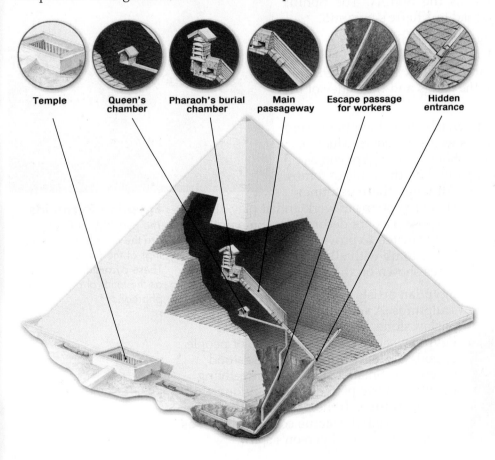

Temple

Queen's chamber

Pharaoh's burial chamber

Main passageway

Escape passage for workers

Hidden entrance

Tombs for the Pharaohs

Tombs of early rulers were underground chambers, or rooms. The burial chamber contained items that the ruler might want in the afterlife.

An **architect** named **Imhotep** designed a new kind of tomb for his pharaoh, with six stone mounds, one on top of the other. The result is known as the Step Pyramid. Later architects made the sides smoother to create a true pyramid.

Three enormous pyramids were built at Giza by **King Khufu**, his son Khafre, and his grandson Menkaure. The tallest of these is the Great Pyramid of Khufu. For more than 4,000 years, this pyramid was the world's tallest building. Nearby stands the famous statue known as the Sphinx. The Sphinx guarded the road to Khafre's pyramid.

The great age of pyramid building ended about 2200 B.C. Pharaohs who ruled after that time carved tombs from the cliffs in the Valley of the Kings and the Valley of the Queens.

Painting and Sculpture Egyptians were skilled artists as well as builders. Much of what we know about life in Egypt comes from paintings found on the walls of tombs. Although these paintings show Egyptians at work and at play, their purpose was not decoration. The paintings were created to provide the person buried in the tomb with all of the objects and pleasures shown on the walls.

Egyptian artists also created wonderful sculptures. A **sculpture** is a statue made of clay, stone, or other materials. Most Egyptian sculptures were statues of people or gods. **Colossal** statues of gods stood in temples. Smaller statues of once-living Egyptians were placed in tombs along with their **mummies**. If the person's mummy was destroyed, the statue could replace it as a home for the dead person's spirit.

Egyptian Pyramids
The pyramids of Egypt are the most famous buildings of the ancient world. These pyramids were built as the tomb of a powerful pharaoh.

Comparing Expository Texts

1. **Craft and Structure** **(a)** Identify a text aid or structural feature that you would find in both an online almanac and a textbook. **(b)** Identify a text aid or structural feature that you would find in an online almanac, but not in a textbook. **(c)** In which text—the almanac or the textbook—is it easier to find specific information? Explain.

Content-Area Vocabulary

2. Use *archaeologists, architect,* and *colossal* in a brief paragraph that shows you understand the meaning of each word.

 **Timed Writing**

Argument: Position Statement

Throughout history, there have been different lists of the Seven Wonders of the World. Take a position on whether or not the Egyptian pyramids should be classified as one of the Seven Wonders of the World. Support your position by integrating details from the texts you have read. **(25 minutes)**

5-Minute Planner

Complete these steps before you begin to write:

1. Read the prompt carefully and completely. Note that the prompt asks you to take a position based on what you have read.

2. Review the two texts. Use text aids and features to locate information about your topic. **TIP:** Relying on text aids and text features alone may lead you to incorrect conclusions. Be sure to review the text completely.

3. Compare the information that is presented in the two texts to connect and clarify main ideas.

4. Write a statement of your opinion, and make notes about the facts you will use to support your position.

5. Use your notes to prepare a quick outline. Then, use your outline to help you organize your response.

Language Study

Word Origins

The English language continues to grow and change. New words enter the language from many sources. The **etymology** of a word describes its **origin** and development. A word's etymology identifies the language in which the word first appeared. It also tells how the word's spelling and meaning have changed over time.

Many English words come from ancient Latin or Greek words or word roots. Some modern words are **allusions,** references to well-known characters, places, or events in history, art, or literature. This chart shows some examples.

Word	Origin	Definition	Example Sentence
prove	Latin word *probare,* which means "test"	to show that something is true	This experiment will prove that light travels faster than sound.
biography	Greek words *bios* ("life") and *graphein* ("to write")	the story of a person's life	The biography of George Washington includes many facts about the American Revolution.
herculean	allusion to Hercules, a hero in ancient Greek myths, known for his great strength	requiring great strength	Moving the heavy box was a herculean task.

Practice A

Find each of the following words in a dictionary. Define each word and explain its origin.

1. solo
2. martial
3. skill
4. marathon
5. edict
6. mentor

Practice B

Each question contains a word that has come into the English language from the Greek or Latin language or from mythology. Use a dictionary to find each italicized word's origin and meaning. Then, use that information to answer each question.

1. What special ability does an *ambidextrous* person have?

2. How did *cereal* get its name?

3. Where will you go if you *circumnavigate* our planet?

4. What does a *dermatologist* treat?

5. Why is the word "goat" a *tetragram*?

6. Why is the word *colossal* used to describe something that is very big?

7. Why is a kangaroo considered a *marsupial*?

8. How would you describe the personality of someone who is *jovial*?

Comprehension and Collaboration

With a partner, research the following characters from Greek mythology. Then, use a dictionary to find an English word that is based on each character's name. Finally, write a few sentences that explain how the word's meaning relates to the character.

- **Helios**
- **Pan**
- **Arachne**

Activity Identify the source of each of the following English words. Then, use a graphic organizer like the one shown to explain how the English word and the source word are related. The first item has been completed as an example.

1. stampede   2. mercurial   3. kindergarten   4. phobia

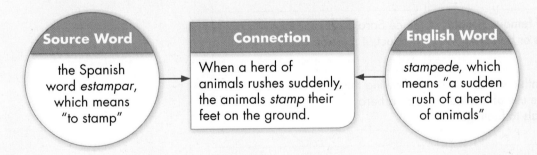

Source Word	Connection	English Word
the Spanish word *estampar*, which means "to stamp"	When a herd of animals rushes suddenly, the animals *stamp* their feet on the ground.	*stampede*, which means "a sudden rush of a herd of animals"

Evaluating Media Messages and Advertisements

A persuasive message encourages the audience to think or act in a certain way. This is especially true of media messages such as advertisements.

Learn the Skills

Identify the source of the message. When you encounter media messages and advertisements, think about who is delivering the "information" and why. Facts supplied by the person or group may be slanted to favor a point of view.

Evaluate the content of the message. A fact is something that can be proved or demonstrated. An *opinion* can be supported but not proved. Notice whether or not the claims in a media message are supported by facts and evidence.

Recognize propaganda. When the information is completely one-sided, it is called *propaganda*. Propaganda is the spreading of misleading ideas. The chart below shows three types of propaganda. These are media techniques that are used in place of factual information.

Technique	Example
Bandwagon appeals rely on the idea that people make choices to be part of a crowd.	Every sixth-grader thinks this, and you should too.
Testimonials portray famous people giving their opinions or behaving in a certain way.	Since Sara Superstar uses this product, it must be good.
Emotional appeals influence an audience through the use of loaded language that appeals to feelings rather than logic.	Following this plan will make you a hero.

Evaluate the delivery of the message. Persuasive messages can be delivered through a variety of media—writing, radio, television, film, or billboards. Ask yourself if the words, sounds, and pictures in a message or ad are meant to make you feel a certain way or *think* a certain way.

Practice the Skills

Presentation of Knowledge and Ideas Use what you have
learned in this workshop to perform the following task.

ACTIVITY: **Evaluate a Persuasive Message**

Evaluate a television commercial by following these steps:
- Identify and explain the commercial's message.
- Analyze the propaganda used in the message.
- Decide whether or not the claims in the commercial are supported
  by evidence.
- Explain how propaganda in the commercial influences your
  emotions.

Use the Evaluation Checklist to help you evaluate the commercial.

Evaluation Checklist

Message

What is the source and content of the message?

Explain the message and its purpose.

Propaganda and Persuasive Techniques

What persuasive techniques are used to influence the viewer? Briefly explain each one used.

❑ Bandwagon appeal ❑ Testimonial ❑ Emotional appeal

Influence on Emotion

How does each technique make you feel? Briefly explain your reasons.

The message made me want to

❑ buy the product. ❑ not buy the product. ❑ Other (explain).

Conclusion

What claims in the commercial are supported by evidence?

What claims are supported by propaganda?

Is the commercial effective? Why or why not?

Technique(s) Used:

Effect of the Message:

Comprehension and Collaboration For three days, view several
types of advertisements. Take notes on the propaganda used
in each one. Also note whether or not the claims in the ads are
supported by facts. Compare your findings with those of a partner.

Writing Process

Write an Informative Text

Comparison-and-Contrast Essay

Defining the Form In a **comparison-and-contrast essay,** an author uses factual details to analyze similarities and differences between two or more subjects. You may use elements of a comparison-and-contrast essay in literary reviews, movie reviews, and comparisons.

Assignment Write a comparison-and-contrast essay in which you examine the similarities and differences between two subjects. Include these elements:

✓ *two subjects that are similar and different*

✓ a *thesis,* or purpose, stated in a *strong opening paragraph*

✓ an *organizational pattern* that clearly shows similarities and differences

✓ facts, descriptions, and examples that *support your assertions* of how the subjects are alike and how they are different

✓ a *well-supported conclusion* that wraps up your essay

✓ error-free writing, including correct usage of *verbs*

To preview the criteria on which your comparison-and-contrast essay may be judged, see the rubric on page 247.

FOCUS ON RESEARCH

When you write a comparison-and-contrast essay, you might have to conduct research in order to:

• find statistics or other data on the two subjects you are comparing.

• obtain background information on the two subjects.

• locate statements that experts have made about the two subjects.

Be sure to note all the sources you use and to cite them in your essay. Refer to the Research Workshop in the Introductory Unit for information on how to cite sources properly.

READING-WRITING CONNECTION
To get a feel for comparison-and-contrast essays, read "Race to the End of the Earth" by William G. Scheller on page 404.

Prewriting/Planning Strategies

Choose subjects that are similar and different in important ways. Use one of these strategies to find a topic:

Use a quicklist to choose your topic. Make a three-column chart. In the first column, jot down people, places, and things that are interesting to you. In the second column, list an adjective to describe each one. Then, in the third column, provide a detail about each. Review your list, looking for ideas that it suggests, such as two brands of frozen pizza or two sports you enjoy. Choose one of those ideas as your topic.

Narrow your topic. You could probably write an entire book comparing and contrasting Mexico and Spain. To make your broad topic more manageable, divide it into smaller subtopics. Then, choose one subtopic, such as Mexican and Spanish food, as the focus of your essay.

Gather details. Conduct research to find relevant details about the subjects you are comparing and contrasting. Be sure to note the source of each detail you plan to use in your essay.

Organize your details. You can see similarities and differences clearly by organizing your details into a Venn diagram like the one shown. In the two outer sections, record details about how each subject is different. In the overlapping area, record similarities. Refer to your diagram as you draft your essay.

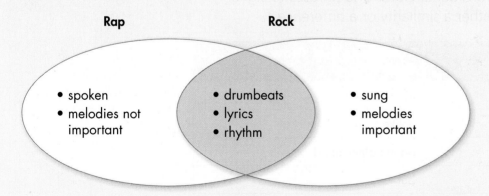

Drafting Strategies

Develop a thesis statement. Your thesis should explain your overall point about the two subjects. It should identify the significance of your comparisons and contrasts. For example, a thesis statement for a comparison-and-contrast essay on baseball and basketball might be: *Teamwork is more essential in basketball than in baseball.*

Draft your introduction. Begin your essay with a strong introductory paragraph that does the following:

- introduces the subjects you are comparing and contrasting
- identifies the features or aspects you will discuss
- states a main idea about your subjects

Use specific details. Develop your topic by citing details. The more you can pinpoint specific similarities and differences, the more interesting and vibrant your essay will be. Compare the following examples:

> **General:** holiday meal
>
> **Concrete:** holiday breakfast of omelets, berries, and cinnamon rolls

Consider your audience. Think about how much your readers are likely to know about the subjects you are comparing and contrasting. Use precise words and provide clear explanations for any technical terms or unfamiliar ideas or events.

Use transitions. Use transitional words and phrases to signal that you are discussing either a similarity or a difference.

Transitions that show similarity	Transitions that show difference
similarly	in contrast
also	unlike
both	on the other hand
like	but
in the same way	however
as well as	instead
too	yet

Organizing a Comparison-and-Contrast Essay

The organization of a comparison-and-contrast essay is extremely important. To clearly show the relationships between the items you are comparing, choose one of these organizational patterns:

- **Block Method:** Present all the details about one subject first. Then, present all the details about the other subject. This method works well when you are writing about more than two things or are covering many different types of details. In following this organization, it is a good idea to refer back to the first subject when you discuss the second. Doing so will help your essay hold together. This technique can also be used to support your thesis.

  ### Example: Relating Back to First Subject
  Velociraptors were carnivores. In this respect, they are similar to tyrannosaurus.

- **Point-by-Point Method:** Discuss each aspect of your subjects in turn. For example, if you are comparing two types of dinosaurs, you could first discuss the diet of each one, then the size and mobility, and so on.

When using the point-by-point organization, think about your thesis when you arrange the details. Suppose you want to emphasize the differences between the two subjects. In that case, discuss the similarities first and then focus on the differences, as this example shows.

Block Method
1. Introduction
2. Tyrannosaurus: diet, size, and mobility
3. Velociraptor: diet, size, and mobility
4. Conclusion

Point-by-Point Method
1. Introduction
2. Diet of tyrannosaurus vs. velociraptor
3. Size and mobility of tyrannosaurus vs. velociraptor
4. Conclusion

Example: From Similarities to Differences
1. Both velociraptor and tyrannosaurus were meat-eaters.
2. Both were able hunters.
3. Tyrannosaurus was much larger then velociraptor.
4. Velociraptor was faster than tyrannosaurus.
5. Differences in size and mobility made them hunt differently.

Revising Strategies

Check organization and balance. Your essay should give equal space to each subject and should be organized consistently. To check the balance of your essay, take a moment to reread it.

- Use a red marker to underline or highlight all the features and details related to one subject. Use a yellow marker for the other subject.
- If one color dominates, add additional features and details related to the other subject.
- If one color appears in large chunks, followed by other places where the colors seem to alternate, revise your organizational plan. For example, you may have made the mistake of starting with block organization and then switching to point-by-point organization.

Use a chart like the one below to help you figure out what features or details are missing from your essay.

	Subject #1	Subject #2
Point 1		
Point 2		
Point 3		
Point 4		

Check subject-verb agreement. Check your draft for correct subject-verb agreement. Make sure that sentences with singular subjects have singular verbs and that sentences with plural subjects have plural verbs.

Example: Unlike football, hockey **is** played on ice. (singular subject, singular verb)
Both football and hockey **are** fast-paced games. (plural subject, plural verb)

Peer Review

Have a classmate read your draft. Ask your reader to give you feedback about the organization and balance, and to show you places where more information would improve your essay.

Correcting Errors With Verbs

Irregular verbs are those in which the past tense and past participle are not formed by adding *-ed* or *-d* to the present tense. **Troublesome verbs** are verb pairs that are easily confused.

Identifying Incorrect Forms of Irregular Verbs Memorize these verb forms that occur frequently in reading and writing.

Examples of Irregular Verbs			
Present	**Present Participle**	**Past**	**Past Participle**
drink	(am) drinking	drank	(have) drunk
do	(am) doing	did	(have) done
bring	(am) bringing	brought	(have) brought

Identifying Incorrect Forms of Troublesome Verbs The two verbs in each of these pairs are often confused:

Lay/Lie *Lay* means "to put or place something." It takes a direct object. Example: *Shelly will lay the guitar on the table*.

Lie means "to rest in a reclining position" or "to be situated." Example: *I like to lie in the hammock*.

Raise/Rise *Raise* means "to lift up" or "to cause to rise." It takes a direct object. Example: *Please raise the curtain*.

Rise means "to get up" or "to go up." It does not take a direct object. Example: *My neighbors rise early in the morning*.

Fixing Errors To fix incorrect irregular verbs, identify which principal part of the verb is needed.

- **Refer to a chart of principal parts of verbs.**
- **Use a dictionary to find the correct form of the verb.**

To fix an incorrectly used troublesome verb:

- **Look up the verb in a glossary or resource of troublesome words.**
- **Use a dictionary to determine which verb to use.**

Grammar in Your Writing
Circle the verbs used in your comparison-and-contrast essay. If any verbs are used incorrectly, fix them using the methods above.

Letters ... Or Numbers?

Have you ever heard the saying, "You can't compare apples and oranges"? Well, I've done it, so I know it's possible. But I'm not here to compare apples and oranges. I'm here to compare something else: numbers and letters. Numbers and letters have so many unusual properties about them. They are probably two of the most difficult things to compare, but I'll tackle them anyway.

We'll start off with their differences. Numbers and letters have a lot of differences, obviously, but I'm only going to name a few. For one thing, letters are used to spell words, and numbers are used to, well, write numbers! Also, numbers go on forever, while letters stop at z, the twenty-sixth letter. No matter how many letters you have in your alphabet, whether it's Hebrew, Spanish, Greek, or anything else, it will always end somewhere. But numbers just keep right on going.

Also, letters can represent numbers, but not the other way around, unless you're a computer programmer. For example, you could have a list of instructions, and the steps could be labeled A, B, C, instead of 1, 2, 3. But you can't say that 586 spells *car*.

Numbers and letters have about as many similarities as they do differences, and they are just as simple. For one thing, words and numbers are both used in everyday speech. For example, you could say, "Mr. Johnson, may I walk your dog?" "But I have two dogs." Just the words themselves that you speak are made up of letters and numbers.

In addition, letters and numbers must be precise. This is tough to explain. Letters cannot just be arranged into any order. They have to spell out a real word. For example, you can't just grab a bunch of letters and stick them together because they look pretty. If you had a word like *sdlkhjiower*, what would it mean? Where would you use it? How would you pronounce it? None of these questions has a real answer because *sdlkhjiower* is not a real word. It's the same with numbers. You need to make sure your answer is precise. Also, you can't just say, "Well, I like 14, so I'm going to make 93 and 27 equal 14." That's not how it works. As with letters, you can't put numbers together just because they look good.

As you see, numbers and letters have many differences, but also many similarities. If you take the time, I'm sure you can find even more on your own.

Jessica's introduction grabs the reader's attention and identifies her topics for comparison.

Jessica uses a point-by-point organization, first addressing differences and then addressing similarities.

Jessica uses examples to explain each point she presents.

In her conclusion, Jessica sums up her ideas and invites readers to consider the topic further.

Editing and Proofreading

Revise to correct errors in grammar, spelling, and punctuation.

Focus on double comparisons. Comparison-and-contrast essays often contain comparative adjectives. Avoid using double comparisons. Never use *-er* or *-est* and *more* or *most* to form the comparative and superlative degrees in the same sentence.

> **Incorrect:** The Great Dane was the *most biggest* dog in the show.
>
> **Correct:** The Great Dane was the *biggest* dog in the show.

Spiral Review
Earlier in this unit, you learned about **principal parts of verbs** (p. 192) and **verb tenses** (p. 214). Check your essay to be sure you have used verbs correctly.

Publishing and Presenting

Consider one of the following ways to share your writing:

Create an illustrated essay. Find photographs to illustrate the similarities and differences you have discussed. Then, share your illustrated essay with classmates.

Make a recording. Practice reading your essay aloud a few times. Read slowly and clearly, emphasizing the strongest points. Then, record and share your essay with a group of classmates.

Reflecting on Your Writing

Writer's Journal Jot down your answer to this question:

How has your writing changed your view on your topic?

Rubric for Self-Assessment

Find evidence in your writing to address each category. Then, use the rating scale to grade your work.

Criteria	Rating Scale			
Purpose/Focus Examines and conveys complex ideas about the similarities and differences between two subjects	*not very* .... *very* 1	2	3	4
Organization Organizes information effectively using the block or point-by-point method	1	2	3	4
Development of Ideas/Elaboration Develops the topic and supports the thesis with relevant facts, definitions, concrete details, quotations, and other examples; establishes and maintains a formal style	1	2	3	4
Language Uses transition words to signal similarities or differences; effectively combines sentences with related ideas	1	2	3	4
Conventions Uses proper grammar, including correct use of verbs	1	2	3	4

SELECTED RESPONSE

I. Reading Literature/Informational Text

Directions: *Read the excerpt from* Something to Declare *by Julia Alvarez. Then, answer each question that follows.*

The first time I received a letter from one of my readers, I was surprised. I had just published my first book of poems, *Homecoming,* which concludes with a sonnet sequence titled "33." My reader wanted to know why I had included forty-one sonnets when the title of the sequence was "33."

I considered not answering. Often, it is the little <u>perplexities</u> and curiosities and quandaries that remain after I have finished reading a book that send me to buy another book by that author. If I want to know more, the best way to find out is to read all the books that the author has written….

Many of the essays in this book began in just that way—as answers to such queries. Jessica Peet, a high-school student, read my first novel, *How the García Girls Lost Their Accents,* in her Vermont Authors class and wanted to know if I considered myself a Vermonter. The Lane Series, our local arts and entertainment series, wanted to know what I might have to say about opera. Share Our Strength was putting together a fund-raising anthology. Did I have anything at all to declare about food?

I could not really say to any of them, "Read my novels or my poems or my stories." These folks wanted what my boarding-school housemother used to call a straight answer. Which is where essays start. Not that they obey housemothers. Not that they list everything you are supposed to list on that Customs Declaration form. (How could the wild, multitudinous, daily things in anyone's head be inventoried in a form?) But that is the pretext of essays: *we have something to declare.*

And so this essay book is dedicated to you, my readers, who have asked me so many good questions and who want to know more than I have told you in my novels and poems. About my experience of immigration, about switching languages, about the writing life, the teaching life, the family life, about all of those combined.

Your many questions boil down finally to this one question: Do you have anything more to declare?

Yes, I do.

1. **Part A** Who is the **narrator** of the passage, and what is the narrator's **point of view**?
   A. Jessica Peet is the narrator; first person
   B. Jessica Peet is the narrator; third person
   C. Julia Alvarez is the narrator; first person
   D. Julia Alvarez is the narrator; third person

   Part B Which phrase clearly shows the narrator's point of view?
   A. "Do you have anything more to declare?"
   B. "Not that they obey housemothers."
   C. "Save Our Strength was putting together a fund-raising anthology"
   D. "The first time I received a letter from one of my readers, I was surprised."

2. Which answer choice best describes the **mood** of this passage?
   A. serious and sorrowful
   B. worried and abrupt
   C. enthusiastic and funny
   D. honest and friendly

3. What is the author's **tone** in this passage?
   A. angry and frustrated
   B. respectful and sincere
   C. mocking and sarcastic
   D. alarmed and concerned

4. Why does the author consider not answering the reader's question about the sonnets in *Homecoming*?
   A. She does not have time to answer every question sent to her by readers.
   B. She would rather answer questions about the writing life.
   C. She would rather write sonnets and essays than answers to questions.
   D. She wants readers to read her books to find answers to their questions.

5. What is the **main idea** of this passage?
   A. The author will share her insights about life in a series of essays.
   B. Writing creatively is more important to the author than writing nonfiction.
   C. Readers expect to learn personal details about the author.
   D. Writing to readers takes the mystery out of creative writing.

6. **Part A** Which phrase is closest in meaning to the underlined word *perplexities*?
   A. confusing or puzzling details
   B. angry or fearful details
   C. creative or imaginative details
   D. scientific or numeric details

   Part B Which other words from the passage help the reader understand the meaning of *perplexities*?
   A. remain, finished, reading
   B. little, curiosities, quandaries
   C. book, send, another
   D. Often, buy, author

⏱ Timed Writing

7. In an essay, explain whether the **author's style** in this passage is formal or informal. Support your ideas with details from the text.

GO ON

II. Reading Informational Text

Directions: *Read this speech. Then, answer each question that follows.*

Do you ever wonder why students are lethargic after lunch, or why they cannot seem to pay attention in afternoon classes? This is most likely due to the high-carbohydrate foods students eat at lunch. Carbs fill us up, but leave us with low energy.

I believe that our school cafeteria needs healthier foods. If you look at the monthly menu, you will see that fried foods, pizza, and pasta dominate the daily specials. Although the daily specials are not our only options, the alternatives are soggy salads, rock-hard bagels, or, even worse, the sugary snacks in the vending machines.

In the news, and in our health classes, we are lectured about eating well. Studies show that eating healthful foods provides teens with the energy to succeed in school, along with a positive self-image. Statistics reveal that there is a growing obesity problem among children in America. So, why are we being tempted by battered onion rings and fatty nachos? Why can't we be tempted by fresh salad bars, grilled chicken sandwiches, and healthy soups? These healthier options will teach us good habits in the long term, and, in the short term, will help us focus in our afternoon classes!

If nutritious foods are served, every student in school will buy them, and you will see an increase in student achievement.

1. **Part A** Which statement best summarizes the author's main idea?

   A. Students are lazy and tired.

   B. Students should not eat lunch.

   C. Students eat foods that make them tired and unfocused.

   D. Teachers are annoyed after lunch.

   Part B Which phrase is a key detail that supports the main idea?

   A. "we are lectured about eating well"

   B. "healthier options will teach us good habits"

   C. "the daily specials are not our only options"

   D. "due to the high-carbohydrate foods students eat at lunch."

2. What is the tone of the speech?

   A. threatening   C. disapproving

   B. funny   D. lighthearted

3. Which of the following claims in the speech is an opinion rather than a fact?

   A. "If nutritious foods are served, every student in school will buy them …"

   B. "Statistics reveal that there is a growing obesity problem among children …"

   C. "Studies show that eating healthy food provides teens with the energy to succeed in school …"

   D. "Carbs fill us up, but leave us with low energy."

III. Writing and Language Conventions

Directions: *Read the passage. Then, answer each question.*

(1) I have read my favorite book, *Charlotte's Web*, four times. (2) Each time I find a new treasure. (3) This time, it was the sadness and beauty of growing up. (4) Fern, a young girl, rescues Wilbur the pig. (5) She is devoted to Wilbur, even when he leaves her farm. (6) Charlotte the spider soon becomes Wilbur's friend. (7) Later, though, Fern's interests change. (8) She becomes happier with her human friends than with the farm animals. (9) Through these changes, Fern shows what lays ahead for all of us. (10) When we leave childhood, we gain much, but we lose much, too.

1. Which **verb tense** does the writer use in sentence 1?
   A. present
   B. present perfect
   C. past
   D. past perfect

2. How could the writer revise sentence 2 to **maintain the verb tense** of sentence 1?
   A. Each time I have found a new treasure.
   B. Each time I am finding a new treasure.
   C. Each time I was finding a new treasure.
   D. Each time I had found a new treasure.

3. Which of these sentences contains a **linking verb?**
   A. sentence 1
   B. sentence 2
   C. sentence 7
   D. sentence 8

4. What is the correct way to rewrite sentence 9 to fix the **troublesome verb?**
   A. Through these changes, Fern shows what lay ahead for all of us.
   B. Through these changes, Fern shows what laid ahead for all of us.
   C. Through these changes, Fern shows what will lay ahead for all of us.
   D. Through these changes, Fern shows what lies ahead for all of us.

5. What **verb tense** does the writer use in sentence 10?
   A. present
   B. present perfect
   C. past
   D. past perfect

CONSTRUCTED RESPONSE

Directions: *Follow the instructions to complete the tasks below as required by your teacher.*

As you work on each task, incorporate both general academic vocabulary and literary terms you learned in Parts 1 and 2.

Writing

TASK 1 Informational Text

Determine the Author's Point of View

Write an essay in which you determine the author's point of view in a nonfiction text from Part 2.

Part 1

- Choose a selection in which the author presents a clear point of view on a topic.
- Take notes on how the author develops a main idea by emphasizing certain evidence or by presenting an interpretation of facts.

Part 2

- Write an essay in which you explain the author's point of view and analyze the author's use of facts and evidence to support his or her perspective.
- Support your ideas by citing specific details from the selection.
- Restate your key findings in the conclusion of your essay.

TASK 2 Informational Text

Analyze Tone

Write an essay in which you analyze tone in a nonfiction work from Part 2.

- From Part 2, choose the selection you will use as the focus of your essay.

- To analyze tone in the selection, begin by determining the author's attitude toward his or her audience and subject.
- Examine the author's word choice by noting the connotative, or associated meanings, of particular words and phrases. Explain how the author's word choice contributes to the tone of the selection.
- Cite additional details, such as sentence structure and length, that further develop the tone.
- In your essay, establish and maintain a formal style.

TASK 3 Informational Text

Determine the Central Idea

Write an essay in which you determine the central idea in a nonfiction work from Part 2.

- Provide a brief summary that presents the most important points in your chosen selection. Do not include your opinions in the summary.
- State the central idea of the selection. Describe how the author presents and develops this idea throughout the selection. Include specific details from the text to support your analysis.
- Look for places in your essay where you can eliminate wordiness or choose more precise language.

Speaking and Listening

TASK 4 **Informational Text**

Trace and Evaluate an Argument

Write and present an essay in which you trace and evaluate the argument in a nonfiction work from Part 2.

- Choose a selection from Part 2 in which the author presents and supports an argument.

- In an essay, trace the argument from its introduction through its conclusion. Note specific claims and evidence the author provides to support the argument.

- Include your evaluation of the argument and the author's use of reasoning and supporting evidence.

- With a small group, take turns presenting your esays orally.

- Listen for slang or informal language in your group members' presentations. Discuss ways to improve your use of formal language.

- Apply the group's feedback to revise your essay.

TASK 5 **Informational Text**

Compare Presentations of Events

Give an oral presentation in which you compare and contrast one author's presentation of events with that of another.

- Choose two nonfiction works from Part 2 that share a similar subject.

- Take notes in which you compare and contrast the ways in which each author presents information and events. For example, one author might tell a personal anecdote about childhood from the first-person perspective, while the other author reflects on childhood from a third-person perspective. Use examples from the texts to support your analysis.

- Present your comparison to a small group of classmates.

- As you speak, use appropriate eye contact. Speak clearly and loudly enough to be understood in a classroom setting.

Research

TASK 6 **Informational Text**

 ## What is important to know?

In Part 2, you have read nonfiction and informational texts about many different ideas and events. Now you will conduct a short research project about a subject from this unit that you would like to learn more about. Use both the Part 2 texts and your research to reflect on this unit's Big Question. Use the following guidelines as you conduct your research:

- Focus your research on ideas and events from one of the texts in Part 2.

- Gather relevant information from at least two reliable print or digital sources.

- Take careful notes and cite your sources accurately.

When you have completed your research, write a brief essay in response to the Big Question. Discuss how your initial thoughts may have been either changed or reinforced. Support your response with examples from the texts in Part 2 and from your research.

"Every day is a new opportunity.
You can **build on yesterday's success**
or put its failures behind and start over again.
That's the way life is, with a **new game every day**,
and that's the way **baseball** is."

BASEBALL

The selections in this unit all deal with the Big Question: **What is important to know?** You gain knowledge every day: by studying, talking with others, meeting new people, or learning a new skill. As you read the texts that follow, you will explore the ways that baseball players and fans gain knowledge about themselves and the world around them by participating in this "great American pastime."

◀ **CRITICAL VIEWING** Can baseball be as rewarding for spectators, such as those in this picture, as it is for players? Explain.

CLOSE READING TOOL

Use the **Close Reading Tool** to practice the strategies you learn in this unit.

READINGS IN PART 3

JACKIE ROBINSON
Justice at Last

Geoffrey C. Ward
and Ken Burns

It was 1945, and World War II had ended. Americans of all races had died for their country. Yet black men were still not allowed in the major leagues. The national pastime was loved by all America, but the major leagues were for white men only.

Branch Rickey of the Brooklyn Dodgers thought that was wrong. He was the only team owner who believed blacks and whites should play together. Baseball, he felt, would become even more thrilling, and fans of all colors would swarm to his ballpark.

Rickey decided his team would be the first to integrate. There were plenty of brilliant Negro league players, but he knew the first black major leaguer would need much more than athletic ability.

Many fans and players were prejudiced—they didn't want the races to play together. Rickey knew the first black player would be cursed and booed. Pitchers would throw at him; runners would spike him. Even his own teammates might try to pick a fight.

But somehow this man had to rise above that. No matter what happened, he must never lose his temper. No matter what was said to him, he must never answer back. If he had even one fight, people might say integration wouldn't work.

When Rickey met Jackie Robinson, he thought he'd found the right man. Robinson was 28 years old, and a superb athlete. In his first season in the Negro leagues, he hit .387. But just as importantly, he had great intelligence and sensitivity. Robinson was college-educated, and knew what joining the majors would mean for blacks. The grandson of a slave, he was proud of his race and wanted others to feel the same.

In the past, Robinson had always stood up for his rights. But now Rickey told him he would have to stop. The Dodgers needed "a man that will take abuse."

At first Robinson thought Rickey wanted someone who was afraid to defend himself. But as they talked, he realized that in this case a truly brave man would have to avoid fighting. He thought for a while, then promised Rickey he would not fight back.

Robinson signed with the Dodgers and went to play in the minors in 1946. Rickey was right—fans insulted him, and so did players. But he performed brilliantly and avoided fights. Then, in 1947, he came to the majors.

Many Dodgers were angry. Some signed a petition demanding to be traded. But Robinson and Rickey were determined to make their experiment work.

On April 15—Opening Day—26,623 fans came out to Ebbets Field. More than half of them were black—Robinson was already their hero. Now he was making history just by being on the field.

The afternoon was cold and wet, but no one left the ballpark. The Dodgers beat the Boston Braves, 5–3.

Robinson went hitless, but the hometown fans didn't seem to care—they cheered his every move.

Robinson's first season was difficult. Fans threatened to kill him; players tried to hurt him. The St. Louis Cardinals said they would strike if he took the field. And because of laws separating the races in certain states, he often couldn't eat or sleep in the same places as his teammates.

Yet through it all, he kept his promise to Rickey. No matter who insulted him, he never retaliated.

Robinson's dignity paid off. Thousands of fans jammed stadiums to see him play. The Dodgers set attendance records in a number of cities.

Slowly his teammates accepted him, realizing that he was the spark that made them a winning team. No one was more daring on the base paths or better with the glove. At the plate, he had great bat control—he could hit the ball anywhere. That season, he was named baseball's first Rookie of the Year.

Jackie Robinson went on to a glorious career. But he did more than play the game well—his bravery taught Americans a lesson. Branch Rickey opened a door, and Jackie Robinson stepped through it, making sure it could never be closed again. Something wonderful happened to baseball—and America—the day Jackie Robinson joined the Dodgers.

ABOUT THE AUTHORS

Geoffrey C. Ward (b. 1940)
The author of many award-winning books, Geoffrey C. Ward is also a screenwriter and a former editor of *American Heritage* magazine. For more than twenty years, Ward has worked with Ken Burns, writing award-winning television documentaries including *Baseball*, *The Civil War*, and *The West*.

Ken Burns (b. 1953)
Ken Burns has co-written, produced, and directed several television documentaries and mini-series and has directed movies that have been nominated for Academy Awards. "Jackie Robinson: Justice at Last" is from a book based on Ward's and Burns's 1994 television documentary *Baseball*. The documentary won numerous awards, including an Emmy.

Close Reading Activities

READ

Comprehension

Reread all or part of the text to help you answer the following questions.

1. Why did Branch Rickey want Jackie Robinson on his team?

2. How did Branch Rickey want Jackie Robinson to act?

3. How did the hometown fans react when Robinson played in his first game with the Dodgers?

Language Study

Selection Vocabulary The following sentences appear in the essay. Write a synonym for each boldfaced word, and then use each word in a sentence of your own.

- Rickey decided his team would be the first to **integrate**.
- Many fans and players were **prejudiced**— they didn't want the races to play together.
- Robinson was 28 years old, and a **superb** athlete.

Diction and Style Study these sentences from the essay, then answer the questions.

> Rickey was right—fans insulted him, and so did players. But he performed brilliantly and avoided fights.

1. **(a)** What does *insulted* mean? **(b)** How is being *insulted* different from being *booed*?

2. **(a)** What does *brilliantly* mean as it is used here? **(b)** What images does the word call to mind? **(c)** Why is *brilliantly* a more effective word choice than *well* would be in this sentence?

Research: Clarify Details This essay may include references that are unfamiliar to you. Choose an unfamiliar detail and briefly research it. Then, explain how your research sheds light on an aspect of the article.

Summarize Write an objective summary of the article. Remember that an objective summary is free from opinion and evaluation.

Conventions Read this passage from the essay. Identify the tense of each verb. Then, explain how that tense indicates when the events took place.

> It was 1945, and World War II had ended. Americans of all races had died for their country. Yet black men were still not allowed in the major leagues. The national pastime was loved by all America, but the major leagues were for white men only.

Academic Vocabulary

These words appear in blue in the instructions and questions on the facing page.

support   opinions   affect

Categorize the words by deciding whether you know each one well, know it a little bit, or do not know it at all. Then, use a dictionary to look up the definitions of the words you do not know.

Literary Analysis

Reread the identified passages. Then, respond to the questions that follow:

> **Focus Passage 1** *(p. 258)*
> When Rickey met Jackie Robinson… he would not fight back.

> **Focus Passage 2** *(p. 259)*
> Robinson's dignity paid off… the day Jackie Robinson joined the Dodgers.

Key Ideas and Details

1. (a) According to the authors, what kind of athlete was Jackie Robinson?
(b) Support: What detail do the authors provide to **support** this claim?

Craft and Structure

2. Draw Conclusions: Why do the authors emphasize the idea that intelligence and sensitivity were as important for Robinson as his physical ability?

3. (a) Analyze: Why do the authors share the thoughts and insights of both Robinson and Rickey in this passage?
(b) Connect: How does this technique help clarify the authors' purpose?

Integration of Knowledge and Ideas

4. Given the historical context, why would "a truly brave man … have to avoid fighting"?

Key Ideas and Details

1. (a) Interpret: How did Robinson's teammates change their **opinions** about him? **(b) Analyze:** What caused them to change?

Craft and Structure

2. How does the authors' choice of the word *jammed* instead of *attended* **affect** the meaning of the second sentence?

3. (a) Interpret: Why do the authors compare Robinson to a spark in the fourth sentence?
(b) Evaluate: Is the metaphor, or comparison, effective? Explain.

Integration of Knowledge and Ideas

4. Interpret: Reread the sentence that begins "Branch Rickey opened a door." In your own words, explain what the authors mean and tell how this sentence expresses a main idea of the essay.

Author's Viewpoint

An author's **viewpoint** is the author's attitude and feelings about a subject. Authors use words with strong connotations, or associations, to express positive or negative viewpoints. Reread the essay and take notes on how the authors express their viewpoint.

1. Baseball (a) What is the authors' attitude toward Branch Rickey and his effect on major league baseball? **(b)** Support your answer with details from the text.

2. What does the title of the selection reveal about the authors' viewpoint?

DISCUSS

From Text to Topic **Group Discussion**

Discuss this passage with a group of classmates. Take notes during the discussion. Contribute your own ideas, and support them with examples from the text.

> But somehow this man had to rise above that. No matter what happened, he must never lose his temper. No matter what was said to him, he must never answer back. If he had even one fight, people might say integration wouldn't work.

WRITE

Writing to Sources **Informative Text**

Assignment

Branch Rickey and Jackie Robinson shared a common goal—to integrate baseball—but they faced different challenges on the way to achieving that goal. Write a **comparison-and-contrast essay** in which you compare the risks and obstacles Branch Rickey faced and overcame with those that Jackie Robinson faced and overcame. Use details from the essay to support your ideas.

Prewriting and Planning Reread the essay to find details about the risks and obstacles Robinson and Rickey each faced. Some risks and obstacles may be suggested but not directly stated. Record your notes in a two-column chart.

Drafting Use the **block method** to organize your essay. Present all the details about one of the men, and then all the details about the other man. Cite specific examples from the essay to support your points.

Revising Reread your essay, making sure you have explained which risks and obstacles were the same for both Robinson and Rickey and which were different. Use transitional words and phrases like these to connect your ideas:

in the same way   similarly   in contrast   on the other hand

Editing and Proofreading Make sure the transitions you use clearly show your comparisons and contrasts. In addition, review your essay to ensure you have correctly used past tense and past perfect tense verbs to express time relationships.

QUESTIONS FOR DISCUSSION

1. Why could a single fight damage the cause of integration?

2. In what way was Robinson's refusal to fight back a way of fighting *for* something?

CONVENTIONS

Make sure the personal pronouns in your essay agree with their antecedents in number, person, and gender. To review pronoun-antecedent agreement, see page 107.

RESEARCH

Research **Investigate the Topic**

Segregation in Sports The courage and wisdom of Jackie Robinson and Branch Rickey helped break down the barrier of racial prejudice in major league baseball. However, another type of segregation in sports exists. Many team sports are segregated by gender: Few sports teams include both men and women.

Assignment

Conduct research to find out how gender segregation is still practiced in amateur and professional baseball and how some people have fought against this bias. Look for articles about gender discrimination in baseball and firsthand accounts of people who have fought the gender barrier. Take clear notes. Share your findings in a short **presentation** to the class.

PREPARATION FOR ESSAY

You may use the knowledge you gain during this research assignment to support your claims in an essay you will write at the end of this section.

Gather Sources Locate authoritative print and electronic sources. Primary sources, such as interviews and letters written by people who have tried to break the gender barrier, provide authentic firsthand information. You may also use secondary sources, such as articles and news accounts by expert authors.

Take Notes Take notes on each source, either electronically or on note cards. Use an organized note-taking strategy.

- Make separate notes for each source. Label each note with the incident(s) it describes.

- Record source information for each note. For Internet sources, record the web address and the date you accessed the site.

Synthesize Multiple Sources Organize information from your sources into a well-structured presentation. Use what you learned to draw conclusions about gender discrimination in baseball. Use your notes to outline your presentation. Create a Works Cited list as described in the Research Workshop in the Introductory Unit of this textbook.

Organize and Present Ideas Review your outline and draft your presentation. Practice delivering your presentation before you present it to a group of classmates. Be prepared to answer questions from your audience.

Daisy Junor of
the South Bend,
Indiana, Blue Sox

Memories of an
All-American
Girl

by Carmen Pauls

Daisy Junor is waiting for me outside her south Regina apartment, a smile on her young-looking, 76-year-old face. She shakes my hand, then holds it in hers. Looking at me, she says, "You've got soft hands. You don't play ball, do you?" Then she gently leads me into her apartment, still holding my hand.

She's right. I don't play baseball. But Daisy does—or did, in the glory days of women's baseball, the 1946–49 seasons of the All-American Girls Professional Baseball League.

The baseball league began in 1943, the brainchild of chewing gum magnate Philip Wrigley. Wrigley, who owned the Chicago Cubs, feared American baseball was going down the tubes. With major-league players going off to fight in World War II, Wrigley was afraid the ball parks might soon be empty.

Wrigley decided to satisfy the craving for America's game with a professional women's baseball league. He sent scouts all over North America, including southern Saskatchewan.

Daisy's team, with players from Regina, Moose Jaw and Estevan, had just won the Western Canada Softball League tournament, and Wrigley's scout came to see them play. Pleased with what he saw, he invited players to come down to Chicago for spring training.

Twenty-two-year-old Daisy had just gotten married, so she turned down the offer. But her sister Ruby went, and was picked to play for the Racine Belles. Over the next couple of years, as her sister and other girls came back to Saskatchewan with glowing reports, Daisy became more and more eager to go.

In the spring of 1946, Daisy heard that the training season would be in Pascagoula, Mississippi, on the Gulf of Mexico. Dave Junor, Daisy's husband, told her he'd never be able to

The Rockford Peaches of the All-American Girls Baseball League pose for a team portrait in 1944.

afford to take her there, so she might as well go. She did, and was signed with the South Bend (Indiana) Blue Sox, as a left-fielder.

"It was a very serious game," Daisy remembers. The girls would play every night, with double-headers on weekends, and only got a day or two off all summer. At home in South Bend, the girls trained every morning and played at night under the hot stadium lights, so there was little time for socializing. In the movie *A League of Their Own*, the girls lived together in a rooming house, but the real players boarded with South Bend baseball fans.

The travel schedule was grueling. The girls headed out to away games every week or two. "We were always coming and going. We were living out of a suitcase most of the time," Daisy recalls. "I always said, 'Gee, it'd be good to have some home-made mashed potatoes.'"

...[T]he girls, from what was sometimes called the "American Glamor League," had a tougher time than their male counterparts. The girls were expected to play ball like men, even though they were wearing short skirts, which caused serious leg burns and bruises during slides.

The girls received lessons on how to charm a date, wear makeup and skirts, and sip tea like a lady.

The All-American Girls were to be every boy's ideal woman as well as the girl next door. "Frankly, I'll tell you, it didn't work with some of them," Daisy says. "Almost all these girls were tomboys, and they all looked so funny in skirts."

But whether it was the posture lessons or their skills on the field, fans loved the All-Americans. Fans would grab a player's glove as a souvenir, or stake out players' homes to catch a glimpse of them. "It was very **exhilarating**," Daisy says. "After the ball game, we could hardly get to the dressing room (because of the requests) for autographs."

Fifty years later, the fans are still coming for autographs. In Arizona, four of Daisy's friends from the league regularly go to local shopping malls to sign and sell autographed baseball cards. "It's almost a living for them," Daisy says. "They say the people just love (them) there."

Daisy herself rarely signs autographs these days. But she's already achieved a sort of **immortality**, with **inductions** into the Saskatchewan Sports Hall of Fame in Regina, the Saskatchewan Baseball Hall of Fame in North Battleford, and the grand-daddy of them all, the Baseball Hall of Fame in Cooperstown, N.Y.

And if you let her get her ball and glove, she'll come play catch with you any time.

◀ **immortality**
(im´ôr tal´i tē) *n.*
ability to live forever

◀ **inductions**
(in duk´shənz) *n.*
introductions; acts of being brought into something

◀ **exhilarating**
(eg zil´ə rāt´ iŋ) *adj.*
exciting; stimulating

ABOUT THE AUTHOR

Carmen Pauls

At the age of eight, Carmen Pauls wrote an essay about the wonders of reading that was published in her local newspaper. Since that time, she has been an award-winning news reporter, screenwriter, and photographer. She currently lives and works in Saskatchewan, Canada.

Close Reading Activities

READ

Comprehension

Reread all or part of the text to help you answer the following questions.

1. Why was the All-American Girls Professional Baseball League formed?

2. Why did women have a "tougher time" than the men playing professional baseball?

3. What was Daisy Junor's role in the women's baseball league?

Research: Clarify Details Choose at least one unfamiliar detail from the article and research it. Then, explain how your research helped you understand the article.

Summarize Write an objective summary of the article. Include main ideas and details, but do not include opinions.

Language Study

Selection Vocabulary Explain how the suffix changes each base word in each boldfaced word from the article. If necessary, use a dictionary to help you answer.

- "It was very **exhilarating**," Daisy says.
- But she's already achieved a sort of **immortality**, with **inductions** into the Saskatchewan Sports Hall of Fame . . .

Literary Analysis

Reread the identified passage. Then, respond to the questions that follow.

> **Focus Passage** (p. 266)
>
> "It was a very serious game… home-made mashed potatoes.'"

Key Ideas and Details

1. **(a) Infer:** What is the main idea of this passage? **(b) Support:** What details in the passage support the main idea?

Craft and Structure

2. **(a) Analyze:** In these paragraphs, the author uses direct quotations from Daisy.

What is the effect of the quotations? **(b) Make a Judgment:** Would the article be as effective if it did not contain quotations? Why or why not?

Integration of Knowledge and Ideas

3. **Evaluate:** The author mentions the movie *A League of Their Own*. Do you think the experiences of Daisy and her teammates would make an interesting subject for a movie? Use details from the passage to support your answer.

Narrative Time Shifts

Narrative time shifts are scenes that jump from the present to the past or even the future.

1. **(a)** Identify the section of the article that takes place in the past. **(b)** What words does the author use to signal shifts in time?

2. What effect does the author achieve by using time shifts in this article?

DISCUSS • RESEARCH • WRITE

From Text to Topic **Partner Discussion**

Discuss this passage with a partner. Take notes during the discussion. Contribute your own ideas, and support them with examples from the text.

> … [T]he girls, from what was sometimes called the "American Glamor League,"… they all looked so funny in skirts."
> (pp. 266–267)

Research **Investigate the Topic**

Women and Baseball The All-American Girls Professional Baseball League inspired the movie *A League of Their Own*, a colorful portrayal of women in baseball during the 1940s.

Assignment

View *A League of Their Own* and conduct additional research to learn more about the history of women in baseball. Take clear notes and carefully identify your sources. Share your findings in an **informal discussion** with the class. As part of your discussion, compare and contrast the experience of reading texts with the experience of viewing a film to learn about a topic.

Writing to Sources **Narrative**

"Memories of an All-American Girl" focuses on one woman's experiences during an extraordinary time in her life.

Assignment

Write an **autobiographical narrative** that describes an opportunity or event that had a positive effect on your life. Follow these steps:

- Introduce the significant opportunity or event.
- Include **visual** descriptions to create vivid images for readers.
- Use transitions to smoothly connect events.
- Conclude by **reflecting** on the impact of the event, and by making a connection between your experience and Daisy Junor's.

QUESTIONS FOR DISCUSSION

1. How were women treated differently from male players?
2. Do you think the women were treated unfairly? Why or why not?

PREPARATION FOR ESSAY

You may use the results of this research project to support your ideas in the essay you will write at the end of this section.

ACADEMIC VOCABULARY

Academic terms appear in blue on these pages. If these words are not familiar to you, use a dictionary to find their definitions. Then, use them as you speak and write about the text.

Preserving a Great American Symbol

Richard Durbin

Mr. Speaker, I rise to condemn the desecration of a great American symbol. No, I am not referring to flagburning; I am referring to the baseball bat.

Several experts tell us that the wooden baseball bat is **doomed** to **extinction**, that major league baseball players will soon be standing at home plate with aluminum bats in their hands.

Baseball fans have been forced to endure countless indignities by those who just cannot leave well enough alone: designated hitters,[1] plastic grass, uniforms that look like pajamas, chicken clowns dancing on the base lines, and, of course, the most heinous sacrilege, lights in Wrigley Field.[2]

Are we willing to hear the crack of a bat replaced by the dinky ping? Are we ready to see the Louisville Slugger replaced by the aluminum ping dinger? Is nothing sacred?

Please do not tell me that wooden bats are too expensive, when players who cannot hit their weight are being paid more money than the President of the United States.

Please do not try to sell me on the notion that these metal clubs will make better hitters.

What will be next? Teflon baseballs? Radar-enhanced gloves? I ask you.

I do not want to hear about saving trees. Any tree in America would gladly give its life for the glory of a day at home plate.

I do not know if it will take a constitutional **amendment** to keep our baseball traditions alive, but if we forsake the great Americana of broken-bat singles and pine tar,[3] we will have certainly lost our way as a nation.

◀ **doomed**
(do͞omd) *v.*
condemned to destruction or death

◀ **extinction**
(ek stiŋk´shən) *n.*
act of bringing to an end; destruction

◀ **amendment**
(ə mend´mənt) *n.*
change made to a law or bill by adding, deleting, or altering its language

---

1. **designated hitter** player who bats in place of the pitcher and does not play any other position. The position was created in 1973 in the American League. Some fans argue that it has changed the game for the worse.
2. **Wrigley Field** historic baseball field in Chicago. It did not have lights for night games until 1988. Some fans regretted the change.
3. **broken-bat singles . . . pine tar** when a batter breaks a wooden bat while hitting the ball and makes it to first base, it is a notable event in a baseball game; pine tar is a substance used to improve the batter's grip on a wooden bat.

ABOUT THE AUTHOR

Richard Durbin (b. 1944)

Richard (Dick) Durbin has been a United States senator from Illinois since 1997. Before being elected to the Senate, Durbin served six terms as a congressman from Illinois in the United States House of Representatives. He gave this humorous speech in the House of Representatives on July 26, 1989.

Close Reading Activities

READ

Comprehension

Reread all or part of the text to help you answer the following questions.

1. What is the purpose of Durbin's speech?

2. What "indignities" have baseball fans already endured?

3. What advantages of aluminum bats does Durbin dismiss?

Language Study

Selection Vocabulary The following phrases come from the selection. Define the boldfaced words. Then, use each word in a sentence of your own.

Literary Analysis

Reread the identified passage. Then, respond to the questions that follow:

> **Focus Passage** (p. 271)
> Baseball fans have been forced … Is nothing sacred?

Key Ideas and Details

1. **(a) Interpret:** What is Durbin's position on the changes in major league baseball? **(b) Analyze:** How does he support his position?

Hyperbole

Hyperbole is a form of figurative language in which an author uses exaggeration to **achieve** an effect. Reread the speech, noting examples of hyperbole.

Research: Clarify Details Choose an unfamiliar reference from the speech and briefly research it. Then, explain how your research helped clarify the speech.

Summarize Write an objective summary of the speech. Objective summaries are free of opinions and evaluation.

- Several experts tell us that the wooden baseball bat is **doomed** to **extinction** . . .
- I do not know if it will take a constitutional **amendment** . . .

Craft and Structure

2. **(a) Analyze:** What effect does Durbin achieve by comparing the "crack" of a wooden bat to the "dinky ping" of an aluminum bat? **(b)** Use details from the speech to explain how the next sentence strengthens this effect.

Integration of Knowledge and Ideas

3. To what type of audience would this speech most appeal? **Cite** details from the text to support your answer.

1. **Analyze:** Identify two examples of hyperbole in the speech, and explain their effects.

2. **Evaluate:** Does Durbin's use of hyperbole strengthen his overall message? Explain.

DISCUSS • RESEARCH • WRITE

From Text to Topic **Panel Discussion**

Discuss the following passage with a group of classmates. Take notes during the discussion. Contribute your own ideas, and support them with examples from the text.

> Please do not try to sell me on the notion that these metal clubs will make better hitters.
> What will be next? Teflon baseballs? Radar-enhanced gloves? I ask you.

Research **Investigate the Topic**

Baseball Traditions For close to a century, baseball has been America's "National Pastime." Many valued traditions have developed around the game and the players, teams, and stadiums associated with it.

Assignment

Conduct research to learn about some of baseball's most well-known traditions and how these traditions affect players and fans today. Consult electronic and print sources. Take clear notes and carefully identify your sources so that you can easily access the information later. Share your findings in an **informal presentation** for the class.

Writing to Sources **Argument**

Some people, like Durbin, argue for preserving traditions such as the wooden bat in baseball. Others argue for the use of new technology such as advanced camera systems for instant replays.

Assignment

Write a **persuasive speech** in which you **argue** for or against the use of new technology in baseball. Follow these steps:

- Identify the issue and clearly state your claim.
- Use statistics, quotations, and other details to support your claim. You may also draw upon information presented in Durbin's speech.
- Conclude your speech by summarizing the impact that new technology will have upon established baseball traditions.

QUESTIONS FOR DISCUSSION

1. What might be the effects of "radar-enhanced gloves"?
2. What does Durbin imply about the effects of technology in sports? What are his reasons for making this argument?

PREPARATION FOR ESSAY

You may use the results of this research project to support your ideas in the essay you will write at the end of this section.

ACADEMIC VOCABULARY

Academic terms appear in blue on these pages. If these words are not familiar to you, use a dictionary to find their definitions. Then, use them as you speak and write about the text.

The Southpaw
Judith Viorst

Dear Richard,

Don't invite me to your birthday party because I'm not coming. And give back the Disneyland sweatshirt I said you could wear. If I'm not good enough to play on your team, I'm not good enough to be friends with.

Your **former** friend,
Janet

P.S. I hope when you go to the dentist he finds 20 cavities.

former ▶
(fôr´ mər) adj.
existing in an
earlier time; past

Dear Janet,

Here is your stupid Disneyland sweatshirt, if that's how you're going to be. I want my comic books now—finished or not. No girl had ever played on the Mapes Street baseball team, and as long as I'm captain, no girl ever will.
Your former friend,
Richard

P.S. I hope when you go for your checkup you need a tetanus shot.

Dear Richard,

I'm changing my goldfish's name from Richard to Stanley. Don't count on my vote for class president next year. Just because I'm a member of the ballet club doesn't mean I'm not a terrific ballplayer.
Your former friend,
Janet

P.S. I see you lost your first game 28-0.

Dear Janet,

I'm not saving any more seats for you on the bus. For all I care you can stand the whole way to school. Why don't you just forget about baseball and learn something nice like knitting?
Your former friend,
    Richard

P.S. Wait until Wednesday.

Dear Richard,

My father said I could call someone to go with us for a ride and hot-fudge sundaes. In case you didn't notice, I didn't call you.
Your former friend,
    Janet

P.S. I see you lost your second game, 34-0.

Dear Janet,

Remember when I took the laces out of my blue-and-white sneakers and gave them to you? I want them back.
Your former friend,
    Richard

P.S. Wait until Friday.

Dear Richard,

Congratulations on your un-broken record. Eight straight loses, wow! I understand you're the laughingstock of New Jersey.
Your former friend,
    Janet

P.S. Why don't you and your team forget about baseball and learn something nice like knitting maybe?

Dear Janet,

Here's the silver horseback riding trophy that you gave me.
I don't think I want to keep it anymore.
Your former friend,
  Richard

P.S. I didn't think you'd be the kind who'd kick a man when
he's down.

Dear Richard,

I wasn't kicking exactly. I was kicking *back*.
Your former friend,
  Janet

P.S. In case you were wondering, my batting average is .345.

Dear Janet,

Alfie is having his tonsils out tomorrow.
We might be able to let you catch next week.
  Richard

Dear Richard,

I pitch.
Janet

Dear Janet,

Joel is moving to Kansas and Danny sprained his wrist.
How about a permanent place in the outfield?
  Richard

Dear Richard,

I pitch.
Janet

Dear Janet,

Ronnie caught the chicken pox and Leo broke his toe and
Elwood has these stupid violin lessons. I'll give you first base,
and that's my final offer.
  Richard

Dear Richard,

Susan Reilly plays first base, Marilyn Jackson catches, Ethel Kahn plays center field, I pitch. It's a package deal.

Janet

P.S. Sorry about your 12-game losing streak.

Dear Janet,

Please! Not Marilyn Jackson.

Richard

Dear Richard,

Nobody ever said that I was **unreasonable**. How about Lizzie Martindale instead?

Janet

Dear Janet,

At least could you call your goldfish Richard again?

Your friend,

Richard

◀ **unreasonable**
(un rē′ zən ə bəl)
adj. not fair;
not sensible

Close Reading Activities

READ

Comprehension

Reread the text to help you answer these questions.

1. What was Janet and Richard's relationship before their argument?

2. Why is Janet angry?

3. What happens to Richard's baseball team?

4. What does Richard finally agree to do?

Research: Clarify Details Choose one unfamiliar reference in the story and research it. Then, write a brief paragraph explaining how your research helped you understand the story.

Summarize Write an objective summary of the story. Objective summaries are free from opinions.

Language Study

Selection Vocabulary Write a synonym for each boldfaced word. Then, use the boldfaced words in sentences.

- Your **former** friend, Janet."
- Nobody ever said that I was **unreasonable**.

Literary Analysis

Reread the identified passage. Then, respond to the questions:

> **Focus Passage** *(pp. 275–276)*
> Congratulations on your un-broken record... We might be able to let you catch next week.

Key Ideas and Details

1. (a) Infer: Why is Richard a "laughingstock"? **(b)** What story details support your inference?

2. Infer: Why does Janet tell Richard her batting average?

Craft and Structure

3. (a) Interpret: What feeling does Janet express when she says, "I wasn't kicking exactly. I was kicking back"?
(b) Evaluate: Would this passage have been as effective if the author had directly stated Janet's feelings? Explain.

Integration of Knowledge and Ideas

4. (a) Describe the format of this story.
(b) Analyze: Why do you think the author chose this structure?

Characterization

Authors use characterization to develop characters and reveal their unique traits, or qualities.

1. What traits are revealed in the notes the two characters write to each other?

2. What character traits help Janet resolve her conflict with Richard?

DISCUSS • RESEARCH • WRITE

From Text to Topic **Group Discussion**

Discuss the first exchange between Janet and Richard with a group of classmates. Take notes during the discussion. Contribute your own ideas, and support them with examples from the text.

> "Dear Richard, Don't invite me to your birthday party… when you go for your checkup you need a tetanus shot." (p. 274)

Research **Investigate the Topic**

Teams and Clubs Youth baseball teams are popular around the world.

Assignment

Conduct research to learn about the worldwide popularity of baseball. Take clear notes that identify your sources so that you can easily access the information later. Share your findings in an **annotated list.**

Writing to Sources **Argument**

"The Southpaw" focuses on a girl's efforts to join a baseball team. People often have to persuade others about the value of their skills and talents.

Assignment

From Janet's perspective, write a formal **persuasive letter** to Richard's team, presenting your qualifications and arguing that you are a good candidate for membership. You can make up additional skills and experience. Follow these steps:

- Present facts and evidence to support your claim that you are qualified to be a member of the team.
- **Anticipate** and respond to any arguments the group might have against your becoming a member.
- **Conclude** by restating your position and summarizing how your membership will benefit the team.

QUESTIONS FOR DISCUSSION

1. In this quarrel, which statements are fair? Which are not?

2. Is this disagreement worthy of breaking up a friendship? Why or why not?

PREPARATION FOR ESSAY

You may use the results of this research project to support your ideas in the essay you will write at the end of this section.

ACADEMIC VOCABULARY

Academic terms appear in blue on these pages. If these words are not familiar to you, use a dictionary to find their definitions. Then, use them as you speak and write.

Red Sox Get Ready to Celebrate 100 Years at Fenway

Larry Fine

BOSTON Fri Apr 20, 2012 5:52 a.m. EDT

(Reuters) - *Major League Baseball's oldest stadium hits the century mark on Friday, and the Boston Red Sox are throwing a grand 100th anniversary bash for fabled Fenway Park.*

Thursday brought the Red Sox faithful an invitation to a remarkable house party, with thousands of fans welcomed into the quirky old ballpark to savor an up-close view of the diamond treasure nestled in the middle of the bustling seaboard city.

Another 100 fans won pairs of Fenway game tickets by finding the prize inside balloons placed around town.

From the towering Green Monster wall in left with its old-time scoreboard, to the triangle in deepest center, to the Pesky Pole[1] down the short right-field line, Fenway Park is an instantly recognizable gem and the scene of a treasure trove of baseball history.

Babe Ruth broke into the major leagues with the Red Sox two years after John "Honey Fitz" Fitzgerald, the eventual grandfather of John F. Kennedy, Jr., tossed out the ceremonial first pitch at Fenway on April 20, 1912, as the proud mayor of Boston.

Ruth was a magnificent left-handed pitcher before evolving into the game's greatest slugger after being sold to the Yankees.

Fittingly, Friday's anniversary game is against the New Yorkers, reprising the inaugural Fenway Park game between the Red Sox and the

inaugural ▶
(in ô´gyə rəl) *adj.*
first in a series

---

1. **Pesky Pole** Fenway Park's right-field foul pole, named after famed Red Sox player Johnny Pesky.

New York Highlanders, who a year later changed their name to the Yankees.

The game will be played at 3:15 p.m., as on April 20, 1912, when the Red Sox won 7–6 in 11 innings, and the teams will dress in throwback uniforms for the contest following a ceremony celebrating the centennial.

The Red Sox and Yankees have been linked throughout the Fenway century.

The sale of Ruth to the Yankees in 1919 by Boston owner Harry Frazee, a theater producer who was short on funds, led to the end of a golden era for the Red

Sox, who had won four World Series crowns in seven years, and the rise of the Yankees.

The move came to be known as The Curse of the Bambino,[2] and Red Sox fans suffered through 86 years of near misses and bad baseball before a delicious deliverance in 2004.

Boston finally got back into the winner's circle by becoming the first MLB team ever to overcome a 3–0 playoffs **deficit**, sweeping the last four games from the Yankees to claim the American League title on their way to winning the World Series with a sweep of the Cardinals.

FENWAY FACELIFTS

Much of the charm of what has been called America's oldest living museum, built two years before the Chicago Cubs' home of Wrigley Field, can be traced to the necessities of fitting a ballpark into a piece of big city real estate.

While the footprint of the stadium remains, Fenway has had numerous facelifts over the decades. The last 10 years have seen some **deft** upgrading that added comfort and additional premium seats to the cozy, 37,000-seat stadium.

Changes were not so subtle in the early years after fires destroyed bleachers and grandstand seats and razed the wooden fence in left.

Tom Yawkey, who bought the club in 1933, began a major overhaul in January 1934 after another major fire.

Concrete bleachers replaced the wood bleachers in center field, and the 37-foot wooden left field wall was replaced by a 37-foot sheet metal structure.

Two years later a 23½-foot tall screen was added on top of the wall to protect the windows of buildings on adjoining Lansdowne Street.

GREEN MONSTER

When the wall's advertisements were covered by green paint in 1947, Fenway Park's signature feature—the Green Monster— was born.

Fenway has been home to such luminaries as Ted Williams, one of major league baseball's greatest hitters, Carl Yazstremski, Luis Tiant, Roger Clemens and Pedro Martinez, and to memories both painful and glorious of fly balls that carried over the Monster for home runs.

deficit ▶
(def´ə sit) *n.* amount that is less than the amount needed

deft ▶
(deft) *adj.* skillful in a quick, sure way

---

2. **The Curse of the Bambino** "The Bambino," one of Ruth's nicknames, means "The Babe" in Italian.

Ted Williams bats against the New York Yankees, 1960

There was 1975, when Carlton Fisk ended one of the greatest World Series games with his 12th inning, Game Six walk-off homer against the Cincinnati Reds down the left field line that he desperately waved fair as he danced down the first base line.

Three years later, a high fly ball from light-hitting Yankees shortstop Bucky Dent barely scraped over the wall for a three-run homer that broke the hearts of the home crowd as the Yankees won a one-game playoff to settle a division race that the Red Sox had led by 14½ games in mid-July.

Just two moments illustrating the agony and ecstasy that have shared the stage in a century of baseball at Fenway Park.

Close Reading Activities

READ

Comprehension

Reread all or part of the text to help you answer the following questions.

1. What are two similarities between the 100th anniversary game and the first game that was played at Fenway Park?

2. Why was 2004 a memorable year for the Boston Red Sox?

3. What is the Green Monster?

Research: Clarify Details Briefly research one unfamiliar detail from the article. Then, explain how your research sheds light on an aspect of the article.

Summarize Write an objective summary of the article. Objective summaries are free from opinion and evaluation.

Language Study

Selection Vocabulary Define these words from the article. Then, use each word in a sentence of your own.

- **inaugural**
- **deficit**
- **deft**

Literary Analysis

Reread the identified passage. Then, respond to the questions that follow:

> **Focus Passage** (p. 283)
>
> There was 1975, when Carlton Fisk … in a century of baseball at Fenway Park.

Key Ideas and Details

1. Which team won each game the author describes in the first and second paragraphs of the bracketed text?

Craft and Structure

2. (a) Analyze: Cite three to four specific terms the author uses to describe events of two notable baseball games.
(b) Draw Conclusions: What can you conclude about the likely audience for this article, based on those details?

Integration of Knowledge and Ideas

3. Analyze: In what way does the last sentence of the passage reflect the overall message of the article? Support your response.

Figurative Language

Writers and speakers use figurative language, such as creative comparisons, to create vivid images and emphasize key points. Note specific comparisons in the article.

1. Baseball (a) What is the writer comparing when he says, "Fenway Park is an instantly recognizable gem and the scene of a treasure trove of baseball history"? **(b)** What idea does this comparison express?

2. Identify one other creative comparison in the article and explain its effect.

DISCUSS • RESEARCH • WRITE

From Text to Topic **Group Discussion**

Compose a quick written response to the following passage. Then share and discuss your response with a small group of classmates. Support your ideas with examples from the text and from your own experience.

> While the footprint of the stadium remains, Fenway has had numerous facelifts over the decades. . . . Two years later a 23½-foot tall screen was added on top of the wall to protect the windows of buildings on adjoining Lansdowne Street. (p. 282)

Research **Investigate the Topic**

Popular Stadiums Fenway Park may be the oldest major league ballpark still in use, but many sports stadiums are well-loved and **unique** in their own ways.

Assignment

Conduct research to identify and learn about a ballpark or sports stadium that interests you. Consult electronic and print resources. Take clear notes and carefully identify your sources so that you can easily access the information later. Share your findings in an **informal presentation** to a group of students.

Writing to Sources **Argument**

Fenway has lasted for more than 100 years, but some fans think the park should be replaced with a newer facility.

Assignment

Write an **argument** in which you take a position on whether or not Fenway Park should be replaced with a new, modern stadium. Follow these steps:

- Introduce Fenway Park and its history.
- Explain the issue and clearly state your **position**.
- Support your claim with evidence from the text.
- Conclude by reflecting on the issue and restating your claim.

QUESTIONS FOR DISCUSSION

1. How has Fenway Park both changed and stayed the same since it opened in 1912?

2. How do the reasons for upgrades made in the 1930s compare with the reasons for more recent upgrades?

PREPARATION FOR ESSAY

You may use the results of this research project to support your ideas in the essay you will write at the end of this section.

ACADEMIC VOCABULARY

Academic terms appear in blue on these pages. If these words are not familiar to you, use a dictionary to find their definitions. Then, use them as you speak and write about the text.

Why We Love Baseball

Players, management and fans chime in on Valentine's Day   By Mark Newman / MLB.com

A record 76 million fans attended Major League Baseball games in 2006, and all signs point toward yet another single-season mark in 2007. On this Valentine's Day, MLB.com decided to investigate this torrid love affair more closely by asking people around the game this simple question: "Why do you love baseball?"

Yankees shortstop Derek Jeter: "I think because everybody can relate. You don't have to be seven feet tall; you don't have to be a certain size to play. Baseball is up and down. I think life's like that sometimes, you know. Back and forth, up and down, you're going through this grind. I think people like watching it. Baseball's like a soap opera every day."

Ernie Banks, Cubs legend and Hall of Famer: "It's just life. When I think about baseball, it's just life. It's really the way life is. It requires a lot of mental capacity to be involved in it. It creates a lot of joy for people and memories for people who follow it. It's a family. You like it because it's a family. You started with it and know all these people—it's family, it's friends, it's fun, it's a beautiful game. All in all, baseball is amazing. I wish everybody could play it for at least two years. I wish everybody—men and women."

Indians manager Eric Wedge: "The game gets inside you. It becomes a part of who you are, and you don't know anything different. It's just something you feel passionate about. If you really feel that strong about something and you feel something that special, it's really hard to put it into words. For me, the love of the game is a given. It's been the one constant that I've known, for as far back as I can remember."

A's general manager Billy Beane: "What I love is that when it is Valentine's Day you're getting real close to going to Arizona, and to me there is something real pure about Spring Training. Most of us are getting out of a long winter, and it's nice to get outside and be in the sunshine in February. To me, Spring Training is my favorite time of year for baseball. It's the most relaxing time as an executive."

Phillies first baseman Ryan Howard: "I think it's just the overall atmosphere: to be able to come out in the summer, nice weather—you can bring your kids and make it a family event. People just can come out and have fun."

Joel Kweskin, 56, White Sox fan based in Charlotte, N.C.: "It's unique unto itself. Football, basketball and hockey are variations of the same concept—back and forth in a linear progression to score a goal. Baseball, however, is mapped out on the field unlike any other sport. A running back or return specialist can run 100 yards, tops; a baserunner legging out an inside-the-park homer runs 20 yards farther. Baseball is the most democratic of sports— any size can play, and because the ball is not controlled by the offense but rather the defense, every player at any given time is involved in a play. Along with the anecdotally accepted **premise** that hitting a pitched baseball is the single most difficult thing to do in sports, so might be fielding a 175-mph line drive or grounder down the line. I love baseball because it is the greatest game ever invented."

◀ **premise**
(pre′məs) n.
something assumed or taken for granted

Devil Rays manager Joe Maddon: "Makes you feel like a kid again every day, you do it every day. And that's what makes it so attractive."

Giants bench coach Ron Wotus: "Baseball has always

been in my blood, and there's nothing like being on grass outdoors, playing the game. It's a great feeling just to hit the ball and have some success. The pace is slower and it's a thinking man's game, and there are so many different facets of it. And because so many people have played it, from Little League on up, they can still give their opinion on what's happening on the field, what kind of pitch should be thrown next."

Former Royals star Willie Wilson: "The first thing is, I don't think there's any criteria for size, so anybody can play. I think people can relate. A lot of people never played football; basketball, you've gotta be tall and be able to jump. But baseball is a game where you pick up a bat and a ball, and you catch it, you swing the bat and you hit the ball. Most people have played softball or some kind of baseball, so they can relate to the sport. For me, that's why I think America just embraces baseball, man."

A's outfielder Milton Bradley: "I just love getting together

with a group of 25 guys and everybody is working together on a common goal. I like competition whatever the sport. Baseball for me is the hardest thing to do. That's why I **ventured** into baseball. It's more difficult than any other sport and I just liked the difficulty of it. I like a challenge."

Cyn Donnelly, 38-year-old Boston author of Red Sox Chick, the most popular fan-written MLBlog: "I love baseball because my parents love baseball and even as a kid I knew it could be something that connected us no matter what else was going on in our lives. I love watching young players come up, I love watching mediocre players do well, even if only for a game. I love watching a struggling player come out of a slump. I love seeing the unexpected, which happens an awful lot in baseball. Unlike any of the other major sports, baseball gives a team many chances to do well. In a three-game series with the opposing team, you can lose one game and still come out of the series up. It makes every minute of the game 'important'. Baseball is a wonderful **diversion** from my real life. Especially when my real life isn't going quite the way I planned."

ventured ▶
(ven´chərd) v. dared to do something risky

diversion ▶
(də vʉr´zhən) n. recreation; distraction from everyday tasks

Royals outfielder David DeJesus: "It's such a team game. You can't rely on one guy to win the game. You build relationships, you make good friends out here, and you're having fun with 25 guys from different places all over the country. I grew up loving it because my Dad always loved it. We practiced together, we watched baseball games together, so it's one of those things I've always been around."

Royals outfielder Joey Gathright: "I can't really put it into words. It's not something I really grew up around in Mississippi. All they do is play football. But, when I was a kid, I was in awe of Rickey Henderson and Ken Griffey Jr., so I just fell in love with those guys and later I fell in love with baseball."

The Lealie family of Spring Valley, Calif.: During the recent FriarFest event, Jazmine, 4, tugged at father Marc all the way into PETCO Park, with 2-year-old brother Quincy bouncing in stride, eyes bright and alive. "Man, she loves this place," said Marc, formerly of Chicago. "I mean, Jazmine really loves PETCO Park, everything about it. These two are Junior Padres now. They come to games every Sunday. Her favorite player is Mike Cameron."

Lorenzo Bundy, manager of Mexico at the Caribbean Series and manager of the Dodgers' Triple-A Las Vegas affiliate: "I love the camaraderie and being around the guys. There is nothing like coming to the park and smelling the grass every day. It's the greatest game in the world … and on any given day anybody can win. That's how the ball bounces and that's fun. They are probably going to have to bury me in this uniform."

ABOUT THE AUTHOR

Mark Newman

Mark Newman has been a vice president of Nascar.com and *Sporting News* and the founder of two Internet firms. As Enterprise Editor at MLB.com, he has interviewed dozens of baseball professionals and fans. Newman is also a lifetime honorary member of the Baseball Writers Association of America.

Close Reading Activities

READ

Comprehension

Reread all or part of the text to help you answer the following questions.

1. What is the connection between the timing of this article and its topic?

2. What observation do multiple speakers make about the physical size requirements of baseball?

3. Identify three reasons speakers give for loving baseball.

Research: Clarify Details Choose at least one unfamiliar detail from this article and briefly research it. Then, explain how your research helps you understand the article.

Summarize Write an objective summary of the article. Describe the nature of the article and state key ideas that are mentioned in at least two comments.

Language Study

Selection Vocabulary Define these words from the article, and then write a paragraph that includes all three words.

- **premise**
- **ventured**
- **diversion**

Literary Analysis

Reread the identified passage. Then, respond to the questions that follow.

> **Focus Passage** *(p. 287)*
>
> **Joel Kweskin, 56 ...** the greatest game ever invented.

Key Ideas and Details

1. What characteristics do football, basketball, and hockey have in common?

Craft and Structure

2. **(a) Infer:** What is the main idea in Joel Kweskin's response? **(b) Connect:** Cite three details Kweskin uses to support his main idea. **(c) Evaluate:** Does Kweskin support his claim effectively? Explain.

Integration of Knowledge and Ideas

3. **Compare and Contrast:** How are Kweskin's remarks similar to and different from the remarks of the speakers quoted earlier in the article?

Word Choice

Word choice can have a powerful effect on the strength and meaning of a writer's or speaker's message. Highly charged words bring to mind strong feelings. Reread this article, noting each speaker's word choice.

1. **Baseball** What do you think Derek Jeter means when he says, "Baseball's like a soap opera ..."? Support your answer.

2. Ron Wotus says, "it's a thinking man's game." What impression about baseball do these words create?

DISCUSS • RESEARCH • WRITE

From Text to Topic **Group Discussion**

Discuss the comment from Eric Wedge with a small group of classmates. Take notes during the discussion. Contribute your own ideas, and support them with examples from the text.

> "The game gets inside you…. as far back as I can remember." (p. 287)

Research **Investigate the Topic**

Baseball in Literature The love of baseball has inspired many works of literature.

Assignment

Conduct research to find poems, novels, memoirs, and essays about baseball. Take clear notes and carefully identify your **sources**. Record your findings in an **annotated bibliography**. Then, write a paragraph in which you compare and contrast the ways in which writers of texts in different genres approach the topic of baseball. Tell which genre you found most useful in your research and explain why.

Writing to Sources **Explanatory Text**

"Why We Love Baseball" presents the reasons why fans and players love baseball. The article makes clear the fact that different people enjoy things for different reasons.

Assignment

Write a **reflective essay** in which you describe your thoughts and feelings about a favorite interest or activity and explain why you like it. Follow these steps:

- Introduce the activity, briefly stating why it is interesting or fun.
- Present the reasons you like the activity, supporting each reason with personal examples, logic, **facts**, or details.
- Use transitional words and phrases to help you move smoothly from point to point.
- Conclude by reflecting upon the impact the activity has had on you. Make a connection between your feelings and the feelings expressed by the people quoted in the Web article.

QUESTIONS FOR DISCUSSION

1. What does Wedge mean by "The game gets inside you"?

2. Does Wedge's argument appeal to emotion or to reason? Which do you think makes a stronger argument? Why?

PREPARATION FOR ESSAY

You may use the results of this **research** project to support your ideas in the essay you will write at the end of this section.

ACADEMIC VOCABULARY

Academic terms appear in blue on these pages. If these words are not familiar to you, use a dictionary to find their definitions. Then, use them as you speak and write about the text.

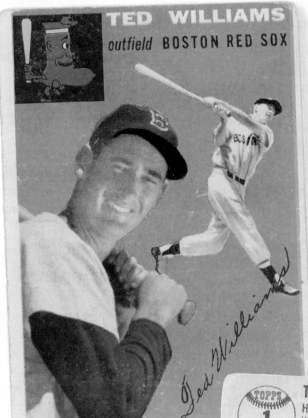

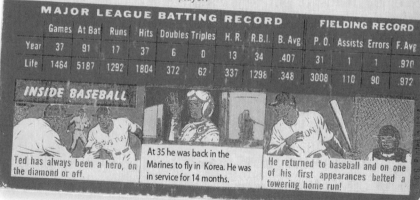

THEODORE SAMUEL WILLIAMS *outfield* **BOSTON RED SOX**

Height: 6' 3"
Weight: 205
Bats Left
Throws Right
Home: So. Miami, Fla.
Born: October 30, 1918

Ted is one of the greatest hitters of all time! In '41, he hit .406, the only time any Big Leaguer hit over .400 since 1930. He led the A.L. in Homers in 1941-42-47-49. Named the Most Valuable Player in '46 and '49, Ted starred in 9 All-Star games, hitting .407. He has the highest Lifetime B.A. of any active player.

MAJOR LEAGUE BATTING RECORD — **FIELDING RECORD**

	Games	At Bat	Runs	Hits	Doubles	Triples	H.R.	R.B.I.	B. Avg	P.O.	Assists	Errors	F. Avg
Year	37	91	17	37	6	0	13	34	.407	31	1	1	.970
Life	1464	5187	1292	1804	372	62	337	1298	.348	3008	110	90	.972

INSIDE BASEBALL

Ted has always been a hero, on the diamond or off.

At 35 he was back in the Marines to fly in Korea. He was in service for 14 months.

He returned to baseball and on one of his first appearances belted a towering home run!

READ • WRITE

Comprehension

Review the baseball card to answer these questions.

1. Identify Ted Williams's team and position.
2. Was Williams still playing baseball when this card was issued? Cite evidence to support your answer.

Critical Analysis

Key Ideas and Details

1. **Interpret:** Does the information on the card emphasize Williams's career as a hitter or as a fielder? Explain.
2. **Draw Conclusions:** Did Williams get on base in the majority of games he played? Support your answer.

Craft and Structure

3. **(a) Interpret:** Describe the tone, or attitude, of the paragraph and captions on the back of the card. **(b) Analyze:** What specific details **reveal** the tone?

Integration of Knowledge and Ideas

4. **Draw Conclusions:** Do you think this baseball card holds a high value for collectors? Explain why or why not.

Writing to Sources **Narrative**

Write a brief **journal entry** from the point of view of a fan who recently watched Ted Williams hit a home run during a Red Sox game. Compare and **contrast** Williams's performance with that of other players. Describe the mood of the crowd and your character's feelings when Williams hit the home run. Use data and details from the baseball card, the other texts in this section, and your own experiences. Follow these steps:

• Describe the setting, characters, and events.
• Include sensory and concrete details to enrich your descriptions.
• Conclude by explaining your character's thoughts about the game and Ted Williams's performance.

Assessment: Synthesis

Speaking and Listening: **Group Discussion**

Baseball and Knowledge The texts in this section vary in genre, length, style, and perspective. However, all of the texts relate in some way to America's love of baseball, as a game and as an institution. The subject of American baseball and the traditions that surround it is fundamentally related to the Big Question this unit addresses: **What is important to know?**

▲ Refer to the selections you read in Part 3 as you complete the activities on this assessment.

Assignment

Conduct discussions. With a small group of classmates, conduct a discussion about people's love and knowledge of baseball. Refer to the texts in this section, other texts you have read, and your personal experience and knowledge to support your ideas. Begin your discussion by addressing the following questions:

- Why is baseball in all its forms—from T-ball to the major leagues—important to Americans of all ages?
- What traditions have grown around baseball, and how do they affect the people who play and love the game?
- How can knowing about the game of baseball, its history, and its traditions help us understand ourselves?

Summarize and present your ideas. After you have fully explored the topic, summarize your discussion for the class.

Criteria for Success

✓ **Organizes the group effectively**
Appoint a group leader and a timekeeper. The group leader should present the discussion questions. The timekeeper should make sure the discussion takes no longer than 20 minutes.

✓ **Maintains focus of discussion**
As a group, stay on topic and avoid straying into other subject areas.

✓ **Involves all participants equally and fully**
No one person should monopolize the conversation. Rather, everyone should take turns speaking and contributing ideas.

✓ **Follows the rules for collegial discussion**
As each group member speaks, others should listen carefully. Build on one another's ideas, and support viewpoints and opinions with sound reasoning and evidence. Express disagreement respectfully.

USE NEW VOCABULARY

As you speak and share ideas, work to use the vocabulary words you have learned in this unit. The more you use new words, the more you will "own" them.

Writing: **Narrative**

Baseball and Knowledge All writing is rooted in the author's knowledge and experience. Sports, such as baseball, play a large role in the lives of many Americans.

Assignment

In an **autobiographical narrative**, describe a situation in which your level of knowledge about a sport affected you either positively or negatively. Focus on a time when you either participated in or observed the sport. Present a sequence of significant events and thoughts that, taken together, create a picture of an experience that had a lasting effect upon you.

Criteria for Success

Purpose/Focus
✓ **Connects specific incidents with larger ideas**
Make meaningful connections between your experiences and the texts you have read in this section.

✓ **Clearly conveys the significance of the story**
Provide a conclusion in which you reflect on what you experienced.

Organization
✓ **Sequences events logically**
Structure your narrative so that individual events build on one another to create a coherent whole.

Development of Ideas/Elaboration
✓ **Supports insights**
Include both personal examples and details from the texts you have read in this section.

✓ **Uses narrative techniques effectively**
Even though an autobiographical narrative is nonfiction, it may include storytelling elements like those found in fiction. Consider using dialogue to help readers "hear" how characters sound.

Language
✓ **Uses description effectively**
Use sensory language and vivid descriptive details.

Conventions
✓ **Does not have errors**
Correct any errors in grammar, spelling, and punctuation.

WRITE TO EXPLORE

Writing is a way to clarify what you feel and think. This means that you may change your mind or get new ideas as you work. Allowing for this will improve your final draft.

Writing to Sources: Explanatory Text

Baseball and Knowledge The related readings in this section represent a wide range of knowledge and insight about the game of baseball, its traditions, and its players. The selections raise questions, such as the following:

- What can we learn about our society from baseball?
- What draws people to a sport such as baseball? Is it the competition, the game itself, a specific team, traditions surrounding the sport, or a combination of these factors?
- How can we benefit from participating in sports such as baseball?

Focus on the question that intrigues you the most, and then complete the following assignment.

Assignment

Write a **comparison-and-contrast essay** in which you explain how two or more authors in this section portray baseball history and tradition. As you analyze each selection, pay particular attention to the details each author includes to support his or her claims. Clearly present, develop, and support your ideas with examples and details from the texts.

INCORPORATE RESEARCH

In your essay, use information you gathered as you completed the brief research assignments related to the selections in this section.

Prewriting and Planning

Choose texts. Review the texts in this section to determine which ones you will cite in your essay. Select at least two selections that will provide strong material to support comparisons and contrasts.

Gather details and identify key ideas. Use a chart like the one shown to develop your key ideas.

Focus Question: What can we learn about our society from baseball?

Text	Passage	Notes
"Jackie Robinson: Justice at Last"	The national pastime was loved by all America, but the major leagues were for white men only.	Authors imply criticism of major league baseball
"Memories of an All-American Girl"	The girls received lessons on how to charm a date, wear makeup and skirts, and sip tea like a lady.	Author reports on an unjust situation objectively, without judging it

Example key idea: While some authors view injustices in baseball as a reflection of society at large, others blame organized baseball for injustices in the sport.

Drafting

Plan your ideas and support. Create an informal outline or list of ideas you want to present. Decide where you will include facts, quotations, and examples to support each point.

Organize to show comparisons and contrasts. Choose an organizational structure that will clearly show similarities and differences. You might use the block method, in which you present all of the details about one of the selections, then all the details about the other selection. Alternatively, you might use the point-by-point method, in which you discuss one feature of both selections, then another feature of both selections, and so on.

Frame and connect ideas. Consider beginning your essay with a compelling story or quotation to capture your readers' interest. Use transitional words and phrases to link the major sections of your essay and to clarify the relationships among your main ideas and supporting details. Write a strong conclusion that sums up your key points.

Revising and Editing

Focus on comparative and superlative adjectives. Review your essay to be sure you have used adjectives correctly. Use comparative adjectives—such as *older* and *more popular*—to compare two things. Use superlative adjectives—such as *oldest* and *most popular*—to compare three or more things.

CITE RESEARCH CORRECTLY

When you quote from a source directly, use quotation marks to indicate that the words are not your own.

Self-Evaluation Rubric

Use the following criteria to evaluate the effectiveness of your essay.

Criteria	Rating Scale			
	not very .... very			
Purpose/Focus Introduces a specific topic; provides a concluding section that follows from and supports the information or explanation presented	1	2	3	4
Organization Organizes complex ideas, concepts, and information to make important connections and distinctions; clearly shows comparisons and contrasts, uses appropriate and varied transitions to link the major sections, create cohesion, and clarify relationships among ideas	1	2	3	4
Development of Ideas/Elaboration Develops the topic with well-chosen, relevant, and sufficient facts, extended definitions, concrete details, quotations, or other information and examples appropriate to the audience's knowledge of the topic	1	2	3	4
Language Uses precise language and domain-specific vocabulary to manage the complexity of the topic; establishes and maintains a formal style and objective tone	1	2	3	4
Conventions Uses correct conventions of grammar, spelling, and punctuation	1	2	3	4

Independent Reading

Titles for Extended Reading

In this unit, you have read texts in a variety of genres, including literary nonfiction. Continue to read on your own. Select works that you enjoy, but challenge yourself to explore new topics, new authors, and works of increasing depth and complexity. The titles suggested below will help you get started.

INFORMATIONAL TEXT

Boy: Tales of Childhood
by Roald Dahl

Read this collection of funny—and true—stories to learn what Roald Dahl found important and fascinating in his own childhood. This **autobiography** shows that life can be just as comical and exciting as fiction.

Zlata's Diary: A Child's Life in Wartime Sarajevo
by Zlata Filipović

During the war in Bosnia and Herzegovina in the early 1990s, Zlata kept a **diary** recording the desperate situations her family faced in Sarajevo. Her diary provides an honest, unique view of what it is like to live during a war.

Adams on Adams
by John Adams   **EXEMPLAR TEXT**

Editor Paul M. Zall explores John Adams's own writings to present this founding father's life and worldview. This **autobiographical** collection includes Adams's "Letter on Thomas Jefferson."

Discoveries: Digging for Answers

Build your knowledge in many subject areas as you read these **essays**, including "Searching for Pompeii," "Identifying Birds," "The Story of American Sign Language," and "The Measure of a Good Cook."

LITERATURE

A Wrinkle in Time
by Madeleine L'Engle
Square Fish, 2007   **EXEMPLAR TEXT**

In this **fantasy novel**, two children, along with a friend, set out on a quest through time and space to find their missing father. In their travels, they become part of a galactic battle between good and evil.

The Number Devil: A Mathematical Adventure
by Hans Magnus Enzensberger
Granta Books, 2000   **EXEMPLAR TEXT**

In this book, which is part math instruction and part good-humored **fantasy**, a boy who dislikes math dreams of meeting a number devil who teaches basic mathematical concepts in an entertaining way.

ONLINE TEXT SET

FOLK TALE
Why Monkeys Live in Trees Julius Lester

EDITORIAL
Jake Wood Baseball Is the Start of Something Special Reginald T. Dogan

POEM
Wilbur Wright and Orville Wright Rosemary and Stephen Vincent Benét

Preparing to Read Complex Texts

Attentive Reading As you read on your own, ask yourself questions like these to enrich your reading experience.

When reading literary nonfiction, ask yourself…

Comprehension: **Key Ideas and Details**

- Is the author writing about a personal experience or a topic he or she has studied? In either case, what are my expectations about the work?
- Are the ideas the author expresses important? Why or why not?
- Did the author live at a different time and place than the present? If so, how does that affect his or her choice of topic and attitude?
- Does the author express beliefs that are very different from mine? If so, how does that affect what I understand and feel about the text?

Text Analysis: **Craft and Structure**

- Does the author organize ideas so that I can understand them? If not, what is unclear?
- Does the author give me a new way of looking at a topic? If so, how? If not, why?
- Is the author an expert on the topic? How do I know?
- Does the author use a variety of evidence that makes sense? If not, what is weak?
- Does the author use words in ways that are both interesting and clear?

Connections: **Integration of Knowledge and Ideas**

- Does the work seem believable? Why or why not?
- Do I agree or disagree with the author's arguments or ideas? Why or why not?
- Does this work remind me of others I have read? If so, how?
- Does this work make me want to read more about this topic or explore a related topic? Why or why not?

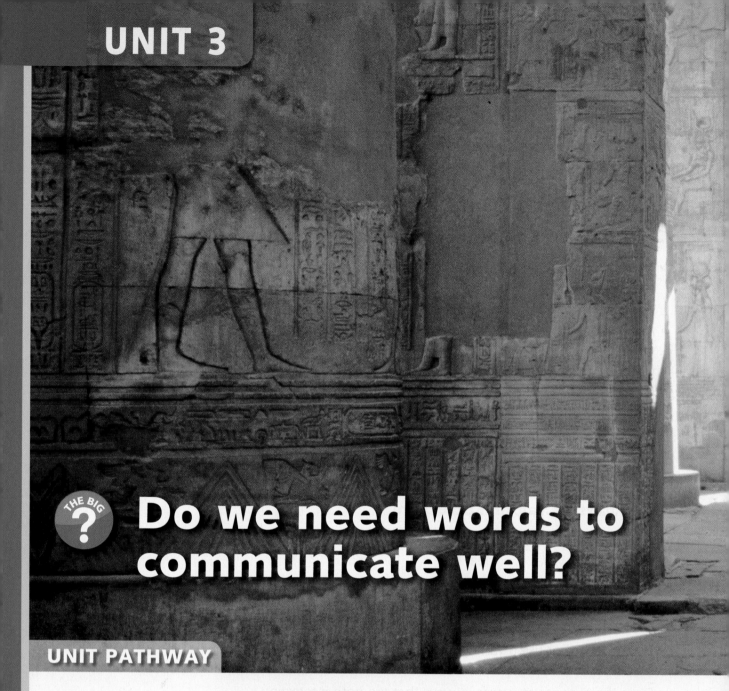

UNIT 3

THE BIG
? **Do we need words to communicate well?**

UNIT PATHWAY

PART 1
SETTING EXPECTATIONS

- INTRODUCING THE BIG QUESTION
- CLOSE READING WORKSHOP

PART 2
TEXT ANALYSIS
GUIDED EXPLORATION

RHYTHM AND RHYME

PART 3
TEXT SET
DEVELOPING INSIGHT

DETERMINATION

PART 4
DEMONSTRATING INDEPENDENCE

- INDEPENDENT READING
- ONLINE TEXT SET

CLOSE READING TOOL

Use this tool to practice the close reading strategies you learn.

STUDENT eTEXT

Bring learning to life with audio, video, and interactive tools.

ONLINE WRITER'S NOTEBOOK

Easily capture notes and complete assignments online.

Find all Digital Resources at **pearsonrealize.com.**

Do we need words to communicate well?

To communicate means to interact with others to promote understanding. Often, we use words to communicate our thoughts and feelings. However, we also use nonverbal communication methods that do not depend on words. An expression such as a smile or a frown can reveal your feelings. A gesture such as a wave or a nod can send a clear message, too.

Exploring the Big Question

Collaboration: One-on-One Discussion Start thinking about the Big Question by identifying various ways that we communicate with one another. List ways that people share thoughts and feelings. Describe examples of communicating information in the following situations:

- thanking someone for a gift
- asking for something you need or want
- persuading someone to change his or her mind
- sharing an important wish or dream
- listening to a friend share a difficult problem

Share ideas with a partner. Highlight examples that use nonverbal communication. Which of these examples are *at least* as effective as using words?

Connecting to the Literature Each reading in this unit will give you additional insight into the Big Question. As you read, consider the different methods authors use to communicate their ideas.

Vocabulary

Acquire and Use Academic Vocabulary The term "academic vocabulary" refers to words you typically encounter in scholarly and literary texts and in technical and business writing. Review the definitions of these academic vocabulary words.

communicate (kə myoo´ ni kāt´) v. share thoughts or feelings, usually in words

correspond (kôr´ ə spänd´) v. communicate with by letter; agree with

quote (kwōt) v. use a speaker's or writer's words

reveal (ri vēl´) v. show; uncover

symbolize (sim´ bə līz´) v. stand for

visual (vizh´ oo əl) adj. able to be seen with the eyes

Gather Vocabulary Knowledge Additional vocabulary words are listed below. Categorize the words by deciding whether you know each one well, know it a little bit, or do not know it at all.

connection	gesture	nonverbal
dialogue	language	share
expression	message	verbal

Then, do the following:

1. Write the definitions of the words you know.
2. If a word sounds familiar but you are not sure of its meaning, write down what you think the word means.
3. Then, using a print or an online dictionary, look up the meanings of the words you do not know or are not certain of. Write down their meanings.
4. Use all of the words in a brief paragraph about the various ways you communicate with others in your daily life.

Close Reading Workshop

In this workshop you will learn an approach to reading that will deepen your understanding of literature and will help you better appreciate author's craft. The workshop includes models for close reading, discussion, research, and writing. After you have reviewed the strategies and models, practice your skills with the Independent Practice selection.

CLOSE READING: POETRY

Use these strategies as you read the poems in this unit.

Comprehension: Key Ideas and Details

- Read first to unlock basic meaning.
- Use context clues to help you determine the meanings of unfamiliar words. Consult a dictionary, if necessary.
- Identify unfamiliar details that you might need to clarify through research.

- Distinguish between what is stated directly and what must be inferred.

Ask yourself questions such as these:
- Who is the speaker in this poem?
- What is the speaker describing?
- What is the tone of the poem?

Text Analysis: Craft and Structure

- Analyze how sound devices, rhythm, and rhyme add meaning to the poem.
- Identify how the poet uses figurative language to express familiar ideas in new ways.
- Consider how the poem's structure relates to its meaning.

Ask yourself questions such as these:
- How do the poet's descriptive words appeal to my senses and help me determine the poem's theme?
- How does the poet's word choice create an atmosphere, or mood?

Connections: Integration of Knowledge and Ideas

- Look for relationships among key ideas. Identify causes and effects, and comparisons and contrasts.
- Connect ideas to determine the poem's theme.
- Compare and contrast this work with other poems you have read.

Ask yourself questions such as these:
- How has this work increased my knowledge of a subject, author, or theme?
- What images are most important to the poem's meaning?

Read

As you read this poem, take note of the annotations that model ways to closely read the text.

Reading Model

"Twelfth Song of Thunder" from the Navajo Mountain Chant [1]

The voice that beautifies the land!
The voice above,
The voice of thunder
Within the dark cloud [2]
5   Again and again it sounds,
The voice that beautifies the land.

The voice that beautifies the land!
The voice below,
The voice of the grasshopper
10   Among the plants [3]
Again and again it sounds,
The voice that beautifies the land. [4]

Key Ideas and Details
1 The title suggests that the Navajo perform a number of chants about nature. This information may lead you to conclude that nature is important to Navajo culture.

Craft and Structure
2 Throughout the poem, the poet uses personification to give the human quality of a voice to elements of nature that are not human.

Integration of Knowledge and Ideas
3 Each stanza focuses on details of the natural world, such as "thunder," "dark cloud," "grasshopper," and "plants." The stanzas work together to convey the poem's larger theme: Nature's beauty is far-reaching.

Craft and Structure
4 The repetition of these lines at the end of each stanza, and the repetition of *voice* throughout the poem creates a musical quality and rhythm that celebrate the sounds of nature.

Discuss

Sharing your own ideas and listening to the ideas of others can deepen your understanding of a text and help you look at a topic in a whole new way. As you participate in collaborative discussions, work to have a genuine exchange in which classmates build upon one another's ideas. Support your points with evidence and ask meaningful questions.

Discussion Model

Student 1: The word *chant* in the title made me think about how the poem is supposed to be read. A chant seems different from a typical poem. When I think of a chant, I think of something with a rhythm that a group of people might speak together.

Student 2: I think you're right. The poem seems like it's meant to be read out loud. The way some words are repeated, like "voice" and "again," gives the chant rhythm, and it seems almost like a song.

Student 3: I also notice the word *twelfth* in the title. That might mean this chant is part of a large ceremony, or maybe one of many chants about thunder or nature. I wonder what that ceremony is about.

Research

Targeted research can clarify unfamiliar details and shed light on various aspects of a text. Consider questions that arise in your mind as you read, and use those questions as the basis for research.

Research Model

Questions: *What is the purpose and history of the Navajo Mountain Chant?*

Key Words for Internet Search: Navajo Mountain Chant + Navajo ceremony

Results: Encyclopedia2, Navajo Mountain Chant; Internet Sacred Text Archive

What I Learned: The Navajo Mountain Chant is a nine-day ceremony that is performed in the late winter, sometime after the season of thunderstorms but before the arrival of spring. The chant marks the change from one season to another. It also is a healing ceremony to cure diseases and mend troubled human relationships.

Write

Writing about a text will deepen your understanding of it and will also allow you to share your ideas more formally with others. The following model essay analyzes the use of various poetic elements in "Twelfth Song of Thunder" and cites evidence to support the main ideas.

Writing Model: Argument

Poetic Elements in "Twelfth Song of Thunder"

"Twelfth Song of Thunder" expresses the theme that the beauty of nature is all around us. The poet develops this theme through the use of poetic elements. Repetition, descriptive language, personification, and rhythm all highlight nature's beauty.

The poet repeats key words, phrases, and lines. The word "voice" appears eight times. The phrase "again and again" is used twice. The line "The voice that beautifies the land" is used four times in the twelve-line poem. This constant repetition focuses the reader's attention on the idea of nature's beauty, and adds a meaningful rhythm that celebrates the sounds of nature.

The poet also uses imagery to appeal to the senses and highlight nature's beauty. The description of the "dark cloud" in line 4 appeals to the reader's sense of sight and helps set the scene. In addition, the mention of the "voice of the grasshopper" in line 9 appeals to the reader's sense of hearing. These examples of imagery suggest that nature's beauty can be appreciated by different senses.

Perhaps the strongest poetic element is the use of personification, or the way in which nonhuman subjects are given human qualities. Thunder clearly makes a sound, and so does a grasshopper, but we do not usually call these sounds "voices." However, the poet does give voices to the thunder and the grasshopper. Giving human characteristics to elements of nature makes a connection that helps us relate to nature.

As with many other chants, this one is meant to be spoken or sung out loud. A Navajo medicine man performs this meaningful chant at sunset on the last day of the nine-day Mountain Chant ceremony to celebrate the seasons and to cure illnesses. The pattern of beats and repetition of words and lines give the chant a powerful musical quality that rejoices in the sounds of nature. The descriptive language and use of personification show the all-reaching beauty of nature.

The writer begins by stating a claim about the theme of the poem. This is an effective way to structure a short response.

Specific details from the poem support the writer's claim.

The writer provides an important example to reinforce a key idea.

In the conclusion, the writer includes evidence from research to make a connection between the purpose and theme of the poem.

As you read the following poems, apply the close reading strategies you have learned. You may need to read the poems multiple times.

Meet the Author

A native of Fresno, California, **Gary Soto** (b. 1952) is an award-winning poet and author of children's books. Much of his work focuses on life in Mexican-American communities and is based on his own childhood and experiences as a young adult.

CLOSE READING TOOL

Read and respond to this selection online using the **Close Reading Tool**.

"Oranges"
by Gary Soto

The first time I walked
With a girl, I was twelve,
Cold, and weighted down
With two oranges in my jacket.
5 December. Frost cracking
Beneath my steps, my breath
Before me, then gone,
As I walked toward
Her house, the one whose
10 Porch light burned yellow
Night and day, in any weather.
A dog barked at me, until
She came out pulling
At her gloves, face bright
15 With rouge[1]. I smiled,
Touched her shoulder, and led
Her down the street, across
A used car lot and a line
Of newly planted trees,
20 Until we were breathing
Before a drugstore. We
Entered, the tiny bell
Bringing a saleslady
Down a narrow aisle of goods.
25 I turned to the candies
Tiered[2] like bleachers,
And asked what she wanted—

---

1. **rouge** (rōo zh) *n.* a reddish cosmetic used to color the cheeks.
2. **tiered** (tē r´d) *adj.* arranged in levels, one above another.

Light in her eyes, a smile
Starting at the corners
30 Of her mouth. I fingered
A nickel in my pocket,
And when she lifted a chocolate
That cost a dime,
I didn't say anything.
35 I took the nickel from
My pocket, then an orange,
And set them quietly on
The counter. When I looked up,
The lady's eyes met mine,
40 And held them, knowing
Very well what it was all
About.
            Outside,
A few cars hissing past,
45 Fog hanging like old
Coats between the trees.
I took my girl's hand
In mine for two blocks,
Then released it to let
50 Her unwrap the chocolate.
I peeled my orange
That was so bright against
The gray of December
That, from some distance,
55 Someone might have thought
I was making a fire in my hands.

"Ode to Family Photographs"

by Gary Soto

This is the pond, and these are my feet.
This is the rooster, and this is more of my feet.

Mamá was never good at pictures.

This is a statue of a famous general who lost an
    arm
5 And this is me with my head cut off.

This is a trash can chained to a gate,
This is my father with his eyes half-closed.

This is a photograph of my sister
And a giraffe looking over her
    shoulder.

10 This is our car's front bumper.
This is a bird with a pretzel in its
    beak.
This is my brother Pedro standing
    on one leg on a rock,
With a smear of chocolate on his
    face.

Mamá sneezed when she looked
15 *Behind the camera: the snapshots*
    are blurry,
The angles dizzy as a spin on a
    merry-go-round.

But we had fun when Mamá picked
    up the camera.
How can I tell?
Each of us laughing hard.
20 Can you see? I have candy in my
    mouth.

Close Reading Activities

Read

Comprehension: Key Ideas and Details

1. **(a) Deduce:** In "Oranges," why does the speaker put the nickel and the orange on the counter? **(b) Interpret:** What does the saleslady's response suggest about her attitude toward the speaker?

2. **(a)** Identify details the speaker uses to describe the girl in "Oranges." **(b) Interpret:** What do these details tell you about his attitude toward the girl?

3. **(a) Identify:** In "Ode to Family Photographs," why does the poet repeat the phrase "This is"? **(b) Interpret:** What is the meaning of the images in lines 5 and 7?

4. **(a)** Describe the speaker's mother's ability as a photographer. **(b) Interpret:** How does the speaker feel about the photographs? How do you know?

Text Analysis: Craft and Structure

5. **(a)** In "Ode to Family Photographs," what is the difference between the sentences in italics and the other lines? **(b) Analyze:** How is the last stanza different from the rest of the poem?

6. **Compare and Contrast:** How are "Oranges" and "Ode to Family Photographs" similar and different? Consider each poem's speaker, descriptive language, and structure.

7. **(a) Analyze:** Find a comparison that is made in one of the poems. **(b) Interpret:** Explain what this comparison means and how it relates to the poem's theme.

Connections: Integration of Knowledge and Ideas

Discuss
In a **small-group discussion**, explore the ways in which descriptive and sensory language develop a mood in each poem.

Research
Briefly research Gary Soto's life and speculate about the influence of his upbringing on the two poems you read. Focus on the following aspects:
a. Soto's Mexican-American heritage
b. his childhood in Central California
Take notes as you research. Then, write a brief **explanation** of why setting is important to Soto's writing.

Write
Common advice for writers is "Write what you know." Write an **essay** in which you evaluate this advice based on an analysis of Soto's poems. Cite details from the poems and from your research to support your analysis.

 Do we need words to communicate well?
What feelings and ideas do the characters in these poems express without words?

"Poetry is **language** at its most distilled and most **powerful**."

—Rita Dove

RHYTHM AND RHYME

As you read the poetry collections in this section, consider ways in which rhyme, rhythm, and other sound devices create meaning. The quotation on the opposite page will help you start thinking about ways in which poets use language and sound to express significant ideas and important themes.

◀ **CRITICAL VIEWING** How do the images in this painting represent the language of poetry?

CLOSE READING TOOL

Use the **Close Reading Tool** to practice the strategies you learn in this unit.

Focus on Craft and Structure

Elements of Poetry

Poetry uses musical elements of **language** to help express thoughts and feelings.

Poetry is a type of literature in which the rhythms and sounds of words are as important as their definitions. When you read most poems, you can hear a **rhythm,** or beat. Other sound devices, such as **rhyme,** add to a poem's musical effect. Rhythm and sound help support a poem's meaning and shape its structure.

Structure Poems are arranged in **lines,** or groups of words, that help create rhythm and emphasis.

Example: Snowflake
A cold little star, spun from the sky, landed on the ground, then vanished.

Poetry looks different from prose because the lengths of individual lines in a poem may vary. In the example above, each of the snowflake's actions is presented on its own line.

The lines of a poem are arranged in units called stanzas. A **stanza** is a group of lines that work together to express a central idea. Like the paragraphs in an essay, the stanzas in a poem divide the text into logical parts.

Speaker When you read a poem, you can "hear" a voice speaking to you. The voice that narrates a poem is called the **speaker.** Like the narrator in a story, the speaker in a poem is an imaginary voice created by the poet. The speaker may present a unique point of view that is not necessarily the point of view of the poet.

Read the poem below, taking special note of its speaker and its structure. Notice the effects of these elements on the poem's meaning.

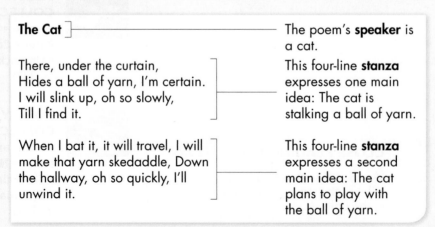

The Cat — The poem's **speaker** is a cat.

There, under the curtain,
Hides a ball of yarn, I'm certain.
I will slink up, oh so slowly,
Till I find it.

This four-line **stanza** expresses one main idea: The cat is stalking a ball of yarn.

When I bat it, it will travel, I will make that yarn skedaddle, Down the hallway, oh so quickly, I'll unwind it.

This four-line **stanza** expresses a second main idea: The cat plans to play with the ball of yarn.

Sound devices add a musical quality to poetry. Poets use the following devices to enhance a poem's mood and meaning.

Rhythm The rhythm of a poem is the beat created by its pattern of stressed and unstressed syllables. A stressed syllable is emphasized when it is spoken. An unstressed syllable is not emphasized. Rhythm can support meaning and make a poem memorable.

Read the following example aloud to hear its rhythm. Stressed syllables are printed in dark type.

Example: Rhythm

The **an**xious **fans** shot **to** their **feet,**
Their **fa**ces **filled** with **fear.**
But **when** the **ball** swished **through** the **net,**
They **cheered** a **migh**ty **cheer!**

In this poem, the regular rhythm is like the bouncing of a basketball. Not all poems have such a predictable rhythmic pattern, however. Poets may vary rhythms to emphasize certain words or to enhance meaning.

Rhyme is the repetition of sounds at the ends of words, as in *pool, rule,* and *fool.* As you read the following example, notice how rhyme connects ideas in the poem.

Example: Rhyme

I was angry with my fri<u>end</u>:
I told my wrath, my wrath did <u>end</u>.
I was angry with my <u>foe</u>:
I told it not, my wrath did <u>grow</u>.
— from "The Poison Tree" by William Blake

The rhyming words *friend* and *end* create a connection between the first two lines of the poem. Together these lines state a sentence with a central idea. Likewise, rhyming words connect the next two lines, which state a second sentence and a new, but related, idea.

Repetition is the use of any element of language—a sound, word, phrase, or sentence—more than once.

Alliteration is the repetition of similar consonant sounds at the beginnings of words.

Onomatopoeia is the use of words to imitate sounds. In the poem below, examples of alliteration are highlighted in color and examples of onomatopoeia are underlined.

Example: Onomatopoeia

Outside, clouds curl before the storm.
I snuggle inside, safe from the <u>whooshing</u> wind.
I watch as the sky darkens,
And put my hand to the cold window.

Analyzing Language, Structure, and Theme in Poetry

Poets choose and arrange words carefully to convey a **theme** about life.

Connotation and Denotation

A word can convey different kinds of meanings. One kind is the word's **denotation,** or dictionary definition. Another kind is the word's **connotation,** or the feelings and associations it evokes in people.

A word with positive connotations is associated with positive feelings and ideas. A word with negative connotations is associated with negative feelings and ideas. Think about the difference between the words *fragrance* and *odor.* Both words literally mean "smell." However, their connotative meanings are very different.

Meaning and Tone Tone is a writer's attitude toward his or her subject. A poem's **tone** can usually be described in one word, such as *joyful* or *lonely.* The connotations of the words in a poem can help convey its tone. Compare the following lines of poetry:

- They rolled over the swells until they slid ashore.
- They slammed over the waves until they hit land.

Both examples convey roughly the same information. However, in the first example, the words *rolled, swells,* and *slid* create a peaceful tone. In the second example, the words *slammed, waves,* and *hit* create an anxious tone.

Figurative Language Poets use **figurative language** to help readers see familiar ideas in fresh new ways. Figurative language is writing or speech that is not meant to be taken literally. Common types of figurative language are described below.

Types of Figurative Language

Simile compares two unlike things using the words *like* or *as.*
> **Example:** The man was as gruff as a grizzly bear.

Metaphor compares two unlike things without using *like* or *as.*
> **Example:** My aching feet were two bricks at the ends of my legs.

Personification gives human qualities to something that is not human.
> **Example:** The flames of the campfire licked the night air.

Hyperbole is an extreme exaggeration.
> **Example:** You've broken my heart into a million pieces!

Imagery Poets use **imagery,** also known as *sensory language,* to create vivid word pictures for readers. Imagery is language that appeals to the five senses of sight, hearing, smell, taste, and touch. The following lines of poetry appeal to the senses of sight and smell:

> The bright crimson roses
> Filled the air with their perfume.

Structure and Theme The **theme** of a poem is the message or insight about life that it conveys. Often, the structure of a poem contributes to its meaning. For example, each stanza may develop a central idea. Combining the central ideas of all the stanzas can lead you to the poem's theme.

As you read the following example, look for the theme of the poem.

Example: Waiting
The hands of the clock
creep
over
the
numbers
until . . .
The bell rings and sets me free.

Notice the different lengths of the poem's two stanzas. The first stanza has six lines, and the second stanza has only one. However, both stanzas contribute to the overall theme of the poem. In the first stanza, beginning with the second line, the poet puts one word on each line. This structure imitates the slow-ticking hands of a clock. The second stanza flows as one sentence. This suggests the speaker's relief upon hearing the bell. Together, the stanzas develop the theme of the poem: Time seems to move slowly when you are waiting for something you want.

Forms of Poetry Poetry comes in many different forms. Following are some of the common forms of poetry, which you will explore in this unit.

A **narrative** poem tells a story in verse. Narrative poetry has elements similar to those in short stories, such as plot and characters.

A **lyric** poem expresses the thoughts and feelings of a single speaker, often in highly musical verse.

A **concrete** poem is shaped to look like its subject. The poet arranges the lines to create a picture on the page.

A **haiku** is a Japanese form of poetry about nature, made up of three lines. The first and third lines have five syllables each. The second line has seven syllables.

A **limerick** is a humorous, rhyming five-line poem with a specific rhythm and pattern of rhyme.

A **free verse** poem does not have a strict structure, regular rhythm, or pattern of rhyme.

Building Knowledge

Poetry Collection 1

? Do we need words to communicate well?

Explore the Big Question as you read the poems in Collection 1. Take notes on ways in which the poems explore relationships between action and communication.

CLOSE READING FOCUS

Key Ideas and Details: **Context Clues**

Context clues are found in the text surrounding an unfamiliar word. These clues help you determine the meaning of a word you may not know. Context clues may be explanations or words with the same meaning. To use context clues, ask questions like these:

- *Which words restate, explain, or contrast with the word?*
- *What word can I use in place of the unfamiliar word?*
- *Does the new sentence I created make sense?*

Craft and Structure: **Rhythm and Rhyme**

Rhythm and rhyme add a musical quality to poems.

- **Rhythm** is the beat, or sound pattern, created by stressed and unstressed syllables.

Jack and **Jill** went **up** the **hill**

(4 stressed / 3 unstressed)

- **Rhyme** is the repetition of sounds at the ends of words, such as *delight* and *excite*. Once a rhyme pattern, or *scheme,* is established, you come to expect rhymes.

As you read, listen for ways in which these sound patterns add layers of meaning and convey each poem's *tone,* or speaker's attitude.

Vocabulary

You will encounter the following words in this collection. Write the words in your notebook. Next to the verb *sympathize*, write its noun and adjective forms.

ravenous	cavernous	deem
beseech	dismal	sympathize

CLOSE READING MODEL

The passages below are from Edgar Allan Poe's "A Dream Within a Dream" and Ogden Nash's "Adventures of Isabel." The annotations to the right of each passage show ways in which you can use close reading skills to understand context clues and analyze rhythm and rhyme.

from "A Dream Within a Dream"

Take this kiss upon the brow!
And, in parting from you now,
Thus much let me avow— [1]
You are not wrong, who deem
That my days have been a dream;

Rhythm and Rhyme
1 The words *brow* and *now* share the end sound "ow," which also occurs at the end of line 3. Lines 1 and 2 have the same rhythm. The rhythm changes slightly in line 3. In some poems, a change in rhythm indicates an important new thought or idea.

from "Adventures of Isabel"

Once in a night as black as pitch [2]
Isabel met a wicked old witch.
The witch's face was cross and wrinkled,
The witch's gums with teeth were sprinkled. [3]

Context Clues
2 The context clues *night* and *black* can help you infer that *pitch* is something that is black. To get more information, you might use a dictionary to learn that pitch is a form of tar.

Rhythm and Rhyme
3 When you read these lines aloud, you can hear the pattern of stressed and unstressed syllables. This rhythm creates a humorous tone.

Meet the Poets

Edgar Allan Poe (1809–1849) led a troubled life. His father deserted him, his mother died before he was three, and his wife died young. Despite his problems, Poe produced some of the world's best-known short stories, essays, and poems.

Ogden Nash (1902–1971), one of America's best-loved poets and humorists, threw away his first poetry attempt. Luckily, he pulled it out of the trash and sent it to the *New Yorker* magazine—which published it immediately. During his forty-year career, Nash wrote more than thirty poetry books.

Maya Angelou (1928–2014) changed her childhood name from Marguerite Johnson, and throughout her life she never stopped exploring who she was. In addition to being a poet and best-selling author, she was an educator, historian, actress, playwright, civil-rights activist, producer, and director.

Lewis Carroll (1832–1898) is the pen name of Charles Lutwidge Dodgson, an English math professor who taught at Oxford University. He wrote two children's classics, *Alice's Adventures in Wonderland* (1865) and *Through the Looking Glass,* (1872), which contains "The Walrus and the Carpenter."

A Dream Within a Dream

Edgar Allan Poe

Take this kiss upon the brow!
And, in parting from you now,
Thus much let me avow—
You are not wrong, who **deem**
5   That my days have been a dream;
Yet if hope has flown away
In a night, or in a day,
In a vision, or in none,
Is it therefore the less *gone*?
10 *All* that we see or seem
Is but a dream within a dream.
I stand amid the roar
Of a surf-tormented shore,
And I hold within my hand
15 Grains of the golden sand—
How few! yet how they creep
Through my fingers to the deep,
While I weep—while I weep!
O God! can I not grasp
20 Them with a tighter clasp?
O God! can I not save
One from the pitiless wave?
Is *all* that we see or seem
But a dream within a dream?

◀ **Vocabulary**
deem (dēm) *v.* hold
an opinion; judge

Spiral Review
IMAGERY How does
the image of the "surf-
tormented shore"
reflect the speaker's
state of mind?

Rhythm and Rhyme
When read aloud, how
many stressed syllables
are there in most lines
of this poem?

Adventures of Isabel

Ogden Nash

Vocabulary ▶
ravenous
(rav′ ə nəs) *adj.*
greedily hungry

cavernous (kav′
ər nəs) *adj.* huge
and hollow;
like a cavern

Isabel met an enormous bear,
Isabel, Isabel, didn't care;
The bear was hungry, the bear was ravenous,
The bear's big mouth was cruel and cavernous.
5 The bear said, Isabel, glad to meet you,
How do, Isabel, now I'll eat you!
Isabel, Isabel, didn't worry,
Isabel didn't scream or scurry.
She washed her hands and
    she straightened her hair up,
10 Then Isabel quietly ate the bear up.

Once in a night as black as pitch
Isabel met a wicked old witch.
The witch's face was cross and wrinkled,
The witch's gums with teeth were sprinkled.
15 Ho ho, Isabel! the old witch crowed,
I'll turn you into an ugly toad!
Isabel, Isabel, didn't worry,
Isabel didn't scream or scurry,
She showed no rage and she showed no rancor,
20 But she turned the witch into milk and drank her.

Isabel met a hideous giant,
Isabel continued self-reliant.
The giant was hairy, the giant was horrid,
He had one eye in the middle of his forehead.
25 Good morning Isabel, the giant said,
I'll grind your bones to make my bread.
Isabel, Isabel, didn't worry,
Isabel didn't scream or scurry.
She nibbled the zwieback that she always fed off,
30 And when it was gone, she cut the giant's head off.

Isabel met a troublesome doctor,
He punched and he poked till he really shocked her.
The doctor's talk was of coughs and chills
And the doctor's satchel bulged with pills.
35 The doctor said unto Isabel,
Swallow this, it will make you well.
Isabel, Isabel, didn't worry,
Isabel didn't scream or scurry.
She took those pills from the pill concocter,
40 And Isabel calmly cured the doctor.

Spiral Review
IMAGERY What do the poem's images suggest about Isabel's personality?

Rhythm and Rhyme
What two-word rhymes are used in lines 29 and 30?

Context Clues
What clues help you understand that a satchel (line 34) is something that holds things?

Life Doesn't Frighten Me

MAYA ANGELOU

Rhythm and Rhyme
The poet uses lists of things to build rhythm and rhyme. What things does she list in the first stanza?

Shadows on the wall
Noises down the hall
Life doesn't frighten me at all
Bad dogs barking loud
5   Big ghosts in a cloud
Life doesn't frighten me at all.

Mean old Mother Goose
Lions on the loose
They don't frighten me at all
10   Dragons breathing flame
On my counterpane[1]
That doesn't frighten me at all.

Context Clues
What words help you understand the meaning of *shoo* in line 14? What does *shoo* mean?

I go boo
Make them shoo
15   I make fun
Way they run
I won't cry
So they fly
I just smile
20   They go wild
Life doesn't frighten me at all.
Tough guys in a fight
All alone at night
Life doesn't frighten me at all.

---

1. **counterpane** *n.* bedspread.

25 Panthers in the park
Strangers in the dark
No, they don't frighten me at all.

That new classroom where
Boys all pull my hair
30 (Kissy little girls
With their hair in curls)
They don't frighten me at all.

Don't show me frogs and snakes
And listen for my scream,
35 If I'm afraid at all
It's only in my dreams.

I've got a magic charm
That I keep up my sleeve,
I can walk the ocean floor
40 And never have to breathe.

Life doesn't frighten me at all
Not at all
Not at all.
Life doesn't frighten me at all.

Rhythm and Rhyme
What repeated words help create rhythm in this poem?

Spiral Review
IMAGERY What common characteristics do most of the images in this poem share?

▶ **Critical Viewing**
Does the girl in this picture accurately reflect the feelings of the speaker?

THE WALRUS AND THE CARPENTER

Lewis Carroll

Context Clues
What words and phrases help you determine the meaning of the word *sulkily* in line 7? What does *sulkily* mean?

The sun was shining on the sea,
    Shining with all his might:
He did his very best to make
    The billows smooth and bright—
5 And this was odd, because it was
    The middle of the night.

The moon was shining sulkily,
    Because she thought the sun
Had got no business to be there
10   After the day was done—
"It's very rude of him," she said,
    "To come and spoil the fun!"

The sea was wet as wet could be,
    The sands were dry as dry.
15 You could not see a cloud, because
    No cloud was in the sky:
No birds were flying overhead—
    There were no birds to fly.

The Walrus and the Carpenter
20   Were walking close at hand:
They wept like anything to see
    Such quantities of sand:
"If this were only cleared away,"
    They said, "it would be grand!"

25 "If seven maids with seven mops
    Swept it for half a year,
Do you suppose," the Walrus said,
    "That they could get it clear?"
"I doubt it," said the Carpenter,
30   And shed a bitter tear.

"O Oysters, come and walk with us!"
    The Walrus did beseech.
"A pleasant walk, a pleasant talk,
    Along the briny beach:
35 We cannot do with more than four,
    To give a hand to each."

The eldest Oyster looked at him,
    But never a word he said:
The eldest Oyster winked his eye,
40   And shook his heavy head—
Meaning to say he did not choose
    To leave the oyster-bed.

◄ **Vocabulary**
beseech (bē sēch′)
v. beg

But four young Oysters hurried up,
　　All eager for this treat:
45　Their coats were brushed, their faces washed,
　　Their shoes were clean and neat—
And this was odd, because, you know,
　　They hadn't any feet.

Four other Oysters followed them,
50　　And yet another four;
And thick and fast they came at last,
　　And more, and more, and more—
All hopping through the frothy waves,
　　And scrambling to the shore.

55　The Walrus and the Carpenter
　　Walked on a mile or so,
And then they rested on a rock
　　Conveniently low:
And all the little Oysters stood
60　　And waited in a row.

"The time has come," the Walrus said,
　　"To talk of many things:
Of shoes—and ships—and sealing wax—
　　Of cabbages—and kings—
65　And why the sea is boiling hot—
　　And whether pigs have wings."

"But wait a bit," the Oysters cried,
    "Before we have our chat;
For some of us are out of breath,
70   And all of us are fat!"
"No hurry!" said the Carpenter.
    They thanked him much for that.

"A loaf of bread," the Walrus said,
    "Is what we chiefly need:
75 Pepper and vinegar besides
    Are very good indeed—
Now, if you're ready, Oysters dear,
    We can begin to feed."

"But not on us!" the Oysters cried,
80   Turning a little blue.
"After such kindness, that would be
    A dismal thing to do!"
"The night is fine," the Walrus said.
    "Do you admire the view?"

85 "It was so kind of you to come!
    And you are very nice!"
The Carpenter said nothing but
    "Cut us another slice.
I wish you were not quite so deaf—
90   I've had to ask you twice!"

Rhythm and Rhyme
In each six-line stanza of this poem, which lines rhyme?

◄ **Vocabulary**
dismal (diz´ məl) *adj.*
causing gloom
or misery

"It seems a shame," the Walrus said,
    "To play them such a trick.
After we've brought them out so far,
    And made them trot so quick!"
95 The Carpenter said nothing but
    "The butter's spread too thick!"

"I weep for you," the Walrus said:
    "I deeply sympathize."
With sobs and tears he sorted out
100   Those of the largest size,
Holding his pocket-handkerchief
    Before his streaming eyes.

"O Oysters," said the Carpenter,
    "You've had a pleasant run!
105 Shall we be trotting home again?"
    But answer came there none—
And this was scarcely odd, because
    They'd eaten every one.

Vocabulary ▶
sympathize (sim′ pə thīz) *v.* share in a feeling; feel compassion

Language Study

Vocabulary For each numbered item below, write a sentence that includes one of the blue vocabulary words.

ravenous   cavernous   deem   beseech   sympathize

1. a child who asks her parents for a pony
2. someone who feels sorry for another person's loss
3. a large cave you discover on a hike
4. a decision to award a prize
5. a person who has not eaten all day

Word Study

WORD STUDY

The **Latin root -mal-** means "bad" or "evil." In "The Walrus and the Carpenter," the two title characters do something **dismal**, or something that causes bad feelings.

Part A Explain how the **Latin root -mal-** contributes to the meanings of *malnourished, malodorous,* and *malicious.* Consult a dictionary if necessary.

Part B Explain your answers to these questions.

1. If a plant is *maladapted* to its environment, will it grow?
2. If a bully's face showed *malice,* would you be frightened?

Close Reading Activities

Literary Analysis

Key Ideas and Details

1. Context Clues Explain how the italicized context clues help you find the meanings of the underlined words.

(a) I stand amid the *roar* / of a <u>surf-tormented</u> *shore*
(b) She *showed no rage* and she *showed no* <u>rancor</u>.
(c) "I *weep* for you," the Walrus said: / I *deeply* <u>sympathize</u>."

2. Context Clues Read this stanza from "Life Doesn't Frighten Me": "I've got a magic *charm* / That I keep up my sleeve, / I can walk the ocean floor / And never have to breathe."

(a) What is a *charm*? **(b)** What context clues help you understand the meaning of the word in this context?

Craft and Structure

3. Rhythm and Rhyme Complete a chart like the one on the right to give examples of rhyming words each poet uses.

4. Rhythm and Rhyme How does each pair of the words listed in the chart affect the tone and meaning of the poem?

5. Rhythm and Rhyme How many stressed syllables are in this line of poetry?
"If seven maids with seven mops / Swept it for half a year"

Integration of Knowledge and Ideas

6. (a) Support: Describe Isabel's personality, using details from "Adventures of Isabel" to support your answer. **(b) Assess:** Is Isabel someone you would want as a friend? Explain.

7. (a) Name three things that do not frighten the speaker of "Life Doesn't Frighten Me." **(b) Infer:** Why does she smile at frightening things?

8.  **Do we need words to communicate well? (a) Infer:** In "The Walrus and the Carpenter," how does the old oyster know to be wary of the Walrus and the Carpenter? **(b) Generalize:** In real life, how might someone know that a situation is dangerous if no one has described the danger in words?

Poetry Collection 1

Poem
"Adventures of Isabel"
worry/scurry

Poem
"A Dream Within a Dream"

Poem
"Life Doesn't Frighten Me"

Poem
"The Walrus and the Carpenter"

ACADEMIC VOCABULARY

As you write and speak about the poems in Poetry Collection 1, use the words related to communication that you explored on page 303 of this text.

Conventions: **Adjectives and Adverbs**

Poetry Collection 1

Adjectives and adverbs are called **modifiers** because they modify, or make clearer, the meaning of another word in the sentence.

An **adjective** describes a person, place, thing, or idea. It modifies a noun or pronoun.

An **adverb** modifies a verb, an adjective, or another adverb.

Adjectives answer the questions, *What kind? Which one? How many? How much?*

Many adverbs end in *-ly*. Adverbs answer the questions, *Where? When? How? To what extent?*

Sentence	Adjective or Adverb	Word It Modifies
The *little* kittens love milk.	*little*: adjective	*kittens* (noun)
They are *cute*.	*cute*: adjective	*They* (pronoun)
He ran *slowly*.	*slowly*: adverb	*ran* (verb)
Maples are *very* tall trees.	*very*: adverb	*tall* (adjective)
He went *extremely* slowly.	*extremely*: adverb	*slowly* (adverb)

Practice A
Write each sentence. Underline each adjective, circle each adverb, and draw an arrow to the word that each modifies.

1. Isabel's doctor gave her the largest bag.
2. The speaker thinks quietly to himself.
3. The girl walked briskly past the dog.
4. The Walrus and the Carpenter have a thrilling idea.

Reading Application Identify two adjectives and two adverbs in "The Walrus and the Carpenter," and state the word each modifies.

Practice B
Identify the modifier in each sentence. Tell whether it is an adjective or an adverb. Then, say what question the modifier answers.

1. The frogs jumped quickly over the snakes.
2. Four oysters crawled across the sand.
3. Slowly, the creature turned to Isabel.
4. The speaker had a nightmare yesterday.

Writing Application Rewrite this sentence four times, using a different adjective and adverb each time: *I saw the (adjective) girl run (adverb).*

Writing to Sources

Explanatory Text One way to respond to literature is to write a **letter to an author**—even if you never send it. Write a letter to the author of one of the poems in Collection 1. In your letter, evaluate the poem's message, tone, rhythm, and rhyme.

- Begin by telling the poet which poem you read and explaining why you are writing about that poem.
- Quote lines, stanzas, or particular words to support your analysis of the poem's message, tone and sound devices.
- Write at least two well-organized paragraphs. Establish and maintain a formal style.
- End with a brief conclusion that summarizes your ideas.
- Use correct business letter format. Review a sample business letter in the Resources section in the back of your textbook.

Grammar Application Use at least three adjectives and two adverbs in your letter.

Research and Technology

Build and Present Knowledge Use library resources to find poems to include in an **illustrated booklet** about facing fears. Follow these steps to complete the assignment:

- Plan to include "Life Doesn't Frighten Me" and other poems you enjoy reading.
- Copy the poems into your booklet, leaving space for illustrations and annotations. Double-check your work to make sure you have copied the poems accurately. Pay particular attention to line breaks and punctuation.
- Illustrate your booklet to capture the spirit of the poems.
- Prepare annotations to summarize selections and point out details for readers. Use these questions as a guide:

  What message(s) do these poems express about facing fears?

  How do the poets use language and literary devices, such as rhyme and rhythm to convey their ideas?

Building Knowledge

Poetry Collection 2

? Do we need words to communicate well?

Explore the Big Question as you read the poems in Collection 2. Note ways in which the poets communicate feelings.

CLOSE READING FOCUS

Key Ideas and Details: **Context Clues**

Context clues are details in a text that give you clues about a word's meaning. When you encounter an unfamiliar word, or a word with multiple meanings, reread and read ahead to look for context clues. This example shows how context clarifies the meaning of the multiple-meaning word *beat*:

> Let the <u>rain</u> beat your <u>head with silver liquid drops</u>.

From the underlined context clues, you can figure out that *beat* is a verb that describes a gentle tap.

Craft and Structure: **Figurative Language**

Figurative language is language that is not meant to be taken literally. Authors and poets use figurative language to state ideas in fresh ways. They may use one or more of the following types of figurative language:

- **Similes** compare two unlike things using *like* or *as*.
- **Metaphors** compare two unlike things by stating that one thing *is* another.
- **Personification** compares an object or animal to a human by giving the object or animal human characteristics.

Vocabulary

You will encounter the following words in the poems in Collection 2. Decide whether you know each word well, know it a little bit, or do not know it at all. After you read, see how your knowledge of each word has increased.

lullaby   sour   pleasant   receive

CLOSE READING MODEL

The passages below are from Sandra Cisneros's "Abuelito Who" and Langston Hughes's "April Rain Song." The annotations to the right of each passage show ways in which you can use close reading skills to understand context clues and analyze figurative language.

from "Abuelito Who"

Abuelito who throws coins like rain [1]

And asks who loves him

Who is dough and feathers

Who is a watch and glass of water [2]

Figurative Language

1 The simile "throws coins like rain" may make you think of many sparkling coins falling with a tinkling sound. The image suggests that Abuelito's generosity pleases the speaker.

Figurative Language

2 The poet uses metaphors to describe Abuelito. He is "dough," "feathers," "a watch," and "a glass of water." These everyday items convey images of familiarity and a feeling of home.

from "April Rain Song"

The rain makes still pools on the sidewalk.

The rain makes running pools in the gutter. [3]

Context Clues

3 You can determine the meaning of the multiple-meaning word *still* by reading ahead. The speaker contrasts the "still pools" with "running pools." This contrast can help you figure out that here *still* means "unmoving."

Meet the Poets

Sandra Cisneros (b. 1954) was born in Chicago, but her family often traveled to Mexico to live with her grandfather, the *abuelito* in her poem "Abuelito Who." The frequent moves left Cisneros with few friends, and she remembers that she "retreated inside" herself, reading books and writing. Cisneros has won several awards for her poetry and short stories.

Langston Hughes (1902–1967), an award-winning poet, dramatist, and novelist, traveled to Africa and Europe as a young man before settling in Harlem in New York City. In the 1920s, he was one of the leaders of the Harlem Renaissance, a period in which African American writers, artists, and musicians produced brilliant works.

Nikki Giovanni (b. 1943), born in Knoxville, Tennessee, has become one of America's most popular poets. Her awards include the National Association for the Advancement of Colored People (NAACP) Image Award for Distinguished Contributions to Arts and Letters. She is a college professor.

Emily Dickinson (1830–1886) spent one year in college, but then became homesick and returned to her parents' house in Amherst, Massachusetts. For her remaining years, she seldom traveled or received guests. Dickinson read many books and wrote more than 1,700 poems, which form a kind of lifelong diary of her deepest thoughts. She is considered one of the leading voices of American poetry.

ABUELITO WHO

SANDRA CISNEROS

Abuelito[1] who throws coins like rain
and asks who loves him
who is dough and feathers
who is a watch and glass of water
5 whose hair is made of fur
is too sad to come downstairs today
who tells me in Spanish you are my diamond
who tells me in English you are my sky
whose little eyes are string
10 can't come out to play
sleeps in his little room all night and day
who used to laugh like the letter k
is sick
is a doorknob tied to a **sour** stick
15 is tired shut the door
doesn't live here anymore
is hiding underneath the bed
who talks to me inside my head
is blankets and spoons and big brown shoes
20 who snores up and down up and down up and down again
is the rain on the roof that falls like coins
asking who loves him
who loves him who?

---

1. **Abuelito** (ä bwä lēˊ tō) *n.* in Spanish, an affectionate term for a grandfather.

Context Clues
What meaning of the word *watch* does the poet use in line 4?

Spiral Review
WORD CHOICE What attitude is suggested by the words the author uses to describe her grandfather?

◄ **Vocabulary**
sour (soŭr) *adj.* having the sharp acid taste of lemon or vinegar

Figurative Language
What type of figurative language does the poet use to describe Abuelito in lines 14–19?

April Rain Song

LANGSTON HUGHES

Vocabulary ▶
lullaby (luľˈə bǐ) *n.*
quiet, gentle song sung
to send a child to sleep

Context Clues
Which meaning of the
word *running* does the
poet use in line 5? How
can you tell?

Let the rain kiss you.
Let the rain beat upon your head with silver liquid drops.
Let the rain sing you a lullaby.

The rain makes still pools on the sidewalk.
5 The rain makes running pools in the gutter.
The rain plays a little sleep-song on our roof
   at night—

And I love the rain.

The World is **NOT** a Pleasant Place to Be

Nikki Giovanni

the world is not a **pleasant** place
to be without
someone to hold and be held by

a river would stop
5 its flow if only
a stream were there
to **receive** it

an ocean would never laugh
if clouds weren't there
10 to kiss her tears

the world is not
a pleasant place to be without
someone

◄ **Vocabulary**
pleasant (plez´ ənt) *adj.*
agreeable; delightful

◄ **Vocabulary**
receive (ri sēv´) *v.* be given

Figurative Language
What type of figurative
language is used in
lines 8–10? What do
you think the poet
means?

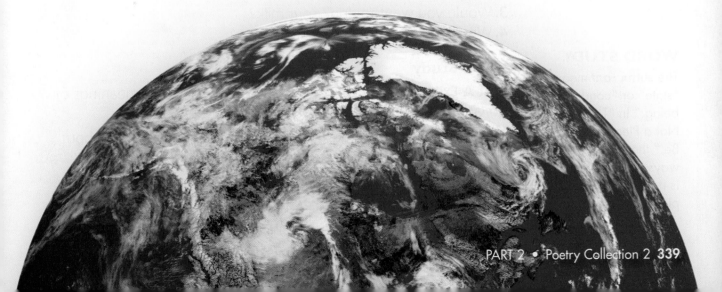

Fame Is a Bee

Emily Dickinson

Figurative Language
What type of figurative language is used to compare fame to a bee?

Fame is a bee.
It has a song—
It has a sting—
Ah, too, it has a wing.

Language Study

Vocabulary The words listed below appear in the poems in Collection 2. Answer each question, explaining your responses.

| lullaby | sour | pleasant | receive |

1. When would a parent be most likely to sing a *lullaby*?
2. Are you *pleasant* after a sleepless night?
3. Would you want to drink *sour* milk?
4. Why do you like to *receive* gifts?

WORD STUDY

The **suffix -ant** means "state" or "condition of being." In "The World Is Not a Pleasant Place to Be," the speaker tells of ways in which the world is not **pleasant** or in a pleasing state.

Word Study

Part A Explain how the **suffix -ant** contributes to the meanings of *vigilant* and *important*. Consult a dictionary if necessary.

Part B Use the context of the sentence and what you know about the suffix -ant to explain your answers to each question.

1. Is an *expectant* person waiting for something?
2. Does a water-*resistant* jacket get soaking wet in the rain?

Close Reading Activities

Literary Analysis

Poetry Collection 2

Key Ideas and Details

1. **Context Clues** In "April Rain Song," what is the meaning of *pools* (line 4)? What context clues in the poem help you determine the meaning?

2. **Context Clues** In "The World Is Not a Pleasant Place to Be," what is the meaning of *flow* (line 5)? What context clues in the poem help you decide?

3. (a) **Make Inferences:** In "Abuelito Who," what is happening with Abuelito? (b) **Interpret:** What words in the poem convey Abuelito's situation?

Craft and Structure

4. **Figurative Language** For each poem, fill in a graphic organizer like the one on the right with examples of the different types of figurative language.

5. **Figurative Language** How does the use of figurative language contribute to the tone of each poem? Cite specific examples from the texts to support your responses.

Title of Poem
Metaphor
Personification
Simile

Integration of Knowledge and Ideas

6. (a) In "April Rain Song," what kind of song does the rain sing? (b) **Infer:** What does the song tell you about the speaker's feelings about rain? (c) **Speculate:** How would the poem be different if it were about the rain that comes with a hurricane?

7. (a) **Interpret:** Fill out a three-column chart in response to the ideas in "Fame Is a Bee." In the first column, list the good things about fame. In the second, list the bad things about fame. (b) **Compare and Contrast:** Trade charts with a partner and discuss how your responses are similar and different. (c) **Assess:** In the third column of your chart, evaluate how your response has or has not changed based on your discussion.

8. **Do we need words to communicate well?**
   (a) In "Abuelito Who" and "April Rain Song," find examples of common things that are described in uncommon ways. (b) Does this technique help the poets communicate their ideas effectively? Explain.

ACADEMIC VOCABULARY

As you write and speak about the poems in Poetry Collection 2, use the words related to communication that you explored on page 303 of this text.

Conventions: Comparisons with Adjectives and Adverbs

Poetry Collection 2

An **adjective** describes a person, a place, a thing, or an idea. An **adverb** describes a verb, an adjective, or another adverb. Adjectives and adverbs are **modifiers** that can be used to compare two or more items or actions.

Type of Modifier	Definition	Adjective Example	Adverb Example
positive	not used to compare	new	calmly
comparative	used to compare *two* examples	newer	more calmly
superlative	used to compare *three* or more examples	newest	most calmly

Comparative and **superlative modifiers** are formed from **positive modifiers.**

1. If a positive adjective contains one or two syllables, you can usually add the ending -*er* or -*est*.

2. If a positive adjective contains three or more syllables, you can usually use the words *more* or *most*.

3. For most adverbs, use the words *more* or *most*.

Practice A

Write sentences about any of the poems in Collection 2, using the comparative or superlative modifiers listed below.

1. sadder
2. quieter
3. most beautiful
4. more easily
5. shortest

Reading Application For each sentence you wrote in Practice A, tell how many examples are being compared.

Practice B

Write each modifier in the form indicated. Then, use each word in an original sentence.

1. softly (superlative)
2. famous (comparative)
3. kind (superlative)
4. frightened (superlative)
5. carefully (comparative)

Writing Application Write one sentence about a poem in Collection 2 using a comparative adjective and one sentence using a superlative adjective.

Writing to Sources

Poetry Write a **poem** using figurative language.

- Think about something that makes you happy—the beach on a sunny day, the stars twinkling in the dark sky, your favorite flavor of ice cream, or anything that comes to your mind.
- Use questions to think about your topic: *What qualities does this thing have? To what can I compare this thing? What vivid words can I use to describe it?* List ideas.
- Review the poems in this collection to see how the poets use figurative and descriptive language.
- Write your poem using precise descriptions, unique comparisons, and figurative language. Experiment with rhyme and rhythm.

Grammar Application In your poem, include at least one comparative adjective and one comparative adverb.

Speaking and Listening

Presentation of Ideas Prepare a **dramatic poetry reading**. Select a poem you have read that is meaningful to you. It may be a poem in Poetry Collection 2 or a different poem.

- First, be sure you know how to pronounce all the words in the poem. Use a dictionary to learn the pronunciations of unfamiliar words.
- Practice reading the poem aloud, using expression and pauses where appropriate. Speak clearly.
- Pay attention to the end-of-line punctuation.
- Vary your volume and pitch to show emotion and to convey tone.
- Memorize your poem.
- Use gestures and body language to enhance your interpretation.
- Ask your classmates to silently read your poem.
- Now, present your dramatic poetry reading to the class.
- Discuss with classmates how reading the poem silently compared and contrasted with hearing it read aloud.

Building Knowledge

Poetry Collection 3

? **Do we need words to communicate well?**

Explore the Big Question as you read the poems in Collection 3. Take notes on the different ways in which the poets communicate experiences.

CLOSE READING FOCUS

Key Ideas and Details: **Paraphrasing**

When you **paraphrase** a literary work, you restate the author's words in your own words. Paraphrasing difficult or confusing passages in a poem helps you identify the main idea and monitor your understanding. Use the following steps to help you paraphrase challenging text:

- Stop and reread any difficult lines or passages.
- Identify unfamiliar words, find their meanings, and replace them with words that mean nearly the same thing.
- Restate the lines in your own words.
- Reread to see whether your paraphrase makes sense.

Craft and Structure: **Forms of Poetry**

Poets use **forms of poetry** suited to the meaning, images, and feelings they want to express. Here are three poetic forms:

- In a **concrete poem**, words are arranged in a shape that reflects the subject of the poem.
- A **haiku** is a Japanese verse form with three lines. Line 1 has five syllables, line 2 has seven, and line 3 has five.
- A **limerick** is a funny poem of five lines. Lines 1, 2, and 5 rhyme and have three beats, or stressed syllables. Lines 3 and 4 rhyme and have two beats.

Vocabulary

You will encounter these words in the poems in Collection 3. Choose one of the words and write at least two of its *synonyms*. After you read, see how your knowledge of each word has increased.

skimming   asphalt   fellow

CLOSE READING MODEL

The passage below is a limerick by an anonymous poet. The annotations to the right of the passage show ways in which you can use close reading skills to paraphrase lines and analyze forms of poetry.

from Limerick

There was a young fellow named Hall, [1]
Who fell in the spring in the fall; [2]
    'Twould have been a sad thing
    If he'd died in the spring,
But he didn't—he died in the fall.

Forms of Poetry

1 You can often identify a limerick from its opening lines. Limericks have an instantly recognizable, bouncy rhythm, and many begin with the words "There was a...."

Paraphrasing

2 This line may be confusing, since both *spring* and *fall* have multiple meanings. When you reread, you can understand that *spring* refers to a spring of water, and *fall* refers to a season of the year. You could paraphrase the line this way: "Who fell into water in autumn."

Meet the Poets

Matsuo Bashō (1644–1694) was born into a family of Japanese landowners. When Bashō was twelve, his father died. Bashō then entered the service of a local lord and began to write poetry. He was an important developer of the haiku form and one of its greatest masters. The Japanese have built a monument near the place where Bashō is believed to have written the haiku in Poetry Collection 3.

Lillian Morrison (b. 1917) played street games and sports as a child in Jersey City, New Jersey. The rhymes and chants she heard on the playground inspired her love of poetry. As an adult, Morrison spent nearly forty years working in the New York Public Library. She has written several books of poetry, including *The Sidewalk Racer and Other Poems of Sports and Motion*. Morrison has said, "I love rhythms, the body movement implicit in poetry, explicit in sports." Many of her poems, such as "The Sidewalk Racer," celebrate the human body in motion.

Dorthi Charles (b. 1960) was a student when she wrote "Concrete Cat." Readers especially enjoy the creative way that Charles presents her subject. This poem is featured in the book *Knock at a Star: A Child's Introduction to Poetry*.

HAIKU

BASHŌ

An old silent pond . . .
A frog jumps into the pond,
splash! Silence again.

The Sidewalk Racer
or On the Skateboard

Lillian Morrison

Vocabulary ▶
skimming (skim´ iŋ)
v. gliding; moving
swiftly and lightly
over a surface

asphalt (as´ fôlt´)
n. brown or black
mixture of substances
used to pave roads

Critical Viewing ▶
What words
might describe the
spirit of both this
skateboarder and the
poem?

Skimming
an asphalt sea
I swerve, I curve, I
sway; I speed to whirring
5 sound an inch above the
    ground; I'm the sailor
     and the sail, I'm the
    driver and the wheel
   I'm the one and only
10   single engine
      human auto
       mobile.

Concrete Cat

Dorthi Charles

```
      A              A
    e   r          e   r

                    stripestripestripestripe
                                             t
    eYe    eYe        stripestripestripe     a
                                              i
whisker        whisker    stripestripestripestripe  l      t  a  i  l
whisker  m   h  whisker      stripestripestripe
         o   t               stripestripestripe
           U
                          stripestripestripestripe


        paw paw        paw paw                    ǝsnoɯ

  dishdish                              litterbox
                                        litterbox
```

Limerick
Anonymous

Vocabulary ▶
fellow (felˊ ō) *n.*
man or boy

Forms of Poetry
What are the stressed syllables in lines 1, 2, and 5?

Critical Viewing ▶
What part of the limerick does this image illustrate?

There was a young fellow named Hall,
Who fell in the spring in the fall;
    'Twould have been a sad thing
    If he'd died in the spring,
5 But he didn't—he died in the fall.

Language Study

Vocabulary The words listed below appear in the poems in Collection 3. Write a sentence that connects the situation in each numbered item below with a vocabulary word.

    skimming   asphalt   fellow

1. children run after an ice cream truck, their bare feet burning
2. a young man walks to school in the rain
3. a girl watches birds glide across a lake

Word Study

WORD STUDY
The **Greek prefix auto-** means "self."

The speaker in "The Sidewalk Racer" compares herself to a "human auto mobile," because she moves by herself under her own power.

Part A Explain how the **Greek prefix auto-** contributes to the meanings of *autobiography* and *automatic.* You may consult a dictionary if necessary.

Part B Use context and what you know about the Greek prefix *auto-* to explain your answer to each question.

1. Why might the inventors of the *automobile* have given their machine that name?
2. If a factory becomes *automated,* do more people work there, or fewer people?

Close Reading Activities

Literary Analysis

Key Ideas and Details

1. **Paraphrase (a)** Paraphrase the haiku in your own words.
   (b) How does paraphrasing the haiku help you clarify your understanding of the poem's main idea? **(c)** How does line length impact the meaning of the haiku?

2. **Paraphrase** Paraphrase lines 6–12 of "The Sidewalk Racer."

3. **Paraphrase** Review "Concrete Cat." Then, write a sentence in which you use your own words to restate the meaning of the poem.

Poetry Collection 3

Craft and Structure

4. **Forms of Poetry (a)** What image appears in each line of the haiku? Record answers in a web like the one on the right. **(b)** How does each line develop the scene in the poem and help you understand its message?

5. **Forms of Poetry** Would "Concrete Cat" be more effective or less effective if it were written in a different shape? Explain.

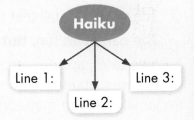

Integration of Knowledge and Ideas

6. **(a) Interpret:** Which words and phrases help show motion in "The Sidewalk Racer?" **(b) Analyze:** How can the speaker be both "the sailor / and the sail"? **(c) Assess:** Which image do you think most successfully conveys the sense of being on a skateboard? Explain.

7. **(a)** What incident does the limerick describe? **(b) Analyze:** How do the double meanings of *spring* and *fall* contribute to the humor in the limerick? **(c) Speculate:** Do you think it would be possible to write a serious limerick? Explain.

8. **Do we need words to communicate well?** With a small group, discuss these questions: **(a)** The poems in this collection use few words to convey meaning. How is the form of a poem as much a part of the meaning as the words of the poem? **(b) Analyze:** Can you separate the form from the meaning in any of these poems? Explain. **(c) Draw Conclusions:** Are poems more effective when they are longer and use more words? Explain, citing evidence from the poems you have read.

ACADEMIC VOCABULARY

As you write and speak about the poems in Poetry Collection 3, use the words related to communication that you explored on page 303 of this text.

Conventions: **Conjunctions and Interjections**

Conjunctions connect sentence parts and help show the relationships between those parts. **Interjections** express feelings. The use of conjunctions helps to improve the flow of your writing. Interjections add liveliness to dialogue and narration.

Poetry Collection 3

Examples of Conjunctions	Examples of Interjections
and, or, but, nor, for, yet, so	*ah, aha, whoa, hey, oh, oops, shh, wow, whew*

A conjunction that joins two independent clauses is preceded by a comma.

The corn grew tall that summer**, and** the harvest was plentiful.

The party was fun**, but** I had to leave early.

In some cases, an interjection is followed by an exclamation point. In other cases, an interjection may be followed by a comma, and an exclamation point may appear at the end of the sentence.

Hey**,** that new song is really great**!**

Aha**!** I've found you at last**!**

Practice A
Fill in the blanks with a conjunction or interjection that completes the sentence.

1. The pond was old, _____ the frog was young.

2. _____, did you hear a splash?

3. The poem is about a cat, _____ it is in the shape of a cat.

4. _____! I love to ride my skateboard.

Reading Application Find three conjunctions in the poems in Collection 3. Explain the relationships between the words, phrases, or clauses that are connected by the conjunctions.

Practice B
Improve these sentences by following the directions in parentheses. Be sure to use commas and exclamation points correctly.

1. Some poems are only three lines long. Others are very long, with many stanzas. (combine with a conjunction)

2. Lily and I like limericks. We decided to write one together. (combine with a conjunction)

3. "Now I understand that poem," Sam said. (add an interjection)

Writing Application Write a paragraph about jumping into a pond. Use at least four conjunctions and two interjections. Circle the conjunctions and underline the interjections.

Writing to Sources

Poetry Write your own haiku, limerick, or concrete **poem.**

- Brainstorm for a list of topics that inspire you. Think about an element of nature, an event from your daily life, an amusing incident, or a visual image that you want to describe.
- Review the poems in this collection as models of the different poetic forms. Decide which of the three forms fits your topic best.
- Write your poem. Choose the correct pattern for the poetic form you have selected. Use a visual layout if you are writing a concrete poem, and use humor, rhythm, and rhyme if you are writing a limerick.
- Make copies of your poem for a small group of classmates. Read the poem aloud as they follow along.

Grammar Application Look for places in your poem where conjunctions can help you connect ideas and improve the rhythm and flow of your writing. Consider using interjections to add liveliness or feeling to your poem.

Research and Technology

Build and Present Knowledge Use a computer word processing program to develop and design a **presentation of a poem**.

- Choose a poem from this collection or another poem that you enjoyed reading.
- Type the poem exactly as the poet wrote it. You may have to set your margins extra wide to accommodate the poem's line breaks, or use tabs to set off indented lines.
- Choose a font or style that is easy to read. Use a larger font size for the title.
- Proofread your poem. Remember to add the poet's name. Use "Anonymous" if the poet is unknown.
- Add pictures or illustrations to enhance the appearance of the poem.
- Post a copy of your poem as part of a class display.

Poetry Collection 4

Do we need words to communicate well?

Explore the Big Question as you read the poems in Collection 4.

CLOSE READING FOCUS

Key Ideas and Details: **Paraphrasing**

Before you **paraphrase** a poem, read it aloud according to its punctuation to help you group words for meaning. Do not automatically stop at the ends of lines. Instead, use the punctuation in the poem to decide where to pause.

- Use a slight pause after a comma.
- Use a longer pause after a colon, semicolon, or dash.
- Your longest pause should come after a period, a question mark, or an exclamation point.
- If there is no punctuation, do not pause at all.

Craft and Structure: **Sound Devices and Tone**

A poet uses **sound devices** to create musical effects, reinforce meaning, and develop **tone**, the poet's attitude toward his or her audience and subject. The following sound devices are commonly used in poetry.

- **Repetition** is the repeated use of any element of language—a sound, word, phrase, or sentence—as in *of the people, by the people, for the people.*
- **Alliteration** is the repetition of initial consonant sounds, such as the *b* sound in *big beautiful bird.*
- **Onomatopoeia** is the use of a word that sounds like what it means, such as *roar* or *buzz.*

Vocabulary

You will encounter the following words in the poems in Collection 4. Write each word, noting whether you think it is a noun, an adjective, or a verb. Use a dictionary to check your responses.

hollowed	dispersed	sculpted
thorny	offense	whirs

CLOSE READING MODEL

The passage below is from Shel Silverstein's poem "No Thank You." The annotations to the right of the passage show ways in which you can use close reading skills to paraphrase the poem and analyze sound devices and tone.

Sound Devices and Tone

1 The speaker repeats the word, "No" at the beginning of each line. This repetition, along with the alliteration in "cute, cuddly kitty-poo" and "midnight meowing mews" creates a bouncy, humorous tone.

from **"No Thank You"**

No I do not want a kitten,
No cute, cuddly kitty-poo,
No more long hair in my cornflakes,
No more midnight meowing mews. [1]

. . .

No I will not take that kitten—
I've had lice and I've had fleas,
I've been scratched and sprayed and bitten,
I've developed allergies. [2]

Paraphrasing

2 When reading this stanza aloud, you would take a long pause after the line that ends with a dash. You would pause only briefly after the lines that end with commas, and take the longest pause after the line that ends with a period.

Meet the Poets

Octavio Paz (1914–1998), a famous Mexican poet, lived in and visited many countries, but always remained deeply committed to his Mexican heritage. In 1990, Paz received the Nobel Prize in Literature.

Shel Silverstein (1932–1999), a Chicago native, was a talented poet, cartoonist, playwright, and songwriter. His popular poetry collections— such as *Where the Sidewalk Ends* and *A Light in the Attic*—show his imaginative sense of humor, which both children and adults enjoy. Silverstein also wrote the classic children's book *The Giving Tree*.

William Shakespeare (1564–1616) is probably the most highly regarded writer in the English language. Born in the English town of Stratford-upon-Avon, Shakespeare went to London as a young man. There he began writing and acting in plays. He wrote at least thirty-seven plays and more than one hundred fifty poems. "The Fairies' Lullaby" comes from the play *A Midsummer Night's Dream*.

Gwendolyn Brooks (1917–2000) wrote many poems about her neighbors in Chicago, the city she lived in for most of her life. She started writing when she was seven years old and published her work in a well-known magazine as a teenager. In 1950, Brooks became the first African American writer to win a Pulitzer Prize.

Wind and water and stone

Octavio Paz

The water **hollowed** the stone,
the wind **dispersed** the water,
the stone stopped the wind.
Water and wind and stone.

5 The wind **sculpted** the stone,
the stone is a cup of water,
the water runs off and is wind.
Stone and wind and water.

The wind sings in its turnings,
10 the water murmurs as it goes,
the motionless stone is quiet.
Wind and water and stone.

One is the other, and is neither:
among their empty names
15 they pass and disappear,
water and stone and wind.

◄ **Vocabulary**
hollowed (häl´ ōd)
v. created a hole
or a space within

dispersed (di spʉrst´)
v. distributed in
many directions

sculpted (sculpt´ əd)
v. shaped or molded

Sound Devices
What effect is created
by the repetition of the
words in the fourth line
of each stanza?

No Thank You

Shel Silverstein

No I do not want a kitten,
No cute, cuddly kitty-poo,
No more long hair in my cornflakes,
No more midnight meowing mews.

5 No more scratchin', snarlin', spitters,
No more sofas clawed to shreds,
No more smell of kitty litter,
No more mousies in my bed.

No I will not take that kitten—
10 I've had lice and I've had fleas,
I've been scratched and sprayed and bitten,
I've developed allergies.

If you've got an ape, I'll take him,
If you have a lion, that's fine,
15 If you brought some walking bacon,
Leave him here, I'll treat him kind.

I have room for mice and gerbils,
I have beds for boars and bats,
But please, *please* take away that kitten—
20 Quick—'fore it becomes a cat.
Well . . . it is kind of cute at that.

Sound Devices
What sound device is used in lines 5 and 6?

Paraphrasing
How do the ellipsis points (. . .) help you understand the poet's meaning?

THE FAIRIES' LULLABY

from **A MIDSUMMER NIGHT'S DREAM**

WILLIAM SHAKESPEARE

Fairies. You spotted snakes with double tongue,
        Thorny hedgehogs, be not seen.
    Newts and blindworms,[1] do no wrong,
        Come not near our fairy Queen.

5   **Chorus.** Philomel,[2] with melody
        Sing in our sweet lullaby;
    Lulla, lulla, lullaby, lulla, lulla, lullaby.
        Never harm,
        Nor spell, nor charm,
10   Come our lovely lady nigh.
    So, good night, with lullaby.

Vocabulary ▶
thorny (thôr′ nē) *adj.*
prickly; full of thorns

Paraphrasing
In reading aloud,
why would you keep
reading at the end of
line 5? How would
you paraphrase lines
5 and 6?

---

1. **newts** (nōōts) **and blindworms** *n.* newts are salamanders, which look like lizards but are related to frogs. Blindworms are legless lizards.
2. **Philomel** (fil′ ə mel′) *n.* nightingale.

Fairies. Weaving spiders, come not here.
        Hence, you long-legged spinners, hence!
     Beetles black, approach not near.
15   Worm nor snail do no **offense**.

Chorus. Philomel, with melody
        Sing in our sweet lullaby;
     Lulla, lulla, lullaby, lulla, lulla, lullaby.
        Never harm,
20   Nor spell, nor charm,
     Come our lovely lady nigh.
     So, good night, with lullaby.

offense (ə fens´)
n. harmful act;
violation of a law

Cynthia in the Snow

Gwendolyn Brooks

Vocabulary ▶

whirs (wŭrz) *v.* flies or moves quickly with a buzzing sound

Sound Devices

What sound device is at work in the words *SUSHES, hushes,* and *flitter-twitters?* What do these words express?

It SUSHES.
It hushes
The loudness in the road.
It flitter-twitters,
5   And laughs away from me.
It laughs a lovely whiteness,
And whitely whirs away,
To be
Some otherwhere,
10 Still white as milk or shirts.
So beautiful it hurts.

Language Study

Vocabulary The words listed below appear in the poems in Collection 4. Answer each numbered question based on the meaning of the italicized vocabulary word.

> hollowed   dispersed   sculpted   offense   whirs

1. Why might a crowd have suddenly *dispersed*?
2. What could you do with a *hollowed* stone?
3. What things can be *sculpted* out of snow?
4. What is an example of a child's minor *offense*?
5. What is an example of something that *whirs*?

Word Study

Part A Explain how the **suffix -y** contributes to the meanings of the words *wordy, grouchy,* and *drowsy.* Consult a dictionary if necessary.

Part B Use context and what you know about the suffix *-y* to explain your answer to each question.

1. If a person is *thirsty,* what should he or she do?
2. When might a child's hands be *sticky*?

WORD STUDY

The **suffix -y** forms adjectives that mean "having," full of," or "characterized by." In "The Fairies' Lullaby," William Shakespeare uses the word **thorny** to describe hedgehogs— small animals that have sharp, thorn-like spines.

Close Reading Activities

Literary Analysis

Key Ideas and Details

1. **Paraphrasing (a)** Paraphrase the final stanza of "Wind and water and stone." **(b)** What ideas become clear after paraphrasing?

2. **Paraphrasing (a)** In "The Fairies' Lullaby," after which words should the chorus pause? **(b)** Paraphrase the chorus's lines.

3. **Paraphrasing (a)** How does punctuation affect the pace, or timing, of the words in "Cynthia in the Snow"? **(b)** How does reading the poem aloud help you paraphrase the poem?

4. **(a)** Name all the creatures the fairies address in "The Fairies' Lullaby." **(b) Classify:** What do all these creatures have in common?

Craft and Structure

5. **Sound Devices and Tone** Complete a chart like the one on the right by listing examples of repetition, alliteration, and onomatopoeia in each poem.

6. **Sound Devices and Tone** What tone do sound devices create in each poem?

Integration of Knowledge and Ideas

7. **(a)** According to the speaker in "Wind and water and stone," what does each of the three natural elements do? **(b) Connect:** What is the three elements' overall effect on nature?

8. **(a)** In "No Thank You," what are three reasons the speaker gives for not wanting a kitten? **(b) Make a Judgment:** Are the reasons convincing? Explain.

9. **(a)** In "Cynthia in the Snow," what five things does the snow do? **(b) Analyze:** What is the speaker's overall reaction to the snow?

10. **Do we need words to communicate well? (a)** Choose two images in the poems that make you think of something familiar in a whole new way. **(b) Interpret:** For each image, explain what the poet communicates by making you think this way.

Poetry Collection 4

"Wind and water and stone"
"No Thank You"
"The Fairies' Lullaby"
"Cynthia in the Snow"

ACADEMIC VOCABULARY

As you write and speak about the poems in Poetry Collection 4, use the words related to communication that you explored on page 303 of this text.

Conventions: Sentence Parts and Types

Poetry Collection 4

> A **sentence** consists of a subject and a predicate, and expresses a complete thought. A sentence always begins with a capital letter.

A **simple subject** is the person, place, or thing about which the sentence is written. A **complete subject** includes the simple subject and any words related to it. A **simple predicate** is the verb that expresses the main action in the sentence. A **complete predicate** includes the verb and any words related to it.

A **compound subject** is made up of two or more nouns that share the same verb and are joined by conjunctions such as *and*.

Sentences can be classified according to their functions.

Type of Sentence	Function	Sample Sentence	End Punctuation
Declarative	states an idea	The sky is blue.	period
Interrogative	asks a question	What time is it?	question mark
Imperative	gives an order or direction	Do not enter this room.	period or exclamation mark
Exclamatory	expresses strong emotion	This is amazing!	exclamation mark

Practice A
Rewrite each sentence, changing it to the type indicated.

1. The speaker of the poem does not want to own a kitten. *(interrogative)*
2. Will you please sing me a lullaby? *(imperative)*
3. I love watching snow fall. *(exclamatory)*
4. How do water and wind change a stone? *(declarative)*

Reading Application Identify three subjects in the poems in this collection. In each case, explain whether the subject is simple or compound.

Practice B
Write a sentence that combines each complete subject below with a complete predicate.

1. the speaker of "No Thank You"
2. the poem "Cynthia in the Snow"
3. the fairies
4. wind and water

Writing Application Write a sentence for each item based on one of the poems you read. **(a)** a declarative sentence with a simple subject, **(b)** an interrogative sentence with a compound subject, **(c)** an exclamatory sentence.

Writing to Sources

Explanatory Text Write a **prose description** inspired by one of the poems you read in Poetry Collection 4. Read your description to the class.

- Review Collection 4, and select the poem you will use as your subject.
- Jot down notes that capture the poem's images and feelings, as well as your reactions to the poem.
- Use words that appeal to the senses of sight, sound, smell, taste, and touch.
- Write a paragraph in which you describe and support your impression of the poem.

Grammar Application Make sure each sentence in your description includes a subject and a predicate. To add interest in your writing, use a variety of sentence types.

Research and Technology

Build and Present Knowledge A **résumé** is a specially formatted summary of information about a person's career and education. Prepare a résumé for one of the poets in this collection.

- Conduct research on the poet of your choice. Focus on specific categories such as schools attended, books written, awards won, and related jobs.
- Search online for examples of résumé formats. Look for writers' résumés to use as models.
- Write a résumé that showcases what you have learned about the poet. Organize your information, using the example résumés you found as a guide. Include categories such as *Education, Publishing History,* and *Honors.*
- Type your résumé using a word-processing program. Use tabs and settings in the program to correctly format the résumé.

Do we need words to communicate well?

Explore the Big Question as you read these poems. Take notes on how the poets paint pictures with words. Then compare and contrast what the two poems suggest about communication.

READING TO COMPARE IMAGERY

Poets E.E. Cummings and Robert Frost use descriptive language that includes vivid images. As you read the poems that follow, consider the effects of each poet's word choice. When you finish reading, compare and contrast the ways in which the two poets use imagery.

"who knows if the moon's"

E.E. Cummings (1894–1962)
As a poet, E.E. (Edward Estlin) Cummings experimented with punctuation, capitalization, spelling, and the arrangement of words on the page. In many poems, his words seem to be scattered on the page. However, the scattered words create the effects he wanted to achieve, especially when the poems are read aloud. Cummings studied painting, which may explain why he became interested in the visual effect of his poems.

"Dust of Snow"

Robert Frost (1874–1963)
Although he was born in California, Robert Frost is often associated with New England. Frost's family moved to Massachusetts when he was eleven years old, and he spent most of his life in the Northeast. Frost began writing poetry in high school. He kept writing while he worked as a farmer, mill worker, newspaper reporter, and teacher. Frost won the Pulitzer Prize four times—more than any other poet.

Comparing Imagery

An **image** is a word picture that appeals to one or more of the five senses of sight, hearing, smell, taste, and touch. Writers use descriptive language and sensory details to develop **imagery**.

- An image can appeal to more than one sense. For example, "soft carpet of yellow prairie flowers" appeals to both touch and sight.

- An image can create a feeling of movement. For example, "the autumn leaves floated gently to the ground" shows the reader how the leaves fell.

- Imagery helps writers express moods or emotions. Mood is the feeling that a poem creates in the reader. A poem can have many moods, including frightening, fanciful, thoughtful, and lonely.

In the poems "who knows if the moon's" and "Dust of Snow," each poet uses imagery to achieve a different effect. As you read each poem, use a chart such as the one below to record the picture the poem creates in your mind, the sense or senses to which each image appeals, and the overall mood or emotion the poet communicates through imagery.

Poem title	Image	Sight	Hearing	Smell	Taste	Touch	Mood

who knows if the moon's

E.E. CUMMINGS

who knows if the moon's
a balloon, coming out of a keen[1] city
in the sky—filled with pretty people?
(and if you and i should

5   get into it, if they
should take me and take you into their balloon,
why then
we'd go up higher with all the pretty people

than houses and **steeples** and clouds:
10   go sailing
away and away sailing into a keen
city which nobody's ever visited, where

always
        it's
15   Spring) and everyone's
in love and flowers pick themselves

---

1. **keen** (kēn) *adj.* slang for *good, fine.*

Imagery
What kind of
movement does
the balloon image
suggest to you?

◄ **Vocabulary**
steeples (stē´ pəlz) *n.*
towers rising above
churches or other
structures

Critical Thinking

1. **Key Ideas and Details** Why might a place where everything is perfect be appealing to Cummings and his readers?

2. **Craft and Structure (a)** What words are repeated in the poem? **(b)** What ideas do these words emphasize?

3. **Craft and Structure** Why do you think lines 13–15 are arranged differently from the other lines in the poem?

4. **Integration of Knowledge and Ideas** Identify an image in the poem and think about how you might capture it in a drawing. **(a)** What information do the words of the poem give you? What information is missing? **(b)** How could you fill in the missing information? **(c)** Describe or draw the picture you would make. **(d)** How are the idea and mood you convey similar to and different from the image in the poem? *[Connect to the Big Question: Do we need words to communicate well?]*

Dust of Snow

Robert Frost

The way a crow
Shook down on me
The dust of snow
From a hemlock[1] tree

5 Has given my heart
A change of mood
And saved some part
Of a day I had rued.

Vocabulary ▶
rued (rōōd) *v.*
regretted

---

1. **hemlock** (hem´ läk´) *n.* evergreen tree; member of the pine family.

Critical Thinking

1. **Key Ideas and Details (a)** What is the action that changes the speaker's mood? **(b) Classify:** Is this action planned or does it occur by chance? Explain.

2. **Key Ideas and Details (a)** Describe the change that the action brings about in the speaker. **(b) Analyze:** Why does the action have this effect? **(c) Generalize:** What lesson do you think the speaker learns from this experience?

3. **Key Ideas and Details** If such small, unexpected natural events happened every day, would they have the same impact on a person? Explain.

4. **Integration of Knowledge and Ideas (a)** Draw a quick sketch of an image like the one described in the poem. **(b)** What parts of the poem could you convey in your picture? **(c)** What parts of the poem are better conveyed in words? *[Connect to the Big Question: Do we need words to communicate well?]*

Comparing Imagery

1. Craft and Structure (a) Choose an image from each poem. To which senses does each image appeal? **(b)** Complete a graphic organizer like the one shown for each poem to analyze the poem's mood. In the center, write a word that describes the mood. Then, in the outer circles, list images, words, or phrases in the poem that help develop that mood.

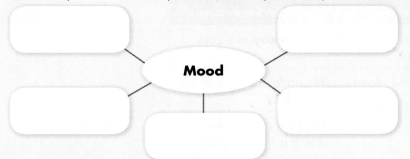

2. Key Ideas and Details In "who knows if the moon's," how does the imagery create a feeling of floating or weightlessness? List details that suggest this movement.

 Timed Writing

Explanatory Text: Essay

Write an essay in which you draw conclusions about the role nature plays in each poem. In your essay, note which descriptive words or phrases contribute to the image of nature, and decide whether the image of nature is positive or negative. **(25 minutes)**

5-Minute Planner

1. Read the prompt carefully and completely.

2. Use these questions to help you get started:
   • In each poem, does nature play a central role, or is it a part of the background for the action?
   • What sensory language contributes to the images of nature?
   • Which words help you tell whether the images of nature are negative or positive?

3. Reread the prompt, and then draft your essay. Include quotations from the two poems.

USE ACADEMIC VOCABULARY

As you write, use academic language, including the following words or their related forms:

achieve

communicate

observe

symbolize

For more information about academic vocabulary, see pages xlvi–l.

Language Study

Words with Multiple Meanings

A **multiple-meaning word** is a word that has more than one basic definition. To determine the meaning intended in a sentence, look at the context—the words surrounding the multiple-meaning word. This chart shows three different definitions and usages for the word *key*. Note how context clues suggest the meaning of *key* in each sentence.

Word	Use	Definition	Example Sentence
key	noun	a device used to open a lock	Use this **key** to unlock the door.
key	noun	a reef or low island	We paddled our boat out to the **key**.
key	adjective	important	The **key** point of the article is that tigers are an endangered species.

Practice A

Use context and your prior knowledge to write the meaning of the italicized word in each sentence. Then, use a print or an online dictionary to verify, or confirm, the meanings.

1. **a.** The old chair was covered with *dust*.

   b. When you take the cookies out of the oven, *dust* them with powdered sugar.

2. **a.** Let's *watch* the news on television at six o'clock.

   b. Check your *watch* to see if we need to leave for home yet.

3. **a.** I think the *content* of that poem is beautiful.

   b. The applause made Mary feel *content* with her performance.

4. **a.** How many people were *present* at the meeting?

   b. I made a birthday *present* for my grandfather.

Practice B

For each word listed, write two sentences that use different meanings of the word. If necessary, look up the meanings in a dictionary.

1. bow
2. set
3. draft
4. cast
5. tip
6. cape
7. current
8. ruler

Activity Look in a dictionary to find five words that have multiple meanings. You may use the five numbered words below, or you may choose words of your own. Write each word on a separate notecard like the one shown. Fill in the left-hand column of the notecard based on one of the word's meanings. Fill in the right-hand column based on another of the word's meanings. Then, trade note cards with a partner. Discuss the different meanings and uses of the words that each of you found.

1. pitcher
2. entry
3. hide
4. line
5. fast

Word: _____	
Part of Speech:	**Part of Speech:**
Definition:	**Definition:**
Example Sentence:	**Example Sentence:**

Problem-and-Solution Proposal

A **problem-and-solution proposal** is a formal plan that suggests a course of action for solving a problem. The following strategies can help you present a convincing problem-and-solution proposal.

Learn the Skills

Organize your ideas. First, identify the problem and make a list of its causes. Use statistics and examples to demonstrate these causes. Then, describe your proposed solution and list the reasons you think the solution will work. Add details that provide evidence and support for each point of your solution.

Establish connections and provide evidence. Use visual aids to show connections or provide evidence. For example, a bar graph or chart can show the connection between the problem you defined and the solution you are proposing. In the example shown, the bar graph illustrates the increase in accidents each year and provides support for the solution of installing a traffic light. Draw your visual aids or create them on a computer.

Plan your delivery. Practice your proposal and prepare any notes and visuals before your presentation so you do not forget your key points.

Remember your listener. Speak slowly and clearly so that your audience will be able to follow your presentation. Adjust your tone for emphasis when you introduce impotant information, then pause after you make a key point. Refer to your visuals at appropriate points during your presentation.

Use standard English. Your argument will be stronger if you use formal, correct language. As you speak, avoid slang and errors in grammar and usage.

Use eye contact and gestures. Make eye contact with members of the audience to keep them engaged, and use gestures to emphasize your points.

Problem: Car accidents have increased each year.
Solution: Replace stop signs with traffic lights.

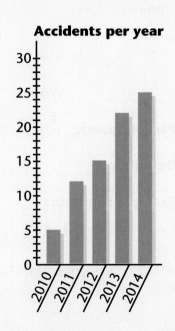

Accidents per year

Practice the Skills

Presentation of Knowledge and Ideas Use what you have learned in this workshop to complete the following activity.

> ACTIVITY: **Present a Problem-and-Solution Proposal**
>
> Find a problem and think of a solution for it. Then, follow the steps below.
>
> • List the causes of the problem.
> • Use statistics and examples to demonstrate the causes.
> • Organize your ideas around your solution.
> • Use visual aids and evidence to support your solution.
> • When delivering your proposal, make eye contact with the audience and use gestures. Be sure to use adequate volume and clear pronunciation.

Use the Speaking Guide to organize and plan your problem-and-solution proposal.

Speaking Guide

Problem: _____

Solution: _____

Supporting Points: _____

Visual Aids

Which visual aid will best support your solution? Briefly explain.

❏ graph   ❏ chart   ❏ table
❏ slide show   ❏ diagram   ❏ video

Delivery of Presentation

Employ the following techniques when you present your proposal.

❏ eye contact   ❏ speaking rate
❏ volume level   ❏ clear pronunciation
❏ natural gestures   ❏ conventions of language

Comprehension and Collaboration Ask a classmate to evaluate your proposal based on the clarity of your presentation and whether or not your proposed solution seems reasonable. Then, evaluate your partner's proposal. If necessary, offer each other suggestions for improvement.

Write an Argument

Argumentative Essay

Defining the Form In an **argumentative essay**, the writer states a claim based on factual evidence. The writer then uses logic, reasoning, and strong support to convince readers to agree with the claim.

Assignment Write an argumentative essay in which you state and support a claim. Include these elements:

- ✓ a *clear thesis statement* that presents a position on an issue that has at least two sides
- ✓ a *clear organization,* including an introduction, a body, and a conclusion
- ✓ facts and examples from *credible sources* that *support your position*
- ✓ *evidence and support* to address the *counterarguments*
- ✓ a *formal style* that takes the subject and audience seriously
- ✓ *precise language* that clearly shows the *relationships between claims and evidence*
- ✓ *correct usage of coordinating conjunctions*

To preview the criteria on which your argumentative essay may be judged, see the rubric on page 383.

FOCUS ON RESEARCH

When you write an argumentative essay, use strong evidence to support your claim. Evidence should be

- *credible,* or from a trustworthy source.
- *accurate,* or recorded correctly from the source.
- *current,* or reflecting up-to-date information.
- *relevant,* or suitable to prove a specific point.

Be sure to cite your sources properly. Refer to the Research Workshop in the Introductory Unit for help on citing sources.

READING-WRITING CONNECTION

To get the feel for argument, read the persuasive speech "Preserving a Great American Symbol" on page 270.

Prewriting/Planning Strategies

Choose a two-sided topic. Select a topic that is important to you and that has two clear sides—one that you can support and one that you can oppose. Use these tips to zero in on an interesting topic:

- **Conduct a media review.** Think about the local issues in the news now. Look at print and online news sources, read letters to the editor, and watch and listen to local television and radio news programs to list all the topics that appeal to you. Then, choose one for your essay.

- **Organize a round table.** Gather classmates for a discussion of places and groups that are important to you. Think of issues that affect the locations and groups you have listed. Jot down any ideas that interest you, and choose a topic.

Narrow your topic to a manageable size. Make sure your topic is not too big to cover in an argumentative essay. Use a graphic organizer like the one shown to narrow your topic.

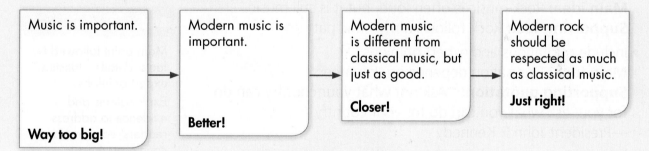

| Music is important.

Way too big! | → | Modern music is important.

Better! | → | Modern music is different from classical music, but just as good.

Closer! | → | Modern rock should be respected as much as classical music.

Just right! |

Build your argument. Plan how you will support your position with facts and strong details. In addition, decide how you will address opposing points of view. Use these tips:

- **Collect evidence.** Identify facts, examples, statistics, quotations, and personal observations that support your position. Take notes on the sources of your information, because you need to credit any ideas or words that are not your own.

- **Anticipate counterarguments.** Look ahead to identify readers' questions and points of view that might differ from your position. Plan to include facts that will successfully address counterarguments and questions.

Drafting Strategies

Write a thesis statement. The evidence you have gathered will help support your position. Prepare a thesis statement—one sentence that names your issue and expresses your position.

Sample Thesis Statements

1. Our school should have recycling bins.
2. Young people should exercise for twenty minutes every day.

Create a clear organization. Review the chart on the right to organize your thoughts. Include your thesis in your introduction. Support your thesis statement in the body of your essay. Organize supporting information into paragraphs. Conclude with a restatement of your thesis.

Support each point. As you develop your evidence, be sure to support it fully.

- Find and use examples.
  Main idea: Vegetables are healthy snacks.
  Supporting example: Carrots are a source of Vitamin A.

- Use facts or statistics.
  Main idea: Rock music is often loud, but it is still music.
  Supporting fact: Rock follows a rhythmic pattern.

- Include quotations and expert opinions.
  Main idea: Our nation depends on volunteers.
  Supporting quotation: "Ask not what your country can do for you; ask what you can do for your country."
  —President John F. Kennedy

Address counterarguments. An effective argumentative essay addresses the opposing point of view. Introduce one or two objections to your position. Use facts or other evidence to show why those objections are not strong enough to overcome your position.

Maintain a formal style. Do not weaken your argument by using slang or informal language. Instead, use a formal, authoritative tone. Maintain that tone by using sophisticated vocabulary and mixing in longer sentences with shorter ones.

Target your audience. As you write, keep in mind your readers' ages and their knowledge about your topic. Use language and details that are appropriate for your audience.

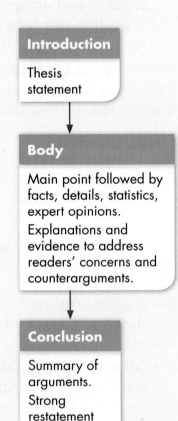

Introduction

Thesis statement

Body

Main point followed by facts, details, statistics, expert opinions. Explanations and evidence to address readers' concerns and counterarguments.

Conclusion

Summary of arguments. Strong restatement of position.

Word Choice

Word choice is the specific language a writer uses to create a strong impression. You can construct an effective argument by using precise language.

Choosing Accurate Words The success of your argument will depend on how credible, or believable, you are. Choose words carefully to make your statements accurate. Avoid using exaggerations. Vivid words create lively writing, but use them only if they are accurate.

> **Fixing Exaggerations**
> The number of families vacationing there has ~~skyrocketed~~ doubled in the last five years.

Another way to make your words accurate is to avoid absolute words. Words such as *all, always, never,* and *only* can lead to generalizations that are too broad. Replace them with words you can defend.

> **Revising Absolute Words**
> ~~All the~~ Some people who object to reality shows have never even seen one.

Using Reasonable Words Strengthen your arguments by appealing to your readers' sense of reason. Highly-charged words can capture readers' interest, but be sure to back up your strongest arguments with words that can be supported by facts.

> **Appealing to Reason, Not Emotion**
> Recycling can save ~~the planet.~~ resources.

Another way to keep your argument based on reason is by staying away from name calling. Stick to arguments that are based on evidence.

> **Fixing Name-Calling**
> Riding a bicycle without wearing a helmet is ~~stupid.~~ risky.

Word Traps to Avoid

✓ Exaggerated words

✓ Absolute words

✓ Emotional words

✓ Name-calling

Checking Your Language Review your essay, focusing on your word choice. Revise words that fall into the word traps in the chart. Choose words that will support your argument and make it more credible.

Revising Strategies

Revise to improve support. Review your draft to find places where you can strengthen the arguments that support your thesis. Follow these steps:

1. Underline your thesis statement.
2. Put a star next to each supporting point. Add more support if you have only one star.
3. If you find a paragraph without support, review your prewriting notes and add evidence. If necessary, conduct additional research to find a fact, statistic, or quotation you can use.
4. Draw attention to a well-supported point by adding powerful language or a colorful comparison that helps readers connect one main point with another.
5. Pay careful attention to how you present counterarguments. Make sure that you fairly state the other point of view. Provide two or more pieces of evidence to explain why you reject that view.
6. Review your conclusion to be sure that it follows logically from the argument you presented in the body of your essay.

Revise sentences to show relationships. Revise your sentences to clarify the relationships between the claims you make and the evidence you provide. Use transition words like the ones on the chart to show the connections among ideas.

because	therefore	as a result
consequently	however	alternatively
on the other hand	in fact	for example

Peer Review

Ask a partner to read your draft and identify places where the support for your argument seems weak. Consider adding details to strengthen your claims. In addition, have your partner review your use of standard English, and suggest any necessary corrections.

Combining Sentences Using Coordinating Conjunctions

Coordinating conjunctions such as *and, but, or,* and *so* are used to connect words, groups of words, or sentences that are similar in form.

Identifying Which Coordinating Conjunction to Use Each coordinating conjunction has a specific purpose. To join a pair of related sentences, first determine the relationship between the ideas in each sentence. Then use the correct coordinating conjunction. Place a comma *after* the first sentence and *before* the coordinating conjunction.

Coordinating Conjunction	Purpose	Use
and	to join similar or related ideas	I live in an apartment, **and** it is on the fourth floor.
but	to highlight differences or contrast	I like soccer, **but** my brother does not.
or	to show choices	You can have your lunch now, **or** you can wait for Molly.
so	to show cause and effect	I enjoy adventure stories, **so** I loved *Treasure Island.*

Fixing Comma Splices You can also use coordinating conjunctions to fix a **comma splice**. In a comma splice, two sentences are incorrectly joined together by only a comma.

   Incorrect: He saw the movie, he liked the movie.
   Correct: He saw the movie, and he liked it.

Using Coordinating Conjunctions Follow these steps:

1. **Identify the relationship between the sentences you wish to combine.**
2. **Choose a coordinating conjunction based on your purpose.**
3. **Join the two sentences using a comma and the coordinating conjunction.**

Grammar in Your Writing

Reread your argumentative essay, looking for short sentences with related ideas. Use coordinating conjunctions to combine sentences.

Modern Rock Is Music, Too

Maybe you think Chopin is really cool—the blissful tones of the piano, played to serenade and mesmerize, the dazzling cadenzas and glistening high notes. For a change, though, why don't you pop in a modern rock CD? Contemporary music gets very little respect, yet most of the people who put it down haven't even listened to it. Modern rock deserves to be regarded and respected as music.

Music can be classified as any group of organized sounds. Yet while the roars of today's lead vocalists don't seem to make sense, even they are organized and related to the message of the song. Is it music? Yes. It follows a precise rhythmic pattern. It repeats. Just because howls from a modern vocalist don't follow any pitches doesn't mean they can't be classified as perfectly good music. You might not like the style, but you cannot deny it is music.

Once you've accepted rock as music, you might say all rock songs are in the same key—E. Just because the lowest string of the guitar is an E doesn't mean modern rock musicians continuously strum that string and open and end a tune with it. Nowadays, as new musicians experiment with different pitches, the common E of rock has almost disappeared.

In a technique called "dropping," guitarists and bassists of modern rock bands have been able to use lower pitches in their songs. In fact, a well-known modern guitarist has successfully created a seven-string guitar. Its seventh string has the default pitch of a B. Although you might have to listen a little harder to hear the evidence, the musicians of contemporary bands know their music. How else could they come up with "dropping" and the seven-string guitar?

I think anyone, even the most classical music lover, can appreciate today's sounds if given a chance. (Notice I didn't say love, just appreciate.) I listen to Chopin and modern rock. I respect both kinds of music because each one has its place. Chopin is like elegant figure skating—rock is like snowboarding. I feel free when I listen to my favorite rock group. Why don't you listen with me?

Isaac clearly establishes the two sides—those who like contemporary music and those who prefer classical. The last sentence in the introduction is the thesis.

Isaac provides evidence that contemporary artists would be considered musical even by classical definitions.

Here, Isaac admits that readers might think that all rock music is written in the same key—an argument he says is no longer true.

Isaac gives details supporting his statement that rock music is no longer written in the key of E. Notice that he has more than one piece of evidence.

A powerful image helps readers understand Isaac's argument.

Editing and Proofreading

Proofread to fix grammar, spelling, and punctuation errors.

Spelling Errors: Irregular Plurals Review these rules and examples, then double-check your work for spelling errors.

- Change the *f* to *v* and add *-es*: *elf, elves; wife, wives*
- Use the same spelling for words that have the same singular and plural forms: *one fish, two fish; one deer, two deer*
- Some words change vowel form to make them plural: *tooth, teeth; mouse, mice; goose, geese; foot, feet*

Spiral Review
Earlier in the unit, you learned about **adjectives and adverbs** (p. 332) and **making comparisons with adjectives** (p. 342). Review your essay to be sure that you have used these modifiers correctly.

Publishing and Presenting

Consider one of the following ways to share your writing:

Deliver a speech. Use your argumentative essay as the basis for a speech that you present to your classmates.

Post your essay. Post your argumentative essay on a community bulletin board or online so that others can read it and discuss your position.

Reflecting on Your Writing

Writer's Journal Jot down your answer to this question:

How did your evidence change or deepen your view on the issue?

Rubric for Self-Assessment

Find evidence in your writing to address each category. Then, use the rating scale to grade your work.

Criteria	Rating Scale
Purpose/Focus In a clear thesis statement, presents a position on an issue that has at least two sides	not very .... very 1　2　3　4
Organization Introduces the topic and makes a clear claim; organizes reasons and evidence clearly and logically; provides a concluding section that follows from the argument presented	1　2　3　4
Development of Ideas/Elaboration Supports the claim with clear reasons and relevant evidence, using credible sources; addresses counterarguments; establishes and maintains a formal style	1　2　3　4
Language Uses precise language to strengthen the argument; uses words, phrases, and clauses to clarify the relationships among claims and reasons	1　2　3　4
Conventions Uses proper grammar, including correct use of coordinating conjunctions	1　2　3　4

Assessment: Skills

SELECTED RESPONSE

I. Reading Literature

Directions: *Read the poem "Wilbur Wright and Orville Wright" by Rosemary and Stephen Vincent Benét. Then, answer each question that follows.*

> Said Orville Wright to Wilbur Wright,
> "These birds are very <u>trying</u>.
> I'm sick of hearing them cheep-cheep
> About the fun of flying.
> 5 A bird has feathers, it is true.
> That much I freely grant.
> But must that stop us, W?"
> Said Wilbur Wright, "It shan't."
>
> And so they built a glider, first,
> 10 And then they built another.
> —There never were two brothers more
> Devoted to each other.
> They ran a dusty little shop
> For bicycle repairing.
> 15 And bought each other soda-pop
> And praised each other's daring.
>
> They glided here, they glided there,
> They sometimes skinned their noses.
> —For learning how to rule the air
> 20 Was not a bed of roses—
> But each would murmer, afterward,
> While patching up his bro,
> "Are we discouraged, W?"
> "Of course we are not, O!"
>
> 25 And finally at Kitty Hawk
> In Nineteen-Three (let's cheer it!)
> The first real airplane really flew
> With Orville there to steer it!
> —And kingdoms may forget their kings
> 30 And dogs forget their bites.
> But, not till Man forgets his wings,
> Will men forget the Wrights.

1. **Part A** What type of **figurative language** is used in the first stanza of the poem?
   A. simile
   B. metaphor
   C. personification
   D. onomatopoeia

   Part B Which lines from the first stanza of the poem use figurative language?
   A. "Said Orville Wright to Wilbur Wright, "These birds are very trying."
   B. "I'm sick of hearing them cheep-cheep About the fun of flying."
   C. "A bird has feathers, it is true. That much I freely grant."
   D. "But must that stop us, W?" Said Wilbur Wright, "It shan't."

2. Which of the following lines could replace line 16 without interrupting the **rhyme scheme**?
   A. And made sure the other came out on top
   B. And showed each other caring
   C. And made sure the other did not stop
   D. And praised the other brother

3. **Part A** What type of **figurative language** is used in the third stanza of the poem?
   A. simile
   B. metaphor
   C. personification
   D. onomatopoeia

   Part B Which lines from the third stanza of the poem contain the example of figurative language?
   A. "They glided here, they glided there, They sometimes skinned their noses."
   B. "—For learning how to rule the air Was not a bed of roses—"
   C. "But each would murmur, afterward, While patching up his bro"
   D. "Are we discouraged, W?" "Of course we are not, O!"

4. Which word best summarizes the **tone** of this poem?
   A. confident
   B. defeated
   C. hysterical
   D. hesitant

5. How do the authors use **repetition** to enhance the poem's mood and meaning?
   A. They repeatedly mention inventions, such as bicycles, gliders, and airplanes.
   B. They repeatedly mention failures, such as skinned noses and a dusty little shop.
   C. They have Wilbur and Orville question each other several times and answer positively.
   D. Over the course of the poem, they make fun of birds and dogs to prove the superiority of humans.

6. "Wilbur Wright and Orville Wright" is an example of which **form of poetry**?
   A. haiku
   B. concrete poem
   C. limerick
   D. narrative poem

7. Which word is closest in meaning to the underlined word *trying* as it is used in the poem?
   A. attempting
   B. bothersome
   C. achieving
   D. happening

⏱ Timed Writing

8. Write an essay or a poem about modern-day flight. Use sound devices such as **repetition**, **alliteration**, and **onomatopoeia** to add to your poem's or essay's mood and meaning.

GO ON

II. Reading Informational Text

Directions: *Read this application. Then, answer each question that follows.*

Application for Adventure Summer Camp

About our camp: Our summer program is for *students entering the 7th or 8th grades.* Applicants must be highly motivated and must see the value in helping others. An adventurous spirit is important because we will be hiking, kayaking, and camping. We will also spend time doing volunteer work in the community.

To apply for our camp: Answer the following questions. Type or print neatly. Provide one brief letter of reference from an adult who is not your parent. A second reference is optional.
No applications will be accepted after March 31.

(1) Name: _____   **(2)** Age: _____   **(3)** Entering grade: _____

(4) Address: _____

(5) Phone number: _____

(6) Hobbies: _____

(7) Why do you want to attend Adventure Camp? _____

(8) What skills make you a good candidate for Adventure Camp?

_____

(9) What type(s) of volunteer work would interest you most?

_____

---

1. Why does some information in the application appear in italics?
   - **A.** to make the application easier to read
   - **B.** to show that the information is important
   - **C.** to make the application more interesting to look at
   - **D.** to show that people do not have to read this information

2. **Part A** What section of the application tells applicants how to apply for Adventure Summer Camp?
   - **A.** The main heading that reads "Application for Adventure Summer Camp."
   - **B.** The section the follows the subhead "About our camp:".
   - **C.** The section that follows the subhead "To apply for our camp:".
   - **D.** The items labeled (1) through (9).

   Part B Based on the instructions in the application, which of the following statements can you infer to be true?
   - **A.** Campers must have at least two hobbies.
   - **B.** Campers need two letters of reference.
   - **C.** Applicants can apply at any time.
   - **D.** There will probably be a choice of volunteer work projects.

III. Writing and Language Conventions

Directions: *Read the passage. Then, answer each question that follows.*

(1) Unfortunately, four saxophone players and two other students recently quit the band because they could not afford to buy or rent needed instruments. (2) Our school band is in desperate need of new instruments. (3) If everyone contributed a mere $5, we could purchase those six instruments. (4) This might be the most important contribution students could make to our school. (5) Most of us spend $5 a week on snacks after school anyway. (6) We should stop buying snacks for just one week. (7) Music enriches the whole school, not just band students. (8) We should work together to solve this problem.

1. What **adverb** modifies the verb *quit* in sentence 1?
   A. not
   B. band
   C. students
   D. recently

2. Which sentence contains an example of a **superlative adjective**?
   A. sentence 2
   B. sentence 3
   C. sentence 4
   D. sentence 5

3. What **compound subject** appears in sentence 1?
   A. four and two
   B. students and they
   C. players and they
   D. players and students

4. How could the writer revise sentence 6 to make it an **imperative sentence?**
   A. Is it not possible to stop buying snacks for just one week?
   B. We will stop buying snacks for one week.
   C. We can stop buying snacks!
   D. Stop buying snacks for one week.

5. How could the writer revise sentence 8 to make it an **interrogative sentence?**
   A. We should work to solve this problem!
   B. Work together to solve this problem.
   C. Shouldn't we work together to solve this problem?
   D. Working together should solve this problem.

6. Which sentence contains a **conjunction?**
   A. sentence 1
   B. sentence 2
   C. sentence 6
   D. sentence 7

CONSTRUCTED RESPONSE

Directions: *Follow the instructions to complete the tasks below as required by your teacher.*

As you work on each task, incorporate both general academic vocabulary and literary terms you learned in Parts 1 and 2.

Writing

TASK 1 Literature

Analyze Figurative Language

Write an essay in which you analyze the figurative language in a poem from Part 2.

- Choose a poem from Part 2 that includes several examples of figurative language, such as simile, metaphor, or personification.
- Determine the meanings of the figurative phrases as they are used in the context of the poem. Analyze the impact of these phrases on the poem's meaning and tone.
- If possible, use a word-processing program to type your essay and prepare it for publication.

TASK 2 Literature

Analyze a Poem's Structure

Write an essay in which you analyze the structure of a poem form Part 2.

- Choose a poem from Part 2 that has three or more stanzas. Select one stanza to analyze.
- In an essay, discuss how your chosen stanza contributes to the development of the poem. Explain why specific images, figures of speech, emotions, or ideas in the stanza are important to the poem as a whole.
- In your conclusion, analyze the ways in which the stanza advances the poem's theme.

TASK 3 Literature

Analyze Sound Devices and Tone

Write an essay in which you analyze the effects of sound devices upon tone in poetry from Part 2.

Part 1

- Review the poetry you studied in Part 2. Find examples of sound devices, such as rhythm, rhyme, repetition, alliteration, and onomatopoeia.
- Take notes about how these sound devices contribute to tone in the poems.

Part 2

- Write an essay in which you analyze the sound devices used in two or more poems from Part 2. Describe the effect of the sound devices on the tone of each poem.
- At the end of your essay, draw a conclusion about the ways in which poets use sound devices to enhance their poems.
- Revise your work to vary sentences and maintain consistency in style and tone.
- Publish your finished essay in the classroom library. Include copies of the poems you analyzed.

Speaking and Listening

TASK 4 Literature

Analyze Sound Devices

Create a multimedia presentation in which you use visuals and audio to enhance the sound devices used in a poem from Part 2.

- Determine the purpose of the sound devices in a poem from Part 2, using evidence from the text to support your analysis.

- Prepare a multimedia presentation of the poem. Choose pictures, video, music, or sound effects that support the poet's use of sound devices and enhance your oral reading of the poem.

- Follow your oral reading with an explanation of your multimedia choices. Accurately use academic vocabulary in your explanation.

TASK 5 Literature

Compare Reading to Listening

Deliver an oral presentation in which you compare the experience of reading a poem from Part 2 with the experience of hearing the poem read aloud.

- With a partner, identify the poem you will discuss.

- Read the poem silently, and then listen to a recording of the poem. If you cannot find a recording of the poem, read the poem aloud to each other.

- Take notes on your experiences, comparing and contrasting what you imagine and feel while reading with what you imagine and feel while listening.

- Organize and present your observations, using adequate volume and clear pronunciation.

Research

TASK 6 Literature

Do we need words to communicate well?

In Part 2, you have read poetry in which speakers use words to communicate. Now you will conduct a short research project on one type of communication that does not require words. Use the following guidelines for your research:

- Focus your research on one type of communication that does not use words.

- Gather relevant information from at least two reliable print or digital sources.

- Take notes as you conduct your research.

- Cite your sources accurately.

When you have completed your research, write a brief essay in response to the Big Question. Use both the literature you have read and your research to reflect on this unit's Big Question. Discuss how your initial ideas have been either changed or reinforced. Support your response with an example from literature and an example from your research.

"You may not **control** all
the events that happen to you,
but you can **decide**
not to be reduced by them."

—Maya Angelou

DETERMINATION

The selections in this unit all deal with the Big Question: **Do we need words to communicate well?** In the texts that follow, you will explore the many ways—both verbal and nonverbal—that people communicate their efforts to achieve their goals. As you read, consider how individuals use determination as they strive for success.

◀ **CRITICAL VIEWING** Does this photograph effectively convey the idea of determination? Why or why not?

CLOSE READING TOOL

Use the **Close Reading Tool** to practice the strategies you learn in this unit.

READINGS IN PART 3

POEM
Simile: Willow and Gingko
Eve Merriam (p. 392)

ANCHOR TEXT

WEB ARTICLE
Angela Duckworth and the Research on "Grit"
Emily Hanford (p. 398)

EXPOSITORY ESSAY
Race to the End of the Earth
William G. Scheller (p. 404)

SHORT STORY
The Sound of Summer Running
Ray Bradbury (p. 410)

LETTER   EXEMPLAR TEXT
from **Letter on Thomas Jefferson**
John Adams (p. 420)

AUTOBIOGRAPHY
Water
Helen Keller (p. 424)

POSTER
Determination (p. 430)

SIMILE: WILLOW AND GINKGO

EVE MERRIAM

crude ▶
(krood) *adj.*
lacking
polish;
not carefully
made

The willow is like an etching,[1]
Fine-lined against the sky.
The ginkgo is like a **crude** sketch,
Hardly worthy to be signed.

5   The willow's music is like a soprano,
Delicate and thin.
The ginkgo's tune is like a chorus
With everyone joining in.

---

1. etching (ech´ iŋ) *n.* print of a drawing made on metal, glass, or wood.

The willow is sleek as a velvet-nosed calf;
10 The ginkgo is leathery as an old bull.
The willow's branches are like silken thread;
The ginkgo's like **stubby** rough wool.

The willow is like a nymph[2] with streaming hair;
Wherever it grows, there is green and gold and fair.
15 The willow dips to the water,
Protected and precious, like the king's favorite
    daughter.

The ginkgo forces its way through gray concrete;
Like a city child, it grows up in the street.
Thrust against the metal sky,
20 Somehow it survives and even **thrives**.

My eyes feast upon the willow,
But my heart goes to the ginkgo.

◀ **stubby**
(stub´ ē) *adj.*
short and
thick; bristly

◀ **thrives**
(thrīvz) *v.*
grows well

---

2. nymph (nimf) *n.* goddess of nature, thought of as a beautiful maiden.

ABOUT THE AUTHOR

Eve Merriam (1916–1992)

As a young child, Eve Merriam fell in love with the music of language. She was also influenced by musical plays that she saw during her childhood. After writing her first poem at age eight, Merriam went on to write award-winning poetry for adults and children. She also wrote and directed theater productions, some of them musicals. Her many books for young readers include *There is No Rhyme for Silver, Out Loud,* and *Rainbow Writing*. "Simile: Willow and Ginkgo" comes from her second collection of poetry, *It Doesn't Always Have to Rhyme*.

Close Reading Activities

READ

Comprehension

Reread all or part of the text to help you answer the following questions.

1. What two objects does the speaker in the poem contrast?

2. Name one thing to which the speaker compares the willow.

3. Name one thing to which the speaker compares the ginkgo.

4. What idea does the speaker express at the end of the poem?

Research: Clarify Details This poem may include references that are unfamiliar to you. Choose an unfamiliar detail and briefly research it. Then, explain how your research helps you understand the poem.

Summarize Write an objective summary of the poem. An objective summary does not include opinions or evaluations.

Language Study

Selection Vocabulary Identify at least one synonym and one antonym for each boldfaced word from the poem. Then, use each word in a sentence of your own.

• The ginkgo is like a **crude** sketch,

• The gingko's like **stubby** rough wool.

• Somehow it survives and even **thrives**.

Diction and Style Study the following lines from the poem. Then, answer the questions.

> *My eyes feast upon the willow,*
> *But my heart goes to the ginkgo.*

1. **(a)** What does the word *feast* mean in these lines? **(b)** What other meanings does *feast* have?

2. **(a)** What does the speaker mean when she says, *"My heart goes to the ginkgo"*? **(b)** Why do you think the poet uses the word *heart* instead of a synonym?

Conventions Identify the adjectives in this stanza. Then, explain how the poet uses the adjectives to contrast the trees.

> The willow is sleek as a velvet-nosed calf;
> The ginkgo is leathery as an old bull.
> The willow's branches are like silken thread;
> The ginkgo's like stubby rough wool.

Academic Vocabulary

The following words appear in blue in the instructions and questions on the facing page.

reveal   communicate   establish

Categorize the words by deciding whether you know each one well, know it a little bit, or do not know it at all. Then, use a print or online dictionary to look up the definitions of the words you do not know well or do not know at all.

Literary Analysis

Reread the identified passages. Then, respond to the questions that follow:

> **Focus Passage 1** (p. 392–393)
>
> The willow is like an etching ... like stubby rough wool.

> **Focus Passage 2** (p. 393)
>
> The willow is like a nymph ... *But my heart goes to the ginkgo.*

Key Ideas and Details

1. Name the categories in which the speaker compares the trees.

2. Analyze: What do the comparisons **reveal** about each tree?

Craft and Structure

3. (a) Summarize: What sensory information does each stanza **communicate**? **(b) Compare and Contrast:** How are the trees different in terms of strength?

4. (a) Analyze: Describe the pattern of rhyming words in these stanzas. **(b)** What is the effect of this rhyme scheme?

Integration of Knowledge and Ideas

5. (a) Synthesize: In these stanzas, is the speaker more positive toward the willow or the ginkgo? **(b) Compare:** How does this tone compare with commonly-held ideas about beauty?

Key Ideas and Details

1. Analyze: What gives the willow "streaming hair"?

2. (a) Analyze: What does "metal sky" mean? **(b) Interpret:** What does this description say about the ginkgo's environment?

Craft and Structure

3. (a) What colors and materials do the fourth and fifth stanzas name? **(b) Analyze:** What do these words suggest about the trees' environments?

4. (a) List the verbs in the fourth and fifth stanzas. **(b) Interpret:** What contrasting moods do these verbs **establish**?

Integration of Knowledge and Ideas

5. (a) In the last two stanzas, how does the speaker's attitude change? **(b) Analyze:** What does this change suggest about the poem's message?

Simile

In a **simile**, the writer uses *like* or *as* to make a comparison. Reread the poem, taking notes on the poet's use of similes.

1. (a) How do the similes in the poem contrast the trees? **(b)** What do comparisons to "silken thread" and "stubby rough wool" show?

2. Determination Explain how the simile that compares the ginkgo to a "city child" relates to the idea of determination.

DISCUSS

From Text to Topic **Group Discussion**

Discuss the following stanza with classmates. Take notes during the discussion. Contribute your own ideas, and support them with examples from the text.

> The willow's music is like a soprano, ... everyone joining in. (p. 392)

WRITE

Writing to Sources **Informative Text**

Assignment

Write an **expository essay** in which you discuss the relationship between environment and determination. Cite evidence from both the poem and your own experience to support your ideas.

Prewriting and Planning Reread the poem to find details that describe how an environment can create the need for determination. The connection might not be stated directly. Instead, it may be implied through the language of the poem. Record your notes.

Drafting Select an organizational structure. Most expository writing includes an introduction, a body, and a conclusion.

- **Introduction** Begin by introducing the poem and stating your thesis.
- **Body** Explain the qualities of a particular environment, and explain how it creates a need for determination.
- **Conclusion** End by drawing a conclusion about the relationship between environment and determination.

Revising Reread your essay. If you have included examples of personal experiences as evidence, make sure it is clear when you are talking about the poem and when you are talking about yourself. Use present-tense verbs to discuss the poem. Use past-tense verbs to discuss your past experiences and present-tense verbs to discuss something that is happening now.

Editing and Proofreading Make sure you have used the correct verb tense in each section. If you are not sure of how to form a tense, look it up in a grammar handbook. Correct any errors you find.

QUESTIONS FOR DISCUSSION

1. Why does the speaker describe the ginkgo's music as a "chorus"?

2. Which is more positive, the description of the willow's music or of the ginkgo's tune? Why?

CONVENTIONS

When you shift from the present to the past, you must use the correct verb tense. Use present-tense verbs (*go, sing, eat*) to discuss the present, and past-tense verbs (*went, sang, ate*) to discuss the past.

RESEARCH

Research **Investigate the Topic**

Survival Skills In this poem, the speaker compares the ginkgo to a "city child" who, through determination, "survives and even thrives." Social scientists have identified certain factors that help children develop the determination they need to succeed. For example, strong family support helps children develop self-esteem and seek positive paths in life.

> ### Assignment
> Conduct research to find out what social scientists have learned about factors that help children use determination to make positive choices and thrive in their environments. Consult credible sources, such as scientific journals. Take clear notes and carefully identify your sources so that you can easily access the information later. Share your findings in a brief **research report**.

PREPARATION FOR ESSAY

You may use the knowledge you gain during this research assignment to support your claims in an essay you will write at the end of this section.

Gather Sources Locate authoritative print and electronic sources. Scientific journals provide the latest social science research. These types of sources are peer-reviewed and usually credible. You may also want to use online sources. Look for sources that feature expert authors and up-to-date information.

Take Notes Take notes on each source, either electronically or on note cards. Use an organized note-taking strategy.

- Use a separate electronic file, sheet of paper, or note card for each source.
- Put quotation marks around each direct quotation from a source. This way, you will not accidentally plagiarize material.
- Record source information for use in your bibliography.

Synthesize Multiple Sources Gather data from your sources and use it to construct an outline. Use your outline to draft a cohesive research report on the factors that help children develop the determination they need to succeed. Create a Works Cited list as described in the Research Workshop in the Introductory Unit of your textbook.

Organize and Present Ideas Review your report and double-check that you have accurately quoted or paraphrased your sources.

Angela Duckworth and the Research on "GRIT"

Emily Hanford

Before she was a psychology professor, Angela Duckworth taught in middle school and high school. She spent a lot of time thinking about something that might seem obvious: The students who tried hardest did the best, and the students who didn't try very hard didn't do very well. Duckworth wanted to know: What is the role of effort in a person's success?

Now Duckworth is an assistant professor at the University of Pennsylvania, and her research focuses on a personality trait she calls "grit." She defines grit as "sticking with things over the very long term until you master them." In a paper, she writes that "the gritty individual approaches achievement as a marathon; his or her advantage is stamina."[1]

---

1. stamina (stam´ ə nə) *n.* endurance; ability to resist fatigue.

Duckworth's research suggests that when it comes to high achievement, grit may be as essential as intelligence. That's a significant finding because for a long time, intelligence was considered *the* key to success.

Intelligence "is probably the best-measured trait that there is in all of human psychology," says Duckworth. "We know how to measure intelligence in a matter of minutes."

But intelligence leaves a lot unexplained. There are smart people who aren't high achievers, and there are people who achieve a lot without having the highest test scores. In one study, Duckworth found that smarter students actually had *less* grit than their peers who scored lower on an intelligence test. This finding suggests that, among the study participants—all students at an Ivy League school—people who are not as bright as their peers "compensate by working harder and with more determination." And their effort pays off: The grittiest students—not the smartest ones—had the highest GPAs.

The Grit Test

Duckworth's work is part of a growing area of psychology research focused on what are loosely called "noncognitive skills."[2] The goal is to identify and measure the various skills and traits other than intelligence that contribute to human development and success.

Duckworth has developed a test called the "Grit Scale." You rate yourself on a series of 8 to 12 items. Two examples: "I have overcome setbacks to conquer an important challenge" and "Setbacks don't discourage me." It's entirely self-reported, so you could game[3] the test, and yet what Duckworth has found is that a person's grit score is highly predictive of achievement under challenging circumstances.

At the elite United States Military Academy, West Point, a cadet's grit score was the best predictor of success in the

---

2. **noncognitive skills** processes that involve emotions and decision-making, rather than cognitive skills such as intelligence, memory, perception, judgment, and reasoning.
3. **game** here, game means "bending the rules" or "cheating."

rigorous ▶
(rig′ ər əs)
adj. difficult;
demanding

rigorous summer training program known as "Beast Barracks." Grit mattered more than intelligence, leadership ability or physical fitness.

At the Scripps National Spelling Bee, the grittiest contestants were the most likely to advance to the finals—at least in part because they studied longer, not because they were smarter or were better spellers....

Learning to Be Gritty

It's not clear what makes some people grittier than others, but Angela Duckworth believes grit is something people can probably learn.

She says every human quality that has been studied has proven to be affected at least in part by a person's environment—even intelligence. In addition, people change over time.

"Think about things about your personality like, 'I'm a pretty extroverted[4] person,'" says Duckworth. "Well, how fixed is that?"

It turns out a personality trait like extroversion can change a lot over a person's life. "If you look at large population data, people get more or less extroverted over time," says

The Scripps Spelling Bee

Duckworth. "There's no reason to think that grit is any different."

She believes grit can wax and wane in response to experiences. In addition, people might be gritty about some things and not others.

"You can see a child be exceptionally self-disciplined about their basketball practicing, and yet when you see them in math class,

---

4. **extroverted** (eks′ trə vurt′ id) *adj.* outgoing; sociable.

they give up at the slightest frustration," says Duckworth.

Donald Kamentz, director of college initiatives at YES Prep, says students he's worked with are some of the grittiest people he's ever met. They "deal with things and **persevere** through situations that most people would find **insurmountable**," he says.

◀ **persevere**
(pʉr′ sə vir′) *v.*
continue although
faced with
difficulties

He's known students who get jobs to pay the bills when their parents are laid off, or figure out how to get the electricity back on when the power company shuts it off.

"And then they go to college and they're struggling with financial aid or their financial aid didn't come through and they don't know what to do," he says. Some of them drop out when confronted with these kinds of challenges. He says they're not gritty enough when it comes to college.

◀ **insurmountable**
(in′ sər mount′ ə bəl) *adj.*
impossible to
overcome

A question for YES Prep and other charter schools in Duckworth's study is not necessarily how to get students to be gritty, but how to get them to be gritty about college completion.

"Which experiences do we give kids to get them in the direction of more grit and not less?" asks Duckworth.

One of the goals of Duckworth's research is to figure this out. Her current project began in the fall of 2011 and is scheduled to wrap up in 2014.

ABOUT THE AUTHOR

Emily Hanford

Emily Hanford began working in radio immediately after graduating from Amherst College in Amherst, Massachusetts. She has worked as a news producer, director, and reporter for several public radio stations. As the senior editor/ producer for the series *North Carolina Voices*, Hanford contributed to a reporting project about high school reform that eventually became the documentary *Put to the Test*. In 2008, Hanford began reporting on education for American RadioWorks.

Close Reading Activities

READ

Comprehension

Reread all or part of the text to help you answer the following questions.

1. What is "grit"?

2. According to Angela Duckworth's research, grit is as **essential** to achievement as which trait?

3. What is the "Grit Scale"?

Research: Clarify Details This article may include references that are unfamiliar to you. Choose an unfamiliar detail and briefly research it. Then, explain how your research clarifies the article.

Summarize Write an objective summary of the article, free from opinion and evaluation.

Language Study

Selection Vocabulary Define each word from the article and use the word in a sentence of your own.

- **rigorous**
- **persevere**
- **insurmountable**

Literary Analysis

Reread the identified passages. Then, respond to the questions that follow:

> **Focus Passage** (pp. 398–399)
>
> Before she was a psychology professor, … had the highest GPAs.

Key Ideas and Details

1. **(a)** What observation sparked Duckworth's interest in "grit"? **(b) Connect:** How does grit affect students' success?

2. **(a) Speculate:** Why might intelligence fail to predict success? **(b) Support:** What examples from the text support this idea?

Craft and Structure

3. **(a)** Does the author use the active or passive voice when she says "for a long time, intelligence was considered *the* key to success"? **(b) Infer:** Why do you think the author phrased the idea this way?

Integration of Knowledge and Ideas

4. **Draw Conclusions:** What do you learn from this passage about the ways in which researchers choose topics for study?

Direct Quotation

A **direct quotation** states a person's exact words. Reread the article, taking notes on Hanford's use of direct quotation.

1. **(a)** Which two people does Hanford quote directly? **(b)** Why does she quote these people?

2. **Determination (a)** Which direct quotation expresses Duckworth's current research question? **(b)** How might this research contribute to the **study** of determination?

DISCUSS • RESEARCH • WRITE

From Text to Topic **Partner Discussion**

Discuss the following passage with a partner. Take notes during the discussion. Contribute your own ideas, and support them with examples from the text.

> Donald Kamentz, director of college initiatives … when it comes to college. (p. 401)

Research **Investigate the Topic**

College Challenges As the article says, problems with financial aid can cause students to drop out of college. Other factors contribute to the drop-out rate as well.

Assignment

Conduct **research** to find out what factors can cause students to drop out of college. Consult government education websites and reputable magazines and journals. Take clear notes and carefully identify your sources so that you can easily access the information later. Share your findings in a **chart**. Create separate categories for factors that are related to determination and factors that are not.

Writing to Sources **Narrative**

People can use "grit" in many different situations.

Assignment

Write an **autobiographical narrative** in which you describe how you used grit to succeed in a situation. Follow these steps:

- Explain the meaning of grit and introduce a situation in which you needed it.

- Describe how you used grit in that situation. Use transitions to create a smooth progression of ideas that build on one another.

- Use literary elements such as description, dialogue, foreshadowing, and suspense to create an engaging narrative.

- Provide a conclusion in which reflect on your "gritty" experience and connect it to the experiences of people described in Hanford's article.

QUESTIONS FOR DISCUSSION

1. What makes some gritty people "not gritty enough when it comes to college"?

2. Why might people be gritty about some things and not others?

PREPARATION FOR ESSAY

You may use the results of this research project to support your ideas in the essay you will write at the end of this section.

ACADEMIC VOCABULARY

Academic terms appear in blue on these pages. If these words are not familiar to you, use a dictionary to find their definitions. Then, use them as you speak and write about the text.

RACE
TO THE END OF
THE EARTH

William G. Scheller

Two explorers competed against each other and a brutal environment to reach the South Pole.

The drifts were so deep and the snow was falling so heavily that the team of five Norwegian explorers could hardly see their sled dogs a few feet ahead of them. Behind rose a monstrous mountain barrier. The men had been the first to cross it. But now they and their dogs were stumbling toward a stark and desolate **plateau** continually blasted by blizzards. The landscape was broken only by the towering peaks of mountains that lay buried beneath a mile of ancient ice. Led by Roald Amundsen, the men were still 300 miles from their goal: the South Pole.

On that same day, a party of 14 British explorers was also struggling across a similarly terrifying landscape toward the same destination. But they were almost twice as far from success. Their commander was Capt. Robert Falcon Scott, a naval officer. Amundsen was Scott's rival.

Preparation Both **expedition** leaders had long been preparing for their race to the South Pole. Amundsen came from a family of hardy sailors, and he had decided at the age of 15 to become a **polar** explorer. He conditioned himself by taking long ski trips across the Norwegian countryside

plateau ▶
(pla tō´) n. raised area of land with a level surface

expedition ▶
(eks´pə dish´ən) n. journey for a particular purpose, such as exploration or scientific study

polar ▶
(pō´lər) adj. near, of, or relating to the North or South Pole

and by sleeping with his windows open in winter.

By the time of his South Pole attempt, Amundsen was an experienced explorer. He had sailed as a naval officer on an expedition in 1897 that charted sections of the Antarctic coast. Between 1903 and 1906 he commanded the ship that made the first voyage through the Northwest Passage, the icy route that threads its way through the Canadian islands separating the Atlantic and Pacific Oceans. During that long journey Amundsen learned how the native people of the Arctic dress and eat to survive in extreme cold. He also learned that the dogsled was the most efficient method of polar transportation. These lessons would serve him well at Earth's frozen southern end.

Robert Scott was an officer in the British Navy. He had decided that leading a daring expedition of discovery would be an immediate route to higher rank. He heard that Great Britain's Royal Geographical Society was organizing such an exploration, and he volunteered in 1899 to be its commander. Now he was in command again.

The two expedition leaders had different styles. Scott followed a British tradition of brave sacrifice. He felt that he and his men should be able to reach the South Pole with as little help as possible from sled dogs and special equipment. He did bring dogs to Antarctica, as well as 19 ponies and three gasoline-powered sledges, or sturdy sleds. But his plan was for his team to "man-haul," or carry, all of their own supplies along the final portion of the route.

Roald Amundsen had spent much time in the far north, and he was a practical man. He'd seen how useful dogs were to Arctic inhabitants. He would be traveling in one of the most dangerous places on Earth, and he knew that sled dogs would be able to get his party all the way to the South Pole and make a safe return.

Amundsen also placed great faith in skis, which he and his Norwegian team members had used since childhood. The British explorers had rarely used skis before this expedition and did not understand their great value.

The two leaders even had different ideas about diet. Scott's men would rely on canned meat. But Amundsen's plan made more sense. He and his men would eat plenty of fresh seal meat. Amundsen may not have fully understood the importance of vitamins, but fresh meat is a better source of vitamin C, which prevents scurvy, a painful and sometimes deadly disease.

The Race Is On! After making long sea voyages from Europe, Scott and Amundsen set up base camps in January on opposite edges of the Ross Ice Shelf. Each team spent the dark winter months making preparations to push on to the Pole when spring would arrive in Antarctica.

Amundsen left base camp on October 20, 1911, with a party of four. Scott, accompanied by nine men, set off from his camp 11 days later. Four others had already gone ahead on the motorized sledges.

FOR SCOTT AND HIS MEN, THE JOURNEY WAS LONG AND BRUTAL.

Scott's Final Diary Entry Things went wrong for Scott from the beginning. The sledges broke down and had to be abandoned. Scott and his men soon met up with the drivers, who were traveling on foot. Blizzards then struck and lasted several weeks into December. Scott's ponies were proving to be a poor choice for Antarctic travel as well. Their hooves sank deep into the snow, and their perspiration froze on their bodies, forming sheets of ice. (Dogs do not perspire; they pant.) On December 9, the men shot the last of the surviving weak and frozen ponies. Two days later Scott sent his remaining dogs back to base camp along with several members of the expedition. Over the next month, most of the men returned to the camp. Scott's plan from here on was for the five men remaining to manhaul supplies the rest of the way to the Pole and back.

For Scott and his men, the journey was long and brutal. To cover only ten miles each day, the team toiled like dogs— like the dogs they no longer had. Food and fuel were in short supply, so the men lacked the energy they needed for such a crushing task.

Robert F. Scott (center) and his team.

Roald Amundsen's careful planning and Arctic experience were paying off. Even so, there's no such thing as easy travel by land in Antarctica. To the men who had just crossed those terrible mountains, the Polar Plateau might have looked easy. But Amundsen's team still had to cross a long stretch they later named the "Devil's Ballroom." It was a thin crust of ice that concealed crevasses, or deep gaps, that could swallow men, sleds, and dogs. Stumbling into one crevasse, a team of dogs dangled by their harnesses until the men could pull them up to safety.

Reaching the Goal On skis, with the "ballroom" behind them and well-fed dogs pulling their supply sleds, Amundsen and his men swept across the ice. The going was smooth for them, and the weather was fine. The Norwegians' only worry was that they'd find Scott had gotten to the Pole first. On the afternoon of December 14, 1911, it was plain that no one was ahead of them. At three o'clock, Amundsen skied in front of the team's sleds, then stopped to look at his navigation instruments. There was no point further south. He was at the South Pole!

Close Reading Activities

READ

Comprehension

Reread all or part of the text to help you answer the following questions.

1. For what were Amundsen and Scott competing?

2. What problems did both men face?

3. What was the outcome of the competition?

Research: Clarify Details This essay may include unfamiliar references. Choose one to briefly research. Then, explain how your research helps you understand the essay.

Summarize Write an objective summary of the essay. Include main ideas, but do not include opinions.

Language Study

Selection Vocabulary: Science Give the scientific meaning of each boldfaced word. Then, give another meaning of each word.

- … a stark and desolate **plateau** continually blasted by blizzards.

- Both **expedition** leaders had long been preparing for their race to the South Pole.

- … dogsled was the most efficient method of **polar** transportation.

Literary Analysis

Reread the identified passage. Then, respond to the questions that follow:

> **Focus Passage** (pp. 405–406)
>
> The two expedition leaders had different styles … sometimes deadly disease.

Key Ideas and Details

1. **(a)** What equipment and supplies did Amundsen and Scott each bring on their expeditions? **(b) Assess:** Which man was better prepared? Why?

2. **(a)** What food did Amundsen and Scott plan to eat on their expeditions? **(b) Evaluate:** What were the disadvantages of Scott's plan?

Craft and Structure

3. **(a) Classify:** How is the passage organized? **(b) Analyze:** Why did the author approach the topic this way?

Integration of Knowledge and Ideas

4. **(a) Infer:** Which explorer does the author seem to admire more? **(b) Support:** Cite **evidence** that supports your choice.

Foreshadowing

Foreshadowing is the use of clues to hint at what might happen later in a narrative.

1. **(a)** Find two examples of foreshadowing in the essay. **(b)** What future event does each example suggest?

2. **Determination** Based on foreshadowing in the essay, would you say that determination always leads to success? Explain.

DISCUSS • RESEARCH • WRITE

From Text to Topic **Group Discussion**

Discuss the following passage with a partner. Take notes during the discussion. Contribute your own ideas, and support them with examples from the text.

> The drifts were so deep and the snow was falling so heavily … their goal: the South Pole. (p. 404)

Research **Investigate the Topic**

Expedition to the South Pole "Race to the End of the Earth" reveals who won the "race" but does not tell what happened to Scott and his team. Specifically, readers do not learn whether Scott and his team ever reached the South Pole.

Assignment

Conduct research to learn more about Scott's background and to find out whether or not Scott's determination ever carried him and his team to the South Pole. Consult credible historical sources. Take clear notes and carefully identify your sources so that you can easily access the information later. Share your findings in a **short research paper**.

Writing to Sources **Narrative**

Scott kept a journal of his adventures and struggles on the expedition.

Assignment

Write a **diary entry,** from Scott's point of view, describing something that happens in the final days of his journey to the South Pole.

- Use first-person pronouns such as *I, me,* and *mine* to convey Scott's **perspective**.
- Describe your experiences using vivid language that appeals to the five senses.
- Expand on information presented in the essay, adding details to build Scott's character, feelings, and personality.
- Use transitions to build suspense and connect your ideas.

QUESTIONS FOR DISCUSSION

1. How does the author emphasize the danger of South Pole expeditions?
2. How does this passage relate to the idea of determination?

PREPARATION FOR ESSAY

You may use the results of this research project to support your ideas in the essay you will write at the end of this section.

ACADEMIC VOCABULARY

Academic terms appear in blue on these pages. If these words are not familiar to you, use a dictionary to find their definitions. Then, use them as you speak and write about the text.

The *Sound* of *Summer* *Running*

from Dandelion Wine

Ray Bradbury

Late that night, going home from the show with his mother and father and his brother Tom, Douglas saw the tennis shoes in the bright store window.

He glanced quickly away, but his ankles were seized, his feet suspended, then rushed. The earth spun; the shop awnings slammed their canvas wings overhead with the thrust of his body running. His mother and father and brother walked quietly on both sides of him. Douglas walked backward, watching the tennis shoes in the midnight window left behind.

"It was a nice movie," said Mother.

Douglas murmured, "It was . . ."

It was June and long past time for buying the special shoes that were quiet as a summer rain falling on the walks. June and the earth full of raw power and everything everywhere in motion. The grass was still pouring in from the country, surrounding the sidewalks, stranding the houses. Any moment the town would capsize, go down and leave not a stir in the clover and weeds. And here Douglas stood, trapped on the dead cement and the red-brick streets, hardly able to move.

"Dad!" He blurted it out. "Back there in that window, those Cream-Sponge Para Litefoot Shoes . . ."

His father didn't even turn. "Suppose you tell me why you need a new pair of sneakers. Can you do that?"

"Well . . ."

It was because they felt the way it feels every summer when you take off your shoes for the first time and run in the grass. They felt like it feels sticking your feet out of the hot covers in wintertime to let the cold wind from the open window blow on them suddenly and you let them stay out a

◀ **seized**
(sēzd) v. grabbed; taken hold of

◀ **suspended**
(sə spend´ əd) v. stopped for a time

long time until you pull them back in under the covers again to feel them, like packed snow. The tennis shoes felt like it always feels the first time every year wading in the slow waters of the creek and seeing your feet below, half an inch further downstream, with refraction, than the real part of you above water.

"Dad," said Douglas, "it's hard to explain."

Somehow the people who made tennis shoes knew what boys needed and wanted. They put marshmallows and coiled springs in the soles and they wove the rest out of grasses bleached and fired in the wilderness. Somewhere deep in the soft loam of the shoes the thin hard sinews of the buck deer were hidden. The people that made the shoes must have watched a lot of winds blow the trees and a lot of rivers going down to the lakes. Whatever it was, it was in the shoes, and it was summer.

Douglas tried to get all this in words.

"Yes," said Father, "but what's wrong with last year's sneakers? Why can't you dig *them* out of the closet?"

Well, he felt sorry for boys who lived in California where they wore tennis shoes all year and never knew what it was to get winter off your feet, peel off the iron leather shoes all full of snow and rain and run barefoot for a day and then lace on the first new tennis shoes of the season, which was better than barefoot. The magic was always in the new pair of shoes. The magic might die by the first of September, but now in late June there was still plenty of magic, and shoes like these could jump you over trees and rivers and houses. And if you wanted, they could jump you over fences and sidewalks and dogs.

"Don't you see?" said Douglas. "I just *can't* use last year's pair."

For last year's pair were dead inside. They had been fine when he started them out, last year. But by the end of summer, every year, you always found out, you always knew, you couldn't really jump over rivers and trees and houses in them, and they were dead. But this was a new year, and he felt that this time, with this new pair of shoes, he could do anything, anything at all.

They walked up on the steps to their house. "Save your money," said Dad. "In five or six weeks—"

"Summer'll be over!"

Lights out, with Tom asleep, Douglas lay watching his feet, far away down there at the end of the bed in the moonlight, free of the heavy iron shoes, the big chunks of winter fallen away from them.

"Reason. I've got to think of reasons for the shoes."

Well, as anyone knew, the hills around town were wild with friends putting cows to riot, playing barometer[1] to the atmospheric changes, taking sun, peeling like calendars each day to take more sun. To catch those friends, you must run much faster than foxes or squirrels. As for the town, it steamed with enemies grown irritable with heat, so remembering every winter argument and insult. *Find friends, ditch enemies!* That was the Cream-Sponge Para Litefoot motto. *Does the world run too fast? Want to catch up? Want to be alert, stay alert? Litefoot, then! Litefoot!*

He held his coin bank up and heard the faint small tinkling, the airy weight of money there.

> *"Reason. I've got to think of reasons for the shoes."*

Whatever you want, he thought, you got to make your own way. During the night now, let's find that path through the forest. . . .

Downtown, the store lights went out, one by one. A wind blew in the window. It was like a river going downstream and his feet wanting to go with it.

In his dreams he heard a rabbit running running running in the deep warm grass.

Old Mr. Sanderson moved through his shoe store as the proprietor of a pet shop must move through his shop where are kenneled animals from everywhere in the world, touching each one briefly along the way. Mr. Sanderson brushed his hands over the shoes in the window, and some of them were like cats to him and some were like dogs; he touched each pair with concern, adjusting laces, fixing tongues. Then he stood in the exact center of the carpet and looked around, nodding.

There was a sound of growing thunder.

---

1. **barometer** (bə räm′ ət ər) *n.* device that measures air pressure, to predict weather changes.

One moment, the door to Sanderson's Shoe Emporium was empty. The next, Douglas Spaulding stood clumsily there, staring down at his leather shoes as if these heavy things could not be pulled up out of the cement. The thunder had stopped when his shoes stopped. Now, with painful slowness, daring to look only at the money in his cupped hand, Douglas moved out of the bright sunlight of Saturday noon. He made careful stacks of nickels, dimes, and quarters on the counter, like someone playing chess and worried if the next move carried him out into sun or deep into shadow.

"Don't say a word!" said Mr. Sanderson.

Douglas froze.

"First, I know just what you want to buy," said Mr. Sanderson. "Second, I see you every afternoon at my window; you think I don't see? You're wrong. Third, to give it its full name, you want the Royal Crown Cream-Sponge Para Litefoot Tennis Shoes: 'Like Menthol On Your Feet!' Fourth, you want credit."

"No!" cried Douglas, breathing hard, as if he'd run all night in his dreams. "I got something better than credit to offer!" he gasped. "Before I tell, Mr. Sanderson, you got to do me one small favor. Can you remember when was the last time you yourself wore a pair of Litefoot sneakers, sir?"

Mr. Sanderson's face darkened. "Oh, ten, twenty, say, thirty years ago. Why . . . ?"

"Mr. Sanderson, don't you think you owe it to your customers, sir, to at least try the tennis shoes you sell, for just one minute, so you know how they feel? People forget if they don't keep testing things. United Cigar Store man smokes cigars, don't he? Candy-store man samples his own stuff, I should think. So . . ."

"You may have noticed," said the old man, "I'm wearing shoes."

"But not sneakers, sir! How you going to sell sneakers unless you can rave about them and how you going to rave about them unless you know them?"

Mr. Sanderson backed off a little distance from the boy's fever, one hand to his chin. "Well . . ."

"Mr. Sanderson," said Douglas, "you sell me something and I'll sell you something just as valuable."

"Is it absolutely necessary to the sale that I put on a pair of the sneakers, boy?" said the old man.

"I sure wish you could, sir!"

The old man sighed. A minute later, seated panting quietly, he laced the tennis shoes to his long narrow feet. They looked detached and alien[2] down there next to the dark cuffs of his business suit. Mr. Sanderson stood up.

"How do they *feel*?" asked the boy.

"How do they feel, he asks; they feel fine." He started to sit down.

"Please!" Douglas held out his hand. "Mr. Sanderson, now could you kind of rock back and forth a little, sponge around, bounce kind of, while I tell you the rest? It's this: I give you my money, you give me the shoes, I owe you a dollar. But, Mr. Sanderson, *but*—soon as I get those shoes on, you know what *happens*?"

"What?"

"Bang! I deliver your packages, pick up packages, bring you coffee, burn your trash, run to the post office, telegraph office, library! You'll see twelve of me in and out, in and out, every minute. Feel those shoes, Mr. Sanderson, *feel* how fast they'd take me? All those springs inside? Feel all the running inside? Feel how they kind of grab hold and can't let you alone and don't like you just *standing* there? Feel how quick I'd be doing the things you'd rather not bother with? You stay in the nice cool store while I'm jumping all around town! But it's not me really, it's the shoes. They're going like mad down alleys, cutting corners, and back! There they go!"

Mr. Sanderson stood amazed with the rush of words. When the words got going the flow carried him; he began to sink deep in the shoes, to flex his toes, limber[3] his arches, test his ankles. He rocked softly, secretly, back and forth in a small breeze from the open door. The tennis shoes silently hushed themselves deep in the carpet, sank as in a jungle grass, in loam and resilient clay. He gave one solemn bounce of his heels in the yeasty dough, in the yielding and welcoming earth. Emotions hurried over his face as if many

---

2. alien (āl′ yən) *adj.* foreign; unfamiliar.
3. limber (lim′ bər) *v.* loosen up (a muscle or limb); make easy to bend.

colored lights had been switched on and off. His mouth hung slightly open. Slowly he gentled and rocked himself to a halt, and the boy's voice faded and they stood there looking at each other in a tremendous and natural silence.

A few people drifted by on the sidewalk outside, in the hot sun.

Still the man and boy stood there, the boy glowing, the man with **revelation** in his face.

"Boy," said the old man at last, "in five years, how would you like a job selling shoes in this emporium?"

"Gosh, thanks, Mr. Sanderson, but I don't know what I'm going to be yet."

"Anything you want to be, son," said the old man, "you'll be. No one will ever stop you."

The old man walked lightly across the store to the wall of ten thousand boxes, came back with some shoes for the boy, and wrote up a list on some paper while the boy was lacing the shoes on his feet and then standing there, waiting.

The old man held out his list. "A dozen things you got to do for me this afternoon. Finish them, we're even Stephen, and you're fired."

"Thanks, Mr. Sanderson!" Douglas bounded away.

"Stop!" cried the old man.

Douglas pulled up and turned.

Mr. Sanderson leaned forward. "How do they *feel*?"

The boy looked down at his feet deep in the rivers, in the fields of wheat, in the wind that already was rushing him out of the town. He looked up at the old man, his eyes burning, his mouth moving, but no sound came out.

"Antelopes?" said the old man, looking from the boy's face to his shoes. "Gazelles?"

The boy thought about it, hesitated, and nodded a quick nod. Almost immediately he vanished. He just spun about with a whisper and went off. The door stood empty. The sound of the tennis shoes faded in the jungle heat.

Mr. Sanderson stood in the sun-blazed door, listening. From a long time ago, when he dreamed as a boy, he remembered the sound. Beautiful creatures leaping under the sky, gone through brush, under trees, away, and only the soft echo their running left behind.

"Antelopes," said Mr. Sanderson. "Gazelles."

He bent to pick up the boy's abandoned winter shoes, heavy with forgotten rains and long-melted snows. Moving out of the blazing sun, walking softly, lightly, slowly, he headed back toward civilization. . . .

ABOUT THE AUTHOR

Ray Bradbury (1920–2012)

As a boy, Ray Bradbury nourished his imagination by attending circuses, watching magicians, and reading science fiction. He once stated, "My life filled up with these wonderful events and people and images, and they stirred my imagination so that by the time I was twelve, I decided to become a writer. Just like that."

Bradbury began publishing short stories in magazines in 1940. His best-known works are the short story collections *The Martian Chronicles* (1950), *The Illustrated Man* (1951), and *The Golden Apples of the Sun* (1953) and the novels *Fahrenheit 451* (1953), *Dandelion Wine* (1957), and *Something Wicked This Way Comes* (1962). Bradbury's stories and novels are known for their sharp social criticism and warnings about human reliance on technology.

Close Reading Activities

READ

Comprehension

Reread all or part of the text to help you answer the following questions.

1. What does Douglas want, and why?

2. Why does Douglas's father refuse to get him what he wants?

3. How does Douglas acquire what he wants?

Research: Clarify Details This story may include details that are unfamiliar to you. Choose one unfamiliar detail, and briefly research it. Then, explain your research clarifies the story.

Summarize Write an objective summary of the story. Do not include your opinions.

Language Study

Selection Vocabulary Write the part of speech of each boldfaced word. Then, use each word in a sentence.

- He glanced quickly away, but his ankles were **seized** …

- … his feet **suspended**, then rushed.

- Still the man and boy stood there, the boy glowing, the man with **revelation** in his face.

Literary Analysis

Reread the identified passage. Then, respond to the questions that follow.

> **Focus Passage** *(pp. 415–416)*
>
> Mr. Sanderson stood amazed … the man with revelation in his face.

Key Ideas and Details

1. What is the "rush of words" Mr. Sanderson hears?

2. What does Mr. Sanderson do as he listens?

Craft and Structure

3. **(a)** What sensory images does Bradbury use to describe how the shoes feel to Mr. Sanderson? **(b) Connect:** To what senses do these images appeal? **(c) Interpret:** What ideas do the images convey?

Integration of Knowledge and Ideas

4. **Draw Conclusions:** What "revelation" comes to Mr. Sanderson after he tries on the shoes?

Symbols

A **symbol** is an object or idea that represents something other than itself. For example, an owl can be a symbol of wisdom. Reread the passage and take notes on the author's use of symbols.

1. What do the tennis shoes **symbolize** for Douglas? Use details in the story to support your interpretation.

2. What do the tennis shoes come to symbolize for Mr. Sanderson? Support your response.

DISCUSS • RESEARCH • WRITE

From Text to Topic **Group Discussion**

Discuss the following passage with a group of classmates. Take notes during the discussion. Contribute your own ideas, and support them with examples from the text.

> He held his coin bank up and heard the faint small tinkling, the airy weight of money there. ...
>
> Whatever you want, he thought, you got to make your own way. During the night now, let's find that path through the forest. ...
>
> Downtown, the store lights went out, one by one. A wind blew in the window. It was like a river going downstream and his feet wanting to go with it.

Research **Investigate the Topic**

Financial Skills Douglas's father teaches him that if you are determined to have something that costs money, you must earn the money to buy it.

Assignment

Conduct research to find out how young people can learn financial, or money-related, skills. Consult the Web sites of state treasurers' offices, as well as financial magazines and books. Take clear notes and carefully identify your sources so that you can easily access the information later. Share your findings in a **presentation** for the class. Explain how determination can help a person learn and use financial skills.

Writing to Sources **Narrative**

"The Sound of Summer Running" vividly describes how an item of clothing has a symbolic meaning for the main character.

Assignment

Write an **autobiographical narrative** in which you tell the story of an object that has a special, symbolic meaning for you.

- Begin by introducing an item that has a symbolic meaning for you.
- In the body of your essay, explain how the item developed its meaning. Use vivid imagery to tell your story.
- Provide a conclusion in which you make connections between your symbolic object and Douglas's shoes.

QUESTIONS FOR DISCUSSION

1. Why does Douglas think that "you got to make your own way"?
2. How does the wind **influence** Douglas's determination?

PREPARATION FOR ESSAY

You may use the knowledge you gain during this research assignment to support your claims in an essay you will write at the end of this section.

ACADEMIC VOCABULARY

Academic terms appear in blue on these pages. If these words are not familiar to you, use a dictionary to find their definitions.

from *Letter on Thomas Jefferson*[1]

John Adams

Mr. Jefferson came into Congress, in June, 1775, and brought with him a reputation for literature, science, and a happy talent of composition. Writings of his were handed about, remarkable for the peculiar **felicity** of expression. Though a silent member in Congress, he was so prompt, frank, **explicit,** and decisive upon committees and in conversation, not even Samuel Adams was more so, that he soon seized upon my heart; and upon this occasion I gave him my vote, and did all in my power to **procure** the votes of others. I think he had one more vote than any other, and that placed him at the head of the committee. I had the next highest number, and that placed me second. The committee met, discussed the subject, and then appointed Mr. Jefferson and me to make the draft, I suppose because we were the two first on the list.

The subcommittee met. Jefferson proposed to me to make the draught. I said, "I will not."

"You should do it."

"Oh! no."

"Why will you not? You ought to do it."

"I will not."

"Why?"

"Reasons enough."

"What can be your reasons?"

"Reason first—You are a Virginian, and a Virginian ought to appear at the head of this business. Reason second—I am obnoxious, suspected, and unpopular. You are much otherwise. Reason third—You can write ten times better than I can."

"Well," said Jefferson, "if you are decided, I will do as well as I can."

"Very well. When you have drawn it up, we will have a meeting."

◄ **felicity**
(fə lis′i tē) *n.* ability to find appropriate expression for one's thoughts

◄ **explicit**
(eks plis′it) *adj.* clear; definite

◄ **procure**
(prō kyoor′) *v.* get or obtain by some effort

ABOUT THE AUTHOR

John Adams
(1735–1826)

John Adams was born in the Massachusetts Bay Colony and attended Harvard University, where he studied law. He was among the men who supported independence from Great Britain for the United States. Adams was a diplomat in France and Holland during the Revolutionary War. He served as George Washington's vice president for two terms and was then elected the new nation's second president.

---

1. **Letter on Thomas Jefferson** John Adams wrote this letter in 1822 telling what happened when a committee appointed him and Thomas Jefferson to write a "Declaration of Independence."

READ

Comprehension

Reread all or part of the text to help you answer the following questions.

1. What does John Adams explain in this letter?

2. How does Adams view Jefferson?

3. How does Adams describe himself?

Research: Clarify Details This letter may include references that are unfamiliar to you. Choose one unfamiliar detail, briefly research it, and then explain how your research **clarifies** the letter.

Summarize Write an objective summary of the letter. Do not include your opinions.

Language Study

Selection Vocabulary Define each boldfaced word, and use the word in a sentence of your own.

• Writings of his were handed about, remarkable for the peculiar **felicity** of expression.

• Though a silent member in Congress, he was so prompt, frank, **explicit**, and decisive …

• … and upon this occasion I gave him my vote, and did all in my power to **procure** the votes of others.

Literary Analysis

Reread the identified passage. Then, respond to the questions that follow.

> **Focus Passage** *(p. 421)*
> Mr. Jefferson came into Congress … the two first on the list.

Key Ideas and Details

1. **(a)** By how many votes was Jefferson elected to head the committee? **(b)** For whom did Adams vote? **(c) Analyze:** Why does Adams reveal this?

Craft and Structure

2. **(a)** What words and phrases does Adams use to describe Jefferson? **(b) Analyze:** What information about Jefferson do these descriptions convey? **(c) Evaluate:** What do you learn about Adams, based on his use of descriptive language?

Integration of Knowledge and Ideas

3. **Make a Judgment:** Based on this passage, do you think Adams and Jefferson were good choices to be co-authors of the Declaration of Independence? Support your answer.

Central Idea

The **central idea** is the key point in a work of nonfiction. Reread the letter, and take notes on how Adams expresses a central idea.

1. What is the letter's central idea?

2. **Determination** How does the central idea show Adams's determination?

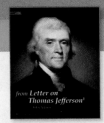

DISCUSS • RESEARCH • WRITE

From Text to Topic **Group Discussion**

Discuss the following passage with a small group of classmates. When it is your turn to speak, respond to the previous speaker and then add your own ideas. Support your ideas with examples from the text.

> I said, "I will not.... You can write ten times better than I can." (p. 421)

Research **Investigate the Topic**

Determination and the Declaration of Independence In some cases, it can take time and determination for a group to reach a consensus, or agreement.

Assignment

Conduct research to learn about the process that the Continental Congress followed in order to write and approve the Declaration of Independence. Consult government sources and first-hand accounts. Share your findings in an **informal speech** to the class. Explain why the Continental Congress needed determination to get the job done.

Writing to Sources **Argument**

In this letter, John Adams compares himself to Thomas Jefferson as he tries to convince Jefferson to draft the Declaration of Independence.

Assignment

Write a **comparison-and-contrast essay** in which you analyze John Adams and Thomas Jefferson. Follow these steps:

- As you reread Adams's letter, record details about each man in a chart or Venn diagram.

- Organize your essay in a way that clearly shows similarities and differences.

- Use transitional words and phrases, such as *similarly* and *on the other hand* to show comparisons and **contrasts**.

- Correct errors in grammar, spelling, and punctuation.

QUESTIONS FOR DISCUSSION

1. Do you think Adams's version of the conversation matches what was really said? Why or why not?

2. How does Adams's version of the conversation characterize Adams himself?

PREPARATION FOR ESSAY

You may use the knowledge you gain during this research assignment to support your claims in an essay you will write at the end of this section.

ACADEMIC VOCABULARY

Academic terms appear in blue on these pages. If these words are not familiar to you, use a dictionary to find their definitions.

Water

Helen Keller

Helen Keller as
a young girl.

The morning after my teacher came she led me into her room and gave me a doll. The little blind children at the Perkins Institution had sent it and Laura Bridgman had dressed it; but I did not know this until afterward.

When I had played with it a little while, Miss Sullivan slowly spelled into my hand the word "d-o-l-l." I was at once interested in this finger play and tried to **imitate** it. When I finally succeeded in making the letters correctly I was flushed with childish pleasure and pride. Running downstairs to my mother I held up my hand and made the letters for doll. I did not know that I was spelling a word or even that words existed; I was simply making my fingers go in monkey-like imitation. In the days that followed I learned to spell in this uncomprehending way a great many words, among them *pin, hat, cup* and a few verbs like *sit, stand* and *walk*. But my teacher had been with me several weeks before I understood that everything has a name.

One day, while I was playing with my new doll, Miss Sullivan put my big rag doll into my lap also, spelled "d-o-l-l" and tried to make me understand that "d-o-l-l" applied to both. Earlier in the day we had had a tussle over the words "m-u-g" and "w-a-t-e-r." Miss Sullivan had tried to impress it upon me that "m-u-g" is *mug* and that "w-a-t-e-r" is *water,* but I **persisted** in confounding the two. In despair she had dropped the subject for the time, only to renew it at the first opportunity. I became impatient at her repeated attempts and, seizing the new doll, I dashed it upon the floor. I was keenly delighted when I felt the

◄ **imitate**
(im´ i tāt´) *v.*
copy; mimic

But my teacher had been with me several weeks before I understood that everything has a name.

◄ **persisted**
(pər sist´ əd) *v.*
refused to give up

fragments of the broken doll at my feet. Neither sorrow nor regret followed my passionate outburst. I had not loved the doll. In the still, dark world in which I lived there was no strong sentiment or tenderness. I felt my teacher sweep the fragments to one side of the hearth,[1] and I had a sense of satisfaction that the cause of my discomfort was removed. She brought me my hat, and I knew I was going out into the warm sunshine. This thought, if a wordless sensation may be called a thought, made me hop and skip with pleasure.

We walked down the path to the well-house, attracted by the fragrance of the honeysuckle with which it was covered. Some one was drawing water and my teacher placed my hand under the spout. As the cool stream gushed over one hand she spelled into the other the word *water*, first slowly, then rapidly. I stood still, my whole attention fixed upon the motions of her fingers. Suddenly I felt a misty consciousness as of something forgotten— a thrill of returning thought; and somehow the mystery of language was revealed to me. I knew then that "w-a-t-e-r" meant the wonderful cool something that was flowing over my hand. That

---

1. hearth (härth) *n.* the stone or brick floor of a fireplace, sometimes extending into the room.

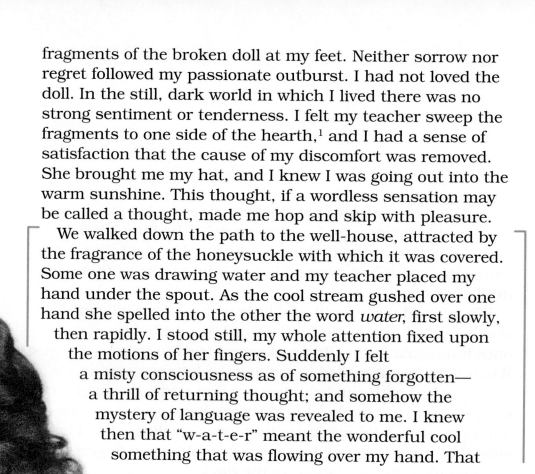

Anne Sullivan
and Helen Keller

living word awakened my soul, gave it light, hope, joy, set it free! There were barriers still, it is true, but barriers that could in time be swept away.

I left the well-house eager to learn. Everything had a name, and each name gave birth to a new thought. As we returned to the house every object which I touched seemed to quiver with life. That was because I saw everything with the strange, new sight that had come to me. On entering the door I remembered the doll I had broken. I felt my way to the hearth and picked up the pieces. I tried vainly to put them together. Then my eyes filled with tears; for I realized what I had done, and for the first time I felt repentance and sorrow.

I learned a great many new words that day. I do not remember what they all were; but I do know that *mother, father, sister, teacher* were among them—words that were to make the world blossom for me, "like Aaron's rod, with flowers." It would have been difficult to find a happier child than I was as I lay in my crib at the close of that eventful day and lived over the joys it had brought me, and for the first time longed for a new day to come.

ABOUT THE AUTHOR

Helen Keller (1880–1968)

A serious illness left Helen Keller blind and deaf before she was two years old. When Keller was nearly seven, her family hired Anne Sullivan, a teacher from the Perkins Institute for the Blind, to help her learn to communicate. In this excerpt from her autobiography, Keller describes her early lessons with Sullivan. Eventually, Keller learned to read by using Braille (raised dots that stand for letters), to type, and to speak. Keller and Sullivan developed a remarkable teacher and student relationship as well as a unique friendship.

Close Reading Activities

READ

Comprehension

Reread all or part of the text to help you answer the following questions.

1. What does Miss Sullivan do after giving Keller the doll?

2. Why does Keller break the new doll?

3. How does Keller learn what the word *water* means?

Research: Clarify Details Choose an unfamiliar detail in the selection and briefly research it. Then, explain how research helps you better understand the autobiography.

Summarize Write an objective summary of the autobiography. An objective summary is free from opionions and evaluations.

Language Study

Selection Vocabulary Name a synonym for each boldfaced word from the selection. Consult a thesaurus if necessary.

• I was at once interested in this finger play and tried to **imitate** it.

• ... "w-a-t-e-r" is *water,* but I **persisted** in confounding the two.

• There were **barriers** still, it is true, but barriers that could in time be swept away.

Literary Analysis

Reread the identified passage. Then, respond to the questions that follow.

> **Focus Passage** *(pp. 426–427)*
>
> We walked down the path… barriers that could in time be swept away.

Key Ideas and Details

1. (a) What event helps Keller recognize the meaning of *w-a-t-e-r*? **(b) Compare and Contrast:** Explain how water from the pump is the same as and different from water in a mug.

Craft and Structure

2. (a) Give three examples of sensory language that Keller uses in this paragraph. **(b) Infer:** What do these examples reveal about the ways in which Keller experiences the world around her?

Integration of Knowledge and Ideas

3. (a) Speculate: How might Keller's life change after the "water" incident? Cite details in the autobiography to support your response.

Author's Purpose

The **author's purpose** is his or her reason for writing. Reread the selection and take notes on how Keller expresses her purpose.

1. What are two possible purposes Keller may have had for writing her autobiography? **Support** your answer.

2. Determination How does writing an autobiography express Keller's determination?

DISCUSS • RESEARCH • WRITE

From Text to Topic **Small Group Discussion**

Discuss the following passage with a group of classmates. Take notes during the discussion. Contribute your own ideas, and support them with examples from the text.

> Running downstairs to my mother I held up my hand and made the letters for doll. … I understood that everything has a name. (p. 425)

Research **Investigate the Topic**

Learning to Communicate In "Water," Helen Keller shows tremendous determination in her quest to learn to communicate.

Assignment

Conduct research to find out how people with visual impairments learn to read, or how people with hearing impairments learn to communicate without speaking. Consult credible health **sources**. Take clear notes and carefully identify your sources so that you can easily access the information later. Share your findings in a **presentation with graphics** for the class.

Writing to Sources **Argument**

"Water" focuses on the moment Anne Sullivan held Helen Keller's hand under running water. In that moment, Keller's world changed.

Assignment

Write an **argumentative essay** in which you argue that the person Helen Keller was before the "water" incident was profoundly different from the person she became after the incident. Follow these steps:

- Reread the text and take notes about Helen's personality and character both before and after the "water" incident.
- Write an introduction in which you state your claim.
- In the body of your essay, use a point-by-point organizational structure to compare and contrast the "before" Helen with the "after" Helen.
- Provide a conclusion in which you summarize your argument and explain how the incident will affect Helen's future.

QUESTIONS FOR DISCUSSION

1. In this passage, how does Keller show determination?

2. How will her determination aid her in years to come?

PREPARATION FOR ESSAY

You may use the results of this research project to support your ideas in the essay you will write at the end of this section.

ACADEMIC VOCABULARY

Academic terms appear in blue on these pages. If these words are not familiar to you, use a dictionary to find their definitions. Then, use them as you speak and write about the text.

DETERMINATION

"Success is not final,
failure is not fatal:
it is the courage to continue
that counts."
—Winston Churchill

VIEW • RESEARCH • DISCUSS

Comprehension

Look at the poster to help you answer the following questions.

1. What is the topic of the poster?
2. According to the poster, what is one possible definition of the topic?

Critical Analysis

Key Ideas and Details

1. **(a)** Describe Churchill's facial expression in the photograph. **(b) Analyze:** What idea or feeling does his expression convey?

2. **(a)** What type of clothing is Churchill wearing? **(b) Interpret:** What does his clothing imply about the **context** of the photograph?

Craft and Structure

3. **(a) Analyze:** How does the poster's title draw the viewer's attention? **(b) Speculate:** If *Kindness* were the title, what image might the poster's designer have chosen to show?

4. **(a)** Identify the parallelism in the **quotation**. **(b) Analyze:** What effect does this construction have on meaning? **(c) Interpret:** What message does the quotation express?

Integration of Knowledge and Ideas

5. **Synthesize:** Why do you think the poster's creator accompanied the quotation with this particular photograph?

Research **Investigate the Topic**

Politics and Determination Winston Churchill was the prime minister of Great Britain from 1940–1945, during World War II.

> **Assignment**
>
> Conduct research to learn how Winston Churchill used his determination to lead Great Britain to victory in WWII. Consult credible historical sources, including both primary and secondary sources. Share your findings in a **report**. With a partner, discuss the **facts** you learned about Churchill through your research.

ACADEMIC VOCABULARY

Academic terms appear in blue on these pages. If these words are not familiar to you, use a dictionary to find their definitions. Then, use them as you speak and write about the text.

Speaking and Listening: Group Discussion

Determination and Communication The texts in this section explore the idea of determination and show that people often express determination through their communication with others. This idea is fundamentally related to the Big Question addressed in this unit: **Do we need words to communicate well?**

Assignment

Conduct discussions. With a small group of classmates, conduct a discussion about issues of determination and communication. Refer to the texts in this section, other texts you have read, and your own prior knowledge to support your ideas. Begin your discussion by addressing the following questions:

- Is determination always a positive trait?
- What are some constructive ways that people can communicate their determination to take an action or reach a goal?
- Do people sometimes communicate their determination in ways that anger, frighten, annoy, or confuse others? How?
- What are nonverbal ways people can show determination?

Summarize and present your ideas. After you have fully explored the topic, summarize your discussion for the class.

▲ Refer to the selections you read in Part 3 as you complete the activities on this assessment.

Criteria for Success

✓ Organizes the group effectively

Appoint a group leader and a timekeeper. The group leader should present the discussion questions. The timekeeper should make sure the discussion takes no longer than 20 minutes.

✓ Maintains focus of discussion

As a group, stay on topic and avoid straying into other subject areas.

✓ Involves all participants equally and fully

No one person should monopolize the conversation. Rather, everyone should take turns speaking and contributing ideas.

✓ Follows the rules for collegial discussion

As each group member speaks, others should listen carefully. Build on one another's ideas and support viewpoints and opinions with sound reasoning and evidence. Express disagreement respectfully.

USE NEW VOCABULARY

As you speak and share ideas, work to use the vocabulary words you have learned in this unit. The more you use new words, the more you will "own" them.

Writing: Narrative

Determination and Communication In many stories, conflict may result from a character's determination to accomplish a goal. Often, the character's success or failure depends on how he or she communicates with others.

Assignment

Write a **fictional narrative** that follows from the events described in Ray Bradbury's story "The Sound of Summer Running." Invent a new challenge for Douglas, and describe how he uses determination in his attempts to succeed. Tell how Douglas communicates his determination to others and how that communication either aids or hinders him.

Criteria for Success

Purpose/Focus

✓ **Connects specific incidents with larger ideas**

Make meaningful connections between Douglas's experiences and other texts you have read in this section.

✓ **Clearly conveys the significance of the story**

Provide a conclusion that makes clear the meaning of Douglas's experiences.

Organization

✓ **Sequences events logically**

Structure your narrative so that individual events build on one another to create a coherent whole.

Development of Ideas/Elaboration

✓ **Supports insights**

Include ideas from other texts you have read and the research you have conducted in this section.

✓ **Uses narrative techniques effectively**

Use dialogue to help readers "hear" how the characters sound. Consider telling your story from the first-person point of view.

Language

✓ **Uses description effectively**

Use sensory language to develop your setting and characters.

Conventions

✓ **Does not have errors**

Eliminate errors in grammar, spelling, and punctuation.

WRITE TO EXPLORE

Writing is a way to clarify what you feel and think. This means that you may change your mind or get new ideas as you work. Allowing for this will improve your final draft.

Writing to Sources: **Argument**

Determination and Communication The related readings in this section present a range of ideas about determination and communication. They raise questions, such as the following, about the value of determination, and a person's ability to communicate his or her determination to others:

- What does it mean to be determined? Is it enough to feel and act determined, or must a person always communicate his or her determination to others?
- What are the different ways that a person can show determination? Are some ways better than others? Why?
- What actions, if any, should people take to turn their determination into success?
- Can there be any drawbacks to having or communicating determination? If so, what are the drawbacks?

Focus on the question that intrigues you the most, and then complete the following assignment.

Assignment

Write an **argumentative essay** in which you state and defend a claim about the values of determination and communication. Build evidence for your claim by analyzing the presentation of determination and communication in two or more texts from this section. Clearly present and develop your ideas, and support them with details from the texts.

Prewriting and Planning

Choose texts. Review the texts in the section to determine which ones you will cite in your essay. Select at least two selections that will provide strong material to support your argument.

Gather details and craft a working thesis, or claim. Use a chart like the one shown to develop your claim. As you reread the texts, gather details that relate to your focus question. Use your notes to develop your claim.

Focus Question: Can there be drawbacks to communicating determination?
In "The Sound of Summer Running," when Douglas says he wants new shoes, he comes into conflict with his father.
In "Letter on Thomas Jefferson," Adams and Jefferson disagree about who should write the draft.
Example Claim: Communicating determination to others can lead to conflict.

Drafting

Organize your ideas and evidence. Create an informal outline or a list of ideas you will to present. Decide where you will include evidence and which evidence you will use to support each point.

Address counterclaims. Strong argumentation takes differing ideas into account and addresses those ideas directly. As you organize your essay, build in sections in which you explain opposing opinions or differing interpretations. Then, write a reasoned, well-supported response to those counterclaims.

Frame and connect ideas. Grab your readers' attention with a strong introduction. Consider beginning with a compelling quotation or a startling fact. In the body of your essay, make sure to show clear connections among your claims, evidence, and counterclaims. Finally, write a strong conclusion in which you sum up your main idea.

Revising and Editing

Strengthen support. Make sure that your claim is clearly stated and that you have supported it with convincing evidence from the texts. Underline main ideas in your essay and confirm that each one is fully supported. Add more evidence as needed.

Review style. Revise to cut wordy passages. Check that you have found the clearest, simplest way to communicate your ideas.

CITE RESEARCH CORRECTLY

Avoid plagiarism by properly crediting the ideas of others. Refer to the Research Workshop in the Introductory Unit of this textbook for information on citing sources.

Self-Evaluation Rubric

Use the following criteria to evaluate the effectiveness of your essay.

Criteria	Rating Scale
Purpose/Focus Introduces a precise claim and distinguishes the claim from alternate or opposing claims; provides a concluding section that follows from and supports the argument presented	*not very .... very* 1 2 3 4
Organization Organizes reasons and evidence clearly and logically; provides a concluding section that follows from the argument presented	1 2 3 4
Development of Ideas/Elaboration Supports the claim with clear reasons and relevant evidence, using credible sources; addresses counterarguments; establishes and maintains a formal style	1 2 3 4
Language Uses precise language to strengthen the argument; uses words, phrases, and clauses to clarify the relationships among claims and reasons	1 2 3 4
Conventions Uses proper grammar, punctuation, and spelling	1 2 3 4

Independent Reading

Titles for Extended Reading

In this unit, you have read texts in a wide variety of genres. Continue to read on your own. Select works that you enjoy, but challenge yourself to explore new authors and works of increasing depth and complexity. The titles suggested below will help you get started.

INFORMATIONAL TEXT

A Short Walk Around the Pyramids & Through the World of Art
by Philip M. Isaacson
Knopf Books for Young Readers   EXEMPLAR TEXT

This **nonfiction art book** takes the reader on a journey through the art world. More than 70 pictures of paintings, crafts, sculptures, architecture, and other works of art accompany Isaacson's lively discussion of art.

Restless Spirit: The Life and Work of Dorothea Lange
by Elizabeth Partridge

Dorothea Lange recorded a **photographic history** of people struggling through some of the most difficult periods in American history.

Free at Last! The Story of Martin Luther King, Jr.
by Angela Bull

This **biography** provides facts on how the slain civil rights leader raised the American social conscience about equality and nonviolence. Read about King's struggle to deliver a message of peace.

LITERATURE

Acolytes
by Nikki Giovanni
William Morrow, 2007   EXEMPLAR TEXT

In this inspiring collection of **poems**, Nikki Giovanni honors men and women who have sacrificed and struggled for freedom, justice, and civil rights.

The Fields of Praise: New and Selected Poems
by Marilyn Nelson
Louisiana State University Press, 1997

In this collection of **poems**, Nelson describes the struggles as well as the joys of the African American experience. In powerful language, she writes about faith, love, tragedy, heartbreak, and pride.

Code Talker
by Joseph Bruchac
Speak, 2006

This **novel** tells the story of Ned Bega, who joins the Marines during World War II. He becomes one of the "code talkers," Navajo soldiers who used their own language as an unbreakable code, and saved many American lives.

ONLINE TEXT SET

PERSONAL ESSAY
The Lady and the Spider Robert Fulghum

SHORT STORY
Dragon, Dragon John Gardner

POEM
Ankylosaurus Jack Prelutsky

Preparing to Read Complex Texts

Attentive Reading As you read on your own, ask yourself questions like these to enrich your reading experience.

When reading poetry, ask yourself…

Comprehension: **Key Ideas and Details**

- Who is the speaker of the poem? What kind of person does the speaker seem to be? How do I know?
- What is the poem about?
- Does any one line or section state the poem's theme, or meaning, directly? If so, what is that line or section?
- If there is no direct statement of a theme, what details help me to see the poem's deeper meaning?

Text Analysis: **Craft and Structure**

- Does the poem have a formal structure, or is it free verse?
- How many stanzas form this poem? What does each stanza tell me?
- Do I notice repetition, rhyme, meter, or other sound devices? How do these elements affect how I read the poem?
- Do any of the poet's word choices seem especially interesting or unusual? Why?
- What images do I notice? Do they create clear word-pictures in my mind? Why or why not?
- Would I like to read this poem aloud? Why or why not?

Connections: **Integration of Knowledge and Ideas**

- Has the poem helped me understand its subject in a new way? If so, how?
- Does the poem remind me of others I have read? If so, how?
- In what ways is the poem different from others I have read?
- What information, ideas, or insights have I gained from reading this poem?
- Do I find the poem moving, funny, or mysterious? How does the poem make me feel?
- Would I like to read more poems by this poet? Why or why not?

How do we decide who we are?

UNIT PATHWAY

PART 1
SETTING EXPECTATIONS

- INTRODUCING THE BIG QUESTION
- CLOSE READING WORKSHOP

PART 2
TEXT ANALYSIS
GUIDED EXPLORATION

ADVENTURE AND IMAGINATION

PART 3
TEXT SET
DEVELOPING INSIGHT

MARK TWAIN

PART 4
DEMONSTRATING INDEPENDENCE

- INDEPENDENT READING
- ONLINE TEXT SET

CLOSE READING TOOL

Use this tool to practice the close reading strategies you learn.

STUDENT eTEXT

Bring learning to life with audio, video, and interactive tools.

ONLINE WRITER'S NOTEBOOK

Easily capture notes and complete assignments online.

Find all Digital Resources at **pearsonrealize.com.**

How do we decide who we are?

Who are you? You might answer this question by stating your name: *I am Angela Reyna.* Instead, you might give a description: *I am a 12-year-old African American girl.* Perhaps you would answer by naming your skills or interests: *I am a good swimmer. I like music and art.*

Many qualities make up who you are: your personality, your values, your hopes and dreams, and your experiences. Some of us may look alike, or we may have similar beliefs. In the end, however, each of us is unique.

How do we come to know exactly who we are?

Exploring the Big Question

Collaboration: One-on-One Discussion Start thinking about the Big Question by identifying ways that we learn about ourselves. Make a list of different situations that have revealed something about you or about another person. Make notes about what you can learn about yourself in each of the following situations:

- being in a contest or other type of competition
- making a mistake
- going to an unfamiliar place
- listening to what others say about you
- getting to know someone who is very different from you
- facing a difficult challenge

Share your examples with a partner. Talk about what each situation can teach a person about himself or herself. Use the vocabulary words in your discussion.

Connecting to the Literature Each reading in this unit will give you additional insight into the Big Question. As you read, consider the ways in which the characters learn more about themselves.

Vocabulary

Acquire and Use Academic Vocabulary The term "academic vocabulary" refers to words you typically encounter in scholarly and literary texts and in technical and business writing. Review the definitions of these academic vocabulary words.

diverse (də vʉrs´) *adj.* many and different; from different backgrounds

perspective (per spek´ tiv) *n.* point of view

reaction (rē´ ak´ shən) *n.* response to something said or done

reflect (ri flekt´) *v.* think or wonder about

respond (ri spänd´) *v.* answer or reply

similar (sim´ ə lər) *adj.* alike

unique (yo͞o nēk´) *adj.* one of a kind

Gather Vocabulary Knowledge Additional vocabulary words are listed below. Categorize the words by deciding whether you know each one well, know it a little bit, or do not know it at all.

appearance	expectations	personality
conscious	ideals	trend
custom	individuality	

Then, do the following:

1. Write the definitions of the words you know.
2. Consult a dictionary to confirm the meanings of the words whose definitions you wrote down. Revise your definitions if necessary.
3. Using a print or an online dictionary, look up the meanings of the words you are unsure of or do not know. Then, write the meanings.
4. Use all of the words in a brief paragraph about expressing individuality.

Close Reading Workshop

In this workshop you will learn an approach to reading that will deepen your understanding of literature and will help you better appreciate the author's craft. The workshop includes models for close reading, discussion, research, and writing activities. After you have reviewed the strategies and models, practice your skills with the Independent Practice selection.

CLOSE READING: DRAMA

Use these strategies as you read the drama in this unit.

Comprehension: Key Ideas and Details

- Read first to unlock basic meaning.
- Identify unfamiliar details that you might need to clarify through research.
- Distinguish between what is stated directly and what must be inferred.

Ask yourself questions such as these:
- Who are the main characters?
- What internal and external conflicts do the characters face?
- When and where does the action take place?

Text Analysis: Craft and Structure

- Think about the genre of the work and how the author presents ideas.
- Analyze how dialogue and stage directions provide information about character and setting.
- Think about how scenes introduce characters, begin or end action, and change setting or mood.

Ask yourself questions such as these:
- How do details in the stage directions help me picture the action?
- How does each scene move the story forward?
- How does dialogue provide clues to characters' personalities?

Connections: Integration of Knowledge and Ideas

- Look for relationships among key ideas.
- Look for characters that represent universal, or common, personality types.
- Compare and contrast this work with other dramas you have read.

Ask yourself questions such as these:
- How has this work increased my knowledge of a subject or a playwright?
- What is the theme of the drama?
- What actors would I choose to play each role in this play?

Read

As you read this excerpt from a drama, take note of the annotations that model ways to closely read the text.

Reading Model

from *Brighton Beach Memoirs* by Neil Simon

STAN. [*half whisper*] Hey! Eugie!

EUGENE. Hi, Stan! [*to audience*] My brother, Stan. He's okay. You'll like him. ¹ [*to* STAN] What are you doing home so early?

STAN. [*looks around, lowers his voice*] ² Is Pop home yet?

EUGENE. No … Did you ask about the tickets?

STAN. What tickets?

EUGENE. For the Yankee game. You said your boss knew this guy who could get passes. You didn't ask him?

STAN. Me and my boss had other things to talk about. [*He sits on steps, his head down, almost in tears*] ² I'm in trouble, Eug. I mean really big trouble.

EUGENE. [*to audience*] This really shocked me. Because Stan is the kind of guy who could talk himself out of *any* kind of trouble. [*to* STAN] What kind of trouble?

STAN. … I got fired today! ³

EUGENE. [*shocked*] Fired? … You mean for good?

STAN. You don't get fired temporarily. It's permanent. It's a lifetime firing. ⁴

EUGENE. Why? What happened? ⁵

Craft and Structure

1 An *aside* is a comment made by a character that the audience can hear but other characters cannot hear. In this aside, Eugene introduces his brother to the audience.

Craft and Structure

2 Stage directions can give important clues about a character's feelings. Stan's body language reveals that he is nervous and upset.

Key Ideas and Details

3 Stan pauses before revealing that he has been fired. His hesitation suggests a conflict: he is worried about how his family will react to his news.

Craft and Structure

4 By stating the obvious, Stan makes the audience laugh. The situation is serious, but the playwright presents it with humor.

Integration of Knowledge and Ideas

5 Eugene asks the same question the audience is thinking. The audience knows only what Eugene knows, which deepens their connection with his character.

Discuss

Sharing your own ideas and listening to the ideas of others can deepen your understanding of a text and help you look at a topic in a whole new way. As you participate in collaborative discussions, work to have a genuine exchange in which classmates build upon one another's ideas. Support your points with evidence and ask meaningful questions.

Discussion Model

Student 1: In most plays I've seen, the characters only talk to each other. It's interesting that Eugene talks to the audience, too, almost as though the audience is a character in the play.

Student 2: Why do you think the playwright did that? It seems as if Eugene's comments to the audience are just extra information, and the dialogue would make sense without them. For example, Eugene says, "this really shocked me," but we can see that he's shocked through his dialogue with Stan.

Student 3: I think Eugene is probably the main character, and that's why he talks to the audience. The audience sees the action and the other characters through his eyes. I wonder what Eugene's role is in the rest of the play, and whether the audience experiences the whole play from his point of view.

Research

Targeted research can clarify unfamiliar details and shed light on various aspects of a text. Consider questions that arise in your mind as you read, and use those questions as the basis for research.

Research Model

Questions: *What is Eugene's role in* Brighton Beach Memoirs*?*

Key Words for Internet Search: "Brighton Beach Memoirs"

What I Learned: In earlier scenes in the play, the audience learns that Eugene is writing his memoirs in a journal. He wants to be a baseball player or a writer. He shares his experiences growing up in the Brighton Beach area of New York City with his family during the Great Depression.

Write

Writing about a text will deepen your understanding of it and will also allow you to share your ideas more formally with others. The following model essay analyzes how the playwright creates meaningful dialogue and cites evidence to support the main ideas.

Writing Model: Informative Essay

Finding Meaning in Dialogue

When Stan gets fired in this scene from *Brighton Beach Memoirs*, playwright Neil Simon gives the audience reasons to laugh. Eugene's comments to the audience reveal his amusing personality while lightening the scene's mood. Most importantly, the dialogue between Eugene and Stan helps the audience understand the brothers' situation and their feelings about each other and their family.

> Stating the main idea at the beginning makes the writer's intentions clear.

Eugene makes comments to the audience that Stan does not hear. For example, he introduces his brother Stan in an aside: "My brother, Stan. He's okay. You'll like him." As the audience, we can form our own opinions about Stan. Eugene's aside, therefore, has another purpose. These lines convey how close Eugene is to his brother.

> Specific details from the play help support the writer's key points.

In his next aside, Eugene shares his amazement when he sees how upset Stan is: "This really shocked me. Because Stan is the kind of guy who can talk himself out of *any* kind of trouble." This amusing comment allows Eugene to lighten the serious mood. Eugene also wants the audience to know more about Stan's personality by sharing a funny detail.

> The writer provides an example to reinforce a main idea.

Similarly, Neil Simon shows Stan's humorous side in his response to Eugene. When Eugene numbly asks, "You mean for good?" Stan wryly responds with, "You don't get fired temporarily." This exchange helps the audience understand that Stan can find humor in the situation, while Eugene still needs to process the bad news.

> This example provides further elaboration and support for the main idea.

Whether Eugene is talking with Stan or commenting to the audience through his asides, his humorous dialogue conveys a sense of realism and give the audience important information. In earlier scenes of the play, the audience learns that the play is about a family who live in the Brighton Beach area of New York City during the Depression. This scene establishes a situation that points to a potential theme: hard times and struggles can bring families together. The dialogue between Eugene and Stan helps the audience understand the conflict that the brothers face.

> In the conclusion, the writer includes evidence from research to support an interpretation of the play's meaning.

As you read the following play, apply the close reading strategies you have learned. You may need to read the drama multiple times.

Gluskabe and Old Man Winter

by Joseph Bruchac

CHARACTERS

Speaking Roles:	Non-speaking Roles:
NARRATOR	SUN
GLUSKABE	FLOWERS
GRANDMOTHER WOODCHUCK	PLANTS
HUMAN BEING	
OLD MAN WINTER	
FOUR OR MORE SUMMER LAND PEOPLE, including the leader	
FOUR CROWS	

Scene I: Gluskabe and Grandmother Woodchuck's Wigwam

GLUSKABE and GRANDMOTHER WOODCHUCK sit inside with their blankets over their shoulders.

NARRATOR: Long ago Gluskabe (gloo-SKAH-bey) lived with his grandmother, Woodchuck, who was old and very wise. Gluskabe's job was to help the people.

GLUSKABE: It is very cold this winter, Grandmother.

GRANDMOTHER WOODCHUCK: *Ni ya yo* (nee yah yo), Grandson. You are right!

GLUSKABE: The snow is very deep, Grandmother.

GRANDMOTHER WOODCHUCK: *Ni ya yo*, Grandson.

GLUSKABE: It has been winter for a very long time, Grandmother.

GRANDMOTHER WOODCHUCK: *Ni ya yo*, Grandson. But look, here comes one of those human beings who are our friends.

HUMAN BEING: *Kwai, Kwai, nidobak* (kwy kwy nee-DOH-bahk). Hello, my friends.

Meet the Author

A professional storyteller and writer from New York State, **Joseph Bruchac** (b. 1942) often draws upon the traditions of his Native American ancestors, the Abenaki people. He has written more than seventy books for children and has performed worldwide as a teller of Native American folk tales.

CLOSE READING TOOL

Read and respond to this selection online using the **Close Reading Tool.**

Gluskabe and **Grandmother Woodchuck:** *Kwai, Kwai, nidoba* (kwy kwy nee-DOH-bah).

Human Being: Gluskabe, I have been sent by the other human beings to ask you for help. This winter has been too long. If it does not end soon, we will all die.

Gluskabe: I will do what I can. I will go to the wigwam of Old Man Winter. He has stayed here too long. I will ask him to go back to his home in the Winter Land to the north.

Grandmother Woodchuck: Be careful, Gluskabe.

Gluskabe: Don't worry, Grandmother. Winter cannot beat me.

Scene II: *The Wigwam of Old Man Winter*

Old Man Winter *sits in his wigwam, "warming" his hands over his fire made of ice. The four balls of summer are on one side of the stage.* **Gluskabe** *enters stage carrying his bag and stands to the side of the wigwam door. He taps on the wigwam.*

Old Man Winter: Who is there!

Gluskabe: It is Gluskabe.

Old Man Winter: Ah, come inside and sit by my fire.

Gluskabe *enters the wigwam.*

Gluskabe: The people are suffering. You must go back to your home in the Winter Land.

Old Man Winter: Oh, I must, eh? But tell me, do you like my fire?

Gluskabe: I do not like your fire. Your fire is not warm. It is cold.

Old Man Winter: Yes, my fire is made of ice. And so are you!

Old Man Winter *throws his white sheet over* **Gluskabe.** **Gluskabe** *falls down.* **Old Man Winter** *stands up.*

Old Man Winter: No one can defeat me!

Old Man Winter *pulls* **Gluskabe** *out of the lodge. Then he goes back inside and closes the door flap. The Sun comes out and shines on* **Gluskabe.** **Gluskabe** *sits up and looks at the Sun.*

Gluskabe: Ah, that was a good nap! But I am not going into Old Man Winter's lodge again until I talk with my grandmother.

Gluskabe *begins walking across the stage toward the four balls.*
Grandmother Woodchuck *enters.*

Grandmother Woodchuck: It is still winter, Gluskabe! Did Old Man Winter refuse to speak to you?

Gluskabe: We spoke, but he did not listen. I will speak to him again; and I will make him listen. But tell me, Grandmother, where does the warm weather come from?

Grandmother Woodchuck: It is kept in the Summer Land.

Gluskabe: I will go there and bring summer back here.

Grandmother Woodchuck: Grandson, the Summer Land people are strange people. Each of them has one eye. They are also greedy. They do not want to share the warm weather. It will be dangerous.

Gluskabe: Why will it be dangerous?

Grandmother Woodchuck: The Summer Land people keep the summer in a big pot. They dance around it. Four giant crows guard the pot full of summer. Whenever a stranger tries to steal summer, those crows fly down and pull off his head!

Gluskabe: Grandmother, I will go to the summer land. I will cover up one eye and look like the people there. And I will take these four balls of sinew with me.

Gluskabe *picks up the four balls, places them in his bag, and puts the bag over his shoulder.*

Scene III: *The Summer Land Village*

The **Summer Land People** *are dancing around the pot full of summer. They are singing a snake dance song, following their leader, who shakes a rattle in one hand.* **Four Crows** *stand guard around the pot as the people dance.*

Summer Land People: *Wee gai wah neh* (wee guy wah ney),

Wee gai wah neh,

Wee gai wah neh, wee gai wah neh,

Wee gai wah neh, wee gai wah neh,

Wee gai wah neh.

GLUSKABE *enters, wearing an eye patch and carrying his bag with the balls in it.*

GLUSKABE: *Kwai, kwai, nidobak!* Hello, my friends.

Everyone stops dancing. They gather around **GLUSKABE.**

LEADER OF THE SUMMER LAND PEOPLE: Who are you?

GLUSKABE: I am not a stranger. I am one of you. See, I have one eye.

SECOND SUMMER LAND PERSON: I do not remember you.

GLUSKABE: I have been gone a long time.

THIRD SUMMER LAND PERSON: He does have only one eye.

FOURTH SUMMER LAND PERSON: Let's welcome him back. Come join in our snake dance.

The singing and dancing begin again: "Wee gai wah neh," etc. **GLUSKABE** *is at the end of the line as the dancers circle the pot full of summer. When* **GLUSKABE** *is close enough, he reaches in, grabs one of the summersticks, and breaks away, running back and forth.*

LEADER OF THE SUMMER LAND PEOPLE: He has taken one of our summersticks!

SECOND SUMMER LAND PERSON: Someone stop him!

THIRD SUMMER LAND PERSON: Crows, catch him!

FOURTH SUMMER LAND PERSON: Pull off his head!

The **CROWS** *swoop after* **GLUSKABE.** *He reaches into his pouch and pulls out one of the balls. As each* **CROW** *comes up to him, he ducks his head down and holds up the ball. The Crow grabs the ball.* **GLUSKABE** *keeps running, and pulls out another ball, repeating his actions until each of the Crows has grabbed a ball.*

FIRST CROW: *Gah-gah!* I have his head.

SECOND CROW: *Gah-gah!* No, I have his head!

THIRD CROW: *Gah-gah!* Look, I have his head!

FOURTH CROW: *Gah-gah!* No, look—I have it too!

LEADER OF THE SUMMER LAND PEOPLE: How many heads did that stranger have?

SECOND SUMMER LAND PERSON: He has tricked us. He got away.

Scene IV: *The Wigwam of Old Man Winter*

GLUSKABE *walks up to* **OLD MAN WINTER'S** *wigwam. He holds the summerstick in his hand and taps on the door.*

OLD MAN WINTER: Who is there!

GLUSKABE: It is Gluskabe.

OLD MAN WINTER: Ah, come inside and sit by my fire.

GLUSKABE *enters, sits down, and places the summerstick in front of* **OLD MAN WINTER.**

GLUSKABE: You must go back to your home in the Winter Land.

OLD MAN WINTER: Oh, I must, eh? But tell me, do you like my fire?

GLUSKABE: Your fire is no longer cold. It is getting warmer. Your wigwam is melting away. You are getting weaker.

OLD MAN WINTER: No one can defeat me!

GLUSKABE: Old Man, you are defeated. Warm weather has returned. Go back to your home in the north.

The blanket walls of **OLD MAN WINTER'S** *wigwam collapse.* **OLD MAN WINTER** *stands up and walks away as swiftly as he can, crouching down as if getting smaller. People carrying the cutouts of the Sun, Flowers, and Plants come out and surround* **GLUSKABE** *as he sits there, smiling.*

NARRATOR: So Gluskabe defeated Old Man Winter. Because he brought only one small piece of summer, winter still returns each year. But, thanks to Gluskabe, spring always comes back again.

Close Reading Activities

Read

Comprehension: Key Ideas and Details

1. Interpret: In Scene I, what signs do you see that Gluskabe will successfully help the people?

2. (a) Find details in the stage directions that establish the seasons at various points in the play. **(b) Connect:** How are these details connected to the main conflict?

3. (a) Distinguish: How does the playwright characterize Old Man Winter? **(b) Infer:** What does this characterization suggest about the winter season?

4. Summarize: Write a brief objective summary of the drama. Cite story details in your writing.

Text Analysis: Craft and Structure

5. (a) What happens in each of the play's four scenes? **(b) Analyze:** Explain how the scenes form a plot with a conflict, rising action, climax, and resolution.

6. (a) Infer: Gluskabe speaks with Grandmother Woodchuck after Old Man Winter defeats him the first time. What

new information about Gluskabe do you learn from this conversation? **(b)** How does the dialogue move the story forward? Explain.

7. (a) What does the last stage direction describe? **(b) Analyze:** How is this stage direction essential to the play's plot?

Connections: Integration of Knowledge and Ideas

Discuss

Conduct a **small-group discussion** about the personification of winter and summer in the drama. Discuss why the Abenaki people might give human characteristics to these elements of nature.

Research

Briefly research several stories of the Abenaki culture. Consider these elements:

a. Gluskabe and other heroes

b. the use of stories as teaching tools

c. the role of nature

Take notes as you conduct your research. Then, write a brief **explanation** of the similarities one or more of the stories share with *Gluskabe and Old Man Winter.*

Write

Many traditional tales helped people make sense of the world. Write an essay in which you describe how *Gluskabe and Old Man Winter* explains an aspect of nature. Cite details from the play to support your analysis.

 How do we decide who we are?

(a) What are Gluskabe's strongest qualities? **(b)** How does he use his strengths to help his people? Cite specific details from the play in your answer.

"**Imagination** will often carry us to **worlds that never were**. But without it, we go nowhere."

—**Carl Sagan**

ADVENTURE AND IMAGINATION

As you read the play in this section, you will explore a fantastic world filled with unusual characters, clever dialogue, and vivid settings. Take note of how the characters' behavior and feelings change as they navigate conflicts and challenges. The quotation on the opposite page will help you start thinking about how adventures—both imaginary and real—can expand your knowledge of yourself and the world around you.

◀ **CRITICAL VIEWING** In what way is the girl in this picture using her imagination? What is the benefit of visiting "worlds that never were"?

READINGS IN PART 2

Drama
The Phantom Tollbooth, Act I
Susan Nanus
(p. 460)

Drama
The Phantom Tollbooth, Act II
Susan Nanus
(p. 490)

CLOSE READING TOOL

Use the **Close Reading Tool** to practice the strategies you learn in this unit.

Focus on Craft and Structure

Elements of Drama

A drama is a story that is written to be performed by actors.

A **drama,** or play, is a story that is performed for an audience. You can read dramas, but they are really meant to be seen and heard. You can watch dramas on stage or on television, movie screens, or computer monitors.

In a drama, you meet **characters,** or fictional people. You watch their lives unfold in a particular **setting,** or time and place. Characters face a **conflict,** or problem, that moves them to act and react. The events that result form the **plot,** a series of actions that build to a **climax.** The climax is the plot's moment of greatest tension. After the climax, the action winds down. The conflict is settled—or left

unsettled—in the **resolution,** or ending. Like most literary works, a drama expresses a **theme,** or insight about life.

The writer of a drama is called a **playwright** or **dramatist.** The written text of a drama is called a **script.** The script includes **dialogue,** or the words the actors speak. It may also include **stage directions** that describe the characters and setting.

Full-length dramas are divided into shorter sections, called **acts.** Each act may contain several **scenes.** A scene is like a little drama all by itself. It presents continuous action in a specific situation.

Elements of Drama	
Stage Directions	Stage directions are the playwright's instructions about how to perform the drama. They may include • details about the way the stage and characters should look; • instructions about where and how actors should move and speak; • details about other staging elements, such as scenery, lighting, sound, and costumes.
Dialogue	Conversation between characters is called dialogue. Through it, audiences learn about plot events and characters' feelings and actions.
Sets/Scenery	Sets and scenery are the constructions onstage that suggest the time and place of the action.
Props	Props are movable items, such as books, coffee mugs, or newspapers. Actors use props to make their actions look realistic.
Acts and Scenes	Acts and scenes are units of action in dramas. Full-length dramas may have several acts, and each act may have several scenes.

Forms of Drama: Past and Present

The oldest surviving dramas come from the ancient Greeks, who divided drama into two types:

- **Comedies** have happy endings. Their humor often comes out of the dialogue and situations. Like modern comedies, ancient comedies entertained but sometimes also expressed serious ideas about human nature.

- **Tragedies** show the downfall of a great person, known as the **tragic hero,** brought down by a fault, or **tragic flaw,** in his or her nature. The ancient tragedies were meant to teach and inspire with stories of legendary figures.

The experience of watching a play in ancient Greece was different from that of today. In ancient Greece, plays were performed in huge, open theaters. Thousands of spectators sat on stone benches that formed a semicircle around the performance space. The actors were all men, and some played more than one role. Each actor wore a mask to indicate his character's gender, age, and social position.

The next important era for drama took place in England in the late 1500s and early 1600s. Then, many audiences attended plays by William Shakespeare—perhaps the greatest playwright of all time. They sat in an open-air wooden playhouse, not as large as the Greek theater. All characters were still played by men, but they used makeup instead of masks.

Shakespeare and other playwrights of his time wrote tragedies that followed the Greek form, as well as comedies with romantic themes.

Today, modern dramas present serious subjects that mix both comedy and tragedy. We can watch a drama with live actors on a stage or watch a performance in a movie theater. We can even watch dramas alone at home in front of our televisions or computers.

Live Theater	Film/Movies	Television Drama	Radio Play
• performed live for an audience • follows a written play **script** • uses scenery and lighting for effect	• recorded on film or digitally and shown in theaters • follows a script called a **screenplay** • uses camera angles for effect	• recorded or performed live • follows a script called a **teleplay** • like film, uses camera angles for effect	• recorded or performed live • follows a script called a **radio play** • uses dialogue and sound effects

Analyzing Dramatic Elements

Most dramas focus on **characters** in **conflict** in order to express a **theme**.

The action in a drama is conveyed through the spoken dialogue and physical actions of its characters. A drama's plot may be full of twists and turns and ups and downs. When you read or watch a drama, you get to go along for the ride.

Keys to Character While some plays feature a narrator who gives the audience important information, most plays do not. Instead, audiences learn about characters from what they say. Playwrights use dialogue to reveal their characters in several ways:

- Characters may speak their inner thoughts, feelings, and conflicts out loud.
- Conversations among characters can reveal their feelings and personality traits.
- Characters may talk about each other. The reader or audience must decide whether to accept such comments as truth.

Most dramatic dialogue takes the form of conversations between or among characters. Sometimes, however, one character holds the spotlight with a special kind of speech.

- A **monologue** is a long, uninterrupted speech spoken by a character to other characters who remain silent. In a monologue, a character may reveal hidden feelings or may persuade another character to take action.
- A **soliloquy** is a speech a character delivers while alone. Sometimes the character speaks to the audience; sometimes only to himself or herself. Through a soliloquy, a character might explore an important question or make a decision.
- An **aside** is a comment made by a character to the audience. Other characters may be present, but an aside is not meant to be heard by anyone but the audience.

When you read a play, stage directions can provide important information about a character's feelings and personality. In the following example, the stage direction (printed in italics) reveals that the character is tired and perhaps frustrated.

> **Example:**
>
> Angela: *(pausing wearily before speaking)* What do you mean by that?

Great plays feature interesting characters whose stories hold the audience or reader's attention. The best dramas feature **complex characters** who have strengths and weaknesses and experience a variety of emotions. Complex characters are often pulled in different directions because of the difficult situations that they face.

Conflict and Plot The problems, or conflicts, characters face are at the core of any drama. As characters respond to challenges and make decisions about how to solve conflicts, their feelings and behavior often change. These changes help move the plot from one event to another.

In drama, as in other types of literature, there are two main types of conflict. **External conflict** occurs between a character and an outside force, such as nature, society, or another character. **Internal conflict** occurs within the mind of a character. It arises when a character is torn between opposing feelings.

Type of Conflict	Examples
External Conflict *A character struggles against an outside force.*	• <u>Against nature</u>: A couple tries to climb a mountain. • <u>Against society</u>: A woman opposes a new city law. • <u>Against another character</u>: Two scientists claim the same discovery.
Internal Conflict *A character struggles against himself or herself.*	• An artist seeks fame but compromises her ideals. • A man has to choose between telling the truth and protecting his brother.

Scenes, or Episodes The events of a play are often presented in separate, connected episodes, or scenes. Every scene has a purpose. It may introduce or change the setting. For example, a scene at a train station may be followed by a scene on a train. A scene may also introduce a character, show a character making a decision, or begin an action that will lead to other actions.

Theme in Drama All the elements of a drama work together to create an illusion of reality, which is known as the *dramatic effect*. Dramatic elements also work to express a **theme,** or central idea about life. The conflict, characters' actions, and the resolution, or outcome of the story, all point to a play's theme. Viewers or readers may interpret that theme in different ways. A strong interpretation will take into account all the play's elements.

Dramatic Subject	Possible Theme
A young girl learns that she can have a full life in spite of her blindness.	With determination, we can overcome limitations.
War forces a family to flee their home and move to a new country.	Political conflicts disrupt innocent people's lives. Still, people survive.

The better a drama is, the more audiences connect with the characters, their situation, and the play's theme. When it is most powerful and effective, drama allows audiences to make discoveries about their own lives by identifying with the imagined lives of others.

Building Knowledge

Meet the Author

Susan Nanus has written scripts for dramas, television miniseries, and movies. Like other screenwriters, she sometimes adapts, or reworks, novels to create screenplays for movies and scripts for stage plays. Her script for *The Phantom Tollbooth* was adapted from a novel by Norton Juster.

For a biography of Norton Juster, see page 488.

? How do we decide who we are?

Explore the Big Question as you read *The Phantom Tollbooth*. Take notes on ways in which the characters learn about themselves.

CLOSE READING FOCUS

Key Ideas and Details: **Summary**

A **summary** of a literary work is a restatement of the work's main ideas and most important points. To summarize a drama, first reread to identify main events. In your summary, include only major events that move the story forward. Present the events in the order in which they happened.

Craft and Structure: **Dialogue in Drama**

A **drama** is a story that is written to be performed. Like short stories, dramas have characters, settings, and a plot that revolves around conflict. In dramas, however, these elements are developed mainly through **dialogue**, the words spoken by the characters. In the **script**, or written form of a drama, each character's name appears before his or her dialogue:

> **KATRINA.** I can't believe you said that!
>
> **WALLACE.** I was only kidding.

As you read this drama, notice how each character's point of view, or personality and beliefs, is developed through dialogue. Also, notice how the dialogue introduces conflict and moves the drama along.

Vocabulary

You will encounter the following words in *The Phantom Tollbooth*, Act I. Write the words, and then circle the two that share the same prefix. Write the meaning of the prefix, and explain how it changes the meaning of each base word.

ignorance	precautionary	unethical
ferocious	misapprehension	unabridged

CLOSE READING MODEL

The passage below is from Susan Nanus's play *The Phantom Tollbooth*, Act I. The annotations to the right of the passage show how you can use close reading skills to summarize a drama and to analyze its dialogue.

from *The Phantom Tollbooth*, Act I

LETHARGARIAN 1. You're . . . in . . . the . . . Dol . . .drums . . . [*Milo looks around.*]

LETHARGARIAN 2. Yes . . . the . . . Dol . . . drums . . . [*A YAWN is heard.*]

MILO. [*Yelling.*] WHAT ARE THE DOLDRUMS?.

LETHARGARIAN 3. The Doldrums, my friend, are where nothing ever happens and nothing ever changes. [1] [*Parts of the Scenery stand up or Six People come out of the scenery colored in the same colors of the trees or the road. They move very slowly and as soon as they move, they stop to rest again.*] Allow me to introduce all of us. We are the Lethargarians at your service.

MILO. [*Uncertainly.*] Very pleased to meet you. I think I'm lost. Can you help me?

LETHARGARIAN 4. Don't say think. [*He yawns.*] It's against the law.

LETHARGARIAN 1. No one's allowed to think in the Doldrums. [*He falls asleep.*] [2]

LETHARGARIAN 2. Don't you have a rule book? It's local ordinance 175389-J. [*He falls asleep.*] [3]

Dialogue in Drama

1 This dialogue introduces aspects of character, setting, and plot. The Lethargarians are characters who appear tired, and speak very slowly. The setting is a place called the Doldrums. Milo's question tells you that he has no idea where he is.

Dialogue in Drama

2 This dialogue presents the surprising news that thinking is not allowed in the Doldrums. This information may hint at a possible conflict later in the plot.

Summary

3 To summarize this entire passage, you might write: "Milo finds himself in a strange land called the Doldrums, whose sleepy, slow-moving citizens, the Lethargarians, are forbidden to think."

The Phantom Tollbooth

Susan Nanus

Based on the book by Norton Juster

Cast (in order of appearance)

- THE CLOCK
- MILO, A BOY
- THE WHETHER MAN
- SIX LETHARGARIANS
- TOCK, THE WATCHDOG (same as the clock)
- AZAZ THE UNABRIDGED, KING OF DICTIONOPOLIS
- THE MATHEMAGICIAN, KING OF DIGITOPOLIS
- PRINCESS SWEET RHYME
- PRINCESS PURE REASON
- GATEKEEPER OF DICTIONOPOLIS

- THREE WORD MERCHANTS
- THE LETTERMAN (fourth word Merchant)
- SPELLING BEE
- THE HUMBUG
- THE DUKE OF DEFINITION
- THE MINISTER OF MEANING
- THE EARL OF ESSENCE
- THE COUNT OF CONNOTATION
- THE UNDERSECRETARY OF UNDERSTANDING
- A PAGE

- KAKAFONOUS A. DISCHORD, DOCTOR OF DISSONANCE
- THE AWFUL DYNNE
- THE DODECAHEDRON
- MINERS OF THE NUMBERS MINE
- THE EVERPRESENT WORDSNATCHER
- THE TERRIBLE TRIVIUM
- THE DEMON OF INSINCERITY
- SENSES TAKER

The Sets

1. MILO'S BEDROOM—with shelves, pennants, pictures on the wall, as well as suggestions of the characters of the Land of Wisdom.

2. THE ROAD TO THE LAND OF WISDOM— a forest, from which the Whether Man and the Lethargarians emerge.

3. DICTIONOPOLIS—a marketplace full of open air stalls as well as little shops. Letters and signs should abound.

4. DIGITOPOLIS—a dark, glittering place without trees or greenery, but full of shining rocks and cliffs, with hundreds of numbers shining everywhere.

5. THE LAND OF IGNORANCE—a gray, gloomy place full of cliffs and caves, with frightening faces. Different levels and heights should be suggested through one or two platforms or risers, with a set of stairs that lead to the castle in the air.

Act I • Scene i

[*The stage is completely dark and silent. Suddenly the sound of someone winding an alarm clock is heard, and after that, the sound of loud ticking is heard.*]

[*LIGHTS UP on the* CLOCK, *a huge alarm clock. The* CLOCK *reads 4:00. The lighting should make it appear that the* CLOCK *is suspended in mid-air (if possible). The* CLOCK *ticks for 30 seconds.*]

CLOCK. See that! Half a minute gone by. Seems like a long time when you're waiting for something to happen, doesn't it? Funny thing is, time can pass very slowly or very fast, and sometimes even both at once. The time now? Oh, a little after four, but what that means should depend on you. Too often, we do something simply because time tells us to. Time for school, time for bed, whoops, 12:00, time to be hungry. It can get a little silly, don't you think? Time is important, but it's what you do with it that makes it so. So my advice to you is to use it. Keep your eyes open and your ears perked. Otherwise it will pass before you know it, and you'll certainly have missed something!

Things have a habit of doing that, you know. Being here one minute and gone the next.

In the twinkling of an eye.

In a jiffy.

In a flash!

I know a girl who yawned and missed a whole summer vacation. And what about that caveman who took a nap one afternoon, and woke up to find himself completely alone. You see, while he was sleeping, someone had invented the wheel and everyone had moved to the suburbs. And then of course, there is Milo. [*LIGHTS UP to reveal* MILO's *Bedroom. The* CLOCK *appears to be on a shelf in the room of a young boy—a room filled with books, toys, games, maps, papers, pencils, a bed, a desk. There is a dartboard with numbers and the face of the* MATHEMAGICIAN, *a bedspread made from* KING AZAZ's *cloak, a kite looking like the Spelling Bee, a punching bag with the* HUMBUG's *face, as well as records, a television,*

◄ Vocabulary
ignorance (ig′ nə rəns) *n.* lack of knowledge, education, or experience

Summary
How would you summarize the point Clock is making?

Comprehension
How do you know what characters and sets are in this play?

Culture Connection

Turnpike Tollbooth

A turnpike is a road that people pay a fee, or toll, to use. Long ago, long spears called "pikes" barred the road. The pikes were turned aside only after travelers paid the toll. A tollbooth is the booth or gate at which tolls are collected. The first record of tolls being collected dates from about 2000 B.C., when tolls were collected on a Persian military road between Babylon and Syria.

Connect to the Literature

How might the tollbooth—an unusual gift—affect Milo's bored state of mind?

Vocabulary ▶
precautionary (pri kô´ shə ner´ ē) *adj.* done to prevent harm or danger

a toy car, and a large box that is wrapped and has an envelope taped to the top. The sound of FOOTSTEPS is heard, and then enter MILO dejectedly. He throws down his books and coat, flops into a chair, and sighs loudly.] Who never knows what to do with himself—not just sometimes, but always. When he's in school, he wants to be out, and when he's out he wants to be in. [*During the following speech,* MILO *examines the various toys, tools, and other possessions in the room, trying them out and rejecting them.*] Wherever he is, he wants to be somewhere else—and when he gets there, so what. Everything is too much trouble or a waste of time. Books—he's already read them. Games—boring. T.V.—dumb. So what's left? Another long, boring afternoon. Unless he bothers to notice a very large package that happened to arrive today.

MILO. [*Suddenly notices the package. He drags himself over to it, and disinterestedly reads the label.*] "For Milo, who has plenty of time." Well, that's true. [*Sighs and looks at it.*] No. [*Walks away.*] Well . . . [*Comes back. Rips open envelope and reads.*]

A VOICE. "One genuine turnpike tollbooth, easily assembled at home for use by those who have never traveled in lands beyond."

MILO. Beyond what? [*Continues reading.*]

A VOICE. "This package contains the following items:" [MILO *pulls the items out of the box and sets them up as they are mentioned.*] "One (1) genuine turnpike tollbooth to be erected according to directions. Three (3) precautionary signs to be used in a precautionary fashion. Assorted coins for paying tolls. One (1) map, strictly up to date, showing how to get from here to there. One (1) book of rules and traffic regulations which may not be bent or broken. Warning! Results are not guaranteed. If not perfectly satisfied, your wasted time will be refunded."

MILO. [*Skeptically.*] Come off it, who do you think you're kidding? [*Walks around and examines tollbooth.*] What am I supposed to do with this? [*The ticking of the* CLOCK *grows loud and impatient.*] Well . . . what else do I have to do. [MILO *gets into his toy car and drives up to the first sign.*]

VOICE. "HAVE YOUR DESTINATION IN MIND."

MILO. [*Pulls out the map.*] Now, let's see. That's funny. I never heard of any of these places. Well, it doesn't matter anyway. Dictionopolis. That's a weird name. I might as well go there. [*Begins to move, following map. Drives off.*]

CLOCK. See what I mean? You never know how things are going to get started. But when you're bored, what you need more than anything is a rude awakening.

[*The* ALARM *goes off very loudly as the stage darkens. The sound of the alarm is transformed into the honking of a car horn, and is then joined by the blasts, bleeps, roars and growls of heavy highway traffic. When the lights come up, Milo's bedroom is gone and we see a lonely road in the middle of nowhere.*]

Scene ii • The Road to Dictionopolis

[*Enter* MILO *in his car.*]

MILO. This is weird! I don't recognize any of this scenery at all. [*A* SIGN *is held up before* MILO, *startling him.*] Huh? [*Reads.*] WELCOME TO EXPECTATIONS. INFORMATION, PREDICTIONS AND ADVICE CHEERFULLY OFFERED. PARK HERE AND BLOW HORN. [MILO *blows horn.*]

WHETHER MAN. [*A little man wearing a long coat and carrying an umbrella pops up from behind the sign that he was holding. He speaks very fast and excitedly.*] My, my, my, my, my, welcome, welcome, welcome, welcome to the Land of Expectations, Expectations, Expectations! We don't get many travelers these days; we certainly don't get many travelers. Now what can I do for you? I'm the Whether Man.

MILO. [*Referring to map.*] Uh . . . is this the right road to Dictionopolis?

Summary
Reread Scene i to identify and summarize the key events.

Dialogue in Drama
What do you learn about the Whether Man from his first speech?

Comprehension
What is in the package Milo opens?

WHETHER MAN. Well now, well now, well now, I don't know of any wrong road to Dictionopolis, so if this road goes to Dictionopolis at all, it must be the right road, and if it doesn't, it must be the right road to somewhere else, because there are no wrong roads to anywhere. Do you think it will rain?

MILO. I thought you were the Weather Man.

WHETHER MAN. Oh, no, I'm the Whether Man, not the weather man. [*Pulls out a SIGN or opens a FLAP of his coat, which reads: "WHETHER."*] After all, it's more important to know whether there will be weather than what the weather will be.

MILO. What kind of place is Expectations?

Dialogue in Drama
What do you learn about the action from this dialogue between Milo and Whether Man?

WHETHER MAN. Good question, good question! Expectations is the place you must always go to before you get to where you are going. Of course, some people never go beyond Expectations, but my job is to hurry them along whether they like it or not. Now what else can I do for you? [*Opens his umbrella.*]

MILO. I think I can find my own way.

WHETHER MAN. Splendid, splendid, splendid! Whether or not you find your own way, you're bound to find some way. If you happen to find my way, please return it. I lost it years ago. I imagine by now it must be quite rusty. You did say it was going to rain, didn't you? [*Escorts* MILO *to the car under the open umbrella.*] I'm glad you made your own decision. I do so hate to make up my mind about anything, whether it's good or bad, up or down, rain or shine. Expect everything, I always say, and the unexpected never happens. Goodbye, goodbye, goodbye, good . . .

[*A loud CLAP of THUNDER is heard.*] Oh dear! [*He looks up at the sky, puts out his hand to feel for rain, and RUNS AWAY.* MILO *watches puzzledly and drives on.*]

Dialogue in Drama
How do Milo's words here move the plot along?

MILO. I'd better get out of Expectations, but fast. Talking to a guy like that all day would get me nowhere for sure. [*He tries to speed up, but finds instead that he is moving slower and slower.*] Oh, oh, now what? [*He can barely move. Behind* MILO, *the* LETHARGARIANS *begin* to enter from all parts of the stage. They are dressed to blend in with the scenery and carry small pillows that look like rocks. Whenever they fall asleep, they rest on the pillows.] Now I really am getting nowhere. I hope I didn't take a wrong turn. [*The car stops. He tries to start it. It won't move. He gets out and begins to tinker with it.*] I wonder where I am.

LETHARGARIAN 1. You're . . . in . . . the . . . Dol . . . drums . . . [MILO *looks around.*]

LETHARGARIAN 2. Yes . . . the . . . Dol . . . drums . . . [*A YAWN is heard.*]

MILO. [*Yelling.*] WHAT ARE THE DOLDRUMS?

LETHARGARIAN 3. The Doldrums, my friend, are where nothing ever happens and nothing ever changes. [*Parts of the Scenery stand up or Six People come out of the scenery colored in the same colors of the trees or the road. They move very slowly and as soon as they move, they stop to rest again.*] Allow me to introduce all of us. We are the Lethargarians at your service.

MILO. [*Uncertainly.*] Very pleased to meet you. I think I'm lost. Can you help me?

LETHARGARIAN 4. Don't say think. [*He yawns.*] It's against the law.

LETHARGARIAN 1. No one's allowed to think in the Doldrums. [*He falls asleep.*]

LETHARGARIAN 2. Don't you have a rule book? It's local ordinance 175389-J. [*He falls asleep.*]

MILO. [*Pulls out rule book and reads.*] Ordinance 175389-J: "It shall be unlawful, illegal and unethical to think, think of thinking, surmise, presume, reason, meditate or speculate while in the Doldrums. Anyone breaking this law shall be severely punished." That's a ridiculous law! Everybody thinks.

ALL THE LETHARGARIANS. We don't!

▼ **Critical Viewing**
What details in this picture show what the Lethargarians are like?

◄ **Vocabulary**
unethical (un eth´ i kəl) *adj.* not conforming to the moral standards of a group

Comprehension
What are the Doldrums?

Lethargarian 2. And most of the time, you don't, that's why you're here. You weren't thinking and you weren't paying attention either. People who don't pay attention often get stuck in the Doldrums. Face it, most of the time, you're just like us. [*Falls, snoring, to the ground.* Milo *laughs.*]

Lethargarian 5. Stop that at once. Laughing is against the law. Don't you have a rule book? It's local ordinance 574381-W.

Milo. [*Opens rule book and reads.*] "In the Doldrums, laughter is frowned upon and smiling is permitted only on alternate Thursdays." Well, if you can't laugh or think, what can you do?

Lethargarian 6. Anything as long as it's nothing, and everything as long as it isn't anything. There's lots to do. We have a very busy schedule . . .

Lethargarian 1. At 8:00 we get up and then we spend from 8 to 9 daydreaming.

Lethargarian 2. From 9:00 to 9:30 we take our early mid-morning nap . . .

Lethargarian 3. From 9:30 to 10:30 we dawdle and delay . . .

Lethargarian 4. From 10:30 to 11:30 we take our late early morning nap . . .

Lethargarian 5. From 11:30 to 12:00 we bide our time and then we eat our lunch.

Lethargarian 6. From 1:00 to 2:00 we linger and loiter . . .

Lethargarian 1. From 2:00 to 2:30 we take our early afternoon nap . . .

Lethargarian 2. From 2:30 to 3:30 we put off for tomorrow what we could have done today . . .

Lethargarian 3. From 3:30 to 4:00 we take our early late afternoon nap . . .

Lethargarian 4. From 4:00 to 5:00 we loaf and lounge until dinner . . .

Lethargarian 5. From 6:00 to 7:00 we dilly-dally . . .

Dialogue in Drama
What does this dialogue reveal about the Doldrums?

Dialogue in Drama
Ellipsis points—three spaced periods—often indicate a pause or an unfinished thought. How does this punctuation help you understand the way the dialogue should be read?

Science Connection

Measuring Time

The Latin poet Ovid coined the phrase "Time flies." Through the ages, telling time has advanced from tracking shadows to measuring vibrations.

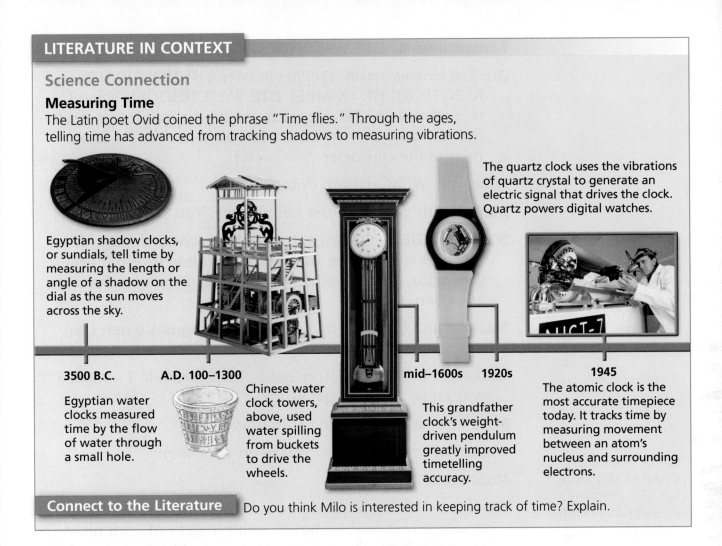

Egyptian shadow clocks, or sundials, tell time by measuring the length or angle of a shadow on the dial as the sun moves across the sky.

The quartz clock uses the vibrations of quartz crystal to generate an electric signal that drives the clock. Quartz powers digital watches.

3500 B.C. **A.D. 100–1300** **mid–1600s** **1920s** **1945**

Egyptian water clocks measured time by the flow of water through a small hole.

Chinese water clock towers, above, used water spilling from buckets to drive the wheels.

This grandfather clock's weight-driven pendulum greatly improved timetelling accuracy.

The atomic clock is the most accurate timepiece today. It tracks time by measuring movement between an atom's nucleus and surrounding electrons.

Connect to the Literature   Do you think Milo is interested in keeping track of time? Explain.

LETHARGARIAN 6. From 7:00 to 8:00 we take our early evening nap and then for an hour before we go to bed, we waste time.

LETHARGARIAN 1. [*Yawning.*] You see, it's really quite strenuous doing nothing all day long, and so once a week, we take a holiday and go nowhere.

LETHARGARIAN 5. Which is just where we were going when you came along. Would you care to join us?

MILO. [*Yawning.*] That's where I seem to be going, anyway. [*Stretching.*] Tell me, does everyone here do nothing?

LETHARGARIAN 3. Everyone but the terrible Watchdog. He's always sniffing around to see that nobody wastes time. A most unpleasant character.

MILO. The Watchdog?

Comprehension
Basically, what do the Lethargarians do all day?

LETHARGARIAN 6. THE WATCHDOG!

ALL THE LETHARGARIANS. [*Yelling at once.*] RUN! WAKE UP! RUN! HERE HE COMES! THE WATCHDOG! [*They all run off and ENTER a large dog with the head, feet, and tail of a dog, and the body of a clock, having the same face as the character THE CLOCK.*]

WATCHDOG. What are you doing here?

MILO. Nothing much. Just killing time. You see . . .

Summary
Would you include the arrival of the Watchdog in a summary of this scene? Why or why not?

WATCHDOG. KILLING TIME! [*His ALARM RINGS in fury.*] It's bad enough wasting time without killing it. What are you doing in the Doldrums, anyway? Don't you have anywhere to go?

MILO. I think I was on my way to Dictionopolis when I got stuck here. Can you help me?

WATCHDOG. Help you! You've got to help yourself. I suppose you know why you got stuck.

MILO. I guess I just wasn't thinking.

WATCHDOG. Precisely. Now you're on your way.

MILO. I am?

Spiral Review
CHARACTER How has Milo changed as a result of visiting the Lethargarians?

WATCHDOG. Of course. Since you got here by not thinking, it seems reasonable that in order to get out, you must start thinking. Do you mind if I get in? I love automobile rides. [*He gets in. They wait.*] Well?

MILO. All right. I'll try. [*Screws up his face and thinks.*] Are we moving?

WATCHDOG. Not yet. Think harder.

MILO. I'm thinking as hard as I can.

WATCHDOG. Well, think just a little harder than that. Come on, you can do it.

Dialogue in Drama
How does the dialogue between Milo and the Watchdog help you understand the problem here?

MILO. All right, all right. . . . I'm thinking of all the planets in the solar system, and why water expands when it turns to ice, and all the words that begin with "q," and . . . [*The wheels begin to move.*] We're moving! We're moving!

WATCHDOG. Keep thinking.

Milo. [*Thinking.*] How a steam engine works and how to bake a pie and the difference between Fahrenheit and Centigrade . . .

Watchdog. Dictionopolis, here we come.

Milo. Hey, Watchdog, are you coming along?

Tock. You can call me Tock, and keep your eyes on the road.

Milo. What kind of place is Dictionopolis, anyway?

Tock. It's where all the words in the world come from. It used to be a marvelous place, but ever since Rhyme and Reason left, it hasn't been the same.

Milo. Rhyme and Reason?

Tock. The two princesses. They used to settle all the arguments between their two brothers who rule over

▲ **Critical Viewing**
Why is a clock part of this character's body?

Comprehension
What does Milo think about to get his car to move?

the Land of Wisdom. You see, Azaz is the king of Dictionopolis and the Mathemagician is the king of Digitopolis and they almost never see eye to eye on anything. It was the job of the Princesses Sweet Rhyme and Pure Reason to solve the differences between the two kings, and they always did so well that both sides usually went home feeling very satisfied. But then, one day, the kings had an argument to end all arguments. . . .

[*The LIGHTS DIM on* Tock *and* Milo, *and come up on* King Azaz *of Dictionopolis on another part of the stage.* Azaz *has a great stomach, a grey beard reaching to his waist, a small crown and a long robe with the letters of the alphabet written all over it.*]

Azaz. Of course, I'll abide by the decision of Rhyme and Reason, though I have no doubt as to what it will be. They will choose *words*, of course. Everyone knows that words are more important than numbers any day of the week.

[*The* Mathemagician *appears opposite* Azaz. *The* Mathemagician *wears a long flowing robe covered entirely with complex mathematical equations, and a tall pointed hat. He carries a long staff with a pencil point at one end and a large rubber eraser at the other.*]

Mathemagician. That's what you think, Azaz. People wouldn't even know what day of the week it is without *numbers*. Haven't you ever looked at a calendar? Face it, Azaz. It's numbers that count.

Azaz. Don't be ridiculous. [*To audience, as if leading a cheer.*] Let's hear it for WORDS!

Mathemagician. [*To audience, in the same manner.*] Cast your vote for NUMBERS!

Azaz. A, B, C's!

Mathemagician. 1, 2, 3's! [*A FANFARE is heard.*]

Azaz And Mathemagician. [*To each other.*] Quiet! Rhyme and Reason are about to announce their decision.

[Rhyme *and* Reason *appear.*]

Rhyme. Ladies and gentlemen, letters and numerals,

Summary
How would you summarize the argument between Azaz and the Mathemagician?

fractions and punctuation marks—may we have your attention, please. After careful consideration of the problem set before us by King Azaz of Dictionopolis [AZAZ *bows.*] and the Mathemagician of Digitopolis [MATHEMAGICIAN *raises his hands in a victory salute.*] we have come to the following conclusion:

REASON. Words and numbers are of equal value, for in the cloak of knowledge, one is the warp and the other is the woof.

RHYME. It is no more important to count the sands than it is to name the stars.

RHYME AND REASON. Therefore, let both kingdoms, Dictionopolis and Digitopolis, live in peace.

[*The sound of CHEERING is heard.*]

AZAZ. Boo! is what I say. Boo and Bah and Hiss!

MATHEMAGICIAN. What good are these girls if they can't even settle an argument in anyone's favor? I think I have come to a decision of my own.

AZAZ. So have I.

AZAZ AND MATHEMAGICIAN. [*To the* PRINCESSES.] You are hereby banished from this land to the Castle-in-the-Air. [*To each other.*] *And as for you, KEEP OUT OF MY WAY!* [*They stalk off in opposite directions.*]

[*During this time, the set has been changed to the Market Square of Dictionopolis. LIGHTS come UP on the deserted square.*]

TOCK. And ever since then, there has been neither Rhyme nor Reason in this kingdom. Words are misused and numbers are mismanaged. The argument between the two kings has divided everyone and the real value of both words and numbers has been forgotten. What a waste!

MILO. Why doesn't somebody rescue the Princesses and set everything straight again?

TOCK. That is easier said than done. The Castle-in-the-Air is very far from here, and the one path which leads to

Summary
Reread this section to summarize the events leading to Rhyme and Reason's banishment.

Comprehension
What conclusion do Reason and Rhyme reach?

Vocabulary ▶
ferocious (fə rō′ shəs)
adj. wild and dangerous

it is guarded by ferocious demons. But hold on, here we are. [*A Man appears, carrying a Gate and a small Tollbooth.*]

GATEKEEPER. AHHHHREMMMM! This is Dictionopolis, a happy kingdom, advantageously located in the foothills of Confusion and caressed by gentle breezes from the Sea of Knowledge. Today, by royal proclamation, is Market Day. Have you come to buy or sell?

MILO. I beg your pardon?

GATEKEEPER. Buy or sell, buy or sell. Which is it? You must have come here for a reason.

MILO. Well, I . . .

GATEKEEPER. Come now, if you don't have a reason, you must at least have an explanation or certainly an excuse.

MILO. [*Meekly.*] Uh . . . no.

GATEKEEPER. [*Shaking his head.*] Very serious. You can't get in without a reason. [*Thoughtfully.*] Wait a minute. Maybe I have an old one you can use. [*Pulls out an old suitcase from the tollbooth and rummages through it.*] No . . . no . . . no . . . this won't do . . . hmmm . . .

MILO. [*To* TOCK.] What's he looking for? [TOCK *shrugs.*]

Dialogue in Drama
What details does the Gatekeeper reveal about Dictionopolis?

GATEKEEPER. Ah! This is fine. [*Pulls out a Medallion on a chain. Engraved in the Medallion is: "WHY NOT?"*] Why not. That's a good reason for almost anything . . . a bit used, perhaps, but still quite serviceable. There you are, sir. Now I can truly say: Welcome to Dictionopolis.

[*He opens the Gate and walks off.* CITIZENS *and* MERCHANTS *appear on all levels of the stage, and* MILO *and* TOCK *find themselves in the middle of a noisy marketplace. As some people buy and sell their wares, others hang a large banner which reads: WELCOME TO THE WORD MARKET.*]

MILO. Tock! Look!

MERCHANT 1. Hey-ya, hey-ya, hey-ya, step right up and take your pick. Juicy tempting words for sale. Get your fresh-picked "if 's," "and's" and "but's"! Just take a look at these nice ripe "where's" and "when's."

Merchant 2. Step right up, step right up, fancy, best-quality words here for sale. Enrich your vocabulary and expand your speech with such elegant items as "quagmire," "flabbergast," or "upholstery."

Merchant 3. Words by the bag, buy them over here. Words by the bag for the more talkative customer. A pound of "happy's" at a very reasonable price . . . very useful for "Happy Birthday," "Happy New Year," "happy days," or "happy-go-lucky." Or how about a package of "good's," always handy for "good morning," "good afternoon," "good evening," and "goodbye."

Milo. I can't believe it. Did you ever see so many words?

Tock. They're fine if you have something to say. [*They come to a Do-It-Yourself Bin.*]

Milo. [*To* Merchant 4 *at the bin.*] Excuse me, but what are these?

Merchant 4. These are for people who like to make up their own words. You can pick any assortment you like or buy a special box complete with all the letters and a book of instructions. Here, taste an "A." They're very good. [*He pops one into* Milo's *mouth.*]

Milo. [*Tastes it hesitantly.*] It's sweet! [*He eats it.*]

Merchant 4. I knew you'd like it. "A" is one of our best-sellers. All of them aren't that good, you know. The "Z," for instance—very dry and sawdusty. And the "X"? Tastes like a trunkful of stale air. But most of the others aren't bad at all. Here, try the "I."

Milo. [*Tasting.*] Cool! It tastes icy.

Merchant 4. [*To* Tock.] How about the "C" for you? It's as crunchy as a bone. Most people are just too lazy to make their own words, but take it from me, not only is it more fun, but it's also *de*-lightful, [*Holds up a "D."*] *e*-lating, [*Holds up an "E."*] and extremely *u*seful! [*Holds up a "U."*]

Milo. But isn't it difficult? I'm not very good at making words.

Comprehension
What is sold in the Dictionopolis marketplace?

Summary
Would you include the scene in the Word Market in a summary of Scene ii? Why or why not?

Vocabulary ▶
misapprehension
(mis′ ap rē hen′ shən)
n. misunderstanding

[*The* SPELLING BEE, *a large colorful bee, comes up from behind.*]

SPELLING BEE. Perhaps I can be of some assistance . . . a-s-s-i-s-t-a-n-c-e. [*The Three turn around and see him.*] Don't be alarmed . . . a-l-a-r-m-e-d. I am the Spelling Bee. I can spell anything. Anything. A-n-y-t-h-i-n-g. Try me. Try me.

MILO. [*Backing off,* TOCK *on his guard.*] Can you spell goodbye?

SPELLING BEE. Perhaps you are under the misapprehension . . . m-i-s-a-p-p-r-e-h-e-n-s-i-o-n that I am dangerous. Let me assure you that I am quite peaceful. Now, think of the most difficult word you can, and I'll spell it.

MILO. Uh . . . o.k. [*At this point,* MILO *may turn to the audience and ask them to help him choose a word or he may think of one on his own.*] How about . . . "Curiosity"?

SPELLING BEE. [*Winking.*] Let's see now . . . uh . . . how much time do I have?

MILO. Just ten seconds. Count them off, Tock.

SPELLING BEE. [*As* TOCK *counts.*] Oh dear, oh dear. [*Just at the last moment, quickly.*] C-u-r-i-o-s-i-t-y.

MERCHANT 4. Correct! [ALL *Cheer.*]

MILO. Can you spell anything?

SPELLING BEE. [*Proudly.*] Just about. You see, years ago, I was an ordinary bee minding my own business, smelling flowers all day, occasionally picking up part-time work in people's bonnets. Then one day, I realized that I'd never amount to anything without an education, so I decided that . . .

HUMBUG. [*Coming up in a booming voice.*] BALDERDASH! [*He wears a lavish coat, striped pants, checked vest, spats and a derby hat.*] Let me repeat . . . BALDERDASH! [*Swings his cane and clicks his heels in the air.*] Well, well, what have we here? Isn't someone going to introduce me to the little boy?

SPELLING BEE. [*Disdainfully.*] This is the Humbug. You can't trust a word he says.

HUMBUG. NONSENSE! Everyone can trust a Humbug. As I

was saying to the king just the other day . . .

SPELLING BEE. You've never met the king. [*To* MILO.] Don't believe a thing he tells you.

HUMBUG. Bosh, my boy, pure bosh. The Humbugs are an old and noble family, honorable to the core. Why, we fought in the Crusades with Richard the Lionhearted, crossed the Atlantic with Columbus, blazed trails with the pioneers. History is full of Humbugs.

SPELLING BEE. A very pretty speech . . . s-p-e-e-c-h. Now, why don't you go away? I was just advising the lad of the importance of proper spelling.

HUMBUG. BAH! As soon as you learn to spell one word, they ask you to spell another. You can never catch up, so why bother? [*Puts his arm around* MILO.] Take my advice, boy, and forget about it. As my great-great-great-grandfather George Washington Humbug used to say . . .

SPELLING BEE. You, sir, are an impostor i-m-p-o-s-t-o-r who can't even spell his own name!

HUMBUG. What? You dare to doubt my word? The word of a Humbug? The word of a Humbug who has direct access to the ear of a King? And the king shall hear of this, I promise you . . .

VOICE 1. Did someone call for the King?

VOICE 2. Did you mention the monarch?

VOICE 3. Speak of the sovereign?

VOICE 4. Entreat the Emperor?

◄ **Critical Viewing**
How does this picture of Spelling Bee compare with his description in the play?

Dialogue in Drama
What does the dialogue between Humbug and Spelling Bee show about their relationship?

Comprehension
What advice does Spelling Bee give Milo?

VOICE 5. Hail his highness?

[*Five tall, thin gentlemen regally dressed in silks and satins, plumed hats and buckled shoes appear as they speak.*]

MILO. Who are they?

SPELLING BEE. The King's advisors. Or in more formal terms, his cabinet.

MINISTER 1. Greetings!

MINISTER 2. Salutations!

MINISTER 3. Welcome!

MINISTER 4. Good Afternoon!

MINISTER 5. Hello!

MILO. Uh . . . Hi.

[*All the* MINISTERS, *from here on called by their numbers, unfold their scrolls and read in order.*]

MINISTER 1. By the order of Azaz the Unabridged . . .

MINISTER 2. King of Dictionopolis . . .

MINISTER 3. Monarch of letters . . .

MINISTER 4. Emperor of phrases, sentences, and miscellaneous figures of speech . . .

MINISTER 5. We offer you the hospitality of our kingdom . . .

MINISTER 1. Country

MINISTER 2. Nation

MINISTER 3. State

MINISTER 4. Commonwealth

MINISTER 5. Realm

MINISTER 1. Empire

MINISTER 2. Palatinate

MINISTER 3. Principality.

MILO. Do all those words mean the same thing?

MINISTER 1. Of course.

MINISTER 2. Certainly.

Vocabulary ▶
unabridged (un´ ə brijd´) *adj.* complete; not shortened

Dialogue in Drama
How does the dialogue of the five Ministers show the importance of words in Dictionopolis?

MINISTER 3. Precisely.

MINISTER 4. Exactly.

MINISTER 5. Yes.

MILO. Then why don't you use just one? Wouldn't that make a lot more sense?

MINISTER 1. Nonsense!

MINISTER 2. Ridiculous!

MINISTER 3. Fantastic!

MINISTER 4. Absurd!

MINISTER 5. Bosh!

MINISTER 1. We're not interested in making sense. It's not our job.

MINISTER 2. Besides, one word is as good as another, so why not use them all?

MINISTER 3. Then you don't have to choose which one is right.

MINISTER 4. Besides, if one is right, then ten are ten times as right.

MINISTER 5. Obviously, you don't know who we are.

[*Each presents himself and* MILO *acknowledges the introduction.*]

MINISTER 1. The Duke of Definition.

MINISTER 2. The Minister of Meaning.

MINISTER 3. The Earl of Essence.

MINISTER 4. The Count of Connotation.

MINISTER 5. The Undersecretary of Understanding.

ALL FIVE. And we have come to invite you to the Royal Banquet.

SPELLING BEE. The banquet! That's quite an honor, my boy. A real h-o-n-o-r.

HUMBUG. DON'T BE RIDICULOUS! Everybody goes to the Royal Banquet these days.

Summary
Briefly restate two ideas included in the Ministers' welcome.

Comprehension
What is the main responsibility of the Ministers?

Spelling Bee. [*To the* Humbug.] True, everybody does go. But some people are invited and others simply push their way in where they aren't wanted.

Humbug. HOW DARE YOU? You buzzing little upstart, I'll show you who's not wanted . . . [*Raises his cane threateningly.*]

Spelling Bee. You just watch it! I'm warning w-a-r-n-i-n-g you! [*At that moment, an ear-shattering blast of TRUMPETS, entirely off-key, is heard, and a* PAGE *appears.*]

Page. King Azaz the Unabridged is about to begin the Royal banquet. All guests who do not appear promptly at the table will automatically lose their place. [*A huge Table is carried out with* King Azaz *sitting in a large chair, carried out at the head of the table.*]

Azaz. Places. Everyone take your places. [*All the characters, including the* Humbug *and the* Spelling Bee, *who forget their quarrel, rush to take their places at the table.* Milo *and* Tock *sit near the king.* Azaz *looks at* Milo.] And just who is this?

Milo. Your Highness, my name is Milo and this is Tock. Thank you very much for inviting us to your banquet, and I think your palace is beautiful!

Minister 1. Exquisite.

Minister 2. Lovely.

Minister 3. Handsome.

Minister 4. Pretty.

Minister 5. Charming.

Azaz. SILENCE! Now tell me, young man, what can you do to entertain us? Sing songs? Tell stories? Juggle plates? Do tumbling tricks? Which is it?

Milo. I can't do any of those things.

Azaz. What an ordinary little boy. Can't you do anything at all?

Milo. Well . . . I can count to a thousand.

Azaz. AARGH, numbers! Never mention numbers here. Only

use them when we absolutely have to. Now, why don't we change the subject and have some dinner? Since you are the guest of honor, you may pick the menu.

Milo. Me? Well, uh . . . I'm not very hungry. Can we just have a light snack?

Azaz. A light snack it shall be!

[Azaz *claps his hands. Waiters rush in with covered trays. When they are uncovered, Shafts of Light pour out. The light may be created through the use of battery-operated flashlights which are secured in the trays and covered with a false bottom. The Guests help themselves.*]

Humbug. Not a very substantial meal. Maybe you can suggest something a little more filling.

Milo. Well, in that case, I think we ought to have a square meal . . .

Azaz. [*Claps his hands.*] A square meal it is! [*Waiters serve trays of Colored Squares of all sizes. People serve themselves.*]

Spelling Bee. These are awful. [Humbug *coughs and all the Guests do not care for the food.*]

Azaz. [*Claps his hands and the trays are removed.*] Time for speeches. [*To* Milo.] You first.

Milo. [*Hesitantly.*] Your Majesty, ladies and gentlemen, I would like to take this opportunity to say that . . .

Azaz. That's quite enough. Mustn't talk all day.

Milo. But I just started to . . .

Azaz. NEXT!

Humbug. [*Quickly.*] Roast turkey, mashed potatoes, vanilla ice cream.

Spelling Bee. Hamburgers, corn on the cob, chocolate pudding p-u-d-d-i-n-g. [*Each Guest names two dishes and a dessert.*]

Azaz. [*The last.*] Pâté de foie gras, soupe à l'oignon, salade endives, fromage et fruits et demi-tasse. [*He claps his

Dialogue in Drama
How do the dialogue and stage directions show that "a light snack" has different meanings for Milo and Azaz?

AARGH, numbers! Never mention numbers here.

Comprehension
What does Azaz forbid Milo to discuss?

hands. *Waiters serve each Guest his Words.*] Dig in. [*To* Milo.] Though I can't say I think much of your choice.

Milo. I didn't know I was going to have to eat my words.

Azaz. Of course, of course, everybody here does. Your speech should have been in better taste.

Minister 1. Here, try some somersault. It improves the flavor.

Minister 2. Have a rigamarole. [*Offers breadbasket.*]

Minister 3. Or a ragamuffin.

Minister 4. Perhaps you'd care for a synonym bun.

Minister 5. Why not wait for your just desserts?

Azaz. Ah yes, the dessert. We're having a special treat today . . . freshly made at the half-bakery.

Milo. The half-bakery?

Azaz. Of course, the half-bakery! Where do you think half-baked ideas come from? Now, please don't interrupt. By royal command, the pastry chefs have . . .

Milo. What's a half-baked idea?

[Azaz *gives up the idea of speaking as a cart is wheeled in and the Guests help themselves.*]

Humbug. They're very tasty, but they don't always agree with you. Here's a good one. [Humbug *hands one to* Milo.]

Milo. [*Reads.*] "The earth is flat."

Spelling Bee. People swallowed that one for years. [*Picks up one and reads.*] "The moon is made of green cheese." Now, there's a half-baked idea.

[*Everyone chooses one and eats. They include: "It Never Rains But Pours," "Night Air Is Bad Air," "Everything Happens for the Best," "Coffee Stunts Your Growth."*]

Azaz. And now for a few closing words. Attention! Let me have your attention! [*Everyone leaps up and Exits, except for* Milo, Tock, *and the* Humbug.] Loyal subjects and friends, once again on this gala occasion, we have . . .

Dialogue in Drama
Identify one pun, or play on words, that adds humor to this dialogue.

Summary
Briefly summarize the events at the banquet.

Milo. Excuse me, but everybody left.

Azaz. [*Sadly.*] I was hoping no one would notice. It happens every time.

Humbug. They're gone to dinner, and as soon as I finish this last bite, I shall join them.

Milo. That's ridiculous. How can they eat dinner right after a banquet?

Azaz. SCANDALOUS! We'll put a stop to it at once. From now on, by royal command, everyone must eat dinner before the banquet.

Milo. But that's just as bad.

Humbug. Or just as good. Things which are equally bad are also equally good. Try to look at the bright side of things.

Milo. I don't know which side of anything to look at. Everything is so confusing, and all your words only make things worse.

Azaz. How true. There must be something we can do about it.

Humbug. Pass a law.

Azaz. We have almost as many laws as words.

Humbug. Offer a reward. [Azaz *shakes his head and looks madder at each suggestion.*] Send for help? Drive a bargain? Pull the switch? Lower the boom? Toe the line?

[*As* Azaz *continues to scowl, the* Humbug *loses confidence and finally gives up.*]

Milo. Maybe you should let Rhyme and Reason return.

Azaz. How nice that would be. Even if they were a bother at times, things always went so well when they were here. But I'm afraid it can't be done.

Humbug. Certainly not. Can't be done.

Milo. Why not?

Humbug. [*Now siding with* Milo.] Why not, indeed?

Azaz. Much too difficult.

> *Things which are equally bad are also equally good.*

Comprehension
Why has everyone left the banquet?

HUMBUG. Of course, much too difficult.

MILO. You could, if you really wanted to.

HUMBUG. By all means, if you really wanted to, you could.

AZAZ. [*To* HUMBUG.] How?

MILO. [*Also to* HUMBUG.] Yeah, how?

HUMBUG. Why . . . uh, it's a simple task for a brave boy with a stout heart, a steadfast dog and a serviceable small automobile.

AZAZ. Go on.

HUMBUG. Well, all that he would have to do is cross the dangerous, unknown countryside between here and Digitopolis, where he would have to persuade the Mathemagician to release the Princesses, which we know to be impossible because the Mathemagician will never agree with Azaz about anything. Once achieving that, it's a simple matter of entering the Mountains of Ignorance from where no one has ever returned alive, an effortless climb up a two thousand foot stairway without railings in a high wind at night to the Castle-in-the-Air. After a pleasant chat with the Princesses, all that remains is a leisurely ride back through those chaotic crags where the frightening fiends have sworn to tear any intruder limb from limb and devour him down to his belt buckle. And finally after doing all that, a triumphal parade! If, of course, there is anything left to parade . . . followed by hot chocolate and cookies for everyone.

AZAZ. I never realized it would be so simple.

MILO. It sounds dangerous to me.

TOCK. And just who is supposed to make that journey?

AZAZ. A very good question. But there is one far more serious problem.

MILO. What's that?

AZAZ. I'm afraid I can't tell you that until you return.

MILO. But wait a minute, I didn't . . .

AZAZ. Dictionopolis will always be grateful to you, my boy, and your dog. [AZAZ *pats* TOCK *and* MILO.]

TOCK. Now, just one moment, sire . . .

AZAZ. You will face many dangers on your journey, but fear not, for I can give you something for your protection. [AZAZ *gives* MILO *a box.*] In this box are the letters of the alphabet. With them you can form all the words you will ever need to help you overcome the obstacles that may stand in your path. All you must do is use them well and in the right places.

MILO. [*Miserably.*] Thanks a lot.

AZAZ. You will need a guide, of course, and since he knows the obstacles so well, the Humbug has cheerfully volunteered to accompany you.

HUMBUG. Now, see here . . . !

AZAZ. You will find him dependable, brave, resourceful and loyal.

HUMBUG. [*Flattered.*] Oh, your Majesty.

Dialogue in Drama
Based on these lines, how does Azaz feel about the power of words?

Comprehension
What does Azaz give Milo for his journey?

Milo. I'm sure he'll be a great help. [*They approach the car.*]

Tock. I hope so. It looks like we're going to need it.

[*The lights darken and the* KING *fades from view.*]

Azaz. Good luck! Drive carefully! [*The three get into the car and begin to move. Suddenly a thunderously loud NOISE is heard. They slow down the car.*]

Milo. What was that?

Tock. It came from up ahead.

Humbug. It's something terrible, I just know it. Oh, no. Something dreadful is going to happen to us. I can feel it in my bones. [*The NOISE is repeated. They all look at each other fearfully as the lights fade.*]

Summary
Reread Scene ii and summarize the main events.

Language Study

Vocabulary The words listed below appear in *The Phantom Tollbooth*, Act I. Write a vocabulary word that fits with each of the numbered word groups. Explain your answers.

ignorance	precautionary	ferocious
misapprehension	unabridged	

1. growling, dangerous _____
2. confusion, disagreement _____
3. inexperience, unawareness _____
4. carefully planned, safe _____
5. complete, entire _____

Word Study

Part A Explain how the **Greek root -eth-** contributes to the meanings of *ethics* and *ethnicity*. Consult a dictionary if necessary.

Part B Use context and what you know about the Greek root *-eth-* to explain your answer to each question.

1. Is it *ethical* to take a book that does not belong to you?
2. Can an *ethicist* tell right from wrong?

WORD STUDY

The **Greek root *-eth-*** means "character" or "custom." In this selection, Milo is told that to think in the land of the Doldrums is **unethical**, meaning that it shows poor character.

Close Reading Activities

Literary Analysis

Key Ideas and Details

1. **Summary (a)** What events would you include in a summary of Act I? **(b)** Explain why they are the most important events.

2. **(a)** Who are Rhyme and Reason? **(b) Analyze Causes and Effects:** What effect does their absence have on Dictionopolis?

3. **(a)** How does Humbug describe the journey that Milo must make? **(b) Predict:** In Act II, Milo will start his journey. What do you think it will be like? **(c) Support:** Give three details from Act I to support your answer.

4. **(a)** What does King Azaz give Milo? **(b) Hypothesize:** Describe a situation in which the gift might help Milo.

Craft and Structure

5. **Dialogue in Drama** Complete a chart like the one on the right to explain what each passage of dialogue below reveals about a character, the setting, and an action. An example has been provided.
   (a) MILO. Well, it doesn't matter anyway. Dictionopolis. That's a weird name. I might as well go there.
   (b) GATEKEEPER. This is Dictionopolis, a happy kingdom, advantageously located in the foothills of Confusion and caressed by gentle breezes from the Sea of Knowledge.
   (c) WATCHDOG. Do you mind if I get in? I love automobile rides.

Dialogue	What it Suggests
Passage (a)	Character: Milo is bored and uninterested.
Passage (b)	Setting:
Passage (c)	Action:

Integration of Knowledge and Ideas

6. **(a) Interpret:** So far, what theme, or insight about life, do you think the author is expressing? **(b) Hypothesize:** Who do you think is the main audience for this theme? **(c) Synthesize:** Why would that audience be interested in the theme?

7. **(a) Apply:** What advice would you give to Milo at the end of Act I? **(b) Support:** Why do you think it would be good advice? Explain your position, citing details from the play.

8. **How do we decide who we are? (a)** Compare and contrast Milo's personality at the beginning and end of Act I. **(b)** What has caused the change in Milo?

ACADEMIC VOCABULARY

As you write and speak about *The Phantom Tollbooth*, Act I, use the words related to identity that you explored on page 441 of this text.

Conventions: Prepositions and Appositives

A **preposition** is a word such as *on, by,* or *from* that relates a noun or pronoun to another word in the sentence.

A **prepositional phrase** begins with the preposition and includes the noun or pronoun, called the **object of the preposition**.

An **appositive** is a noun or pronoun that identifies or explains another noun or pronoun next to it in the sentence.

An **appositive phrase** includes an appositive and its modifiers. If an appositive or an appositive phrase is not essential to the meaning of the sentence, it is set off with commas or dashes.

Prepositions/Prepositional Phrases	Appositives/Appositive Phrases
Jenny stood *near* the stage.	Jenny, *a young girl*, stood near the stage. (not essential)
After the performance, the audience clapped and cheered.	My friend *Maria* clapped and cheered. (essential)

Practice A

Rewrite each sentence, circling each preposition and underlining each object of the preposition.

1. Milo sat on his bed.
2. After school, Milo was bored.
3. In the play, the clock spoke.
4. Milo traveled to the land of Dictionopolis.
5. Tock rode with the others.

Reading Application Reread the first act of *The Phantom Tollbooth* and identify at least three prepositional phrases.

Practice B

Rewrite each sentence, circling the appositive or appositive phrase. Underline the noun or pronoun it identifies or explains.

1. Milo, a young boy, stared into space.
2. The Whether Man, a little man wearing a coat, was not a weather man.
3. The novel *The Phantom Tollbooth* has been popular for decades.
4. A dog with a clock for a body, the Watchdog, hopped into the car.

Writing Application Write three sentences based on *The Phantom Tollbooth*, containing appositive or prepositional phrases.

Writing to Sources

Informative Text Write a brief **summary** of *The Phantom Tollbooth*, Act I.

- Review the play to decide which events, characters, and ideas are important.
- Present events in the order in which they occur, giving your summary a beginning, a middle, and an end.
- Provide enough information for readers to understand the main ideas and natural flow of the drama.
- Leave out unimportant details, and do not include opinions or evaluations.

Grammar Application Be sure that you have used prepositions and appositives correctly in your summary. If an appositive phrase is not essential, set it off with commas.

Research and Technology

Build and Present Knowledge Work with a small group to research and prepare a **multimedia presentation** on a topic related to drama. Because the audience for your presentation will be your class, choose your topic with your classmates' interests in mind. You might select from among these topics: actors, theaters, stage sets, playwrights, comedies, or serious dramas.

Follow these steps to complete the assignment:

- Keep the backgrounds and interests of your audience in mind. Choose a topic your audience will find interesting.
- Conduct research on your topic, using reputable online or print resources. To ensure accuracy, confirm facts in at least two different sources.
- Include printouts, slides, photos, or drawings to illustrate the facts you present. Your illustrations should be lively to capture your audience's attention.
- Use other graphics, such as diagrams, timelines, and charts.
- Use audio aids, such as recordings and sound effects.

Practice your presentation, and then deliver it to the class.

Building Knowledge

Meet the Author

Norton Juster (b. 1929) designed buildings and other structures during his career as an architect. He took up creative writing in his spare time "as a relaxation" from architecture. When he began writing *The Phantom Tollbooth,* the novel on which this drama is based, he thought it was just a short story for his own pleasure. Yet before long, Juster says, "it had created its own life, and I was hooked." The novel has been translated into several languages and adapted for an animated film.

How do we decide who we are?

Explore the Big Question as you read *The Phantom Tollbooth*, Act II. Take notes on ways in which the play explores how experiences can change a person.

CLOSE READING FOCUS

Key Ideas and Details: **Compare and Contrast**

When you **compare** two things, you tell how they are alike. When you **contrast** two things, you tell how they are different. As you read drama, picture the action to compare and contrast characters, situations, and events. Pay attention to the dialogue and the descriptions of how characters speak and act.

Craft and Structure: **Stage Directions**

A dramatic script contains two types of information. Lines of dialogue tell readers what the characters say. **Stage directions** are the words in a drama that the characters do not say. These directions tell performers how to move and speak. They also help readers picture the action, sounds, and scenery. Stage directions are usually printed in italics and set between brackets, as in this example.

> **CARLOS.** [*To* ISABEL.] Remember, don't make a sound! [*He tiptoes offstage.*]

Remember to read the stage directions when you read a play, or you may miss important information.

Vocabulary

You will encounter the following words in *The Phantom Tollbooth*, Act II. Decide whether you know each word well, know it a little bit, or do not know it at all. After you read the play, see how your knowledge of each word has increased.

dissonance	deficiency	admonishing
iridescent	malicious	transfixed

CLOSE READING MODEL

The passage below is from Susan Nanus's play *The Phantom Tollbooth*, Act II. The annotations to the right of the passage show ways in which you can use close reading skills to compare and contrast characters, situations, and events, as well as analyze stage directions.

from *The Phantom Tollbooth*, Act II

MILO. [*Suspiciously.*] Just what kind of doctor are you? **1**

DISCHORD. Well, you might say, I'm a specialist. I specialize in noises, from the loudest to the softest, and from the slightly annoying to the terribly unpleasant. For instance, have you ever heard a square-wheeled steamroller ride over a street full of hardboiled eggs? [*Very loud CRUNCHING SOUNDS are heard.*] **2**

MILO. [*Holding his ears.*] But who would want all those terrible noises?

DISCHORD. [*Surprised at the question.*] Everybody does. Why, I'm so busy I can hardly fill all the orders for noise pills, racket lotion, clamor salve and hubbub tonic. That's all people seem to want these days. Years ago, everyone wanted pleasant sounds and business was terrible. But then the cities were built and there was a great need for honking horns, screeching trains, clanging bells and all the rest of those wonderfully unpleasant sounds we use so much today. **3** I've been working overtime ever since and my medicine here is in great demand. All you have to do is take one spoonful every day, and you'll never have to hear another beautiful sound again. Here, try some.

HUMBUG. [*Backing away.*] If it's all the same to you, I'd rather not. **4**

Stage Directions
1 The italic words in brackets signal a stage direction. This one tells you that Milo is suspicious of Dischord.

Stage Directions
2 These stage directions call for a sound effect. Someone backstage might create the effect by playing a recording or using objects that create a crunching sound.

Compare and Contrast
3 Dischord contrasts what his business was like years ago to what his business is like now that the cities are bustling.

Compare and Contrast
4 When you compare Dischord to a real-life doctor, his ideas about medicine may be the opposite of what you expect. Real-life doctors do not try to cure something positive such as the ability to hear beautiful sounds.

The Phantom Tollbooth

Susan Nanus
Based on the book by Norton Juster

Review and Anticipate

In Act I, Milo is lifted from his boredom into a strange king-dom that is in conflict over the importance of letters and numbers. After traveling through Dictionopolis, he agrees to rescue the princesses who can settle the conflict. As Act II opens, Milo enters Digitopolis with Tock and Humbug—char-acters who will help him rescue the princesses.

Act II • Scene i

The set of Digitopolis glitters in the background, while Up-stage Right near the road, a small colorful Wagon sits, look-ing quite deserted. On its side in large letters, a sign reads: "KAKAFONOUS A. DISCHORD Doctor of Dissonance." Enter MILO, TOCK, *and* HUMBUG, *fearfully. They look at the wagon.*

TOCK. There's no doubt about it. That's where the noise was coming from.

HUMBUG. [*To* MILO.] Well, go on.

MILO. Go on what?

HUMBUG. Go on and see who's making all that noise in there. We can't just ignore a creature like that.

Stage Directions
What information about setting do these stage directions provide?

Vocabulary ▶
dissonance (dis ´ ə nəns) *n.* harsh or unpleasant combination of sounds

Milo. Creature? What kind of creature? Do you think he's dangerous?

Humbug. Go on, Milo. Knock on the door. We'll be right behind you.

Milo. O.K. Maybe he can tell us how much further it is to Digitopolis.

[Milo *tiptoes up to the wagon door and KNOCKS timidly. The moment he knocks, a terrible CRASH is heard inside the wagon, and Milo and the others jump back in fright. At the same time, the Door Flies Open, and from the dark interior, a Hoarse Voice inquires.*]

Voice. Have you ever heard a whole set of dishes dropped from the ceiling onto a hard stone floor? [*The Others are speechless with fright. Milo shakes his head. Voice happily.*] Have you ever heard an ant wearing fur slippers walk across a thick wool carpet? [Milo *shakes his head again.*] Have you ever heard a blindfolded octopus unwrap a cellophane-covered bathtub? [Milo *shakes his head a third time.*] Ha! I knew it. [*He hops out, a little man, wearing a white coat, with a stethoscope around his neck, and a small mirror attached to his forehead, and with very huge ears, and a mortar and pestle in his hands. He stares at Milo, Tock and Humbug.*] None of you looks well at all! Tsk, tsk, not at all. [*He opens the top or side of his Wagon, revealing a dusty interior resembling an old apothecary shop, with shelves lined with jars and boxes, a table, books, test tubes and bottles and measuring spoons.*]

Milo. [*Timidly.*] Are you a doctor?

Dischord. [Voice.] I am KAKAFONOUS A. DISCHORD, DOCTOR OF DISSONANCE! [*Several small explosions and a grinding crash are heard.*]

Humbug. [*Stuttering with fear.*] What does the "A" stand for?

Dischord. AS LOUD AS POSSIBLE! [*Two screeches and a bump are heard.*] Now, step a little closer and stick out your tongues. [Dischord *examines them.*] Just as I expected. [*He opens a large dusty book and thumbs through the pages.*] You're all suffering from a severe lack of noise. [Dischord *begins running around, collecting bottles, reading the labels to himself as he goes along.*]

Stage Directions
What information about sound effects do you learn from these stage directions?

Comprehension
Why are Milo, Tock, and Humbug frightened?

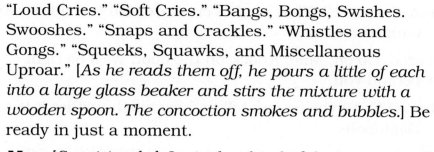
"Loud Cries." "Soft Cries." "Bangs, Bongs, Swishes. Swooshes." "Snaps and Crackles." "Whistles and Gongs." "Squeeks, Squawks, and Miscellaneous Uproar." [*As he reads them off, he pours a little of each into a large glass beaker and stirs the mixture with a wooden spoon. The concoction smokes and bubbles.*] Be ready in just a moment.

MILO. [*Suspiciously.*] Just what kind of doctor are you?

DISCHORD. Well, you might say, I'm a specialist. I specialize in noises, from the loudest to the softest, and from the slightly annoying to the terribly unpleasant. For instance, have you ever heard a square-wheeled steamroller ride over a street full of hard-boiled eggs? [*Very loud CRUNCHING SOUNDS are heard.*]

MILO. [*Holding his ears.*] But who would want all those terrible noises?

DISCHORD. [*Surprised at the question.*] Everybody does. Why, I'm so busy I can hardly fill all the orders for noise pills, racket lotion, clamor salve and hubbub tonic. That's all people seem to want these days. Years ago, everyone wanted pleasant sounds and business was terrible. But then the cities were built and there was a great need for honking horns, screeching trains, clanging bells and all the rest of those wonderfully unpleasant sounds we use so much today. I've been working overtime ever since and my medicine here is in great demand. All you have to do is take one spoonful every day, and you'll never have to hear another beautiful sound again. Here, try some.

HUMBUG. [*Backing away.*] If it's all the same to you, I'd rather not.

MILO. I don't want to be cured of beautiful sounds.

TOCK. Besides, there's no such sickness as a lack of noise.

DISCHORD. How true. That's what makes it so difficult to cure. [*Takes a large glass bottle from the shelf.*] Very well, if you want to go all through life suffering from a noise **deficiency**, I'll just give this to Dynne for his lunch. [*Uncorks the bottle and pours the liquid into it. There is a rumbling and then a loud*

Vocabulary ▶
deficiency (dē fish′ ən sē) *n.* shortage or lack

explosion accompanied by smoke, out of which DYNNE, *a smog-like creature with yellow eyes and a frowning mouth, appears.*]

DYNNE. [*Smacking his lips.*] Ahhh, that was good, Master. I thought you'd never let me out. It was really cramped in there.

DISCHORD. This is my assistant, the awful Dynne. You must forgive his appearance, for he really doesn't have any.

MILO. What is a Dynne?

DISCHORD. You mean you've never heard of the awful Dynne? When you're playing in your room and making a great amount of noise, what do they tell you to stop?

MILO. That awful din.

DISCHORD. When the neighbors are playing their radio too loud late at night, what do you wish they'd turn down?

TOCK. That awful din.

DISCHORD. And when the street on your block is being repaired and the drills are working all day, what does everyone complain of?

HUMBUG. [*Brightly.*] The dreadful row.

DYNNE. The Dreadful Rauw was my grandfather. He perished in the great silence epidemic of 1712. I certainly can't understand why you don't like noise. Why, I heard an explosion last week that was so lovely, I groaned with appreciation for two days. [*He gives a loud groan at the memory.*]

DISCHORD. He's right, you know! Noise is the most valuable thing in the world.

MILO. King Azaz says words are.

DISCHORD. NONSENSE! Why, when a baby wants food, how does he ask?

DYNNE. [*Happily.*] He screams!

DISCHORD. And when a racing car wants gas?

DYNNE. [*Jumping for joy.*] It chokes!

Stage Directions
How does this stage direction help you imagine what Dynne is like?

Compare and Contrast
How are Dischord's opinions different from most people's regarding sounds?

Comprehension
What caused people to want noise and hubbub rather than pleasant sounds?

DISCHORD. And what happens to the dawn when a new day begins?

DYNNE. [*Delighted.*] It breaks!

DISCHORD. You see how simple it is? [*To* DYNNE.] Isn't it time for us to go?

MILO. Where to? Maybe we're going the same way.

Compare and Contrast
How are these rounds different from the daily rounds of people such as mail carriers?

DYNNE. I doubt it. [*Picking up empty sacks from the table.*] We're going on our collection rounds. Once a day, I travel throughout the kingdom and collect all the wonderfully horrible and beautifully unpleasant sounds I can find and bring them back to the doctor to use in his medicine.

DISCHORD. Where are you going?

MILO. To Digitopolis.

DISCHORD. Oh, there are a number of ways to get to Digitopolis, if you know how to follow directions. Just take a look at the sign at the fork in the road. Though why you'd ever want to go there, I'll never know.

MILO. We want to talk to the Mathemagician.

HUMBUG. About the release of the Princesses Rhyme and Reason.

Stage Directions
How do these stage directions help you understand what Dischord is doing?

DISCHORD. Rhyme and Reason? I remember them. Very nice girls, but a little too quiet for my taste. In fact, I've been meaning to send them something that Dynne brought home by mistake and which I have absolutely no use for. [*He rummages through the wagon.*] Ah, here it is . . . or maybe you'd like it for yourself. [*Hands* MILO *a Package.*]

MILO. What is it?

DISCHORD. The sounds of laughter. They're so unpleasant to hear, it's almost unbearable. All those giggles and snickers and happy shouts of joy, I don't know what Dynne was thinking of when he collected them. Here, take them to the Princesses or keep them for yourselves, I don't care. Well, time to move on. Goodbye now and good luck! [*He has shut the wagon by now and gets in. LOUD NOISES begin to erupt as* DYNNE *pulls the wagon offstage.*]

Milo. [*Calling after them.*] But wait! The fork in the road . . . you didn't tell us where it is . . .

Tock. It's too late. He can't hear a thing.

Humbug. I could use a fork of my own, at the moment. And a knife and a spoon to go with it. All of a sudden, I feel very hungry.

Milo. So do I, but it's no use thinking about it. There won't be anything to eat until we reach Digitopolis. [*They get into the car.*]

Humbug. [*Rubbing his stomach.*] Well, the sooner the better is what I say. [*A SIGN suddenly appears.*]

DIGITOPOLIS	5 Miles
	1,600 Rods
	8,800 Yards
	26,400 Feet
	316,800 Inches
	633,600 Half Inches **AND THEN SOME**

◀ **Critical Viewing**
How are the different measurements on this sign related?

Voice. [*A strange voice from nowhere.*] But which way will get you there sooner? That is the question.

Tock. Did you hear something?

Milo. Look! The fork in the road and a signpost to Digitopolis! [*They read the Sign.*]

Humbug. Let's travel by miles, it's shorter.

Milo. Let's travel by half inches. It's quicker.

Tock. But which road should we take? It must make a difference.

Milo. Do you think so?

Tock. Well, I'm not sure, but . . .

Humbug. He could be right. On the other hand, he could also be wrong. Does it make a difference or not?

Voice. Yes, indeed, indeed it does, certainly, my yes, it does make a difference.

Comprehension
What does Dischord give to Milo, and why?

Stage Directions
Why would the information presented here be important to a group performing the play?

[*The* DODECAHEDRON *appears, a 12-sided figure with a different face on each side, and with all the edges labeled with a small letter and all the angles labeled with a large letter. He wears a beret and peers at the others with a serious face. He doffs his cap and recites:*]

DODECAHEDRON. *My angles are many.*
My sides are not few.
I'm the Dodecahedron.
Who are you?

MILO. What's a Dodecahedron?

DODECAHEDRON. [*Turning around slowly.*] See for yourself. A Dodecahedron is a mathematical shape with 12 faces. [*All his faces appear as he turns, each face with a different expression. He points to them.*] I usually use one at a time. It saves wear and tear. What are you called?

MILO. Milo.

DODECAHEDRON. That's an odd name. [*Changing his smiling face to a frowning one.*] And you have only one face.

MILO. [*Making sure it is still there.*] Is that bad?

DODECAHEDRON. You'll soon wear it out using it for everything. Is everyone with one face called Milo?

MILO. Oh, no. Some are called Billy or Jeffery or Sally or Lisa or lots of other things.

DODECAHEDRON. How confusing. Here everything is called exactly what it is. The triangles are called triangles, the circles are called circles, and even the same numbers have the same name. Can you imagine what would happen if we named all the twos Billy or Jeffery or Sally or Lisa or lots of other things? You'd have to say Robert plus John equals four, and if the fours were named Albert, things would be hopeless.

MILO. I never thought of it that way.

Vocabulary ▶
admonishing (ad män´ ish iŋ) *adj.* disapproving

DODECAHEDRON. [*With an admonishing face.*] Then I suggest you begin at once, for in Digitopolis, everything is quite precise.

MILO. Then perhaps you can help us decide which road we should take.

DODECAHEDRON. [*Happily.*] By all means. There's nothing to it. [*As he talks, the three others try to solve the problem on a Large Blackboard that is wheeled onstage for the occasion.*] Now, if a small car carrying three people at 30 miles an hour for 10 minutes along a road 5 miles long at 11:35 in the morning starts at the same time as 3 people who have been traveling in a little automobile at 20 miles an hour for 15 minutes on another road exactly twice as long as half the distance of the other, while a dog, a bug, and a boy travel an equal distance in the same time or the same distance in an equal time along a third road in mid-October, then which one arrives first and which is the best way to go?

HUMBUG. Seventeen!

MILO. [*Still figuring frantically.*] I'm not sure, but . . .

DODECAHEDRON. You'll have to do better than that.

MILO. I'm not very good at problems.

DODECAHEDRON. What a shame. They're so very useful. Why, did you know that if a beaver 2 feet long with a tail a foot and a half long can build a dam 12 feet high and 6 feet wide in 2 days, all you would need to build Boulder Dam is a beaver 68 feet long with a 51 foot tail?

HUMBUG. [*Grumbling as his pencil snaps.*] Where would you find a beaver that big?

DODECAHEDRON. I don't know, but if you did, you'd certainly know what to do with him.

MILO. That's crazy.

DODECAHEDRON. That may be true, but it's completely accurate, and as long as the answer is right, who cares if the question is wrong?

TOCK. [*Who has been patiently doing the first problem.*] All three roads arrive at the same place at the same time.

DODECAHEDRON. Correct! And I'll take you there myself. [*The blackboard rolls off, and all four get into the car and drive off.*] Now you see how important problems are. If you hadn't done this one properly, you might have gone the wrong way.

...as long as the answer is right, who cares if the question is wrong?

MILO. But if all the roads arrive at the same place at the same time, then aren't they all the right road?

DODECAHEDRON. [*Glaring from his upset face.*] Certainly not! They're all the wrong way! Just because you have a choice, it doesn't mean that any of them has to be right. [*Pointing in another direction.*] That's the way to Digitopolis and we'll be there any moment. [*Suddenly the lighting grows dimmer.*] In fact, we're here. Welcome to the Land of Numbers.

HUMBUG. [*Looking around at the barren landscape.*] It doesn't look very inviting.

MILO. Is this the place where numbers are made?

DODECAHEDRON. They're not made. You have to dig for them. Don't you know anything at all about numbers?

MILO. Well, I never really thought they were very important.

DODECAHEDRON. NOT IMPORTANT! Could you have tea for two without the 2? Or three blind mice without the 3? And how would you sail the seven seas without the 7?

MILO. All I meant was . . .

DODECAHEDRON. [*Continues shouting angrily.*] If you had high hopes, how would you know how high they were? And did you know that narrow escapes come in different widths? Would you travel the whole world wide without ever knowing how wide it was? And how could you do anything at long last without knowing how long the last was? Why, numbers are the most beautiful and valuable things in the world. Just follow me and I'll show you. [*He motions to them and pantomimes walking through rocky terrain with the others in tow. A Doorway similar to the Tollbooth appears and the* DODECAHEDRON *opens it and motions the others to follow him through.*] Come along, come along. I can't wait for you all day. [*They enter the doorway and the lights are dimmed very low, as to simulate the interior of a cave. The SOUNDS of scrapings and tapping, scuffling and digging are heard all around them. He hands them Helmets with flashlights attached.*] Put these on.

▼ Critical Viewing
Which qualities of Dodecahedron are the most interesting to you? Why?

MILO. [*Whispering.*] Where are we going?

DODECAHEDRON. We're here. This is the numbers mine. [*LIGHTS UP A LITTLE, revealing Little Men digging and chopping, shoveling and scraping.*] Right this way and watch your step. [*His voice echoes and reverberates. Iridescent and glittery numbers seem to sparkle from everywhere.*]

MILO. [*Awed.*] Whose mine is it?

VOICE OF MATHEMAGICIAN. By the four million eight hundred and twenty-seven thousand six hundred and fifty-nine hairs on my head, it's mine, of course! [*ENTER the MATHEMAGICIAN, carrying his long staff which looks like a giant pencil.*]

HUMBUG. [*Already intimidated.*] It's a lovely mine, really it is.

MATHEMAGICIAN. [*Proudly.*] The biggest number mine in the kingdom.

MILO. [*Excitedly.*] Are there any precious stones in it?

MATHEMAGICIAN. Precious stones! [*Then softly.*] By the eight million two hundred and forty-seven thousand three hundred and twelve threads in my robe, I'll say there are. Look here. [*Reaches in a cart, pulls out a small object, polishes it vigorously and holds it to the light, where it sparkles.*]

MILO. But that's a five.

MATHEMAGICIAN. Exactly. As valuable a jewel as you'll find anywhere. Look at some of the others. [*Scoops up others and pours them into MILO's arms. They include all numbers from 1 to 9 and an assortment of zeros.*]

DODECAHEDRON. We dig them and polish them right here, and then send them all over the world. Marvelous, aren't they?

TOCK. They are beautiful. [*He holds them up to compare them to the numbers on his clock body.*]

MILO. So that's where they come from. [*Looks at them and carefully hands them back, but drops a few which smash and break in half.*] Oh, I'm sorry!

MATHEMAGICIAN. [*Scooping them up.*] Oh, don't worry about that. We use the broken ones for fractions. How about some lunch? [*Takes out a little whistle and blows it. Two miners rush in carrying an immense cauldron which is bubbling and steaming. The workers put down their tools and gather around to eat.*]

HUMBUG. That looks delicious! [TOCK *and* MILO *also look hungrily at the pot.*]

MATHEMAGICIAN. Perhaps you'd care for something to eat?

MILO. Oh, yes, sir!

TOCK. Thank you.

HUMBUG. [*Already eating.*] Ummm . . . delicious! [*All finish their bowls immediately.*]

MATHEMAGICIAN. Please have another portion. [*They eat and finish.* MATHEMAGICIAN *serves them again.*] Don't stop now. [*They finish.*] Come on, no need to be bashful. [*Serves them again.*]

MILO. [*To* TOCK *and* HUMBUG *as he finishes again.*] Do you want to hear something strange? Each one I eat makes me a little hungrier than before.

MATHEMAGICIAN. Do have some more. [*He serves them again. They eat frantically, until the* MATHEMAGICIAN *blows his whistle again and the pot is removed.*]

HUMBUG. [*Holding his stomach.*] Uggghhh! I think I'm starving.

MILO. Me, too, and I ate so much.

DODECAHEDRON. [*Wiping the gravy from several of his mouths.*] Yes, it was delicious, wasn't it? It's the specialty of the kingdom . . . subtraction stew.

▲ **Critical Viewing**
Which details in the picture suggest that this is Mathemagician?

Tock. [*Weak from hunger.*] I have more of an appetite than when I began.

Mathemagician. Certainly, what did you expect? The more you eat, the hungrier you get, everyone knows that.

Milo. They do? Then how do you get enough?

Mathemagician. Enough? Here in Digitopolis, we have our meals when we're full and eat until we're hungry. That way, when you don't have anything at all, you have more than enough. It's a very economical system. You must have been stuffed to have eaten so much.

Dodecahedron. It's completely logical. The more you want, the less you get, and the less you get, the more you have. Simple arithmetic, that's all. [Tock, Milo *and* Humbug *look at him blankly.*] Now, look, suppose you had something and added nothing to it. What would you have?

Milo. The same.

Dodecahedron. Splendid! And suppose you had something and added less than nothing to it? What would you have then?

Humbug. Starvation! Oh, I'm so hungry.

Dodecahedron. Now, now, it's not as bad as all that. In a few hours, you'll be nice and full again . . . just in time for dinner.

Milo. But I only eat when I'm hungry.

Mathemagician. [*Waving the eraser of his staff.*] What a curious idea. The next thing you'll have us believe is that you only sleep when you're tired.

[*The mine has disappeared as well as the Miners.*]

Humbug. Where did everyone go?

Mathemagician. Oh, they're still in the mine. I often find that the best way to get from one place to another is to erase everything and start again. Please make yourself at home.

Compare and Contrast
How are the meals that characters eat in Digitopolis different from real-life meals?

Comprehension
What is the easiest way for Mathemagician to get from one place to another?

Cultural Connection

Plumb Line

A plumb line is a cord that has a weight, often called a *plumb* or *plumb bob,* at one end. The word *plumb* comes from the Old French word *plomb,* which means "lead." Not surprisingly, the weight on a plumb line is frequently made of lead. The weight keeps the line straight and makes it a useful tool for measuring heights and straight lines.

Connect to the Literature

For what purpose does Mathemagician use a plumb line? Would this work in real life? Why or why not?

[*They find themselves in a unique room, in which all the walls, tables, chairs, desks, cabinets and blackboards are labeled to show their heights, widths, depths and distances to and from each other. To one side is a gigantic notepad on an artist's easel, and from hooks and strings hang a collection of rulers, measures, weights and tapes, and all other measuring devices.*]

MILO. Do you always travel that way? [*He looks around in wonder.*]

MATHEMAGICIAN. No, indeed! [*He pulls a plumb line from a hook and walks.*] Most of the time I take the shortest distance between any two points. And of course, when I have to be in several places at once . . . [*He writes 3 x 1 = 3 on the notepad with his staff.*] I simply multiply. [THREE FIGURES *looking like the* MATHEMAGICIAN *appear on a platform above.*]

MILO. How did you do that?

MATHEMAGICIAN AND THE THREE. There's nothing to it, if you have a magic staff. [THE THREE FIGURES *cancel themselves out and disappear.*]

HUMBUG. That's nothing but a big pencil.

MATHEMAGICIAN. True enough, but once you learn to use it, there's no end to what you can do.

MILO. Can you make things disappear?

MATHEMAGICIAN. Just step a little closer and watch this. [*Shows them that there is nothing up his sleeve or in his hat. He writes:*] 4 + 9 - 2 x 16 + 1 = 3 x 6 - 67 + 8 x 2 - 3 + 26 - 1 - 34 + 3 - 7 + 2 - 5 = [*He looks up expectantly.*]

HUMBUG. Seventeen?

MILO. It all comes to zero.

MATHEMAGICIAN. Precisely. [*Makes a theatrical bow and rips off paper from notepad.*] Now, is there anything else you'd like to see? [*At this point, an appeal to the audience to see if anyone would like a problem solved.*]

MILO. Well . . . can you show me the biggest number there is?

MATHEMAGICIAN. Why, I'd be delighted. [*Opening a closet door.*] We keep it right here. It took four miners to dig it out. [*He shows them a huge "3" twice as high as the* **MATHEMAGICIAN.**]

MILO. No, that's not what I mean. Can you show me the longest number there is?

MATHEMAGICIAN. Sure. [*Opens another door.*] Here it is. It took three carts to carry it here. [*Door reveals an "8" that is as wide as the "3" was high.*]

MILO. No, no, that's not what I meant either. [*Looks helplessly at* TOCK.]

TOCK. I think what you would like to see is the number of the greatest possible magnitude.

MATHEMAGICIAN. Well, why didn't you say so? [*He busily measures them and all other things as he speaks, and marks it down.*] What's the greatest number you can think of? [*Here, an appeal can also be made to the audience or* MILO *may think of his own answers.*]

MILO. Uh . . . nine trillion, nine hundred and ninety-nine billion, nine hundred ninety-nine million, nine-hundred ninety-nine thousand, nine hundred and ninety-nine. [*He puffs.*]

MATHEMAGICIAN. [*Writes that on the pad.*] Very good. Now add one to it. [MILO *or audience does.*] Now add one again. [MILO *or audience does so.*] Now add one again. Now add one again. Now add . . .

MILO. But when can I stop?

MATHEMAGICIAN. Never. Because the number you want is always at least one more than the number you have, and it's so large that if you started saying it yesterday, you wouldn't finish tomorrow.

HUMBUG. Where could you ever find a number so big?

MATHEMAGICIAN. In the same place they have the smallest number there is, and you know what that is?

Compare and Contrast
Based on Mathemagician's actions here, how does he see numbers differently from Milo?

Comprehension
What does Mathemagician teach Milo about numbers?

MILO. The smallest number . . . let's see . . . one one-millionth?

MATHEMAGICIAN. Almost. Now all you have to do is divide that in half and then divide that in half and then divide that in half and then divide that . . .

MILO. Doesn't that ever stop either?

MATHEMAGICIAN. How can it when you can always take half of what you have and divide it in half again? Look. [*Pointing offstage.*] You see that line?

MILO. You mean that long one out there?

MATHEMAGICIAN. That's it. Now, if you just follow that line forever, and when you reach the end, turn left, you will find the Land of Infinity. That's where the tallest, the shortest, the biggest, the smallest and the most and the least of everything are kept.

MILO. But how can you follow anything forever? You know, I get the feeling that everything in Digitopolis is very difficult.

Compare and Contrast
Do real-life situations support Mathemagician's statement about being wrong? Explain.

MATHEMAGICIAN. But on the other hand, I think you'll find that the only thing you can do easily is be wrong, and that's hardly worth the effort.

MILO. But . . . what bothers me is . . . well, why is it that even when things are correct, they don't really seem to be right?

MATHEMAGICIAN. [*Grows sad and quiet.*] How true. It's been that way ever since Rhyme and Reason were banished. [*Sadness turns to fury.*] And all because of that stubborn wretch Azaz! It's all his fault.

MILO. Maybe if you discussed it with him . . .

MATHEMAGICIAN. He's just too unreasonable! Why just last month, I sent him a very friendly letter, which he never had the courtesy to answer. See for yourself. [*Puts the letter on the easel. The letter reads:*]

4738 1919,

667 394107 5841 62589 85371 14

39588 7190434 203 27689 57131 481206.

5864 98053,

62179875073

MILO. But maybe he doesn't understand numbers.

MATHEMAGICIAN. Nonsense! Everybody understands numbers. No matter what language you speak, they always mean the same thing. A seven is a seven everywhere in the world.

MILO. [*To* TOCK *and* HUMBUG.] Everyone is so sensitive about what he knows best.

TOCK. With your permission, sir, we'd like to rescue Rhyme and Reason.

MATHEMAGICIAN. Has Azaz agreed to it?

TOCK. Yes, sir.

MATHEMAGICIAN. THEN I DON'T! Ever since they've been banished, we've never agreed on anything, and we never will.

MILO. Never?

MATHEMAGICIAN. NEVER! And if you can prove otherwise, you have my permission to go.

MILO. Well then, with whatever Azaz agrees, you disagree.

MATHEMAGICIAN. Correct.

MILO. And with whatever Azaz disagrees, you agree.

MATHEMAGICIAN. [*Yawning, cleaning his nails.*] Also correct.

MILO. Then, each of you agrees that he will disagree with whatever each of you agrees with, and if you both disagree with the same thing, aren't you really in agreement?

MATHEMAGICIAN. I'VE BEEN TRICKED! [*Figures it over, but comes up with the same answer.*]

TOCK. And now may we go?

MATHEMAGICIAN. [*Nods weakly.*] It's a long and dangerous journey. Long before you find them, the demons will know you're there. Watch out for them, because if you

> *A seven is a seven everywhere in the world.*

Stage Directions
What does this stage direction suggest about the Mathemagician's opinion of himself?

Comprehension
How does Milo outsmart Mathemagician?

ever come face to face, it will be too late. But there is one other obstacle even more serious than that.

MILO. [*Terrified.*] What is it?

MATHEMAGICIAN. I'm afraid I can't tell you until you return. But maybe I can give you something to help you out. [*Claps hands. ENTER the* DODECAHEDRON, *carrying something on a pillow. The* MATHEMAGICIAN *takes it.*] Here is your own magic staff. Use it well and there is nothing it can't do for you. [*Puts a small, gleaming pencil in* MILO's *breast pocket.*]

HUMBUG. Are you sure you can't tell about that serious obstacle?

MATHEMAGICIAN. Only when you return. And now the Dodecahedron will escort you to the road that leads to the Castle-in-the-Air. Farewell, my friends, and good luck to you. [*They shake hands, say goodbye, and the* DODECAHEDRON *leads them off.*] Good luck to you! [*To himself.*] Because you're sure going to need it. [*He watches them through a telescope and marks down the calculations.*]

DODECAHEDRON. [*He re-enters.*] Well, they're on their way.

MATHEMAGICIAN. So I see. . . [DODECAHEDRON *stands waiting.*] Well, what is it?

DODECAHEDRON. I was just wondering myself, your Numbership. What actually is the serious obstacle you were talking about?

MATHEMAGICIAN. [*Looks at him in surprise.*] You mean you really don't know?

BLACKOUT

Scene ii • The Land of Ignorance

LIGHTS UP on RHYME *and* REASON, *in their castle, looking out two windows.*

RHYME. *I'm worried sick, I must confess*
I wonder if they'll have success
All the others tried in vain,
And were never seen or heard again.

REASON. Now, Rhyme, there's no need to be so pessimistic.

Stage Directions
BLACKOUT means that all the lights focused on the stage are turned off. How does this add suspense here?

Stage Directions
What effect does the stage direction LIGHTS UP have on the action?

Milo, Tock, and Humbug have just as much chance of succeeding as they do of failing.

RHYME. *But the demons are so deadly smart*
They'll stuff your brain and fill your heart
With petty thoughts and selfish dreams
And trap you with their nasty schemes.

REASON. Now, Rhyme, be reasonable, won't you? And calm down, you always talk in couplets when you get nervous. Milo has learned a lot from his journey. I think he's a match for the demons and that he might soon be knocking at our door. Now come on, cheer up, won't you?

RHYME. I'll try.

[*LIGHTS FADE on the* PRINCESSES *and COME UP on the little Car, traveling slowly.*]

MILO. So this is the Land of Ignorance. It's so dark. I can hardly see a thing. Maybe we should wait until morning.

VOICE. They'll be mourning for you soon enough. [*They look up and see a large, soiled, ugly bird with a dangerous beak and a* malicious *expression.*]

MILO. I don't think you understand. We're looking for a place to spend the night.

BIRD. [*Shrieking.*] It's not yours to spend!

MILO. That doesn't make any sense, you see . . .

BIRD. Dollars or cents, it's still not yours to spend.

MILO. But I don't mean . . .

BIRD. Of course you're mean. Anybody who'd spend a night that doesn't belong to him is very mean.

TOCK. Must you interrupt like that?

BIRD. Naturally, it's my job. I take the words right out of your mouth. Haven't we met before? I'm the Everpresent Wordsnatcher.

MILO. Are you a demon?

BIRD. I'm afraid not. I've tried, but the best I can manage to be is a nuisance. [*Suddenly gets nervous as he looks beyond the three.*] And I don't have time to waste with you. [*Starts to leave.*]

◄ **Vocabulary**
malicious (mə lish´ əs)
adj. having or showing bad intentions

Compare and Contrast
How is the bird like other characters Milo meets?

Comprehension
How does Reason reassure Rhyme?

Tock. What is it? What's the matter?

Milo. Hey, don't leave. I wanted to ask you some
questions. . . . Wait!

Bird. Weight? Twenty-seven pounds. Bye-bye. [*Disappears.*]

Milo. Well, he was no help.

Man. Perhaps I can be of some assistance to you? [*There
appears a beautifully dressed man, very polished and
clean.*] Hello, little boy. [*Shakes* Milo's *hand.*] And how's
the faithful dog? [*Pats* Tock.] And who is this handsome
creature? [*Tips his hat to* Humbug.]

Humbug. [*To others.*] What a pleasant surprise to meet
someone so nice in a place like this.

Man. But before I help you out, I wonder if first you could
spare me a little of your time, and help me with a few
small jobs?

Humbug. Why, certainly.

Tock. Gladly.

Milo. Sure, we'd be happy to.

Man. Splendid, for there are just three tasks. First, I
would like to move this pile of sand from here to there.
[*Indicates through pantomime a large pile of sand.*] But
I'm afraid that all I have is this tiny tweezers. [*Hands
it to* Milo, *who begins moving the sand one grain at a
time.*] Second, I would like to empty this well and fill
that other, but I have no bucket, so you'll have to use
this eyedropper. [*Hands it to* Tock, *who begins to work.*]
And finally, I must have a hole in this cliff, and here is
a needle to dig it. [Humbug *eagerly begins. The man leans
against a tree and stares vacantly off into space. The
LIGHTS indicate the passage of time.*]

Milo. You know something? I've been working steadily for
a long time, now, and I don't feel the least bit tired or
hungry. I could go right on the same way forever.

Man. Maybe you will. [*He yawns.*]

Milo. [*Whispers to* Tock.] Well, I wish I knew how long it
was going to take.

Stage Directions
How do these stage
directions move the
action along?

Tock. Why don't you use your magic staff and find out?

Milo. [*Takes out pencil and calculates. To* Man.] Pardon me, sir, but it's going to take 837 years to finish these jobs.

Man. Is that so? What a shame. Well then you'd better get on with them.

Milo. But . . . it hardly seems worthwhile.

Man. WORTHWHILE! Of course they're not worthwhile. I wouldn't ask you to do anything that was worthwhile.

Tock. Then why bother?

Man. Because, my friends, what could be more important than doing unimportant things? If you stop to do enough of them, you'll never get where you are going. [*Laughs villainously.*]

Milo. [*Gasps.*] Oh, no, you must be . . .

Man. Quite correct! I am the Terrible Trivium, demon of petty tasks and worthless jobs, ogre of wasted effort and monster of habit. [*They start to back away from him.*] Don't try to leave, there's so much to do, and you still have 837 years to go on the first job.

Milo. But why do unimportant things?

Man. Think of all the trouble it saves. If you spend all your time doing only the easy and useless jobs, you'll never have time to worry about the important ones which are so difficult. [*Walks toward them whispering.*] Now do come and stay with me. We'll have such fun together. There are things to fill and things to empty, things to take away and things to bring back, things to pick up and things to put down . . . [*They are* transfixed *by his soothing voice. He is about to embrace them when a* Voice *screams.*]

Voice. Run! Run! [*They all wake up and run with the Trivium behind. As the voice continues to call out directions, they follow until they lose the Trivium.*] RUN! RUN! This way! This way! Over here! Over here! Up here! Down there! Quick, hurry up!

Tock. [*Panting.*] I think we lost him.

Compare and Contrast
In what ways are Man and the Everpresent Wordsnatcher different?

Compare and Contrast
How is Terrible Trivium similar to the Lethargarians, who appear in Act I?

◄ **Vocabulary**
transfixed (trans fikst´) *v.* made motionless by horror or fascination

Comprehension
What does the Terrible Trivium ask Milo, Tock, and Humbug to do?

▲ Critical Viewing
How does this image show that Milo, Tock, and Humbug need one another in order to succeed?

Voice. Keep going straight! Keep going straight! Now step up! Now step up!

Milo. Look out! [*They all fall into a Trap.*] But he said "up!"

Voice. Well, I hope you didn't expect to get anywhere by listening to me.

Humbug. We're in a deep pit! We'll never get out of here.

Voice. That is quite an accurate evaluation of the situation.

Milo. [*Shouting angrily.*] Then why did you help us at all?

Voice. Oh, I'd do as much for anybody. Bad advice is my specialty. [*A Little Furry Creature appears.*] I'm the demon of Insincerity. I don't mean what I say; I don't mean what I do; and I don't mean what I am.

Milo. Then why don't you go away and leave us alone!

Insincerity. (VOICE) Now, there's no need to get angry. You're a very clever boy and I have complete confidence in you. You can certainly climb out of that pit . . . come on, try. . .

Milo. I'm not listening to one word you say! You're just telling me what you think I'd like to hear, and not what is important.

Insincerity. Well, if that's the way you feel about it . . .

Milo. That's the way I feel about it. We will manage by ourselves without any unnecessary advice from you.

Insincerity. [*Stamping his foot.*] Well, all right for you! Most people listen to what I say, but if that's the way you feel, then I'll just go home. [*Exits in a huff.*]

HUMBUG. [*Who has been quivering with fright.*] And don't you ever come back! Well, I guess we showed him, didn't we?

MILO. You know something? This place is a lot more dangerous than I ever imagined.

TOCK. [*Who's been surveying the situation.*] I think I figured a way to get out. Here, hop on my back. [MILO *does so.*] Now, you, Humbug, on top of Milo. [*He does so.*] Now hook your umbrella onto that tree and hold on. [*They climb over* HUMBUG, *then pull him up.*]

HUMBUG. [*As they climb.*] Watch it! Watch it, now. Ow, be careful of my back! My back! Easy, easy . . . oh, this is so difficult. Aren't you finished yet?

TOCK. [*As he pulls up* HUMBUG.] There. Now, I'll lead for a while. Follow me, and we'll stay out of trouble. [*They walk and climb higher and higher.*]

HUMBUG. Can't we slow down a little?

TOCK. Something tells me we better reach the Castle-in-the-Air as soon as possible, and not stop to rest for a single moment. [*They speed up.*]

MILO. What is it, Tock? Did you see something?

TOCK. Just keep walking and don't look back.

MILO. You *did* see something!

HUMBUG. What is it? Another demon?

TOCK. Not just one, I'm afraid. If you want to see what I'm talking about, then turn around. [*They turn around. The stage darkens and hundreds of Yellow Gleaming Eyes can be seen.*]

HUMBUG. Good grief! Do you see how many there are? Hundreds! The Overbearing Know-it-all, the Gross Exaggeration, the Horrible Hopping Hindsight, . . . and look over there! The Triple Demons of Compromise! Let's get out of here! [*Starts to scurry.*] Hurry up, you two! Must you be so slow about everything?

MILO. Look! There it is, up ahead! The Castle-in-the-Air! [*They all run.*]

HUMBUG. They're gaining!

Compare and Contrast
How is the way these new creatures make their entrance different from the way other characters appear onstage?

Comprehension
Why are Milo and the others running?

Milo. But there it is!

Humbug. I see it! I see it!

[*They reach the first step and are stopped by a little man in a frock coat, sleeping on a worn ledger. He has a long quill pen and a bottle of ink at his side. He is covered with ink stains over his clothes and wears spectacles.*]

Tock. Shh! Be very careful. [*They try to step over him, but he wakes up.*]

Senses Taker. [*From sleeping position.*] Names? [*He sits up.*]

Humbug. Well, I . . .

Senses Taker. *NAMES?* [*He opens book and begins to write, splattering himself with ink.*]

Humbug. Uh . . . Humbug, Tock and this is Milo.

Senses Taker. Splendid, splendid. I haven't had an "M" in ages.

Milo. What do you want our names for? We're sort of in a hurry.

Senses Taker. Oh, this won't take long. I'm the official Senses Taker and I must have some information before I can take your sense. Now if you'll just tell me: [*Handing them a form to fill. Speaking slowly and deliberately.*] When you were born, where you were born, why you were born, how old you are now, how old you were then, how old you'll be in a little while . . .

Milo. I wish he'd hurry up. At this rate, the demons will be here before we know it!

Senses Taker. . . . Your mother's name, your father's name, where you live, how long you've lived there, the schools you've attended, the schools you haven't attended . . .

Humbug. I'm getting writer's cramp.

Tock. I smell something very evil and it's getting stronger every second. [*To* Senses Taker.] May we go now?

Senses Taker. Just as soon as you tell me your height, your weight, the number of books you've read this year . . .

Milo. We have to go!

Senses Taker. All right, all right, I'll give you the short form. [*Pulls out a small piece of paper.*] Destination?

Milo. But we have to . . .

Senses Taker. *DESTINATION?*

Milo, Tock AND **Humbug.** The Castle-in-the-Air! [*They throw down their papers and run past him up the first few stairs.*]

Senses Taker. Stop! I'm sure you'd rather see what I have to show you. [*Snaps his fingers; they freeze.*] A circus of your very own. [*CIRCUS MUSIC is heard.* Milo *seems to go into a trance.*] And wouldn't you enjoy this most wonderful smell? [Tock *sniffs and goes into a trance.*] And here's something I know you'll enjoy hearing . . . [*To* Humbug. *The sound of CHEERS and APPLAUSE for* Humbug *is heard, and he goes into a trance.*] There we are. And now, I'll just sit back and let the demons catch up with you.

[Milo *accidentally drops his package of gifts. The Package of Laughter from* Dr. Dischord *opens and the Sounds of Laughter are heard. After a moment,* Milo, Tock *and* Humbug *join in laughing and the spells are broken.*]

Milo. There was no circus.

Tock. There were no smells.

Humbug. The applause is gone.

Senses Taker. I warned you I was the Senses Taker. I'll steal your sense of Purpose, your sense of Duty, destroy your sense of Proportion—and but for one thing, you'd be helpless yet.

Milo. What's that?

Stage Directions
Without these stage directions, would you be able to picture the action here? Explain.

Comprehension
What happens to Senses Taker when Milo drops the Package of Laughter?

SENSES TAKER. As long as you have the sound of laughter, I cannot take your sense of Humor. Agh! That horrible sense of humor.

HUMBUG. HERE THEY COME! LET'S GET OUT OF HERE!

[*The demons appear in nasty slithering hordes, running through the audience and up onto the stage, trying to attack* TOCK, MILO *and* HUMBUG. *The three heroes run past the* SENSES TAKER *up the stairs toward the Castle-in-the-Air with the demons snarling behind them.*]

MILO. Don't look back! Just keep going! [*They reach the castle. The two princesses appear in the windows.*]

PRINCESSES. Hurry! Hurry! We've been expecting you.

MILO. You must be the Princesses. We've come to rescue you.

HUMBUG. And the demons are close behind!

TOCK. We should leave right away.

PRINCESSES. We're ready anytime you are.

MILO. Good, now if you'll just come out. But wait a minute—there's no door! How can we rescue you from the Castle-in-the-Air if there's no way to get in or out?

HUMBUG. Hurry, Milo! They're gaining on us.

REASON. Take your time, Milo, and think about it.

MILO. Ummm, all right . . . just give me a second or two. [*He thinks hard.*]

HUMBUG. I think I feel sick.

MILO. I've got it! Where's that package of presents? [*Opens the package of letters.*] Ah, here it is. [*Takes out the letters and sticks them on the door, spelling:*] E-N-T-R-A-N-C-E. Entrance. Now, let's see. [*Rummages through and spells in smaller letters:*] P-u-s-h. Push. [*He pushes and a*

Compare and Contrast
Based on Milo's actions here, how has he changed since leaving his bedroom?

door opens. The PRINCESSES *come out of the castle. Slowly, the demons ascend the stairway.*]

HUMBUG. Oh, it's too late. They're coming up and there's no other way down!

MILO. Unless . . . [*Looks at* TOCK.] Well . . . Time flies, doesn't it?

TOCK. Quite often. Hold on, everyone, and I'll take you down.

HUMBUG. Can you carry us all?

TOCK. We'll soon find out. Ready or not, here we go! [*His alarm begins to ring. They jump off the platform and disappear. The demons, howling with rage, reach the top and find no one there. They see the* PRINCESSES *and the heroes running across the stage and bound down the stairs after them and into the audience. There is a mad chase scene until they reach the stage again.*]

HUMBUG. I'm exhausted! I can't run another step.

MILO. We can't stop now . . .

TOCK. Milo! Look out there! [*The armies of* AZAZ *and* MATHEMAGICIAN *appear at the back of the theater, with the Kings at their heads.*]

AZAZ. [*As they march toward the stage.*] Don't worry, Milo, we'll take over now.

MATHEMAGICIAN. Those demons may not know it, but their days are numbered!

SPELLING BEE. Charge! C-H-A-R-G-E! Charge! [*They rush at the demons and battle until the demons run off howling. Everyone cheers. The* FIVE MINISTERS OF AZAZ *appear and shake* MILO's *hand.*]

MINISTER 1. Well done.

MINISTER 2. Fine job.

MINISTER 3. Good work!

MINISTER 4. Congratulations!

MINISTER 5. CHEERS! [*Everyone cheers again. A fanfare interrupts. A* PAGE *steps forward and reads from a large scroll:*]

Stage Directions
How do these stage directions help you know what the characters are feeling?

Comprehension
What does Milo do to get into the Castle-in-the-Air?

PAGE. *Henceforth, and forthwith,*
Let it be known by one and all,
That Rhyme and Reason
Reign once more in Wisdom.

[*The* PRINCESSES *bow gratefully and kiss their brothers, the Kings.*]

And furthermore,
The boy named Milo,
The dog known as Tock,
And the insect hereinafter referred to as the Humbug
Are hereby declared to be Heroes of the Realm.

[*All bow and salute the heroes.*]

MILO. But we never could have done it without a lot of help.

REASON. That may be true, but you had the courage to try, and what you can do is often a matter of what you *will* do.

AZAZ. That's why there was one very important thing about your quest we couldn't discuss until you returned.

MILO. I remember. What was it?

AZAZ. Very simple. It was impossible!

MATHEMAGICIAN. *Completely* impossible!

HUMBUG. Do you mean . . . ? [*Feeling faint.*] Oh . . . I think I need to sit down.

AZAZ. Yes, indeed, but if we'd told you then, you might not have gone.

Compare and Contrast
Do you think there are real-life situations in which Mathemagician's statement might hold true? Explain.

MATHEMAGICIAN. And, as you discovered, many things are possible just as long as you don't know they're impossible.

MILO. I think I understand.

RHYME. I'm afraid it's time to go now.

REASON. And you must say goodbye.

MILO. To everyone? [*Looks around at the crowd. To* TOCK *and* HUMBUG.] Can't you two come with me?

HUMBUG. I'm afraid not, old man. I'd like to, but I've arranged for a lecture tour which will keep me occupied for years.

TOCK. And they do need a watchdog here.

MILO. Well, O.K., then. [MILO *hugs the* HUMBUG.]

HUMBUG. [*Sadly.*] Oh, bah.

MILO. [*He hugs* TOCK, *and then faces everyone.*] Well, goodbye. We all spent so much time together, I know I'm going to miss you. [*To the* PRINCESSES.] I guess we would have reached you a lot sooner if I hadn't made so many mistakes.

REASON. You must never feel badly about making mistakes, Milo, as long as you take the trouble to learn from them. Very often you learn more by being wrong for the right reasons than you do by being right for the wrong ones.

MILO. But there's so much to learn.

RHYME. That's true, but it's not just learning that's important. It's learning what to do with what you learn and learning why you learn things that matters.

MILO. I think I know what you mean, Princess. At least, I hope I do. [*The car is rolled forward and* MILO *climbs in.*] Goodbye! Goodbye! I'll be back someday! I will! Anyway, I'll try. [*As* MILO *drives the set of the Land of Ignorance begins to move offstage.*]

AZAZ. Goodbye! Always remember. Words! Words! Words!

MATHEMAGICIAN. And numbers!

AZAZ. Now, don't tell me you think numbers are as important as words?

MATHEMAGICIAN. Is that so? Why I'll have you know . . . [*The set disappears, and* MILO'S *Room is seen onstage.*]

MILO. [*As he drives on.*] Oh, oh, I hope they don't start all over again. Because I don't think I'll have much time in the near future to help them out. [*The sound of loud ticking is heard.* MILO *finds himself in his room. He gets out of the car and looks around.*]

THE CLOCK. Did someone mention time?

Compare and Contrast
With which piece of advice—Reason's or Rhyme's—do you agree more? Explain.

Spiral Review
CHARACTER How do the words "I think I know what you mean" indicate that Milo has grown and learned from his experiences?

MILO. Boy, I must have been gone for an awful long time. I wonder what time it is. [*Looks at clock.*] Five o'clock. I wonder what day it is. [*Looks at calendar.*] It's still today! I've only been gone for an hour! [*He continues to look at his calendar, and then begins to look at his books and toys and maps and chemistry set with great interest.*]

CLOCK. An hour. Sixty minutes. How long it really lasts depends on what you do with it. For some people, an hour seems to last forever. For others, just a moment, and so full of things to do.

MILO. [*Looks at clock.*] Six o'clock already?

CLOCK. In an instant. In a trice. Before you have time to blink. [*The stage goes black in less than no time at all.*]

Language Study

Vocabulary The words listed below appear in *The Phantom Tollbooth*, Act II. For each numbered prompt below, write a sentence that includes a vocabulary word.

dissonance   deficiency   admonishing   iridescent   malicious

1. a necktie that looks red or blue from different angles
2. the sounds that two yowling cats make
3. the act of spreading unkind gossip
4. a look that a babysitter might give a rude child
5. a person's lack of enough vitamin C

WORD STUDY

The **prefix *trans-*** means "across" or "through." In *The Phantom Tollbooth*, Act II, Milo is **transfixed** by a soothing voice. He looks as if he has been fixed into place by something that has pierced through him.

Word Study

Part A Explain how the **prefix *trans-*** contributes to the meanings of *transform* and *transatlantic*. Consult a dictionary if necessary.

Part B Use context and what you know about the prefix *trans-* to explain your answers to these questions.

1. Is a *transcontinental* trip a short one?
2. Can a person *transfer* money from one bank to another?

Close Reading Activities

Literary Analysis

Key Ideas and Details

Compare and Contrast Create two Venn diagrams like the one shown on the right. Then, use details from Act II to compare and contrast these characters:

1. Rhyme and Reason

2. Humbug and Tock

3. **(a)** What does the Terrible Trivium want Milo, Tock, and Humbug to do? **(b) Deduce:** What will be the result if they follow his directions? **(c) Interpret:** What important lesson does Milo learn through his experience with the Terrible Trivium?

4. **(a)** How is the Senses Taker's spell broken? **(b) Draw Conclusions:** What does Milo learn about humor from his encounter with the Senses Taker?

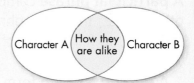

Craft and Structure

5. **Stage Directions (a)** Describe one place in the play where stage directions are necessary for helping you understand what is happening. **(b)** Find one place in the play that has no stage directions. Write your own stage directions for that section of the play. Explain how your stage directions clarify the action.

Integration of Knowledge and Ideas

6. **(a) Apply:** Do you agree that the speed of time depends on what you are doing? **(b) Support:** Support your answer with examples from your own experience.

7. **Evaluate:** If you were Milo, would you want to return to the Lands Beyond? Why or why not? Support your position with details from the play.

8. **How do we decide who we are?** With a small group, discuss the following question: In your opinion, which of Milo's experiences will lead him to the most important new interest or hobby? Explain your answer.

ACADEMIC VOCABULARY

As you write and speak about *The Phantom Tollbooth*, Act II, use the words related to identity that you explored on page 441 of this text.

Conventions: **Participles and Gerunds**

A **participle** is a verb form that acts as an adjective. A **present participle** ends in *-ing*: *relaxing* music. A **past participle** of a regular verb ends in *-ed* or *-d*: *a relaxed* position.

A **participial phrase** combines a present or past participle with other words; the entire phrase acts as an adjective: *Relaxing on the patio,* Jo fell asleep. (phrase modifies *Jo*)

A **gerund** is a verb form that ends in *-ing* and is used as a noun: *I like relaxing.*

A **gerund phrase** combines a gerund with other words; the entire phrase acts as a noun: *Relaxing in your spare time* is important. (phrase is subject of sentence)

Practice A
Rewrite each sentence, circling all the participles and participial phrases, and underlining all the gerunds and gerund phrases.

1. Milo finished eating the numbers.
2. In the Doldrums, thinking was a prohibited activity.
3. Tired from traveling, they rested.
4. Milo, returning to his room, had an amazed feeling.

Reading Application Write a paragraph about *The Phantom Tollbooth* using at least one present participle, one past participle, one gerund, and one gerund phrase. Circle the participles and underline the gerund and gerund phrase.

Practice B
Complete each sentence with a gerund, a gerund phrase, a participle, or a participial phrase. Identify the part of speech for each one.

1. The Senses Taker was good at _____.
2. King Azaz delays _____ that the mission is impossible.
3. _____, Milo almost quit.
4. _____ Tock, Milo said goodbye to his friends.

Writing Application Write two sentences about the play for each of these words: *learning, counting, seeing*. In the first sentence, use the word as a participle; in the second, as a gerund.

Writing to Sources

Argument Imagine that you are a drama critic, and write a **review** of *The Phantom Tollbooth*. Follow these steps:

- Review Acts I and II. Take notes on the strengths and weaknesses of the plot and characters.
- Begin your review by stating your overall evaluation of the play. Then, logically organize the relevant examples from your notes to support your position and claims.
- Conclude by telling readers whether or not you recommend that they see this play.

Grammar Application Reread your review to be sure that you have used participles, participial phrases, gerunds, and gerund phrases correctly.

Speaking and Listening

Comprehension and Collaboration Now that you have read *The Phantom Tollbooth,* access the audio version of the play on your eText. Listen to the recording as a class. Then, hold a **group discussion** by forming small groups and talking about how the experience of reading the play was similar to and different from the experience of listening to it.

Use the following list of questions to guide your discussion. Choose a speaker to present your group's findings to the class.

- Did hearing the voices of different characters make the play easier to understand? Why or why not?
- What was the effect of hearing speakers emphasize certain words or phrases? Did the same words or phrases seem to require emphasis when you were reading the play? Why or why not?
- Did listening to the play help you imagine the action, or were you better able to imagine events and characters by reading about them? Explain your response.

Listen carefully to your classmates' arguments. Which of their claims were supported with strong evidence and reasons? Which claims were not?

How do we decide who we are?

Explore the Big Question as you read a scene from *You're a Good Man, Charlie Brown* and a drama review of a performance of that play.

READING TO COMPARE AUTHOR'S PURPOSE ACROSS GENRES

Playwright Clark Gesner and theater critic Matthew MacDermid write in two different genres, or forms of writing. Like all authors, however, each one writes with a purpose. When you finish reading, compare and contrast the ways that each author's writing supports his purpose.

from **You're a Good Man, Charlie Brown**

Clark Gesner (1938–2002)
Clark Gesner wrote *You're a Good Man, Charlie Brown* because he loved Charles Schulz's *Peanuts* comic strip. The production opened off-Broadway in 1967 and was immediately successful. Since then, it has become one of the most frequently produced musical comedies in the United States.

"Happiness is a Charming Charlie Brown at Orlando Rep"

Matthew MacDermid
Matthew MacDermid is a stage manager and theater critic. He has reviewed productions appearing in central Florida for *Talkin' Broadway*, an online theater resource. *Talkin' Broadway* provides current news about theater openings, revivals, and trends. It also provides a forum for interactive discussions on theatrical topics.

Comparing Author's Purpose Across Genres

An **author's purpose** is the author's main reason for writing a work. The purpose may be to inform, to entertain, to persuade, or to express emotions. Sometimes, an author may have more than one purpose for writing.

- When writing to **inform**, an author gives factual information on a subject to educate his or her audience.

- When writing to **persuade**, an author gives reasons, facts, and evidence to sway his or her readers to share the author's opinion.

- When writing to **entertain**, an author writes purely for the enjoyment of his or her audience.

- When writing to **express emotions**, an author uses words to convey the joy, sorrow, anger, or hope he or she feels.

An author chooses the genre, or specific form of writing, that will best enable him or her to achieve a specific purpose. For example, to fulfill the purpose of informing, an author might write an expository essay. To fulfill the purpose of entertaining, an author might write a short story, play, or humorous essay. Genre and purpose are usually closely related in functional texts, which convey information that is meant to be used in a specific way.

The scene by Clark Gesner is from a musical comedy, and the article by Matthew MacDermid is a review of a production of that show. The two selections are related, but the authors write in different genres and have different purposes for writing. As you read, use a chart like this one to note details from each selection that help you identify each author's unique purpose.

Selection	Details	Author's Purpose
from *You're a Good Man, Charlie Brown*		
"Happiness is a Charming Charlie Brown at Orlando Rep"		

from You're a Good Man, Charlie Brown

Clark Gesner

Based on the comic strip *Peanuts* by Charles M. Schulz

▲ **Critical Viewing**
What do you already know about Charlie Brown and *Peanuts*?

SCHROEDER. I'm sorry to have to say it right to your face, Lucy, but it's true. You're a very crabby person. I know your crabbiness has probably become so natural to you now that you're not even aware when you're being crabby, but it's true just the same. You're a very crabby person and you're crabby to just about everyone you meet. (LUCY *remains silent—just barely*) Now I hope you don't mind my saying this, Lucy, and I hope you'll take it in the spirit that it's meant. I think we should all be open to any opportunity to learn more about ourselves. I think Socrates was very right when he said that one of the first rules for anyone in life is "Know thyself." (LUCY *has begun whistling quietly to herself*) Well, I guess I've said about enough. I hope I haven't offended you or anything. (*He makes an awkward exit*)

LUCY. (*Sits in silence, then shouts offstage* at SCHROEDER) Well, what's Socrates got to do with it anyway, huh? Who was *he* anyway? Did he ever get to be king, huh! Answer me that, did he ever get to be king! (*Suddenly to herself, a real question*) *Did* he ever get to be king? (*She shouts offstage, now a question*) Who was Socrates, anyway? (*She gives up the rampage and plunks herself down*) "Know thyself," hmph. (*She thinks a moment, then makes a silent resolution to herself, exits and quickly returns with a clipboard and pencil.* CHARLIE BROWN *and* SNOOPY *have entered, still with baseball equipment*)

CHARLIE BROWN. Hey, Snoopy, you want to help me get my arm back in shape? Watch out for this one, it's a new fastball.

LUCY. Excuse me a moment, Charlie Brown, but I was wondering if you'd mind answering a few questions.

CHARLIE BROWN. Not at all, Lucy. What kind of questions are they?

LUCY. Well, I'm conducting a survey to enable me to know myself better, and first of all I'd like to ask: on a scale of zero to one hundred, using a standard of fifty as average, seventy-five as above average and ninety as exceptional, where would you rate me with regards to crabbiness?

CHARLIE BROWN. (*Stands in silence for a moment, hesitating*) Well, Lucy, I . . .

LUCY. Your ballots need not be signed and all answers will be held in strictest confidence.

CHARLIE BROWN. Well still, Lucy, that's a very hard question to answer.

Author's Purpose
What does your reaction to Lucy's behavior here tell you about the author's purpose?

You're a very crabby person and you're crabby to just about everyone you meet.

Lucy. You may have a few moments to think it over if you want, or we can come back to that question later.

Charlie Brown. I think I'd like to come back to it, if you don't mind.

Lucy. Certainly. This next question deals with certain character traits you may have observed. Regarding personality, would you say that mine is *A* forceful, *B* pleasing, or *C* objectionable? Would that be *A*, *B*, or *C*? What would your answer be to that, Charlie Brown, forceful, pleasing or objectionable, which one would you say, hmm? Charlie Brown, hmm?

Vocabulary ▶
objectionable (əb jek´ shən ə bəl) *adj.* disagreeable

Charlie Brown. Well, I guess I'd have to say forceful, Lucy, but . . .

Lucy. "Forceful." Well, we'll make a check mark at the letter *A* then. Now, would you rate my ability to get along with other people as poor, fair, good or excellent?

Charlie Brown. I think that depends a lot on what you mean by "get along with other people."

Lucy. You know, make friends, sparkle in a crowd, that sort of thing.

Charlie Brown. Do you have a place for abstention?

Lucy. Certainly, I'll just put a check mark at "None of the above." The next question deals with physical appearance. In referring to my beauty, would you say that I was "stunning," "mysterious," or "intoxicating"?

Charlie Brown. (*Squirming*) Well, gee, I don't know, Lucy. You look just fine to me.

Lucy. (*Making a check on the page*) "Stunning." All right, Charlie Brown, I think we should get back to that first question. On a scale of zero to one hundred, using a standard of fifty as average, seventy-five as . . .

Charlie Brown. (*Loud interruption*) I . . . (*quieter*) . . . remember the question, Lucy.

Lucy. Well?

Vocabulary ▶
tentatively (ten´ tə tiv lē) *adv.* in a hesitant way

Charlie Brown. (*Tentatively*) Fifty-one?

LUCY. (*Noting it down*) Fifty-one is your crabbiness rating for me. Very well then, that about does it. Thank you very much for helping with this survey, Charlie Brown. Your cooperation has been greatly appreciated. (*She shakes hands with* CHARLIE BROWN)

CHARLIE BROWN. (*Flustered*) It was a pleasure, Lucy, any time. Come on, Snoopy.

LUCY. Oh, just a minute, there is one more question. Would you answer "Yes" or "No" to the question: "Is Lucy Van Pelt the sort of person that you would like to have as president of your club or civic organization?"

CHARLIE BROWN. Oh, yes, by all means, Lucy.

LUCY. (*Making note*) Yes. Well, thank you very much. That about does it, I think. (CHARLIE BROWN exits, *but* SNOOPY *pauses, turns, and strikes a dramatic "thumbs down" pose to* LUCY) WELL, WHO ASKED YOU! (SNOOPY *makes a hasty exit.* LUCY *stands center stage, figuring to herself on the clipboard and mumbling*) Now let's see. That's a fifty-one, "None of the above," and . . . (*She looks up*) Schroeder was right. I can already feel myself being filled with the glow of self-awareness. (PATTY *enters. She is heading for the other side of the stage, when* LUCY *stops her*) Oh, Patty, I'm conducting a survey and I wonder if . . .

PATTY. A hundred and ten, *C,* "Poor," "None of the above," "No," and what are you going to do about the dent you made in my bicycle! (PATTY *storms off.* LUCY *watches her go, then looks at the audience*)

LUCY. It's amazing how fast word of these surveys gets around. (LINUS *wanders in and plunks himself down in front of the TV.* LUCY *crosses to him, still figuring*)

LUCY. Oh, Linus, I'm glad you're here. I'm conducting a survey and there are a few questions I'd like to ask you.

LINUS. Sure, go ahead.

LUCY. The first question is: on a scale of zero to one hundred, with a standard of fifty as average, seventy-five as above average and ninety as exceptional, where would you rate me with regards to crabbiness?

◄ **Vocabulary**
civic (siv´ ik) *adj.* representing a city or group of citizens

In referring to my beauty, would you say that I was "stunning," "mysterious," or "intoxicating"?

Spiral Review
Dialogue What does Patty's response show about her feelings for Lucy?

Comprehension
What is the subject of Lucy's survey?

Linus. (*Slowly turns his head to look at her, then turns back to the TV*) You're my big sister.

Lucy. That's not the question.

Linus. No, but that's the answer.

Lucy. Come on, Linus, answer the question.

Linus. (*Getting up and facing* Lucy) Look, Lucy, I know very well that if I give any sort of honest answer to that question you're going to slug me.

Lucy. Linus. A survey that is not based on honest answers is like a house that is built on a foundation of sand. Would I be spending my time to conduct this survey if I didn't expect complete candor in all the responses? I promise not to slug you. Now what number would you give me as your crabbiness rating?

Linus. (*After a few moments of interior struggle*) Ninety-five. (Lucy *sends a straight jab to his jaw which lays him out flat*)

Author's Purpose
What further details does the author provide here to help you understand his purpose?

Lucy. No decent person could be expected to keep her word with a rating over ninety. (*She stalks off, busily figuring away on her clipboard*) Now, I add these two columns and that gives me my answer. (*She figures energetically, then finally sits up with satisfaction*) There, it's all done. Now, let's see what we've got. (*She begins to scan the page. A look of trouble skims over her face. She rechecks the figures. Her eternal look of self-confidence wavers, then crumbles*) It's true. I'm a crabby person. I'm a very crabby person and everybody knows it. I've been spreading crabbiness wherever I go. I'm a supercrab. It's a wonder anyone will still talk to me. It's a wonder I have any friends at all—(*She looks at the figures on the paper*) or even associates. I've done nothing but make life miserable for everyone. I've done nothing but breed unhappiness and resentment. Where did I go wrong? How could I be so selfish? How could . . . (Linus *has been listening. He comes and sits near her*)

Linus. What's wrong, Lucy?

Lucy. Don't talk to me, Linus. I don't deserve to be spoken to. I don't deserve to breathe the air I breathe. I'm no good, Linus. I'm no good.

Linus. That's not true, Lucy.

Lucy. Yes it is. I'm no good, and there's no reason at all why I should go on living on the face of this earth.

Linus. Yes there is.

Lucy. Name one. Just tell me one single reason why I should still deserve to go on living on this planet.

Linus. Well, for one thing, you have a little brother who loves you. (Lucy *looks at him. She is silent. Then she breaks into a great, sobbing "Wah!"*) Every now and then I say the right thing.

(Lucy *continues sobbing as she and* Linus *exit. A brief musical interlude, a change of light, and* Schroeder *and* Sally *come onstage*)

> No decent person could be expected to keep her word with a rating over ninety.

Critical Thinking

1. **Key Ideas and Details (a)** What does Schroeder say that causes Lucy to develop the survey? **(b) Compare and Contrast:** How are Charlie Brown's answers different from Patty's responses? **(c) Interpret:** What do the different answers suggest about their contrasting feelings and personalities?

2. **Key Ideas and Details (a)** How does Snoopy react to Lucy? **(b) Infer:** What do Snoopy's gestures tell you about his feelings for Lucy?

3. **Key Ideas and Details (a)** Why is Linus afraid to tell Lucy the truth? **(b) Cause and Effect:** What happens when he tells the truth? **(c) Paraphrase:** Explain what Lucy means by the statement "No decent person could be expected to keep her word with a rating over ninety."

4. **Integration of Knowledge and Ideas (a)** What conclusion does Lucy draw about herself after the survey? **(b)** What does Linus say to try to change her mind? **(c)** What lesson might Lucy and the audience learn about "who we are"? Explain. *[Connect to the Big Question: How do we decide who we are?]*

Happiness is a Charming Charlie Brown at Orlando Rep

Matthew MacDermid

David Hsieh, courtesy of www.reacttheatre.org

A t the conclusion of *You're A Good Man, Charlie Brown*—the classic musical based on Charles M. Schulz's "Peanuts" comic strip—the well-known characters of Charlie Brown, Sally Brown, Lucy, Linus, Schroeder and Snoopy sing of the simple joys in life that bring them happiness. The melody by Clark M. Gesner, along with the charming lyrics (such as "playing the drum in your own school band" and "being alone every now and then") make for a rather touching moment, allowing children and adults of all ages to ponder where they find happiness. At the Orlando Repertory Theatre, which is opening its fourth season with the revised version of this long-running Off-Broadway hit, happiness is alive and evident in a wonderful production **evoking** the original script's charm and the contemporary flair of new orchestrations by Michael Gibson, as well as additional dialogue and music by Michael Mayer and Andrew Lippa, respectively.

Vocabulary ▶
evoking (ē vōk´ iŋ)
v. calling forth

You're A Good Man, Charlie Brown is really a series of comic strip vignettes taken directly from Schulz's funny pages. Delightful musical numbers are added to comment on the situations, allowing charismatic performers to bring cartoon characters to three-dimensional life. The Rep's cast is an outstanding blend of fresh, wide-eyed professional talent headed by the outstanding Michael Swickard as Charlie Brown. His round eyes and round head perfectly embody the lovable loser constantly battling his affection for the little red headed girl across the school yard and his inability to properly fly a kite. Karla Sue Schultz, as Charlie's sister Sally, establishes youth, naivete and a terrific sense of humor backed by a great voice in sketches about jumping rope and coat-hanger sculptures. She is especially effective in one of Lippa's new numbers, "My New Philosophy." Ronald E. Hornsby's Schroeder has less showy material, even with the new number "Beethoven's Birthday," but does his best with what he is given.

However, three performers take their characters to a higher level, stealing the spotlight with every opportunity and even chewing a bit of the scenery along the way. Shannon Bilo is a wonder as Lucy, with a clarion belt and expert comic timing that seems to go for days. Mark Catlett is outstanding as her kid brother Linus, sucking his thumb and doing the tango with his blanket, all the while exuding the mind-numbing intelligence of such a youngster. And Chris Layton stops the show with his rousing Snoopy, channeling the showbiz legends of yesteryear (including Carol Channing) in his celebratory "Suppertime."

Technically, this production remains on par with its performers, a perfect blend of design excellence from Alvin DeLeon's scenery, Simone Smith's costumes, Sam Hazell's props, David M. Upton's lighting and James E. Cleveland's sound. Justin S. Fischer's musical direction is also terrific, with his five-piece band perfectly executing Gibson's fresh orchestrations.

Myles Thoroughgood's musical staging is character driven and lovely, providing each performer with a

◄ **Vocabulary**
embody (em bäd′ ē) *v.* give bodily form to; represent

Author's Purpose
What do you think the author's purpose is for writing this article?

Comprehension
How does the critic feel about the overall production?

Vocabulary ▶
abundantly (ə bun´
dənt lē) *adv.* in an
exceptional way

signature dance move that surfaces throughout. Jeffrey Revels' direction isn't quite up to the standard of everything else. While his work is mostly excellent, it is somewhat inconsistent, with several scene buttons falling flat and a couple that actually seem to bring the show to a halt. But what is good is great, and his decisions in casting have **abundantly** affected the success of his production.

The Orlando Repertory Theatre has produced one of their best productions to date with this *Charlie Brown*. It runs in the 328-seat Edyth Busch Theatre, in the Rep complex at 1001 E. Princeton Street in Orlando, through October 1st.

Cast:
Charlie Brown—Michael Swickard
Lucy—Shannon Bilo
Snoopy—Chris Layton
Linus—Mark Catlett
Sally—Karla Sue Schultz
Schroeder—Ronald E. Hornsby

Critical Thinking

1. **Key Ideas and Details (a)** How does the play relate to the comic strip? **(b) Interpret:** According to the review, what make the play's subject suitable for theater?

2. **Key Ideas and Details (a)** How are the author's opinions of each actor's performance similar? **(b) Contrast:** How are his opinions different? **(c) Analyze:** Which actor seems to be his favorite? Explain.

3. **Key Ideas and Details (a)** Which member of the production does the author criticize? **(b) Summarize:** What weaknesses does the author cite as part of his criticism?

4. **Integration of Knowledge and Ideas** If you were an actor in this production, how much value would you give to this review? Why? *[Connect to the Big Question: How do we decide who we are?]*

Writing to Sources

Comparing Author's Purpose

1. **(a)** What purpose did Clark Gesner have for writing his play *You're a Good Man, Charlie Brown?* **(b)** Explain what details helped you determine the author's purpose.

2. **(a)** What purpose did Matthew MacDermid have for writing his review? **(b)** Explain how details in the review helped you determine the author's purpose.

3. Complete a Venn diagram like the one below to show how the drama scene and the review are alike and different.

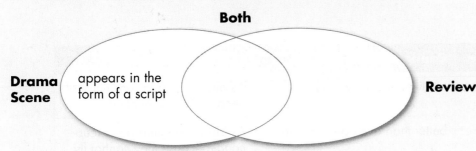

Both

Drama Scene

appears in the form of a script

Review

⏱ Timed Writing

Explanatory Text: Essay
In an essay, compare and contrast each author's purpose for writing and the way in which each genre—play and review—presents its topic. Provide textual evidence to support your understanding. **(30 minutes)**

5-Minute Planner

1. Read the prompt carefully and completely. Consider these questions to get started.

   - How does each selection convey ideas and information?

   - What type of information does each author provide?

   - What kind of audience is each genre—play and review—most likely to reach? Explain.

2. Use your notes on the selections and your answers to the questions above to formulate a response.

3. Reread the prompt, and then draft your essay.

USE ACADEMIC VOCABULARY

As you write, use academic language, including the following words or their related forms:

opinion

reflect

respond

specific

For more information about academic vocabulary, see pages xlvi–l.

Language Study

Connotation and Denotation

A word's **denotation** is its definition. You can find denotations in a dictionary. The associations or feelings that a word suggests are called its **connotation**. Connotations can be positive, negative, or neutral. For example, the words *inexpensive, cheap,* and *economical* are synonyms that mean "low-priced." However, *cheap* suggests something that is poorly constructed. It has a negative connotation. *Economical* suggests something that saves money. It has a positive connotation. *Inexpensive* does not carry either positive or negative feelings. It has a neutral connotation.

Word	Denotation	Connotation	Example Sentence
unusual	not common or ordinary	not like others (neutral)	As birds, penguins are *unusual* because they cannot fly.
exceptional		better than average (positive)	As birds, penguins are *exceptional* because they cannot fly.
strange		different in an unwelcome way (negative)	As birds, penguins are *strange* because they cannot fly.

Practice A

Each of the following words has a positive, neutral, or negative connotation. For each word pair, identify which word has a more positive connotation. Use a dictionary if you need help checking a word's denotation.

1. bright, dazzling
2. argue, discuss
3. clever, sly
4. challenging, dangerous

Practice B

Each of these words has a neutral connotation. Provide a synonym for each one, using a dictionary or thesaurus if necessary. Then, label each of your synonyms *negative, positive,* or *neutral,* depending on its connotation. Finally, use five of your synonyms to write sentences that clearly show either a positive or a negative connotation.

1. ask
2. quiet
3. get
4. food
5. walk
6. car
7. laugh
8. curiosity
9. write
10. anticipate

Activity Each of the following words has a neutral connotation. Use a thesaurus to locate synonyms for each word. Find a synonym with a positive connotation and one with a negative connotation. Use a graphic organizer like this one to organize your synonyms. The first one has been completed as an example.

smell   warm   house   think   different

Synonyms with Negative Connotations		Synonyms with Positive Connotations
stink	← smell →	fragrance

Delivering a Persuasive Speech

The purpose of a **persuasive speech** is to convince an audience to think or act in a certain way. The speaker presents a claim, or argument, and uses strategies to convince the audience that his or her claim is valid. The following strategies will help you deliver an effective persuasive speech.

Learn the Skills

Develop your argument. Select a topic that is important to you and that has at least two sides. Identify which side you support. Then, list the reasons you support that side. Include evidence such as facts, statistics, or quotations from experts to strengthen your claim.

Organize your ideas. Rank your reasons and evidence in order of importance. When you deliver your speech, save your most important reason for last.

Start strong. Begin with a startling comparison or an anecdote that will capture your audience's attention. Then, provide a clear statement of your position.

Convince your listeners. Your audience will hear your presentation only once, so make sure they hear each and every word. To convince your audience, use speaking strategies that will highlight your strongest support.

- Speak loudly and slowly enough to be heard and understood.
- Make eye contact with your audience.
- Vary the volume and tone of your voice to emphasize key points.

Repeat key points. After explaining your ideas, repeat your most important idea in a single sentence. Pause afterward to allow your listeners to process what you say.

Use visuals. A picture, graphic, or chart can provide a dramatic illustration of a point you are making. Use your visuals to provide relevant evidence.

Practice the Skills

Presentation of Knowledge and Ideas Use what you have learned in this workshop to perform the following task.

ACTIVITY: **Deliver a Persuasive Speech**

Plan, write, and deliver your speech. Ask classmates to use the feedback form to give you advice on how you can improve your delivery. As you deliver your speech, remember these points:

- Provide strong evidence
- Engage listeners
- Repeat key points
- Use visuals

As your classmates deliver their persuasive speeches, consider whether or not they have been successful in convincing you to accept their views. Use the following form to evaluate their presentations.

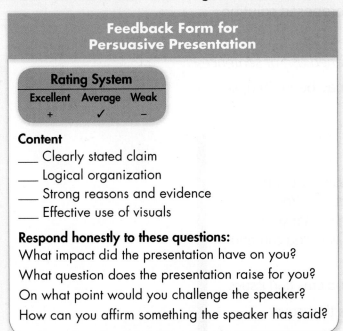

Feedback Form for Persuasive Presentation

Rating System

Excellent	Average	Weak
+	✓	–

Content
___ Clearly stated claim
___ Logical organization
___ Strong reasons and evidence
___ Effective use of visuals

Respond honestly to these questions:
What impact did the presentation have on you?
What question does the presentation raise for you?
On what point would you challenge the speaker?
How can you affirm something the speaker has said?

Comprehension and Collaboration After you have delivered your speeches, get into small groups and discuss the responses to the feedback forms. Was your position clear? Was your evidence strong? Was the organization logical? Were visuals used effectively? As a group, discuss your classmates' most successful speeches and examine why they worked so well.

Write an Argument

Problem-and-Solution Essay

Defining the Form In a **problem-and-solution essay,** the writer identifies and explains a problem and then proposes one or more possible solutions. The writer's goal is to persuade readers that the problem needs to be solved and that the proposed solution will solve the problem.

Assignment Think about a problem that affects your school, your community, or the world. Propose one or more solutions to the problem. Include these elements:

✓ a *thesis* stating the problem and your idea for a solution

✓ a *detailed explanation* of the problem

✓ a *step-by-step description* of your proposed solution

✓ *persuasive evidence* that supports your proposed solution

✓ *a consistent, logical organization*

✓ error-free writing, including *correct and varied use of sentences*

To preview the criteria on which your essay may be judged, see the rubric on page 545.

FOCUS ON RESEARCH

To write an effective problem-and-solution essay, you must explain the nature and seriousness of the problem. You must also present evidence to support the claim that your solution will solve the problem in a practical way. You can find information in these sources:

• government agencies that study various problems and issues

• print or online newspapers and magazines that cover public issues

• Web sites of national or local groups that focus on particular issues

Consider how objective, or fair-minded, each source is. Does the source reflect only one narrow point of view? If so, you might need to find other sources that look at the issue from a broader perspective.

Prewriting/Planning Strategy

Narrow your scope. Begin by choosing a topic you consider interesting and important. Be sure to narrow the scope of your problem to a manageable size. For example, pollution is a serious problem. Solutions to ending all air pollution are beyond the scope of this assignment. You could, however, discuss steps individuals can take to use less energy or recycle products instead of throwing them out. Use the examples in the chart for guidance on narrowing a topic.

Broad Topic	Narrower Topic	Narrow Topics
Problems in public schools	Improving student performance	• Strategies for building reading skills • Successful methods for teaching math • Effective tutoring programs • Ways to motivate students to learn

Determine your audience. Think about the audience you will address in your essay. Do you want to persuade public officials to adopt your solution? Do you hope to convince community leaders, such as school principals? Will you address your essay to your peers? Defining your audience will help you determine what kind of evidence to present, and which points to emphasize in your solution.

Gather information. Once you have identified a problem, you will need to gather information about it and about your proposed solution. Look for these types of evidence:

- facts or statistics about the extent of the problem
- quotations from experts about the scope or seriousness of the problem
- information that shows why your solution is a practical one
- examples of other people or groups who have succeeded in putting a solution like yours in place to solve a similar problem

If possible, interview experts who can comment on your solution.

Drafting Strategies

State your thesis. Begin your essay with a clear thesis—one sentence that states both the problem and your proposed solution.

Explain the problem. Before presenting your solution in detail, you need to define the problem fully. Explain the situation using the evidence you gathered in your research. Along with discussing the scope of the problem, you might briefly describe its causes and effects.

Detail your solution. After you explain the problem, develop your solution with examples and details. Provide relevant evidence that shows why your solution will work. In addition, address possible objections to your solution. See the chart for suggestions.

Possible Objection	Response
The solution is not practical.	Give a real-life example in which a similar solution solved the problem.
The solution is expensive.	Compare the cost of the solution to the cost of the problem.
People will not support the solution.	Interview people about the solution and quote responses in favor of it.

After addressing possible objections, discuss the effects of your proposed solution.

Develop your conclusion. In your conclusion, remind readers about the nature of the problem. Then restate your solution and summarize why you think it will work.

Consider your audience. To achieve your overall purpose of persuading others to accept your proposed solution, keep your audience—your readers—in mind as you draft. Choose details that will show how the problem and solution affects your audience. To make your argument more convincing, establish and maintain a formal style.

Support Your Ideas

Providing Support In drafting your problem-and-solution essay, your first step is to explain the causes and effects of the problem and to explain why the problem needs to be solved. Your next step is to convince readers that your ideas for a solution will work. To do this, support your ideas with facts, details, examples, and explanations. Ask yourself the following questions about your solution:

- Is my solution practical? Can it really be done? If so, how?
- Has my solution ever been tried? If so, what was the result?
- Have experts considered my solution in the past? What did they say?
- What are the disadvantages of my solution?

For each of your proposed solutions, use a chart like the one below to determine whether or not you have adequate support for your ideas. The following example examines an idea that solves this problem: *Many students do not get adequate nutrition from their diets.*

Idea 1

Serve healthy food in the lunchroom.

Detail	Explanation	Fact	Example
A peanut butter and banana sandwich on whole-wheat bread, a slice of watermelon, and a glass of milk provide protein, complex carbohy-drates, calcium, and potassium.	Studies show that students who get better nutrition at even one meal a day do better in school and get sick less often.	When other school districts switched to healthier lunch menus, student grades improved and students were out sick less often.	Healthy food can be tasty. For example, a strawberry-yogurt fruit smoothie is loaded with nutrients and good taste.

Revising Strategy

Revise the introduction for effect. Your readers do not necessarily see the problem or the solution as you do. You need to convince them your ideas are valid. Revise your opening paragraph to highlight the problem. You might use startling statistics, a powerful quotation from an expert, or the details of a dramatic event linked to the problem. This type of strong beginning will capture your readers' attention and make them eager to hear your proposed solution to the problem.

Revise to add support. Make sure to offer strong support for your position. Take the point of view of someone who has to be convinced about your solution. Then reread your explanation of the solution. Does every point make sense? Are the points connected logically? Is there evidence that supports each step in the solution? Revise to correct any problems in these areas. Use the chart below as a guide to your revisions.

Weakness	Possible Corrections
Poor explanation of a step	• Rewrite to clarify what the step entails • Revise to explain how the step addresses one part of the problem
Lack of logic in steps	• Reorder the steps if they are not in sequence • If necessary, add an intermediate step
Lack of evidence	• Add more statistics, examples, facts, or quotations from your research

Peer Review

Ask a partner to read your draft and identify places where you lack support for your definition of the problem or for your solution. Consider adding more details. Ask your partner to read your draft and mark instances where standard English is not used. Make any necessary corrections.

Combining Sentences for Variety

To add variety to your sentences, include prepositional phrases, appositive phrases, participial phrases, and gerund phrases.

Type of Phrase	Use	Example
Prepositional phrase	• as an adjective • as an adverb	The boy **in the red jacket** is my brother. The book fell **off the table**.
Appositive phrase	• as a noun phrase	Jim, a **7-year-old boy**, agreed.
Participial phrase	• as an adjective	**Arriving on Friday**, the package was late.
Gerund phrase	• as a noun	**Playing the guitar** is relaxing.

Combining Sentences for Variety

To add variety to your sentence patterns, include prepositional phrases, appositive phrases, participial phrases, or gerund phrases.

Combining Short Sentences The examples show how to use these four kinds of phrases to pack information into your sentences.

- **Using a Prepositional Phrase**
  Separate: The bus moved slowly. The road was wet.
  Combined: The bus moved slowly *along the wet road*.

- **Using an Appositive Phrase**
  Separate: Henry likes to ride a bike. He is a healthy 89-year-old.
  Combined: Henry, *a healthy 89-year-old,* likes to ride a bike.

- **Using a Participial Phrase**
  Separate: We ran out of water. We were thirsty.
  Combined: *Having run out of water,* we were thirsty.

- **Using a Gerund Phrase**
  Separate: Do not order beef. It would be a mistake.
  Combined: *Ordering beef* would be a mistake.

Fixing Choppy Sentences To fix choppy sentences, follow these steps:
  1. **Look for the relationship among ideas.**
  2. **Combine sentences to stress these connections among ideas.**

Grammar in Your Writing
Read your problem-and-solution essay, looking for pairs of short, related sentences. Using the examples as a guide, combine some for variety.

Panther Problems

The Florida panther is one of our state's most interesting animals, but sadly, it is also one of the rarest. There are currently only about sixty panthers in Florida. Panther numbers don't grow because of shrinking panther habitat and increasing traffic in areas populated by panthers. To save panthers from extinction, we must make sure there is enough land set aside for panthers to live on and that they have safe ways to move through the areas in which they live.

A grown panther needs approximately 275 square miles to roam and hunt. If too many adult panthers occupy the same territory, they fight and injure or kill one another. In addition, panthers hunt other wild animals, such as deer, for food. To be a good habitat for a panther, an area must have prey animals for the panther to hunt. Because of development, the "wild" areas that panthers used to call home are now filled with houses and stores rather than food and hiding places. It is unlikely that development will suddenly stop or even slow down. Therefore, experts must plan ahead and set aside one or two large protected areas where panthers can live, rather than many smaller areas.

Loss of habitat isn't the only problem caused by development. More houses means more roads, and that means more problems for panthers. According to the Florida Game and Freshwater Fish Commission, 42% of panther deaths in a recent twenty-five-year period were road kills. Underpasses have been built to allow panthers and other animals to cross a territory without crossing a road. In an area known as Alligator Alley, one large underpass was built. Since then, there have been no reported killings of panthers by cars. The success of the underpass in this area shows that we can protect panthers without halting progress.

The two solutions suggested here would meet the needs of humans and panthers. The solutions are costly, but they have been proven effective, and they are the least disruptive to the human community. Saving the Florida panther is a complex issue, but if we put our heads together, I'm confident we will make the right decisions.

Shamus states his thesis in the first paragraph and suggests a two-step solution to the problem.

The problem is explained in more detail so that readers will understand the value of the proposed solution.

Transition words such as "because" and "therefore" show cause-and-effect relationships.

Each part of the problem and its solution is addressed in a separate paragraph. Statistics provide evidence that a solution is needed and that the proposed solution is the right one.

Editing and Proofreading

Proofread your draft to correct errors in spelling, grammar, and punctuation.

Focus on words with suffixes. **Suffixes** are word parts that are added to the ends of base words. To spell a word with a suffix, remember the following rules:

Suffixes that begin with a consonant *(-ful, -tion,-ly)*: Change final *y* to *i* in the base word, unless a vowel precedes the *y*.

Suffixes beginning with a vowel: Change final *y* to *i* in the base word, unless a vowel precedes the *y*. Usually, drop the final *e* in the base word.

Spiral Review
Earlier in the unit, you learned about **prepositions and appositives** (p. 486) and **participles and gerunds** (p. 520). Review your essay to be sure that you have used these elements correctly.

Publishing and Presenting

Consider one of the following ways to share your writing:

Present a proposal. Use your problem-and-solution essay as the basis for a presentation.

Submit your paper for publication. Send a clean copy to your school paper or local newspaper. Include a cover letter.

Reflecting on Your Writing

Writer's Journal Jot down your answer to this question: *Who can implement the solutions proposed in your essay?*

Rubric for Self-Assessment

Find evidence in your writing to address each category. Then, use the rating scale to grade your work.

Criteria	Rating Scale
Purpose/Focus Presents a clear problem and proposed solution; supports the solution with clear reasons and relevant evidence, using credible sources; addresses possible objections to the solution	*not very* .... *very* 1　　2　　3　　4
Organization Introduces the problem and solution; has a concluding section that follows logically from the argument presented	1　　2　　3　　4
Development of Ideas/Elaboration Organizes reasons and evidence clearly and logically; establishes and maintains a formal style	1　　2　　3　　4
Language Uses precise language to strengthen the argument; uses words, phrases, and clauses to clarify the relationships among ideas	1　　2　　3　　4
Conventions Varies sentence patterns for meaning, interest, and style	1　　2　　3　　4

SELECTED RESPONSE

I. Reading Literature

Directions: *Read Augusta Stevenson's dramatic version of Aesop's fable "The Crow and the Fox." Then, answer each question that follows.*

[MADAM CROW *sits in a tree. Enter her daughter* MISS CROW, *carrying a large piece of cheese in her mouth.*]

MADAM. O joy! O joy! We'll dine as if we were queen and princess!

[*Miss Crow flies to Madam Crow. Enter* MASTER FOX.]

Fox. I bid you good morning, dear madam.

MADAM. Good morning to you, dear sir.

Fox. [*Sitting under tree*] With your permission, I'll speak with your daughter.

MADAM. She'll be pleased to listen, that she will—you are so clever.

Fox. [*Modestly*] Nay, madam, not so clever, only thoughtful. [*He sighs.*]

MADAM. You have something on your mind.

Fox. [*Sighing again*] Yes, dear madam,—I am thinking of your daughter.

MADAM. Then speak! Speak now, sir!—at once, sir!

Fox. I speak. O sweet Miss Crow, how beautiful your wings are!

MADAM. [*Pleased*] Do you hear that, daughter?

[MISS CROW *nods, spreading her wings proudly.*]

Fox. I speak again. How bright your eye, dear maid! How graceful your neck!

MADAM. Bend your neck, child! Now bend it well that he may better see your grace.

[MISS CROW *bends neck twice.*]

Fox. But oh, that such a sweet bird should be dumb!—should be so utterly dumb!

[*He weeps gently in his little pocket handkerchief.*]

MADAM. [*Looks surprised and insulted. Ruffles her feathers <u>indignantly</u>*] Do you think, sir, she cannot *caw* as well as the rest of us?

Fox. I must think so, dear madam. Alas! [*Weeping again.*]

MADAM. You shall think so no longer! Caw, child, as you never have before!

Miss Crow. [*Opening mouth; dropping cheese*] Caw! Caw!

[*Fox quickly snaps up the cheese.*]

Fox. Thank you, Miss Crow. Dear madam, whatever I said of her beauty, I said nothing of her brains. [*He goes, waving his handkerchief.*]

---

1. Which answer choice is the best **summary** of the drama?

A. The evil fox is able to steal the crows' cheese even though the crows stand up to him.

B. The fox and the crows make a deal and share a piece of cheese.

C. Two kind crows donate their cheese to a lonely and hungry fox.

D. The clever fox tricks the silly crows into dropping the cheese.

2. Why do the **stage directions** in the play include descriptions such as *[Modestly]* and *[Pleased]*?

A. so actors will know where to stand

B. so the audience will know where to look

C. so actors will know how to speak their lines

D. so actors will know what to wear

3. **Part A** What does Master Fox's **dialogue** tell you about his character?

A. He says what he does not mean, showing he is sly and tricky.

B. He talks hesitantly to the crows, showing he is shy.

C. He accuses Miss Crow, showing he is suspicious.

D. He speaks uncertainly, showing that he is confused.

Part B Which phrase from the passage best shows the fox's character?

A. "I bid you good morning, dear madam."

B. "How bright your eye, dear maid! How graceful your neck!"

C. "I speak again."

D. "With your permission, I'll speak to your daughter."

4. Which of these is most likely the **author's purpose** for writing this play?

A. to entertain   C. to inform

B. to persuade   D. to explain

5. Which of these would most likely serve as a prop in this **drama**?

A. a handkerchief   C. a flower

B. a mirror   D. feathers

6. What is the **theme,** or insight, conveyed by this drama?

A. Flattery and kind words can be used dishonestly.

B. Mammals need to be smarter than birds.

C. Remember to put your cheese down before you caw.

D. Even if you see a fox crying, do not offer him a handkerchief.

7. **Part A** Which word is closest in meaning to the underlined word *indignantly*?

A. urgently   C. energetically

B. excitedly   D. angrily

Part B Which of the following context clues help you understand the meaning of *indignantly*?

A. "Weeping again" and "weeps gently"

B. "insulted" and "Ruffles her feathers"

C. "'I must think so,'" and "'Alas!'"

D. "'Do you think," and "she cannot *caw*"

⏱ Timed Writing

8. In an essay, tell what the **stage directions** and **dialogue** in this passage reveal about Madam Crow. Support your analysis with details from the passage.

GO ON

II. Reading Informational Text

Directions: *Read the passage from a persuasive letter below. Then, answer each question that follows.*

It is important that our school begin a recycling program. Our trash cans are brimming with bottles and cans that students carelessly toss away. The school community wastes thousands of pieces of paper every day, all of which is discarded. Recycling can reduce this waste. My family has reduced our waste by 30% by recycling.

Recycling has countless benefits for the school community and for the environment. Every ton of paper that is recycled will save 3.3 cubic yards of landfill space. Soda bottles can be turned into clothing or other useful items, instead of clogging landfills. Recycling will teach us all the value of working together to achieve a common goal. Some students have already voiced interest in this program.

Currently, this school has no environmental initiative in place. Our town's Department of Public Works is willing to donate recycling bins in our cafeteria for bottles and cans, and bins for paper recycling in each classroom. Once a week, a recycling truck will pick up the recyclables, just as the garbage truck comes to pick up the trash. That leaves the school community to place their paper, bottles, and cans in the appropriate bins, instead of the trash cans. This program will prove to have many benefits.

1. **Part A** What is the main claim made by the author of the persuasive letter?
   A. A recycling program is needed in the school.
   B. Recycling trucks help play a role in reducing the amount of trash in school.
   C. The town is wiling to donate recycling bins.
   D. Recycling trucks will pick up the recyclables.

Part B Which of the following statements from the letter best supports the claim?
   A. "Some students have already voiced interest in this program."
   B. "Soda bottles can be turned into clothing."
   C. "Recycling has countless benefits for the school community and for the environment."
   D. "Once a week, a recycling truck will pick up the recyclables, just as the garbage truck comes to pick up the trash."

III. Writing and Language Conventions

Directions: *Read the letter. Then, answer each question.*

Mr. Allan Reeves
13 Riverside Circle
New York, New York 10007
Dear Mr. Reeves:
   (1) I just finished reading your book *Common Denominators*. (2) I can't believe how awesome it was! (3) I read the story of the people lost at sea. (4) I was struck by their courage. (5) I wondered if I could survive such a frightening situation. (6) I hope you continue to write stories of courage and survival against the odds. (7) I think these stories inspire others, especially young readers. (8) I know they inspire me.
   Sincerely yours,
   Savion Miller

1. Which sentence contains an **appositive**?
A. sentence 5
B. sentence 6
C. sentence 1
D. sentence 8

2. Which sentence contains a **prepositional phrase**?
A. sentence 5
B. sentence 6
C. sentence 7
D. sentence 8

3. Which word in sentence 1 is a **gerund**?
A. just
B. finished
C. reading
D. book

4. Which of the following revisions best combines sentences 3 and 4 using a **participial phrase?**
A. Reading the story of the people lost at sea, I was struck by their courage.
B. I read the story of the people lost at sea, struck by their courage.
C. Reading the story of the people lost at seas made me struck by their courage.
D. I read the story of the people lost at sea, and I was struck by their courage.

STOP

CONSTRUCTED RESPONSE

Directions: *Follow the instructions to complete the tasks below as required by your teacher.*

As you work on each task, incorporate both general academic vocabulary and literary terms you learned in Parts 1 and 2.

Writing

TASK 1 Literature

Analyze a Character

Write an essay in which you describe how a character in a drama changes as the plot unfolds.

- From one of the dramas in Part 2, identify a character who undergoes changes between the beginning and the end of the play.
- Describe the points at which the character does something or learns something that contributes to the change.
- Compare and contrast the character at the beginning of the play with the character at the end of the play. State clearly the ways in which the character has changed.
- Use evidence from the play to support your analysis.
- Use appropriate transitions to show relationships between your ideas.

TASK 2 Literature

Analyze a Scene

Write an essay in which you analyze how a particular scene fits into the overall structure of The Phantom Tollbooth.

- Select a scene from the drama and explain how this scene contributes to the play as a whole. For example, it might move the plot forward, introduce a conflict, develop a character, express an aspect of the theme, or do a combination of these functions.
- Support your claims with relevant details and examples from the text.
- Maintain a consistent style and tone in your writing.

TASK 3 Literature

Summarize and Determine Theme

Write a summary of one of the dramatic selections in Part 2 and state the work's theme.

Part 1

- Choose a drama selection from Part 2.
- Identify the major events in the drama, and determine why each of these events is important. Make notes of your findings.

Part 2

- Write an essay in which you summarize the drama.
- State the theme of the drama. Your summary of important events and main points should lead to and support your statement of the theme.

Speaking and Listening

TASK 4 ▸ Literature
Analyze Plot Development

Give an oral presentation in which you analyze the plot of a drama from Part 2.

- Describe how the play's plot unfolds in episodes. Determine the conflicts—both internal and external—and the stages at which the conflicts are introduced (exposition), are developed (rising action), reach their greatest tension (climax), begin to be settled (falling action), and are resolved (resolution).

- Visually display the key episodes in a plot diagram. You might draw a poster or create a brief slide show.

- Accurately use academic vocabulary in your presentation.

TASK 5 ▸ Literature
Analyze Setting

Lead a small group discussion about the importance of setting in several scenes from The Phantom Tollbooth.

- Come to the discussion prepared. Choose at least three scenes in which setting contributes to a conflict, influences characters, or helps convey a theme. Create a list of questions to get the discussion started.

- During the discussion, pose additional questions and respond to specific questions from members of your group. Use examples from the drama to support your ideas.

- At the end of your discussion, review and summarize the main points that your group made.

Research

TASK 6 ▸ Literature

How do we decide who we are?

In the selections in Part 2, dramatic characters change and grow as a result of their experiences. Conduct a short research project on different situations that help people learn about themselves and others, such as learning new skills, visiting new places, getting to know people with varied backgrounds, or facing difficult challenges.

Use both the literature you have read and your research to reflect on this unit's Big Question. Review the following guidelines before you begin your research:

- Focus your research on one way people learn about themselves and others.

- Gather relevant information from at least two reliable print or digital sources.

- Take notes as you conduct your research.

- Cite your sources.

When you have completed your research, write a brief essay in response to the Big Question. Discuss how your initial ideas have been either changed or reinforced. Support your response with examples from both the literature in Part 2 and from your research.

The PRINCE and the PAUPER

Adapted from a book by Mark Twain

pauper ▶
(pô′ pər) *n.* someone who is very poor

CHARACTERS

Edward, Prince of Wales	Justice
Tom Canty, *the Pauper*	Constable
Lord Hertford	Jailer
Lord St. John	Sir Hugh Hendon
King Henry VIII	Two Prisoners
Herald	Two Guards
Miles Hendon	Three Pages
John Canty, *Tom's father*	Lords and Ladies
Hugo, *a young thief*	Villagers
Two Women	

SCENE 1

TIME. 1547.

SETTING. *Westminster Palace, England. Gates leading to courtyard are at right. Slightly to the left, off courtyard and inside gates, interior of palace anteroom is visible. There is a couch with a rich robe draped on it, screen at rear, bellcord, mirror, chairs, and a table with bowl of nuts, and a large golden seal on it. Piece of armor hangs on one wall. Exits are rear and downstage.*

AT RISE, TWO GUARDS—*One at right, one at left—stand in front of gates, and several* VILLAGERS *hover nearby, straining to see into courtyard where* PRINCE *may be seen through fence, playing.* TWO WOMEN *enter right.*

1ST WOMAN. I have walked all morning just to have a glimpse of Westminster Palace.

2ND WOMAN. Maybe if we can get near enough to the gates, we can have a glimpse of the young prince. *(*TOM CANTY, *dirty and ragged, comes out of crowd and steps close to gates.)* I have always dreamed of seeing a real prince! *(Excited, he presses his nose against gates.)*

1ST GUARD. Mind your manners, you young beggar! *(Seizes* TOM *by collar and sends him sprawling into crowd.* VILLAGERS *laugh, as* TOM *slowly gets to his feet.)*

PRINCE. *(Rushing to gates)* How dare you treat a poor subject of the King in such a manner! Open the gates and let him in! *(As* VILLAGERS *see* PRINCE, *they take off their hats and bow low.)*

VILLAGERS. *(Shouting together)* Long live the Prince of Wales! *(*GUARDS *open gates and* TOM *slowly passes through, as if in a dream.)*

PRINCE. *(To* TOM*)* You look tired, and you have been treated cruelly. I am Edward, Prince of Wales. What is your name?

TOM. *(Looking around in awe)* Tom Canty, Your Highness.

PRINCE. Come into the palace with me, Tom. *(*PRINCE *leads* TOM *into anteroom.* VILLAGERS *pantomime conversation, and all but a few exit.)* Where do you live, Tom?

TOM. In the city, Your Highness, in Offal[1] Court.

PRINCE. Offal Court? That is an odd name. Do you have parents?

TOM. Yes, Your Highness.

PRINCE. How does your father treat you?

TOM. If it please you, Your Highness, when I am not able to beg a penny for our supper, he treats me to beatings.

---

1. **offal** (ô′ fəl) scraps left over when an animal is butchered.

PRINCE. *(Shocked)* What! Beatings? My father is not a calm man, but he does not beat me. *(Looks at* TOM *thoughtfully)* You speak well and have an easy grace. Have you been schooled?

TOM. Very little, Your Highness. A good priest who shares our house in Offal Court has taught me from his books.

PRINCE. Do you have a pleasant life in Offal Court?

TOM. Pleasant enough, Your Highness, save when I am hungry. We have Punch and Judy shows,[2] and sometimes we lads have fights in the street.

PRINCE. *(Eagerly)* I should like that. Tell me more.

TOM. In summer, we run races and swim in the river, and we love to wallow in the mud.

PRINCE. *(Sighing, wistfully)* If I could wear your clothes and play in the mud just once, with no one to forbid me, I think I could give up the crown!

TOM. *(Shaking his head)* And if I could wear your fine clothes just once, Your Highness …

PRINCE. Would you like that? Come, then. We shall change places. You can take off your rags and put on my clothes—and I will put on yours. *(He leads* TOM *behind screen, and they return shortly, each wearing the other's clothes.)* Let's look at ourselves in this mirror. *(Leads* TOM *to mirror)*

TOM. Oh, Your Highness, it is not proper for me to wear such clothes.

PRINCE. *(Excitedly, as he looks in mirror)* Heavens, do you not see it? We look like brothers! We have the same features and bearing. If we went about together, dressed alike, there is no one who could say which is the Prince of Wales and which Tom Canty!

TOM. *(Drawing back and rubbing his hand)* Your Highness, I am frightened …

PRINCE. Do not worry. *(Seeing* TOM *rub his hand)* Is that a bruise on your hand?

TOM. Yes, but it is a slight thing, Your Highness.

---

2. **Punch and Judy shows** public puppet shows presented in England in the sixteenth century.

PRINCE. *(Angrily)* It was shameful and cruel of that guard to strike you. Do not stir a step until I come back. I command you! *(He picks up golden Seal of England and carefully puts it into piece of armor. He then dashes out to gates.)* Open! Unbar the gates at once! *(2ND GUARD opens gates, and as PRINCE runs out, in rags, 1ST GUARD seizes him, boxes him on the ear, and knocks him to the ground.)*

1ST GUARD. Take that, you little beggar, for the trouble you have made for me with the Prince. *(VILLAGERS roar with laughter.)*

PRINCE. *(Picking himself up, turning on GUARD furiously)* I am Prince of Wales! You shall hang for laying your hand on me!

1ST GUARD. *(Presenting arms; mockingly)* I salute Your Gracious Highness! *(Then, angrily, 1ST GUARD shoves PRINCE roughly aside.)* Be off, you mad bag of rags! *(PRINCE is surrounded by VILLAGERS, who hustle him off.)*

VILLAGERS. *(Ad lib, as they exit, shouting)* Make way for His Royal Highness! Make way for the Prince of Wales! Hail to the Prince! *(Etc.)*

TOM. *(Admiring himself in mirror)* If only the boys in Offal Court could see me! They will not believe me when I tell them about this. *(Looks around anxiously)* But where is the Prince? *(Looks cautiously into courtyard. TWO GUARDS immediately snap to attention and salute. He quickly ducks back into anteroom as HERTFORD and ST. JOHN enter at rear.)*

HERTFORD. *(Going toward TOM, then stopping and bowing low)* My Lord, you look distressed. What is wrong?

TOM. *(Trembling)* Oh, I beg of you, be merciful. I am no Prince, but poor Tom Canty of Offal Court. Please let me see the Prince, and he will give my rags back to me and let me go unhurt. *(Kneeling)* Please, be merciful and spare me!

HERTFORD. *(Puzzled and disturbed)* Your Highness, on your knees? To me? *(Bows quickly, then, aside to ST. JOHN)* The Prince has gone mad! We must inform the King. *(To TOM)* A moment, Your Highness. *(HERTFORD and ST. JOHN exit rear.)*

TOM. Oh, there is no hope for me now. They will hang me for certain! *(HERTFORD and ST. JOHN re-enter, supporting*

KING. TOM *watches in awe as they help him to couch, where he sinks down wearily.)*

KING. *(Beckoning* TOM *close to him)* Now, my son, Edward, my prince. What is this? Do you mean to deceive me, the King, your father, who loves you and treats you so kindly?

TOM. *(Dropping to his knees)* You are the King? Then I have no hope!

KING. *(Stunned)* My child, you are not well. Do not break your father's old heart. Say you know me.

TOM. Yes, you are my lord the King, whom God preserve.

KING. True, that is right. Now, you will not deny that you are Prince of Wales, as they say you did just a while ago?

TOM. I beg you, Your Grace, believe me. I am the lowest of your subjects, being born a pauper, and it is by a great mistake that I am here. I am too young to die. Oh, please, spare me, sire!

KING. *(Amazed)* Die? Do not talk so, my child. You shall not die.

TOM. *(Gratefully)* God save you, my king! And now, may I go?

KING. Go? Where would you go?

TOM. Back to the alley where I was born and bred to misery.

KING. My poor child, rest your head here. *(He holds* TOM'S *head and pats his shoulder, then turns to* HERTFORD *and* ST. JOHN.*)* Alas, I am old and ill, and my son is mad. But this shall pass. Mad or sane, he is my heir and shall rule England. Tomorrow he shall be installed and confirmed in his princely dignity! Bring the Great Seal!

HERTFORD. *(Bowing low)* Please, Your Majesty, you took the Great Seal from the Chancellor two days ago to give to His Highness the Prince.

KING. So I did. *(To* TOM*)* My child, tell me, where is the Great Seal?

TOM. *(Trembling)* Indeed, my lord, I do not know.

affliction ▶
(ə flik´ shən) *n.* pain, illness, suffering

KING. Ah, your affliction hangs heavily upon you. 'Tis no matter. You will remember later. Listen, carefully! *(Gently, but firmly)* I command you to hide your affliction in all ways that be within your power. You shall deny to no one that you are the true prince, and if your memory should

fail you upon any occasion of state, you shall be advised by your uncle, the Lord Hertford.

TOM. *(Resigned)* The King has spoken. The King shall be obeyed.

KING. And now, my child, I go to rest. *(He stands weakly, and HERTFORD leads him off, rear.)*

TOM. *(Wearily, to ST. JOHN)* May it please your lordship to let me rest now?

ST. JOHN. So it please Your Highness, it is for you to command and us to obey. But it is wise that you rest, for this evening you must attend the Lord Mayor's banquet in your honor. *(He pulls bellcord, and THREE PAGES enter and kneel before TOM.)*

TOM. Banquet? *(Terrified, he sits on couch and reaches for cup of water, but 1ST PAGE instantly seizes cup, drops on one knee, and serves it to him. TOM starts to take off his boots, but 2ND PAGE stops him and does it for him. He tries to remove his cape and gloves, and 3RD PAGE does it for him.)* I wonder that you do not try to breathe for me also! *(Lies down cautiously. PAGES cover him with robe, then back away and exit.)*

ST. JOHN. *(To HERTFORD, as he enters)* Plainly, what do you think?

HERTFORD. Plainly, this. The King is near death, my nephew the Prince of Wales is clearly mad and will mount the throne mad. God protect England, for she will need it!

ST. JOHN. Does it not seem strange that madness could so change his manner from what it used to be? It troubles me, his saying he is not the Prince.

HERTFORD. Peace, my lord! If he were an impostor and called himself Prince, that would be natural. But was there ever an impostor,

who being called Prince by the King and court, denied it? Never! This is the true Prince gone mad. And tonight all London shall honor him. *(HERTFORD and ST. JOHN exit. TOM sits up, looks around helplessly, then gets up.)*

TOM. I should have thought to order something to eat. *(Sees bowl of nuts on table)* Ah! Here are some nuts! *(Looks around, sees Great Seal in armor, takes it out, looks at it curiously.)* This will make a good nutcracker. *(He takes bowl of nuts, sits on couch and begins to crack nuts with Great Seal and eat them, as curtain falls.)*

SCENE 2

TIME. *Later that night.*

SETTING. *A street in London, near Offal Court. Played before the curtain.*

AT RISE. PRINCE *limps in, dirty and tousled. He looks around wearily. Several VILLAGERS pass by, pushing against him.*

PRINCE. I have never seen this poor section of London. I must be near Offal Court. If I can only find it before I drop! *(JOHN CANTY steps out of crowd, seizes PRINCE roughly.)*

CANTY. Out at this time of night, and I warrant you haven't brought a farthing home! If that is the case and I do not break all the bones in your miserable body, then I am not John Canty!

PRINCE. *(Eagerly)* Oh, are you his father?

CANTY. *His* father? I am *your* father, and—

PRINCE. Take me to the palace at once, and your son will be returned to you. The King, my father, will make you rich beyond your wildest dreams. Oh, save me, for I am indeed the Prince of Wales.

CANTY. *(Staring in amazement)* Gone stark mad! But mad or not, I'll soon find where the soft places lie in your bones. Come home! *(Starts to drag PRINCE off)*

PRINCE. *(Struggling)* Let me go! I am the Prince of Wales, and the King shall have your life for this!

CANTY. *(Angrily)* I'll take no more of your madness! *(Raises stick to strike, but PRINCE struggles free and runs off, and CANTY runs after him)*

SETTING. *Same as Scene 1, with addition of dining table, set with dishes and goblets, on raised platform. Throne-like chair is at head of table.*

AT RISE. *A banquet is in progress.* TOM, *in royal robes, sits at head of table, with* HERTFORD *at his right and* ST. JOHN *at his left.* LORDS *and* LADIES *sit around table eating and talking softly.*

TOM. *(To* HERTFORD) What is this, my Lord? *(Holds up a plate)*

HERTFORD. Lettuce and turnips, Your Highness.

TOM. Lettuce and turnips? I have never seen them before. Am I to eat them?

HERTFORD. *(Discreetly)* Yes, Your Highness, if you so desire. *(*TOM *begins to eat food with his fingers. Fanfare of trumpets is heard, and* HERALD *enters, carrying scroll. All turn to look.)*

HERALD. *(Reading from scroll)* His Majesty, King Henry VIII, is dead! The King is dead! *(All rise and return to* TOM, *who sits, stunned.)*

ALL. *(Together)* The King is dead. Long live the King! Long live Edward, King of England! *(All bow to* TOM. HERALD *bows and exits.)*

HERTFORD. *(To* TOM) Your Majesty, we must call the council. Come, St. John. *(*HERTFORD *and* ST. JOHN *lead* TOM *off at rear.* LORDS *and* LADIES *follow, talking among themselves. At gates, down right,* VILLAGERS *enter and mill about.* PRINCE *enters right, pounds on gates and shouts.)*

PRINCE. Open the gates! I am the Prince of Wales! Open, I say! And though I am friendless with no one to help me, I will not be driven from my ground.

MILES HENDON. *(Entering through crowd)* Though you be Prince or not, you are indeed a gallant lad and not friendless. Here I stand to prove it, and you might have a worse friend than Miles Hendon.

1ST VILLAGER. 'Tis another prince in disguise. Take the lad and dunk him in the pond! *(He seizes* PRINCE, *but* MILES *strikes him with the flat of his sword. Crowd, now angry, presses forward threateningly, when fanfare of trumpets is heard off-stage.* HERALD, *carrying scroll, enters up left at gates.)*

HERALD. Make way for the King's messenger! *(Reading from scroll)* His Majesty, King Henry VIII is dead! The King is dead! *(He exits right, repeating message, and VILLAGERS stand in stunned silence.)*

PRINCE. *(Stunned)* The King is dead!

1ST VILLAGER. *(Shouting)* Long live Edward, King of England!

VILLAGERS. *(Together)* Long live the King! *(Shouting, ad lib)* Long live King Edward! Heaven protect Edward, King of England! *(Etc.)*

MILES. *(Taking PRINCE by the arm)* Come, lad, before the crowd remembers us. I have a room at the inn, and you can stay there. *(He hurries off with stunned PRINCE. TOM, led by HERTFORD, enters courtyard up rear. VILLAGERS see them.)*

VILLAGERS. *(Together)* Long live the King! *(They fall to their knees as curtains close.)*

SCENE 4

SETTING. *Miles's room at the inn. At right is table set with dishes and bowls of food, a chair at each side. At left is bed, with table and chair next to it, and a window. Candle is on table.*

AT RISE. MILES *and* PRINCE *approach table.*

MILES. I have had a hot supper prepared. I'll bet you're hungry, lad.

PRINCE. Yes, I am. It's kind of you to let me stay with you, Miles. I am truly Edward, King of England, and you shall not go unrewarded. *(Sits at table)*

MILES. *(To himself)* First he called himself Prince, and now he is King. Well, I will humor him. *(Starts to sit)*

Prince. *(Angrily)* Stop! Would you sit in the presence of the King?

Miles. *(Surprised, standing up quickly)* I beg your pardon, Your Majesty. I was not thinking. *(Stares uncertainly at PRINCE, who sits at table, expectantly. MILES starts to uncover dishes of food, serves PRINCE and fills glasses.)*

PRINCE. Miles, you have a gallant way about you. Are you nobly born?

MILES. My father is a baronet,[3] Your Majesty.

PRINCE. Then you must also be a baronet.

MILES. *(Shaking his head)* My father banished me from home seven years ago, so I fought in the wars. I was taken prisoner, and I have spent the past seven years in prison. Now I am free, and I am returning home.

PRINCE. You have been shamefully wronged! But I will make things right for you. You have saved me from injury and possible death. Name your reward and if it be within the compass of my royal power, it is yours.

MILES. *(Pausing briefly, then dropping to his knee)* Since Your Majesty is pleased to hold my simple duty worthy of reward, I ask that I and my successors may hold the privilege of sitting in the presence of the King.

PRINCE. *(Taking* MILES'S *sword, tapping him lightly on each shoulder)* Rise and seat yourself. *(Returns sword to* MILES, *then rises and goes over to bed)*

MILES. *(Rising)* He should have been born a king. He plays the part to a marvel! If I had not thought of this favor, I might have had to stand for weeks. *(Sits down and begins to eat)*

PRINCE. Sir Miles, you will stand guard while I sleep. *(Lies down and instantly falls asleep)*

MILES. Yes, Your Majesty. *(With a rueful look at his uneaten supper, he stands up.)* Poor little chap. I suppose his mind has been disordered with ill usage. *(Covers* PRINCE *with his cape)* Well, I will be his friend and watch over him. *(Blows out candle, then yawns, sits on chair next to bed, and falls asleep.* JOHN CANTY *and* HUGO *appear at window, peer around room, then enter cautiously through window. They lift the sleeping* PRINCE, *staring nervously at* MILES.*)*

CANTY. *(In loud whisper)* I swore the day he was born he would be a thief and a beggar, and I won't lose him now. Lead the way to the camp, Hugo! *(CANTY and* HUGO *carry* PRINCE *off right, as* MILES *sleeps on and curtain falls.)*

---

3. **baronet** a member of the English upper class.

TIME. *Two weeks later.*

SETTING. *Country village street.*

BEFORE RISE. VILLAGERS *walk about.* CANTY, HUGO, *and* PRINCE *enter.*

CANTY. I will go in this direction. Hugo, keep my mad son with you, and see that he doesn't escape again! *(Exits)*

HUGO. *(Seizing* PRINCE *by the arm)* He won't escape! I'll see that he earns his bread today, or else!

PRINCE. *(Pulling away)* I will not beg with you, and I will not steal! I have suffered enough in this miserable company of thieves!

HUGO. You shall suffer more if you do not do as I tell you! *(Raises clenched fist at* PRINCE*)* Refuse if you dare! *(*WOMAN *enters, carrying wrapped bundle in a basket on her arm.)* Wait here until I come back. *(*HUGO *sneaks along after* WOMAN, *then snatches her bundle, runs back to* PRINCE, *and thrusts it into his arms.)* Run after me and call, "Stop, thief!" But be sure you lead her astray! *(Runs off.* PRINCE *throws down bundle in disgust.)*

WOMAN. Help! Thief! Stop, thief! *(Rushes at* PRINCE *and seizes him, just as several* VILLAGERS *enter)* You little thief! What do you mean by robbing a poor woman? Somebody bring the constable! *(*MILES *enters and watches.)*

1ST VILLAGER. *(Grabbing* PRINCE*)* I'll teach him a lesson, the little villain!

PRINCE. *(Struggling)* Take your hands off me! I did not rob this woman!

MILES. *(Stepping out of crowd and pushing man back with the flat of his sword)* Let us proceed gently, my friends. This is a matter for the law.

PRINCE. *(Springing to* MILES'S *side)* You have come just in time, Sir Miles. Carve this rabble to rags!

MILES. Speak softly. Trust in me and all shall go well.

CONSTABLE. *(Entering and reaching for* PRINCE*)* Come along, young rascal!

MILES. Gently, good friend. He shall go peaceably to the Justice.

PRINCE. I will not go before a Justice! I did not do this thing!

MILES. *(Taking him aside)* Sire, will you reject the laws of the realm, yet demand that your subjects respect them?

PRINCE. *(Calmer)* You are right, Sir Miles. Whatever the King requires a subject to suffer under the law, he will suffer himself while he holds the station of a subject. *(CONSTABLE leads them off right. VILLAGERS follow. Curtain)*

* * * * *

SETTING. *Office of the* JUSTICE. *A high bench is at center.*

AT RISE. JUSTICE *sits behind bench.* CONSTABLE *enters with* MILES *and* PRINCE, *followed by* VILLAGERS. WOMAN *carries wrapped bundle.*

CONSTABLE. *(To* JUSTICE*)* A young thief, your worship, is accused of stealing a dressed pig from this poor woman.

JUSTICE. *(Looking down at* PRINCE, *then* WOMAN*)* My good woman, are you absolutely certain this lad stole your pig?

WOMAN. It was none other than he, your worship.

JUSTICE. Are there no witnesses to the contrary? *(All shake their heads.)* Then the lad stands convicted. *(To* WOMAN*)* What do you hold this property to be worth?

WOMAN. Three shillings and eight pence, your worship.

JUSTICE. *(Leaning down to* WOMAN*)* Good woman, do you know that when one steals a thing above the value of thirteen pence, the law says he shall hang for it?

WOMAN. *(Upset)* Oh, what have I done? I would not hang the poor boy for the whole world! Save me from this, your worship. What can I do?

JUSTICE. *(Gravely)* You may revise the value, since it is not yet written in the record.

WOMAN. Then call the pig eight pence, your worship.

JUSTICE. So be it. You may take your property and go. *(WOMAN starts off, and is followed by CONSTABLE. MILES follows them cautiously down right.)*

CONSTABLE. *(Stopping* WOMAN*)* Good woman, I will buy your pig from you. *(Takes coins from pocket)* Here is eight pence.

WOMAN. Eight pence! It cost me three shillings and eight pence!

CONSTABLE. Indeed! Then come back before his worship and answer for this. The lad must hang!

WOMAN. No! No! Say no more. Give me the eight pence and hold your peace. *(CONSTABLE hands her coins and takes pig. WOMAN exits, angrily. MILES returns to bench.)*

JUSTICE. The boy is sentenced to a fortnight in the common jail. Take him away, Constable! *(JUSTICE exits. PRINCE gives MILES a nervous glance.)*

MILES. *(Following CONSTABLE)* Good sir, turn your back a moment and let the poor lad escape. He is innocent.

CONSTABLE. *(Outraged)* What? You say this to me? Sir, I arrest you in—

MILES. Do not be so hasty! *(Slyly)* The pig you have purchased for eight pence may cost you your neck, man.

CONSTABLE. *(Laughing nervously)* Ah, but I was merely jesting with the woman, sir.

MILES. Would the Justice think it a jest?

CONSTABLE. Good sir! The Justice has no more sympathy with a jest than a dead corpse! *(Perplexed)* Very well, I will turn my back and see nothing! But go quickly! *(Exits)*

MILES. *(To PRINCE)* Come, my liege. We are free to go. And that band of thieves shall not set hands on you again, I swear it!

PRINCE. *(Wearily)* Can you believe, Sir Miles, that in the last fortnight, I, the King of England, have escaped from thieves and begged for food on the road? I have slept in a barn with a calf! I have washed dishes in a peasant's kitchen, and narrowly escaped death. And not once in all of my wanderings did I see a courier searching for me! Is it no matter for commotion and distress that the head of state is gone?

MILES. *(Sadly, aside)* Still busy with his pathetic dream. *(To PRINCE)* It is strange indeed my liege. But come, I will take you to my father's home in Kent. We are not far away. There you may rest in a house with seventy rooms! Come, I am all impatience to be home again! *(They exit, MILES in cheerful spirits, PRINCE looking puzzled, as curtains close.)*

SCENE 6

SETTING. *Village jail. Bare stage, with barred window on one wall.*

AT RISE. TWO PRISONERS, *in chains, are onstage. JAILER shoves MILES and PRINCE, in chains, onstage. They struggle and protest.*

MILES. But I tell you I *am* Miles Hendon! My brother, Sir Hugh, has stolen my bride and my estate!

JAILER. Be silent! Impostor! Sir Hugh will see that you pay well for claiming to be his dead brother and for assaulting him in his own house! *(Exits)*

MILES. *(Sitting, with head in hands)* Oh, my dear Edith … now wife to my brother Hugh, against her will, and my poor father … dead!

1ST PRISONER. At least you have your life, sir. I am sentenced to be hanged for killing a deer in the King's park.

2ND PRISONER. And I must hang for stealing a yard of cloth to dress my children.

PRINCE. *(Moved; to PRISONERS)* When I mount my throne, you shall all be free. And the laws that have dishonored you shall be swept from the books. *(Turning away)* Kings should go to school to learn their own laws and be merciful.

1ST PRISONER. What does the lad mean? I have heard that the King is mad, but merciful.

2ND PRISONER. He is to be crowned at Westminster[4] tomorrow.

PRINCE. *(Violently)* King? What King, good sir?

1ST PRISONER. Why, we have only one, his most sacred majesty, King Edward the Sixth.

2ND PRISONER. And whether he be mad or not, his praises are on all men's lips. He has saved many innocent lives, and now he means to destroy the cruelest laws that oppress the people.

PRINCE. *(Turning away, shaking his head)* How can this be? Surely it is not that little beggar boy! *(SIR HUGH enters with JAILER.)*

SIR HUGH. Seize the impostor!

MILES. *(As JAILER pulls him to his feet)* Hugh, this has gone far enough!

SIR HUGH. You will sit in the public stocks for two hours, and the boy would join you if he were not so young. See to it, jailer, and after two hours, you may release them. Meanwhile, I ride to London for the coronation! *(SIR HUGH exits and MILES is hustled out by JAILER.)*

---

4. **Westminster** Westminster Abbey, church in London that hosts coronations and other important ceremonies.

PRINCE. Coronation! What does he mean? There can be no coronation without me! *(Curtain falls.)*

SCENE 7

TIME. *Coronation Day.*

SETTING. *Outside gates of Westminster Abbey, played before curtain. Painted screen or flat at rear represents Abbey. Throne is center. Bench is near it.*

AT RISE. LORDS *and* LADIES *crowd Abbey. Outside gates,* GUARDS *drive back cheering* VILLAGERS, *among them* MILES.

MILES. *(Distraught)* I've lost him! Poor little chap! He has been swallowed up in the crowd! *(Fanfare of trumpets is heard, then silence.* HERTFORD, ST. JOHN, LORDS *and* LADIES *enter slowly, in a procession followed by* PAGES, *one of whom carries crown on small cushion.* TOM *follows procession, looking about nervously. Suddenly,* PRINCE, *in rags, steps out from crowd, his hand raised.)*

PRINCE. I forbid you to set the crown of England upon that head. I am the King!

HERTFORD. Seize the little vagabond!

TOM. I forbid it! He *is* the King! *(Kneels before* PRINCE*)* Oh, my lord the King, let poor Tom Canty be the first to say, "Put on your crown and enter into your own right again." *(*HERTFORD *and several* LORDS *look closely at both boys.)*

HERTFORD. This is strange indeed. *(To* TOM*)* By your favor, sir, I wish to ask certain questions of this lad.

PRINCE. I will answer truly whatever you may ask, my lord.

HERTFORD. But if you have been well trained, you may answer my questions as well as our lord the King. I need a definite proof. *(Thinks a moment)* Ah! Where lies the Great Seal of England? It has been missing for weeks, and only the true Prince of Wales can say where it lies.

TOM. Wait! Was the seal round and thick, with letters engraved on it? *(*HERTFORD *nods.)* I know where it is, but it was not I who put it there. The rightful King shall tell you. *(To* PRINCE*)* Think, my King, it was the very last thing you did that day before you rushed out of the palace wearing my rags.

PRINCE. *(Pausing)* I recall how we exchanged clothes, but have no recollection of hiding the Great Seal.

TOM. *(Eagerly)* Remember when you saw the bruise on my hand, you ran to the door, but first you hid this thing you call the Seal.

PRINCE. *(Suddenly)* Ah! I remember! *(To* ST. JOHN*)* Go, my good St. John, and you will find the Great Seal in the armor that hangs on the wall in my chamber. *(ST. JOHN hesitates, but at a nod from* TOM*, hurries off.)*

TOM. *(Pleased)* Right, my King! Now the scepter of England is yours again. *(ST. JOHN returns in a moment with Great Seal.)*

ALL. *(Shouting)* Long live Edward, King of England! *(TOM takes off his cape and throws it over* PRINCE'S *rags. Trumpet fanfare is heard.* ST. JOHN *takes crown and places it on* PRINCE. *All kneel.)*

HERTFORD. Let the small impostor be flung into the Tower![5]

PRINCE. *(Firmly)* I will not have it so. But for him, I would not have my crown. *(To* TOM*)* My poor boy, how was it that you could remember where I hid the Seal, when I could not?

TOM. *(Embarrassed)* I did not know what it was, my King, and I used it to … to crack nuts. *(All laugh, and* TOM *steps back.* MILES *steps forward, staring in amazement.)*

MILES. Is he really the King? Is he indeed the sovereign of England, and not the poor and friendless Tom o' Bedlam[6] I thought he was? *(He sinks down on bench.)* I wish I had a bag to hide my head in!

1ST GUARD. *(Rushing up to him)* Stand up, you mannerless clown! How dare you sit in the presence of the King!

PRINCE. Do not touch him! He is my trusty servant, Miles Hendon, who saved me from shame and possible death. For his service, he owns the right to sit in my presence.

MILES. *(Bowing, then kneeling)* Your Majesty!

---

5. **Tower** the Tower of London, site of a prison and place of execution.
6. **Bedlam** English asylum for the mentally ill.

PRINCE. Rise, Sir Miles. I command that Sir Hugh Hendon, who sits within this hall, be seized and put under lock and key until I have need of him. *(Beckons to* TOM*)* From what I have heard, Tom Canty, you have governed the realm with royal gentleness and mercy in my absence. Henceforth, you shall hold the honorable title of King's Ward! *(*TOM *kneels and kisses* PRINCE'S *hand.)* And because I have suffered with the poorest of my subjects and felt the cruel force of unjust laws, I pledge myself to a reign of mercy for all! *(All bow low, then rise.)*

ALL. *(Shouting)* Long live the King! Long live Edward, King of England! *(Curtain)*

THE END

from

The Prince and the Pauper

Mark Twain

Chapter I. The birth of the Prince and the Pauper.

In the ancient city of London, on a certain autumn day in the second quarter of the sixteenth century, a boy was born to a poor family of the name of Canty, who did not want him. On the same day another English child was born to a rich family of the name of Tudor, who did want him. All England wanted him too. England had so longed for him, and hoped for him, and prayed God for him, that, now that he was really come, the people went nearly mad for joy. Mere acquaintances hugged and kissed each other and cried. Everybody took a holiday, and high and low, rich and poor, feasted and danced and sang, and got very mellow;[1] and they kept this up for days and nights together. By day, London was a sight to see, with gay banners waving from every balcony and housetop, and splendid pageants marching along. By night, it was again a sight to see, with its great bonfires at every corner, and its troops of revellers making merry around them. There was no talk in all England but of the new baby, Edward Tudor, Prince of Wales, who lay lapped[2] in silks and satins, unconscious of all this fuss, and not knowing that great lords and ladies were tending him and watching over him—and not caring, either. But there was no talk about the other baby, Tom Canty, lapped in his poor rags, except among the family of paupers whom he had just come to trouble with his presence.

---

1. **mellow** joyful or lighthearted.
2. **lapped** wrapped up or enfolded.

Chapter III. Tom's meeting with the Prince.

Tom got up hungry, and sauntered hungry away, but with his thoughts busy with the shadowy splendours of his night's dreams. He wandered here and there in the city, hardly noticing where he was going, or what was happening around him. People jostled him, and some gave him rough speech; but it was all lost on the musing boy. By-and-by he found himself at Temple Bar,[3] the farthest from home he had ever travelled in that direction. He stopped and considered a moment, then fell into his imaginings again, and passed on outside the walls of London. The Strand[4] had ceased to be a country-road then, and regarded itself as a street, but by a strained construction; for, though there was a tolerably compact row of houses on one side of it, there were only some scattered great buildings on the other, these being palaces of rich nobles, with ample and beautiful grounds stretching to the river—grounds that are now closely packed with grim acres of brick and stone.

Tom discovered Charing Village presently, and rested himself at the beautiful cross built there by a bereaved king of earlier days; then idled down a quiet, lovely road, past the great cardinal's stately palace, toward a far more mighty and majestic palace beyond—Westminster. Tom stared in glad wonder at the vast pile of masonry, the wide-spreading wings, the frowning bastions and turrets,[5] the huge stone gateway, with its gilded bars and its magnificent array of colossal granite lions, and other the signs and symbols of English royalty. Was the desire of his soul to be satisfied at last? Here, indeed, was a king's palace. Might he not hope to see a prince now—a prince of flesh and blood, if Heaven were willing?

At each side of the gilded[6] gate stood a living statue—that is to say, an erect and stately and motionless man-at-arms, clad from head to heel in shining steel armour. At a respectful distance were many country folk, and people from the city,

◀ **sauntered**
(sôn´ tərd) *v.*
walked in a slow, relaxed manner

---

3. **Temple Bar** historic gate to the city of London.
4. **The Strand** street in London.
5. **bastions and turrets** projections and towers from the top or sides of a building.
6. **gilded** covered in gold.

waiting for any chance glimpse of royalty that might offer. Splendid carriages, with splendid people in them and splendid servants outside, were arriving and departing by several other noble gateways that pierced the royal enclosure.

Poor little Tom, in his rags, approached, and was moving slowly and timidly past the sentinels, with a beating heart and a rising hope, when all at once he caught sight through the golden bars of a spectacle that almost made him shout for joy. Within was a comely boy, tanned and brown with sturdy outdoor sports and exercises, whose clothing was all of lovely silks and satins, shining with jewels; at his hip a little jewelled sword and dagger; dainty buskins on his feet, with red heels; and on his head a jaunty crimson cap, with drooping plumes fastened with a great sparkling gem. Several gorgeous gentlemen stood near—his servants, without a doubt. Oh! he was a prince—a prince, a living prince, a real prince—without the shadow of a question; and the prayer of the pauper-boy's heart was answered at last.

Tom's breath came quick and short with excitement, and his eyes grew big with wonder and delight. Everything gave way in his mind instantly to one desire: that was to get close to the prince, and have a good, devouring look at him. Before he knew what he was about, he had his face against the gate-bars. The next instant one of the soldiers snatched him rudely away, and sent him spinning among the gaping crowd of country gawks and London idlers. The soldier said,—

"Mind thy manners, thou young beggar!"

The crowd jeered and laughed; but the young prince sprang to the gate with his face flushed, and his eyes flashing with indignation, and cried out,—

"How dar'st thou use a poor lad like that? How dar'st thou use the King my father's meanest subject so? Open the gates, and let him in!"

You should have seen that fickle crowd snatch off their hats then. You should have heard them cheer, and shout, "Long live the Prince of Wales!"

The soldiers presented arms with their halberds,[7] opened the gates, and presented again as the little Prince of Poverty passed in, in his fluttering rags, to join hands with the Prince of Limitless Plenty.

Edward Tudor said—

"Thou lookest tired and hungry: thou'st been treated ill. Come with me."

Half a dozen attendants sprang forward to—I don't know what; interfere, no doubt. But they were waved aside with a right royal gesture, and they stopped stock still where they were, like so many statues. Edward took Tom to a rich apartment in the palace, which he called his cabinet. By his command a repast was brought such as Tom had never encountered before except in books. The prince, with princely delicacy and breeding, sent away the servants, so that his humble guest might not be embarrassed by their critical presence; then he sat near by, and asked questions while Tom ate.

"What is thy name, lad?"

"Tom Canty, an' it please thee, sir."

---

7. **halberds** (hal′ bərds) weapons used in the fifteenth and sixteenth centuries.

ABOUT THE AUTHOR

Mark Twain (1835–1910)

Mark Twain, who was born Samuel Langhorne Clemens, grew up along the Mississippi River in Hannibal, Missouri. He became a riverboat pilot at the age of twenty-three. Later, when he became an author, he adopted the pen name Mark Twain, a term used by riverboat pilots that means "two fathoms (twelve feet) deep." In addition to piloting riverboats and writing novels, Twain also worked as a journalist in the American West and travelled the world giving lectures. During his lifetime, he gained fame as both a writer and a very entertaining stage presence. Today, Twain's most popular novel is *Tom Sawyer*, but the book that most critics consider to be his masterpiece is *The Adventures of Huckleberry Finn*.

Close Reading Activities

READ

Comprehension

Reread to answer these questions.

1. In the play, who changes places?

2. What happens at the end of the play?

3. In the novel, how does Tom meet the Prince?

4. In the novel, what does the Prince do for Tom?

Language Study

Selection Vocabulary Define each boldfaced word and use it in a sentence. Then, identify each word's connotation—the feelings it suggests—as either negative, neutral, or positive.

- I am the lowest of your subjects, being born a **pauper**, and it is by a great mistake that I am here.
- Ah, your **affliction** hangs heavily upon you.
- Tom got up hungry, and **sauntered** hungry away, but with his thoughts busy with the shadowy splendours of his night's dreams.

Diction and Style Read this sentence from the novel excerpt and answer the questions that follow.

> The soldiers presented arms ... as the little Prince of Poverty passed in, in his fluttering rags, to join hands with the Prince of Limitless Plenty.

1. (a) What words describe Tom's clothing? **(b)** What image do these words convey?

Research: Clarify Details Research an unfamiliar detail in these works and explain how your research sheds light on the work.

Summarize Write an objective summary of *The Prince and the Pauper*. Include only the main ideas and details. Do not include your opinions.

2. (a) What proper nouns describe the two boys? **(b)** What important idea about the boys do these words suggest?

Conventions Identify the appositive phrase in the lines from the play that appear below. **(a)** What noun does the phrase identify or explain? **(b)** Why does the Prince include this information?

> PRINCE. Take me to the palace at once, and your son will be returned to you. The King, my father, will make you rich beyond your wildest dreams.

Academic Vocabulary

The following words appear in blue in the questions on the facing page.

respond   technique   similar

Copy the words in your notebook. Which word is a literary term? Which is an action? Which can be used to link words and describe nouns?

Literary Analysis

Reread the identified passages. The first is from the play; the second is from the novel excerpt. Then, respond to the questions that follow:

> **Focus Passage 1** *(pp. 559–560)*
>
> **ST. JOHN.** Does it not seem strange ... *crack nuts with Great Seal and eat them, as curtain falls).*

> **Focus Passage 2** *(p. 574)*
>
> "Mind thy manners ... "Long live the Prince of Wales!"

Key Ideas and Details

1. What troubles St. John?

2. Does Tom seem to feel at home in the palace? What details support your answer?

Craft and Structure

3. (a) What does Hertford say to reassure St. John? **(b) Interpret:** How do Hertford's remarks add humor to the play?

4. (a) At the end of the scene, what action of Tom's do the stage directions describe? **(b) Interpret:** What is funny about Tom's action?

Integration of Knowledge and Ideas

5. Draw Conclusions: Which man has greater insight, Hertford or St. John? Support your answer.

6. Synthesize: What does this passage suggest about the life of a real prince?

Key Ideas and Details

1. (a) Who is the young beggar? **(b)** What does he want to do?

Craft and Structure

2. (a) Compare and Contrast: How does the crowd **respond** both before and after the prince speaks? **(b) Interpret:** What does this response tell you about the crowd?

3. (a) Infer: In this passage, who does the narrator address as "you"? **(b) Analyze:** What effect does Twain achieve by using this **technique**?

Integration of Knowledge and Ideas

4. Draw Conclusions: What does this passage suggest about human nature? **(b) Deduce:** Does Twain want his audience to laugh, to think, or both? Explain.

Theme

A **theme** is a central insight about life. As you reread the play, list details that reveal one or more themes.

1. (a) What does Miles do for the Prince? **(b)** In the end, how is Miles rewarded?

2. (a) What does the constable do that he should not do? **(b)** What is the outcome for the constable and for the Prince?

3. (a) How does Tom behave toward the Prince throughout the play? **(b)** What is the outcome for Tom?

4. What theme do these **similar** events show?

DISCUSS

From Text to Topic **Partner Discussion**

Discuss the following passage with a partner. Contribute your own ideas, and support them with examples from the text. Take notes during your discussion.

> **PRINCE.** *(Violently)* King? What King, good sir?
>
> **1ST PRISONER.** Why, we only have one, his most sacred majesty, King Edward the Sixth.
>
> **2ND PRISONER.** And whether he be mad or not, his praises are on all men's lips. He has saved many innocent lives, and now he means to destroy the cruelest laws that oppress the people.
>
> **PRINCE.** *(Turning away, shaking his head)* How can this be? Surely it is not that little beggar boy! (p. 568)

QUESTIONS FOR DISCUSSION

1. What does this passage suggest about the real qualifications of a king?

2. What does the Prince's surprise imply about differences between Tom and himself?

WRITE

Writing to Sources **Informative Text**

> **Assignment**
>
> Write a **comparison-and-contrast essay** in which you analyze the two main characters in *The Prince and the Pauper*.

Prewriting and Planning Reread both the play and the novel excerpt, looking for details that describe each boy's personality, behavior, and motivations. Record your notes in a Venn diagram.

Drafting Select a strategy for developing your ideas. Most comparison-and-contrast writing follows either a block or point-by-point organization (see p. 243 for information on these organizational patterns).

Cite specific examples from the texts to support your points.

Revising Reread your essay, making sure you clearly explain similarities and differences. Add or revise transitional words or phrases, such as those below, to connect your ideas.

in the same way	*also*	*similarly*	*likewise*
in contrast	*on the contrary*	*on the other hand*	*nevertheless*

Editing and Proofreading Make sure your transitional words and phrases show comparisons and contrasts.

CONVENTIONS

Check your use of pronouns to make sure each pronoun has a clear antecedent. For example, if you refer to a character as *him*, make sure the identity of that character is clear.

RESEARCH

Research **Investigate the Topic**

The Palace of Westminster In *The Prince and the Pauper*, Mark Twain presents ideas about identity, partly by describing royalty and royal settings. One of the most famous royal settings in England is the Palace of Westminster.

> ### Assignment
>
> Conduct research to learn about the Palace of Westminster and its long history. Find out about the structure itself, as well as the associations this important site has had with British royalty and other key figures in British history. Consult credible print and Internet sources. Take clear notes so that you can easily access the information later. Share your findings in an **illustrated timeline**. In addition, write a paragraph in which you tell why you think Mark Twain chose the Palace of Westminster as a primary setting for his novel.

PREPARATION FOR ESSAY

You may use the knowledge you gain during this research assignment to support your claims in an essay you will write at the end of this section.

Gather Sources Locate authoritative print and electronic sources. Look for expert authors and up-to-date facts. Follow links to new information, but remember to evaluate new sites for credibility.

Take Notes Take notes on each of your sources, either electronically or on note cards. Use an organized note-taking strategy.

- Clearly identify all the sources you consult. Note that many Web sites offer information on how to correctly cite them.
- Copy and paste only citation information, URLs, and exact words that you plan to quote.
- Paraphrase and summarize all other information on separate note cards or in separate files that clearly state each source.

Synthesize Multiple Sources Assemble data from your sources, including drawings, photographs, and diagrams. Use your notes and visuals to create your illustrated timeline. Create a Works Cited list as described in the Research Workshop in the Introductory Unit of this textbook.

Organize and Present Ideas Present your outline and paragraph to a small group of classmates. Be prepared to answer questions from your audience.

Stage Fright

MARK TWAIN

compulsion ▶
(kəm pul′ shən) *n.*
driving force

My heart goes out in sympathy to anyone who is making his first appearance before an audience of human beings. By a direct process of memory I go back forty years, less one month—for I'm older than I look. I recall the occasion of my first appearance. San Francisco knew me then only as a reporter, and I was to make my bow to San Francisco as a lecturer. I knew that nothing short of **compulsion** would get me to the theater. So I bound myself by a hard-and-fast contract so that I could not escape. I got to the theater forty-five minutes before the hour set for the lecture. My knees were shaking so that I didn't know whether I could stand up. If there is an awful, horrible malady[1] in the world, it is stage fright—and seasickness. They are a pair. I had stage fright then for the first and last time. I was only seasick once, too. It was on a little ship on which there were two hundred other passengers. I—was—sick. I was so sick that there wasn't any left for those other two hundred passengers.

---

1. malady (mal′ ə dē) *n.* illness.

It was dark and lonely behind the scenes in that theater, and I peeked through the little peek holes they have in theater curtains and looked into the big auditorium. That was dark and empty, too. By and by it lighted up, and the audience began to arrive.

I had got a number of friends of mine, stalwart[2] men, to sprinkle themselves through the audience armed with big clubs. Every time I said anything they could possibly guess I intended to be funny, they were to pound those clubs on the floor. Then there was a kind lady in a box up there, also a good friend of mine, the wife of the governor. She was to watch me intently, and whenever I glanced toward her she was going to deliver a gubernatorial laugh that would lead the whole audience into applause.

At last I began. I had the manuscript tucked under a United States flag in front of me where I could get at it in case of need. But I managed to get started without it. I walked up and down—I was young in those days and needed the exercise—and talked and talked.

Right in the middle of the speech I had placed a gem. I had put in a moving, pathetic part which was to get at the hearts and souls of my hearers. When I delivered it, they did just what I hoped and expected. They sat silent and **awed**. I had touched them. Then I happened to glance up at the box where the governor's wife was—you know what happened.

◀ **awed**
(ôd) *adj.* filled with feelings of fear and wonder

Well, after the first **agonizing** five minutes, my stage fright left me, never to return. I know if I was going to be hanged I could get up and make a good showing, and I intend to. But I shall never forget my feelings before the agony left me, and I got up here to thank you for her for helping my daughter, by your kindness, to live through her first appearance. And I want to thank you for your appreciation of her singing, which is, by the way, hereditary.

◀ **agonizing**
(ag´ ə nīz´in) *adj.* making great efforts or struggling; being in great pain

---

2. **stalwart** (stôl´ wərt) *adj.* strong; sturdy.

Close Reading Activities

READ

Comprehension

Reread to answer the following questions.

1. Where is Twain when he experiences stage fright?

2. What plan does Twain make before he speaks?

3. What happens after the first five minutes?

Research: Clarify Details Research at least one unfamiliar detail in this speech and explain how your research sheds light on the work.

Summarize Write an objective summary of the speech. Remember that an objective summary does not include opinions or evaluations.

Language Study

Selection Vocabulary Define each boldfaced word, then list related words in different parts of speech. Use a dictionary if you need help.

• I knew that nothing short of **compulsion** would get me to the theater.

• They sat silent and **awed**.

• Well, after the first **agonizing** five minutes, my stage fright left me, never to return.

Literary Analysis

Reread the passage and answer the questions:

> **Focus Passage** *(p. 580)*
> My heart goes out in sympathy ... those other two hundred passengers.

Key Ideas and Details

1. For whom does Twain feel sympathy? Why?

Craft and Structure

2. **(a) Connect:** To what does Twain compare stage fright? **(b) Interpret:** What idea does he suggest by making this comparison?

3. **(a)** How does Twain use *hyperbole*, or exaggeration, to describe his experience on the "little ship"? **(b) Draw Conclusions:** What is the effect of this hyperbole?

Integration of Knowledge and Ideas

4. What is Twain's **opinion** of stage fright? Support your answer with details from the passage.

Humor

Humor is writing that is intended to make readers laugh. Reread the speech, and take notes on how Twain uses humor.

1. **(a)** What does Twain say about his age? **(b)** Why is his remark funny?

2. **(a)** What does the governor's wife do? **(b)** Why is her action funny?

3. **(a)** In the last line of the speech, what does Twain say about his daughter's talent? **(b)** Why is this funny?

DISCUSS • RESEARCH • WRITE

From Text to Topic **Panel Discussion**

Discuss the following passage with a small group of classmates. Take notes during the discussion. Contribute your own ideas, and support them with examples from the text.

> At last I began. I had the manuscript tucked under a United States flag in front of me where I could get at it in case of need. But I managed to get started without it.

Research **Investigate the Topic**

Stage Fright In his speech, Twain says he feels sympathy for anyone going on stage for the first time.

Assignment

Conduct research to learn more about stage fright. Use a library database to find health studies about the human body's reaction to stage fright. Take clear notes and carefully identify your sources so that you can easily access the information later. Share your findings in a **brief research report**. Tell whether or not Twain describes a **common** reaction to stage fright in his speech.

Writing to Sources **Informative Text**

Mark Twain relates his own experience with stage fright. Develop a how-to essay to help people deal with stage fright.

Assignment

Write a **how-to essay** in which you include advice that Twain either follows himself or implies in his speech. Follow these steps:

- Introduce the topic, and organize your ideas by using bullets or numbers.
- Develop the topic with information from your research, from personal experience, and from Twain's speech.
- Use transitions to show the relationships among ideas.
- Establish and maintain a formal style.

QUESTIONS FOR DISCUSSION

1. What is Twain worried about?

2. For what **purpose** does he put the manuscript under a U.S. flag? Why is that funny?

PREPARATION FOR ESSAY

You may use the results of this research to support your ideas in the essay you will write at the end of this section.

ACADEMIC VOCABULARY

Academic terms appear in blue on these pages. If these words are not familiar to you, use a dictionary to find their definitions. Then, use them as you speak and write about the text.

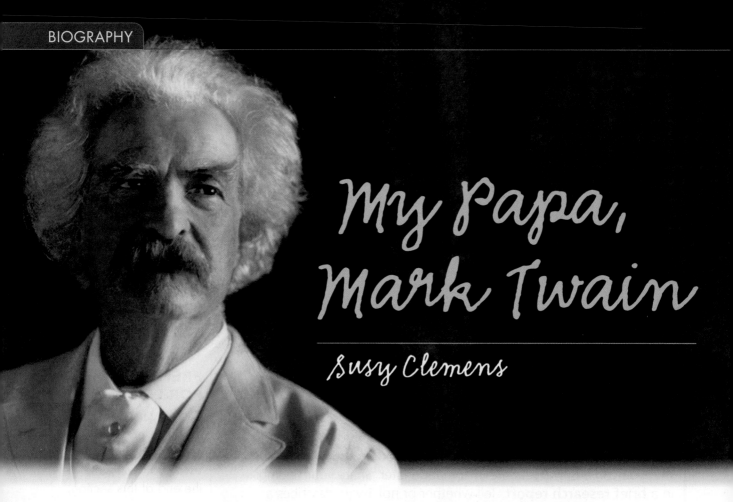

My Papa, Mark Twain

Susy Clemens

We are a very happy family.

We consist of Papa, Mamma, Jean, Clara and me. It is papa I am writing about, and I shall have no trouble in not knowing what to say about him, as he is a *very* **striking** character.

striking ▶
(strĭ´kĭŋ) *adj.* very noticeable or impressive; unusual

   Papa's appearance has been described many times, but very incorrectly. He has beautiful gray hair, not any too thick or any too long, but just right; a Roman nose which greatly improves the beauty of his features; kind blue eyes and a small mustache. He has a wonderfully shaped head and profile. He has a very good figure—in short, he is an extrodinarily fine looking man. All his features are perfect except that he hasn't extrodinary teeth. His complexion is very fair, and he doesn't ware a beard. He is a very good man and a very funny one. He has got a temper, but we all of us have in this family. He is the loveliest man I ever saw or ever hope to see—and oh, so absentminded.

Papa's favorite game is billiards, and when he is tired and wishes to rest himself he stays up all night and plays billiards, it seems to rest his head. He smokes a great deal almost **incessantly**. He has the mind of an author exactly, some of the simplest things he can't understand. Our burglar alarm is often out of order, and papa had been obliged to take the mahogany room off from the alarm altogether for a time, because the burglar alarm had been in the habit of ringing even when the mahogany-room window was closed. At length he thought that perhaps the burglar alarm might be in order, and he decided to try and see; accordingly he put it on and then went down and opened the window; **consequently** the alarm bell rang, it would even if the alarm had been in order. Papa went despairingly upstairs and said to mamma, "Livy the mahogany room won't go on. I have just opened the window to see."

"Why, Youth," mamma replied. "If you've opened the window, why of course the alarm will ring!"

"That's what I've opened it for, why I just went down to see if it would ring!"

Mamma tried to explain to papa that when he wanted to go and see whether the alarm would ring while the window was closed he *mustn't* go and open the window—but in vain, papa couldn't understand, and got very impatient with mamma for trying to make him believe an impossible thing true.

Papa has a peculiar gait we like, it seems just to suit him, but most people do not; he always walks up and down the room while thinking and between each coarse at meals.

Papa is very fond of animals particularly of cats, we had a dear little gray kitten once that he named "Lazy" (papa always wears gray to match his hair and eyes) and he would carry him around on his shoulder, it was a mighty pretty sight! the gray cat sound asleep against papa's gray coat and hair. The names that he has give our different cats are really remarkably funny, they are named Stray Kit, Abner, Motley, Fraeulein, Lazy, Buffalo Bill, Soapy Sall, Cleveland, Sour Mash, and Pestilence and Famine.

Papa uses very strong language, but I have an idea not nearly so strong as when he first married mamma. A lady

◀ **incessantly**
(in ses´ ənt lē)
adv. constantly;
continually

◀ **consequently**
(kän´ si kwent´ lē)
adv. as a result

acquaintance of his is rather apt to interrupt what one is saying, and papa told mamma he thought he should say to the lady's husband "I am glad your wife wasn't present when the Deity said Let there be light."

Papa said the other day, "I am a mugwump[1] and a mugwump is pure from the marrow out." (Papa knows that I am writing this biography of him, and he said this for it.) He

He could listen to himself talk for hours ...

doesn't like to go to church at all, why I never understood, until just now, he told us the other day that he couldn't bear to hear anyone talk but himself, but that he could listen to himself talk for hours without getting tired, of course he said this in joke, but I've no dought it was founded on truth.

One of papa's latest books is "The Prince and the Pauper" and it is unquestionably the best book he has ever written, some people want him to keep to his old style, some gentleman wrote him, "I enjoyed Huckleberry Finn immensely and am glad to see that you have returned to your old style." That enoyed me, that enoyed me greatly, because it trobles me to have so few people know papa, I mean realy know him, they think of Mark Twain as a humorist joking at everything; "And with a mop of reddish brown hair which sorely needs the barbar brush, a roman nose, short stubby mustache, a sad care-worn face, with maney crows' feet" etc. That is the way people picture papa, I have wanted papa to write a book that would reveal something of his kind sympathetic nature, and "The Prince and the Pauper" partly does it. The book is full of lovely charming ideas, and oh the language! It is perfect. I think that one of the most touching scenes in it is where the pauper is riding on horseback with his nobles in the "recognition procession" and he sees his mother oh and then what followed! How she runs to his side, when she sees him throw up his hand palm outward, and is rudely pushed off by one of the King's officers, and then how the little pauper's conscience troubles him when he remembers the shameful words that were falling from his lips when she was turned from his side "I know you not woman" and how his

---

1. **mugwump** (mug ́ wump ́) *n.* Republican who refused to support the party candidates in the 1884 election.

grandeurs were stricken valueless and his pride consumed to ashes. It is a wonderfully beautiful and touching little scene, and papa has described it so wonderfully. I never saw a man with so much variety of feeling as papa has; now the "Prince and the Pauper" is full of touching places, but there is always a streak of humor in them somewhere. Papa very seldom writes a passage without some humor in it somewhere and I don't think he ever will.

Clara and I are sure that papa played the trick on Grandma about the whipping that is related in "The Adventures of Tom Sawyer": "Hand me that switch." The switch hovered in the air, the peril was desperate—"My, look behind you Aunt!" The old lady whirled around and snatched her skirts out of danger. The lad fled on the instant, scrambling up the high board fence and disappeared over it.

We know papa played "Hookey" all the time. And how readily would papa pretend to be dying so as not to have to go to school! Grandma wouldn't make papa go to school, so she let him go into a printing office to learn the trade. He did so, and gradually picked up enough education to enable him to do about as well as those who were more studious in early life.

ABOUT THE AUTHOR

Susy Clemens (1872–1896)

Olivia Susan Clemens, called Susy, was the oldest daughter of Mark Twain and his wife Olivia. Susy was born in Elmira, New York, and grew up in her family's luxurious home in Hartford, Connecticut. There, her parents entertained famous people of the time—and Susy had the opportunity to meet them. Her upbringing and education helped bring out her talents in dramatics, music, and writing.
Her father was so pleased with portions of what Susy wrote about him that he used them in his own autobiography. It is said that Susy was her father's favorite daughter. After she died at age twenty-four, Twain's writing turned darker and more serious.

Close Reading Activities

READ

Comprehension

Reread to answer the following questions.

1. What conclusion does Clemens draw about her father's looks?

2. What is Clemens's opinion of *The Prince and the Pauper?*

3. What is her opinion of her father's education?

Research: Clarify Details Choose at least one unfamiliar detail in the selection, and research it. Explain how your research sheds light on the biography.

Summarize Write an objective summary of the biography. Include only the most important ideas and details.

Language Study

Selection Vocabulary Use each boldfaced word in a sentence that shows it you know the word's meaning.

• … I shall have no trouble in not knowing what to say about him, as he is a very **striking** character.

• He smokes a great deal almost **incessantly**.

• Accordingly he put it on and then went down and opened the window; **consequently** the alarm bell rang.

Literary Analysis

Reread the passage and answer the questions:

> **Focus Passage** *(pp. 585–586)*
> Papa uses … it was founded on truth.

Key Ideas and Details

1. What does Clemens say about her father's use of strong language?

2. Does Twain support Clemens in her writing of his biography? Explain.

Craft and Structure

3. **(a)** What remark did Twain make to his wife? **(b)** Why does Clemens include this anecdote in her biography?

4. **(a)** What does Twain say about talking? **(b)** How are his words both hyperbole —or exaggeration— and fact?

Integration of Knowledge and Ideas

5. What key ideas about Mark Twain does this passage reveal?

Point of View

Point of view is the perspective from which a story is told. Reread the biography, and take notes on the author's perspective.

1. **Identify** two details of Clemens's life that show her perspective.

2. How might the author's point of view be different if someone outside Twain's family had written this biography?

3. How **credible** is Susy Clemens as a biographer? Explain.

DISCUSS • RESEARCH • WRITE

From Text to Topic **Partner Discussion**

Discuss the following passage with a partner. Take notes during the discussion. Contribute your own ideas, and support them with examples from the text.

> I never saw a man with so much variety of feeling as papa has; now "The Prince and the Pauper" is full of touching places, but there is always a streak of humor in them somewhere. Papa very seldom writes a passage without some humor in it somewhere and I don't think he ever will.

Research **Investigate the Topic**

Twain According to Others Research to learn what other biographers have written about Mark Twain.

Assignment

Use library databases and other resources to find a reliable biography of Mark Twain. Read at least one chapter, and compare the biographer's portrayal of Twain with Susy Clemens's portrayal. Take clear notes and carefully identify your source so that you can easily access the information later. Share your findings in an **informal speech** for the class.

Writing to Sources **Argument**

In this selection, Mark Twain's biographer is his own daughter.

Assignment

Write an **argument** in which you make a claim stating whether or not a person's family member can make a good biographer for that person. Follow these steps:

- Introduce your claim and organize your reasons clearly.
- Use evidence from "My Papa, Mark Twain" to support your claim.
- Consider and address opposing views.
- Establish and maintain a formal style.
- Provide an effective conclusion. For example, you might end with your most **convincing** point.

QUESTIONS FOR DISCUSSION

1. How is this passage typical of the entire biography?
2. How is Susy Clemens like a traditional biographer? How is she different?

PREPARATION FOR ESSAY

You may use the results of this research project to support your ideas in the essay you will write at the end of this section.

ACADEMIC VOCABULARY

Academic terms appear in blue on these pages. If these words are not familiar to you, use a dictionary to find their definitions. Then, use them as you speak and write about the text.

Mark Twain's First "Vacation"

**from an interview in the *New York World*,
7 September 1902**

"Do you know what it means to be a boy on the banks of the Mississippi, to see the steamboats go up and down the river, and never to have had a ride on one? Can you form any conception of what that really means? I think not.

"Well, I was seven years old and my dream by night and my longing by day had never been realized. But I guess it came to pass. That was my first vacation." A pause.

"One day when the big packet[1] that used to stop at Hannibal rung up to the mooring at my native town, a small chunk of a lad might have been seen kiting[2] on to the deck and in a jiffy disappearing from view beneath a yawl[3] that was placed bottom up. I was the small chunk of a lad.

"They called it a life-boat," said Mr. Clemens, "but it was one of that kind of life-boats that wouldn't save anybody. Well, the packet started along all right, and it gave me great thrills of joy to be on a real sure-enough steamboat. But just then it commenced to rain. Now, when it rains in the Mississippi country it rains. After the packet had started I had crawled from beneath it and was enjoying the motion of the swift-moving craft. But the rain drove me to cover and that was beneath the yawl. No. It was not a life boat, for the manner in which that rain came pouring down upon me from the bottom of that yawl made me wonder if I was

---

1. **packet** boat that travels up and down a river or coast carrying people or goods.
2. **kiting** climbing up on.
3. **yawl** small boat, or dinghy.

ever to return home again. To add to the fun the red-hot cinders from the big stacks[4] came drifting down and stung my legs and feet with a remorseless **vigor**, and if it hadn't been a steamboat that I was on I would have wanted to be safe at home in time for supper. Well, it kept on raining and storming generally until toward evening, when, seventeen miles below Hannibal,[5] I was discovered by one of the crew." A very **deliberate** pause.

"They put me ashore at Louisiana." Another pause.

"I was sent home by some friends of my father's. My father met me on my return." A twinkle in the steel-blue eyes. "I remember that quite **distinctly**."

Then as an afterthought: "My mother had generally attended to that part of the duties of the household, but on that occasion my father assumed the entire responsibility." Reminiscently: "That was my first vacation and its ending"—he bit his cigar, "and I remember both."

◄ **vigor**
(vig´ ər) *n.* active force or strength

◄ **deliberate**
(di lib´ ər it) *adj.* intended or carefully planned

◄ **distinctly**
(di stiŋkt´ lē) *adv.* clearly or plainly

---

4. **stacks** smokestacks.
5. **Hannibal** town in Missouri on the Mississippi River, where Mark Twain grew up.

Close Reading Activities

READ

Comprehension

Reread to answer the following questions.

1. What did Twain do when he was seven?
2. Where did he spend his time on the packet?
3. How did his adventure end?

Research: Clarify Details Choose at least one unfamiliar detail in the selection, and briefly research it. Explain how your research sheds light on the interview.

Summarize Write an objective summary of the interview. Remember to leave out your opinions and evaluations.

Language Study

Selection Vocabulary Write a synonym for each boldfaced word. Then write a sentence using each boldfaced word.

- To add to the fun the red-hot cinders from the big stacks came drifting down and stung my legs and feet with a remorseless **vigor** …
- A very **deliberate** pause.
- I remember that quite **distinctly**.

Literary Analysis

Reread the passage and answer the questions:

> **Focus Passage** (p. 591)
>
> "I was sent home by some friends of my father's … and I remember both."

Key Ideas and Details

1. Who met Twain when he got home?
2. What two things does Twain remember clearly about his adventure?

Craft and Structure

3. **(a)** Who usually performed the "duties" when Twain had done something wrong? **(b) Infer:** What does Twain mean by "duties"? **(c) Speculate:** Why does Twain use this *euphemism*, or vague and mild word, instead of directly stating what the "duties" were?

Integration of Knowledge and Ideas

4. **Analyze:** What makes this passage funny?

Plot

Plot is the sequence of events in a narrative. Reread the interview, and take notes on how Twain develops a plot.

1. **(a)** What is the **conflict** in Twain's story? **(b)** How does Twain develop the conflict?

2. **(a)** What is the climax of Twain's story? **(b)** Why is it exciting?

3. What makes Twain a good storyteller? Cite details from the interview to support your answer.

DISCUSS • RESEARCH • WRITE

From Text to Topic **Group Discussion**

Discuss the following passage with a group of classmates. Take notes during the discussion. Contribute your own ideas, and support them with examples from the text.

> Well, it kept on raining and storming generally until toward evening, when, seventeen miles below Hannibal, I was discovered by one of the crew." A very deliberate pause.
>
> "They put me ashore at Louisiana." Another pause.
>
> "I was sent home by some friends of my father's. My father met me on my return." A twinkle in the steel-blue eyes. "I remember that quite distinctly."

Research **Investigate the Topic**

Twain's First Riverboat Journey Make a poster based on "Mark Twain's First 'Vacation'."

Assignment

Conduct research to find out about riverboats on the Mississippi River before the Civil War. Use maps to speculate on Twain's journey. Take clear notes and carefully identify your sources so that you can easily access the information later. Share your findings in a **visual presentation** for the class.

Writing to Sources **Narrative**

Mark Twain tells his story by looking back on an event that occurred when he was seven years old.

Assignment

Write a **narrative** that **retells** "Mark Twain's First 'Vacation'" from the point of view of Twain's father. Follow these steps:

- Reread the interview to find details to use in your narrative.
- Develop a narrative with a clear sequence of events.
- Write from Twain's father's point of view, imagining how he might feel and react to the events.
- Use dialogue, and appropriate pacing in your narrative.
- Provide a satisfying conclusion.

QUESTIONS FOR DISCUSSION

1. What details does the interviewer add to the text? What effect do these details **achieve**?

2. How is the format of this interview different from other interviews you have read?

PREPARATION FOR ESSAY

You may use the results of this research project to support your ideas in the essay you will write at the end of this section.

ACADEMIC VOCABULARY

Academic terms appear in blue on these pages. If these words are not familiar to you, use a dictionary to find their definitions. Then, use them as you speak and write about the text.

According to Mark Twain

It is better to remain silent and be thought a fool than to open one's mouth and remove all doubt.

A person who won't read has no advantage over one who can't read.

If you tell the truth, you don't have to remember anything.

Action speaks louder than words but not nearly as often.

Always do right. This will gratify some people and astonish the rest.

Never put off till tomorrow what you can do the day after tomorrow.

A lie can travel halfway around the world while the truth is putting on its shoes.

To believe yourself brave is to be brave; it is the one only essential thing.

Everybody's private motto: It's better to be popular than right.

READ • RESEARCH • WRITE

Comprehension

Reread all or part of the text to help you answer the following questions.

1. In your own words, what does Twain say about keeping silent?
2. In your own words, what does Twain say about truth and lies?
3. According to Twain, how do people respond when someone does the right thing?

Critical Analysis

Key Ideas and Details

1. **Analyze:** On what topics does Twain give advice?

Craft and Structure

2. **(a) Distinguish:** Identify one quotation that uses hyperbole, or exaggeration. **(b) Draw Conclusions:** How does hyperbole make the advice more memorable or entertaining?

3. **(a) Analyze:** In which quotation does Twain seem to make fun of, or satirize, traditional advice? **(b) Deduce:** How does Twain use humor to **modify** the advice?

Integration of Knowledge and Ideas

4. **Compare and Contrast:** How is Twain's advice similar to and different from other common sayings you have heard?

Research **Investigate the Topic**

Twain's Quotations Conduct research to find additional quotations from Twain. Classify the quotations according to the literary devices Twain uses, such as word choice and hyperbole. Make a generalization about how Twain creates humor in his advice.

Writing to Sources **Argument**

Write a brief **argument** supporting one side of this claim: Mark Twain's advice about believing yourself brave is completely serious/ is completely humorous. Support your claim with an analysis of the exact words of the **quotation**. As you write, **establish** and maintain a formal style.

ACADEMIC VOCABULARY

Academic terms appear in blue on these pages. If these words are not familiar to you, use a dictionary to find their definitions. Then, use them as you speak and write about the text.

An Encounter With An Interviewer

Mark Twain

The nervous, dapper, "peart"[1] young man took the chair I offered him, and said he was connected with the Daily Thunderstorm, and added:

"Hoping it's no harm, I've come to interview you."

"Come to what?"

"Interview you."

"Ah! I see. Yes—yes. Um! Yes—yes."

I was not feeling bright that morning. Indeed, my powers seemed a bit under a cloud. However, I went to the bookcase, and when I had been looking six or seven minutes I found I was obliged to refer to the young man. I said:

"How do you spell it?"

"Spell what?"

"Interview."

"Oh, my goodness! what do you want to spell it for?"

"I don't want to spell it; I want to see what it means."

"Well, this is astonishing, I must say. I can tell you what it means, if you—if you—"

"Oh, all right! That will answer, and much obliged to you, too."

"In, in, ter, ter, inter—"

"Then you spell it with an h."

"Why certainly!"

"Oh, that is what took me so long."

"Why, my dear sir, what did you propose to spell it with?"

"Well, I—I—hardly know. I had the Unabridged, and I was ciphering around in the back end, hoping I might tree her among the pictures.[2] But it's a very old edition."

"Why, my friend, they wouldn't have a picture of it in even the latest e— My dear sir, I beg your pardon, I mean no harm in the world, but you do not look as—as—intelligent as I had expected you would. No harm—I mean no harm at all."

"Oh, don't mention it! It has often been said, and by

◄ **astonishing**
(ə stän´ ish iŋ)
adj. amazing or surprising

---

1. **peart** (pirt) pert; lively.
2. **Unabridged . . . among the pictures** Twain says he was hoping to find the word in the back of a dictionary, where it might be illustrated with a picture.

people who would not flatter and who could have no
inducement to flatter, that I am quite remarkable in that
way. Yes—yes; they always speak of it with rapture."

"I can easily imagine it. But about this interview. You
know it is the custom, now, to interview any man who has
become notorious."

"Indeed, I had not heard of it before. It must be very
interesting. What do you do it with?"

"Ah, well—well—well—this is disheartening. It ought to be
done with a club in some cases; but customarily it consists
in the interviewer asking questions and the interviewed
answering them. It is all the rage now. Will you let me ask
you certain questions calculated to bring out the salient
points of your public and private history?"

"Oh, with pleasure—with pleasure. I have a very bad
memory, but I hope you will not mind that. That is to say,
it is an irregular memory—singularly irregular. Sometimes
it goes in a gallop, and then again it will be as much as a
fortnight[3] passing a given point. This is a great grief to me."

"Oh, it is no matter, so you will try to do the best you can."

"I will. I will put my whole mind on it."

"Thanks. Are you ready to begin?"

"Ready."

Q. How old are you?

A. Nineteen, in June.

Q. Indeed. I would have taken you to be thirty-five or six.
Where were you born?

A. In Missouri.

Q. When did you begin to write?

A. In 1836.

Q. Why, how could that be, if you are only nineteen now?

A. I don't know. It does seem curious, somehow.

Q. It does, indeed. Whom do you consider the most
remarkable man you ever met?

A. Aaron Burr.[4]

Q. But you never could have met Aaron Burr, if you are only
nineteen years!

---

3. **fortnight** two weeks.
4. **Aaron Burr** vice president of the United States from 1801–1805.

A. Now, if you know more about me than I do, what do you ask me for?

Q. Well, it was only a suggestion; nothing more. How did you happen to meet Burr?

A. Well, I happened to be at his funeral one day, and he asked me to make less noise, and—

Q. But, good heavens! if you were at his funeral, he must have been dead, and if he was dead how could he care whether you made a noise or not?

A. I don't know. He was always a particular kind of a man that way.

Q. Still, I don't understand it at all, You say he spoke to you, and that he was dead.

A. I didn't say he was dead.

Q. But wasn't he dead?

A. Well, some said he was, some said he wasn't.

Q. What did you think?

A. Oh, it was none of my business! It wasn't any of my funeral.

Q. Did you—However, we can never get this matter straight. Let me ask about something else. What was the date of your birth?

A. Monday, October 31, 1693.

Q. What! Impossible! That would make you a hundred and eighty years old. How do you account for that?

A. I don't account for it at all.

Q. But you said at first you were only nineteen, and now you make yourself out to be one hundred and eighty. It is an awful discrepancy.

A. Why, have you noticed that? (Shaking hands.) Many a time it has seemed to me like a discrepancy, but somehow I couldn't make up my mind. How quick you notice a thing!

Q. Thank you for the compliment, as far as it goes. Had you, or have you, any brothers or sisters?

A. Eh! I—I—I think so—yes—but I don't remember.

Q. Well, that is the most extraordinary statement I ever heard!

A. Why, what makes you think that?

Q. How could I think otherwise? Why, look here! Who is this a picture of on the wall? Isn't that a brother of yours?

Well, some said he was, some said he wasn't.

A. Oh, yes, yes, yes! Now you remind me of it; that was a brother of mine. That's William—Bill we called him. Poor old Bill!

Q. Why? Is he dead, then?

A. Ah! well, I suppose so. We never could tell. There was a great mystery about it.

Q. That is sad, very sad. He disappeared, then?

A. Well, yes, in a sort of general way. We buried him.

Q. Buried him! Buried him, without knowing whether he was dead or not?

A. Oh, no! Not that. He was dead enough.

Q. Well, I confess that I can't understand this. If you buried him, and you knew he was dead.

A. No! no! We only thought he was.

Q. Oh, I see! He came to life again?

A. I bet he didn't.

Q. Well, I never heard anything like this. Somebody was dead. Somebody was buried. Now, where was the mystery?

A. Ah! that's just it! That's it exactly. You see, we were twins—defunct—and I—and we got mixed in the bathtub when we were only two weeks old, and one of us was drowned. But we didn't know which. Some think it was Bill. Some think it was me.

Q. Well, that is remarkable. What do you think?

A. Goodness knows! I would give whole worlds to know. This solemn, this awful mystery has cast a gloom over

my whole life. But I will tell you a secret now, which I never have revealed to any creature before. One of us had a peculiar mark—a large mole on the back of his left hand; that was me. That child was the one that was drowned!

Q. Very well, then, I don't see that there is any mystery about it, after all.

A. You don't? Well, I do. Anyway, I don't see how they could ever have been such a blundering lot as to go and bury the wrong child. But, 'sh!—don't mention it where the family can hear of it. Heaven knows they have heartbreaking troubles enough without adding this.

Q. Well, I believe I have got material enough for the present, and I am very much obliged to you for the pains you have taken. But I was a good deal interested in that account of Aaron Burr's funeral. Would you mind telling me what particular circumstance it was that made you think Burr was such a remarkable man?

A. Oh! it was a mere trifle![5] Not one man in fifty would have noticed it at all. When the sermon was over, and the procession all ready to start for the cemetery, and the body all arranged nice in the hearse, he said he wanted to take a last look at the scenery, and so he got up and rode with the driver.

Then the young man reverently withdrew. He was very pleasant company, and I was sorry to see him go.

---

5. trifle something of little importance.

Close Reading Activities

READ

Comprehension

Reread and answer the questions.

1. Who are readers meant to believe is narrating this story?

2. What is the interviewer's attitude toward the narrator at the beginning of the story?

3. What is the interviewer's attitude toward the narrator at the end of the story?

Research: Clarify Details Research an unfamiliar detail from the story and explain how what you learned sheds light on an aspect of the story.

Summarize Write an objective summary of the story. Leave out your opinions and evaluations.

Language Study

Selection Vocabulary Use each boldfaced word in a sentence of your own. For the words with suffixes, explain what each suffix means.

• Well, this is **astonishing**, I must say.

• Yes, yes; they always speak of it with **rapture**.

• You know, it is the custom, now, to interview any man who has become **notorious**.

Literary Analysis

Reread the identified passage:

> **Focus Passage** (p. 598)
>
> "I can easily imagine it … This is a great grief to me."

Key Ideas and Details

1. **(a)** Who is the speaker in each paragraph? **(b) Analyze:** How can you tell?

Craft and Structure

2. **(a)** What does the interviewer say about the way that interviews ought to be done? **(b) Interpret:** What does this remark suggest about interviews in general?

3. **(a)** What does the narrator say about his memory? **(b) Interpret:** What do these remarks suggest about the quality of his interview answers?

Integration of Knowledge and Ideas

4. Based on this passage, what is Mark Twain's opinion of interviews? Cite details in the text that support your response.

Tone

Tone is the writer's attitude toward his or her audience and subject. Reread "An Encounter With An Interviewer," and take notes on the elements that develop tone.

1. **(a)** Whom does the narrator say is the most remarkable man he has ever met? **(b)** Why is this a ridiculous answer?

2. How does the narrator's tone show his attitude toward interviews?

DISCUSS • RESEARCH • WRITE

From Text to Topic **Small Group Discussion**

Discuss the following passage with a small group of classmates. Take notes during the discussion. Contribute your own ideas, and support them with examples from the text.

> Q. Well, I believe I have got material enough for the present …
> I was sorry to see him go. (p. 601)

Research **Investigate the Topic**

Real Twain Interviews After he became famous, Mark Twain was interviewed many times. Find out how Twain, as an interview subject, was similar to or different from the narrator of this story.

Assignment

Conduct research to locate one or more **interviews** that Twain gave during his lifetime. Consult Mark Twain Web sites and library resources. Take clear notes and carefully identify your sources so that you can easily access the information later. Share your findings in an **oral presentation** to the class. Compare and contrast the real Twain with the narrator of the story.

Writing to Sources **Argument**

In "An Encounter With An Interviewer," the narrator gently makes fun of interviews and interviewers.

Assignment

Write an **argument** in which you use evidence from Twain's story to argue that interviews are a bothersome, inaccurate, or otherwise poor means of gathering information. Follow these steps:

- State your claim and organize the reasons that support it in order of importance.
- **Refer** to evidence from "An Encounter With An Interviewer" as you support your claims.
- Use precise words to clearly convey the main points of your argument.
- Provide a concluding section or statement.

QUESTIONS FOR DISCUSSION

1. Is the narrator really sorry to see the interviewer go? How can you tell?

2. Why does the narrator **pose** as an unreliable interview subject?

PREPARATION FOR ESSAY

You may use the results of this research project to support your ideas in the essay you will write at the end of this section.

ACADEMIC VOCABULARY

Academic terms appear in blue on these pages. If these words are not familiar to you, use a dictionary to find their definitions. Then, use them as you speak and write about the text.

Speaking and Listening: Group Discussion

Mark Twain and Identity The texts in this section all comment in some way, either seriously or humorously, on choices that affect who we are. Even when Mark Twain pokes fun at these choices, his work addresses the Big Question for this unit: **How do we decide who we are?**

Assignment

Conduct discussions. With a small group of classmates, conduct a discussion about Mark Twain and what his work seems to say about identity. Refer to the texts in this section, other texts you have read, and your personal experience and knowledge to support your ideas. Begin your discussion by addressing the following questions:

- How does Twain use humor to present serious ideas? What does this reveal about Twain as a person?

- Does Twain seem to believe that people can change for the better?

- In what ways do Twain's characters represent people in general?

- Twain is considered one of the greatest American writers and humorists of all time. Why do you think that is so?

Summarize and present your ideas. After you have fully explored the topic, summarize your discussion for the class.

▲ Refer to the selections you read in Part 3 as you complete the activities on this assessment.

Criteria for Success

✓ **Organizes the group effectively**
Appoint a group leader and a timekeeper. The group leader should present the discussion questions. The timekeeper should make sure the discussion takes no longer than 20 minutes.

✓ **Maintains focus of discussion**
As a group, stay on topic and avoid straying into other subject areas.

✓ **Involves all participants equally and fully**
No one person should monopolize the conversation. Rather, everyone should take turns speaking and contributing ideas.

✓ **Follows the rules for collegial discussion**
As each group member speaks, others should listen carefully. Express disagreement respectfully.

USE NEW VOCABULARY

As you speak and share ideas, work to use the vocabulary words you have learned in this unit. The more you use new words, the more you will "own" them.

Writing: **Narrative**

Mark Twain and Identity In Mark Twain's *The Prince and the Pauper*, two boys exchange identities. Their deception leads to problems, but in the end, each boy learns important lessons.

Assignment

Write a **fictional narrative**, or short story, in which a case of mistaken identity creates a conflict that eventually lead the main character to learn an important lesson. Refer to the research you conducted on Twain and his work to help you develop the conflict and resolution in your story.

Criteria for Success

Purpose/Focus

✓ **Connects specific incidents with larger ideas**
Make meaningful connections between the character's choices or experiences and the texts you have read in this section.

✓ **Clearly conveys the significance of the story**
Provide a conclusion in which the character learns an important lesson.

Organization

✓ **Sequences events logically**
Structure your narrative so that individual events build on one another to create a coherent whole.

Development of Ideas/Elaboration

✓ **Supports insights**
Include details based on the texts you have read in this section.

✓ **Uses narrative techniques effectively**
Use pacing to build suspense in your story.

Language

✓ **Uses description effectively**
Use descriptive details that help readers picture settings and characters.

Conventions

✓ **Does not have errors**
Correct errors in grammar, spelling, and punctuation.

WRITE TO EXPLORE

Writing is a way to clarify what you feel and think. This means that you may change your mind or get new ideas as you work. Allowing for this will improve your final draft.

Writing to Sources: **Informative Text**

Mark Twain and Identity The related readings in this section show that in his writing, Mark Twain used humor to express important ideas about human nature. The selections raise questions, such as the following, about the reasons people behave as they do:

- Why do people make poor choices? Do all poor choices lead to disaster? Does a positive outcome ever result from a poor choice?
- Is the use of humor an effective way to make a serious point or teach an important lesson?
- What are some reasons people poke fun at others? Why do they poke fun at themselves?

Focus on the question or questions that intrigue you the most, and then complete the following assignment.

> **Assignment**
>
> Write an **informative essay** in which you explore and analyze some of Mark Twain's ideas about human nature. Clearly present, develop, and support your ideas with examples and details from the texts.

Prewriting and Planning

Choose texts. Review the texts in the section to determine which ones you will cite in your essay. Select at least two texts that will provide strong material to support your ideas.

Gather details and identify key ideas. Use a chart like the one shown to develop your key ideas.

Focus Question: Why do people make poor choices?

Text	Passage	Notes
The Prince and the Pauper	**TOM.** ...and sometimes we lads have fights in the streets. **PRINCE.** *(Eagerly)* I should like that ...	It is human nature to want something different from what you have, but when the Prince chooses Tom's life, he is sorry.
"According to Mark Twain"	Never put off till tomorrow what you can do the day after tomorrow.	People decide to put off things they should be doing. Twain humorously suggests delaying even further.

Example Claim: Twain suggests that people sometimes make poor choices before they consider the possible consequences.

INCORPORATE RESEARCH

Make sure to introduce each supporting fact and example in a way that shows a clear connection between the researched material and the point it supports in your essay.

Drafting

Define and develop your focus. Review your prewriting notes to find a main idea or focus for your essay. Then write one strong sentence that states your focus. Include this sentence in your introduction, and elaborate on it in the body of your essay.

Use examples to provide support. Use examples from the selections in this section and from your research to help you support your main argument or claims. For example, refer to a specific scene, character, or image that illustrates one of your key points. Be sure to use quotation marks if you include the exact words of a text or source.

Revising and Editing

Revise to organize around your strongest idea. Review your draft and circle your strongest point—the key argument or quotation that pulls your essay together. Consider moving this point to the end, just before your concluding statement. Then, revise your last paragraph to add a transition sentence that clearly explains the connection between this point and your other ideas.

CITE RESEARCH CORRECTLY

Review your draft to make sure your citations are formatted properly. Refer to the Research Workshop in the Introductory Unit for information on how to cite sources.

Self-Evaluation Rubric

Use the following criteria to evaluate the effectiveness of your essay.

Criteria	Rating Scale			
	not very .... *very*			
Purpose/Focus Introduces a specific topic; provides a concluding section that follows from and supports the information or explanation presented	1	2	3	4
Organization Organizes complex ideas, concepts, and information to make important connections and distinctions; uses appropriate and varied transitions to link the major sections, create cohesion, and clarify relationships among ideas	1	2	3	4
Development of Ideas/Elaboration Develops the topic with well-chosen, relevant and sufficient facts, extended definitions, concrete details, quotations or other information and examples appropriate to the audience's knowledge of the topic	1	2	3	4
Language Uses precise language and domain-specific vocabulary to manage the complexity of the topic; establishes and maintains a formal style and objective tone	1	2	3	4
Conventions Uses correct conventions of grammar, spelling, and punctuation	1	2	3	4

Independent Reading

Titles for Extended Reading

In this unit, you have read texts in a variety of genres. Continue to read on your own. Select works that you enjoy, but challenge yourself to explore new authors and works of increasing depth and complexity. The titles suggested below will help you get started.

INFORMATIONAL TEXT

Welcome to the Globe!
The Story of Shakespeare's Theatre
by Linda Martin

 The Globe Theatre in London is where Shakespeare's plays were performed. This illustrated **nonfiction book** teaches the history of this famous theatre.

Small Things Considered:
Why There Is No Perfect Design
by Henry Petroski   EXEMPLAR TEXT

This **nonfiction book** explores the fascinating world of design. It includes the article "The Evolution of the Grocery Bag" and other essays that describe the thinking behind the design of everyday items such as telephone keypads and toothbrushes.

Tiger Tales
by Deborah Chancellor

 This **nonfiction** book uncovers the truth about how the number of wild tigers and other animal populations are decreasing because of hunting.

LITERATURE

You're a Good Man, Charlie Brown
by Clark Gesner
Random House, Inc., 1967

This **musical comedy** is based on the hugely popular cartoon series *Peanuts* by Charles Schulz and features Snoopy, Lucy, Linus, and the gang.

James and the Giant Peach: A Play
by Roald Dahl

 James goes on an adventure inside a giant peach in this **play** based on Roald Dahl's beloved children's story. Complete with ideas for props and costumes, this play is one you could stage with your friends.

Seven Plays of Mystery and Suspense

 This collection of **plays** will delight lovers of mystery and suspense stories. Expect to be on the edge of your seat as you read.

The Collected Poems of
Langston Hughes
by Langston Hughes
Vintage, 1995   EXEMPLAR TEXT

 This complete collection of Hughes's **poems** contains his life's work. Hughes celebrates African American life and shares the beauty of his language and the wisdom of his insights.

ONLINE TEXT SET

SPEECH
My Heart is in the Highlands Jane Yolen

NOVEL EXCERPT
from **Roll of Thunder, Hear My Cry** Mildred D. Taylor

POEM
Alphabet Naomi Shihab Nye

Preparing to Read Complex Texts

Attentive Reading As you read on your own, ask yourself questions like these to enrich your reading experience.

When reading drama, ask yourself…

Comprehension: **Key Ideas and Details**

- Who is the main character? What struggles does this character face?
- What other characters are important? How do these characters relate to the main character?
- Where and when does the play take place? Do the time and place of the setting affect the characters? If so, how?
- Do the characters, settings, and events seem real? Why or why not?
- How does the play end? How does the ending make me feel?

Text Analysis: **Craft and Structure**

- Does the playwright include background information? If so, how does this help me understand what I am reading?
- How many acts are in this play? What happens in each act?
- Does the dialogue sound like real speech? Are there passages that seem especially real? Are there any that seem false?
- What do the stage directions tell me about the ways characters move, speak, and feel? In what other ways do I learn about the characters?
- At what point in the play do I feel the most suspense? Why?
- What speech or passage in the play do I like the most? Why?
- Does the playwright seem to have a positive or a negative point of view? How do I think the playwright's point of view affects the story?

Connections: **Integration of Knowledge and Ideas**

- How does this play compare with others I have read or seen?
- What new ideas have I gained from reading this play?
- If I were to be in this play, what role would I want?
- Would I recommend this play to others? Why or why not?

UNIT 5

THE BIG ?

How much do our communities shape us?

UNIT PATHWAY

PART 1
SETTING EXPECTATIONS

- INTRODUCING THE BIG QUESTION
- CLOSE READING WORKSHOP

PART 2
TEXT ANALYSIS
GUIDED EXPLORATION

SHARED LESSONS

PART 3
TEXT SET
DEVELOPING INSIGHT

PEOPLE AND ANIMALS

PART 4
DEMONSTRATING INDEPENDENCE

- INDEPENDENT READING
- ONLINE TEXT SET

CLOSE READING TOOL

Use this tool to practice the close reading strategies you learn.

STUDENT eTEXT

Bring learning to life with audio, video, and interactive tools.

ONLINE WRITER'S NOTEBOOK

Easily capture notes and complete assignments online.

Find all Digital Resources at **pearsonrealize.com.**

How much do our communities shape us?

The word *community* usually refers to a group of people who have common needs and interests. In fact, this word comes from a Latin word that means "common." People in a community may live near each other, or they may live far apart. One type of community is a neighborhood. Another can be an organization whose members live in different areas. People in communities often share languages and values. They may exchange information, support one another, and work together to solve problems. While individual members contribute to the shape of a community, the opposite is also true: a community can shape its members.

Exploring the Big Question

Collaboration: One-on-One Discussion Start thinking about the Big Question by examining different types of communities. Briefly describe how the following groups are influenced by their communities:

- students in a classroom
- workers in a factory
- members of a sports team
- citizens of a town
- members of a choir or theater group

Share your lists and descriptions with a partner. Talk about your own experiences as a member of a community. Use the vocabulary words in your discussion.

Connecting to the Literature Each reading in this unit will give you additional insight into the Big Question. As you read, pause to consider the ways in which characters benefit from the support of their communities.

Vocabulary

Acquire and Use Academic Vocabulary The term "academic vocabulary" refers to words you typically encounter in scholarly and literary texts and in technical and business writing. Review the definitions of these academic vocabulary words.

common (käm´ən) *adj.* ordinary; shared

influence (in´flo͞o əns) *v.* sway or persuade

involve (in välv´) *v.* include

isolate (ī´sə lāt´) *v.* set apart

participation (pär tis´ə pā´ shən) *n.* taking part in an event or activity

support (sə pôrt´) *v.* stand behind; back up

Gather Vocabulary Knowledge Additional vocabulary words are listed below. Categorize the words by deciding whether you know each one well, know it a little bit, or do not know it at all.

belief	culture	group
community	family	history
connection	generation	values

Then, do the following:

1. Write the definitions of the words you know.
2. Consult a dictionary to confirm the meanings of the words whose definitions you wrote down. Revise your definitions if necessary.
3. Using a print or an online dictionary, look up the meanings of the words you do not know. Then, write the meanings.
4. Write true or false statements about each word. For example, *A persuasive advertisement may <u>influence</u> what you buy. (true) If I <u>support</u> Mayor Green, I will not vote for him. (false)*
5. Exchange your sentences with a partner to test each other on your knowledge of the words. Label each statement *true* or *false* and offer a brief explanation for each answer.

Close Reading Workshop

In this workshop you will learn an approach to reading that will deepen your understanding of literature and will help you better appreciate the author's craft. The workshop includes models for close reading, discussion, research, and writing activities. After you have reviewed the strategies and models, practice your skills with the Independent Practice selection.

CLOSE READING: FOLK LITERATURE

Use these strategies as you read the works of folk literature in this unit.

Comprehension: Key Ideas and Details

- Read first to unlock basic meaning.
- Use context clues to help you determine the meanings of unfamiliar words.
- Identify unfamiliar details that you might need to clarify through research.

Ask yourself questions such as these:
- Who are the main characters? What are their distinctive traits?
- Where and when is the story set? What is interesting or unusual about the setting?
- What is the conflict in the story?

Text Analysis: Craft and Structure

- Identify elements of folk literature, including the use of fantasy, exaggeration, and repeated narrative patterns.
- Examine how the literary work presents a culturally perspective or a universal theme.

Ask yourself questions such as these:
- What details in the story reflect the background, customs, and beliefs of the culture from which the story comes?
- What insight or lesson does the story present?

Connections: Integration of Knowledge and Ideas

- Recognize common characters, settings, and conflicts among various works of folk literature.
- Compare and contrast this work with other works you have read that express the same or similar themes.

Ask yourself questions such as these:
- How has this work increased my knowledge of folk literature?
- Why have people retold this story as part of a cultural tradition?

Read

As you read this piece of folk literature, take note of the annotations that model ways to closely read the text.

from *Black Ships Before Troy: The Story of the Iliad* by Rosemary Sutcliff

In the high and far-off days when men were heroes and walked with the gods, Peleus, king of the Myrmidons, took for his wife a sea nymph called Thetis, Thetis of the Silver Feet. Many guests came to their wedding feast, and among the mortal guests came all the gods of high Olympus. **1**

But as they sat feasting, one who had not been invited was suddenly in their midst: Eris, the goddess of discord, had been left out because wherever she went she took trouble with her; yet here she was, all the same, and in her blackest mood, to avenge the insult. **2**

All she did—it seemed a small thing—was to toss down on the table a golden apple. Then she breathed upon the guests once, and vanished.

The apple lay gleaming among the piled fruits and the brimming wine cups; and bending close to look at it, everyone could see the words "To the fairest" traced on its side. **3**

Then the three greatest of the goddesses each claimed that it was hers. Hera claimed it as wife to Zeus, the All-father, and queen of all the gods. Athene claimed that she had the better right, for the beauty of wisdom such as hers surpassed all else. Aphrodite only smiled, and asked who had a better claim to beauty's prize than the goddess of beauty herself.

They fell to arguing among themselves; the argument became a quarrel, and the quarrel grew more and more bitter, and each called upon the assembled guests to judge between them. But the other guests refused, for they knew well enough that, whichever goddess they chose to receive the golden apple, they would make enemies of the other two. **4**

In the end, the three took the quarrel home with them to Olympus. The other gods took sides, some with one and some with another, and the ill will between them dragged on for a long while. More than long enough in the world of men for a

Key Ideas and Details

1 The opening lines describe a time "when men were heroes and walked with the gods." These fantastic details help identify the story as a myth.

Craft and Structure

2 The goddess Eris is an outcast, a familiar character type in folk literature. Though uninvited, she comes to the feast seeking revenge. This event sets the plot in motion.

Integration of Knowledge and Ideas

3 You may connect the apple and the words "the fairest" to the fairy tale "Snow White," in which an evil queen tricks Snow White into eating a poisoned apple. This may lead you to predict that a conflict has been set in motion.

Craft and Structure

4 The idea that it is dangerous to anger the gods is a familiar theme in classical mythology.

child born when the quarrel first began, to grow to manhood and become a warrior or a herdsman. But the immortal gods do not know time as mortals know it. **5**

Now on the northeast coast of the Aegean Sea, there was a city of men. Troy was its name, a great city surrounded by strong walls, and standing on a hill hard by the shore. It had grown rich on the tolls that its kings demanded from merchant ships passing up the nearby straits to the Black Sea cornlands and down again. Priam, who was now king, was lord of wide realms and long-maned horses, and he had many sons about his hearth. And when the quarrel about the golden apple was still raw and new, a last son was born to him and his wife Queen Hecuba, and they called him Paris.

There should have been great rejoicing, but while Hecuba still carried the babe within her, the soothsayers had foretold that she would give birth to a firebrand that should burn down Troy. And so, when he was born and named, the king bade a servant carry him out into the wilderness and leave him to die. The servant did as he was bid; but a herdsman searching for a missing calf found the babe and brought him up as his own. **6**

The boy grew tall and strong and beautiful, the swiftest runner and the best archer in all the country around. **7** So his boyhood passed among the oak woods and the high hill-pastures that rose toward Mount Ida. And there he met and fell in love with a wood nymph called Oenone, who loved him in return. She had the gift of being able to heal the wounds of mortal men, no matter how sorely they were hurt.

Among the oak woods they lived together and were happy—until one day the three jealous goddesses, still quarreling about the golden apple, chanced to look down from Olympus, and saw the beautiful young man herding his cattle on the slopes of Mount Ida.

They knew, for the gods know all things, that he was the son of Priam, king of Troy, though he himself did not know it yet; but the thought came to them that he would not know who they were, and therefore he would not be afraid to judge between them. They were growing somewhat weary of the argument by then.

So they tossed the apple down to him, and Paris put up his hands and caught it. After it the three came down, landing before him so lightly that their feet did not bend the mountain grasses, and bade him choose between them, which was the fairest and had best right to the prize he held in his hand. **8**

Key Ideas and Details

5 A baby boy grows to manhood as the goddesses continue to quarrel. This distorted passage of time could only occur in an exaggerated world of fantasy.

Craft and Structure

6 This paragraph presents common elements of folk literature. Details such as a soothsayer's warning and a character's lack of knowledge about his true identity appear in many other folk stories.

Key Ideas and Details

7 Many characters in folk literature have exaggerated traits. In addition to being "tall and strong and beautiful," Paris is "the swiftest runner" and "the best archer" in the land.

Craft and Structure

8 The goddesses are "weary of the argument." They decide to use Paris—without his knowledge—to settle the issue. The gods' manipulation of human "destiny" is a common idea in mythology.

First Athene, in her gleaming armor, fixed him with sword-gray eyes and promised him supreme wisdom if he would name her.

Then Hera, in her royal robes as queen of heaven, promised him vast wealth and power and honor if he awarded her the prize.

Lastly, Aphrodite drew near, her eyes as blue as deep-sea water, her hair like spun gold wreathed around her head, and, smiling honey-sweet, whispered that she would give him a wife as fair as herself if he tossed the apple to her.

And Paris forgot the other two with their offers of wisdom and power, forgot also, for that moment, dark-haired Oenone in the shadowed oak woods; and he gave the golden apple to Aphrodite. **9**

Integration of Knowledge and Ideas
9 The repetition of the word *forgot* emphasizes a common theme in folk literature: when faced with temptation, a person can forget everything he or she once valued.

Discuss

Sharing your own ideas and listening to the ideas of others can deepen your understanding of a text and help you look at a topic in a whole new way. As you participate in collaborative discussions, work to have a genuine exchange in which classmates build upon one another's ideas. Support your points with evidence and ask meaningful questions.

Student 1: I wonder why the three goddesses keep trying to decide which of them is "the fairest." Do they think that being "the fairest" is better than being queen of the gods, the goddess of wisdom, or the goddess of beauty?

Student 2: I think they don't have anything better to do. They're immortal. All that time stretches out in front of them, so they make their arguments last as long as they can. Also, in a lot of myths the gods act like human beings. Sometimes they're stubborn.

Student 3: That's true. Another point, though, is that what the gods do in myths usually has major consequences for human beings. I think their contest will cause some kind of problem for Paris, his family in Troy, or both.

Research

Targeted research can clarify unfamiliar details and shed light on various aspects of a text. Consider questions that arise in your mind as you read, and use those questions as the basis for research.

Research Model

Questions: *How do the consequences of Paris's choice affect his future or the future of his family?*

Key Words for Internet Search: Paris AND Troy

Result: history of the Trojan War

What I Learned: When Aphrodite asks Paris to choose her as "the fairest," she promises to give him the most beautiful woman in the world, Helen of Sparta. Helen is already married to the king of Sparta in Greece, but Paris kidnaps her. The Greeks go to Troy to avenge her kidnapping, which sets off the Trojan War.

Write

Writing about a text will deepen your understanding of it and will also allow you to share your ideas more formally with others. The following model essay identifies a theme in the work and cites evidence to support the main ideas.

Writing Model: Explanatory Text

Don't Blame Paris

In this excerpt from Rosemary Sutcliff's *Black Ships Before Troy*, three goddesses take advantage of Paris, a human who does not have the knowledge to understand what is going on. Although Paris makes a choice that ultimately leads to a terrible war, he cannot be blamed because the goddesses tricked him into making that choice.

> In the introductory paragraph, the writer states a claim and explains the essay's title.

The author first introduces a mythological setting in which gods and humans live together. The conflict begins when "the three greatest of the goddesses"—Hera, Athene, and Aphrodite—quarrel about who should win the prize of a golden apple, and be declared "the fairest." Their argument continues for a long time because "the immortal gods do not know time as mortals know it." During the argument, a boy named Paris grows up without knowing that he is the son of King Priam of Troy, and that it was foretold he would someday destroy his father's city.

> Important background information helps readers understand the topic.

The author describes the goddesses' argument as their reason for interfering in Paris's life. Their quarrel brings out petty human emotions in the goddesses, and their pride, bitterness, and jealousy prevent them from resolving the conflict. Because they "know all things," the goddesses realize that Paris does not know their identities so they can use him to decide the winner of their contest. If Paris had been raised by his true parents, they might have taught him to recognize the goddesses and to beware of their possible trickery.

> The writer interprets story details to draw a conclusion that supports the main idea.

Paris, however, is does not suspect the goddesses. When asked to choose "the fairest," he picks Aphrodite because she offers him a beautiful wife. This is Helen of Sparta, who is already married to a Greek king. Paris's choice sets in motion a chain of events that lead to war: Paris captures Helen for his wife, which causes the Greeks to seek revenge. However, these events are not Paris's fault. The goddesses use deception to influence Paris's actions. The myth presents an important theme of classical mythology: the gods often use humans for their own personal gain. Therefore, the gods, and not Paris, are the cause of the deadly war.

> The writer incorporates information from research in this statement of cause and effect.

> The concluding statement restates the writer's claim.

As you read the following story, apply the close reading strategies you have learned. You may need to read the story multiple times.

Black Cowboy, Wild Horses: A True Story

by Julius Lester

Meet the Author

Julius Lester (b. 1939), a native of St. Louis, Missouri, has been a folk singer, a civil rights photographer, a writer, and a professor of African American Studies and Judaic Studies. His works include novels, stories, poetry, nonfiction, and a memoir.

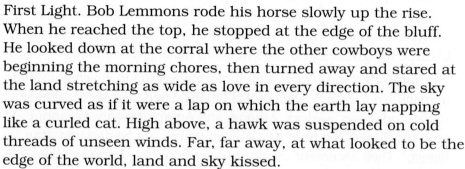

CLOSE READING TOOL

Read and respond to this selection online using the **Close Reading Tool**.

First Light. Bob Lemmons rode his horse slowly up the rise. When he reached the top, he stopped at the edge of the bluff. He looked down at the corral where the other cowboys were beginning the morning chores, then turned away and stared at the land stretching as wide as love in every direction. The sky was curved as if it were a lap on which the earth lay napping like a curled cat. High above, a hawk was suspended on cold threads of unseen winds. Far, far away, at what looked to be the edge of the world, land and sky kissed.

He guided Warrior, his black stallion, slowly down the bluff. When they reached the bottom, the horse reared, eager to run across the vastness of the plains until he reached forever. Bob smiled and patted him gently on the neck. "Easy. Easy," he whispered. "We'll have time for that. But not yet."

He let the horse trot for a while, then slowed him and began peering intently at the ground as if looking for the answer to a question he scarcely understood.

It was late afternoon when he saw them—the hoofprints of mustangs, the wild horses that lived on the plains. He stopped, dismounted, and walked around carefully until he had seen all the prints. Then he got down on his hands and knees to examine them more closely.

Some people learned from books. Bob had been a slave and never learned to read words. But he could look at the ground and read what animals had walked on it, their size and weight, when they had passed by, and where they were going. No one he knew could bring in mustangs by themselves, but Bob could make horses think he was one of them—because he was.

He stood, reached into his saddlebag, took out an apple, and gave it to Warrior, who chewed with noisy enthusiasm. It was a herd of eight mares, a colt, and a stallion. They had passed there two days ago. He would see them soon. But he needed to smell of sun, moon, stars, and wind before the mustangs would accept him.

The sun went down and the chilly night air came quickly. Bob took the saddle, saddlebag, and blanket off Warrior. He was cold, but could not make a fire. The mustangs would smell the smoke in his clothes from miles away. He draped a thick blanket around himself, then took the cotton sack of dried fruit, beef jerky, and nuts from his saddlebag and ate. When he was done, he lay his head on his saddle and was quickly asleep. Warrior grazed in the tall, sweet grasses.

As soon as the sun's round shoulders came over the horizon, Bob awoke. He ate, filled his canteen, and saddling Warrior, rode away. All day he followed the tracks without hurrying.

Near dusk, clouds appeared, piled atop each other like mountains made of fear. Lightning flickered from within them like candle flames shivering in a breeze. Bob heard the faint but distinct rumbling of thunder. Suddenly lightning vaulted from cloud to cloud across the curved heavens.

Warrior reared, his front hooves pawing as if trying to knock the white streaks of fire from the night sky. Bob raced Warrior to a nearby **ravine** as the sky exploded sheets of light. And there, in the distance, beneath the ghostly light, Bob saw the herd of mustangs. As if sensing their presence, Warrior rose into the air once again, this time not challenging the heavens but almost in greeting. Bob thought he saw the mustang stallion rise in response as the earth shuddered from the sound of thunder.

Then the rain came as hard and stinging as **remorse**. Quickly Bob put on his poncho, and turning Warrior away from the wind and the rain, waited. The storm would pass soon. Or it wouldn't. There was nothing to do but wait.

Finally the rain slowed and then stopped. The clouds thinned, and there, high in the sky, the moon appeared as white as grief. Bob slept in the saddle while Warrior grazed on the wet grasses.

The sun rose into a clear sky and Bob was awake immediately. The storm would have washed away the tracks, but they had been going toward the big river. He would go there and wait.

By mid-afternoon he could see the ribbon of river shining in the distance. He stopped, needing only to be close enough to see the horses when they came to drink. Toward evening he saw a trail of rolling, dusty clouds.

◄ **Vocabulary**
ravine (rə vēn´) *n.* long, deep hollow in the earth's surface

◄ **Vocabulary**
remorse (ri môrs´) *n.* guilt over a wrong one has done

In front was the mustang herd. As it reached the water, the stallion slowed and stopped. He looked around, his head raised, nostrils flared, smelling the air. He turned in Bob's direction and sniffed the air again.

Bob tensed. Had he come too close too soon? If the stallion smelled anything new, he and the herd would be gone and Bob would never find them again. The stallion seemed to be looking directly at him. Bob was too far away to be seen, but he did not even blink his eyes, afraid the stallion would hear the sound. Finally the stallion began drinking and the other horses followed. Bob let his breath out slowly. He had been accepted.

The next morning he crossed the river and picked up the herd's trail. He moved Warrior slowly, without sound, without dust. Soon he saw them grazing. He stopped. The horses did not notice him. After a while he moved forward, slowly, quietly. The stallion raised his head. Bob stopped.

When the stallion went back to grazing, Bob moved forward again. All day Bob watched the herd, moving only when it moved but always coming closer. The mustangs sensed his presence. They thought he was a horse.

So did he.

The following morning Bob and Warrior walked into the herd. The stallion eyed them for a moment. Then, as if to test this newcomer, he led the herd off in a gallop. Bob lay flat across Warrior's back and moved with the herd. If anyone had been watching, they would not have noticed a man among the horses.

When the herd set out early the next day, it was moving slowly. If the horses had been going faster, it would not have happened.

The colt fell to the ground as if she had stepped into a hole and broken her leg. Bob and the horses heard the chilling sound of the rattles. Rattlesnakes didn't always give a warning before they struck. Sometimes, when someone or something came too close, they bit with the fury of fear.

The horses whinnied and pranced nervously, smelling the snake and death among them. Bob saw the rattler, as beautiful as a necklace, sliding silently through the tall grasses. He made no move to kill it. Everything in nature had the right to protect itself, especially when it was afraid.

The stallion galloped to the colt. He pushed at her. The colt struggled to get up, but fell to her side, shivering and kicking feebly with her thin legs. Quickly she was dead.

Already vultures circled high in the sky. The mustangs milled aimlessly. The colt's mother whinnied, refusing to leave the side of her colt. The stallion wanted to move the herd from there, and pushed the mare with his head. She refused to budge, and he nipped her on the rump. She skittered away. Before she could return to the colt, the stallion bit her again, this time harder. She ran toward the herd. He bit her a third time, and the herd was off. As they galloped away, Bob looked back. The vultures were descending from the sky as gracefully as dusk.

It was time to take over the herd. The stallion would not have the heart to fight fiercely so soon after the death of the colt. Bob galloped Warrior to the front and wheeled around, forcing the stallion to stop quickly. The herd, confused, slowed and stopped also.

Bob raised Warrior to stand high on his back legs, fetlocks pawing and kicking the air. The stallion's eyes widened. He snorted and pawed the ground, surprised and uncertain. Bob charged at the stallion.

Both horses rose on hind legs, teeth bared as they kicked at each other. When they came down, Bob charged Warrior at the stallion again, pushing him backward. Bob rushed yet again.

The stallion neighed loudly, and nipped Warrior on the neck. Warrior snorted angrily, reared, and kicked out with his forelegs, striking the stallion on the nose. Still maintaining his balance, Warrior struck again and again. The mustang stallion cried out in pain. Warrior pushed hard against the stallion. The stallion lost his footing and fell to the earth. Warrior rose, neighing triumphantly, his front legs pawing as if seeking for the rungs on which he could climb a ladder into the sky.

The mustang scrambled to his feet, beaten. He snorted weakly. When Warrior made as if to attack again, the stallion turned, whinnied weakly, and trotted away.

Bob was now the herd's leader, but would they follow him? He rode slowly at first, then faster and faster. The mustangs followed as if being led on ropes.

Throughout that day and the next he rode with the horses. For Bob there was only the bulging of the horses' dark eyes, the quivering of their flesh, the rippling of muscles and bending of bones in their bodies. He was now sky and plains and grass and river and horse.

When his food was almost gone, Bob led the horses on one last ride, a dark surge of flesh flashing across the plains like black lightning. Toward evening he led the herd up the steep hillside, onto the bluff, and down the slope toward the big corral. The cowboys heard him coming and opened the corral gate. Bob led the herd, but at the last moment he swerved Warrior aside, and the mustangs flowed into the fenced enclosure. The cowboys leaped and shouted as they quickly closed the gate.

Bob rode away from them and back up to the bluff. He stopped and stared out onto the plains. Warrior reared and whinnied loudly.

"I know," Bob whispered. "I know. Maybe someday."

Maybe someday they would ride with the mustangs, ride to that forever place where land and sky kissed, and then ride on. Maybe someday.

Close Reading Activities

Read

Comprehension: Key Ideas and Details

1. (a) Identify examples of Bob Lemmons's legendary ability. **(b) Infer:** What danger does Bob face in approaching the mustangs too soon?

2. (a) How does Bob depend on Warrior? **(b) Connect:** Why does it seem that Warrior's goals match Bob's goals?

3. (a) What does Bob do after he leads the mustangs to the corral? **(b) Interpret:** What do his actions suggest about the life of a legendary hero?

4. Summarize: Write a brief, objective summary of the story. Cite story details in your writing.

Text Analysis: Craft and Structure

5. (a) Describe the setting, including the weather. **(b) Interpret:** How does the setting affect the story's development?

6. Evaluate: The author states that Bob "could make horses think he was one

of them—because he was." Why is this exaggeration meaningful?

7. (a) Why does Bob decide not to kill the rattler? **(b) Generalize:** What central idea about Bob does his decision convey?

Connections: Integration of Knowledge and Ideas

Discuss
Conduct a **small-group discussion** about the character of Bob. Identify qualities that make him seem like a real person, as well as exaggerated abilities that make him seem like a legend. Then compare the character of Bob to other legendary characters you know.

Research
Bob Lemmons was a real-life "mustanger" who worked to gain the trust of wild horses. Research Lemmons's life and the methods he used to gather horses. Consider the following:

a. Lemmons's personal history and motivations

b. the job of capturing wild horses in the old West

c. horse training tactics that are practiced today

Take notes as you perform your research. Then, write a brief **explanation** of why Bob Lemmons makes a good legendary character.

Write
Warrior plays an important role in the story. Write an **essay** in which you analyze Warrior as a character from folk literature. Consider, for example, the stallion's heroic traits and unusual abilities. Support your analysis with story details.

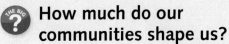 **How much do our communities shape us?**

(a) What is Bob Lemmons's "community"? **(b)** How does this community influence Bob's life and personality? Explain.

"Alone we can do so little; **together** we can do **so much**.

—**Helen Keller**

SHARED LESSONS

As you read the folk literature in this section, explore the ways in which tales from the oral tradition can reveal the values, beliefs, and customs of the cultures from which they originated. The quotation on the opposite page will help you start thinking about ways in which learning from past mistakes or experiences can help you understand common themes about life.

◀ **CRITICAL VIEWING** How can a person benefit from sharing his or her experiences with others in a situation such as the one shown in the photo?

READINGS IN PART 2

FABLE • RUSSIAN FOLK TALE
The Tiger Who Would Be King • The Ant and the Dove
James Thurber • Leo Tolstoy
(p. 634) • (p. 636)

GREEK MYTH
Arachne
Olivia E. Coolidge
(p. 642)

FOLK TALE
The Stone
Lloyd Alexander
(p. 652)

FOLK TALE
Why the Tortoise's Shell Is Not Smooth
Chinua Achebe
(p. 668)

CLOSE READING TOOL

Use the **Close Reading Tool** to practice the strategies you learn in this unit.

Elements of Folk Literature

Folk literature is a genre of writing that has its origins in the **oral tradition.**

The Oral Tradition Long before writing or books were invented, people told stories. These stories were passed along by word of mouth from one generation to the next. You may have experienced a similar sharing of stories among your family or friends. The passing along of stories is known as the **oral tradition.** Folk literature—including folk tales, fairy tales, fables, wise sayings, folk songs, legends, and myths—originated in the stories of the oral tradition.

Theme is the central message or insight in a literary work. The themes in folk literature have survived the test of time and place. This is because many themes in folk literature are universal.

Universal themes express ideas, values, and insights into human nature that people from different cultures and eras have found meaningful and important. For example, universal themes might warn of the dangers of greed or the value of kindness. Sometimes, the theme of a folk story is **culturally specific.** Such themes reflect the background, customs, and beliefs of a particular culture.

Purposes of Folk Literature The **purpose** of a literary work is the reason it is created. In folk literature, that purpose may be to teach a lesson, to explain something in nature, or simply to entertain. In folk literature, the purpose may be tied closely to the theme.

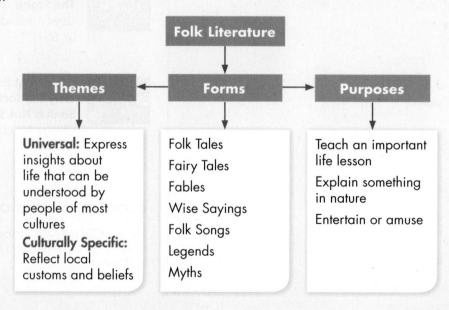

Folk Literature

Themes ↔ **Forms** → **Purposes**

Themes
Universal: Express insights about life that can be understood by people of most cultures
Culturally Specific: Reflect local customs and beliefs

Forms
Folk Tales
Fairy Tales
Fables
Wise Sayings
Folk Songs
Legends
Myths

Purposes
Teach an important life lesson
Explain something in nature
Entertain or amuse

The Oral Tradition in Print

Once writing and books were invented, stories from the oral tradition were collected and put into print. Today, collections of folk literature are generally classified by type.

Folk Tales are stories that often deal with heroes, adventure, magic, or romance. They were told not only to entertain but also to communicate the shared ideas of a culture.

Fables are brief stories or poems that teach lessons, or morals. These morals are usually stated directly at the ends of the fables. The main characters are often animals with human characteristics.

Folk songs present the ideas, values, feelings, and beliefs of a culture in musical form. With simple melodies and repeated lines, they tell stories of war, adventure, and romance.

Myths are fictional tales that explore the actions of gods and heroes or explain why things are a certain way in the natural world. Every ancient culture has its own **mythology.** The mythology of ancient Greece and Rome is known as **classical mythology.**

Legends are traditional, familiar stories about the past. Legends usually have some basis in fact. However, over time and through many retellings, the factual details have often been changed, making the legends more fiction than fact.

Characteristics of Folk Literature The different types of folk literature have many common characteristics.

Characteristic	Definition
Fantasy	writing that is highly imaginative and contains elements not found in real life
Personification	type of figurative language in which a nonhuman subject is given human characteristics
Hyperbole	exaggeration or overstatement that is often used to create a comic effect
Irony	involves surprises, unexpected events, and interesting or amusing contradictions
Dialect	form of language spoken by people of a particular region or group

Analyzing Structure and Theme in Folk Literature

Works of folk literature express **themes**—central messages that provide insights into life and human nature.

For modern readers, folk literature is a source of entertainment and insights. Elements of adventure, romance, and drama provide the entertainment. However, it is the themes—the deeper meanings of these stories—that provide insights into human nature.

Stated and Implied Theme

Themes in folk literature are expressed in many different ways. In a fable, the theme is often stated at the end of the story as a moral, or lesson. Look at the following example.

Example: The Boy Who Cried Wolf

While watching his father's sheep, a boy decided to trick the local villagers. "Wolf! Wolf!" he cried, loud enough for all to hear. When the villagers ran to help him, they discovered that there was no wolf. The boy continued playing this trick for several days. Then one day, a wolf actually appeared. The boy cried, "Wolf! Wolf!" but the villagers thought the boy was playing his trick again. They ignored his pleas for help. As a result, the wolf ate the sheep.

Moral: If you always tell lies, no one will believe you when you tell the truth.

Not all themes in folk literature are so clearly stated, however. Sometimes, a theme is implied, or suggested.

In these cases, readers must analyze the characters, setting, and events in the story to determine what the theme is.

Symbols and Theme A symbol is a person, place, or object that represents something beyond its literal meaning. For example, a mirror might symbolize vanity in a fairy tale or folk tale. As you read, pay attention to objects that seem to represent important ideas. Understanding the deeper meaning of a symbol can help you determine a story's theme.

Common Themes in Folk Literature

Here are some common themes in folk literature:

- Often, those who seem foolish are actually wise.
- Too much pride can lead to a fall.
- Wisdom comes through suffering.
- The virtues of kindness, generosity, and modesty are stronger than their opposites—cruelty, greed, and pride.
- An unappealing outward appearance may disguise a noble soul.

Folk literature has several unique characteristics and structural devices that contribute to the development of theme. Keep these in mind as you read.

Simple Diction Diction is an author's choice of words, phrases, and sentence structure. The simple diction in much of folk literature is characterized by plain, common words, everyday language, and simple sentence construction. The use of simple diction helps convey theme in a way that people of all backgrounds can easily recognize and understand.

Repetition The repetition of events, lines of dialogue, descriptions, and sound patterns is a familiar element in folk literature. A **refrain,** often found in folk songs and poems, is the repetition of a phrase, line, or verse at regular intervals in the text. Repetition adds a pleasing rhythm to a story. In addition, it probably helped listeners and storytellers of the past remember the details of a story or song.

Patterns In folk literature, the story structure often follows a familiar and regular pattern. For example, many folk stories begin with simple phrases such as *Once upon a time...* or *Long ago, in a far-off land....* Another pattern often found in folk literature is the introduction of "threes"— for example, three characters or three events. The fairy tale "Rumpelstiltskin" is a good example of the use of "threes."

Patterns in "Rumpelstiltskin"
• A young girl must spin <u>three</u> rooms of straw into gold.
• She has <u>three</u> days to complete her task.
• She gets <u>three</u> tries to guess the name of the odd little man who helps her.

Archetypes An **archetype** is an element that recurs regularly in literature and has similar meanings to people of different cultures and eras. Oral storytellers used archetypes to explore universal themes such as the dangers of greed and the importance of courage. Here are some common archetypes found in folk literature:

Common Archetypes in Folk Literature	
Plot	• dangerous journey • quest to prove one's honor • search for a valuable item
Characters	• enchanted princess • superhuman heroes and villains • trickster, or wise fool • talking animals
Ideas	• good vs. evil • magic in the normal world • hero or heroine aided by supernatural forces • evil disguised as good

Meet the Author

James Thurber (1894–1961) wrote for his high school and college newspapers in Ohio. After military service in World War I, Thurber began writing and cartooning. Much of his early work appeared in *The New Yorker* magazine. Although failing eyesight forced him to give up drawing, Thurber kept making people laugh through his writing.

Leo Tolstoy (1828–1910) was born into a wealthy family in Russia and inherited the family estate. By the time he was fifty, he had written some of the world's most famous novels, including *War and Peace*. In midlife, Tolstoy began to reject his life of luxury. He surrendered the rights to many of his works and gave his property to his family. This world-famous writer died alone in a remote train station in Russia.

How much do our communities shape us?

Explore the Big Question as you read "The Tiger Who Would Be King" and "The Ant and the Dove."

CLOSE READING FOCUS

Key Ideas and Details: **Cause and Effect**

A **cause** is an event, an action, or a feeling that produces a result. The result is called an **effect**. Sometimes an effect is the result of several causes. Other times, one cause can produce several different effects. To help you identify the relationship between an event and its causes, reread important passages in a literary work, looking for connections.

Craft and Structure: **Fables and Folk Tales**

Fables and **folk tales** are part of the oral tradition, in which stories and poems were passed from generation to generation by word of mouth.

- **Fables** are brief stories that often have animal characters. A fable teaches a lesson, or moral, that is usually stated at the end of the story.
- **Folk tales** often have clever characters who outsmart their superiors. These stories may contain elements of magic and adventure.

Some fables and folk tales have *ironic*, or surprising, endings because they do not turn out as you expect. The twist ending helps you see the story's theme, or message. As you read a fable or folk tale, notice how the setting, characters, and events introduce and develop the story's theme.

Vocabulary

You will encounter the following words in these tales. Write the words in your notebook, underlining the verbs.

prowled	inquired	repulse
monarch	startled	repaid

CLOSE READING MODEL

The passages below are from the fable "The Tiger Who Would Be King" and the folk tale "The Ant and the Dove." The annotations to the right of the passages show ways in which you can use close reading skills to analyze cause and effect and to interpret fables and folk tales.

from "The Tiger Who Would Be King"

One morning the tiger woke up in the jungle and told his mate that he was king of beasts.

"Leo, the lion, is king of beasts," she said. [1]

"We need a change," said the tiger. "The creatures are crying for a change."

The tigress listened but she could hear no crying, except that of her cubs.

"I'll be king of beasts by the time the moon rises," said the tiger. [2]

Fables and Folk Tales

1 A tiger announces that he is king of beasts, and his mate responds. The fact that these animals think and speak like humans can help you identify the story as a fable or folk tale.

Cause and Effect

2 Although the tigress does not hear the animals "crying for a change," the tiger insists he will replace the lion as king. You might predict that the tiger's plan to become king will become the cause of a conflict.

from "The Ant and the Dove"

A few days later a hunter was about to catch the dove in his net. When the ant saw what was happening, it walked right up to the man and bit him on the foot. Startled, the man dropped the net. [3] And the dove, thinking that you never can tell how or when a kindness may be repaid, flew away. [4]

Cause and Effect

3 The man's attempt to catch the dove causes the ant to bite the man. The effect of the bite is that the man drops the net.

Fables and Folk Tales

4 To discover the moral or theme of a folk tale, look for direct statements that reflect a general truth or an important idea about life.

THE TIGER WHO WOULD BE KING

JAMES THURBER

One morning the tiger woke up in the jungle and told his mate that he was king of beasts.

"Leo, the lion, is king of beasts," she said.

"We need a change," said the tiger. "The creatures are crying for a change."

The tigress listened but she could hear no crying, except that of her cubs.

"I'll be king of beasts by the time the moon rises," said the tiger. "It will be a yellow moon with black stripes, in my honor."

"Oh, sure," said the tigress as she went to look after her young, one of whom, a male, very like his father, had got an imaginary thorn in his paw.

The tiger prowled through the jungle till he came to the lion's den. "Come out," he roared, "and greet the king of beasts! The king is dead, long live the king!"

Inside the den, the lioness woke her mate. "The king is here to see you," she said.

"What king?" he inquired, sleepily.

"The king of beasts," she said.

Vocabulary ▶
prowled (proʊld)
v. moved around quietly and secretly

inquired (in kwīrd´)
v. asked

"I am the king of beasts," roared Leo, and he charged out of the den to defend his crown against the pretender.

It was a terrible fight, and it lasted until the setting of the sun. All the animals of the jungle joined in, some taking the side of the tiger and others the side of the lion. Every creature from the aardvark to the zebra took part in the struggle to overthrow the lion or to **repulse** the tiger, and some did not know which they were fighting for, and some fought for both, and some fought whoever was nearest, and some fought for the sake of fighting.

"What are we fighting for?" someone asked the aardvark.

"The old order," said the aardvark.

"What are we dying for?" someone asked the zebra.

"The new order," said the zebra.

When the moon rose, fevered and gibbous,[1] it shone upon a jungle in which nothing stirred except a macaw[2] and a cockatoo,[3] screaming in horror. All the beasts were dead except the tiger, and his days were numbered and his time was ticking away. He was **monarch** of all he surveyed, but it didn't seem to mean anything.

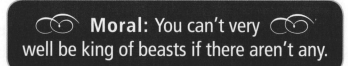

Moral: You can't very well be king of beasts if there aren't any.

LITERATURE IN CONTEXT

Language Connection

Allusions

James Thurber uses an allusion in his description of the tigress who attends to her male cub with an imaginary thorn in his paw. An *allusion* is a reference to a person, place, or thing in another artistic work. Thurber makes an allusion to the fable of a shepherd who boldly relieves a lion from the pain caused by a thorn in his paw. Later, when the shepherd is in danger, the lion remembers the shepherd's kindness and saves him.

Connect to Literature

Why does Thurber allude to the fable about the lion and the shepherd?

◀ **Vocabulary**
repulse (ri puls´)
v. drive back;
repel an attack

monarch (män´ ərk)
n. single or sole ruler

Fables and Folk Tales
What conflict or problem does this fable address?

---

1. **gibbous** (gib´ əs) *adj.* more than half but less than completely illuminated.
2. **macaw** (mə kô´) *n.* bright-colored, harsh-voiced parrot of Central or South America.
3. **cockatoo** (kok´ ə tü´) *n.* crested parrot with white feathers tinged with yellow or pink.

The Ant and the Dove
Russian Folk Tale · Leo Tolstoy

Spiral Review
CHARACTERS How are the characters in this story typical of fables?

Vocabulary ▶
startled (stärt′ əld) *adj.* surprised

repaid (ri pād′) *v.* did or gave in return

A thirsty ant went to the stream to drink. Suddenly it got caught in a whirlpool and was almost carried away.

At that moment a dove was passing by with a twig in its beak. The dove dropped the twig for the tiny insect to grab hold of. So it was that the ant was saved.

A few days later a hunter was about to catch the dove in his net. When the ant saw what was happening, it walked right up to the man and bit him on the foot. Startled, the man dropped the net. And the dove, thinking that you never can tell how or when a kindness may be repaid, flew away.

Language Study

Vocabulary Respond to each item below based on your knowledge of the italicized vocabulary words.

> **prowled   inquired   repulse   monarch   startled**

1. Explain why a wolf might have *prowled* near a river.
2. Provide two reasons why garbage might *repulse* people.
3. Identify three things that a *startled* person might do.
4. Explain why you might have *inquired* about a friend's health.
5. Explain why the United States does not have a *monarch*.

WORD STUDY

The **suffix -ment** means the "act," "art," or "process of." A word ending in -ment is usually a noun. "The Ant and the Dove" is a story about the **repayment** of a favor, or the act of paying back a favor.

Word Study

Part A Explain how the **suffix -ment** contributes to the meanings of *argument* and *payment*. Consult a dictionary if necessary.

Part B Use context and what you know about the suffix -ment to explain your answer to each question.

1. When do you give your friends *encouragement*?
2. How do you get a *measurement*?

Literary Analysis

Key Ideas and Details

1. **Cause and Effect (a)** In "The Tiger Who Would Be King," identify two causes of the fight in the jungle. **(b)** What is the effect of the fight?

2. **(a)** What does the dove in "The Ant and the Dove" do for the ant? **(b) Make Inferences:** How does this action save the ant?

3. **Cause and Effect** What is the end effect of the dove's action in "The Ant and the Dove?"

Craft and Structure

4. **Fables and Folk Tales** Make a chart like the one on the right to identify the elements of fables and folk tales in the two stories.

5. **Fables and Folk Tales (a)** What is **ironic**, or surprising, about the ending of "The Tiger Who Would Be King"? **(b)** What theme does the ending suggest?

Title	
Characters	Moral or Theme

Integration of Knowledge and Ideas

6. **(a)** Which two animals fight to rule in "The Tiger Who Would Be King"? **(b) Make Inferences:** Some of the animals join the fight for the sake of fighting. What does this suggest about them? **(c) Apply:** What human qualities does Thurber show in these animals?

7. **Relate:** Does "The Ant and the Dove" remind you of any other stories you have read? Explain.

8. **How much do our communities shape us?** With a small group, discuss the following questions: **(a)** In "The Tiger Who Would Be King," what action in the community could have saved the animals? Support your answer with details. **(b) Draw Conclusions:** Explain why the animals did not take that action.

ACADEMIC VOCABULARY

As you write and speak about "The Tiger Who Would Be King" and "The Ant and the Dove," use the words related to cooperation that you explored on page 613 of this text.

Conventions: **Subject Complements**

A **subject complement** is a noun, a pronoun, or an adjective that appears with a linking verb and tells something about the subject of the sentence.

A **predicate noun** renames or identifies the subject. A **predicate adjective** describes the subject.

Predicate Noun	Predicate Adjective
Lucy is an excellent *doctor*.	This toast tastes *burnt*.
To us, he seems a *fool*.	Frank seemed *glad* about the news.
The caterpillar became a *butterfly*.	You've grown *tall* this summer!
Her piggy bank was a small *cat*.	If the cheese smells *moldy*, don't eat it.

Practice A

Identify the predicate noun or predicate adjective in each sentence.

1. The lion is king of the beasts.
2. The tiger grows angry.
3. The tigress was busy with her cubs.
4. The argument became a war.
5. His roar sounds fierce.
6. The tiger became the king.

Reading Application In "The Tiger Who Would Be King," find at least two predicate nouns and two predicate adjectives. Copy the sentences with subject complements and label each complement *predicate noun* or *predicate adjective*.

Practice B

Identify the predicate noun or predicate adjective in each sentence. Then, rewrite each sentence, replacing the predicate noun or predicate adjective to change the meaning of the sentence.

1. The ant is helpful to the dove.
2. The man became a hunter.
3. The ant's action was kind.
4. The dove seems thankful now.

Writing Application Write a description of one of the fables. Use at least two predicate adjectives and two predicate nouns in your description. Circle the predicate adjectives and the predicate nouns you use.

Writing to Sources

Narrative Text Write a **fable** that teaches the same lesson as one of the selections you read.

- First, reread the selection to determine what lesson it teaches. Then, brainstorm for situations in which characters could learn that lesson.

- Decide who your characters will be, then use dialogue and description to develop the characters.

- Use effective pacing in your fable. To slow the pace as you introduce scenes, use longer sentences and more details. To move faster and create tension, use short sentences.

- Use transitions to clearly show how story events lead to the lesson learned.

- Provide a moral at the end that logically follows from the events.

Grammar Application Review your fable to identify and correct errors in grammar and punctuation.

Speaking and Listening

Presentation of Ideas Prepare an **oral report** on either James Thurber or Leo Tolstoy.

- Research the author's life using the Internet or print sources. Answer questions you have about the author's background and key published works. Add questions or change your focus, if necessary, as your research develops.

- Take notes on the key points you want to share in your report. Then, use your notes to compose an interesting oral presentation. Include information that tells how some of the author's other works are similar to and different from the one you read in your textbook.

- Prepare visual aids, such as pictures, timelines, and graphs to grab your audience's attention and to support your ideas.

- Practice delivering your presentation. Speak expressively, emphasizing key points. When you are ready, share your report with the class.

Building Knowledge

Meet the Author

Olivia E. Coolidge (1908–2006) lived in both Europe and the United States. She taught English, Latin, and Greek, but was best known as a writer. In addition to writing about subjects from classical mythology, such as the Trojan War, she wrote about colonial times in American history. Coolidge was known for the accuracy of her historical fiction and for her attention to detail. She said that she enjoyed writing about legends and myths because they express ancient values that are still important in the modern world.

How much do our communities shape us?

Explore the Big Question as you read "Arachne." Take notes on ways in which the myth expresses the values of ancient Greek society.

CLOSE READING FOCUS

Key Ideas and Details: **Cause and Effect**

A **cause** is an event, action, or emotion that makes something happen. An **effect** is what happens. When an effect occurs, it can then become the cause of another event. In most stories, the plot unfolds as a series of linked events—causes and effects—that are organized into sentences, paragraphs, and scenes.

As you read, look for clue words such as *because, so,* and *as a result* that signal cause-and-effect relationships. Then, ask questions such as "What happened?" and "Why did this happen?" to help you follow the structure of cause-and-effect.

Craft and Structure: **Myths**

Myths are fictional tales that describe the actions of gods or heroes. Every culture has its own myths. A myth can do one or more of the following:

- Tell how the universe or a culture began
- Explain something in nature, such as thunder
- Express a theme, or insight—often one that emphasizes the importance of a value, such as honesty or bravery

The characters, plot, and imagery in a myth often provide a glimpse into the culture from which the myth came.

Vocabulary

You will encounter the following words in "Arachne." Which word is an adverb? How can you tell?

obscure	humble	mortal
indignantly	obstinacy	strive

CLOSE READING MODEL

The passage below is from Olivia E. Coolidge's retelling of the myth "Arachne." The annotations to the right of the passage show ways in which you can use close reading skills to analyze cause and effect and interpret myths.

from **"Arachne"**

"Stupid old woman," said Arachne indignantly, "who gave you a right to speak in this way to me? It is easy to see that you were never good for anything in your day, or you would not come here in poverty and rags to gaze at my skill. If Athene resents my words, let her answer them herself. I have challenged her to a contest, but she, of course, will not come. It is easy for the gods to avoid matching their skill with that of men." [1]

At these words the old woman threw down her staff and stood erect. The wondering onlookers saw her grow tall and fair and stand clad in long robes of dazzling white. They were terribly afraid as they realized that they stood in the presence of Athene. Arachne herself flushed red for a moment, for she had never really believed that the goddess would hear her. [2] Before the group that was gathered there she would not give in; so pressing her pale lips together in obstinacy and pride, she led the goddess to one of the great looms and set herself before the other. [3]

Myths

1 Arachne says she has challenged Athene, and complains that the gods avoid competition with humans. These details help you infer that Athene is a goddess and that this tale is a myth. Arachne's boastful attitude suggests that the myth might convey an important idea about pride.

Cause and Effect

2 Blushing red is an effect, caused by Arachne's realization that she has insulted Athene. Here, the word *for* means "because" and signals a cause-and-effect relationship.

Cause and Effect

3 Arachne is too proud to give in. This feeling of pride causes her to compete against Athene.

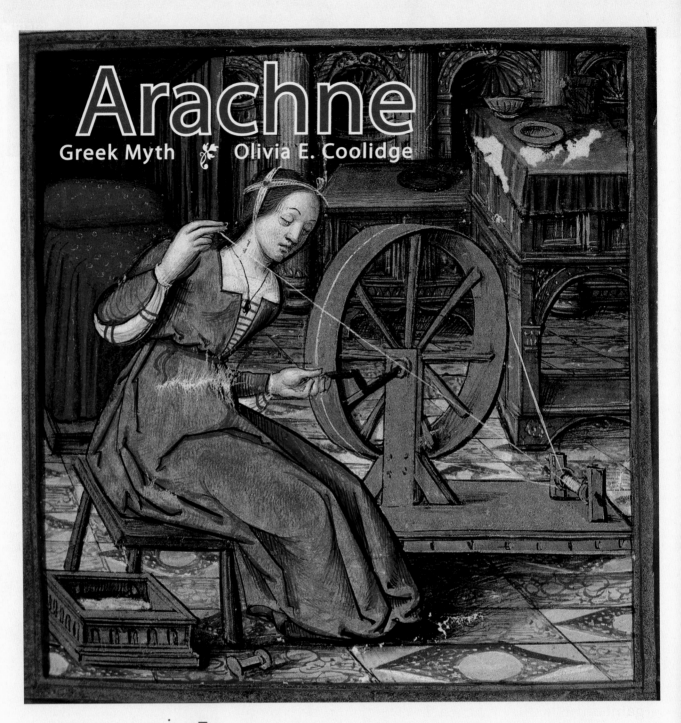

Arachne

Greek Myth ❧ **Olivia E. Coolidge**

A rachne [ə rak´ nē] was a maiden who became famous throughout Greece, though she was neither wellborn nor beautiful and came from no great city. She lived in an obscure little village, and her father was a humble dyer of wool.

In this he was very skillful, producing many varied shades, while above all he was famous for the clear, bright scarlet which is made from shellfish, and which was the most glorious of all the colors used in ancient Greece. Even more skillful than her father was Arachne. It was her task to spin the fleecy wool into a fine, soft thread and to weave it into cloth on the high, standing loom within the cottage. Arachne was small and pale from much working. Her eyes were light and her hair was a dusty brown, yet she was quick and graceful, and her fingers, roughened as they were, went so fast that it was hard to follow their flickering movements. So soft and even was her thread, so fine her cloth, so gorgeous her embroidery, that soon her products were known all over Greece. No one had ever seen the like of them before.

At last Arachne's fame became so great that people used to come from far and wide to watch her working. Even the graceful nymphs[1] would steal in from stream or forest and peep shyly through the dark doorway, watching in wonder the white arms of Arachne as she stood at the loom and threw the shuttle from hand to hand between the hanging threads, or drew out the long wool, fine as a hair, from the distaff[2] as she sat spinning. "Surely Athene[3] herself must have taught her," people would murmur to one another. "Who else could know the secret of such marvelous skill?"

Arachne was used to being wondered at, and she was immensely proud of the skill that had brought so many to look on her. Praise was all she lived for, and it displeased her greatly that people should think anyone, even a goddess, could teach her anything. Therefore when she heard them murmur, she would stop her work and turn round indignantly to say, "With my own ten fingers I gained this skill, and by hard practice from early morning till night. I never had time to stand looking as you people do while another maiden worked. Nor if I had, would I give Athene credit because the girl was more skillful than I. As

Cause and Effect
What causes Arachne's work to be known all over Greece?

Spiral Review
SETTING In this paragraph, what do you learn about the world of this story?

---

1. **nymphs** (nimfz) *n.* minor nature goddesses, represented as beautiful maidens living in rivers, trees, and mountains.
2. **distaff** (dis´ taf) *n.* stick on which flax or wool is wound for spinning.
3. **Athene** (ə thē´ nə) *n.* Greek goddess of wisdom, skills, and warfare.

Cause and Effect
What do you think will be the effect of Arachne's bragging?

Vocabulary ▶
mortal (môr′ təl) *adj.* referring to humans, who eventually die

indignantly (in dig′ nənt lē) *adv.* in a way that expresses anger

obstinacy (äb′ stə nə sē) *n.* stubbornness

strive (strīv) *v.* struggle; compete

for Athene's weaving, how could there be finer cloth or more beautiful embroidery than mine? If Athene herself were to come down and compete with me, she could do no better than I."

One day when Arachne turned round with such words, an old woman answered her, a gray old woman, bent and very poor, who stood leaning on a staff and peering at Arachne amid the crowd of onlookers. "Reckless girl," she said, "how dare you claim to be equal to the immortal gods themselves? I am an old woman and have seen much. Take my advice and ask pardon of Athene for your words. Rest content with your fame of being the best spinner and weaver that mortal eyes have ever beheld."

"Stupid old woman," said Arachne indignantly, "who gave you a right to speak in this way to me? It is easy to see that you were never good for anything in your day, or you would not come here in poverty and rags to gaze at my skill. If Athene resents my words, let her answer them herself. I have challenged her to a contest, but she, of course, will not come. It is easy for the gods to avoid matching their skill with that of men."

At these words the old woman threw down her staff and stood erect. The wondering onlookers saw her grow tall and fair and stand clad in long robes of dazzling white. They were terribly afraid as they realized that they stood in the presence of Athene. Arachne herself flushed red for a moment, for she had never really believed that the goddess would hear her. Before the group that was gathered there she would not give in; so pressing her pale lips together in obstinacy and pride, she led the goddess to one of the great looms and set herself before the other. Without a word both began to thread the long woolen strands that hang from the rollers, and between which the shuttle[4] moves back and forth. Many skeins lay heaped beside

---

4. **shuttle** (shut′ əl) *n.* instrument used in weaving to carry thread back and forth.

them to use, bleached white, and gold, and scarlet, and other shades, varied as the rainbow. Arachne had never thought of giving credit for her success to her father's skill in dyeing, though in actual truth the colors were as remarkable as the cloth itself.

Soon there was no sound in the room but the breathing of the onlookers, the whirring of the shuttles, and the creaking of the wooden frames as each pressed the thread up into place or tightened the pegs by which the whole was held straight. The excited crowd in the doorway began to see that the skill of both in truth was very nearly equal, but that, however the cloth might turn out, the goddess was the quicker of the two. A pattern of many pictures was growing on her loom. There was a border of twined branches of the olive, Athene's favorite tree, while in the middle, figures began to appear. As they looked at the glowing colors, the spectators realized that Athene was weaving into her pattern a last warning to Arachne. The central figure was the goddess herself competing with Poseidon for possession of the city of Athens; but in the four corners were mortals who had tried to strive with gods and pictures of the awful fate that had overtaken them. The goddess ended a little before Arachne and stood back from her marvelous work to see what the maiden was doing.

Never before had Arachne been matched against anyone whose skill was equal, or even nearly equal to her own. As she stole glances from time to time at Athene and saw the goddess working swiftly, calmly, and always a little faster than herself, she became angry instead of frightened, and an evil thought came into her head. Thus as Athene stepped back a pace to watch Arachne finishing her work, she saw that the maiden had taken for her design a pattern of scenes which showed evil or unworthy actions of the gods, how they had deceived fair maidens, resorted to trickery, and appeared on earth from time to time in the form of poor and humble people. When the goddess saw this insult glowing in bright colors on Arachne's loom, she did not wait while the cloth was

LITERATURE IN CONTEXT

Culture Connection

Athene

As goddess of wisdom and warfare, Athene was a key figure in Greek mythology. Athene protected her favorites, such as Odysseus and Heracles (or Hercules), and punished those who displeased her, including Arachne and Ajax, a famous Greek warrior. According to one story, the people of a major Greek city wanted to name their city after either Poseidon, the sea god, or Athene, depending on who gave them the more useful gift. Poseidon created horses, and Athene created olive trees. The gods judged Athene's gift more useful, so Athens was named for her. To honor Athene, the city built a great temple, called the Parthenon.

Connect to the Literature

Which of Athene's character traits does this myth illustrate?

Comprehension

Why is Arachne upset when people say Athene must have taught her to spin?

judged, but stepped forward, her gray eyes blazing with anger, and tore Arachne's work across. Then she struck Arachne across the face. Arachne stood there a moment, struggling with anger, fear, and pride. "I will not live under this insult," she cried, and seizing a rope from the wall, she made a noose and would have hanged herself.

The goddess touched the rope and touched the maiden. "Live on, wicked girl," she said. "Live on and spin, both you and your descendants. When men look at you they may remember that it is not wise to strive with Athene." At that the body of Arachne shriveled up, and her legs grew tiny, spindly, and distorted. There before the eyes of the spectators hung a little dusty brown spider on a slender thread.

All spiders descend from Arachne, and as the Greeks watched them spinning their thread wonderfully fine, they remembered the contest with Athene and thought that it was not right for even the best of men to claim equality with the gods.

Myths
Why is Arachne's design disrespectful to the gods?

Myths
What traits of spiders does this myth explain?

Language Study

Vocabulary The words in blue appear in "Arachne." Rewrite each sentence below, using a vocabulary word so that the new sentence has the opposite meaning of the original.

obscure	humble	indignantly	obstinacy	strive

1. Everyone in the class had heard of the famous novel.
2. Her agreeable nature makes her easy to get along with.
3. Mr. Vallone was a rich and famous tailor.
4. "No, thank you," she said in a cheerful way.
5. The two brothers always try to help each other.

Word Study

Part A Explain how the **Latin root -mort-** contributes to the meanings of *immortal* and *mortician*. Consult a dictionary if necessary.

Part B Use context and what you know about the Latin root *-mort-* to explain your answer to each question.

1. If an ancient Greek warrior received a *mortal* wound, would he recover?
2. How strongly embarrassed is someone who is *mortified*?

WORD STUDY

The **Latin root -mort-** means "death." Unlike a god or goddess, who cannot die, Arachne is a **mortal**—a human being, who will not live forever.

Close Reading Activities

Literary Analysis

Key Ideas and Details

1. **Cause and Effect** What is the effect of Arachne's skill as a weaver?

2. **Cause and Effect** What causes Athene to visit Arachne?

3. **Cause and Effect** Complete the chart on the right to show other causes and effects in "Arachne."

4. **(a)** What does Arachne value more than anything else? **(b) Interpret:** Why does Arachne refuse to accept the advice of the old woman? **(c) Analyze:** What character traits does Arachne reveal through her behavior?

5. **(a)** What design does Athene weave? **(b) Make Inferences:** What is Athene's original intention toward Arachne? **(c) Deduce:** What makes Athene angry?

Craft and Structure

6. **Myths** What does this myth explain about spiders?

7. **Myths** What beliefs and values about behavior are taught through the theme of this myth?

Integration of Knowledge and Ideas

8. **(a) Make a Judgment:** Do you think it was fair of Athene to turn Arachne into a spider? **(b) Defend:** Share and defend your judgment with a partner. Then decide together on a single answer to share with the class.

9. **Compare and Contrast:** Think of another myth you have read. Then, explain the ways in which "Arachne" is similar to and different from that myth.

Causes	Effects
Arachne challenges Athene.	
	Arachne's design shows unworthy actions of the gods.
Athene touches the rope and touches Arachne.	

10. **THE BIG ?** **How much do our communities shape us?** Discuss the following questions with a partner or in a small group. **(a) Interpret:** In ancient Greece, what important life lesson might this myth have taught its audience? **(b) Synthesize:** What cultural values do the story and its lesson suggest?

ACADEMIC VOCABULARY

As you write and speak about "Arachne," use the words related to values that you explored on page 613 of this text.

Conventions: Direct and Indirect Objects

A **direct object** is a noun or pronoun that receives the action of the verb and answers the question *Who* or *What?* An **indirect object** names the person or thing to whom or for whom an action is done, and answers the question *To or for whom?* or *To or for what?*

Sentence	Question	Answer	Direct/Indirect Object
Elsa baked bread.	Baked *what?*	*bread*	*bread* (direct object)
Mimi brought us a surprise.	Brought *what?* Brought *to whom?*	*surprise* *us*	*surprise* (direct object) *us* (indirect object)

An indirect object appears between the verb and the direct object.

If a noun or pronoun is followed by a preposition such as *to* or *for*, the noun or pronoun after the preposition becomes the object of the preposition. It is not an indirect object.

Example: I threw the ball <u>to *Jack*</u>.

Practice A
Find the direct object and either the indirect object or the prepositional phrase in the following sentences. Then, rewrite each sentence with a different direct object.

1. Arachne's father taught her the art of weaving.
2. The goddess gave Arachne a warning.
3. Arachne showed her anger to the crowd.

Reading Application Identify at least three examples of direct objects in "Arachne."

Practice B
Use the following verbs to write sentences that contain direct objects, indirect objects, and prepositional phrases. Label each direct object, indirect object, and prepositional phrase.

1. give   2. bought   3. made

Writing Application Use direct and indirect objects and prepositional phrases to write three sentences about myths. Use these sentences as models: *People tell their children myths. People tell myths to their children.*

Writing to Sources

Explanatory Text Write a brief **comparison-and-contrast essay** in which you analyze ways in which the characters of Arachne and Athene are alike and different.

- Reread the myth to find details that describe the personality, appearance, motivations, and actions of each character. Record your notes in a two-column chart or Venn diagram.
- Choose an organizational structure—such as the block or point-by-point method (see p. 243)—that will help you present your ideas clearly.
- Use language that expresses your meaning precisely and is appropriately formal for academic work.
- Support your ideas with details from the myth.

Grammar Application Use direct and indirect objects in your essay to add information to your sentences.

Research and Technology

Build and Present Knowledge Imagine that you are writing an essay that explains how "Arachne" reflects the cultural values of ancient Greece. Find two reliable research sources that provide information on that topic. Then write an **annotated bibliography entry** for each source.

- Use a library catalog or do a keyword search on the Internet to find reliable sources of information.
- Sources should be well-known for accuracy and recently published. Consult Web sites that have *.edu, .gov,* or *.org* at the ends of their addresses.
- Write down publication information from two sources.
- Read each source. Paraphrase, or restate, key ideas in your own words in order to avoid plagiarism.
- Write an annotated bibliography entry for each source. Include the publication information, your paraphrases, and an explanation of why the source is reliable and valuable.

Meet the Author

Lloyd Alexander (1924–2007) shocked his parents by telling them he wanted to become a writer. "My family pleaded with me to forget literature and do something sensible, such as find some sort of useful work," he recalled. He eventually became a successful author, after working in a bank, serving in World War II, and writing for a magazine. He wrote more than forty books for children and young adults.

How much do our communities shape us?

Explore the Big Question as you read "The Stone." Take notes on ways in which the story explores how one individual's actions can impact his family and community.

CLOSE READING FOCUS

Key Ideas and Details: **Setting a Purpose**

Setting a purpose, or reason, for reading gives you a focus as you read. Once you have set your purpose, adjust your reading rate to help you accomplish that purpose.

- When you are reading to learn facts, read slowly and carefully. Pause periodically to think about what you have read. Your reading rate should also be slow when you read descriptive passages that are heavy with details.
- When you are reading for enjoyment, you can read faster. For example, you might read dialogue quickly to imitate the flow of conversation.

Craft and Structure: **Universal Theme**

The theme of a literary work is its central idea or message about life and human nature. A **universal theme** is a message that is expressed regularly in many cultures and time periods. Examples of universal themes include the importance of courage, the power of love, and the danger of greed. You can find a story's universal theme by examining its conflict and the actions of the main character. Notice the changes he or she undergoes and the effects of those changes.

Vocabulary

You will encounter the following words in this story. Write synonyms for the words you know.

feeble	vanished	plight
jubilation	rue	sown

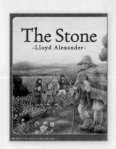

CLOSE READING MODEL

The passage below is from Lloyd Alexander's folk tale "The Stone." The annotations to the right of the passage show ways in which you can use close reading skills to set a purpose for reading and to analyze universal themes.

from "The Stone"

There was a cottager named Maibon, and one day he was driving down the road in his horse and cart when he saw an old man hobbling along, so frail and feeble he doubted the poor soul could go many more steps. Though Maibon offered to take him in the cart, the old man refused; and Maibon went his way home, shaking his head over such a pitiful sight, **1** and said to his wife, Modrona:

"Ah, ah, what a sorry thing it is to have your bones creaking and cracking, and dim eyes, and dull wits. **2** When I think this might come to me, too! A fine, strong-armed, sturdy-legged fellow like me? One day to go tottering, and have his teeth rattling in his head, and live on porridge, like a baby? There's no fate worse in all the world."

"There is," answered Modrona, "and that would be to have neither teeth nor porridge. **3** "Get on with you, Maibon, and stop borrowing trouble. Hoe your field or you'll have no crop to harvest, and no food for you, nor me, nor the little ones." **4**

Setting a Purpose
1 At this point, your purpose for reading might be to find out if Maibon will see the old man again.

Universal Theme
2 Maibon thinks the old man's signs of age are "a sorry thing," and he dreads growing old himself. The fear of getting older and closer to death appears in many stories. You may recognize it as a universal theme.

Setting a Purpose
3 When you come to the conversation between Maibon and Modrona, you may decide to read more quickly, so that their dialogue sounds like a real-life conversation.

Universal Theme
4 Madrona tells Maibon to "stop borrowing trouble." In other words, Madrona wants Maibon to be happy with what he has. You may recognize this idea as a universal theme.

The Stone

·Lloyd Alexander·

There was a cottager named Maibon, and one day he was driving down the road in his horse and cart when he saw an old man hobbling along, so frail and feeble he doubted the poor soul could go many more steps. Though Maibon offered to take him in the cart, the old man refused; and Maibon went his way home, shaking his head over such a pitiful sight, and said to his wife, Modrona:

"Ah, ah, what a sorry thing it is to have your bones creaking and cracking, and dim eyes, and dull wits. When I think this might come to me, too! A fine, strong-armed, sturdy-legged fellow like me? One day to go tottering, and have his teeth rattling in his head, and live on porridge, like a baby? There's no fate worse in all the world."

"There is," answered Modrona, "and that would be to have neither teeth nor porridge. Get on with you, Maibon, and stop borrowing trouble. Hoe your field or you'll have no crop to harvest, and no food for you, nor me, nor the little ones."

◄ **Vocabulary**
feeble (fē´ bəl)
adj. weak

Comprehension
Why is Maibon upset?

◄ **Critical Viewing**
What impression of old age is conveyed by this picture?

Setting a Purpose
At what rate would you read this descriptive passage? Why?

Sighing and grumbling, Maibon did as his wife bade him. Although the day was fair and cloudless, he took no pleasure in it. His ax-blade was notched, the wooden handle splintery; his saw had lost its edge; and his hoe, once shining new, had begun to rust. None of his tools, it seemed to him, cut or chopped or delved[1] as well as they once had done.

"They're as worn out as that old codger I saw on the road," Maibon said to himself. He squinted up at the sky. "Even the sun isn't as bright as it used to be, and doesn't warm me half as well. It's gone threadbare as my cloak. And no wonder, for it's been there longer than I can remember. Come to think of it, the moon's been looking a little wilted around the edges, too.

"As for me," went on Maibon, in dismay, "I'm in even a worse state. My appetite's faded, especially after meals. Mornings, when I wake, I can hardly keep myself from yawning. And at night, when I go to bed, my eyes are so heavy I can't hold them open. If that's the way things are now, the older I grow, the worse it will be!" •

In the midst of his complaining, Maibon glimpsed something bouncing and tossing back and forth beside a fallen tree in a corner of the field. Wondering if one of his piglets had squeezed out of the sty and gone rooting for

---

1. **delved** (delvd) *v.* dug.

acorns, Maibon hurried across the turf. Then he dropped his ax and gaped in astonishment.

There, struggling to free his leg which had been caught under the log, lay a short, thickset figure: a dwarf with red hair bristling in all directions beneath his round, close-fitting leather cap. At the sight of Maibon, the dwarf squeezed shut his bright red eyes and began holding his breath. After a moment, the dwarf's face went redder than his hair; his cheeks puffed out and soon turned purple. Then he opened one eye and blinked rapidly at Maibon, who was staring at him, speechless.

"What," snapped the dwarf, "you can still see me?"

"That I can," replied Maibon, more than ever puzzled, "and I can see very well you've got yourself tight as a wedge under that log, and all your kicking only makes it worse."

At this, the dwarf blew out his breath and shook his fists. "I can't do it!" he shouted. "No matter how I try! I can't make myself invisible! Everyone in my family can disappear—Poof! Gone! Vanished! But not me! Not Doli! Believe me, if I could have done, you never would have found me in such a plight. Worse luck! Well, come on. Don't stand there goggling like an idiot. Help me get loose!"

At this sharp command, Maibon began tugging and heaving at the log. Then he stopped, wrinkled his brow, and scratched his head, saying:

"Well, now, just a moment, friend. The way you look, and all your talk about turning yourself invisible—I'm thinking you might be one of the Fair Folk."

"Oh, clever!" Doli retorted. "Oh, brilliant! Great clodhopper! Giant beanpole! Of course I am! What else! Enough gabbling. Get a move on. My leg's going to sleep."

"If a man does the Fair Folk a good turn," cried Maibon, his excitement growing, "it's told they must do one for him."

"I knew sooner or later you'd come round to that," grumbled the dwarf. "That's the way of it with you ham-handed, heavy-footed oafs. Time was, you humans got along well with us. But nowadays, you no sooner see a Fair Folk than it's grab, grab, grab! Gobble, gobble, gobble! Grant my wish! Give me this, give me that! As if we had nothing better to do!

"Yes, I'll give you a favor," Doli went on. "That's the rule,

◄ **Vocabulary**
vanished (va´ nisht) v. disappeared

plight (plīt) n. awkward, sad, or dangerous situation

Universal Theme
What problem does Maibon face?

Comprehension
What is unusual about Doli?

I'm obliged to. Now, get on with it."

Hearing this, Maibon pulled and pried and chopped away at the log as fast as he could, and soon freed the dwarf.

Doli heaved a sigh of relief, rubbed his shin, and cocked a red eye at Maibon, saying:

"All right. You've done your work, you'll have your reward. What do you want? Gold, I suppose. That's the usual. Jewels? Fine clothes? Take my advice, go for something practical. A hazelwood twig to help you find water if your well ever goes dry? An ax that never needs sharpening? A cook pot always brimming with food?"

"None of those!" cried Maibon. He bent down to the dwarf and whispered eagerly, "But I've heard tell that you Fair Folk have magic stones that can keep a man young forever. That's what I want. I claim one for my reward."

Universal Theme
Why is Doli frustrated by Maibon and other humans?

Doli snorted. "I might have known you'd pick something like that. As to be expected, you humans have it all muddled. There's nothing can make a man young again. That's even beyond the best of our skills. Those stones you're babbling about? Well, yes, there are such things. But greatly overrated. All they'll do is keep you from growing any older."

"Just as good!" Maibon exclaimed. "I want no more than that!"

Doli hesitated and frowned. "Ah—between the two of us, take the cook pot. Better all around. Those stones—we'd sooner not give them away. There's a difficulty—"

"Because you'd rather keep them for yourselves," Maibon broke in. "No, no, you shan't cheat me of my due. Don't put me off with excuses. I told you what I want, and that's what I'll have. Come, hand it over and not another word."

Doli shrugged and opened a leather pouch that hung from his belt. He spilled a number of brightly colored pebbles into his palm, picked out one of the larger stones, and handed it to Maibon. The dwarf then jumped up, took to his heels, raced across the field, and disappeared into a thicket.

Laughing and crowing over his good fortune and his cleverness, Maibon hurried back to the cottage. There, he told his wife what had happened, and showed her the stone he had claimed from the Fair Folk.

"As I am now, so I'll always be!" Maibon declared, flexing his arms and thumping his chest. "A fine figure of a man! Oho, no gray beard and wrinkled brow for me!"

Instead of sharing her husband's jubilation, Modrona flung up her hands and burst out:

"Maibon, you're a greater fool than ever I supposed! And selfish into the bargain! You've turned down treasures! You didn't even ask that dwarf for so much as new jackets for the children! Nor a new apron for me! You could have had the roof mended. Or the walls plastered. No, a stone is what you ask for! A bit of rock no better than you'll dig up in the cow pasture!"

Crestfallen[2] and sheepish, Maibon began thinking his wife was right, and the dwarf had indeed given him no more than a common field stone.

"Eh, well, it's true," he stammered, "I feel no different than I did this morning, no better nor worse, but every way the same. That redheaded little wretch! He'll rue the day if I ever find him again!"

So saying, Maibon threw the stone into the fireplace. That night he grumbled his way to bed, dreaming revenge on the dishonest dwarf.

Next morning, after a restless night, he yawned, rubbed his eyes, and scratched his chin. Then he sat bolt upright in bed, patting his cheeks in amazement.

"My beard!" he cried, tumbling out and hurrying to tell his wife. "It hasn't grown! Not by a hair! Can it be the dwarf didn't cheat me after all?"

"Don't talk to me about beards," declared his wife as

◀ Vocabulary
jubilation
(jōō′ bə lā′ shən) *n.* great joy; triumph

rue (rōō) *v.* feel sorrow or regret for something

Setting a Purpose
How does your reading rate change when you read dialogue? Explain.

Comprehension
Why does Maibon's wife say he's a fool?

---

2. **crestfallen** (krest′ fôl′ ən) *adj.* made sad or humble; disheartened.

Maibon went to the fireplace, picked out the stone, and clutched it safely in both hands. "There's trouble enough in the chicken roost. Those eggs should have hatched by now, but the hen is still brooding on her nest."

"Let the chickens worry about that," answered Maibon. "Wife, don't you see what a grand thing's happened to me? I'm not a minute older than I was yesterday. Bless that generous-hearted dwarf!"

"Let me lay hands on him and I'll bless him," retorted Modrona. "That's all well and good for you. But what of me? You'll stay as you are, but I'll turn old and gray, and worn and wrinkled, and go doddering into my grave! And what of our little ones? They'll grow up and have children of their own. And grandchildren, and great-grandchildren. And you, younger than any of them. What a foolish sight you'll be!"

But Maibon, gleeful over his good luck, paid his wife no heed, and only tucked the stone deeper into his pocket. Next day, however, the eggs had still not hatched.

"And the cow!" Modrona cried. "She's long past due to calve, and no sign of a young one ready to be born!"

"Don't bother me with cows and chickens," replied Maibon. "They'll all come right, in time. As for time, I've got all the time in the world!"

Having no appetite for breakfast, Maibon went out into the field. Of all the seeds he had sown there, however, he was surprised to see not one had sprouted. The field, which by now should have been covered with green shoots, lay bare and empty. •

"Eh, things do seem a little late these days," Maibon said to himself. "Well, no hurry. It's that much less for me to do. The wheat isn't growing, but neither are the weeds."

Some days went by and still the eggs had not hatched, the cow had not calved, the wheat had not sprouted. And now Maibon saw that his apple tree showed no sign of even the smallest, greenest fruit.

"Maibon, it's the fault of that stone!" wailed his wife. "Get rid of the thing!"

"Nonsense," replied Maibon. "The season's slow, that's all."

Nevertheless, his wife kept at him and kept at him so much that Maibon at last, and very reluctantly, threw the stone out the cottage window. Not too far, though, for he

Vocabulary ▶
sown (sōn) v. planted; scattered with seeds

▶ **Critical Viewing**
Find three details that suggest that the people in this picture lead a life similar to that of Maibon and his wife.

had it in the back of his mind to go later and find it again.

Next morning he had no need to go looking for it, for there was the stone sitting on the window ledge.

"You see?" said Maibon to his wife. "Here it is back again. So, it's a gift meant for me to keep."

"Maibon!" cried his wife. "Will you get rid of it! We've had nothing but trouble since you brought it into the house. Now the baby's fretting and fuming. Teething, poor little thing. But not a tooth to be seen! Maibon, that stone's bad luck and I want no part of it!"

Protesting it was none of his doing that the stone had come back, Maibon carried it into the vegetable patch. He dug a hole, not a very deep one, and put the stone into it.

Next day, there was the stone above ground, winking and glittering.

"Maibon!" cried his wife. "Once and for all, if you care for your family, get rid of that cursed thing!"

Seeing no other way to keep peace in the household, Maibon regretfully and unwillingly took the stone and threw it down the well, where it splashed into the water and sank from sight.

But that night, while he was trying vainly to sleep, there came such a rattling and clattering that Maibon clapped his hands over his ears, jumped out of bed, and went stumbling into the yard. At the well, the bucket was jiggling back and forth and up and down at the end of the rope;

Comprehension
What is the stone doing to everything on Maibon's farm?

Literature Connection

Rocks and Roles

Stones play a role in many stories. For example, in Aesop's fable "The Crow and the Pitcher," a thirsty crow tries to drink from a pitcher, but the water is too far down for his beak to reach. After much thought, the crow solves his problem by dropping pebbles into the pitcher until the water rises enough that he can drink it. The moral: Necessity is the mother of invention.

In "The Stone," a rock causes problems rather than solving them when Maibon makes foolish choices.

Connect to the Literature

How might Maibon have used his stone wisely?

Setting a Purpose

At what rate would you read dialogue such as this? Why?

and in the bottom of the bucket was the stone.

Now Maibon began to be truly distressed, not only for the toothless baby, the calfless cow, the fruitless tree, and the hen sitting desperately on her eggs, but for himself as well.

"Nothing's moving along as it should," he groaned. "I can't tell one day from another. Nothing changes, there's nothing to look forward to, nothing to show for my work. Why sow if the seeds don't sprout? Why plant if there's never a harvest? Why eat if I don't get hungry? Why go to bed at night, or get up in the morning, or do anything at all? And the way it looks, so it will stay for ever and ever! I'll shrivel from boredom if nothing else!"

"Maibon," pleaded his wife, "for all our sakes, destroy the dreadful thing!"

Maibon tried now to pound the stone to dust with his heaviest mallet; but he could not so much as knock a chip from it. He put it against his grindstone without so much as scratching it. He set it on his anvil and belabored it with hammer and tongs, all to no avail.

At last he decided to bury the stone again, this time deeper than before. Picking up his shovel, he hurried to the field. But he suddenly halted and the shovel dropped from his hands. There, sitting cross-legged on a stump, was the dwarf. •

"You!" shouted Maibon, shaking his fist. "Cheat! Villain! Trickster! I did you a good turn, and see how you've repaid it!"

The dwarf blinked at the furious Maibon. "You mortals are an ungrateful crew. I gave you what you wanted."

"You should have warned me!" burst out Maibon.

"I did," Doli snapped back. "You wouldn't listen. No, you yapped and yammered, bound to have your way. I told you we didn't like to give away those stones. When you mortals get hold of one, you stay just as you are—but so does everything around you. Before you know it, you're mired in time like a rock in the mud. You take my advice.

Get rid of that stone as fast as you can."

"What do you think I've been trying to do?" blurted Maibon. "I've buried it, thrown it down the well, pounded it with a hammer—it keeps coming back to me!"

"That's because you really didn't want to give it up," Doli said. "In the back of your mind and the bottom of your heart, you didn't want to change along with the rest of the world. So long as you feel that way, the stone is yours."

"No, no!" cried Maibon. "I want no more of it. Whatever may happen, let it happen. That's better than nothing happening at all. I've had my share of being young, I'll take my share of being old. And when I come to the end of my days, at least I can say I've lived each one of them."

"If you mean that," answered Doli, "toss the stone onto the ground, right there at the stump. Then get home and be about your business."

Spiral Review
REPETITION What feeling is created by Maibon's repeated attempts to get rid of the stone?

Universal Theme
What message about change does Doli try to share with Maibon?

Maibon flung down the stone, spun around, and set off as fast as he could. When he dared at last to glance back over his shoulder, fearful the stone might be bouncing along at his heels, he saw no sign of it, nor of the redheaded dwarf.

Maibon gave a joyful cry, for at that same instant the fallow field was covered with green blades of wheat, the branches of the apple tree bent to the ground, so laden they were with fruit. He ran to the cottage, threw his arms around his wife and children, and told them the good news. The hen hatched her chicks, the cow bore her calf. And Maibon laughed with glee when he saw the first tooth in the baby's mouth.

Never again did Maibon meet any of the Fair Folk, and he was just as glad of it. He and his wife and children and grandchildren lived many years, and Maibon was proud of his white hair and long beard as he had been of his sturdy arms and legs.

"Stones are all right, in their way," said Maibon. "But the trouble with them is, they don't grow."

Language Study

Vocabulary The words listed below appear in "The Stone." Explain your answers to the numbered questions.

| feeble | plight | jubilation | rue | sown |

1. How could you solve a hungry person's *plight*?
2. Would you react with *jubilation* if you lost a contest?
3. Would you ask your *feeble* uncle to carry your suitcase?
4. Do you *rue* the day you met your best friend?
5. Can seeds be *sown* in the desert?

WORD STUDY

The **Latin root -van-** means "empty." In this story, the stone **vanished**, or disappeared, leaving an empty space.

Word Study

Part A Explain how the **Latin root -van-** contributes to the meanings of *vainly* and *evanescence*. Consult a dictionary if necessary.

Part B Use context to explain your answers to these questions:

1. What are the dangers of having too much *vanity*?
2. Would you feel insulted if someone described you as *vain*?

Close Reading Activities

Literary Analysis

Key Ideas and Details

1. **Setting a Purpose** Choose two passages from the folk tale. In a chart like the one on the right, tell your **reading rate** for each passage.

2. **Setting a Purpose** Use the information in your chart to explain when and why you changed your reading rate as you read.

3. **(a)** How does Maibon get the stone? **(b) Make Inferences:** Why does he choose the stone over other gifts? **(c) Interpret:** Why is Maibon unable to get rid of the stone?

Passage
Reading Rate

Craft and Structure

4. **Universal Theme** What lesson is Doli trying to teach Maibon when he says that the stones are greatly overrated?

5. **Universal Theme** What universal theme is revealed in the folk tale, just after Doli explains why the stone would not go away?

6. **Universal Theme** Which of Maibon's actions best supports the theme? Why?

Integration of Knowledge and Ideas

7. **(a) Analyze:** What new belief finally allows Maibon to rid himself of the stone? **(b) Connect:** What emotion does Maibon show at the end of the story? **(c) Support:** Why do you think the author uses this detail?

8. **Apply:** Many messages in advertisements and on consumer products promote youthfulness. Do you think this is a good message? Why or why not?

9. **How much do our communities shape us?** With a small group, discuss the following questions:
   (a) Hypothesize: How might the stone have affected Maibon's neighbors if he had kept it? **(b) Synthesize:** Based on this story, what obligations do you think each individual has to his or her neighbors or community? Explain.

ACADEMIC VOCABULARY

As you write and speak about "The Stone," use the words related to family and community that you explored on page 613 of this text.

Conventions: Independent and Dependent Clauses

A **clause** is a group of words with its own subject and verb.

An **independent clause** has a subject and a verb and can stand by itself as a complete sentence. A **dependent**, or **subordinate, clause** has a subject and a verb but cannot stand alone as a sentence. Many dependent clauses begin with subordinating conjunctions, such as *if, when, because,* or *since*. Others, sometimes called **relative clauses,** usually begin with relative pronouns, such as *who, whom, whose, which,* or *that*.

I can hear you independent clause	because you are speaking loudly. dependent clause
There is the brave person independent clause	who saved my dog's life. dependent clause

Put a comma after a dependent clause that opens a sentence. Elsewhere, if the dependent clause is **nonrestrictive,** or not necessary to understand the main idea of the sentence, set it off with commas, dashes, or parentheses.

Example: *When he left Nevada,* Dan moved to Vermont.

Example: Dan, *who grew up in Nevada,* moved to Vermont last year.

Practice A
Add an independent clause to each dependent clause to make a complete sentence.

1. whose leg is caught under a log
2. that is brimming with food
3. When Maibon makes his wish
4. because she is angry
5. if Doli helps him

Reading Application Scan "The Stone" to find two independent and two dependent clauses.

Practice B
Add a dependent clause to each of the following independent clauses to make a new sentence. State whether the dependent clause is *subordinate* or *relative*.

1. Modrona scolds him
2. Maibon searches for Doli
3. Maibon was proud of his hair
4. Wishes can cause trouble

Writing Application Write a sentence about "The Stone" that contains an independent and a dependent clause.

Writing to Sources

Narrative Text Write a **plot proposal**—a plan of story events—that illustrates the universal theme of "The Stone."

- Review "The Stone" to identify the universal theme your new story will convey.
- Brainstorm for a situation that illustrates the theme. Use your imagination and your own experience to develop your idea. Decide how the setting, characters, and plot will work together to reveal the theme.
- Write a brief description of the plot.
- When you finish writing, check to be sure that your proposal clearly illustrates the universal theme.
- Proofread your proposal to check for correct capitalization, spelling, and punctuation.

Grammar Application Use independent and dependent clauses correctly in your plot proposal. Set off nonrestrictive clauses with commas, dashes, or parentheses.

Research and Technology

Build and Present Knowledge With a small group, prepare a **written and visual report** on human aging. Follow these steps to complete the assignment:

- Decide how to divide the responsibilities of the assignment among your group members.
- Type keywords, such as "human aging process," into an Internet Web browser to find information from multiple sources.
- Get together as a group to discuss what you have learned. Then, create an outline to organize your information.
- Decide how to pair pictures and other graphics with facts.
- Practice your presentation in your group before presenting to the rest of the class. In your presentation, connect the information you learned through your research to descriptions of aging that appear in "The Stone."

Meet the Author

Chinua Achebe (1930–2013) liked to retell stories from his native country of Nigeria. Achebe attended the local mission school where his father taught, and then went to universities in Nigeria and England. He won acclaim with his novel, *Things Fall Apart* (1958), about changing times in Africa. He moved to the United States when the political climate in Nigeria made it too dangerous for him to stay. He once wrote, "Any good story, any good novel, should have a message."

? How much do our communities shape us?

Explore the Big Question as you read "Why the Tortoise's Shell Is Not Smooth." Take notes on ways in which the story explores what happens when a community's rules are broken.

CLOSE READING FOCUS

Key Ideas and Details: **Purpose for Reading**

Your **purpose for reading** is the reason you read a text. Sometimes you choose a text based on a purpose you already have. Other times, you set a purpose based on the kind of text you are about to read. Setting a purpose helps you focus your reading. For example, you might read to learn about a subject, to gain understanding, or simply to be entertained. Preview the text by looking at the title, the pictures, and the beginnings of paragraphs before you read. This will help you set a purpose or decide whether the text will fit a purpose you already have.

Craft and Structure: **Personification**

Figurative language is language that is used imaginatively rather than literally. **Personification** is figurative language in which a nonhuman subject is described as if it had human qualities. In the example, *rain kisses her cheek*, the rain behaves like a person.

Writers use personification to make text lively or to emphasize an important point. In folk tales, personification is often used to give human qualities to animal characters. The animals' behavior illustrates human traits and problems in a humorous way.

Vocabulary

You will encounter the following words in this story. Decide whether you know each word well, know it a little bit, or do not know it at all. After you read, see how your knowledge of each word has increased.

cunning	famine	orator
custom	eloquent	compound

CLOSE READING MODEL

The passage below is from Chinua Achebe's folk tale "Why the Tortoise's Shell Is Not Smooth." The annotations to the right of the passage show ways in which you can use close reading skills to set a purpose and analyze personification.

from "Why the Tortoise's Shell Is Not Smooth" [1]

Low voices, broken now and then by singing, reached Okonkwo from his wives' huts as each woman and her children told folk stories. Ekwefi and her daughter, Ezinma, sat on a mat on the floor. It was Ekwefi's turn to tell a story.

"Once upon a time," she began, "all the birds were invited to a feast in the sky. [2] They were very happy and began to prepare themselves for the great day. They painted their bodies with red cam wood and drew beautiful patterns on them with dye. [3]

"Tortoise saw all these preparations and soon discovered what it all meant. Nothing that happened in the world of the animals ever escaped his notice; he was full of cunning. As soon as he heard of the great feast in the sky his throat began to itch at the very thought. [4] There was a famine in those days and Tortoise had not eaten a good meal for two moons. His body rattled like a piece of dry stick in his empty shell. So he began to plan how he would go to the sky." [4]

Purpose for Reading

1 Previewing the title tells you that this folk tale explains something in nature. You might set a purpose to learn why, according to the tale, the tortoise's shell is not smooth.

Purpose for Reading

2 You may recognize the words, "Once upon a time" as a traditional beginning for many fairy tales and folk tales. At this point, you might decide that your purpose is to read for enjoyment.

Personification

3 The birds are "very happy" and paint their bodies the way humans in an African village might decorate themselves for a special occasion. The personification of animals is a common feature of folk tales.

Personification

4 Tortoise plots to join the feast in a way a human might. Imagining Tortoise with human characteristics helps you understand his cunning.

Why the
TORTOISE'S SHELL
Is Not SMOOTH
—
Chinua Achebe

Low voices, broken now and again by singing, reached Okonkwo (ō kōn´ kwō) from his wives' huts as each woman and her children told folk stories. Ekwefi (e kwe´ fē) and her daughter, Ezinma (e zēn´ mä), sat on a mat on the floor. It was Ekwefi's turn to tell a story.

Purpose for Reading
What purpose for reading does this story's title present?

"Once upon a time," she began, "all the birds were invited to a feast in the sky. They were very happy and began to prepare themselves for the great day. They painted their bodies with red cam wood[1] and drew beautiful patterns on them with dye.

"Tortoise saw all these preparations and soon discovered what it all meant. Nothing that happened in the world of the animals ever escaped his notice; he was full of **cunning**. As soon as he heard of the great feast in the sky his throat began to itch at the very thought. There was a **famine** in those days and Tortoise had not eaten a good meal for two moons. His body rattled like a piece of dry stick in his empty shell. So he began to plan how he would go to the sky."

"But he had no wings," said Ezinma.

"Be patient," replied her mother. "That is the story. Tortoise had no wings, but he went to the birds and asked to be allowed to go with them.

"'We know you too well,' said the birds when they had heard him. 'You are full of cunning and you are ungrateful. If we allow you to come with us you will soon begin your mischief.'

"'You do not know me,' said Tortoise. 'I am a changed man. I have learned that a man who makes trouble for others is also making it for himself.'

◀ **Vocabulary**
cunning (kun´ iŋ) *n.*
slyness; deception

famine (fam´ in) *n.*
shortage of food

Comprehension
Why is the tortoise hungry?

---

1. **red cam** (cam) **wood** hard West African wood that makes red dye.

"Tortoise had a sweet tongue, and within a short time all the birds agreed that he was a changed man, and they each gave him a feather, with which he made two wings.

"At last the great day came and Tortoise was the first to arrive at the meeting place. When all the birds had gathered together, they set off in a body. Tortoise was very happy as he flew among the birds, and he was soon chosen as the man to speak for the party because he was a great orator.

"'There is one important thing which we must not forget,' he said as they flew on their way. 'When people are invited to a great feast like this, they take new names for the occasion. Our hosts in the sky will expect us to honor this age-old custom.'

"None of the birds had heard of this custom but they knew that Tortoise, in spite of his failings in other directions, was a widely traveled man who knew the customs of different peoples. And so they each took a new name. When they had all taken, Tortoise also took one. He was to be called *All of you*. ●

"At last the party arrived in the sky and their hosts were very happy to see them. Tortoise stood up in his many-colored plumage and thanked them for their invitation. His speech was so eloquent that all the birds were glad they had brought him, and nodded their heads in approval of all he said. Their hosts took him as the king of the birds, especially as he looked somewhat different from the others.

"After kola nuts had been presented and eaten, the people of the sky set before their guests the most delectable dishes Tortoise had ever seen or dreamed of. The soup was brought out hot from the fire and in the very pot in which it had been cooked. It was full of meat and fish. Tortoise began to sniff aloud. There was pounded yam and also yam pottage[2] cooked with palm oil and fresh fish. There were also pots of palm wine. When everything had been set before the guests, one of the people of the sky came forward and tasted a little from each pot. He then invited the birds to eat. But Tortoise jumped to his feet and asked: 'For whom have you prepared this feast?'

---

2. yam (yam) **pottage** (pät´ ij) *n.* thick stew made of sweet potatoes.

"'For all of you,' replied the man.

"Tortoise turned to the birds and said: 'You remember that my name is *All of you*. The custom here is to serve the spokesman first and the others later. They will serve you when I have eaten.'

"He began to eat and the birds grumbled angrily. The people of the sky thought it must be their custom to leave all the food for their king. And so Tortoise ate the best part of the food and then drank two pots of palm wine, so that he was full of food and drink and his body grew fat enough to fill out his shell.

"The birds gathered round to eat what was left and to peck at the bones he had thrown all about the floor. Some of them were too angry to eat. They chose to fly home on an empty stomach. But before they left, each took back the feather he had lent to Tortoise. And there he stood in his hard shell full of food and wine but without any wings to fly home. He asked the birds to take a message for his wife, but they all refused. In the end Parrot, who had felt more angry than the others, suddenly changed his mind and agreed to take the message.

"'Tell my wife,' said Tortoise, 'to bring out all the soft things in my house and cover the compound with them so that I can jump down from the sky without very great danger.'

"Parrot promised to deliver the message, and then flew away. But when he reached Tortoise's house he told his wife to bring out all the hard things in the house.

"When people are invited to a great feast like this, they take new names for the occasion."

And so she brought out her husband's hoes, machetes, spears, guns, and even his cannon. Tortoise looked down from the sky and saw his wife bringing things out, but it was too far to see what they were. When all seemed ready he let himself go. He fell and fell and fell until he began to fear that he would never stop falling. And then like the sound of his cannon he crashed on the compound."

"Did he die?" asked Ezinma.

"No," replied Ekwefi. "His shell broke into pieces. But there was a great medicine man in the neighborhood. Tortoise's wife sent for him and he gathered all the bits of shell and stuck them together. That is why Tortoise's shell is not smooth."

Purpose for Reading
Did you achieve your purpose for reading this folk tale? Why or why not?

Language Study

Vocabulary The words listed below appear in the folk tale. Use one of the words to complete each *analogy* item below. In an analogy, pairs of words share a relationship.

cunning	famine	orator	eloquent	compound

1. *speech* is to *speaker* as *oration* is to _____
2. *tiresome* is to *boring* as *persuasive* is to _____
3. *eating* is to *feast* as *starving* is to _____
4. *attractiveness* is to *beauty* as *craftiness* is to _____
5. *tree* is to *forest* as *building* is to _____

Word Study

Part A Explain how the **suffix -ary** contributes to the meaning of *primary* and *legendary*. Consult a dictionary if necessary.

Part B Explain your answer to each question.

1. Does a *cautionary* tale instruct you to be careful?
2. Are science fiction authors likely to be *visionary* writers?

WORD STUDY
The **suffix -ary** means "related to" or "connected with." In this folk tale, the birds think it is **customary**, or related to the usual practice, for the king to eat all the food at a feast.

Close Reading Activities

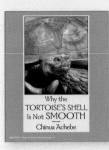

Literary Analysis

Key Ideas and Details

1. **Purpose for Reading (a)** What was your purpose for reading this folk tale? **(b)** How might your purpose be different if you were reading a nonfiction article about tortoises?

2. **Purpose for Reading** How well did previewing the title and pictures give you a sense of what the folk tale would be about? Explain.

3. **(a) Analyze Causes and Effects:** Why does Tortoise want to go to the great feast? **(b) Make Inferences:** Why do the birds not want to take him at first?

4. **(a) Analyze Causes and Effects:** Why do the birds eventually decide to help Tortoise go to the feast? **(b) Deduce:** Why do they choose him to speak for the group? **(c) Assess:** How does Tortoise make use of this privilege?

5. **(a) Interpret:** Explain how Tortoise's new name allows him to eat before the birds eat. **(b) Draw Conclusions:** What lesson do the birds learn about Tortoise?

Craft and Structure

6. **Personification** Complete a chart like the one on the right to analyze one of the animal characters. Use details from the text to support your entries.

7. **Personification (a)** In the text, find three examples of personification in the description of Tortoise's character. **(b)** What effect does the use of personification have on the story?

Character's Name:	
Animal Qualities:	
Human Qualities:	

Integration of Knowledge and Ideas

8. At the end of the folk tale, the birds learn that Tortoise has not changed. **(a) Interpret:** Based on the ending, what lesson do you think this folk tale teaches? **(b) Hypothesize:** Why do you think the author has written about this lesson? Cite details from the text to support your answer.

9. **THE BIG ?** **How much do our communities shape us?**
   (a) Synthesize: What unwritten community rules does Tortoise break? Explain. **(b) Speculate:** How do you think the birds will treat Tortoise after this incident? Explain.

ACADEMIC VOCABULARY

As you write and speak about "Why the Tortoise's Shell Is Not Smooth," use the words related to communities that you explored on page 613 of this text.

Conventions: **Simple, Compound, and Complex Sentences**

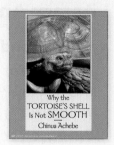

> Sentences can be classified according to the number and kinds of their clauses—groups of words with their own subjects and verbs.

An **independent clause** can stand alone as a sentence because it expresses a complete thought. A **dependent clause** cannot stand alone because it does not express a complete thought. A dependent clause usually begins with a relative pronoun, such as *who, which,* or *that,* or a subordinating conjunction, such as *because, if,* or *when.* This chart shows how clauses are used to create the three types of sentence structures.

Simple Sentences	Compound Sentences	Complex Sentences
A single independent clause	Two or more independent clauses	One independent clause and one or more dependent clauses
<u>The dog barked.</u> <u>He and I walked home.</u> <u>The girl in the front row is the class president.</u>	<u>Brad cooked the meal,</u> <u>Kai set the table,</u> and <u>I washed dishes.</u> <u>I like baseball,</u> but <u>he prefers soccer.</u>	<u>The other travelers,</u> (who were very tired), <u>climbed onto the bus.</u> (Because the storm came), <u>our game was postponed.</u>

Practice A

Copy each sentence, underlining independent clauses and circling dependent clauses. Then tell what kind of sentence each is.

1. Tortoise, who was very hungry, longed to join the feast.

2. Tortoise tried to trick the birds.

3. Tortoise crashed, and his shell broke.

Reading Application In the folk tale, find and record a simple, a compound, and a complex sentence.

Practice B

Add to each group of words to make the kind of sentence indicated.

1. The people of the sky (simple)

2. The birds went to the feast (compound)

3. who thought of a sneaky plan (complex)

Writing Application Write a brief summary of "Why the Tortoise's Shell Is Not Smooth." Include simple, compound, and complex sentences.

Writing to Sources

Informative Text Write an **invitation** to the feast in the sky in "Why the Tortoise's Shell Is Not Smooth." Choose the best format for your invitation. For example, you may write a letter, create a card, or develop a poster. Follow these steps to include important information:

- Review the folk tale to find details to include in your invitation.
- Identify the event and explain its purpose.
- Include the date, time, and location of the event.
- Provide directions for getting to the location.
- Ask your guests to let you know if they will attend.
- Include a phone number or an e-mail address for replies.

Grammar Application Proofread your invitation, and correct any grammatical errors you find.

Speaking and Listening

Comprehension and Collaboration With a group, present a **dramatic reading** of "Why the Tortoise's Shell Is Not Smooth." Act out the scene in which Tortoise asks the birds if he can go with them to the feast.

Follow these steps to complete the assignment:

- Assign a role to each member of your group.
- Act out the parts of the characters using exact words from the folk tale.
- Practice reading fluently and with appropriate pacing, intonation, and expression.
- Vary the tone and volume of your voice to show different levels of feeling. Use gestures to bring the words to life.
- Have classmates watch your dramatic reading and provide feedback. Then, practice and deliver the reading again.

How much do our communities shape us?

Explore the Big Question as you read these selections. Take notes on the ways that each main character reacts to being in an unusual community.

READING TO COMPARE FANTASY

Authors Rudyard Kipling and Roald Dahl use elements of fantasy in the stories that follow. You may be familiar with fantasy from movies about superheroes or space travel. Sometimes the fantastic elements or special effects dominate these movies. Other times, the fantastic elements serve as a background for stories about very believable human characters. When you finish reading these selections, compare how the two authors make use of fantasy.

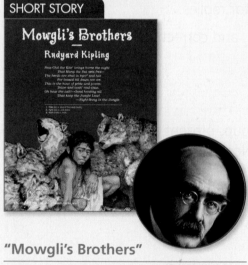

SHORT STORY

Mowgli's Brothers
Rudyard Kipling

FICTION

from James and the Giant Peach

"Mowgli's Brothers"

Rudyard Kipling (1865–1936)
Rudyard Kipling was born in India to British parents. When he was very young, his Indian nurses told him folk tales that featured talking animals. These stories inspired the characters in many of Kipling's works, such as *The Jungle Book*, in which "Mowgli's Brothers" appears. As a boy, Kipling was sent to school in England. At age sixteen, he returned to India as a journalist. His work as a reporter, writer, and poet earned him the 1907 Nobel Prize.

from *James and the Giant Peach*

Roald Dahl (1916–1990)
As a boy growing up in Wales, Roald Dahl loved books and stories. When he was eight years old, he began keeping a diary, and hid it in a box tied to a high tree branch. Years later, Dahl began his writing career by describing his experiences in the Royal Air Force during World War II. Dahl became interested in writing stories for children while making up bedtime stories for his daughters. "I have a passion for teaching kids to become readers," he once said.

Comparing Elements of Fantasy

Fantasy is imaginative writing that contains elements not found in real life. Many fantastic stories balance imagination with realistic elements—characters, events, or situations that are true to life. These realistic details help readers relate to an inventive or unusual story. This blend of the impossible and the possible makes fantasy an enjoyable genre. Use these questions to identify the fantastic and realistic elements in the stories that follow:

- Which elements of the story's setting could not exist in real life? Which elements could exist?
- Which elements of a character's behavior could not occur in real life? Which elements could occur?
- Which elements of the situation could not happen in real life? Which elements could happen?

Create a chart like the one below. Then, record the fantastic and realistic elements in each story.

Title:		
Element	Fantastic or Realistic	Why?

Fantasy and Theme

Although works of fantasy are not realistic, they can convey serious **themes**. In "Mowgli's Brothers," for example, readers learn about the importance of belonging. In the excerpt from *James and the Giant Peach*, readers learn that communities can be imperfect but still valuable. The lessons are true even though the stories are not.

Fantasy elements can actually make a message stronger or highlight a story's lesson. Through the appeal of fantasy, the lessons reach readers effectively. As you read, think about each story's message and how the fantasy genre helps make the message understandable.

Mowgli's Brothers
—
Rudyard Kipling

Now Chil the Kite[1] brings home the night
That Mang the Bat sets free—
The herds are shut in byre[2] and hut
For loosed till dawn are we.
This is the hour of pride and power,
Talon and tush[3] and claw.
Oh hear the call!—Good hunting all
That keep the Jungle Law!
—Night-Song in the Jungle

---

1. **Kite** (kīt) *n.* bird of the hawk family.
2. **byre** (bīr) *n.* cow barn.
3. **tush** (tush) *n.* tusk.

It was seven o'clock of a very warm evening in the Seeonee hills[4] when Father Wolf woke up from his day's rest, scratched himself, yawned, and spread out his paws one after the other to get rid of the sleepy feeling in their tips. Mother Wolf lay with her big gray nose dropped across her four tumbling, squealing cubs, and the moon shone into the mouth of the cave where they all lived. "Augrh!" said Father Wolf, "it is time to hunt again"; and he was going to spring downhill when a little shadow with a bushy tail crossed the threshold and whined: "Good luck go with you, O Chief of the Wolves; and good luck and strong white teeth go with the noble children, that they may never forget the hungry in this world."

It was the jackal—Tabaqui the Dishlicker—and the wolves of India despise Tabaqui because he runs about making mischief, and telling tales, and eating rags and pieces of leather from the village rubbish-heaps. But they are afraid of him too, because Tabaqui, more than anyone else in the jungle, is apt to go mad, and then he forgets that he was ever afraid of anyone, and runs through the forest biting everything in his way. Even the tiger runs and hides when little Tabaqui goes mad, for madness is the most disgraceful thing that can overtake a wild creature. We call it hydrophobia, but they call it *dewanee*—the madness—and run.

"Enter, then, and look," said Father Wolf, stiffly; "but there is no food here."

"For a wolf, no," said Tabaqui; "but for so mean a person as myself a dry bone is a good feast. Who are we, the Gidur log [the jackal-people], to pick and choose?" He scuttled to the back of the cave, where he found the bone of a buck with some meat on it, and sat cracking the end merrily.

"All thanks for this good meal," he said, licking his lips. "How beautiful are the noble children! How large are their eyes! And so young too! Indeed, indeed, I might have remembered that the children of Kings are men from the beginning." ●

Now, Tabaqui knew as well as anyone else that there is nothing so unlucky as to compliment children to their faces; and it pleases him to see Mother and Father Wolf look uncomfortable.

---

4. **Seeonee** (sē ō′ nē) **hills** hills in central India.

Elements of Fantasy
What element of fantasy is introduced in this paragraph? Explain.

Elements of Fantasy
What is fantastic about Tabaqui's behavior? What is realistic about it?

Comprehension
Why do the wolves despise Tabaqui?

Tabaqui sat still, rejoicing in the mischief that he had made: then he said spitefully:

"Shere Khan, the Big One, has shifted his hunting-grounds. He will hunt among these hills for the next moon, so he has told me."

Shere Khan was the tiger who lived near the Waingunga River, twenty miles away.

"He has no right!" Father Wolf began angrily—"By the Law of the Jungle he has no right to change his quarters without due warning. He will frighten every head of game within ten miles, and I—I have to kill for two, these days."

"His mother did not call him Lungri [the Lame One] for nothing," said Mother Wolf, quietly. "He has been lame in one foot from his birth. That is why he has only killed cattle. Now the villagers of the Waingunga are angry with him, and he has come here to make our villagers angry. They will scour the Jungle for him when he is far away, and we and our children must run when the grass is set alight. Indeed, we are very grateful to Shere Khan!"

"Shall I tell him of your gratitude?" said Tabaqui.

"Out!" snapped Father Wolf. "Out and hunt with thy master. Thou hast done harm enough for one night."

"I go," said Tabaqui, quietly. "Ye can hear Shere Khan below in the thickets. I might have saved myself the message."

Father Wolf listened, and below in the valley that ran down to a little river, he heard the dry, angry, snarly, singsong whine of a tiger who has caught nothing and does not care if all the Jungle knows it.

"The fool!" said Father Wolf. "To begin a night's work with that noise! Does he think that our buck are like his fat Waingunga bullocks?"[5]

"H'sh! It is neither bullock nor buck he hunts tonight," said Mother Wolf. "It is Man." The whine had changed to a sort of humming purr that seemed to come from every quarter of the compass. It was the noise that bewilders woodcutters and gypsies sleeping in the open, and makes them run sometimes into the very mouth of the tiger.

"Man!" said Father Wolf, showing all his white teeth. "Faugh! Are there not enough beetles and frogs in the tanks

---

5. **bullocks** (bŏŏl′ əks) *n.* steers.

that he must eat Man and on our ground too!"

The Law of the Jungle, which never orders anything without a reason, forbids every beast to eat Man except when he is killing to show his children how to kill, and then he must hunt outside the hunting-grounds of his pack or tribe. The real reason for this is that man-killing means, sooner or later, the arrival of white men on elephants, with guns, and hundreds of brown men with gongs and rockets and torches. Then everybody in the jungle suffers. The reason the beasts give among themselves is that Man is the weakest and most defenseless of all living things, and it is unsportsmanlike to touch him. They say too—and it is true—that man-eaters become mangy,[6] and lose their teeth.

The purr grew louder, and ended in the full-throated "Aaarh!" of the tiger's charge.

Then there was a howl—an untigerish howl—from Shere Khan. "He has missed," said Mother Wolf. "What is it?"

Father Wolf ran out a few paces and heard Shere Khan muttering and mumbling savagely, as he tumbled about in the scrub.

"The fool has had no more sense than to jump at a woodcutter's campfire, and has burned his feet," said Father Wolf, with a grunt. "Tabaqui is with him."

"Something is coming up hill," said Mother Wolf, twitching one ear. "Get ready."

The bushes rustled a little in the thicket, and Father Wolf dropped with his haunches under him, ready for his leap. Then, if you had been watching, you would have seen the most wonderful thing in the world—the wolf checked in mid-spring. He made his bound before he saw what it was he was jumping at, and then he tried to stop himself. The result was that he shot up straight into the air for four or five feet, landing almost where he left ground.

"Man!" he snapped. "A man's cub. Look!"

Directly in front of him, holding on by a low branch, stood a naked brown baby who could just walk—as soft and as dimpled a little atom[7] as ever came to a wolf's cave at night. He looked up into Father Wolf's face, and laughed.

Elements of Fantasy
Do you think Father Wolf's behavior here could occur in real life? Why or why not?

Comprehension
Why does the Law of the Jungle generally forbid man-killing?

---

6. **mangy** (mān′ jē) *adj.* having mange, a skin disease of mammals that causes sores and loss of hair.

7. **atom** (at′ əm) *n.* tiny piece of matter.

"Is that a man's cub?" said Mother Wolf. "I have never seen one. Bring it here."

A wolf accustomed to moving his own cubs can, if necessary, mouth an egg without breaking it, and though Father Wolf's jaws closed right on the child's back not a tooth even scratched the skin, as he laid it down among the cubs.

"How little! How naked, and—how bold!" said Mother Wolf, softly. The baby was pushing his way between the cubs to get close to the warm hide. "Ahai! He is taking his meal with the others. And so this is a man's cub. Now, was there ever a wolf that could boast of a man's cub among her children?"

"I have heard now and again of such a thing, but never in our Pack or in my time," said Father Wolf. "He is altogether without hair, and I could kill him with a touch of my foot. But see, he looks up and is not afraid."

The moonlight was blocked out of the mouth of the cave, for Shere Khan's great square head and shoulders were thrust into the entrance. Tabaqui, behind him, was squeaking: "My lord, my lord, it went in here!"

"Shere Khan does us great honor," said Father Wolf, but his eyes were very angry. "What does Shere Khan need?"

"My quarry. A man's cub went this way," said Shere Khan. "Its parents have run off. Give it to me."

Shere Khan had jumped at a woodcutter's campfire, as Father Wolf had said, and was furious from the pain of his burned feet. But Father Wolf knew that the mouth of the cave was too narrow for a tiger to come in by. Even where he was, Shere Khan's shoulders and forepaws were cramped for want of room, as a man's would be if he tried to fight in a barrel.

"The Wolves are a free people," said Father Wolf. "They take orders from the Head of the Pack, and not from any striped cattle-killer. The man's cub is ours—to kill if we choose."

"Ye choose and ye do not choose! What talk is this of choosing? By the bull that I killed, am I to stand nosing into your dog's den for my fair dues? It is I, Shere Khan, who speak!"

The tiger's roar filled the cave with thunder. Mother Wolf shook herself clear of the cubs and sprang forward, her eyes, like two green moons in the darkness, facing the blazing eyes of Shere Khan.

Vocabulary ▶
quarry (kwôr′ ē) *n.* prey; anything being hunted or pursued

"And it is I, Raksha [The Demon], who answer. The man's cub is mine, Lungri—mine to me! He shall not be killed. He shall live to run with the Pack and to hunt with the Pack; and in the end, look you, hunter of little naked cubs— frog-eater—fish-killer— he shall hunt thee! Now get hence, or by the Sambhur that I killed (I eat no starved cattle), back thou goest to thy mother, burned beast of the Jungle, lamer than ever thou camest into the world! Go!"

Father Wolf looked on amazed. He had almost forgotten the days when he won Mother Wolf in fair fight from five other wolves, when she ran in the Pack and was not called The Demon for compliment's sake. Shere Khan might have faced Father Wolf, but he could not stand up against Mother Wolf, for he knew that where he was she had all the advantage of the ground, and would fight to the death. So he backed out of the cave-mouth growling, and when he was clear he shouted:

"Each dog barks in his own yard! We will see what the Pack will say to this fostering of man-cubs. The cub is mine, and to my teeth he will come in the end, O bush-tailed thieves!"

Mother Wolf threw herself down panting among the cubs, and Father Wolf said to her gravely:

"Shere Khan speaks this much truth. The cub must be shown to the Pack. Wilt thou still keep him, Mother?"

"Keep him!" she gasped. "He came naked, by night, alone and very hungry; yet he was not afraid! Look, he has pushed one of my babies to one side already. And that lame butcher would have killed him and would have run off to the Waingunga while the villagers here hunted through all our

▲ Critical Viewing
Do you think this tiger is friendly to humans? Why or why not?

◄ Vocabulary
fostering (fôs′ tər iŋ)
n. taking care of

Comprehension
How does Mother Wolf respond to Shere Kahn's demands?

right in your assembly; but the Law of the Jungle says that if there is a doubt which is not a killing matter in regard to a new cub, the life of that cub may be bought at a price. And the Law does not say who may or may not pay that price. Am I right?"

"Good! good!" said the young wolves, who are always hungry. "Listen to Bagheera. The cub can be bought for a price. It is the Law."

"Knowing that I have no right to speak here, I ask your leave."

"Speak then," cried twenty voices.

"To kill a naked cub is shame. Besides, he may make better sport for you when he is grown. Baloo has spoken in his behalf. Now to Baloo's word I will add one bull, and a fat one, newly killed, not half a mile from here, if ye will accept the man's cub according to the Law. Is it difficult?"

There was a clamor of scores of voices, saying: "What matter? He will die in the winter rains. He will scorch in the sun. What harm can a naked frog do us? Let him run with the Pack. Where is the bull, Bagheera? Let him be accepted." And then came Akela's deep bay, crying: "Look well—look well, O Wolves!"

Mowgli was still deeply interested in the pebbles, and he did not notice when the wolves came and looked at him one by one. At last they all went down the hill for the dead bull, and only Akela, Bagheera, Baloo, and Mowgli's own wolves were left. Shere Khan roared still in the night, for he was

▲ **Critical Viewing**
How do you think the other animals might behave toward a panther like the one shown? Explain.

very angry that Mowgli had not been handed over to him.

"Ay, roar well," said Bagheera, under his whiskers; "for the time comes when this naked thing will make thee roar to another tune, or I know nothing of man."

"It was well done," said Akela. "Men and their cubs are very wise. He may be a help in time."

"Truly, a help in time of need; for none can hope to lead the Pack forever," said Bagheera.

Akela said nothing. He was thinking of the time that comes to every leader of every pack when his strength goes from him and he gets feebler and feebler till at last he is killed by the wolves and a new leader comes up—to be killed in his turn.

"Take him away," he said to Father Wolf, "and train him as befits one of the Free People."

And that is how Mowgli was entered into the Seeonee wolf-pack at the price of a bull and on Baloo's good word.

Elements of Fantasy
Which behavior described here is not likely to occur in real life?

Spiral Review
Theme How do Akela's thoughts suggest a possible theme?

Critical Thinking

1. **Key Ideas and Details** **(a)** How is Mowgli similar to the wolf cubs? How is he different? **(b) Analyze:** What qualities in Mowgli does Mother Wolf find appealing?

2. **Key Ideas and Details** **(a)** Who pays for Mowgli's life? **(b) Evaluate:** Are this character's reasons based on his own self-interest or on what is good for the pack? **(c) Support:** What examples from the story support your answer?

3. **Key Ideas and Details** **(a)** Describe how the wolves in the pack make decisions. **(b) Take a Position:** Do you think the process is effective? Explain.

4. **Integration of Knowledge and Ideas** "Mowgli's Brothers" takes place in a community that has many rules. **(a)** What is the purpose of the rules? **(b)** In what ways do the rules shape the actions of the characters? *[Connect to the Big Question: How much do our communities shape us?]*

from

James and the Giant Peach

Roald Dahl

It was quite a large hole, the sort of thing an animal about the size of a fox might have made.

James knelt down in front of it and poked his head and shoulders inside.

He crawled in.

He kept on crawling.

This isn't just a hole, he thought excitedly. It's a tunnel!

The tunnel was damp and murky, and all around him there was the curious bittersweet smell of fresh peach. The floor was soggy under his knees, the walls were wet and sticky, and peach juice was dripping from the ceiling. James opened his mouth and caught some of it on his tongue. It tasted delicious.

He was crawling uphill now, as though the tunnel were leading straight toward the very center of the gigantic fruit. Every few seconds he paused and took a bite out of the wall. The peach flesh was sweet and juicy, and marvelously refreshing.

He crawled on for several more yards, and then suddenly—bang—the top of his head bumped into something extremely hard blocking his way. He glanced up. In front of him there was a solid wall that seemed at first as though it were made of wood. He touched it with his fingers. It certainly felt like wood, except that it was very jagged and full of deep grooves.

"Good heavens!" he said.

"I know what this is! I've come to the stone in the middle of the peach!" •

Then he noticed that there was a small door cut into the face of the peach stone. He gave a push. It swung open. He crawled through it, and before he had time to glance up and see where he was, he heard a voice saying, "Look who's here!" And another one said, "We've been waiting for you!"

James stopped and stared at the speakers, his face white with horror.

He started to stand up, but his knees were shaking so much he had to sit down again on the floor. He glanced behind him, thinking he could bolt back into the tunnel the way he had come, but the doorway had disappeared. There was now only a solid brown wall behind him.

◀ **Critical Viewing**
Which details of this picture are fantastic? Which are realistic?

Elements of Fantasy
Identify one fantastic element and one realistic element in this paragraph.

Comprehension
What clues help James guess what the solid wall really is?

Vocabulary ▶
intently (in tent´ lē) *adv.*
with great attention
or determination

James's large frightened eyes traveled slowly around the room.

The creatures, some sitting on chairs, others reclining on a sofa, were all watching him **intently**.

Creatures?

Or were they insects?

An insect is usually something rather small, is it not? A grasshopper, for example, is an insect.

So what would you call it if you saw a grasshopper as large as a dog? As large as a large dog. You could hardly call that an insect, could you?

There was an Old-Green-Grasshopper as large as a large dog sitting on a stool directly across the room from James now.

And next to the Old-Green-Grasshopper, there was an enormous Spider.

And next to the Spider, there was a giant Ladybug with nine black spots on her scarlet shell.

Each of these three was squatting upon a magnificent chair.

On a sofa nearby, reclining comfortably in curled-up positions, there was a Centipede and an Earthworm.

On the floor over in the far corner, there was something thick and white that looked as though it might be a Silkworm. But it was sleeping soundly and nobody was paying any attention to it.

Every one of these "creatures" was at least as big as James himself, and in the strange greenish light that shone down from somewhere in the ceiling, they were absolutely terrifying to behold.

"I'm hungry!" the Spider announced suddenly, staring hard at James.

"I'm famished!" the Old-Green-Grasshopper said.

"So am I!" the Ladybug cried.

The Centipede sat up a little straighter on the sofa.

"Everyone's famished!" he said. "We need food!"

Four pairs of round black glassy eyes were all fixed upon James.

The Centipede made a wriggling movement with his body as though he were about to glide off the sofa—but he didn't.

There was a long pause—and a long silence.

The Spider (who happened to be a female spider) opened her mouth and ran a long black tongue delicately over her lips. "Aren't you hungry?" she asked suddenly, leaning forward and addressing herself to James.

Poor James was backed up against the far wall, shivering with fright and much too terrified to answer.

"What's the matter with you?" the Old-Green-Grasshopper asked. "You look positively ill!"

"He looks as though he's going to faint any second," the Centipede said.

"Oh, my goodness, the poor thing!" the Ladybug cried. "I do believe he thinks it's him that we are wanting to eat!"

There was a roar of laughter from all sides.

"Oh dear, oh dear!" they said. "What an awful thought!"

"You mustn't be frightened," the Ladybug said kindly. "We wouldn't dream of hurting you. You are one of us now, didn't you know that? You are one of the crew. We're all in the same boat."

Elements of Fantasy
Identify one fantastic detail in this paragraph.

Spiral Review
Folk Tale How are the characters in this modern story similar to those in many folk tales? Explain.

Comprehension
Why do the creatures laugh at James's fright?

◀ **Critical Viewing**
What part of the story do you think this picture shows?

Elements of Fantasy
Could a conversation such as this one occur in real life? Explain.

"We've been waiting for you all day long," the Old-Green-Grasshopper said. "We thought you were never going to turn up. I'm glad you made it."

"So cheer up, my boy, cheer up!" the Centipede said. "And meanwhile I wish you'd come over here and give me a hand with these boots. It takes me hours to get them all off by myself."

James decided that this was most certainly not a time to be disagreeable, so he crossed the room to where the Centipede was sitting and knelt down beside him.

"Thank you so much," the Centipede said. "You are very kind."

"You have a lot of boots," James murmured.

"I have a lot of legs," the Centipede answered proudly. "And a lot of feet. One hundred, to be exact."

"There he goes again!" the Earthworm cried, speaking for the first time. "He simply cannot stop telling lies about his legs! He doesn't have anything like a hundred of them! He's only got forty-two! The trouble is that most people don't bother to count them. They just take his word. And anyway, there is nothing marvelous, you know, Centipede, about having a lot of legs."

"Poor fellow," the Centipede said, whispering in James's ear. "He's blind. He can't see how splendid I look."

"In my opinion," the Earthworm said, "the really marvelous thing is to have no legs at all and to be able to walk just the same."

"You call that walking!" cried the Centipede. "You're a slitherer, that's all you are! You just slither along!"

"I glide," said the Earthworm primly.

"You are a slimy beast," answered the Centipede.

"I am not a slimy beast," the Earthworm said. "I am a useful and much loved creature. Ask any gardener you like. And as for you . . ."

"I am a pest!" the Centipede announced, grinning broadly and looking round the room for approval.

"He is so proud of that," the Ladybug said, smiling at James. "Though for the life of me I cannot understand why."

"I am the only pest in this room!" cried the Centipede, still grinning away. "Unless you count Old-Green-Grasshopper over there. But he is long past it now. He is too old to be a pest any more."

The Old-Green-Grasshopper turned his huge black eyes upon the Centipede and gave him a withering look. "Young fellow," he said, speaking in a deep, slow, scornful voice, "I have never been a pest in my life. I am a musician."

"Hear, hear!" said the Ladybug.

"James," the Centipede said. "Your names is James, isn't it?"

▲ **Critical Viewing**
Which characters are represented in this picture?

Comprehension
How do the Centipede and the Earthworm get along?

Vocabulary ▶
colossal (kə läs´ əl) *adj.*
very large; huge

"Yes."

"Well, James, have you ever in your life seen such a marvelous colossal Centipede as me?"

"I certainly haven't," James answered. "How on earth did you get to be like that?"

"Very peculiar," the Centipede said. "Very, very peculiar indeed. Let me tell you what happened. I was messing about in the garden under the old peach tree and suddenly a funny little green thing came wriggling past my nose. Bright green it was, and extraordinarily beautiful, and it looked like some kind of a tiny stone or crystal . . ."

"Oh, but I know what that was!" cried James.

"It happened to me, too!" said the Ladybug.

"And me!" Miss Spider said. "Suddenly there were little green things everywhere! The soil was full of them!"

"I actually swallowed one!" the Earthworm declared proudly.

"So did I!" the Ladybug said.

"I swallowed three!" the Centipede cried. "But who's telling this story anyway? Don't interrupt!"

"It's too late to tell stories now," the Old-Green-Grasshopper announced. "It's time to go to sleep."

"I refuse to sleep in my boots!" the Centipede cried. "How many more are there to come off, James?"

"I think I've done about twenty so far," James told him.

"Then that leaves eighty to go," the Centipede said.

"Twenty-two, not eighty!" shrieked the Earthworm. "He's lying again."

The Centipede roared with laughter.

"Stop pulling the Earthworm's leg," the Ladybug said.

This sent the Centipede into hysterics. "Pulling his leg!" he cried, wriggling with glee and pointing at the Earthworm.

"Which leg am I pulling? You tell me that?"

James decided that he rather liked the Centipede. He was obviously a rascal, but what a change it was to hear somebody laughing once in a while. He had never heard Aunt Sponge or Aunt Spiker laughing aloud in all the time he had been with them.

"We really must get some sleep," the Old-Green-Grasshopper said. "We've got a tough day ahead of us tomorrow. So would you be kind enough, Miss Spider, to make the beds?" •

Elements of Fantasy
Which aspects of this good-natured teasing are realistic and which are fantastic?

A few minutes later, Miss Spider had made the first bed. It was hanging from the ceiling, suspended by a rope of threads at either end so that actually it looked more like a hammock than a bed. But it was a magnificent affair, and the stuff that it was made of shimmered like silk in the pale light.

"I do hope you'll find it comfortable," Miss Spider said to the Old-Green-Grasshopper. "I made it as soft and silky as I possibly could. I spun it with gossamer. That's a much better quality thread than the one I use for my own web."

"Thank you so much, my dear lady," the Old-Green-Grasshopper said, climbing into the hammock. "Ah, this is just what I needed. Good night, everybody. Good night."

Then Miss Spider spun the next hammock, and the Ladybug got in.

After that, she spun a long one for the Centipede, and an even longer one for the Earthworm.

"And how do you like your bed?" she said to James when it came to his turn. "Hard or soft?"

"I like it soft, thank you very much," James answered.

Elements of Fantasy
Would you call Miss Spider's bed-making behavior fantastic or realistic? Why?

Comprehension
How did the creatures get to be big?

"For goodness' sake stop staring round the room and get on with my boots!" the Centipede said. "You and I are never going to get any sleep at this rate! And kindly line them up neatly in pairs as you take them off. Don't just throw them over your shoulder."

James worked away frantically on the Centipede's boots. Each one had laces that had to be untied and loosened before it could be pulled off, and to make matters worse, all the laces were tied up in the most complicated knots that had to be unpicked with fingernails. It was just awful. It took about two hours. And by the time James had pulled off the last boot of all and had lined them up in a row on the floor—twenty-one pairs altogether—the Centipede was fast asleep.

Critical Thinking

1. **Key Ideas and Details (a)** What is James's first reaction when he encounters the creatures in the peach? **(b) Infer:** How does he interpret their actions and words at first?

2. **Key Ideas and Details (a)** What does the Centipede ask James to do? **(b) Infer:** What words would you use to describe the Centipede's personality? **(c) Analyze:** As a group, how do the creatures seem to get along? Give examples from the text to support your answer.

3. **Key Ideas and Details (a)** By bedtime, do you think James is beginning to like the creatures? Why or why not? **(b) Speculate:** What do you think will happen to James and his new friends? Why?

4. **Integration of Knowledge and Ideas** If James stays with the creatures for a year, how do you think his reaction to them might change? Explain. *[Connect to the Big Question: How much do our communities shape us?]*

Writing to Sources

Comparing Elements of Fantasy

1. Integration of Knowledge and Ideas For each selection, complete a chart like the one shown to list the fantastic and realistic elements in each category.

Category	Fantastic Element	Realistic Element
Animals		
Human		
Setting		
Situation		

 **Timed Writing**

Explanatory Text: Essay

In an essay, compare and contrast the use of fantastic and realistic elements in "Mowgli's Brothers" and the excerpt from *James and the Giant Peach*. Use the information in your charts and the questions below to get started. **(30 minutes)**

5-Minute Planner

1. Read the prompt carefully and completely.

2. Organize your ideas by answering these questions:

- In which story do the animals seem more realistic? Why?
- Is the boy in either story fantastic in some way? If so, how?
- Which story's setting seems more realistic?
- Could either situation happen in real life? Explain.
- What might be the author's reason for including fantastic elements?
- Do the fantastic elements help readers understand the message of the story? Explain.

3. Reread the prompt, and then draft your essay.

USE ACADEMIC VOCABULARY

As you write, use academic language, including the following words or their related forms:

conflict

convince

encounter

unique

For more information about academic vocabulary, see pages xlvi–l.

Idioms

An **idiom** is an expression that has a different meaning from the literal meanings of the words it contains. For example, if a baseball game was postponed because it was "raining cats and dogs," it was postponed because it was raining very hard.

Some idioms are very common and easily understood. Others, however, can be confusing. Look for context clues in sentences that contain an idiom. For example, the sentence above contains the context clue that the game was "postponed." When you add your own background knowledge you can determine that a baseball game would be *postponed* if it was raining too hard to play.

Idioms usually develop in some specialized field where they originally make sense. Look at these common idioms and their sources:

Idiom	Source	Meaning
to watch like a hawk	wildlife	to look at something very closely
to hit the nail on the head	carpentry	to do or say something in exactly the right way
to be on an even keel	sailing	to be balanced, steady, and heading in the right direction

Practice A

Identify the idiom in each sentence.

1. We all worked like ants to finish the class art project.
2. Tom dropped the ball when he forgot to buy a birthday gift for Ana.
3. The members of the soccer team cut down on their snacks.
4. I think I might be coming down with a cold.
5. She let the cat out of the bag when she revealed the secret.

Practice B

Identify the idiom in each sentence. Then, use context clues to figure out the meaning of the idiom. Restate the idiom in your own words.

1. I didn't want to apologize to my sister, but I had to face the music.
2. Kyle wanted to play a role he could sink his teeth into.
3. Leila was putting out fires all day at work until she came home and relaxed.
4. Mrs. Fine's grandchild was the apple of her eye.
5. When Gerald lost the chess match, he was fit to be tied.

Activity Think of three idioms you know. Then, using note cards like the one shown, describe the source of each idiom. For example, your example may be an idiom that relates to an animal, nature, or a kind of food. Next, explain the meaning of each idiom. Finally, write a sentence using each idiom.

Idiom:
Source:
Meaning:
Example sentence:

Comprehension and Collaboration

With a partner, conduct online research to find idioms from another language, such as Spanish or Japanese. Try to find at least five examples. Share your findings with others in the class.

Speaking and Listening

Oral Response to Literature

After you have read a literary work, you may be asked to deliver an oral response to literature. An oral response includes many of the characteristics of a written response.

Learn the Skills

The first step toward preparing a successful oral response is to read the literary work carefully and thoughtfully to develop an interpretation.

Developing your response

- **Organize around clear ideas.** Organize your response around a number of clear ideas, premises, or images. Your introduction should include a thesis statement that expresses your interpretation of the work. The body of the speech should present clearly related and logically organized ideas. Conclude your response by restating your interpretation and sharing your opinion.

- **Create clear transitions among ideas.** Make sure your listeners can follow the flow of your ideas. To do so, use transitional words and phrases. Introduce examples and details with words and phrases such as *for example, for instance, namely,* and *particularly.* Indicate emphasis with words like *above all* and *chiefly.*

- **Use examples and quotations from the text.** To develop your interpretation, use examples from the literature, including direct quotations, to support your opinion.

Delivering your response

- **Use nonverbal elements.** Use nonverbal cues such as eye contact and hand gestures to help the audience follow your main ideas and to emphasize *salient,* or important, points.

- **Use effective rate, volume, and tone.** Use a strong, clear voice that can be heard in the back of the room. Speak slowly and enunciate every word. Do not be afraid to pause before reading a quotation or introducing a new thought.

Practice the Skills

Presentation of Knowledge and Ideas Use what you have learned in this workshop to perform the following task.

> ### ACTIVITY: Oral Response to Literature
>
> Present an oral response to literature to your class. Follow the steps below.
> - Choose a work of literature on which to base your response.
> - Organize your interpretation using the strategies in this workshop.
> - Present your response to the class.
> - Use a Speaking Guide like the one below.

Use a Speaking Guide like the one below to prepare and organize your presentation.

Speaking Guide

Preparing the response:

Novel, short story, or collection title: _____

Author: _____

Main points: _____

Supporting details: _____

Interpretation: _____

Delivering the response:

Before you present, practice these tips:

❑ Hold up the book in which the literary work appears.

❑ When reading a passage or a quotation, read directly from the work. Use sticky notes to mark pages before the presentation.

❑ Use props. Hold up an object mentioned in your presentation.

Speaking techniques:

❑ Employ eye contact and use natural gestures.

❑ Use an appropriate speaking rate and volume.

❑ Use a clear voice and enunciate your words.

❑ Use correct conventions of language.

Comprehension and Collaboration Evaluate and discuss a classmate's presentation. Listen to and interpret the verbal and nonverbal cues in the presentation. After paraphrasing the major ideas and supporting evidence, ask the speaker questions to clarify his or her purpose, perspective, or any other confusing points.

Writing Process

Write an Explanatory Text

Cause-and-Effect Essay

Defining the Form A **cause-and-effect essay** is a piece of expository writing that explains the reasons or the results for something that happens. You might use elements of this form in social studies reports, scientific lab reports, or news reports.

Assignment Write a cause-and-effect essay to explain the reasons leading to an event or situation and the results of that event or situation. Your essay should feature the following elements:

✓ a *thesis* that states the causes and effects of a situation

✓ *relevant facts and details* that support the thesis statement

✓ a *coherent* organizational pattern that emphasizes cause-and-effect relationships and has a *clear introduction* and *logical conclusion*

✓ a *formal style* and effective *word choice*

✓ *transitions* that make connections between ideas

✓ error-free writing, including correct use of *commas, parentheses, and dashes*

To preview the criteria on which your cause-and-effect essay may be judged, see the rubric on page 709.

FOCUS ON RESEARCH

When you write a cause-and-effect essay, you might conduct research to:

• learn background information about the event or situation.

• locate facts, statistics, or other details that describe the scope and nature of the causes and effects.

• find quotations from experts about the significance of the causes and effects.

Cite your source when you use a direct quotation. The Research Workshop in the Introductory Unit explains how to cite sources properly.

READING-WRITING CONNECTION

To get the feel for cause-and-effect writing, read the essay "Birds Struggle to Recover from Egg Thefts of 1800s" by Edie Lau on page 148.

Prewriting/Planning Strategies

Brainstorm. In a group, discuss possible topics. You may wish to begin with a general idea such as "historical events" or a fill-in-the-blank exercise such as "What causes_____?" Review the results and choose an idea from the list as your topic.

Browse media sources. Look through the newspaper or a favorite magazine for topics that interest you. Circle key words or ideas and consider their causes or effects. Choose a topic based on your findings.

Use a topic web. Create a topic web like the one shown to help you evaluate and narrow your topic. First, write your topic inside a circle. Then, write connected ideas, or subtopics, inside circles surrounding your topic. Label each idea "cause" or "effect." When you have finished, review your completed web. To narrow your topic, focus on a single one of your subtopics.

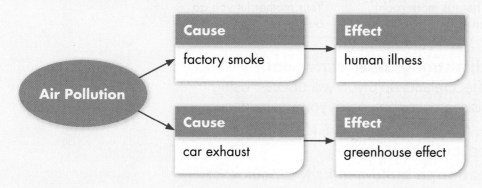

Use a T-chart in research. To find facts and examples that explain cause-and-effect relationships, you may need to conduct research. Use a T-chart to organize your ideas.

Fact	Example

Drafting Strategies

Organize details. You may have identified a single cause and a single effect, or multiple causes for a single effect. This chart shows an example of a single cause with several effects. Select an organization for your essay from the following two common patterns.

- **Many Causes/Single Effect** If a number of unrelated events leads to a single result, focus one paragraph on each cause.
- **Single Cause/Many Effects** If one cause produces several effects, focus one paragraph on each effect.

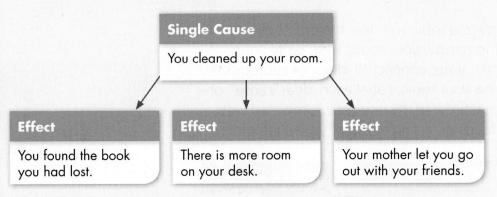

Single Cause

You cleaned up your room.

Effect

You found the book you had lost.

Effect

There is more room on your desk.

Effect

Your mother let you go out with your friends.

Focus your writing with a strong thesis statement. Consider the cause-and-effect relationship you will discuss. Using your notes, craft one thesis sentence that states your main idea.

Example: If the city builds a new sports stadium, local businesses will get the benefit of increased sales.

Include enough information to build a link. Make sure that your sentences show readers exactly how the events or situations are linked in cause-and-effect relationships. Provide supporting details that are precise rather than vague.

Vague: If your skin is damaged, you are at risk for illness.

Clear: If you are fair-skinned and spend a lot of time in the sun without wearing sunscreen, you are more likely to get skin cancer.

Connect with transitions. Choose transitional words and phrases that show clear cause-and-effect relationships.

To show a cause: *Because* of the flood, many homes were damaged.

To show an effect: *As a result*, people have to rebuild.

Using Commas, Parentheses, and Dashes

A **comma** signals readers to pause. It is used to separate words or groups of words in a series.

> **Examples:** School supplies include pencils, erasers, and notebooks.
> I went home, studied for my test, and went to bed.

Commas are also used to set off introductory and nonessential elements in a sentence. A nonessential, or **nonrestrictive,** element is one that is not needed to convey the sentence's main idea.

Set off Nonessential Appositive Phrase	Set off Introductory Phrase	Set off Nonessential Element
The fire truck, *a huge vehicle,* shone in the sunlight.	*In the moonlight,* the tree glowed a ghostly white.	The store, which I love, is in the Riverside mall.

Parentheses also separate nonessential words, phrases, or clauses from the rest of the sentence. However, parentheses suggest the information is even less important than information set off by commas.

> **Example:** On Saturday (Jeff's birthday) we are leaving the city.

Like commas and parentheses, **dashes** also separate words, phrases, or clauses from the rest of the sentence, but they indicate a more sudden and stronger interruption in thought.

> **Example:** Take the sauce off the burner—be careful, it's hot—and pour it into a bowl.

Fixing Errors in Usage

1. Use commas to set off introductory and nonessential elements and to separate items in a series. In a series, include a comma after the last item before the *and*.

2. Reread any sentence that includes parentheses or dashes to be sure they are used correctly.

Grammar In Your Writing

Choose two paragraphs in your cause-and-effect essay. Underline every sentence that contains commas, parentheses, or dashes. Correct any usage errors you find.

Revising Strategies

Test for logical organization. Examine the connections between your paragraphs. Follow these steps to be sure the topic sentences in each paragraph support the thesis of your essay.

1. Highlight the topic sentence of each paragraph.
2. Label each connection to the topic as *cause* or *effect*.
3. Read the topic sentences in the order in which they appear.
4. If necessary, reorder sentences or paragraphs for clarity.
5. Write a concluding statement that follows from the topic sentences of your essay.

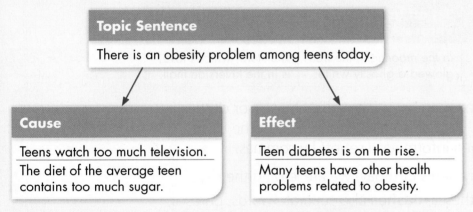

Topic Sentence

There is an obesity problem among teens today.

Cause

Teens watch too much television.
The diet of the average teen contains too much sugar.

Effect

Teen diabetes is on the rise.
Many teens have other health problems related to obesity.

Confirm the link. Make sure your essay describes events that are truly connected by cause and effect, not related only because one event happened after another.

Chronology:	We finished the dishes, then started our homework.
Cause and Effect:	I studied so hard for the test that I was able to do well.

Confirm accuracy. Compare your notes against your draft to ensure that your writing correctly reflects the facts.

Add graphics. Some cause-and-effect relationships are complicated for readers to grasp through words alone. Visual aids, such as diagrams or flowcharts, make complex processes easier to understand. Look for places to add graphics in your essay.

Peer Review

Share your essay with a partner. Ask your reader to tell you whether all of your cause-and-effect relationships are reliable, logical, and clearly explained.

Revising Choppy Sentences

You can combine choppy sentences in your writing by using subject complements and direct and indirect objects. (For more on these sentence elements, see pages 638 and 648.)

Sentence Combining Using Complements This chart shows how combining these elements can eliminate choppy sentences.

Complement	Choppy Sentences	Compound Element
predicate adjective	Tennis is **fast-paced**. It is **fun**.	Tennis is **fast-paced** and **fun**.
predicate noun	One great sport is **tennis**. Another is **badminton**.	Two great sports are **tennis** and **badminton**.
direct object	Playing tennis well requires **equipment**. It requires **practice**.	Playing tennis well requires **equipment** and **practice**.
indirect object	Al gave **me** a tennis lesson. Al gave **Jo** a tennis lesson, too.	Al gave **Jo** and **me** a tennis lesson.

Punctuation Tip You may want to include interesting details that are not essential. Set off nonessential elements with **commas**, **dashes**, or **parentheses**.

> **Example:** Tennis, which requires practice, is a fun sport.

> **Example:** Tennis is fun—both to watch and to play.

> **Example:** Tennis requires equipment (rackets, balls, and shoes) as well as practice.

Fixing Choppy Sentences In a pair of sentences, look at any direct objects, indirect objects, and subject complements after each verb. Then, combine the sentences with compound objects or complements when it makes sense to do so.

Grammar in Your Writing

Reread the draft of your cause-and-effect essay aloud. Listen for pairs of choppy sentences that can be combined with direct or indirect objects or subject complements.

Don't Get Burned

Sunscreen should always be worn when you are out in the sun because the sun can be very dangerous to your skin. If your skin is exposed to the sun's ultraviolet rays without sunscreen, it will turn red, burn, and hurt. Many people believe that burning their skin is one step closer to their desire of getting a tan. They do not realize that both burning and tanning your skin can damage it. Once you burn or tan and the redness or color begins to fade, the damaged skin may begin to peel, leaving a new, unhealthy, thin, and sensitive layer of skin.

What you do to your skin as a child and as a young adult will affect your skin for your full life. Sunscreen can help. Doctors recommend that children apply sunscreen often and at least 30 minutes before going out in the sun. Adults, children, and young adults will benefit from using sunscreens with sun protection factor (SPF) numbers of 15 or more. The SPF numbers give some idea of how long you can stay out in the sun without burning. For example, an SPF of 15 should protect you for approximately 150 minutes—nearly two and a half hours— in the sun. While some sunscreens say they are waterproof, they do not give you total protection from water and sweat. As a result, it is also recommended that sunscreen be applied often.

Nobody's skin is immune to skin cancer. If your skin is damaged a lot by the sun during your childhood and adult years, your chances of getting skin cancer are greater than they are for people who have taken better steps toward protection. Some signs of skin cancer are leathery scab-like patches of skin that may be discolored, bleed, or burn. If you have been burned several times in a short period of time, you should be checked by a doctor because some forms of skin cancer cannot be detected.

So, think twice the next time you are at the beach or the pool without sunscreen, hoping to absorb the sun. Be careful and apply sunscreen to protect yourself from skin damage. Remember that even though a tan may look nice for a few days, it may cause you health problems and unhealthy-looking skin in the future.

Bryson begins by stating his thesis, the cause-and-effect relationship he will show.

Details about the sun's ability to damage the skin help support the writer's purpose.

The writer uses examples to make doctors' recommendations clear.

Each paragraph focuses on a cause or an effect related to Bryson's thesis.

Editing and Proofreading

Correct errors in grammar, spelling, and punctuation.

Focus on spelling. In words with multiple syllables, use a dictionary to help you spell the unstressed vowel sound. The sound, known as a *schwa*, is an open neutral sound like you hear in the words *ago*, *ag**e**nt*, and *san**i**ty*. The *schwa* sound can be spelled with almost any vowel. In a dictionary, the *schwa* is represented with the symbol ə.

Spiral Review
Earlier in the unit, you learned about **subject complements** (p. 638) and about **direct and indirect objects** (p. 648). Review your essay to be sure that you have used complements correctly.

Publishing and Presenting

Consider one of the following ways to share your writing:

Make a movie proposal. Treat your cause-and-effect essay like a script for a short film. Create a storyboard that shows what different scenes might look like.

Make an oral presentation. Read your essay aloud to classmates or family members. Then, invite questions and discussion.

Reflecting on Your Writing

Writer's Journal Jot down your answers to this question:

How do you view your topic differently now that you have analyzed its related causes and effects?

Rubric for Self-Assessment

Find evidence in your writing to address each category. Then, use the rating scale to grade your work.

Criteria	Rating Scale
Purpose/Focus Develops an informative and explanatory text that analyzes clear cause-and-effect relationships	*not very* .... *very* 1 2 3 4
Organization Introduces the topic clearly; organizes information to show cause and effect; provides a concluding statement that follows from the information presented	1 2 3 4
Development of Ideas/Elaboration Presents a clear thesis statement; develops the topic with relevant facts, definitions, concrete details, quotations, and examples	1 2 3 4
Language Uses appropriate transitions to clarify relationships among ideas and concepts	1 2 3 4
Conventions Uses proper capitalization, spelling, and punctuation, including correct use of commas, parentheses, and dashes	1 2 3 4

SELECTED RESPONSE

I. Reading Literature

Directions: *Read the passage from "A Crippled Boy," by My-Van Tran. Then, answer each question that follows.*

Long, long ago there was a boy called Theo. He was crippled in both legs and could hardly walk. Since he could not work, he had no choice but to live on rice and vegetables which kind people gave him…

…To amuse himself Theo practiced throwing pebbles at targets. Hour after hour he would spend practicing his aim…

One day Theo was under his favorite banyan tree. To his surprise, he heard a drumbeat… It happened that the King was out for a country walk with some of his officials and was passing by Theo's tree…

Theo was very frightened and tried to get away; but he could not crawl very far. The King asked Theo what he had been doing. Theo told the King his story.

Then the King asked Theo to <u>demonstrate</u> his skill at pebble throwing… The King was impressed and asked Theo to return with him to the palace where the King said, "I have a little job for you to do."

The following day, before the King had a meeting with his mandarins, he ordered Theo to sit quietly behind a curtain. The King had ordered a few holes to be made in the curtain so that Theo could see what was going on.

"Most of my mandarins talk too much," the King explained. "They never bother to listen to me or let me finish my sentence. So if anybody opens his mouth to speak while I am talking, just throw a pebble into his mouth. This will teach him to shut up."

Sure enough, just as the meeting was about to start one mandarin opened his big mouth, ready to speak.

Oops! Something got into his mouth and he quickly closed it.

Another mandarin opened his mouth to speak but strangely enough he, too, shut his mouth without saying a word.

A miracle had happened. Throughout the whole meeting all the mandarins kept their silence.

For once the King could speak as much as he wanted without being interrupted. The King was extremely pleased with his success and the help that Theo had given him.

After that he always treasured Theo's presence and service…

1. Many **folk tales** feature characters who have unusual skills or abilities. Who posesses a special skill in this story?
   A. Theo
   B. the King
   C. the King's officials
   D. the mandarins

2. **Part A** What is a **universal theme** that this folk tale expresses?
   A. It is good to work for a King.
   B. Some people talk too much.
   C. Skill and practice will be rewarded.
   D. Some people are luckier than others.

   Part B Which phrase from the passage best supports the answer to Part A?
   A. "Hour after hour he would spend practicing his aim"
   B. "I have a little job for you to do."
   C. "just as the meeting was about to start one mandarin opened his big mouth"
   D. "Most of my mandarins talk too much."

3. **Part A** In folk literature, **irony** involves surprises, unexpected events, and interesting contradictions. What ironic situation occurs in the story?
   A. Theo relies on others to support him.
   B. At first, Theo is frightened of the King.
   C. The King feels that his mandarins talk too much and never listen to him.
   D. Although Theo cannot work in his village, he does valued work for the King.

   Part B Which phrase from the passage best supports the answer to Part A?
   A. "he had no choice but to live on rice and vegetables which kind people gave him"
   B. "The King had ordered a few holes to be made in the curtain"

   C. "The King was impressed and asked Theo to return with him to the palace"
   D. "The King was out for a country walk"

4. What is the **cause** of Theo's accuracy at throwing pebbles?
   A. Theo cannot walk.
   B. Theo practices for hours every day.
   C. Theo likes to sit under a banyan tree.
   D. Theo is helped by kind people.

5. What **effect** does the King hope that Theo's pebble-throwing skill will have?
   A. Theo will no longer be scared of the King.
   B. People will give Theo more food.
   C. Theo will no longer have to live alone.
   D. People will learn to stop talking while the King is speaking.

6. What elements of this **folk tale** are specific to the culture from which it originates?
   A. pebble-throwing and practicing aim
   B. the King and the mandarins
   C. a boy who cannot walk and kind people
   D. a drumbeat and a country walk

7. Which phrase is closest in meaning to the underlined word *demonstrate*?
   A. show clearly
   B. protest
   C. officials
   D. a disability

Timed Writing

8. Write an original story that has the same **universal theme** as "A Crippled Boy."

GO ON

II. Reading Informational Text

Directions: *Read the excerpt from an online article. Then, answer each question that follows.*

To plan for a trip to Washington, D.C., Lucinda has prepared an outline of sites she wants to visit at the National Mall. She expects to see and learn many new things on this enriching trip.

I. Memorials and Monuments
A. Lincoln Memorial
1. built in 1922 and pictured on the penny
2. 36 columns representing the states of the Union when Lincoln died

B. Vietnam Veterans Memorial
1. called "the wall"
2. inscribed with the names of about 58,000 American armed troops killed during the Vietnam War

C. Washington Monument
1. 555.5-foot obelisk near east end of reflecting pool
2. designed by architect Robert Mills

II. Museums
A. United States Holocaust Memorial Museum
1. most visited site in the mall
2. remembers victims of the Holocaust

B. Freer Gallery
1. museum of American and Asian Art

C. Hirshorn Museum and Sculpture Garden
1. one of the best collections of modern art in the world
2. includes art by Edward Hopper and Georgia O'Keeffe
3. has an outdoor sculpture garden

1. According to Lucinda's outline, what is she most interested in visiting?

A. museums, memorials, and monuments
B. Washington, D.C.
C. art museums
D. areas with interesting architecture

2. What item could Lucinda add to section II under the letter D.?

A. Jefferson Memorial
B. United States Botanic Gardens
C. National Museum of American History
D. The White House

3. What other information would connect to and clarify the main ideas in the outline?

A. a travel guide that contains information about each place
B. a street map of Washington, D.C.
C. a documentary about U.S. presidents
D. a U.S. history textbook

III. Writing and Language Conventions

Directions: *Read the following excerpt from a multimedia report. Then, answer each question that follows.*

Script for Multimedia Report: Maui

(1) **Visual:** photo of beach in Maui (2) Maui has 120 miles of coastline. (3) Maui has over 30 miles of beaches. (4) Maui is a large island. (5) **Visual:** photo of Maui taken from the air (6) The most interesting thing to do in Maui is hike up the Haleakala Crater. (7) Haleakala is the largest dormant volcano on earth. (8) At the top, the fog is very thick, and it is surprisingly cold. (9) **Visual:** photo of crater (10) Because Maui has a diverse landscape, there are enough activities to keep anyone busy.

---

1. Which revision to sentences 2 and 3 uses a compound **direct object** to eliminate choppy sentences?
   - **A.** Maui has 120 miles of coastline, and it also has over 30 miles of beaches.
   - **B.** Maui has 120 miles of coastline, but it has only 30 miles of beaches.
   - **C.** Maui's coastlines and beaches are over 120 miles and 30 miles.
   - **D.** Maui has 120 miles of coastline and over 30 miles of beaches.

2. Which portion of sentence 10 is a **dependent clause**?
   - **A.** Because Maui has a diverse landscape
   - **B.** there are enough
   - **C.** activities to keep
   - **D.** anyone busy

3. What kind of **sentence** is sentence 7?
   - **A.** complex sentence with one dependent clause
   - **B.** compound sentence
   - **C.** simple sentence
   - **D.** complex sentence with two dependent clauses

4. Identify the **predicate noun** in sentence 4.
   - **A.** Maui
   - **B.** is
   - **C.** large
   - **D.** island

STOP

CONSTRUCTED RESPONSE

Directions: *Follow the instructions to complete the tasks below as required by your teacher.*

As you work on each task, incorporate both general academic vocabulary and literary terms you learned in Parts 1 and 2.

Writing

TASK 1 Literature

Analyze a Key Scene

Write an essay in which you analyze how a key scene in a literary work from Part 2 helps to communicate the work's theme.

- Identify and describe an important scene from a selection in Part 2.
- State the theme of the work.
- Explain how the scene you chose contributes to the development of the theme. Include details from the scene that help readers understand the message of the work.
- Sum up your analysis in the conclusion of your essay.

TASK 2 Literature

Analyze Structure and Theme

Write an essay in which you analyze how structural devices help develop theme in two works of folk literature.

- Identify a work of folk literature from Part 2 that features a structural device such as repetition, patterns, or archetypes.
- Write an essay in which you analyze how the structural device helps develop the work's theme. Explain whether or not the device makes the work more effective, supporting your claims with evidence from the text.

- Identify a second work of folk literature that features a different structural device. Analyze the device's role in the development of theme, and evaluate the effectiveness of the device.
- Compare and contrast the effectiveness of the structural devices in the two stories you chose.
- Make sure to use complete sentences that convey your ideas clearly.

TASK 3 Literature

Evaluate Theme

Write an essay in which you evaluate the theme of a work that contains fantasy.

Part 1

- Identify a story in Part 2 in which the theme is affected by the use of fantasy. Review the story, taking notes on the fantastic elements and the theme.

Part 2

- Write an essay in which you analyze the ways in which the fantastic elements strengthen the theme in the work.
- Cite specific examples from the text to support your ideas.
- Use a formal writing style and tone.

Speaking and Listening

TASK 4 Literature

Compare Uses of Personification

Lead a discussion in which you analyze and compare the portrayals of animal characters in one or more literary works from Part 2.

- Come to the discussion prepared with general ideas about the reasons folk tales and fables often include animals with human qualities. In addition, prepare specific questions about the similarities and differences between at least two animal characters from Part 2.
- Pose your questions and respond to the ideas contributed by your group members.
- Review the key ideas expressed by the group and state any new ideas you arrive at during the discussion.

TASK 5 Literature

Analyze Theme

Prepare and present an oral presentation in which you evaluate the theme of a work of literature from Part 2.

- State the theme of the work you selected.
- Explain how the theme is conveyed through particular details in the work. Consider character, plot, setting, elements of fantasy, and cultural details.
- Organize your presentation by sequencing your ideas in a way that will help your audience follow your reasoning.
- If you have the technology available, prepare a slide show to accompany your oral presentation. Alternatively, create a poster or other visual display.

Research

TASK 6 Literature

 ## How much do our communities shape us?

In Part 2 of this unit, you have read literature that examines the ways in which people and groups are shaped by their communities. Now you will conduct a short research project to explore the ways people shape the communities they live in. Use both literature you have read and your research to reflect on this unit's Big Question. Review the following guidelines before you begin your research:

- Focus your research on people or groups who have worked to make changes that improved their communities.

- Gather relevant information from at least two reliable print or digital sources.
- Take notes as you research the improvements people and groups have made to their communities.
- Cite your sources accurately.

When you have completed your research, write a response to the Big Question. Discuss how your initial ideas have changed or been reinforced. Support your response with an example from literature and an example from your research.

"You can judge a man's **true character** by the way he **treats** his fellow animals."
—**Paul McCartney**

PEOPLE AND ANIMALS

The selections in this unit all deal with the Big Question: **How much do our communities shape us?** Members of a community often benefit from working together. In the texts that follow, humans and animals cooperate in a variety of ways to help one another. As you read, think about the ways that mutual support can be beneficial to all the creatures that share a community.

◄ **CRITICAL VIEWING** What is the relationship between the girl and the dog in this photograph? How can you tell?

CLOSE READING TOOL

Use the **Close Reading Tool** to practice the strategies you learn in this unit.

READINGS IN PART 3

ANCHOR TEXT

MYTH
Prologue from **The Whale Rider**
Witi Ihimaera (p. 718)

MAGAZINE ARTICLE
The Case of the Monkeys That Fell From the Trees
Susan E. Quinlan (p. 726)

WEB ARTICLE
Rescuers to Carry Oxygen Masks for Pets
Associated Press (p. 734)

INFOGRAPHIC
2012 Pet Ownership Statistics
American Pet Products Association (p. 738)

SHORT STORY
The Old Woman Who Lived With the Wolves
Chief Luther Standing Bear (p. 740)

NEWS RELEASE
Satellites and Sea Lions
NASA (p. 746)

NARRATIVE ESSAY
Turkeys
Bailey White (p. 750)

Prologue from # The Whale Rider

Witi Ihimaera

yearning ▶
(yʉr′ niŋ) *n.* feeling of wanting something very much

In the old days, in the years that have gone before us, the land and sea felt a great emptiness, a **yearning.** The mountains were like a stairway to heaven, and the lush green rainforest was a rippling cloak of many colors. The sky was iridescent, swirling with the patterns of wind and clouds; sometimes it reflected the prisms of rainbow or southern aurora.[1] The sea was ever-changing, shimmering and seamless to the sky. This was the well at the bottom of the world, and when you looked into it you felt you could see to the end of forever.

---

1. **southern aurora** (ô rôr′ ə) *n.* streamers or arches of light appearing above Earth in the Southern Hemisphere.

This is not to say that the land and sea were without life, without vivacity. The tuatara, the ancient lizard with its third eye, was sentinel here, unblinking in the hot sun, watching and waiting to the east. The moa browsed in giant wingless herds across the southern island. Within the warm stomach of the rainforests, kiwi,[2] weka,[3] and the other birds foraged for *huhu* and similar succulent insects. The forests were loud with the clatter of tree bark, chatter of cicada, and murmur of fish-laden streams. Sometimes the forest grew suddenly quiet, and in wet bush could be heard the filigree of fairy laughter like a sparkling glissando.[4]

The sea, too, teemed with fish, but they also seemed to be waiting. They swam in brilliant shoals, like rains of glittering dust, throughout the greenstone depths—*hapuku, manga, kahawai, tamure, moki,* and *warehou*—herded by shark or *mango ururoa.* Sometimes from far off a white shape would be seen flying through the sea, but it would only be the serene flight of the *tarawhai,* the stingray with the spike on its tail.

Waiting. Waiting for the seeding. Waiting for the gifting. Waiting for the blessing to come.

◀ **teemed**
(tēmd) *v.* was full of

---

2. **kiwi** (kē´ wē) *n.* small, flightless New Zealand bird.
3. **weka** (wā´ kä) *n.* flightless New Zealand wading bird.
4. **glissando** (gli sän´ dō) *n.* quick sliding up or down the musical scale.

Suddenly, looking up at the surface, the fish began to see the dark bellies of the canoes from the east. The first of the Ancients were coming, journeying from their island kingdom beyond the horizon. Then, after a period, canoes were seen to be returning to the east, making long cracks on the surface sheen. The land and the sea sighed with gladness:

We have been found.

The news is being taken back to the place of the Ancients.

Our blessing will come soon.

In that waiting time, earth and sea began to feel the sharp pangs of need, for an end to the yearning. The forests sent sweet perfumes upon the eastern winds and garlands of *pohutukawa* upon the eastern tides.

The sea flashed continuously with flying fish, leaping high to look beyond the horizon and to be the first to announce the coming; in the shallows, the chameleon sea horses pranced at attention. The only reluctant ones were the fairy people, who retreated with their silver laughter to caves in glistening waterfalls.

The sun rose and set, rose and set. Then one day, at its noon apex, the first sighting was made. A spume on the horizon. A dark shape rising from the greenstone depths of the ocean, awesome, leviathan, breaching through the surface and hurling itself skyward before falling seaward again. Underwater the muted thunder boomed like a great door opening far away, and both sea and land trembled from the impact of that downward plunging.

Suddenly the sea was filled with awesome singing, a song with eternity in it, a song to the land:

You have called and I have come,
bearing the gift of the Gods.

The dark shape rising, rising again. A whale, gigantic. A sea monster. Just as it burst through the sea, a flying fish leaping high in its ecstasy saw water and air streaming like thunderous foam from that noble beast and knew, ah yes, that the time had come. For the sacred sign was on the monster, a swirling tattoo imprinted on the forehead.

Then the flying fish saw that astride the head, as it broke skyward, was a man. He was wondrous to look upon, the whale rider. The water streamed away from him and he opened his mouth to gasp in the cold air. His eyes were shining with

apex ▶
(ā′ peks′) *n.*
highest point

splendor. His body dazzled with diamond spray. Upon that beast he looked like a small tattooed figurine, dark brown, glistening, and erect. He seemed, with all his strength, to be pulling the whale into the sky.

Rising, rising. And the man felt the power of the whale as it propelled itself from the sea. He saw far off the land long sought and now found, and he began to fling small spears seaward and landward on his magnificent journey toward the land.

Some of the spears in midflight turned into pigeons, which flew into the forests. Others, on landing in the sea, changed into eels. And the song in the sea drenched the air with ageless music, and land and sea opened themselves to him, the gift long waited for: *tangata*, man. With great gladness and thanksgiving, the man cried out to the land,

Karanga mai, karanga mai, karanga mai.

Call me. But there was one spear, so it is told, the last, that, when the whale rider tried to throw it, refused to leave his hand. Try as he might, the spear would not fly.

So the whale rider uttered a prayer over the wooden spear, saying, "Let this spear be planted in the years to come, for there are sufficient spear already implanted. Let this be the one to flower when the people are troubled and it is most needed."

And the spear then leaped from his hands with gladness and soared through the sky. It flew across a thousand years. When it hit the earth, it did not change but waited for another hundred and fifty years to pass until it was needed.

The flukes of the whale stroked majestically at the sky.

Hui e, haumi e, taiki e.

Let it be done.

> Try as he might, the spear would not fly.

ABOUT THE AUTHOR

Witi Ihimaera (b. 1944)

Witi Ihimaera was raised in the Maori culture of New Zealand. He became interested in writing at an early age and recalls scribbling stories across a wall of his room at his family farm. Ihimaera is the first Maori to publish both a novel and a collection of short stories. He says that he sees writing as a way to express his experience of being a Maori. *The Whale Rider,* a book that he wrote in just three weeks in 1987, inspired the successful 2002 movie *The Whale Rider.*

Close Reading Activities

READ

Comprehension

Reread to answer the following questions.

1. What feeling did the land and sea have in the old days?

2. What amazing sight rose from the sea?

3. What happened when the whale rider tried to throw the last spear?

Language Study

Selection Vocabulary Use each boldfaced word from the myth in an original sentence that shows its meaning.

- … the land and sea felt a great emptiness, a **yearning**.
- The sea, too, **teemed** with fish, but they also seemed to be waiting.
- Then one day, at its noon **apex**, the first sighting was made.

Diction and Style Reread the sentence and answer the questions that follow.

> The forests were loud with the clatter of tree bark, chatter of cicada, and murmur of fish-laden streams.

1. **(a)** To which of the five senses does this passage appeal? **(b)** What specific words relate to this sense?

2. Based on its **sensory** language, what is the main idea of the passage?

Research: Clarify Details Research one unfamiliar detail from the myth. Then, explain how your research sheds light on an aspect of the myth.

Summarize Write an objective summary of the myth. Do not include your opinions or evaluations.

Conventions Identify the independent and dependent clauses in this passage. Then, explain how the clauses add sentence variety.

> It flew across a thousand years. When it hit the earth, it did not change but waited for another hundred and fifty years to pass until it was needed.

Academic Vocabulary

The following words appear in blue in the instructions and questions on the facing page.

sensory   observe   reveal

Copy the words into your notebook. For each word, find at least one related word that is built on the same root (for example, appreciate/appreciation).

Literary Analysis

Reread the identified passages. Then, respond to the questions that follow.

> **Focus Passage 1** *(p. 720)*
> Suddenly, looking up at the surface, the fish began … *Our blessing will come soon.*

Key Ideas and Details

1. (a) What do the fish **observe** about the directions in which the canoes move?
(b) Infer: Why are the land and sea excited about the arrival of the Ancients?

2. Interpret: Why are the land and the sea happy to see the Ancients leave?

Craft and Structure

3. (a) In the passage, find an example of personification—figurative language in which a nonhuman subject is given human characteristics. **(b) Assess:** What is the effect of this personification?

Integration of Knowledge and Ideas

4. Speculate: How might the events described in the passage bring a blessing to the land and sea?

> **Focus Passage 2** *(p. 721)*
> Rising, rising. And the man felt … the spear would not fly.

Key Ideas and Details

1. Interpret: Why does the man cry out to the land?

2. Analyze: How is the last spear different from the other spears?

Craft and Structure

3. Generalize: The narrator says the man is on a "magnificent journey." What meaning does the word *magnificent* give to the passage?

4. Analyze: How do the phrases "song in the sea" and "ageless music" contribute to the atmosphere of the passage?

Integration of Knowledge and Ideas

5. Infer: What information does this passage **reveal** about the culture that first told the story of the whale rider?

Myth

A **myth** is a fictional tale that often explains how elements of nature originated. Myths are part of the oral tradition. Reread the myth, and take notes on ways the author explains elements of nature.

1. People and Animals (a) What does this myth explain? **(b)** Do you think the whale rider is a mortal or a god?

Use details from the myth to support your answer.

2. What values does this myth teach?

DISCUSS

From Text to Topic **Partner Discussion**

Discuss the following passage with a partner. Take notes during the discussion. Contribute your own ideas, and support them with examples from the text.

> The sun rose and set, rose and set…. trembled from the impact of that downward plunging. (p. 720)

WRITE

Writing to Sources **Informative Text**

> ### Assignment
>
> Write a **cause-and-effect essay** in which you analyze events in the Prologue from *The Whale Rider*. In particular, consider the actions of both the Ancients and the whale rider. Explore how these actions affect the land, the sea, and the people.

Prewriting and Planning Reread the myth, looking for details that describe the land and sea at different points in the story: before the canoes arrive, after the canoes return to the east, and after the whale and whale rider change them. Record your notes in a web or chart.

Drafting In your draft, cite specific examples from the myth to support your points. Make sure the information you provide clearly shows how events are linked in cause-and-effect relationships. If your supporting details seem vague or unclear, review the myth to find additional information to include in your essay.

Revising Reread your essay, making sure you have used transitional words and phrases that clarify cause-and-effect relationships. Choose from among the examples below.

because	*as a result*	*so*
due to	*for this reason*	*consequently*

Editing and Proofreading Check to see that you have used a variety of sentence structures, including simple and complex sentences. Revise to correct any errors in grammar, spelling, or punctuation.

QUESTIONS FOR DISCUSSION

1. What characteristics of whales might inspire people to develop myths about them?
2. Would this passage have the same impact if a different type of creature had appeared in the sea? Why or why not?

CONVENTIONS

Use a comma after a dependent clause at the beginning of a sentence.

RESEARCH

Research **Investigate the Topic**

The Role of Myths The whale and the whale rider in this myth represent certain beliefs and values of the Maori culture.

Assignment

Conduct research to find out about the role of myths in society, and to learn what myths from different cultures have in common. Focus your research on myths that have both human and animal characters. Take clear notes and carefully identify your sources. Share your findings in an **oral presentation** for the class.

PREPARATION FOR ESSAY

You may use the knowledge you gain during this research assignment to support your claims in an essay you will write at the end of this section.

Gather Sources Locate authoritative sources. Search print sources, such as anthologies and reference books. Conduct key word searches, using terms such as *creation myths*, to locate appropriate Web sites. Look for sources with expert authors.

Take Notes Take notes on each of your sources, either electronically or on note cards. Use an organized note-taking strategy.

- Use two columns, with key words in the first column and details in the second, or use an outline with general headings followed by specific details.
- Record source information to use in citations.
- Write legibly so that you can read your notes later.

Synthesize Multiple Sources Assemble data from your sources and organize it into a cohesive presentation. Use your notes to construct an outline for your presentation. Follow accepted conventions to cite all of the sources you used in developing your presentation. See the Citing Sources pages in the Introductory Unit of this textbook for additional guidance.

Organize and Present Ideas Review your outline and practice delivering your presentation. Be prepared to answer questions from your audience.

The Case of the Monkeys
That Fell From the Trees
Susan E. Quinlan

When the **incidents** began in August 1972, biologist Ken Glander and his wife, Molly, had been studying the eating habits of a troop of howling monkeys in northwestern Costa Rica for nearly three months. Then, over a two-week period, seven monkeys from various troops in the area fell out of trees and died. Another fell but climbed back up.

◀ **incidents**
(in ́sə dənts ́)
n. events;
occurrences

One morning the Glanders watched a female howling monkey with a ten-day-old baby turn in tight circles on a tree branch. **Abruptly,** she fell off the branch. For a moment she hung upside down, suspended by her long tail. Then her grip failed and she plunged thirty-five feet to the forest floor. Dazed but still alive, she climbed back up, carrying her clinging infant. She stopped on a thick branch and sat there without eating for the next twenty-four hours.

◀ **abruptly**
(ə brupt ́ lē)
adv. suddenly

Normally, howling monkeys are skilled, nimble climbers. They often leap ten feet or more between tree limbs, and they almost never fall. Why were monkeys suddenly falling from trees?

Glander wondered if a disease or parasite[1] might be involved. He asked scientists in the microbiology department at the University of Costa Rica to examine some of the dead monkeys and look for clues. The scientists found no signs of disease or parasites. Nor had the monkeys starved. All had died in apparently healthy condition. Glander began to think they had been poisoned. But who or what would poison wild monkeys? Glander had several green, leafy suspects in mind, all of them tropical forest trees.

Many tropical trees have similar-looking leaves and trunks, so it is difficult to determine their species.[2] But tropical plant expert Paul Opler had identified all the trees in the Glanders' study area. Several poisonous species were present. Suspiciously, some of the monkeys that fell had been feeding in trees known to have poisonous leaves. Yet Glander knew this proved nothing.

---

1. **parasite** (par ́ə sīt) plant, animal, or insect that lives on or in another living thing, called "the host." The parasite gets its food from the blood or tissue of the host.
2. **species** (spē ́ sēz) group of plants or animals, scientifically classified because of similar traits.

All plants produce chemicals called secondary compounds, many of which are poisonous. Plants make these chemicals for a variety of purposes. Some ward off plant-eating animals, especially insects. But howling monkeys eat nothing except plants, so they could not survive unless they were able to digest or tolerate plant poisons. Other scientists had observed howlers eating leaves from many kinds of trees, including poisonous species, without any signs of **distress.** As a result, most scientists assumed that howling monkeys had an unlimited food supply in their lush tropical forest homes. Glander wasn't so sure.

distress ▶
(di stres´) *n.* serious pain or sadness

The monkeys that fell from the trees strengthened his belief that howling monkeys could not eat leaves from just any tree. He suspected that certain trees were monkey killers, but he needed evidence before he could point fingers. He and Molly began collecting the data they needed to make a case.

Their days started around 4 or 5 a.m. That's when the monkeys awoke, often greeting the day with roars and growls. The monkeys soon set off, alternating bouts of feeding with periods of crawling, leaping, and climbing through the treetops. Wherever the monkeys went, the Glanders followed on foot.

That's when the monkeys awoke, often greeting the day with roars and growls.

At midday, the monkeys settled down. Draping themselves over large branches, their arms and legs dangling, the howlers slept with their tails wrapped around branches to anchor them in place. Late in the day, when the air cooled a few degrees, the monkeys stirred. They climbed and fed until settling down for the night at sunset.

For twelve months, the Glanders endured long days, mosquitoes, heavy rains, and temperatures that sometimes soared over 100°F. They did this in order to make their observations of the monkey troop as continuous as possible. Throughout each day, they recorded how many minutes the monkeys spent sleeping, eating, and moving. They recorded which of 1,699 individually numbered trees the monkeys slept in and ate from, and exactly which parts the monkeys ate—leaves, fruits, flowers, or stems.

Each day, the scientists collected samples of leaves from every tree the monkeys fed in that day, and leaves from nearby trees of the same species. The monkeys had visited these trees but did not feed in them. The Glanders tagged the leaves with wire labels, noting the tree, the date, and the time that the sample was collected.

Next, they dried the leaves in an oven, then packed them in zippered plastic bags for later study.

The Glanders soon noticed that the howlers ate new leaves whenever they could, only occasionally eating fruits, flowers, or mature leaves. In certain trees, the monkeys plucked off the leaves, then stripped and tossed away the leaf blades. They ate only the remaining leaf stems. Other scientists thought this messy feeding behavior meant that howling monkeys could afford to be wasteful in a forest where food was so abundant. Glander wasn't convinced.

After thousands of hours of field work, including nearly two thousand hours of observing monkeys, Glander reviewed all the records he and Molly had gathered. Their careful data showed that howlers had not eaten leaves from just any trees in the forest. Indeed, the monkeys had rarely eaten leaves from the most common tree species. Instead, they spent most of their feeding time in a few uncommon kinds of trees. All told, the monkeys had eaten from only 331 of the 1,699 trees in the area. More surprisingly, they had spent three-quarters of their feeding time in just 88 trees. The data showed that the monkeys selected only certain tree species for feeding.

Glander discovered something even more surprising. The monkeys had not eaten leaves from all the trees of favored species. Instead, they ate leaves from just a few individual trees of most species. For example, the monkeys traveled through most of the 149 madera negra trees in the area, but they ate mature leaves from only three of these. This pattern fascinated Glander, because the madera negra is one of the most toxic[3] trees in the forest. Its leaves are used to make rat poison.

To learn more, Glander chemically analyzed all the leaves he and Molly had collected from the madera negra trees in the study area during their field studies. The results were startling. The three individual trees from which the monkeys had eaten mature leaves showed no traces of poison alkaloids.[4] But leaves collected from the other madera negras were packed with these poisons. Somehow, the monkeys had picked out those very few trees whose leaves were not poisonous.

---

3. **toxic** (täk´ sik) poisonous.
4. **alkaloids** (al´ kə lɔidz) group of chemical substances, some poisonous, found in plants.

Chemical analyses of mature leaves from other kinds of trees revealed a similar pattern. The howling monkeys had consistently selected the most nutritious, most digestible, and least poisonous leaves available in their patch of forest. Glander noted that howlers ate only the leaf stems in some trees because the stems contained fewer poisons than the leaves. His data showed that instead of being sloppy eaters awash in a sea of food, howling monkeys are cautious, picky eaters in a forest filled with poisons.

But the mystery of the monkeys that fell from the trees was not solved. If howling monkeys can identify and avoid the most toxic leaves, why would they ever become poisoned and fall? Glander uncovered more clues by studying plants and their poisons.

The concentration of poison is not uniform among those plants that produce poisonous secondary compounds. The kinds and amounts of poison present vary widely among plant species, among individual plants of a single species, and even within the parts of a single plant. In fact, individual plants make varying amounts of poisons at different times of year and under different growing conditions. Some plants produce more poisons after their leaves or twigs are eaten by plant-eating animals. These same plants make fewer poisons if they are not damaged by plant-eaters. Due to these constant changes, Glander realized that monkeys could not simply learn which trees had poisonous leaves and which had edible ones. Their task was far more complicated. How did the monkeys do it?

Again, Glander found an answer in his field records. Howlers had fed in 331 of the trees in the study area, but they made only one stop in 104 of these trees. In each case, a solitary adult monkey visited the tree briefly, ate just a little bit, and then moved on. Glander thinks these monkeys were "sampling" the leaves for poisons. If the plant parts were toxic, they probably tasted bad or made the monkey who sampled them feel slightly ill. He suspects that each monkey troop finds out which trees currently have the least poisonous leaves by regularly and carefully sampling from trees throughout the area. By using this technique, the monkeys would avoid eating too many of the most toxic plant poisons.

Considering the ever-changing toxicity of the leaves in a forest, however, Glander reasoned that individual monkeys may sometimes make mistakes. They may eat too many of the wrong leaves. More importantly, when edible leaves are scarce due to unusual conditions, monkeys may be forced to eat leaves they wouldn't otherwise choose. Glander first saw monkeys falling from trees during a severe drought[5] year, when the howlers' food choices were quite limited. Because some poisons produced by tropical plants affect animal muscles and nerves, eating the wrong leaves could certainly cause illness, dizziness, and deadly falls.

Today, after more than thirty years of studying monkeys, Ken Glander is convinced that the falling monkeys he and Molly observed were poisoned by eating leaves from the wrong trees at the wrong time. His work shows that a tropical forest is like a pantry filled with a mixture of foods and poisons. Only the most selective eaters can avoid the poisons and find enough edible food to survive.

However, the monkeys' poison-filled pantry has a silver lining. Poison chemicals used in small amounts often have medicinal value. Many human medicines contain plant poisons, including aspirin, quinine, atropine, morphine, digitoxin (a heart medicine), and cancer-fighting vincristine and paclitaxel. In fact, an estimated one-fourth of all medicines prescribed in the United States today come from plants.

Glander and other researchers have gathered some evidence that howlers and other monkeys sometimes select poisonous leaves for medicinal purposes, such as ridding themselves of parasites. Glander thinks scientists searching for new medicines for people might get some useful tips from howlers. The monkeys' behavior might help scientists select those plants most worth sampling.

---

5. **drought** (drout) period of little or no rain.

ABOUT THE AUTHOR

Susan E. Quinlan (b. 1954)

Susan E. Quinlan and her husband, Bud Lehnhausen, have worked together for more than twenty-five years conducting wildlife research and teaching natural history courses.

A biologist, writer, and educator, Quinlan is inspired by her love of wildlife. "I write about nature and the work of scientists because I want to share my fascination in these topics with young readers," she says.

Close Reading Activities

READ

Comprehension

Reread as needed to answer the questions.

1. What mystery do Ken and Molly Glanders want to solve?

2. How do the Glanders gather information?

3. How do the monkeys know which leaves to eat?

4. What do the Glanders conclude?

Research: Clarify Details Conduct research to learn about one unfamiliar detail from the article. Explain how your research sheds light on the article.

Summarize Write an objective summary of the article. Remember to leave out your opinions and evaluations.

Language Study

Selection Vocabulary Define each boldfaced word and use it in a sentence of your own.

• When the **incidents** began in August 1972 …

• **Abruptly**, she fell off the branch.

• Other scientists have observed howlers eating leaves from many kinds of trees, including poisonous species, without any signs of **distress**.

Literary Analysis

Reread the identified passage. Then, respond to the questions that follow.

> **Focus Passage** *(p. 729)*
>
> After thousands of hours of field work, … species for feeding.

Key Ideas and Details

1. What does the Glanders' **study** reveal about the monkeys' eating habits?

Craft and Structure

2. (a) Classify: What specific types of details does the author provide in this passage?
(b) Evaluate: What do these details suggest about the Glanders' research?

Integration of Knowledge and Ideas

3. Speculate: What makes the Glanders' long hours of **observation** and recording worthwhile in the end?

Expository Writing

Expository texts explain concepts or provide information on real people, places, or events.

1. (a) Who are the real people in the article?
(b) What facts lead them to **investigate** a problem?

2. After collecting leaves, what do the researchers do?

3. People and Animals What does the Glanders' work show about the relationship between scientists and animals?

DISCUSS • RESEARCH • WRITE

From Text to Topic **Panel Discussion**

Conduct a panel discussion with four or five classmates. Take notes during the discussion. Contribute your own ideas, and support them with examples from the text.

> Glander and other researchers have gathered some evidence that howlers and other monkeys sometimes select poisonous leaves for medicinal purposes, such as ridding themselves of parasites. Glander thinks scientists searching for new medicines for people might get some useful tips from howlers.

Research **Investigate the Topic**

The Scientific Method Scientists follow particular steps in order to ask and answer scientific questions. The steps can vary, but they usually follow a process known as the scientific method.

Assignment

Conduct research to find out more about the scientific method and how and when it was developed. Consult online encyclopedias or print sources. Take notes and carefully identify your sources. Share your findings in an **annotated chart**. Include a paragraph in which you explain how scientists can use the scientific method in their research about animals.

Writing to Sources **Informative Text**

This article describes how the Glanders investigated an incident they observed. They spent a year studying howler monkeys and kept extensive field records before arriving at their conclusion.

Assignment

Write an **explanation** of the Glanders' method of investigating why the howling monkeys fell from trees in Costa Rica. Follow these steps:

- Introduce the Glanders' question and explain their method clearly.
- Use relevant facts and concrete details from the article.
- Clarify relationships. For example, use words that show order—such as *first* and *next*—to present the steps the Glanders followed.
- Provide a conclusion that explains how the steps led to answers about the falling monkeys.

QUESTIONS FOR DISCUSSION

1. How might information learned through scientific research lead Glander and others to new research questions?
2. What does the passage reveal about a way in which howlers are like people?

PREPARATION FOR ESSAY

You may use the results of this research project to support your ideas in the essay you will write at the end of this section.

ACADEMIC VOCABULARY

Academic terms appear in blue on these pages. If these words are not familiar to you, use a dictionary to find their definitions. Then, use them as you speak and write about the text.

Rescuers to Carry
Oxygen Masks for Pets

By Associated Press
Updated: 9/3/2006

APPLETON, Wis. Pets here will be breathing a little easier now that local rescuers will be carrying oxygen masks designed for animals.

Six Appleton fire trucks and 13 ambulances will be equipped with masks intended for use on dogs, cats and other small animals.

Alderman Richard Thompson initiated the program after he saw a newspaper photograph of a firefighter in Superior giving mouth-to-mouth **resuscitation** to a cat rescued from a house fire.

"A pet is family to most people," he said. "I know I wouldn't want to lose Maggie, my collie, or Lucy, my Tabby cat, to a fire, carbon monoxide poisoning or who knows what else."

The money to pay for each $49 mask came from donations by local animal lovers.

"It was something to see," Thompson said. "There was no organized solicitation effort. People and community groups just read or heard about the program and stepped up to the plate."

The masks, which come in three sizes, will be distributed to each of six fire stations and to the Appleton Police Department K-9 unit, he said.

The Madison Fire Department carries similar masks on its seven ambulances, said Lori Wirth, the department's community education officer.

The Madison department also bought its masks with money raised from **unsolicited** donations, she said. In fact, the department raised so much money it was able to buy mask kits for several neighboring communities.

Wirth said the department's firefighters haven't had to use the masks yet but they're trained and willing.

"What we've done so far is use the masks as a way to remind people to get out of their residence in the event of a fire and don't go searching for pets," she said. "Firefighters will care for any pets we find in the event they suffer from smoke **inhalation**."

◄ **resuscitation**
(ri sus´ə tā´ shən)
n. act of bringing back to life or consciousness; act of reviving

◄ **unsolicited**
(un´sə lis´it´ əd) *adj.*
not requested

◄ **inhalation**
(in´hə lā´shən) *n.*
breathing in

Close Reading Activities

READ

Comprehension

Answer these questions.

1. Why did Richard Thompson start the program described in this article?

2. How do the cities of Appleton and Madison, Wisconsin, raise money for the oxygen masks?

Research: Clarify Details Choose at least one unfamiliar detail from the Web article and briefly research it. Then, explain how your research sheds light on the article.

Summarize Write an objective summary of the article.

Language Study

Selection Vocabulary Identify the suffix two of the boldfaced words share. Explain how this suffix changes the part of speech of the root word. Then use each word in a sentence.

• … a firefighter in Superior giving mouth-to-mouth **resuscitation** to a cat …

• The Madison department also bought its masks with money raised from **unsolicited** donations, she said.

• Firefighters will care for any pets we find in the event they suffer from smoke **inhalation**.

Literary Analysis

Reread the identified passage.

Focus Passage (p. 735)

"A pet is family to most people," he said.
… stepped up to the plate."

Key Ideas and Details

1. **(a) Infer:** According to Thompson, who would be interested in this program?
(b) Analyze: How is Thompson like those people?

2. How did individuals **support** the program?

Craft and Structure

3. **(a)** What does "stepped up to the plate" mean? **(b) Analyze:** How does the use of this expression affect the tone of article?

Integration of Knowledge and Ideas

4. **Draw Conclusions:** What does the first **quotation** add to the article as a whole?

Text Features

Text features give structure to a text and help readers find information. Text features include headlines, bylines, headings, and captions. Reread the article and take notes on the text features.

1. Identify three text features in the article and explain what information each feature provides.

2. **People and Animals** What do the text features show about animals in Appleton?

Rescuers to Carry
Oxygen Masks for Pets

DISCUSS • RESEARCH • WRITE

From Text to Topic **Partner Discussion**

Discuss the following passage with a partner. Take notes during the discussion. Contribute your own ideas, and support them with examples from the text.

> "What we've done so far is use the masks as a way to remind people to get out of their residence in the event of a fire and don't go searching for pets," she said. "Firefighters will care for any pets we find in the event they suffer from smoke inhalation."

Research **Investigate the Topic**

Oxygen Masks Why do animals need oxygen after a fire?

Assignment

Conduct research to find out why people and animals may need oxygen after being exposed to a fire, and why pets need specialized oxygen masks. Consult online sources and look for **authorities** you can trust. Take clear notes and carefully identify your sources. Share your findings in a **short research paper**.

Writing to Sources **Narrative**

Alderman Thompson says, "A pet is family to most people." Many families in the U.S. have pets.

Assignment

Write a **nonfiction narrative** in which you describe the actions someone took to make sure a pet was safe. You may base the narrative on your own experience or on a situation you witnessed or read about. Follow these steps:

- Introduce your narrative with evidence from the article that explains why people care for pets.
- Use vivid words to precisely describe both the pet and the situation.
- Explain the specific steps that ensured the pet's safety.
- Write a strong conclusion, in which you reflect on what the people involved learned from the experience.

QUESTIONS FOR DISCUSSION

1. What did the Madison Fire Department hope would happen after it provided pet oxygen masks to firefighters?
2. How might use of the masks help accomplish this goal?

PREPARATION FOR ESSAY

You may use the results of this research project to support your ideas in the essay you will write at the end of this section.

ACADEMIC VOCABULARY

Academic terms appear in blue on these pages. If these words are not familiar to you, use a dictionary to find their definitions. Then, use them as you speak and write about the text.

2012 PET OWNERSHIP STATISTICS

Number of Households That Own a Pet (Millions)

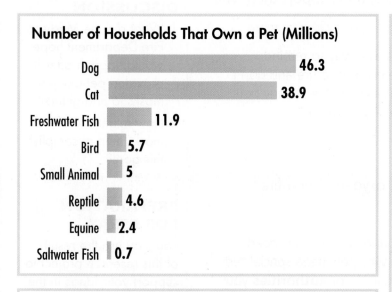

- Dog — **46.3**
- Cat — **38.9**
- Freshwater Fish — **11.9**
- Bird — **5.7**
- Small Animal — **5**
- Reptile — **4.6**
- Equine — **2.4**
- Saltwater Fish — **0.7**

Estimated 2011 Sales Within the U.S. Market

For 2011, it estimated that $50.84 billion was spent on our pets in the U.S.

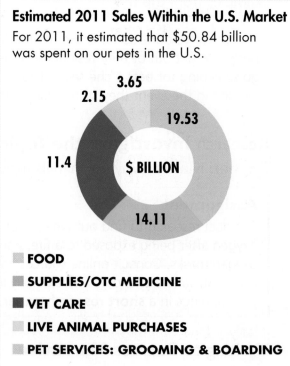

3.65
2.15
19.53
11.4
$ BILLION
14.11

- ■ **FOOD**
- ■ **SUPPLIES/OTC MEDICINE**
- ■ **VET CARE**
- ■ **LIVE ANIMAL PURCHASES**
- ■ **PET SERVICES: GROOMING & BOARDING**

According to the 2011–2012 APPA National Pet Owners Survey, basic annual expenses for dog and cat owners in dollars include:

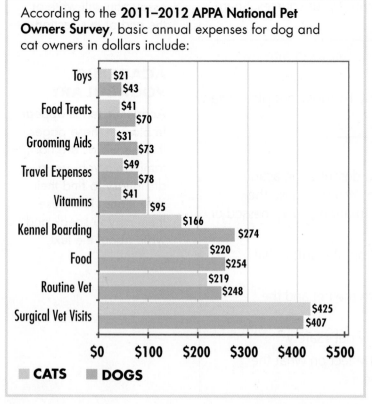

	CATS	DOGS
Toys	$21	$43
Food Treats	$41	$70
Grooming Aids	$31	$73
Travel Expenses	$49	$78
Vitamins	$41	$95
Kennel Boarding	$166	$274
Food	$220	$254
Routine Vet	$219	$248
Surgical Vet Visits	$425	$407

■ **CATS** ■ **DOGS**

Close Reading Activities

READ • DISCUSS • WRITE

Comprehension

Study the infographic to answer these questions.

1. (a) According to the first graph, what is the most commonly owned pet? **(b)** What is the least commonly owned pet?

2. What is similar about the **subject** of the graph on the bottom left and the subject of the graph on the right?

Critical Analysis

Key Ideas and Details

1. (a) In general, who spends more money each year—a cat owner or a dog owner? **(b) Analyze:** What is the exception to your **generalization** about which pet is more expensive?

Craft and Structure

2. Interpret: What is the purpose of the color key that accompanies the graph on the right?

Integration of Knowledge and Ideas

3. (a) Speculate: Which animals might be included under the heading "Small Animals" in the first graph? **(b) Infer:** Why are all the "small animals" grouped together under one heading?

From Text to Topic **Class Discussion**

Discuss the infographic with classmates. Explore questions such as the following in your conversation.

1. Why might kennel boarding be more of an expense for dog owners than for cat owners?

2. How can you **explain** the large difference between the number of people who own freshwater fish and saltwater fish?

Writing to Sources **Argument**

Write a brief **argument** in which you claim either that the benefits of owning a pet outweigh the costs, or that the costs of owning a pet outweigh the benefits. Include some information from the graphs. You may also refer to your own experiences or to other selections you have read in this section.

ACADEMIC VOCABULARY

Academic terms appear in blue on these pages. If these words are not familiar to you, use a dictionary to find their definitions. Then, use them as you speak and write about the text.

THE OLD WOMAN
WHO LIVED WITH
THE WOLVES

Chief Luther Standing Bear

The Sioux were a people who traveled
about from place to place a great deal within the borders of
their own country. They did not trespass upon the territory
of their neighbor Indians, but liked to make their home
first here and then there upon their own ground, just as
they pleased. It was not like moving from one strange town
to another, but wherever they settled it was home. Taking
down and putting up the tipis was not hard for them to do.

The reasons for their moving were many. Perhaps the
grass for their ponies ran short, or the water in the creek
became low. Maybe the game had gone elsewhere, and
maybe the people just moved the camp to a fresh green spot,
for the Sioux loved pure water, pure air, and a clean place
on which to put their tipis.

One day, long ago, a Sioux village was on the march. There
were many people in the party, and many children. A great
number of horses carried the tipis, and herds of racing and
war horses were being taken care of by the young men. In
this crowd was a young woman who carried with her a pet
dog. The dog was young and playful, just past the puppy

age. The young woman was very fond of her pet, as she had cared for it since it was a wee little thing with eyes still closed. She romped along with the pup, and the way seemed short because she played with it and with the young folks when not busy helping her mother with the packing and unpacking.

One evening Marpiyawin missed her dog. She looked and she called, but he was not to be found. Perhaps someone liked her playful pet and was keeping him concealed, but after a search she became satisfied that no one in camp was hiding him. Then she thought that perhaps he had lain down to sleep somewhere along the way and had been left behind. Then, lastly, she thought that the wolves had enticed him to join their pack. For oftentimes the Sioux dogs were coaxed away and ran with the wolf-pack, always returning, however, in a few days or weeks to the village.

So Marpiyawin, thinking the matter over, decided that she would go back over the way her people had journeyed and that somewhere she would find her dog. She would then bring him back to camp with her. Without a word to anyone, she turned back, for she had no fear of becoming lost. Nothing could befall her, so why should she fear? As she walked back, she came to the foothills at the base of the mountains where her village people had spent the summer. As she slept that night, the first snowfall of the autumn came so silently that it did not awaken her. In the morning everything was white with snow, but it was not far to the place where the village had been in camp and so determined was she to find her dog that she decided to keep going. Marpiyawin now felt that her pet had gone back to the old camping-ground, as dogs often do, and was now there howling and crying to be found.

That afternoon the snow fell thicker and faster and Marpiyawin was forced to seek shelter in a cave, which was rather dark, but warm and comfortable. She was not hungry, for in her little rawhide[1] bag was still some wasna.[2] She was tired, however, so it was not long till she fell asleep,

◀ **coaxed**
(kōkst) *v.* persuaded by gentle urging

---

1. **rawhide** (rô′ hīd) *n.* rough leather.
2. **wasna** (wäs′ nuh) *n.* meat and berries pounded and pressed together in flat strips to make a nutritious food that is easy to carry.

and while she slept she had a most wonderful vision. In her dream the wolves talked to her and she understood them, and when she talked to them they understood her too. They told her that she had lost her way, but that she should trust them and they would not see her suffer from cold or hunger. She replied that she would not worry, and when she awoke it was without fear, even though in the cave with her were the wolves sitting about in a friendly manner.

The blizzard raged outside for many days, still she was contented, for she was neither cold nor hungry. For meat the wolves supplied her with tender rabbits and at night they kept her body warm with their shaggy coats of fur. As the days wore on, she and the wolves became fast friends.

traversed ▶
(trə vʉrst′) v.
went across

But clear days finally came and the wolves offered to lead her back to her people, so they set out. They traversed many little valleys and crossed many creeks and streams; they walked up hills and down hills, and at last came to one from which she could look down upon the camp of her people. Here she must say "Good-bye" to her friends and companions—the wolves. This made her feel very sad, though she wanted to see her people again. Marpiyawin thanked all the wolves for their kindness to her and asked what she might do for them. All they asked was that, when the long winter months came and food was scarce, she bring to the top of the hill some nice fat meat for them to eat. This she gladly promised to do and went down the hill toward the camp of her people.

mystified ▶
(mist′ tə fīd′) v.
made someone feel confused or unable to understand something

As Marpiyawin neared the village, she smelled a very unpleasant odor. At first it mystified her, then she realized it was the smell of human beings. At once the knowledge came to her that the smell of humans was very different from the smell of animals. This was why she now knew that animals so readily track human beings and why the odor of man is oftentimes so offensive to them. She had been with the wolves so long that she had lost the odor of her people and now was able to see that, while man often considers the animal offensive, so do animals find man offensive.

Marpiyawin came to the camp of her people and they were happy to see her, for they had considered her lost and thought she had been taken by an enemy tribe. But she pointed to the top of the hill in the distance, and there sat her friends, their forms black against the sky. In great surprise her people looked, not knowing what to say. They thought she must have just escaped a great danger. So she explained to them that she had been lost and would have perished had not the wolves saved her life. She asked them to give her some of their fat meat that she might carry it to the top of the hill. Her people were so grateful and happy that a young man was sent about the camp telling of the safe return of Marpiyawin and collecting meat from each tipi. Marpiyawin took the meat, placed the bundle on her back, and went up the hill, while the village people looked on in wonder. When she reached the hilltop she spread the meat on the ground and the wolves ate it.

THEY THOUGHT SHE MUST HAVE ESCAPED A GREAT DANGER.

Ever after that, when the long winter months came and food was scarce, and hard to find, Marpiyawin took meat to her friends the wolves. She never forgot their language and oftentimes in the winter their voices calling to her would be heard throughout the village. Then the people would ask the old woman what the wolves were saying. Their calls would be warnings that a blizzard was coming, or that the enemy was passing close, and to send out a scout or to let the old woman know that they were watching her with care.

And so Marpiyawin came to be known to the tribe as "The Old Woman Who Lived with the Wolves," or, in the Sioux language as, "Win yan wan si k'ma nitu ompi ti."

ABOUT THE AUTHOR

CHIEF LUTHER STANDING BEAR (1868–1939)

A member of the Oglala Sioux, Chief Standing Bear was originally named *Ota K'Te* (Plenty Kill). He later called himself Standing Bear because it was his father's name. He graduated from the Carlisle Indian School in Pennsylvania and became a writer who fought for Native American rights. In his work, Chief Standing Bear describes the customs and beliefs of the Sioux, including their special relationship with nature. In *Land of the Spotted Eagle,* he wrote, "Earth was bountiful and we were surrounded with the blessings of the great mystery."

Close Reading Activities

READ

Comprehension

Answer the following questions.

1. Why do the Sioux move from place to place?

2. How does Marpiyawin get separated from the rest of her tribe?

3. How does Marpiyawin survive harsh conditions?

Research: Clarify Details Research an unfamiliar detail from the story, and explain how the information you learn sheds light on the story.

Summarize Write an objective summary of the story. Remember to leave out your opinions and evaluations.

Language Study

Selection Vocabulary Define each boldfaced word from the story. Then use the word in a sentence of your own.

• … Sioux dogs were **coaxed** away and ran with the wolf-pack …

• They **traversed** many little valleys and crossed many creeks …

• At first it **mystified** her, then she realized it was the smell of human beings.

Literary Analysis

Reread the identified passage. Then, respond to the questions that follow.

> **Focus Passage** (pp. 741–742)
> That afternoon the snow fell thicker … sitting about in a friendly manner.

Key Ideas and Details

1. **(a)** How does Marpiyawin come to spend time with the wolves? **(b) Interpret:** Why is she not afraid of the wolves?

Craft and Structure

2. **(a)** What **sensory** images does the author provide in the passage? **(b) Interpret:** How do these images help you understand Marpiyawin's situation?

Integration of Knowledge and Ideas

3. **Draw Conclusions:** What does Marpiyawin's experience with the wolves **indicate** about the relationship of the Sioux people to nature?

Conflict and Resolution

In an **external conflict**, a character struggles against an outside force. An **internal conflict** takes place inside a character. The **resolution** is the outcome of a conflict. Reread the short story, and take notes on the conflict and resolution.

1. Which type of conflict develops when Marpiyawin becomes lost?

2. **People and Animals** How does Marpiyawin's trust in animals help her **resolve** the conflict?

DISCUSS • RESEARCH • WRITE

From Text to Topic **Group Discussion**

Discuss the following passage with a group of classmates. Take notes during the discussion. Contribute your own ideas, and support them with examples from the text.

> The blizzard ranged outside … toward the camp of her people. (p. 742)

Research **Investigate the Topic**

Humans and Animals For thousands of years, humans have raised, kept, and farmed with animals. Animals have helped humans survive in difficult times, just as the wolves helped Marpiyawin in this story.

Assignment

Conduct research to find out when and how people domesticated, or tamed, dogs, sheep, cows, and horses. How did both humans and animals benefit? Consult online databases and reference sources. Take clear notes and carefully identify your sources so that you can easily access the information later. Share your findings in an **informal speech** to the class.

Writing to Sources **Informative Text**

"The Old Woman Who Lived With Wolves" is about one community of people living close to nature.

Assignment

Write an **informative essay** in which you make a claim about how the Sioux in the story benefit from Marpiyawin's experiences with the wolves. Follow these steps:

- Introduce your claim about the benefits of Marpiyawin's experiences upon her people. Organize the reasons that support your claim.
- Develop your essay with details and examples from the story.
- Use transition words and phrases such as *for this reason* and *because* to clarify the relationships between your claim and supporting details.

QUESTIONS FOR DISCUSSION

1. What does Marpiyawin learn from living with the wolves?
2. How are the communities of the wolves and the Sioux alike?

PREPARATION FOR ESSAY

You may use the results of this research project to support your ideas in the essay you will write at the end of this section.

ACADEMIC VOCABULARY

Academic terms appear in blue on these pages. If these words are not familiar to you, use a dictionary to find their definitions. Then, use them as you speak and write about the text.

SATELLITES AND SEA LIONS:
Working Together to Improve Ocean Models

NASA News Release
Updated 2/6/07

The best oceanographers in the world never studied at a university. Yet they know how to **navigate** expertly along oceanic fronts, the invisible boundaries between waters of different temperatures and densities. These ocean experts can find rich fishing in places and at depths that others would assume are barren. They regularly visit the most interesting and dynamic parts of the sea.

Sea lions, seals, sharks, tuna, and other top ocean predators share some of their experiences with human researchers, thanks to electronic tags. Besides tracking the animals, these sensors also collect oceanographic data, such as temperature and salinity. Scientists are beginning to incorporate this rich store of information into ocean models providing new insights into the inner workings of the ocean and the lives of its creatures.

"Our goal is to produce a three-dimensional model of the ocean," says oceanographer Dr. Yi Chao. Chao uses data from satellites, ships, buoys and floats to map the currents, heat content and different water densities beneath the ocean surface. When Chao heard Dr. Dan Costa, a professor of **marine** biology at the University of California, Santa Cruz, present some of his animal tagging data at a scientific meeting a few years ago, he saw an opportunity to improve his ocean models. Costa recognized a chance to get a clearer picture of the place where his research subjects live. …

The research collaboration now includes Dr. Barbara Block, a professor of marine sciences at Stanford University, Palo Alto, Calif., and the scientists have added tagging data collected from tuna and sharks to their studies. Together with a group called TOPP, for Tagging of Pacific Pelagics, they are now working to expand the use of environmental and biological data collected by ocean inhabitants.

navigate ▶
(nav´ə gāt´) *v.*
find the way

marine ▶
(mə rēn´) *adj.*
relating to the ocean or ocean life

"We are at the forefront of knowing how animals use the ocean," says Costa. "But we want to understand the environment better. We still see the ocean primarily as deep or shallow or near-shore or offshore. But just as there are different habitats on land, the ocean has fine-scale features that are very important to animals," he explains. "We want to be able to look at the ocean and say the equivalent of 'this is a grassland' or 'this is a forest.'"

In late January, Costa and his research group headed up the California coast to begin tagging elephant seals and collecting tags that were deployed last spring. The work is strictly regulated to ensure that the animals are protected from harm, and it requires a permit from the National Marine Fisheries Service. . . .

"Marine scientists have been tracking marine animals for years," says Chao. "It's an interesting challenge, though, to use the data. There are all sorts—from tuna, sharks, seals—you name it. Some of these data sets have small errors, others much larger errors. Figuring out how to put these in our system is a challenge," he says. "But five years from now, we should be able to see the ocean the way a turtle sees it."

"As we are getting more data from the sea and improving our computer models," says Chao, "we should be able to make routine ocean forecasts, similar to what **meteorologists** have been doing in the past few decades. People who open the newspaper or turn on the TV in the morning will see the updated ocean forecast and make appropriate decisions as they plan their activities on the sea."

What is most important about using marine animals as ocean sensors is that the work benefits the animals, Costa explains. "Collaborations between biologists like Barbara Block and me and physical oceanographers like Yi are critical for understanding why the animals go where they go," he says, "as we need to know and understand the ocean physics and its relationship to climate processes. Further, the ability to understand how climate change is affecting the world oceans is not only of benefit to humans, but is vital for trying to figure out what is going to happen to habitats of marine animals."

◀ **meteorologists** (mēt′ē ə räl′ə jist) *n.* scientists who study the atmosphere and weather

Close Reading Activities

READ

Comprehension

Reread as needed to answer these questions.

1. What is the main idea of the news release?

2. How can the research described in the news release benefit animals in the future?

Language Study

Selection Vocabulary Define each boldfaced word below. Then, use the word in a sentence of your own.

• Yet they know how to **navigate** expertly along oceanic fronts …

Literary Analysis

Reread the passage and answer the questions.

> **Focus Passage** *(p. 747)*
>
> "Marine scientists have been tracking … as they plan their activities on the sea."

Key Ideas and Details

1. **(a)** What kinds of animals are the scientists studying? **(b) Interpret:** What data are the scientists collecting, and why?

Expository Writing

Expository writing explains or informs. Reread the selection, noting reasons the news release is an example of expository writing.

1. What topic does the news release explain?

Research: Clarify Details Research at least one unfamiliar detail from the news release and explain how the information you learn sheds light on the text.

Summarize Write an objective summary of the news release. Remember to leave out your opinions and judgments.

• … Dr. Barbara Block, a professor of **marine** sciences at Stanford University …

• … similar to what **meteorologists** have been doing in the past few decades.

2. **Infer:** Will it be easy for scientists to use the data to make ocean forecasts? Cite textual evidence to support your answer.

Craft and Structure

3. **Deduce:** What do the quotations from Chao add to the passage?

Integration of Knowledge and Ideas

4. **(a)** What effect will the computer models have on people's everyday lives? **(b) Infer:** Why is this kind of modeling useful?

2. **People and Animals** How does the news release present information that shows how the scientists' work will benefit people and animals?

DISCUSS • RESEARCH • WRITE

From Text to Topic **Class Discussion**

Discuss the following passage with your class. Take notes during the discussion. Contribute your own ideas, and support them with examples from the text.

> What is most important about using marine animals … what is going to happen to habitats of marine animals." (p. 747)

Research **Investigate the Topic**

Oceanographers All oceanographers study the ocean. However, there are different fields of study within oceanography. For example, chemical oceanographers study the chemical composition of oceans and the **interaction** that take place between the oceans and the atmosphere.

Assignment

Conduct research to find out about different types of scientists who study the ocean and its creatures. Consult **credible** online and print sources about oceanographers. Take clear notes and carefully identify your sources so that you can easily locate the information later. Share your findings in a **visual report**.

Writing to Sources **Argument**

The news release focuses on ways that scientists have learned about animals and oceans by working **collaboratively**.

Assignment

Write a **persuasive letter** to NASA in which you argue for increased spending on marine study. Promote collaboration among scientists on new research about ocean animals. Follow these steps:

- Present your claim about supporting new research.
- Acknowledge and refute the opposing position.
- Support your claim with reasons and evidence from the text.
- Use transitional words and phrases to clarify the relationships among the reasons and evidence that support your claim.
- Conclude with a statement that summarizes your argument.

QUESTIONS FOR DISCUSSION

1. How does sharing information lead people to a better understanding of animals?

2. What information about climate can the researchers learn from animals?

PREPARATION FOR ESSAY

You may use the results of this research project to support your ideas in the essay at the end of this section.

ACADEMIC VOCABULARY

Academic terms appear in blue on these pages. If these words are not familiar to you, use a dictionary to find their definitions. Then, use them as you speak and write about the text.

Turkeys
Bailey White

Something about my mother attracts ornithologists.[1] It all started years ago when a couple of them discovered she had a rare species of woodpecker coming to her bird feeder. They came in the house and sat around the window, exclaiming and taking pictures with big fancy cameras. But long after the red cockaded woodpeckers had gone to roost, the ornithologists were still there. There always seemed to be three or four of them wandering around our place and staying for supper.

In those days, during the 1950's, the big concern of ornithologists in our area was the wild turkey. They were rare, and the pure-strain wild turkeys had begun to

---

1. **ornithologists** (ôr´ nə thäl´ ə jists) *n.* people who study birds.

interbreed with farmers' domestic stock. The species was being degraded. It was extinction by dilution, and to the ornithologists it was just as tragic as the more dramatic demise of the passenger pigeon or the Carolina parakeet.

One ornithologist had devised a formula to compute the ratio of domestic to pure-strain wild turkey in an individual bird by comparing the angle of flight at takeoff and the rate of acceleration. And in those sad days, the turkeys were flying low and slow.

It was during that time, the spring when I was six years old, that I caught the measles. I had a high fever, and my mother was worried about me. She kept the house quiet and dark and crept around silently, trying different methods of cooling me down.

◀ **dilution**
(di lōō´ shən)
n. process of weakening by mixing with something else

◀ **demise**
(di mīz´) *n.* end of existence; death

Even the ornithologists stayed away—but not out of fear of the measles or respect for a household with sickness. The fact was, they had discovered a wild turkey nest. According to the formula, the hen was pure-strain wild—not a taint of the sluggish domestic bird in her blood—and the ornithologists were camping in the woods, protecting her nest from predators and taking pictures.

One night our phone rang. It was one of the ornithologists. "Does your little girl still have measles?" he asked.

"Yes," said my mother. "She's very sick. Her temperature is 102."

"I'll be right over," said the ornithologist.

In five minutes a whole carload of them arrived. They marched solemnly into the house, carrying a cardboard box. "A hundred and two, did you say? Where is she?" they asked my mother.

They crept into my room and set the box down on the bed. I was barely conscious, and when I opened my eyes, their worried faces hovering over me seemed to float out of the darkness like giant, glowing eggs. They snatched the covers off me and felt me all over. They consulted in whispers.

"Feels just right, I'd say."

"A hundred two—can't miss if we tuck them up close and she lies still."

I closed my eyes then, and after a while the ornithologists drifted away, their pale faces bobbing up and down on the black wave of fever.

The next morning I was better. For the first time in days I could think. The memory of the ornithologists with their whispered voices was like a dream from another life. But when I pulled down the covers, there staring up at me with googly eyes and wide mouths were sixteen fuzzy baby turkeys, and the cracked chips and caps of sixteen brown speckled eggs.

I was a sensible child. I gently stretched myself out. The eggshells crackled, and the turkey babies fluttered and cheeped and snuggled against me. I laid my aching head back on the pillow and closed my eyes. "The ornithologists," I whispered. "The ornithologists have been here."

It seems the turkey hen had been so disturbed by the elaborate protective measures that had been undertaken on her behalf that she had abandoned her nest on the night the eggs were due to hatch. It was a cold night. The ornithologists, not having an incubator on hand, used their heads and came up with the next best thing.

The baby turkeys and I gained our strength together. When I was finally able to get out of bed and feebly creep around the house, the turkeys peeped and cheeped around my ankles, scrambling to keep up with me and tripping over their own big spraddle-toed feet. When I went outside for the first time, the turkeys tumbled after me down the steps and scratched around in the yard while I sat in the sun.

Finally, in late summer, the day came when they were ready to fly for the first time as adult birds. The ornithologists gathered. I ran down the hill, and the turkeys ran too. Then, one by one, they took off. They flew high and fast. The ornithologists made Vs with their thumbs and forefingers, measuring angles. They consulted their stopwatches and paced off distances. They scribbled in their tiny notebooks. Finally they looked at each other. They sighed. They smiled. They jumped up and down and hugged each other. "One hundred percent pure wild turkey!" they said.

Nearly forty years have passed since then. Now there's a vaccine for measles. And the woods where I live are full of pure wild turkeys. I like to think they are all descendants of those sixteen birds I saved from the **vigilance** of the ornithologists.

◀ **vigilance**
(vij´ ə ləns)
n. watchfulness

ABOUT THE AUTHOR

Bailey White (b. 1950)

Baily White's father, Robb, wrote children's stories and television and movie scripts. Inspired by her father's love of words, White began writing in her teen years. Her mother, Rosalie, was a farmer. Through her mother, White gained an admiration for nature. As a teacher in Thomasville, Georgia, White did not expect to become famous. However, she became an essayist on National Public Radio, where she shared her observations with listeners across the country. White's collection of essays, *Mama Makes Up Her Mind and Other Dangers of Southern Living,* was on the bestseller list for 55 weeks.

Close Reading Activities

READ

Comprehension

Reread as needed to answer the questions.

1. In the essay, what problem threatens the wild turkeys?

2. What are the ornithologists doing in the woods?

3. What is the final result of the ornithologists' plan to save the eggs?

Research: Clarify Details Research at least one unfamiliar detail and explain how the information you learn sheds light on an aspect of the narrative essay.

Summarize Write an objective summary of the essay. Do not include your opinions or evaluations.

Language Study

Selection Vocabulary Define each boldfaced word and use it in a sentence of your own.

- It was extinction by **dilution** …

- … the more dramatic **demise** of the passenger pigeon or the Carolina parakeet.

- … those sixteen birds I saved from the **vigilance** of the ornithologists.

Literary Analysis

Reread the identified passage. Then, respond to the questions that follow.

> **Focus Passage** (p. 752)
> "Feels just right … brown speckled eggs.

Key Ideas and Details

1. **Analyze:** What key detail is **crucial** to the success of the ornithologists' plan?

2. **Interpret:** What risks do the ornithologists take by following their plan?

Craft and Structure

3. **(a)** What words and phrases does White use to describe the feeling of having a fever? **(b) Evaluate:** Does White convey the feeling effectively? Why or why not?

Integration of Knowledge and Ideas

4. **Draw Conclusions:** What does the ornithologists' plan show about the ways in which scientists use problem-solving skills?

Author's Influences

An **author's influences** are factors that affect his or her writing. These factors include the author's cultural background and the time in which he or she lives. Reread the narrative essay, and take notes on the factors that influenced the author.

1. **(a)** Where and when did the events take place? **(b)** What details of White's situation made these events possible?

2. **People and Animals** How does the author feel about the event nearly forty years later?

DISCUSS • RESEARCH • WRITE

From Text to Topic **Class Discussion**

Discuss the following passage with a group of classmates. Take notes during the discussion. Contribute your own ideas, and support them with examples from the text.

> Finally, in late summer, the day came … "One hundred percent pure wild turkey!" they said. (p. 753)

Research **Investigate the Topic**

Wild Turkeys When the events that White describes took place, wild turkeys were threatened with extinction. Today, these turkeys have made a comeback. There are five different types of wild turkeys in North America.

Assignment

Conduct research to find out about wild turkeys and how people helped them make a comeback. Consult print and online resources. Carefully identify your sources so that you can easily access the information later. Share your findings in an **informal presentation** for the class.

Writing to Sources **Argument**

Bailey White and the ornithologists are responsible for helping to save sixteen wild turkeys. Some scientists and activists, called *conservationists,* work to keep animals from becoming extinct.

Assignment

Write a **persuasive essay** from the point of view of a conservationist who wants to save the wild turkey. Argue for the value of saving the species using information from the narrative essay to support your claims. Follow these steps:

- Introduce your claim.
- Support your claim with logical reasoning and information from the text.
- Use transition words, phrases, and clauses to connect your claim and reasons.
- Provide a strong concluding statement.

QUESTIONS FOR DISCUSSION

1. How is the behavior of the humans and turkeys related?
2. What idea about humans and animals is revealed in this passage?

PREPARATION FOR ESSAY

You may use the results of this research project to support your ideas in the essay you will write at the end of this section.

ACADEMIC VOCABULARY

Academic terms appear in blue on these pages. If these words are not familiar to you, use a dictionary to find their definitions. Then, use them as you speak and write about the text.

Assessment: Synthesis

Speaking and Listening: **Small Group Discussion**

People, Animals, and Communities The texts in this section vary in genre, length, style, and perspective. However, all of the texts comment in some way on the idea that animals can make valuable contributions to human communities. The issues surrounding the many ways animals and people can help one another are fundamentally related to the Big Question addressed in this unit: **How much do our communities shape us?**

> **Assignment**
>
> **Conduct discussions.** With a small group of classmates, conduct a discussion about issues surrounding people, animals, and communities. Refer to the texts in this section, other texts you have read, and your personal experience and knowledge to support your ideas. Begin your discussion by addressing the following questions:
>
> • How do people help abandoned or injured animals?
>
> • How can people benefit from caring for animals? How can animals benefit from being cared for by people?
>
> • How can animals help people and their communities?
>
> **Summarize and present your ideas.** After you have fully explored the topic, summarize your discussion and present your findings to the class as a whole.

▲ Refer to the selections you read in Part 3 as you complete the activities on this assessment.

Criteria for Success

✓ **Organizes the group effectively**
Appoint a group leader and a timekeeper. The group leader should present the discussion questions. The timekeeper should make sure the discussion takes no longer than 20 minutes.

✓ **Maintains focus of discussion**
As a group, stay on topic and avoid straying into other subject areas.

✓ **Involves all participants equally and fully**
No one person should monopolize the conversation. Rather, everyone should take turns speaking and contributing ideas.

✓ **Follows the rules for collegial discussion**
As each group member speaks, others should listen carefully. Build on one another's ideas and support viewpoints and opinions with sound reasoning and evidence. Express disagreement respectfully.

USE NEW VOCABULARY

As you speak and share ideas, work to use the vocabulary words you have learned in this unit. The more you use new words, the more you will "own" them.

Writing: **Narrative**

People, Animals, and Communities Many kinds of communities help animals, and many groups of animals help people. For example, people may help animals by forming groups to support wildlife preservation or working together at animal shelters. Animals may help people by working to herd other animals, providing transportation, or aiding people with disabilities.

Assignment

Write a nonfiction **narrative** that describes a situation in which people and animals help each other. Your narrative may be based on a personal experience or on a situation with which you are familiar. Use sensory language and dialogue to bring your narrative to life. Include relevant facts and examples from the texts in this section.

Criteria for Success

Purpose/Focus
✓ **Connects specific incidents with larger ideas**
Make meaningful connections between the situations you describe and the texts you have read in this section.

Organization
✓ **Organize ideas and information logically**
Structure your narrative so that your facts, details, or examples relate to the topic to create a coherent whole.

Development of Ideas/Elaboration
✓ **Supports insights**
Include both personal examples and details from the texts you have read in this section.

✓ **Uses narrative techniques effectively**
Consider using dialogue to help readers "hear" how characters sound.

Language
✓ **Uses description effectively**
Effectively uses descriptive details.

Conventions
✓ **Does not have errors**
Eliminate errors in grammar, spelling, and punctuation.

WRITE TO EXPLORE

Writing is a way to clarify what you feel and think. As you write, you may change your mind or get new ideas as you work. Allowing for this exploration of ideas will improve the quality of your writing.

Writing to Sources: **Explanatory Text**

People, Animals, and Communities The related readings in this section present a range of ideas about the ways that people and animals help one another in communities. The selections raise questions, such as the following, about community values and beliefs:

- What part can animals play in a culture's values and beliefs?
- How can observation and scientific research help both people and animals?
- What role do pets play in family life?
- How can people and animals aid in one another's survival?

Focus on the question that intrigues you the most, and then complete the following assignment.

Assignment
Write an **explanatory essay** in which you explain how people and animals help one another and shape communities. Build evidence by analyzing the communities of people and animals in two or more texts from this section. Clearly present, develop, and support your ideas with examples and details from the texts.

INCORPORATE RESEARCH

In your essay, use information you gathered as you completed the brief research assignments related to the selections in this section.

Prewriting and Planning

Choose texts. Review the texts in the section to determine which ones you will cite in your essay. Select at least two texts that will provide strong material to support your exposition.

Gather details and craft a working thesis, or topic. Use a chart like the one shown to develop your informative essay.

Focus Question: How can people and animals help each other survive?

Text	Passage	Notes
Prologue from The Whale Rider	The news is being taken back to the place of the Ancients. Our blessing will come soon.	The land and sea are glad because they have waited for people to come.
"The Old Woman Who Lived With the Wolves"	As the days wore on, she and the wolves became fast friends. But clear days finally came and the wolves offered to lead her back to her people.	The girl belongs to a community of people and becomes part of a community of wolves.

Example Thesis: Communities of people and animals both benefit when one group shares resources with the other.

Drafting

Write a strong introduction. Your introduction is the first thing your audience will read. Include a sentence or two that clearly presents your topic, and then identify the main points you will make in your essay.

Develop your ideas. Decide which facts from your reading and research are relevant to your topic. If appropriate, write an extended definition. Review your notes to find the strongest details, quotations, and examples that support your ideas.

Use the SEE technique. For each main idea you identify, use the SEE technique to add depth to your essay. In a paragraph, first write a **S**tatement. Next, write a sentence that **E**xtends the idea. Finally, write a sentence that **E**laborates on the extension.

Revising and Editing

Use the appropriate verb tense. Make sure that your topic or thesis is clearly stated and that you have supported it with convincing evidence from the texts. Underline main ideas in your paper and confirm that each one is supported. Add additional details or examples, if necessary.

Review style. Check that you have found the clearest, simplest way to communicate your ideas. Omit unnecessary words.

CITE RESEARCH CORRECTLY

Avoid plagiarism by properly crediting the ideas of others. See the Citing Sources pages in the Introductory Unit of this textbook for guidance.

Self-Evaluation Rubric

Use the following criteria to evaluate the effectiveness of your essay.

Criteria	Rating Scale
Purpose/Focus Introduces a specific topic; provides a concluding section that follows from and supports the information or explanation presented	*not very .... very* 1 2 3 4
Organization Organizes complex ideas, concepts, and information to make important connections and distinctions; uses appropriate and varied transitions to link the major sections, create cohesion, and clarify relationships among ideas	1 2 3 4
Development of Ideas/Elaboration Develops the topic with well-chosen, relevant and sufficient facts, extended definitions, concrete details, quotations or other information and examples appropriate to the audience's knowledge of the topic	1 2 3 4
Language Uses precise language and domain-specific vocabulary to manage the complexity of the topic; establishes and maintains a formal style and objective tone	1 2 3 4
Conventions Uses correct conventions of grammar, spelling, and punctuation	1 2 3 4

Independent Reading

Titles for Extended Reading

In this unit, you have read texts in a variety of genres that originated in the oral tradition. Continue to read on your own. Select works that you enjoy, but challenge yourself to explore new writers and works of increasing depth and complexity. The titles suggested below will help you get started.

INFORMATIONAL TEXT

Discoveries: Finding Connections

This collection of **essays** explores the importance of communities in "The Maori Culture of New Zealand," "Natural Disasters," "The Delta Blues," and "Numbers: The Universal Language."

Understanding the Holy Land
by Mitch Frank

The Israeli-Palestinian conflict may be familiar to you, but how much do you really know? This **nonfiction book** explains why this conflict is important and how it affects the rest of the world.

The Circuit
by Francisco Jiménez

In this **autobiography**, Jiménez tells of his difficult early years as part of a family of migrant farm workers. To him, life consisted of constant moving around and work, with school wedged in around harvesting jobs.

LITERATURE

**Black Ships Before Troy:
The Story of the Iliad**
by Rosemary Sutcliff
Laurel Leaf, 2005   **EXEMPLAR TEXT**

Sutcliff retells the grand **epic** of the Greeks' ten-year-long battle against the city of Troy in exciting and vivid detail. She breathes life into classical and mythical characters and also re-creates some of the brutal realities of battle.

Sleeping Ugly
by Jane Yolen

This funny **fairy tale** turns the original version upside down. Princess Miserella is beautiful but mean. Plain Jane is homely but sweet. To this pair of opposites, Jane Yolen adds a magical mix-up and an unsuspecting prince.

Myths and Stories from the Americas

This collection of **myths** and **folk tales** includes stories of creation, tricksters, love, and adventure from North America, Hawaii, the Caribbean, Central America, and South America.

This Big Sky
by Pat Mora

This book of fourteen **poems** combines Mora's vivid imagery with cut-paper collages to bring the awe-inspiring American Southwest to life for the reader.

ONLINE TEXT SET

AUTOBIOGRAPHY
The Market Square Dog James Herriot

SHORT STORY
Aaron's Gift Myron Levoy

REFLECTIVE ESSAY
Childhood and Poetry Pablo Neruda

Preparing to Read Complex Texts

Attentive Reading As you read on your own, ask yourself questions like these to enrich your reading experience.

When reading texts from the oral tradition, ask yourself ...

Comprehension: **Key Ideas and Details**

- From what culture does this text come? What do I know about that culture?
- What type of text am I reading? For example, is it a myth, a legend, or a tall tale? What characters and events do I expect to find in this type of text?
- What elements of the culture do I see in the text? For example, do I notice beliefs, foods, or settings that have meaning for the people of this culture?

Text Analysis: **Craft and Structure**

- Who is retelling or presenting this text? Do I think the author has changed the text from the original? If so, how?
- Does the text include characters and tell a story? If so, are the characters and plot interesting?
- What do I notice about the language used in the text? Which aspects seem similar to or different from the language used in modern texts?
- Does the text include symbols? If so, do they have a special meaning in the original culture of the text? Do they also have meaning in modern life?

Connections: **Integration of Knowledge and Ideas**

- What does this text teach me about the culture from which it comes?
- What, if anything, does this text teach me about people in general?
- How does this text compare with others I have read?
- Do I know of any modern versions of this text? How are they similar to or different from this one?
- If I were researching this culture for a report, would I include passages from this text? If so, what would those passages show?

Resources

Literary Terms

ALLITERATION *Alliteration* is the repetition of initial consonant sounds. Writers use alliteration to draw attention to certain words or ideas, to imitate sounds, and to create musical effects.

ALLUSION An *allusion* is a reference to a well-known person, event, place, literary work, or work of art. Understanding what a literary work is saying often depends on recognizing its allusions and the meanings they suggest.

ANALOGY An *analogy* makes a comparison between two or more things that are similar in some ways but otherwise unalike.

ANECDOTE An *anecdote* is a brief story about an interesting, amusing, or strange event. Writers tell anecdotes to entertain or to make a point.

ANTAGONIST An *antagonist* is a character or a force in conflict with a main character, or protagonist.

See *Conflict* and *Protagonist.*

ARGUMENT See *Persuasion.*

ATMOSPHERE *Atmosphere,* or *mood,* is the feeling created in the reader by a literary work or passage.

AUTHOR'S INFLUENCES An *author's influences* are things that affect his or her writing. These factors include the author's time and place of birth and cultural background, as well as world events that took place during the author's lifetime.

AUTHOR'S STYLE *Style* is an author's typical way of writing. Many factors determine an author's style, including diction; tone; use of characteristic elements such as figurative language, dialect, rhyme, meter, or rhythmic devices; typical grammatical structures and patterns; typical sentence length; and typical methods of organization.

AUTOBIOGRAPHY An *autobiography* is the story of the writer's own life, told by the writer. Autobiographical writing may tell about the person's whole life or only a part of it.

Because autobiographies are about real people and events, they are a form of nonfiction. Most autobiographies are written in the first person.

See *Biography, Nonfiction,* and *Point of View.*

BIOGRAPHY A *biography* is a form of nonfiction in which a writer tells the life story of another person. Most biographies are written about famous or admirable people. Although biographies are nonfiction, the most effective ones share the qualities of good narrative writing.

See *Autobiography* and *Nonfiction.*

CHARACTER A *character* is a person or an animal that takes part in the action of a literary work. The main, or *major,* character is the most important character in a story, poem, or play. A *minor* character is one who takes part in the action but is not the focus of attention.

Characters are sometimes classified as flat or round. A *flat character* is one-sided and often stereotypical. A *round character,* on the other hand, is fully developed and exhibits many traits—often both faults and virtues. Characters can also be classified as dynamic or static. A *dynamic character* is one who changes or grows during the course of the work. A *static character* is one who does not change.

See *Characterization, Hero/Heroine,* and *Motive.*

CHARACTERIZATION *Characterization* is the act of creating and developing a character. Authors use two major methods of characterization—*direct* and *indirect.* When using *direct* characterization, a writer states the *character's traits,* or characteristics.

When describing a character *indirectly,* a writer depends on the reader to draw conclusions about the character's traits. Sometimes the writer tells what other participants in the story say and think about the character.

See *Character* and *Motive.*

CHARACTER TRAITS *Character traits* are the qualities, attitudes, and values that a character has or displays—for example, dependability, intelligence, selfishness, or stubbornness.

CLIMAX The *climax,* also called the turning point, is the high point in the action of the plot. It is the moment of greatest tension, when the outcome of the plot hangs in the balance.

See *Plot.*

COMEDY A *comedy* is a literary work, especially a play, that is light, is often humorous or satirical, and ends happily. Comedies frequently depict ordinary characters faced with temporary difficulties and conflicts. Types of comedy include *romantic comedy,* which involves problems between lovers, and the *comedy of manners,* which satirically challenges social customs of a society.

CONCRETE POEM A *concrete poem* is one with a shape that suggests its subject. The poet arranges the letters, punctuation, and lines to create an image, or picture, on the page.

CONFLICT A *conflict* is a struggle between opposing forces. Conflict is one of the most important elements of stories, novels, and plays because it causes the action. There are two kinds of conflict: external and internal. An *external conflict* is one in which a character struggles against some outside force, such as another person. Another kind of external conflict may occur between a character and some force in nature.

An *internal conflict* takes place within the mind of a character. The character struggles to make a decision, take an action, or overcome a feeling.

See *Plot.*

CONNOTATIONS The *connotation* of a word is the set of ideas associated with it in addition to its explicit meaning. The connotation of a word can be personal, based on individual experiences. More often, cultural connotations—those recognizable by most people in a group—determine a writer's word choices.

See also *Denotation.*

DENOTATION The *denotation* of a word is its dictionary meaning, independent of other associations that the word may have. The denotation of the word *lake,* for example, is "an inland body of water." "Vacation spot" and "place where the fishing is good" are connotations of the word *lake.*

See also *Connotation.*

DESCRIPTION A *description* is a portrait, in words, of a person, place, or object. Descriptive writing uses images that appeal to the five senses—sight, hearing, touch, taste, and smell.

See *Image.*

DEVELOPMENT See *Plot.*

DIALECT *Dialect* is the form of a language spoken by people in a particular region or group. Dialects differ in pronunciation, grammar, and word choice. The English language is divided into many dialects. British English differs from American English.

DIALOGUE A *dialogue* is a conversation between characters. In poems, novels, and short stories, dialogue is usually set off by quotation marks to indicate a speaker's exact words.

In a play, dialogue follows the names of the characters, and no quotation marks are used.

DRAMA A *drama* is a story written to be performed by actors. Although a drama is meant to be performed, one can also read the script, or written version, and imagine the action. The *script* of a drama is made up of dialogue and stage directions. The *dialogue* is the words spoken by the actors. The *stage directions,* usually printed in italics, tell how the actors should look, move, and speak. They also describe the setting, sound effects, and lighting.

Dramas are often divided into parts called *acts.*

The acts are often divided into smaller parts called *scenes.*

DYNAMIC CHARACTER See *Character.*

ESSAY An *essay* is a short nonfiction work about a particular subject. Most essays have a single major focus and a clear introduction, body, and conclusion.

There are many types of essays. An *informal essay* uses casual, conversational language. A *historical essay* gives facts, explanations, and insights about historical events. An *expository essay* explains an idea by breaking it down. A *narrative essay* tells a story about a real-life experience. An *informational essay* explains a process. A *persuasive essay* offers an opinion and supports it.

See *Exposition, Narration,* and *Persuasion.*

EXPOSITION In the plot of a story or a drama, the *exposition,* or introduction, is the part of the work that introduces the characters, setting, and basic situation.

See *Plot.*

EXPOSITORY WRITING *Expository writing* is writing that explains or informs.

EXTENDED METAPHOR In an *extended metaphor,* as in a regular metaphor, a subject is spoken or written of as though it were something else. However, extended metaphor differs from regular metaphor in that several connected comparisons are made.

See *Metaphor.*

EXTERNAL CONFLICT See *Conflict.*

FABLE A *fable* is a brief story or poem, usually with animal characters, that teaches a lesson, or moral. The moral is usually stated at the end of the fable.

See *Irony* and *Moral.*

FANTASY A *fantasy* is highly imaginative writing that contains elements not found in real life. Examples of fantasy include stories that involve supernatural elements, stories that resemble fairy tales, stories that deal with imaginary places and creatures, and science-fiction stories.

See *Science Fiction.*

FICTION *Fiction* is prose writing that tells about imaginary characters and events. Short stories and novels are works of fiction. Some writers base their fiction on actual events and people, adding invented characters, dialogue, settings, and plots. Other writers rely on imagination alone.

See *Narration, Nonfiction,* and *Prose.*

FIGURATIVE LANGUAGE *Figurative language* is writing or speech that is not meant to be taken literally. The many types of figurative language are known as *figures of speech.* Common figures of speech include metaphor, personification, and simile. Writers use figurative language to state ideas in vivid and imaginative ways.

See *Metaphor, Personification, Simile,* and *Symbol.*

FIGURE OF SPEECH See *Figurative Language.*

FLASHBACK A *flashback* is a scene within a story that interrupts the sequence of events to relate events that occurred in the past.

FLAT CHARACTER See *Character.*

FOLK TALE A *folk tale* is a story composed orally and then passed from person to person by word of mouth. Folk tales originated among people who could neither read nor write. These people entertained one another by telling stories aloud—often dealing with heroes, adventure, magic, or romance. Eventually, modern scholars collected these stories and wrote them down.

Folk tales reflect the cultural beliefs and environments from which they come.

See *Fable, Legend, Myth,* and *Oral Tradition.*

FOOT See *Meter.*

FORESHADOWING *Foreshadowing* is the author's use of clues to hint at what might happen later in the story. Writers use foreshadowing to build their readers' expectations and to create suspense.

FREE VERSE *Free verse* is poetry not written in a regular, rhythmical pattern, or meter. The poet is free to write lines of any length or with any number of stresses, or beats. Free verse is therefore less constraining than *metrical verse,* in which every line must have a certain length and a certain number of stresses.

See *Meter.*

GENRE A *genre* is a division or type of literature. Literature is commonly divided into three major genres: poetry, prose, and drama. Each major genre is, in turn, divided into lesser genres, as follows:

1. *Poetry:* lyric poetry, concrete poetry, dramatic poetry, narrative poetry, epic poetry

2. *Prose:* fiction (novels and short stories) and nonfiction (biography, autobiography, letters, essays, and reports)

3. *Drama:* serious drama and tragedy, comic drama, melodrama, and farce

See *Drama, Poetry,* and *Prose.*

HAIKU The *haiku* is a three-line Japanese verse form. The first and third lines of a haiku each have five syllables. The second line has seven syllables. A writer of haiku uses images to create a single, vivid picture, generally of a scene from nature.

HERO/HEROINE A *hero* or *heroine* is a character whose actions are inspiring, or noble. Often heroes and heroines struggle to overcome the obstacles and problems that stand in their way. Note that the term *hero* was originally used only for male characters, while heroic female characters were always called *heroines.* However, it is now acceptable to use *hero* to refer to females as well as to males.

HISTORICAL FICTION In *historical fiction,* real events, places, or people are incorporated into a fictional or made-up story.

IMAGERY See *Images.*

IMAGES *Images* are words or phrases that appeal to one or more of the five senses. Writers use images to describe how their subjects look, sound, feel, taste, and smell. Poets often paint images, or word pictures, that appeal to your senses. These pictures help you experience the poem fully.

INTERNAL CONFLICT See *Conflict.*

IRONY *Irony* is a contradiction between what happens and what is expected. The three main types of irony are *situational irony, verbal irony,* and *dramatic irony.*

JOURNAL A *journal* is a daily, or periodic, account of events and the writer's thoughts and feelings about those events. Personal journals are not normally written for publication, but sometimes they do get published later with permission from the author or the author's family.

LEGEND A *legend* is a widely told story about the past—one that may or may not have a foundation in fact. Every culture has its own legends—its familiar, traditional stories.

See *Folk Tale, Myth,* and *Oral Tradition.*

LETTERS A *letter* is a written communication from one person to another. In personal letters, the writer shares information and his or her thoughts and feelings with one other person or group. Although letters are not normally written for publication, they sometimes do get published later with the permission of the author or the author's family.

LIMERICK A *limerick* is a humorous, rhyming, five-line poem with a specific meter and rhyme scheme. Most limericks have three strong stresses in lines 1, 2, and 5 and two strong stresses in lines 3 and 4. Most follow the rhyme scheme *aabba.*

LYRIC POEM A *lyric poem* is a highly musical verse that expresses the observations and feelings of a single speaker. It creates a single, unified impression.

MAIN CHARACTER See *Character.*

MEDIA ACCOUNTS *Media accounts* are reports, explanations, opinions, or descriptions written for television, radio, newspapers, and magazines. While some media accounts report only facts, others include the writer's thoughts and reflections.

METAPHOR A *metaphor* is a figure of speech in which something is described as though it were something else. A metaphor, like a simile, works by pointing out a similarity between two unlike things.

See *Extended Metaphor* and *Simile.*

METER The *meter* of a poem is its rhythmical pattern. This pattern is determined by the number of *stresses,* or beats, in each line. To describe the meter of a poem, read it while emphasizing the beats in each line. Then, mark the stressed and unstressed syllables, as follows:

M̆y fáth | ĕr wás | t̆he fírst | t̆o héar |

As you can see, each strong stress is marked with a slanted line (´) and each unstressed syllable with a horseshoe symbol (˘). The weak and strong stresses are then divided by vertical lines (|) into groups called *feet.*

MINOR CHARACTER See *Character.*

MOOD See *Atmosphere.*

MORAL A *moral* is a lesson taught by a literary work. A fable usually ends with a moral that is directly stated. A poem, novel, short story, or essay often suggests a moral that is not directly stated. The moral must be drawn by the reader, based on other elements in the work.

See *Fable.*

MOTIVATION See *Motive.*

MOTIVE A *motive* is a reason that explains or partially explains a character's thoughts, feelings, actions, or speech. Writers try to make their characters' motives, or motivations, as clear as possible. If the motives of a main character are not clear, then the character will not be believable.

Characters are often motivated by needs, such as food and shelter. They are also motivated by feelings, such as fear, love, and pride. Motives may be obvious or hidden.

MYTH A *myth* is a fictional tale that explains the actions of gods or heroes or the origins of elements of nature. Myths are part of the oral tradition. They are composed orally and then passed from generation to generation by word of mouth. Every ancient culture has its own mythology, or collection of myths. Greek and Roman myths are known collectively as *classical mythology.*

See *Oral Tradition.*

NARRATION *Narration* is writing that tells a story. The act of telling a story is also called narration. Each piece is a *narrative.* A story told in fiction, nonfiction, poetry, or even in drama is called a narrative.

See *Narrative, Narrative Poem,* and *Narrator.*

NARRATIVE A *narrative* is a story. A narrative can be either fiction or nonfiction. Novels and short stories are types of fictional narratives. Biographies and autobiographies are nonfiction narratives. Poems that tell stories are also narratives.

See *Narration* and *Narrative Poem.*

NARRATIVE POEM A *narrative poem* is a story told in verse. Narrative poems often have all the elements of short stories, including characters, conflict, and plot.

NARRATOR A *narrator* is a speaker or a character who tells a story. The narrator's perspective is the way he or she sees things. A *third-person narrator* is one who stands outside the action and speaks about it. A *first-person narrator* is one who tells a story and participates in its action.

See *Point of View.*

NONFICTION *Nonfiction* is prose writing that presents and explains ideas or that tells about real people, places, objects, or events. Autobiographies, biographies, essays, reports, letters, memos, and newspaper articles are all types of nonfiction.

See *Fiction.*

NOVEL A *novel* is a long work of fiction. Novels contain such elements as characters, plot, conflict, and setting. The writer of novels, or novelist, develops these elements. In addition to its main plot, a novel may contain one or more subplots, or independent, related stories. A novel may also have several themes.

See *Fiction* and *Short Story.*

NOVELLA A fiction work that is longer than a short story but shorter than a novel.

ONOMATOPOEIA *Onomatopoeia* is the use of words that imitate sounds. *Crash, buzz, screech, hiss, neigh, jingle,* and *cluck* are examples of onomatopoeia. *Chickadee, towhee,* and *whippoorwill* are onomatopoeic names of birds.

Onomatopoeia can help put the reader in the activity of a poem.

ORAL TRADITION *Oral tradition* is the passing of songs, stories, and poems from generation to generation by word of mouth. Folk songs, folk tales, legends, and myths all come from the oral tradition. No one knows who first created these stories and poems.

See *Folk Tale, Legend,* and *Myth.*

OXYMORON An *oxymoron* (pl. *oxymora*) is a figure of speech that links two opposite or contradictory words, to point out an idea or situation that seems contradictory or inconsistent but on closer inspection turns out to be somehow true.

PERSONIFICATION *Personification* is a type of figurative language in which a nonhuman subject is given human characteristics.

PERSPECTIVE See *Narrator* and *Point of View.*

PERSUASION *Persuasion* is used in writing or speech that attempts to convince the reader or listener to adopt a particular opinion or course of action. Newspaper editorials and letters to the editor use persuasion. So do advertisements and campaign speeches given by political candidates. An *argument* is a logical way of presenting a belief, conclusion, or stance. A good argument is supported with reasoning and evidence.

See *Essay.*

PLAYWRIGHT A *playwright* is a person who writes plays. William Shakespeare is regarded as the greatest playwright in English literature.

PLOT *Plot* is the sequence of events in which each event results from a previous one and causes the next. In most novels, dramas, short stories, and narrative poems, the plot involves both characters and a central conflict. The plot usually begins with an exposition that introduces the setting, the characters, and the basic situation. This is followed by the *inciting incident,* which introduces the central conflict. The conflict then increases during the *development* until it reaches a high point of interest or suspense, the *climax.* The climax is followed by the *falling action,* or end, of the central conflict. Any events that occur during the *falling action* make up the *resolution,* or *denouement.*

Some plots do not have all of these parts. Some stories begin with the inciting incident and end with the resolution.

See *Conflict.*

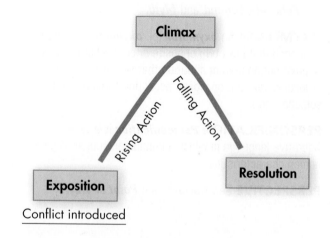

Conflict introduced

POETRY *Poetry* is one of the three major types of literature, the others being prose and drama. Most poems make use of highly concise, musical, and emotionally charged language. Many also make use of imagery, figurative lan-

guage, and special devices of sound such as rhyme. Major types of poetry include lyric poetry, narrative poetry, and concrete poetry.

See *Concrete Poem, Genre, Lyric Poem,* and *Narrative Poem.*

POINT OF VIEW *Point of view* is the perspective, or vantage point, from which a story is told. The storyteller is either a narrator outside the story or a character in the story. *First-person point of view* describes a story told by a character who uses the first-person pronoun "I."

The two kinds of *third-person point of view,* limited and omniscient, are called "third person" because the narrator uses third-person pronouns such as "he" and "she" to refer to the characters. There is no "I" telling the story.

In stories told from the *omniscient third-person point of view,* the narrator knows and tells about what each character feels and thinks.

In stories told from the *limited third-person point of view,* the narrator relates the inner thoughts and feelings of only one character, and everything is viewed from this character's perspective.

See *Narrator.*

PROBLEM See *Conflict.*

PROSE *Prose* is the ordinary form of written language. Most writing that is not poetry, drama, or song is considered prose. Prose is one of the major genres of literature and occurs in two forms—fiction and nonfiction.

See *Fiction, Genre,* and *Nonfiction.*

PROTAGONIST The *protagonist* is the main character in a literary work. Often, the protagonist is a person, but sometimes it can be an animal.

See *Antagonist* and *Character.*

REFRAIN A *refrain* is a regularly repeated line or group of lines in a poem or a song.

REPETITION *Repetition* is the use, more than once, of any element of language—a sound, word, phrase, clause, or sentence. Repetition is used in both prose and poetry.

See *Alliteration, Meter, Plot, Rhyme,* and *Rhyme Scheme.*

RESOLUTION The *resolution* is the outcome of the conflict in a plot.

See *Plot.*

RHYME *Rhyme* is the repetition of sounds at the ends of words. Poets use rhyme to lend a songlike quality to their verses and to emphasize certain words and ideas. Many traditional poems contain **end rhymes,** or rhyming words at the ends of lines.

Another common device is the use of **internal rhymes,** or rhyming words within lines. Internal rhyme also emphasizes the flowing nature of a poem.

See *Rhyme Scheme.*

RHYME SCHEME A *rhyme scheme* is a regular pattern of rhyming words in a poem. To indicate the rhyme scheme of a poem, one uses lowercase letters. Each rhyme is assigned a different letter, as follows in the first stanza of "Dust of Snow" by Robert Frost:

The way a crow	*a*
Shook down on me	*b*
The dust of snow	*a*
From a hemlock tree	*b*

Thus, the stanza has the rhyme scheme **abab.**

RHYTHM *Rhythm* is the pattern of stressed and unstressed syllables in spoken or written language.

See *Meter.*

ROUND CHARACTER See *Character.*

SCENE A *scene* is a section of uninterrupted action in the act of a drama.

See *Drama.*

SCIENCE FICTION *Science fiction* combines elements of fiction and fantasy with scientific fact. Many science-fiction stories are set in the future.

SENSORY LANGUAGE *Sensory language* is writing or speech that appeals to one or more of the five senses.

See *Images.*

SETTING The *setting* of a literary work is the time and place of the action. The setting includes all the details of a place and time—the year, the time of day, even the weather. The place may be a specific country, state, region, community, neighborhood, building, institution, or home. Details such as dialects, clothing, customs, and modes of transportation are often used to establish setting. In most stories, the setting serves as a backdrop—a context in which the characters interact. Setting can also help create a feeling, or atmosphere.

See *Atmosphere.*

SHORT STORY A *short story* is a brief work of fiction. Like a novel, a short story presents a sequence of events, or plot. The plot usually deals with a central conflict faced by a main character, or protagonist. The events in a short story usually communicate a message about life or human nature. This message, or central idea, is the story's theme.

See *Conflict, Plot,* and *Theme.*

SIMILE A *simile* is a figure of speech that uses **like** or **as** to make a direct comparison between two unlike ideas. Everyday speech often contains similes, such as "pale as a ghost," "good as gold," "spread like wildfire," and "clever as a fox."

SPEAKER The *speaker* is the imaginary voice a poet uses when writing a poem. The speaker is the character who tells the poem. This character, or voice, often is not identified by name. There can be important differences between the poet and the poem's speaker.

See *Narrator.*

STAGE DIRECTIONS *Stage directions* are notes included in a drama to describe how the work is to be performed or staged. Stage directions are usually printed in italics and enclosed within parentheses or brackets. Some stage directions describe the movements, costumes, emotional states, and ways of speaking of the characters.

STAGING *Staging* includes the setting, lighting, costumes, special effects, music, dance, and so on that go into putting on a stage performance of a drama.

See *Drama.*

STANZA A *stanza* is a group of lines of poetry that are usually similar in length and pattern and are separated by spaces. A stanza is like a paragraph of poetry—it states and develops a single main idea.

STATIC CHARACTER See *Character.*

SURPRISE ENDING A *surprise ending* is a conclusion that is unexpected. The reader has certain expectations about the ending based on details in the story. Often, a surprise ending is **foreshadowed,** or subtly hinted at, in the course of the work.

See *Foreshadowing* and *Plot.*

SUSPENSE *Suspense* is a feeling of anxious uncertainty about the outcome of events in a literary work. Writers create suspense by raising questions in the minds of their readers.

SYMBOL A *symbol* is anything that stands for or represents something else. Symbols are common in everyday life. A dove with an olive branch in its beak is a symbol of peace. A blindfolded woman holding a balanced scale is a symbol of justice. A crown is a symbol of a king's status and authority.

SYMBOLISM *Symbolism* is the use of symbols. Symbolism plays an important role in many different types of literature. It can highlight certain elements the author wishes to emphasize and also add levels of meaning.

THEME The *theme* is a central message, concern, or purpose in a literary work. A theme can usually be expressed as a generalization, or a general statement, about human beings or about life. The theme of a work is not a summary of its plot. The theme is the writer's central idea.

Although a theme may be stated directly in the text, it is more often presented indirectly. When the theme is stated indirectly, or implied, the reader must figure out what the theme is by looking carefully at what the work reveals about people or about life.

TONE The *tone* of a literary work is the writer's attitude toward his or her audience and subject. The tone can often be described by a single adjective, such as *formal* or *informal, serious* or *playful, bitter,* or *ironic.* Factors that contribute to the tone are word choice, sentence structure, line length, rhyme, rhythm, and repetition.

TRAGEDY A *tragedy* is a work of literature, especially a play, that results in a catastrophe for the main character. In ancient Greek drama, the main character is always a significant person—a king or a hero—and the cause of the tragedy is a tragic flaw, or weakness, in his or her character. In modern drama, the main character can be an ordinary person, and the cause of the tragedy can be some evil in society itself. The purpose of tragedy is not only to arouse fear and pity in the audience but also, in some cases, to convey a sense of the grandeur and nobility of the human spirit.

TURNING POINT See *Climax.*

UNIVERSAL THEME A *universal theme* is a message about life that is expressed regularly in many different cultures and time periods. Folk tales, epics, and romances often address universal themes like the importance of courage, the power of love, or the danger of greed.

Tips for Literature Circles

As you read and study literature, discussions with other readers can help you understand and enjoy what you have read. Use the following tips.

• Understand the purpose of your discussion

Your purpose when you discuss literature is to broaden your understanding of a work by testing your own ideas and hearing the ideas of others. Keep your comments focused on the literature you are discussing. Starting with one focus question will help to keep your discussion on track.

• Communicate effectively

Effective communication requires thinking before speaking. Plan the points that you want to make and decide how you will express them. Organize these points in logical order and use details from the work to support your ideas. Jot down informal notes to help keep your ideas focused.

Remember to speak clearly, pronouncing words slowly and carefully. Also, listen attentively when others are speaking, and avoid interrupting.

• Consider other ideas and interpretations

A work of literature can generate a wide variety of responses in different readers. Be open to the idea that many interpretations can be valid. To support your own ideas, point to the events, descriptions, characters, or other literary elements in the work that led to your interpretation. To consider someone else's ideas, decide whether details in the work support the interpretation he or she presents. Be sure to convey your criticism of the ideas of others in a respectful and supportive manner.

• Ask questions

Ask questions to clarify your understanding of another reader's ideas. You can also use questions to call attention to possible areas of confusion, to points that are open to debate, or to errors in the speaker's points. To move a discussion forward, summarize and evaluate conclusions reached by the group members.

When you meet with a group to discuss literature, use a chart like the one shown to analyze the discussion.

Work Being Discussed:	
Focus Question:	
Your Response:	Another Student's Response:
Supporting Evidence:	Supporting Evidence:

Tips for Improving Reading Fluency

When you were younger, you learned to read. Then, you read to expand your experiences or for pure enjoyment. Now, you are expected to read to learn. As you progress in school, you are given more and more material to read. The tips on these pages will help you improve your reading fluency, or your ability to read easily, smoothly, and expressively.

Keeping Your Concentration

One common problem that readers face is the loss of concentration. When you are reading an assignment, you might find yourself rereading the same sentence several times without really understanding it. The first step in changing this behavior is to notice that you do it. Becoming an active, aware reader will help you get the most from your assignments. Practice using these strategies:

- Cover what you have already read with a note card as you go along. Then, you will not be able to reread without noticing that you are doing it.

- Set a purpose for reading beyond just completing the assignment. Then, read actively by pausing to ask yourself questions about the material as you read.

- Use the Reading Strategy instruction and notes that appear with each selection in this textbook.

- Stop reading after a specified period of time (for example, 5 minutes) and summarize what you have read. To help you with this strategy, use the Reading Check questions that appear with each selection in this textbook. Reread to find any answers you do not know.

Reading Phrases

Fluent readers read phrases rather than individual words. Reading this way will speed up your reading and improve your comprehension. Here are some useful ideas:

- Experts recommend rereading as a strategy to increase fluency. Choose a passage of text that is neither too hard nor too easy. Read the same passage aloud several times until you can read it smoothly. When you can read the passage fluently, pick another passage and keep practicing.

- Read aloud into a tape recorder. Then, listen to the recording, noting your accuracy, pacing, and expression. You can also read aloud and share feedback with a partner.

- Use *Hear It!* Prentice Hall Literature Audio program CDs to hear the selections read aloud. Read along silently in your textbook, noticing how the reader uses his or her voice and emphasizes certain words and phrases.

Understanding Key Vocabulary

If you do not understand some of the words in an assignment, you may miss out on important concepts. Therefore, it is helpful to keep a dictionary nearby when you are reading. Follow these steps:

- Before you begin reading, scan the text for unfamiliar words or terms. Find out what those words mean before you begin reading.

- Use context—the surrounding words, phrases, and sentences—to help you determine the meanings of unfamiliar words.

- If you are unable to understand the meaning through context, refer to the dictionary.

Paying Attention to Punctuation

When you read, pay attention to punctuation. Commas, periods, exclamation points, semicolons, and colons tell you when to pause or stop. They also indicate relationships between groups of words. When you recognize these relationships you will read with greater understanding and expression. Look at the chart below

Punctuation Mark	Meaning
comma	brief pause
period	pause at the end of a thought
exclamation point	pause that indicates emphasis
semicolon	pause between related but distinct thoughts
colon	pause before giving explanation or examples

Using the Reading Fluency Checklist

Use the checklist below each time you read a selection in this textbook. In your Language Arts journal or notebook, note which skills you need to work on and chart your progress each week.

Reading Fluency Checklist
❏ Preview the text to check for difficult or unfamiliar words.
❏ Practice reading aloud.
❏ Read according to punctuation.
❏ Break down long sentences into the subject and its meaning.
❏ Read groups of words for meaning rather than reading single words.
❏ Read with expression (change your tone of voice to add meaning to the word).

Reading is a skill that can be improved with practice. The key to improving your fluency is to read. The more you read, the better your reading will become.

Types of Writing

Good writing can be a powerful tool used for many purposes. Writing can allow you to defend something you believe in or show how much you know about a subject. Writing can also help you share what you have experienced, imagined, thought, and felt. The three main types of writing are argument, informative/explanatory, and narrative.

Argument

When you think of the word *argument*, you might think of a disagreement between two people, but an argument is more than that. An argument is a logical way of presenting a belief, conclusion, or stance. A good argument is supported with reasoning and evidence.

Argument writing can be used for many purposes, such as to change a reader's point of view or opinion or to bring about an action or a response from a reader.

There are three main purposes for writing a formal argument:

- to change the reader's mind
- to convince the reader to accept what is written
- to motivate the reader to take action, based on what is written

The following are some types of argument writing:

Advertisements An advertisement is a planned message meant to be seen, heard, or read. It attempts to persuade an audience to buy a product or service, accept an idea, or support a cause. Advertisements may appear in print, online, or in broadcast form.

Several common types of advertisements are public service announcements, billboards, merchandise ads, service ads, and political campaign literature.

Persuasive Essay A persuasive essay presents a position on an issue, urges readers to accept that position, and may encourage a specific action. An effective persuasive essay

- Explores an issue of importance to the writer
- Addresses an issue that is arguable
- Uses facts, examples, statistics, or personal experiences to support a position
- Tries to influence the audience through appeals to the readers' knowledge, experiences, or emotions
- Uses clear organization to present a logical argument

Forms of persuasion include editorials, position papers, persuasive speeches, grant proposals, advertisements, and debates.

Informative/Explanatory

Informative/explanatory writing should rely on facts to inform or explain. Informative/explanatory writing serves some closely related purposes: to increase readers' knowledge of a subject, to help readers better understand a procedure or process, or to provide readers with an enhanced comprehension of a concept. It should also feature a clear introduction, body, and conclusion. The following are some examples of informative/explanatory writing:

Cause-and-Effect Essay A cause-and-effect essay examines the relationship between events, explaining how one event or situation causes another. A successful cause-and-effect essay includes

- A discussion of a cause, event, or condition that produces a specific result
- An explanation of an effect, outcome, or result
- Evidence and examples to support the relationship between cause and effect
- A logical organization that makes the explanation clear

Comparison-and-Contrast Essay A comparison-and-contrast essay analyzes the similarities and differences between or among two or more things. An effective comparison-and-contrast essay

- Identifies a purpose for comparison and contrast
- Identifies similarities and differences between or among two or more things, people, places, or ideas
- Gives factual details about the subjects
- Uses an organizational plan suited to the topic and purpose

Descriptive Writing Descriptive writing creates a vivid picture of a person, place, thing, or event. Most descriptive writing includes

- Sensory details—sights, sounds, smells, tastes, and physical sensations
- Vivid, precise language
- Figurative language or comparisons

- Adjectives and adverbs that paint a word picture

- An organization suited to the subject

Types of descriptive writing include descriptions of ideas, observations, travel brochures, physical descriptions, functional descriptions, remembrances, and character sketches.

Problem-and-Solution Essay A problem-and-solution essay describes a problem and offers one or more solutions to it. It describes a clear set of steps to achieve a result. An effective problem-and-solution essay includes

- A clear statement of the problem, with its causes and effects summarized for the reader

- The most important aspects of the problem

- A proposal of at least one realistic solution

- Facts, statistics, data, or expert testimony to support the solution

- A clear organization that makes the relationship between problem and solution obvious

Research Writing Research writing is based on information gathered from outside sources. A research paper—a focused study of a topic—helps writers explore and connect ideas, make discoveries, and share their findings with an audience. An effective research paper

- Focuses on a specific, narrow topic, which is usually summarized in a thesis statement

- Presents relevant information from a wide variety of sources

- Uses a clear organization that includes an introduction, body, and conclusion

- Includes a bibliography or works-cited list that identifies the sources from which the information was drawn

Other types of writing that depend on accurate and insightful research include multimedia presentations, statistical reports, annotated bibliographies, and experiment journals.

Workplace Writing Workplace writing is probably the format you will use most after you finish school. In general, workplace writing is fact-based and meant to communicate specific information in a structured format. Effective workplace writing

- Communicates information concisely

- Includes details that provide necessary information and anticipate potential questions

- Is error-free and neatly presented

Common types of workplace writing include business letters, memorandums, résumés, forms, and applications.

Narrative

Narrative writing conveys experience, either real or imaginary, and uses time to provide structure. It can be used to inform, instruct, persuade, or entertain. Whenever writers tell a of story, they are using narrative writing. Most types of narrative writing share certain elements, such as characters, a setting, a sequence of events, and, often, a theme. The following are some types of narration:

Autobiographical Writing Autobiographical writing tells a true story about an important period, experience, or relationship in the writer's life. Effective autobiographical writing includes

- A series of events that involve the writer as the main character

- Details, thoughts, feelings, and insights from the writer's perspective

- A conflict or an event that affects the writer

- A logical organization that tells the story clearly

- Insights that the writer gained from the experience

Types of autobiographical writing include autobiographical sketches, personal narratives, reflective essays, eyewitness accounts, and memoirs.

Short Story A short story is a brief, creative narrative. Most short stories include

- Details that establish the setting in time and place

- A main character who undergoes a change or learns something during the course of the story

- A conflict or a problem to be introduced, developed, and resolved

- A plot, the series of events that make up the action of the story

- A theme or message about life

Types of short stories include realistic stories, fantasies, historical narratives, mysteries, thrillers, science-fiction stories, and adventure stories.

Writing Friendly Letters

Writing Friendly Letters

A friendly letter is much less formal than a business letter. It is a letter to a friend, a family member, or anyone with whom the writer wants to communicate in a personal, friendly way. Most friendly letters are made up of five parts:

- ✔ the heading
- ✔ the salutation, or greeting
- ✔ the body
- ✔ the closing
- ✔ the signature

The purpose of a friendly letter is often one of the following:

- ✔ to share personal news and feelings
- ✔ to send or to answer an invitation
- ✔ to express thanks

Model Friendly Letter

In this friendly letter, Betsy thanks her grandparents for a birthday present and gives them some news about her life.

11 Old Farm Road
Topsham, Maine 04011

April 14, 20—

Dear Grandma and Grandpa,

Thank you for the sweater you sent me for my birthday. It fits perfectly, and I love the color. I wore my new sweater to the carnival at school last weekend and got lots of compliments.

The weather here has been cool but sunny. Mom thinks that "real" spring will never come. I can't wait until it's warm enough to go swimming.

School is going fairly well. I really like my Social Studies class. We are learning about the U.S. Constitution, and I think it's very interesting. Maybe I will be a lawyer when I grow up.

When are you coming out to visit us? We haven't seen you since Thanksgiving. You can stay in my room when you come. I'll be happy to sleep on the couch. (The TV is in that room!!)

Well, thanks again and hope all is well with you.

Love,

Betsy

The **heading** includes the writer's address and the date on which he or she wrote the letter.

The **body** is the main part of the letter and contains the basic message.

Some common **closings** for personal letters include "Best wishes," "Love," "Sincerely," and "Yours truly."

Writing Business Letters

Formatting Business Letters

Business letters follow one of several acceptable formats. In **block format,** each part of the letter begins at the left margin. A double space is used between paragraphs. In **modified block format,** some parts of the letter are indented to the center of the page. No matter which format is used, all letters in business format have a heading, an inside address, a salutation or greeting, a body, a closing, and a signature. These parts are shown and annotated on the model business letter below, formatted in modified block style.

Model Business Letter

In this letter, Yolanda Dodson uses modified block format to request information.

Students for a Cleaner Planet
c/o Memorial High School
333 Veteran's Drive
Denver, CO 80211

January 25, 20—

Steven Wilson, Director
Resource Recovery Really Works
300 Oak Street
Denver, CO 80216

Dear Mr. Wilson:

Memorial High School would like to start a branch of your successful recycling program. We share your commitment to reclaiming as much reusable material as we can. Because your program has been successful in other neighborhoods, we're sure that it can work in our community. Our school includes grades 9–12 and has about 800 students.

Would you send us some information about your community recycling program? For example, we need to know what materials can be recycled and how we can implement the program.

At least fifty students have already expressed an interest in getting involved, so I know we'll have the people power to make the program work. Please help us get started.

Thank you in advance for your time and consideration.

Sincerely,

Yolanda Dodson

Yolanda Dodson

The **heading** shows the writer's address and organization (if any) and the date.

The **inside address** indicates where the letter will be sent.

A **salutation** is punctuated by a colon. When the specific addressee is not known, use a general greeting such as "To whom it may concern:"

The **body** of the letter states the writer's purpose. In this case, the writer requests information.

The **closing** "Sincerely" is common, but "Yours truly" or "Respectfully yours" are also acceptable. To end the letter, the writer types her name and provides a **signature.**

Parts of Speech

Nouns A **noun** is the name of a person, place, or thing. A **common noun** names any one of a class of people, places, or things. A **proper noun** names a specific person, place, or thing.

Pronouns A **pronoun** is a word that stands for a noun or for a word that takes the place of a noun. A **personal pronoun** refers to (1) the person speaking, (2) the person spoken to, or (3) the person, place, or thing spoken about.

	Singular	Plural
First Person	I, me, my, mine	we, us, our, ours
Second Person	you, your, yours	you, your, yours
Third Person	he, him, his, she, her, hers, it, its	they, them, their, theirs

A **reflexive pronoun** is a word that ends in -*self* or -*selves* and names the person or thing receiving the action when that person or thing is the same as the one performing the action.

A **demonstrative pronoun** directs attention to a specific person, place, or thing.

These are the juiciest pears I have ever tasted.

An **interrogative pronoun** is used to begin a question.

Who is the author of "Jeremiah's Song"?

An **indefinite pronoun** refers to a person, place, or thing, often without specifying which one.

Everyone bought something.

Verbs A **verb** is a word that expresses time while showing an action, a condition, or the fact that something exists. An **action verb** indicates the action of someone or something. A **linking verb** connects the subject of a sentence with a noun or a pronoun that renames or describes the subject. A **helping verb** can be added to another verb to make a single verb phrase.

Adjectives An **adjective** describes a noun or a pronoun or gives a noun or a pronoun a more specific meaning. Adjectives answer the questions *what kind, which one, how many,* or *how much.*

The articles *the, a,* and *an* are adjectives. *An* is used before a word beginning with a vowel sound.

A noun may sometimes be used as an adjective.

family home   *science* fiction

A **proper adjective** is (1) a proper noun used as an adjective or (2) an adjective formed from a proper noun. When *this, that, these,* or *those* appears immediately before a noun, that word is functioning as a **demonstrative adjective.**

Adverbs An **adverb** modifies a verb, an adjective, or another adverb. Adverbs answer the questions *where, when, in what way,* or *to what extent.*

Prepositions A **preposition** relates a noun or a pronoun following it to another word in the sentence.

Conjunctions A **conjunction** connects other words or groups of words. A **coordinating conjunction** connects similar kinds or groups of words. **Correlative conjunctions** are used in pairs to connect similar words or groups of words.

both Granpa *and* Grandma   *neither* they *nor* I

A **subordinating conjunction** is a word used to join two complete ideas by making one of the ideas dependent on the other.

Interjections An interjection is a word that expresses feeling or emotion and functions independently of a sentence.

Phrases, Clauses, and Sentences

Sentences A **sentence** is a group of words with two main parts: a complete subject and a complete predicate. Together, these parts express a complete thought.

A **fragment** is a group of words that does not express a complete thought.

Subject The **subject** of a sentence is the word or group of words that tells whom or what the sentence is about. The **simple subject** is the essential noun, pronoun, or group of words acting as a noun that cannot be left out of the complete subject. A **complete subject** is the simple subject plus any modifiers.

A **compound subject** is two or more subjects that have the same verb and are joined by a conjunction.

Neither the horse nor the driver looked tired.

Predicate The **predicate** of a sentence is the verb or verb phrase that tells what the complete subject of the sentence does or is. The **simple predicate** is the essential verb or verb phrase that cannot be left out of the complete predicate. A **complete predicate** is the simple predicate plus any modifiers or complements.

Pony express riders carried packages more than 2,000 miles.

A **compound predicate** is two or more verbs that have the same subject and are joined by a conjunction.

She *sneezed and coughed* throughout the trip.

Complement A **complement** is a word or group of words that completes the meaning of the predicate of a sentence. Five different kinds of complements can be found in English sentences: *direct objects, indirect objects, objective complements, predicate nominatives,* and *predicate adjectives.*

A **direct object** is a noun, pronoun, or group of words acting as a noun that receives the action of a transitive verb.

    We watched the *liftoff.*

An **indirect object** is a noun, pronoun, or group of words that appears with a direct object and names the person or thing that something is given to or done for.

    He sold the *family* a mirror.

An **objective complement** is an adjective or noun that appears with a direct object and describes or renames it.

    I called Meg my *friend.*

A **subject complement** is a noun, pronoun, or adjective that appears with a linking verb and tells something about the subject. A subject complement may be a *predicate nominative* or a *predicate adjective.*

A **predicate nominative** is a noun or pronoun that appears with a linking verb and renames, identifies, or explains the subject.

    Kiglo was the *leader.*

A **predicate adjective** is an adjective that appears with a linking verb and describes the subject of a sentence.

    Roko became *tired.*

Sentence Types A **simple sentence** consists of a single independent clause. A **compound sentence** consists of two or more independent clauses joined by a comma and a coordinating conjunction or by a semicolon. A **complex sentence** consists of one independent clause and one or more subordinate clauses. A **compound-complex sentence** consists of two or more independent clauses and one or more subordinate clauses. A **declarative sentence** states an idea and ends with a period. **Interrogative Sentence** An interrogative sentence asks a question and ends with a question mark. An **imperative sentence** gives an order or a direction and ends with either a period or an exclamation mark. An **exclamatory sentence** conveys a strong emotion and ends with an exclamation mark.

Phrases A **phrase** is a group of words, without a subject and a verb, that functions in a sentence as one part of speech. A **prepositional phrase** is a group of words that includes a preposition and a noun or a pronoun that is the object of the preposition. An **adjective phrase** is a prepositional phrase that modifies a noun or a pronoun by telling what kind or which one. An **adverb phrase** is a prepositional phrase that modifies a verb, an adjective, or an adverb by pointing out *where, when, in what manner,* or *to what extent.* An **appositive phrase** is a noun or a pronoun with modifiers, placed next to a noun or a pronoun to add information and details. A **participial phrase** is a participle modified by an adjective or an adverb phrase or accompanied by a complement. The entire phrase acts as an adjective.

    Running at top speed, he soon caught up with them.

An **infinitive phrase** is an infinitive with modifiers, complements, or a subject, all acting together as a single part of speech.

    At first I was too busy enjoying my food *to notice how the guests were doing.*

Gerunds A **gerund** is a noun formed from the present participle of a verb ending in *–ing.* Like other nouns, gerunds can be used as subjects, direct objects, predicate nouns, and objects of prepositions.

Gerund Phrases A **gerund phrase** is a gerund with modifiers or a complement, all acting together as a noun.

Clauses A **clause** is a group of words with its own subject and verb. An **independent clause** can stand by itself as a complete sentence.

A **subordinate clause** has a subject and a verb but cannot stand by itself as a complete sentence; it can only be part of a sentence.

    "Although it was late"

Using Verbs, Pronouns, and Modifiers

Principal Parts A **verb** has **four principal parts:** the *present,* the *present participle,* the *past,* and the *past participle.* Regular verbs form the past and past participle by adding -ed to the present form.

Irregular verbs form the past and past participle by changing form rather than by adding *-ed.*

Verb Tense A **verb tense** tells whether the time of an action or condition is in the past, the present, or the future. Every verb has six tenses: *present, past, future, present perfect, past perfect,* and *future perfect.* The **present tense** shows actions that happen in the present. The **past tense** shows actions that have already happened. The **future tense** shows actions that will happen. The **present perfect tense** shows actions that begin in the past and continue to the present. The **past perfect tense** shows a past action or condition that ended before another past action. The **future perfect tense** shows a future action or condition that will have ended before another begins.

Pronoun Case The **case** of a pronoun is the form it takes to show its use in a sentence. There are three pronoun cases: *nominative, objective,* and *possessive.* The **nominative case** is used to name or rename the subject of the sentence. The nominative case pronouns are *I, you, he, she, it, we, you, they.* The **objective case** is used as the direct object, indirect object, or object of a preposition. The objective case pronouns are *me, you, him, her, it, us, you, them.* The **possessive case** is used to show ownership. The possessive pronouns are *my, your, his, her, its, our, their, mine, yours, his, hers, its, ours, theirs.*

Subject-Verb Agreement To make a subject and a verb agree, make sure that both are singular or both are plural. Two or more singular subjects joined by *or* or *nor* must have a singular verb. When singular and plural subjects are joined by *or* or *nor*, the verb must agree with the closest subject.

Pronoun-Antecedent Agreement Pronouns must agree with their antecedents in number and gender. Use singular pronouns with singular antecedents and plural pronouns with plural antecedents. Many errors in pronoun-antecedent agreement occur when a plural pronoun is used to refer to a singular antecedent for which the gender is not specified.

Incorrect: Everyone did their best.

Correct: Everyone did his or her best.

The following indefinite pronouns are singular: *anybody, anyone, each, either, everybody, everyone, neither, nobody, no one, one, somebody, someone.*

The following indefinite pronouns are plural: *both, few, many, several.*

The following indefinite pronouns may be either singular or plural: *all, any, most, none, some.*

Modifiers The **comparative** and **superlative** degrees of most adjectives and adverbs of one or two syllables can be formed in either of two ways: Use *–er* or *more* to form a comparative degree and *–est* or *most* to form the superlative degree of most one- and two-syllable modifiers.

More and *most* can also be used to form the comparative and superlative degrees of most one- and two-syllable modifiers. These words should not be used when the result sounds awkward, as in "A greyhound *is more* fast than a beagle."

Glossary of Common Usage

accept, except: *Accept* is a verb that means "to receive" or "to agree to." *Except* is a preposition that means "other than" or "leaving out." Do not confuse these two words.

affect, effect: *Affect* is normally a verb meaning "to influence" or "to bring about a change in." *Effect* is usually a noun, meaning "result."

among, between: *Among* is usually used with three or more items. *Between* is generally used with only two items.

bad, badly: Use the predicate adjective *bad* after linking verbs such as *feel, look,* and *seem.* Use *badly* whenever an adverb is required.

beside, besides: *Beside* means "at the side of" or "close to." *Besides* means "in addition to."

can, may: The verb *can* generally refers to the ability to do something. The verb *may* generally refers to permission to do something.

different from, different than: *Different from* is generally preferred over *different than.*

farther, further: Use *farther* when you refer to distance. Use *further* when you mean "to a greater degree or extent" or "additional."

fewer, less: Use *fewer* for things that can be counted. Use *less* for amounts or quantities that cannot be counted.

good, well: Use the predicate adjective *good* after linking verbs such as *feel, look, smell, taste,* and *seem.* Use well whenever you need an adverb.

its, it's: The word *its* with no apostrophe is a possessive pronoun. The word *it's* is a contraction for *it is.* Do not confuse the possessive pronoun *its* with the contraction *it's,* standing for "it is" or "it has."

lay, lie: Do not confuse these verbs. *Lay* is a transitive verb meaning "to set or put something down." Its principal parts are *lay, laying, laid, laid. Lie* is an intransitive verb meaning "to recline." Its principal parts are *lie, lying, lay, lain.*

like, as: *Like* is a preposition that usually means "similar to" or "in the same way as." *Like* should always be followed by an object. Do not use *like* before a subject and a verb. Use *as* or *that* instead.

of, have: Do not use *of* in place of have after auxiliary verbs like *would, could, should, may, might,* or *must.*

raise, rise: *Raise* is a transitive verb that usually takes a direct object. *Rise* is intransitive and never takes a direct object.

set, sit: *Set* is a transitive verb meaning "to put (something) in a certain place." Its principal parts are s*et, setting, set, set. Sit* is an intransitive verb meaning "to be seated." Its principal parts are *sit, sitting, sat, sat.*

than, then: The conjunction *than* is used to connect the two parts of a comparison. Do not confuse *than* with the adverb *then,* which usually refers to time.

that, which, who: Use the relative pronoun *that* to refer to things or people. Use *which* only for things and *who* only for people.

when, where, why: Do not use *when, where,* or *why* directly after a linking verb such as *is.* Reword the sentence.

Faulty: Suspense is when an author increases the reader's tension.

Revised: An author uses suspense to increase the reader's tension.

who, whom: In formal writing, remember to use *who* only as a subject in clauses and sentences and *whom* only as an object.

Capitalization and Punctuation

Capitalization

1. Capitalize the first word of a sentence.
2. Capitalize all proper nouns and adjectives.
3. Capitalize a person's title when it is followed by the person's name or when it is used in direct address.
4. Capitalize titles showing family relationships when they refer to a specific person, unless they are preceded by a possessive noun or pronoun.
5. Capitalize the first word and all other key words in the titles of books, periodicals, poems, stories, plays, paintings, and other works of art.
6. Capitalize the first word and all nouns in letter salutations and the first word in letter closings.

Punctuation

End Marks

1. Use a **period** to end a declarative sentence, an imperative sentence, and most abbreviations.
2. Use a **question mark** to end a direct question or an incomplete question in which the rest of the question is understood.
3. Use an **exclamation mark** after a statement showing strong emotion, an urgent imperative sentence, or an interjection expressing strong emotion.

Commas

1. Use a comma before the conjunction to separate two independent clauses in a compound sentence.
2. Use commas to separate three or more words, phrases, or clauses in a series.
3. Use commas to separate adjectives of equal rank. Do not use commas to separate adjectives that must stay in a specific order.
4. Use a comma after an introductory word, phrase, or clause.
5. Use commas to set off parenthetical and nonessential expressions.
6. Use commas with places and dates made up of two or more parts.
7. Use commas after items in addresses, after the salutation in a personal letter, after the closing in all letters, and in numbers of more than three digits.

Semicolons

1. Use a semicolon to join independent clauses that are not already joined by a conjunction.
2. Use a semicolon to join independent clauses or items in a series that already contain commas.

Colons

1. Use a colon before a list of items following an independent clause.
2. Use a colon in numbers giving the time, in salutations in business letters, and in labels used to signal important ideas.

Quotation Marks

1. A **direct quotation** represents a person's exact speech or thoughts and is enclosed in quotation marks.
2. An **indirect quotation** reports only the general meaning of what a person said or thought and does not require quotation marks.
3. Always place a comma or a period inside the final quotation mark of a direct quotation.
4. Place a question mark or an exclamation mark inside the final quotation mark if the end mark is part of the quotation; if it is not part of the quotation, place it outside the final quotation mark.

Titles

1. Underline or italicize the titles of long written works, movies, television and radio shows, lengthy works of music, paintings, and sculptures.
2. Use quotation marks around the titles of short written works, episodes in a series, songs, and titles of works mentioned as parts of collections.

Hyphens

1. Use a **hyphen** with certain numbers, after certain prefixes, with two or more words used as one word, and with a compound modifier that comes before a noun.

Apostrophes

1. Add an **apostrophe** and s to show the possessive case of most singular nouns.
2. Add an apostrophe to show the possessive case of plural nouns ending in *s* and *es.*
3. Add an apostrophe and s to show the possessive case of plural nouns that do not end in *s* or *es.*
4. Use an apostrophe in a contraction to indicate the position of the missing letter or letters.

diversion (də vʉr´zhən) 1. *n.* recreation. 2. *n.* distraction from everyday tasks

doomed (do͞omd) *v.* condemned to destruction or death

drone (drōn) *n.* continuous humming sound

E

eloquent (el´ ə kwənt) *adj.* persuasive and expressive

embody (em bäd´ ē) *v.* 1. give bodily form to; 2. represent

encounter (en koun´tər) *v.* come upon or meet with, usually unexpectedly

endured (en do͝ord´) *v.* suffered through

enroll (en rōl´) *v.* place oneself on a register or list

entrepreneurs (än´ trə prə n ərz´) *n.* people who organize and manage a business

essential (ə sen´shəl) *adj.* necessary

establish (ə stab´lish) *v.* show to be true

evaluate (ē val´yo͞o āt´) *v.* find the importance or value

evidence (ev´ə dəns) *n.* proof

evident (ev´ ə dənt) *adj.* easy to see; very clear

evoking (ē vōk´ iŋ) *v.* calling forth

exact (eg zakt´) *v.* demand with force or authority

examine (eg zam´ ən) *v.* study or look at closely

exhausted (eg zôst´ əd) *adj.* very tired

exhilarating (eg zil´ə rāt´ iŋ) *adj.* exciting; stimulating

exodus (eks´ ə dəs) *n.* departure of a large group of people

expectations (ek´spek tā´shənz) *n.* feelings that something is about to happen

expedition (eks´pə dish´ən) *n.* journey for a particular purpose, such as exploration or scientific study

explain (ek splān´) *v.* give the reason for or cause of

explicit (eks plis´it) *adj.* clear or definite

expression (ek spresh´ən) *n.* figure of speech

extinction (ek stiŋk´shən) *n.* act of bringing to an end; destruction

exuded (eg zyo͞od´ əd) *v.* gave off; oozed

F

facts (faktz) *n.* truths known from experience or observation

faltered (fol´ tərd) *v.* lost strength; weakened

family (fam´ə lē) *n.* a group of people who share ancestry or who function as a social unit within a household

famine (fam´ in) *n.* a shortage of food

feeble (fē´ bəl) *adj.* weak

felicity (fə lis´i tē) *n.* ability to find appropriate expression for one's thoughts

fellow (fel´ ō) *n.* man or boy

ferocious (fə rō´ shəs) *adj.* wild and dangerous

flickering (flik´ər iŋ) *v.* burning unsteadily

former (fôr´ mər) *adj.* existing in an earlier time; past

fostering (fôs´ tər iŋ) *n.* taking care of

G

game (gām) *n.* contest; type of play in which there is usually one winner

generalization (jen´ər ə li zā´shən) *n.* broad statement

generation (jen´ər ā´shən) *n.* people living at the same time and/or of about the same age

gesture (jes´chər) *n.* motion of the hand or body to show or point

gnawing (nô´ iŋ) *v.* biting and cutting with the teeth

group (gro͞op) *n.* collection or set, as of people

grudgingly (gruj´ iŋ lē) *adv.* in an unwilling or resentful way

guess (ges) *n.* estimate based on little or no information

H

history (his´tə rē) *n.* record of past events

hollowed (häl´ ōd) *v.* created a hole or a space within

homey (hōm´ ē) *adj.* comfortable; having a feeling of home

humble (hum´bəl) *adj.* modest; not proud

I

ideals (ī dē´əlz) *n.* models or standards of excellence or perfection

identify (ī den´tə fī´) *v.* find or determine

ignorance (ig´ nə rəns) *n.* lack of knowledge, education, or experience

ignore (ig nôr´) *v.* pay no attention to

imitate (im´ i tāt´) *v.* copy; mimic

immortality (im´ôr tal´i tē) *n.* ability to live forever

inaugural (in ô´ gyə rəl) *adj.* first in a series

incessantly (in ses´ ənt lē) *adv.* constantly; continually

incidents (in ´sə dənts´) *n.* events; occurrences

indicate (in´di kāt´) *v.* point out

indicated (in´di kāt əd) *v.* pointed out

indignantly (in dig´ nənt lē) *adv.* in a way that expresses anger

individuality (in´də vij´o͞o al´ə tē) *n.* way in which a person or thing stands apart or is different

inductions (in duk´shənz) *n.* 1. introductions; 2. acts of being brought into something

inevitably (in ev´ i tə blē) *adv.* unavoidably

influence (in´flo͞o əns) *v.* 1. sway or persuade; 2. have a power or effect on something

inhalation (in´hə lā´shən) *n.* breathing in

inquired (in kwīrd´) *v.* asked

inscribed (in skrībd´) *adj.* written on

instinctively (in stiŋk´ tiv lē) *adv.* done automatically, without thinking

insurmountable (in´sər mount´ə bəl) *adj.* impossible to overcome

integrate (in´ tə grāt) *v.* 1. remove all barriers and allow free association; 2. bring together as a whole

intently (in tent´ lē) *adv.* with great attention or determination

interaction (in´tər ak´shən) *n.* influence of people or things on one another

interviews (in´tər vo͞os) *n.* conversations conducted by reporters to ask questions

investigate (in ves´tə gāt´) *v.* search and examine to learn the facts about something

invincible (in vin´ sə bəl) *adj.* incapable of being harmed or defeated

involve (in välv´) *v.* include

iridescent (ir´ ə des´ ənt) *adj.* showing different colors when seen from different angles

isolate (ī´sə lāt´) *v.* set apart

issue (ish´o͞o) *n.* problem or point on which there is disagreement

J

jubilation (jo͞o´ bə lā´ shən) *n.* 1. great joy; 2. triumph

judge (juj) *v.* 1. form an opinion about; 2. decide on

K

knowledge (näl´ij) *n.* 1. result of learning; 2. awareness

L

language (laŋ´gwij) *n.* form of communication between people

liable (lī´ ə bəl) *adj.* likely to do something or to happen

limit (lim´it) *n.* as far as something can go; farthest extreme

lose (lo͞oz) *v.* fail in a game or a dispute

lullaby (lul´ə bī´) *n.* quiet, gentle song sung to send a child to sleep

M

malicious (mə lish´ əs) *adj.* having or showing bad intentions

marine (mə rēn´) *adj.* relating to the ocean or ocean life

mauled (môld) *v.* badly injured by being attacked

measure (mezh´ ər) *v.* find the value of

melancholy (mel´ ən käl´ ē) *adj.* sad; gloomy

message (mes´ij) *n.* written or spoken communication

meteorologists (mēt´ē ə räl´ə jistz) *n.* scientists who study the atmosphere and weather

migrated (mī´ grāt əd) *v.* moved from one place to another

misapprehension (mis´ ap rē hen´ shən) *n.* misunderstanding

mistook (mis to͝ok´) *v.* 1. identified incorrectly; 2. misunderstood

modify (mäd´ə fi) *v.* change the form or quality of

monarch (män´ ərk) *n.* single or sole ruler

monotonous (mə nät´ n əs) *adj.* unchanging

mortal (môr´ təl) *adj.* referring to humans, who eventually die

mystified (mist´ tə fīd´) *v.* made someone feel confused or unable to understand something

N

narrow (nar´ō) *adj.* limited in extent, not wide

navigate (nav´ə gāt´) *v.* find the way

negotiate (ni gō´shē āt´) *v.* settle or come to an agreement

nonverbal (nän´vʉr´bəl) *adj.* not involving or using words or speech

notorious (nō tôr´ē əs) *adj.* famous for negative behavior or qualities

O

objectionable (əb jek´ shən ə bəl) *adj.* disagreeable

obscure (əb skyo͝or´) *adj.* not well known

observant (əb zʉrv´ ənt) *adj.* quick to notice; alert

observation (əb zʉr vā´ shən) *n.* act or practice of noting and recording facts and events for scientific study

observe (əb zʉrv´) *v.* see or notice

obstinacy (äb´ stə nə sē) *n.* stubbornness

offense (ə fens´) *n.* 1. harmful act; 2. violation of a law

opinion (ə pin´yən) *n.* personal belief

opinions (ə pin´yənz) *n.* personal beliefs

orator (ôr´ ət ər) *n.* person who speaks well in public

P

participation (pär tis´ə pā´ shən) *n.* taking part in an event or activity

passage (pas´ij) *n.* brief portion of a written work

pauper (pô´pər) *n.* someone who is very poor

persevere (pʉr´sə vir´) *v.* continue although faced with difficulties

persisted (pər sist´ əd) *v.* refused to give up

personality (pʉr´sə nal´ə tē) *n.* the sum of behaviors and feelings that define an individual

perspective (per spek´ tiv) *n.* point of view

plateau (pla tō´) *n.* raised area of land with a level surface

pleasant (plez´ ənt) *adj.* agreeable; delightful

plight (plīt) *n.* awkward, sad, or dangerous situation

polar (pō´lər) *adj.* near, of, or relating to the North or South Pole

pose (pōz) *v.* act; pretend

position (pə zish´ən) *n.* stand taken on a question or issue

precautionary (pri kô´ shə ner´ ē) *adj.* done to prevent harm or danger

prejudiced (prej´ ə dist) *adj.* having unfair feelings of dislike for a specific group

prelude (prā´ lood´) *n.* introduction to a main event

premise (pre´məs) *n.* something assumed or taken for granted

privation (prī vā´ shən) *n.* lack of necessities

process (prä´ses) *n.* series of actions that bring about a result

procure (prō kyoor´) *v.* get or obtain by some effort

prowled (prould) *v.* moved around quietly and secretly

pulsating (pul´ sāt´ iŋ) *adj.* beating or throbbing in a steady rhythm

purpose (pʉr´ pəs) *n.* function; reason why something is done

pursue (pər soo´) *v.* 1. be involved in; 2. follow

Q

quarry (kwôr´ ē) *n.* prey; anything being hunted or pursued

question (kwes´ chən) *v.* 1. doubt; 2. wonder about

quotation (kwō´ tā´ shən) *n.* the words of a source

quote (kwōt) *v.* use the exact words of a speaker or writer

R

rapture (rap´chər) *n.* expression of joy

ravenous (rav´ ə nəs) *adj.* greedily hungry

reaction (rē´ ak´ shən) *n.* response to something said or done

receive (ri sēv´) *v.* be given

refer (ri fʉr´) 1. *v.* turn to for information such as to a book or an expert. 2. *v.* direct attention to an earlier event

reflect (ri flekt´) *v.* think or wonder about seriously

reflecting (ri flekt´ŋ) *v.* 1. thinking seriously; 2. recollecting or realizing after some thought; 3. expressing thoughts about

repaid (ri pād´) *v.* did or gave in return

repulse (ri puls´) *v.* 1. drive back; 2. repel an attack

research (rē´sʉrch´) *n.* 1. collection of information about a subject; 2. the study of a topic

resident (rez´ i dənt) *adj.* relating to or concerning those who live in a particular place; *n.* inhabitant; one who lives in a particular place

resist (ri zist´) *v.* oppose actively; refuse to give in

resolutions (rez´ ə loo´ shənz) *n.* 1. intentions; 2. things decided

resolve (ri zälv´) *v.* 1. settle; 2. bring to an end

respond (ri spänd´) *v.* answer or reply

resuscitation (ri sus´ə tā´ shən) *n.* act of bringing back to life or consciousness

retells (rē telz) *v.* 1. tells again; 2. relates

reunion (rē yoon´ yən) *n.* gathering of people who have been separated

reveal (ri vēl´) *v.* 1. show; 2. make known

revelation (rev´ ə lā´ shən) *n.* a sudden rush of understanding

rigorous (rig´ər əs) *adj.* difficult; demanding

routine (roo tēn´) *n.* usual way in which something is done

rue (roo) *v.* feel sorrow or regret for something

rued (rood) *v.* regretted

S

sauntered (sôn´ tərd) *v.* walked in a slow, relaxed manner

savoring (sā´ vər iŋ) *v.* 1. enjoying; 2. tasting with delight

scouring (skour´ iŋ) *v.* cleaning or polishing by vigorous rubbing

sculpted (sculpt´ əd) *v.* shaped or molded

seized (sēzd) *v.* grabbed; taken hold of

sensory (sen´sər ē) *adj.* related to the sense of sight, hearing, smell, taste, or touch

share (sher) *v.* communicate with, such as an idea or an experience

similar (sim´ə lər) *adj.* alike

similarities (sim´ə lər´ə tēz´) *n.* qualities of being alike

skimming (skim´ iŋ) v. gliding; moving swiftly and lightly over a surface

sour (sour) adj. having the sharp acid taste of lemon or vinegar

source (sôrs) n. book, person, Web site, or other content that supplies information

sources (sôrs əz) n. books, people, Web sites, or other content that supply information

sown (sōn) v. planted; scattered with seeds

spasm (spaz´ əm) n. sudden short burst of energy or activity

specific (spə sif´ ik) adj. precise or particular

splendor (splen´dər) n. 1. gorgeous appearance; 2. magnificence

startled (stärt´ əld) adj. surprised

starvation (star vā´ shən) n. state of extreme hunger

steeples (stē´ pəlz) n. towers rising above churches or other structures

striking (strī´ kiŋ) adj. 1. very notice-able or impressive; 2. unusual

strive (strīv) 1. v. struggle; 2. v. compete

stubby (stub´ ē) adj. 1. short and thick; 2. bristly

study (stud´ ē) 1. v. look into deeply or examine; 2. n. research or investigation of a subject; 3. report based on research or investigation into a claim

subject (sub´jikt´) n. topic

summit (sum´ it) n. highest part

superb (sə pʉrb´) adj. extremely fine; excellent

support (sə pôrt´) v. 1. stand behind; 2. provide evidence for; 3. help

survival (sər vī´vəl) n. act of lasting or continuing to live

suspended (sə spend´ əd) v. stopped for a time

symbolize (sim´ bə līz´) v. stand for

sympathize (sim´ pə thīz) v. 1. share in a feeling; 2. feel compassion

T

technique (tek nēk´) n. author's way of using words

teemed (tēmd) v. was full of

tentatively (ten´ tə tiv lē) adv. in a hesitant way

testify (tes´ tə fī´) v. make a statement of fact or belief under oath; bear witness

thorny (thôr´ nē) adj. 1. prickly; 2. full of thorns

thrives (thrīvz) v. grows well

timidly (tim´ id lē) adv. in a way that shows fear or shyness

tongues (tuŋz) n. languages or dialects

trace (trās) n. mark left behind by something

transfixed (trans fikst´) v. made motionless by horror or fascination

transport (trans pôrt´) v. carry from one place to another

traversed (trə vʉrst´) v. went across

trend (trend) n. tendency or general direction

trudged (trudj´d) v. walked as if tired or with effort

U

unabridged (un´ ə brijd´) adj. complete; not shortened

undulating (un´ jə lā tiŋ) adj. moving in waves, like a snake

unethical (un eth´ i kəl) adj. not conforming to the moral standards of a group

unique (yoo nēk´) adj. 1. one of a kind; 2. unusual

unreasonable (un rē´ zən ə bəl) adj. 1. not fair; 2. not sensible

unsolicited (un´sə lis´it´ əd) adj. not requested

V

values (val´yooz) n. beliefs of a person or group

vanished (va´ nisht) v. disappeared

ventured (ven´chərd) v. dared to do something risky

verbal (vʉr´bəl) adj. involving or using words or speech

vigilance (vij´ ə ləns) n. watchfulness

vigor (vig´ər) n. active force or strength

vigorously (vig´ ər əs lē) adv. force-fully or energetically

visual (vizh´ oo əl) adj. able to be seen with the eyes

vow (vou) n. promise or a pledge

W

whirs (wʉrz) v. flies or moves quickly with a buzzing sound

win (win) v. gain a victory or come out ahead

winced (winst) v. pulled back slightly, as if in pain

Y

yearning (yʉr´ niŋ) n. feeling of wanting something very much

Spanish Glossary

El vocabulario académico aparece en **azul**.

A

abruptly / súbitamente *adv.* repentinamente; inesperadamente

abundantly / abundantemente *adv.* en grandes cantidades

accompanied / acompañó *v.* 1. fue en compañía de otro; 2. se unió; se juntó

achieve / lograr *v.* alcanzar lo que se desea

acquired / adquirió *v.* obtuvo posesión de

admonishing / amonestado *adj.* desaprobado

affect / afectar *v.* influenciar

affliction / aflicción *s.* dolor, malestar o sufrimiento

agonizing / agonizante *adj.* que causa gran dolor, angustia o sufrimiento

alter / alterar *v.* cambiar

ambassador / embajador *s.* representante especial; comúnmente un representante oficial de una nación en otra nación

amendment / enmienda *s.* cambio realizado a una propuesta o ley al agregarle quitarle algo o al cambiarle el lenguaje

anticipate / anticipar *v.* esperar

anxious / ansioso *adj.* deseoso

apex / cumbre *s.* punto más alto

appearance / apariencia *s.* aspecto de una persona o cosa

applications / solicitudes *s.* formularios que se completan para hacer una petición

archaeologists / arqueólogos *s.* personas que estudian la historia humana por medio del análisis de artefactos antiguos y otras ruinas y restos

architect / arquitecto *s.* persona que diseña edificios

argue / discutir *v.* 1. dar razones a favor o en contra de algo; 2. debatir

asphalt / asfalto *s.* mezcla marrón o negra de sustancias que se usa para pavimentar carreteras

assess / evaluar *v.* estimar el valor o la importancia de algo

associate / socio *s.* persona que forma parte de una compañía o asociación; amigo

astonishing / increíble *adj.* sorprendente; extraordinario

astray / descarriado *adv.* alejado del camino correcto

authorities / autoridades *s.* personas que son respetadas por su conocimiento acerca de un tema

awed / sobrecogido *adj.* con sentimientos de temor y asombro

B

barriers / barreras *s.* algo que dificulta el progreso; obstáculo

battle / lucha *s.* pelea; gran disputa

belief / creencia *s.* idea conforme

beseech / suplicar *v.* rogar

bound / sujetó *v.* amarró

C

cavernous / cavernoso *adj.* 1. enorme y hueco; 2. como una caverna

challenge / desafiar 1. *v.* retar 2. desafío *s.* un reto; el acto de cuestionar

chaotic / caótico *adj.* completamente confuso

choral / coral *adj.* relacionado con un grupo de cantantes o un coro

cite / citar *v.* 1. referirse a; 2. mencionar a manera de ejemplo

civic / cívico *adj.* en representación de una ciudad o de un grupo de ciudadanos

clarifies / clarifica *v.* facilita la comprensión; hace fácil de entender

coaxed / convenció *v.* persuadió de manera sutil

collaboratively / en forma colaborativa *adv.* juntos

colossal / colosal *adj.* extremadamente grande

common / común *adj.* ordinario; frecuente y esperado

communicate / comunicar *v.* compartir pensamientos o sentimientos, usualmente con palabras

community / comunidad *s.* grupo de personas que tienen un interés en común o que viven cerca el uno del otro

compete / competir *v.* 1. contender; 2. participar en un deporte, juego o concurso

compound / complejo de edificios *s.* varias edificaciones y el terreno que las rodea

compulsion / compulsión *s.* impulso irresistible

concept / concepto *s.* idea general o noción

conclude /concluir *v.* 1. finalizar, terminar; 2. darle clausura a algo que se ha escrito

condemnation / condenación *s.* expresión de fuerte desaprobación

conflict / conflicto *s.* problema

connection / conexión *s.* enlace o vínculo

conscious / consciente *adj.* que está despierto o tiene presente

consequently / consecuentemente *adv.* como resultado de

conservatively / de manera conservadora *adv.* moderadamente; cautelosamente

context / contexto *s.* palabras alrededor de una palabra o frase y que influencian el sentido de ésta

contrast / contraste 1. *s.* diferencia 2. *v.* mostrar las diferencias entre dos o más cosas

contrasts / contrastes *s.* diferencias notables entre personas o cosas

contribute / contribuir *v.* 1. ayudar a obtener un resultado; 2. abastecer

convince / convencer *v.* persuadir al apoyar un argumento con evidencia

convincing / convincente *adj.* que persuade al apoyar un argumento con evidencia

correspond / corresponder *v.* 1. comunicarse con; 2. equivaler a

credible / creíble *adj.* confiable

crucial / crucial *adj.* importante

crude / crudo *adj.* 1. sin pulir; 2. hecho sin cuidado

culture / cultura *s.* el conjunto de costumbres de un grupo o de una comunidad

cunning / astucia *s.* 1. malicia; 2. ingenio

custom / costumbre *s.* lo que se hace comúnmente; manera común de hacer algo; hábito

D

decisively / decisivamente *adv.* con determinación

deem / considerar *v.* 1. tener una opinión sobre; 2. juzgar

defend / defender *v.* 1. resguardar de un ataque; 2. proteger

defiance / desafío *s.* resistencia abierta hacia la autoridad

deficiency / deficiencia *s.* escasez o carencia

deficit / déficit *s.* cantidad que es menor que la cantidad necesitada

deft / diestro *adj.* hábil, de manera rápida y confiada

deliberate / deliberado *adj.* con intención o cuidadosamente planeado

demented / demente *adj.* loco

demise / fallecimiento *s.* fin de la existencia; muerte

determine / determinar *v.* fijar los términos de algo o tomar una decisión

diagnosis / diagnóstico *s.* identificación de una condición médica

dialogue / diálogo *s.* conversación; intercambio de palabras

dilution / dilución *s.* proceso mediante el cual se diluyen componentes al mezclarlos

dismal / sombrío *adj.* que causa tristeza o melancolía

dispersed / dispersó *v.* distribuyó en varias direcciones

dispute / disputa *s.* argumento; debate o pelea

dissonance / disonancia *s.* conjunto desagradable de sonidos

distinctly / nítidamente *adv.* claramente; sencillamente

distinguish / distinguir *v.* diferenciar; considerar por separado

distorted / distorsionado *adj.* torcido de tal manera que perdió la forma original

distress / angustia *s.* dolor o tristeza marcados

diverse / diverso *adj.* 1. muchos y variados; 2. de orígenes diferentes

diversion / diversión *s.* 1. recreación; 2. distracción de las labores cotidianas

doomed / condenado *v.* destinado al fracaso, a la destrucción o muerte

drone / zumbido *s.* sonido continuado y bronco

E

eloquent / elocuente *adj.* vívido, persuasivo y expresivo

embody / encarnar *v.* 1. dar forma corporal; 2. representar

encounter / encontrar *v.* dar con algo o unirse con alguien, a veces inesperadamente

endured / aguantó *v.* soportó una situación difícil

enroll / matricularse *v.* inscribirse o registrarse

entrepreneurs / emprendedores *s.* personas que crean y manejan empresas

essential / esencial *adj.* necesario

establish / establecer *v.* mostrar que es cierto

evaluate / evaluar *v.* encontrar la importancia o valor de

evidence / evidencia *s.* prueba que apoya una aseveración o argumento

evident / evidente *adj.* aparente; muy claro

evoking / evocando *v.* recordando

exact / exigir *v.* pedir con fuerza o autoridad

examine / examinar *v.* estudiar a fondo; observar detenidamente

exhausted / agotado *adj.* muy cansado

exhilarating / estimulante *adj.* emocionante; excitante

exodus / éxodo *s.* partida de un gran grupo de personas

expectations / expectativas *s.* sensación de que algo está por ocurrir

expedition / expedición *s.* viaje con un propósito particular, como para exploración o para estudios científicos

explain / explicar *v.* dar razón o causa de algo

explicit / explícito *adj.* claro; definido

expression / expresión *s.* figura retórica

extinction / extinción *s.* desaparición; destrucción

exuded / exudó *v.* emitió; rezumó

F

facts / hechos *s.* verdades conseguidas a través de la observación o la experiencia

faltered / flaqueó *v.* perdió la fuerza; se debilitó

family / familia *s.* grupo de personas con antepasados comunes o que funcionan como una unidad social dentro de un hogar

famine / hambruna *s.* escasez de alimentos

feeble / débil *adj.* flojo

felicity / acierto *s.* habilidad para encontrar la expresión apropiada para los pensamientos de uno

fellow / tipo *s.* hombre o joven

ferocious / feroz *adj.* salvaje y peligroso

flickering / parpadeando *v.* titilando

former / anterior *adj.* que existió en tiempos anteriores; pasado

fostering / criando *v.* cuidando de

G

game / juego *s.* concurso; tipo de diversión en la que usualmente hay un ganador

generalization / generalización *s.* afirmación amplia

generation / generación *s.* personas que viven en en mismo período de tiempo y/o son de la misma edad

gesture / gesto *s.* movimiento de la mano o del cuerpo para demostrar o señalar

gnawing / mordiendo *v.* apretando y cortando con los dientes

group / grupo *s.* conjunto o agrupación, como de personas

grudgingly / a regañadientes *adv.* de mala gana o con resentimiento

guess / conjetura *s.* estimado basado en poca o ninguna información

H

history / historia *s.* récord de sucesos del pasado

hollowed / ahuecó *v.* abrió una cavidad o un espacio dentro de algo

homey / hogareño *adj.* cómodo; que genera el sentimiento de estar en el hogar

humble / humilde *adj.* modesto; sin vanidad

I

ideals / ideales *s.* modelos o estándares de excelencia o perfección

identify / identificar *v.* encontrar o determinar

ignorance / ignorancia *s.* falta de conocimiento, educación o experiencia

ignore / ignorar *v.* no prestar atención a

imitate / imitar *v.* copiar; emular

immortality / inmortalidad *s* vida eterna sin posibilidad de morir

inaugural / inaugural *adj.* primero de una serie

incessantly / sin cesar *adv.* constante; continuo

incidents / incidentes *s.* eventos; ocurrencias

indicate / indicar *v.* señalar

indicated / indicado *v.* señalado

indignantly / con indignación *adv.* expresando ira o desprecio

individuality / individualidad *s.* forma en la que alguien o algo se diferencia de otros

inductions / iniciaciones *s.* 1. introducciones; actos requeridos para ingresar a algo

inevitably / inevitablemente *adv.* de tal manera que no se puede eludir

influence / influenciar 1. *v.* persuadir; 2. tener poder o efecto sobre algo

inhalation / inhalación *s.* aspiración de aire, vapores, etc.

inquired / inquirido *v.* preguntado

inscribed / inscrito *adj.* que lleva escrito o grabado

instinctively / instintivamente *adv.* automáticamente, sin pensar

insurmountable / insuperable *adj.* imposible de superar

integrate / integrar *v.* 1. eliminar las barreras y permitir la libre asociación; 2. unificar

intently / atentamente *adv.* con gran atención o determinación

interaction / interacción *s.* influencia recíproca entre dos o más personas

interviews / entrevistas *s.* conversaciones conducidas por reporteros para hacer preguntas y luego informar sobre las respuestas

investigate / investigar *v.* buscar y examinar para descubrir algo

invincible / invencible *adj.* incapaz de ser lastimado o vencido

involve / involucrar *v.* incluir

iridescent / iridiscente *adj.* que muestra colores distintos cuando se observa desde diferentes ángulos

isolate / aislar *v.* considerar por separado; apartar

issue / asunto *s.* problema o punto acerca del cual hay un desacuerdo

J

jubilation / júbilo *s.* 1. gran alegría; 2. triunfo

judge / juzgar *v.* 1. formar una opinión sobre; 2. pronunciar juicio

K

knowledge / conocimiento *s.* 1. el resultado del aprendizaje; 2. el tener presente

L

language / lenguaje *s.* sistema de comunicación entre personas

liable / responsable *adj.* que es probable que haga algo

limit / límite *s.* punto en el que no se puede seguir; extremo máximo

lose / perder *v.* fallar o fracasar en un juego o una disputa

lullaby / canción de cuna *s.* canción dulce, delicada y lenta utilizada para dormir a los niños

M

malicious / malicioso *adj.* que tiene o demuestra malas intenciones

marine / marina *adj.* con relación a la vida marítima y al océano

mauled / magullado *v.* herido gravemente al ser atacado

measure / evaluar *v.* hallar el valor de

melancholy / melancólico *adj.* que tiene una tristeza vaga y profunda

message / mensaje *s.* comunicación escrita o verbal

meteorologists / meteorólogos *s.* científicos que estudian la atmósfera y el clima

migrated / migró *v.* se fue de un lugar a otro

misapprehension / malentendido *s.* mala interpretación

mistook / se equivocó 1. *v.* identificó incorrectamente; 2. malentendió

modify / modificar *v.* cambiar la forma o cualidad de algo

monarch / monarca *s.* soberano de un estado

monotonous / monótono *adj.* que no cambia; sin variedad

mortal / mortal *adj.* referente a seres que mueren eventualmente

mystified / desconcertó *v.* hizo sentir confuso o incapaz de entender algo

N

narrow / estrecho *adj.* de extension limitada; que no es ancho

navigate / navegar *v.* buscar el camino

negotiate / negociar *v.* decidir; llegar a un acuerdo

nonverbal / no verbal *adj.* que no involucra o usa palabras o el habla

notorious / infame *adj.* famoso por tener comportamiento o cualidades negativas

O

objectionable / inaceptable *adj.* desagradable

obscure / críptico *adj.* no muy conocido; oscuro; enigmático

observant / observador *adj.* que se da cuenta rápidamente; alerta; vigilante

observation / observación *s.* acto o práctica de tomar notas y de registrar eventos para estudios científicos

observe / observar *v.* notar o ver

obstinacy / obstinación *s.* terquedad

offense / ofensa *s.* 1. acto perjudicial; 2. violación de la ley

opinion / opinión *s.* punto de vista personal o creencia

opinions / opiniones *s.* puntos de vista personales; creencias

orator / orador *s.* persona que habla bien en público

P

participation / participación *s.* el acto de tomar parte en un evento o actividad

passage / pasaje *s.* breve pedazo de un escrito

pauper / indigente *s.* alguien que es muy pobre

persevere / perseverar *v.* continuar a pesar de las complicaciones y adversidades

persisted / persistió *v.* se rehusó a darse por vencido

personality / personalidad *s.* el conjunto de comportamientos y sentimientos que definen a un individuo

perspective / perspectiva *s.* punto de vista

plateau / meseta *s.* zona elevada de la tierra con una superficie plana

pleasant / placentero *adj.* agradable; apacible

plight / situación grave *s.* condición difícil, triste o peligrosa

polar / polar *adj.* cerca de o con relación al Polo norte o Polo sur

pose / posar *v.* actuar; fingir; aparentar

position / postura *s.* posición adoptada frente a una pregunta o a un asunto

precautionary / preventivo *adj.* hecho para evitar daño o peligro

prejudiced / prejuiciado *adj.* que tiene sentimientos hostiles e irracionales contra un grupo específico

prelude / preludio *s.* introducción a un evento principal

premise / premisa *s.* algo que se asume o que se da por entendido

privation / privación *s.* falta de recursos

process / proceso *s.* serie de acciones que llevan a un resultado

procure / conseguir *v.* obtener a través de esfuerzo

prowled / rondó *v.* se movió por un lugar silenciosamente y en secreto

pulsating / pulsante *adj.* latiendo o palpitando a cierto ritmo

purpose / propósito *n.* función; razón por la cual se hace algo

pursue / perseguir *v.* 1. tratar de alcanzar algo; 2. seguir

Q

quarry / presa *s.* cualquier cosa que está siendo cazada o perseguida

question / cuestionar *v.* 1. dudar; 2. preguntarse acerca de algo

quotation / cita *s.* las palabras de una fuente

quote / citar *v.* usar las palabras exactas de un escritor o un orador

R

rapture / éxtasis *s.* expresión de intensa alegría

ravenous / hambriento *adj.* que tiene mucha hambre

reaction / reacción *s.* respuesta o acción que responde a algo dicho o hecho

receive / recibir *v.* tomar lo que es dado

refer / referir 1. *v.* consultar a un experto, un libro, etc., para obtener información; 2. dirigir la atención a un suceso previo

reflect / reflexionar *v.* pensar o considerar algo en forma seria y detenida

reflecting / reflexionando *v.* 1. pensando seriamente; 2. recordando o dándose cuenta después de pensar un rato; 3. expresando ideas acerca de

repaid / retribuyó *v.* hizo o dio a cambio de algo

repulse / repeler *v.* 1. rechazar un ataque; 2. alejar algo con fuerza

research / investigación *s.* 1. recolección de información acerca de algo o alguien; 2. el estudio de un tema

resident / residente 1. *adj.* relativo a los que viven en un lugar en particular; 2. *s.* habitante; alguien que vive en un lugar en particular

resist / resistir *v.* oponerse activamente; negarse a ceder

resolutions / resoluciones *s.* 1. intenciones; 2. cosas que se deciden

resolve / resolver *v.* 1. decidir; 2. finalizar

respond / responder *v.* replicar; contestar

resuscitation / resucitación *s.* acto de traer de nuevo a la vida o a un estado consciente

retells / recuenta *v.* 1. vuelve a decir; 2. relata

reunion / reunión *s.* congregación de personas que han estado separadas

reveal / revelar *v.* 1. mostrar; 2. descubrir; dar a conocer

revelation / revelación *s.* comprensión repentina

rigorous / riguroso *adj.* difícil; exigente; estricto

routine / rutina *n.* forma usual en la que se hace algo

rue / lamentar *v.* sufrir una pena o arrepentirse

rued / lamentó *v.* se arrepintió de algo

S

sauntered / paseó *v.* caminó de manera lenta y relajada

savoring / saboreando *v.* 1. disfrutando; 2. degustando o apreciando con placer

scouring / fregando *v.* limpiando o frotando vigorosamente

sculpted / esculpió *v.* dio forma o moldeó

seized / incautado *v.* tomado a la fuerza

sensory / sensorial *adj.* con relación a los sentidos: vista, oído, gusto, olfato y tacto

share / compartir *v.* comunicar una idea o experiencia

similar / similar *adj.* semejante

similarities / similitudes *s.* cualidades parecidas

skimming / rasando *v.* deslizándose; moviéndose rápida y ligeramente por una superficie

sour / ácido *adj.* con el sabor fuerte y ácido de limón o vinagre

source / fuente *n.* libro, persona, sitio Web u otro recurso que se usa para conseguir información

sources / fuentes *s.* libros, personas, páginas Web o cualquier otro medio que pueda dar información

sown / sembrado *v.* plantado; regado con semillas

spasm / arranque *s.* ímpetu de energía o inicio repentino de una actividad

specific / específico *adj.* preciso o particular

splendor / esplendor *s.* 1. belleza impresionante; 2. magnificencia; brillo intenso

startled / sobresaltado *adj.* sorprendido

starvation / inanición *s.* falta extrema de alimento

steeples / torres *s.* edificaciones que se elevan encima de las iglesias o en otras estructuras

striking / destacado *adj.* 1. muy notable o impresionante; 2. inusual

strive / esforzarse *v.* 1. luchar; 2. competir

stubby / regordete *adj.* bajo y grueso

study / estudiar 1. *v.* mirar o examinar algo con cuidado; 2. **estudio** *s.* investigación de un tema con diferentes propósitos; 3. reporte basado en la investigación de un tema

subject / tema *s.* materia

summit / cumbre *s.* la parte más alta

superb / espléndido *adj.* extremadamente fino; excelente

support / apoyar *v.* 1. dar respaldo a; confirmar; 2. basar; 3. ayudar

survival / supervivencia *s.* el acto de durar o de continuar con vida

suspended / suspendido *v.* detenido por un cierto periodo de tiempo

symbolize / simbolizar *v.* atribuir; representar

sympathize / compadecer *v.* 1. compartir un sentimiento; 2. sentir compasión

T

technique / técnica *s.* forma en la que un autor utiliza las palabras

teemed / estar repleto *v.* estar lleno de

tentatively / tentativamente *adv.* de forma vacilante

testify / testificar *v.* hacer una declaración de lo que se cree verdad bajo juramento; dar testimonio de hechos

thorny / espinoso *adj.* lleno de espinas

thrives / prospera *v.* crece muy bien

timidly / tímidamente *adv.* con temor o modestia

tongues / lenguas *s.* idiomas o dialectos

trace / rastro *s.* huella que deja algo o alguien a su paso

transfixed / cautivado *v.* paralizado a causa de horror o fascinación

transport / transportar *v.* llevar de un lugar a otro

traversed / atravesó *v.* cruzó

trend / tendencia *s.* inclinación o dirección general

trudged / marchó fatigosamente *v.* caminó de manera cansada o con mucho esfuerzo

U

unabridged / íntegra *adj.* completa; no acortada

undulating / ondulado *adj.* que se mueve en oleadas, como una serpiente

unethical / poco ético *adj.* que no respeta los estándares morales de un grupo

unique / único *adj.* 1. sin otro de su especie; 2. inusual

unreasonable / irracional *adj.* 1. injusto ; 2. inaceptable; insensato

unsolicited / no solicitado *adj.* no pedido

V

values / valores *s.* creencias de una persona o de un grupo

vanished / desaparecido *v.* desvanecido; esfumado

ventured / se atrevió *v.* se arriesgó a hacer algo

verbal / verbal *adj.* que involucra o usa palabras o el habla

vigilance / vigilancia *s.* supervisión

vigor / vigor *s.* fuerza; fortaleza

vigorously / vigorosamente *adv.* con fuerza o energía

visual / visual *adj.* que se puede ver o entender por medio de la vista

vow / juramento *s.* promesa o compromiso

W

whirs / runrunea *v.* vuela o se mueve rápidamente emitiendo un zumbido

win / ganar *v.* vencer; terminar por delante

winced / se retorció *v.* se movió hacia atrás un poco, por causa de dolor

Y

yearning / anhelo *n.* fuerte deseo de tener o alcanzar algo

Index of Skills

Literary Analysis

Act, in drama, 454, R2

Action, in drama, 456

Address (formal speech), 181

Advertisement, 181, R12

Alliteration, 134, 315, 354, R1

Allusion, 236, 635, R1

Analogy, 672, R1

Anecdote, 183, 195, 205, R1

Antagonist, R1

Anti-bandwagon approach, lxvi

Archetype, 631

Argument, lxiv-lxix, 181, 376, R1, R6, R12

Argumentative (persuasive) essay, 181, 376, R12

Aside, 456

Assertion (claim), lxiv, lxv

Atmosphere, R1

Author's influences, 206, 754, R1

Author's purpose, 146, 180, 182, 428, 523

Author's style, R1

Author's viewpoint, 104, 180, 182, 184, 261, 588, R6

Autobiographical sketch, 181, R13

Autobiography/autobiographical narrative, 181, 185, R1, R13

Bandwagon approach/appeal, lxvi, 238

Biography, 179, R1

Cause, 632, 640

Cause-and-effect essay, 702, R12

Central (key/main) idea, 183, 206, 216, 422

Character, 14, 17, 454, 456, 631, R1

Characterization, 14, 17, 28, 278, 456, R1

Character motivation, 14, 456, R5

Character trait, 14, 17, 456, R1

Chronological order/organization, 100

Claim (assertion), lxiv, lxv

Classical mythology, 629, R5

Climax, 15, 18, 104, 454, R1, R6

Comedy, 455, R2

Comedy of manners, R2

Compare, 488

Comparison-and-contrast essay, 240, R12

Conclusion, 58

Concrete poem, 317, 344, R2

Conflict, 14, 15, 16, 17, 18, 44, 104, 454, 456, 457, 592, 744, R2, R6

Connotation, 182, 316, 534, R2

Contrast, 488

Culturally specific theme, 628

Denotation, 316, 534, R2

Denouement, R6

Description/descriptive writing, R2, R12

Development (rising action), 15, 18, 104, R6

Dialect, 629, R2

Dialogue, 454, 458, R2

Diary, 181

Diction (word choice), 180, 182, 290, 631

Direct characterization, 17, 28, R1

Direct quotation, 183, 402

Drama (play), 442–443, 453, 454–457, 458, R2, R3

Dramatist (playwright), 454

Dynamic character, R1

Editorial, 181

Effect, 632, 640

Emotional appeal, lxvi, 238

Endorsement, lxvi

End rhyme, R7

Episode, 457

Essay, 181, 240, 376, 538, 702, R2
   argumentative, 181, 376, R12
   cause-and-effect, 702, R12
   comparison-and-contrast, 240, R12
   expository/informational, 181, R2
   historical, R2
   informal, R2
   narrative, 181, R2
   persuasive, 181, 376, R2 , R12
   problem-and-solution, 538, R13
   reflective, 181

Example, 183

Explanatory writing, 180, 181, 732, 748, R3, R12

Exposition (as a plot element), 15, 18, 104, R2, R6

Expository essay, 181

Expository writing/text, 180, 181, 732, 748, R3, R12

Extended metaphor, R3

External conflict, 14, 16, 44, 457, 744, R2

Fable, 629, 632, R3

Fact, 183, 194

Fairy tale, 628

Falling action, 15, 18, 104, R6

Fantasy, 629, 677, R3

Fiction, 4–5, 13, 14–17, R3

Figurative language/figure of speech, 183, 284, 316, 334, R3
   idiom, 698–699

First-person point of view/narrator, 104, 184, R5, R6

Flashback, 73, 268, R3

Flat character, R1

Folk literature, 614–617, 627, 628–631, R3, R5
   characteristics, 628–631
   patterns, 631
   structure, 631
   themes, common, 630
   types, 628, 629

Folk song, 629

Folk tale, 629, 632, R3

Foot (metrical), R4

Foreshadowing, 73, 408, R3, R7

Free verse, 317, R3

Functional text, 181

Genre, R3

Grounds (evidence), lxiv, lxv

Haiku, 317, 344, R3

Hero/heroine, R4

Historical essay, R2

Historical fiction, R4

Humor, 582

Hyperbole, lxvi, 272, 316, 629

Idiom, 698

Imagery/image (sensory detail), 104, 152, 180, 316, 367, R4

Inciting incident, R6

Indirect characterization, 17, 28, R1

Informal essay, R2

Informational essay, 181, R2

Informative/informational text, 180, 181, 732, 748, R3, R12

Internal conflict, 14, 16, 44, 457, 744, R2

Internal rhyme, R7

Irony, 629, 632, R4
   ironic ending, 632

Journal, R4

Justification, lxiv, lxv

Key (central/main) idea, 183, 206, 216, 422

Comprehension Skills

Argument, analyzing, lxiv–lxvii
  persuasive address, model, lxv
  persuasive speech, model, lxvii

Author's influences, examining, 206

Author's purpose, recognizing and comparing, 182, 428, 523, 533

Cause and effect, identifying, 632, 640

Central (key, main) idea, identifying, 4, 164, 183, 206, 216, 304, 422, 442, 614

Claims, evaluating, lxiv, 194

Close Reading Workshop, lx–lxi, 4–11, 164–177, 304–311, 442–451, 614–625
  drama models, 443, 459, 489
  fiction/short story models, 5, 19, 29, 45, 59
  folk literature models, 615–617, 633, 641, 651, 667
  nonfiction models, 165, 185, 195, 207, 217
  poetry models, 305, 319, 335, 345, 355

Comparing and contrasting texts, 72–97, 230–235, 366–371, 423, 488, 521, 522–533, 676–697
  author's purpose, 532–533
  expository/informational texts, 230–235
  fantasy, 676–697
  foreshadowing and flashback, 72–97
  imagery, 366–371

Complex texts, comprehending, lviii–lxiii, 159, 299, 437, 609, 761

Conclusions, drawing, 58

Context clues, using, lx, lxi, 318, 334

Craft and structure, analyzing, 4, 164, 304, 442, 615

Details, identifying important, 4, 164, 183, 193, 206, 216, 304, 422, 442, 614

Events, identifying and organizing, 193

Expository/informational texts, analyzing and comparing, 230

Fact and opinion, distinguishing, 194, 238

Fantasy, recognizing and comparing, 677

Fluency, tips for improving, R10–R11

Foreshadowing and flashback, recognizing and comparing, 73

Imagery, comparing, 367

Independent reading, lviii–lix, lxiii, 8–11, 158–159, 168–177, 298–299, 308–311, 436–437, 446–451, 608–609, 620–625, 760–761
  Independent Practice, lvii–lix, lxiii, 8–11, 168–177, 308–311, 446–451, 620–625

Inferences, making, 28, 44

Informational/expository texts, analyzing and comparing, 230

Key (main, central) idea, identifying, 4, 164, 183, 206, 216, 304, 422, 442, 614

Knowledge and ideas, integrating, 4, 164, 304, 442, 614

Main (key, central) idea, identifying, 4, 164, 183, 206, 216, 304, 422, 442, 614

Multidraft reading, lviii–lix

Paraphrasing, lx, 344, 354

Predictions, making, 18, 184

Prior knowledge, using, 44

Pronoun antecedents, identifying, to comprehend text, lx

Purpose, author's, recognizing and comparing, 182, 428, 523, 533

Purpose for reading, setting, 650, 666

Questions, asking, lxii–lxiii, 4, 164, 304, 442, 615, R9

Rhetorical devices, analyzing, lxvi–lxvii

Summarizing, lvi–lvii, 458

Text aids and features, using, 230, 736

Writing

Applications

Anecdote, personal, 205

Argument, lxviii–lxix, 57, 147, 153, 156–157, 235, 273, 285, 376–383, 423, 521, 538–545, 589, 595, 603, 739, 749, 755
  Student Model, 382, 544
  Writing Process, 376–383, 538–545

Argumentative essay, 156–157, 376–383, 423, 429, 434, 755, R19
  Student Model, 382, R19
  Writing Process, 376–383

Autobiographical narrative, 193, 205, 269, 295, 403

Cause-and-effect essay, 130, 702–709, 724
  Student Model, 708
  Writing Process, 702–709

Comparison-and-contrast essay, 11, 97, 240–247, 262, 296–297, 371, 423, 429, 533, 578, 649, 697
  Student Model, 246
  Writing Process, 240–247

Description, 71, 365
  character, 71

Descriptive essay, 143

Diary/journal entry, 137, 215, 293, 409

Editorial, 147

Essay, 11, 97, 130, 156–157, 177, 229, 291, 296–297, 311, 371, 419, 471, 533, 583, 625, 697, 724, 755

Explanation, 733

Explanatory/informative text, 27, 43, 71, 97, 229, 240–247, 262, 296–297, 333, 371, 396, 487, 533, 583, 649, 697, 702–709, 724, 733, 745, 758–759
  Student Model, 246, 708
  Writing Process, 240–247, 702–709

Expository essay, 296–297, 396, 745, 758–759

Fable, 639

Fictional narrative, 102–109, 135, 155, 433, 605
  Student Model, 108
  Writing Process, 102–109

Historical fiction, 155

How-to essay, 583

Informative/explanatory text, 27, 43, 71, 97, 229, 240–247, 262, 296–297, 333, 371, 487, 533, 578, 583, 675, 697, 702–709, 733, 745, 758–759
  Student Model, 246, 708
  Writing Process, 240–247, 702–709

Invitation, 675

Journal/diary entry, 137, 215, 293, 409

Letter, 43, 279, 333, 675, R14–R15
  business, R15
  friendly, R14
  invitation, 675
  of recommendation, 43
  persuasive, 279, 749
  to author, 333

List, of reasons, 27

Narrative, 102–109, 135, 155, 193, 205, 269, 295, 403, 433, 593, 605, 639, 665, 736, 757
  Student Model, 108
  Writing Process, 102–109

Nonfiction narrative, 193, 205, 269, 295, 737, 757

Persuasive essay, 156–157, 376–383, 423, 429, 434, 755, R19
  Student Model, 382, R19

Persuasive letter, 279, 749

Persuasive speech, 57, 273

Plot proposal, 665

Poem, 343, 353
  haiku, limerick, or concrete poem, 353
  poem using figurative language, 343

Position statement, 235

Strategies

Language Conventions

Vocabulary

Assessment

Index of Authors and Titles

The following authors and titles appear in the print and online versions of Pearson Literature.

Additional Selections: Author and Title Index

The following authors and titles appear in the Online Literature Library.

Acknowledgments

Grateful acknowledgment is made to the following for copyrighted material:

Airmont Publishing Company, Inc. "Water" by Helen Keller from *The Story of My Life*. Copyright © 1965 by Airmont Publishing Company, Inc. Used by permission of Airmont Publishing Company, Inc.

Ricardo E. Alegría "The Three Wishes" selected and adapted by Ricardo E. Alegría from *The Three Wishes: A Collection of Puerto Rican Folktales*. Copyright © 1969 by Ricardo E. Alegría. Used by permission of Ricardo E. Alegría.

American Red Cross National Headquarters "Red Cross Helps Florida Residents Recover From Tornadoes" by Arindam Mukherjee, December 29, 2006 posted on *www.redcross.org*. Used by permission courtesy of the American National Red Cross. All rights reserved in all countries.

The Associated Press "Rescuers to Carry Oxygen Masks for Pets" from *www.postcrescent.com*. Copyright © 2007 The Associated Press. Used with permission. All rights reserved.

Atheneum Books for Young Readers, an imprint of Simon & Schuster "Stray" by Cynthia Rylant from *Every Living Thing*. Copyright © 1985 by Cynthia Rylant. Used by permission of Atheneum Books for Young Readers, an imprint of Simon & Schuster Children's Publishing Division.

The Bancroft Library, Administrative Offices "Letter from a Concentration Camp" by Yoshiko Uchida from *The Big Book For Peace*. Text copyright © 1990 by Yoshiko Uchida. Courtesy of the Bancroft Library University of California, Berkeley. Used with permission.

Bantam Doubleday Dell Publishing "Black Ships Before Troy: The Story of The Iliad" by Rosemary Sutcliff from *Delacorte Press*. Copyright © 1993 by Frances Lincoln Limited.

Susan Bergholz Literary Services "Abuelito Who" by Sandra Cisneros from *My Wicked Wicked Ways*. Copyright © 1987 by Sandra Cisneros. Published by Third Woman Press and in hardcover by Alfred A. Knopf. Used by permission of Third Woman Press and Susan Bergholz Literary Services, New York. "Names/Nombres" by Julia Alvarez from *Nuestro, March, 1985*. Copyright © 1985 by Julia Alvarez. First published in *Nuestro. March, 1985*. "Something to Declare" (Introduction) by Julia Alvarez. Copyright © 1998 by Julia Alvarez. From *Something To Declare*, published by Plume, an imprint of Penguin Group (USA), in 1999 and originally in hardcover by Algonquin Books of Chapel Hill. "Eleven" from *Woman Hollering Creek* by Sandra Cisneros. Copyright © 1991 by Sandra Cisneros. Published by Vintage Books, a division of Random House, Inc., New York and originally in hardcover by Random House, Inc. Used by permission of Susan Bergholz Literary Services, New York, NY and Lamy, NM. All rights reserved.

Robert Bly "Friends All of Us" from *Childhood and Poetry* by Pablo Neruda. Reprinted from *Neruda and Vallejo: Selected Poems*, by Robert Bly, Beacon Press, Boston, 1993. Used by permission.

BOA Editions, Ltd. c/o The Permissions Company "Alphabet" by Naomi Shihab Nye from *Fuel*. Copyright © 1998 by Naomi Shihab Nye. All rights reserved. Used by permission of BOA Editions Ltd., www.boaeditions.org.

Georges Borchardt, Inc. "Dragon, Dragon" from *Dragon, Dragon And Other Tales* by John Gardner. Copyright © 1975 by Boskydell Artists, Ltd. Used by permission of Georges Borchardt, Inc., for the Estate of John Gardner.

Brandt & Hochman Literary Agents, Inc. "Wilbur Wright and Orville Wright" by Stephen Vincent Benét, from *A Book of Americans* by Rosemary and Stephen Vincent Benét. Copyright © 1933 by Rosemary and Stephen Vincent Benét. Copyright © renewed 1961 by Rosemary Carr Benét. "Lob's Girl" from *A Whisper in the Night* by Joan Aiken. Delacorte Press. Copyright © 1984 by Joan Aiken Enterprises, Ltd. Used by permission of Brandt & Hochman Literary Agents, Inc.

John Brewton, George M. Blackburn & Lorraine A. Blackburn "Limerick (Accidents--More or Less Fatal)" from *Laughable Limericks*. Copyright © 1965 by Sara and John E. Brewton. Used by permission of Brewton, Blackburn and Blackburn.

Brooks Permissions "Cynthia In the Snow" from *Bronzeville Boys and Girls* by Gwendolyn Brooks. Copyright © 1956 by Gwendolyn Brooks. Used by consent of Brooks Permissions.

The Center for Social Organization of Schools "Chinese and African Americans in the Gold Rush." © Johns Hopkins University. Reprinted with the permission of the Center for Social Organization of Schools, Johns Hopkins University School of Education.

Curtis Brown Ltd. From *The Pigman & Me (Learning the Rules)* by Paul Zindel. Copyright © 1992 by Paul Zindel. First published by HarperCollins. "Adventures of Isabel" by Ogden Nash from *Parents Keep Out*. Originally published by *Nash's Pall Mall Magazine*. Copyright © 1936 by Ogden Nash. All rights reserved. "Greyling" by Jane Yolen from *Greyling: A Picture Story from the Islands*. Copyright © 1968, 1996 by Jane Yolen. First published by Penguin Putnam. Used by permission of Curtis Brown, Ltd.

Diana Chang (Diana C. Herrmann) "Saying Yes" by Diana Chang. Copyright by Diana Chang. Used by permission of the author.

Chronicle Books "Oranges" from *New and Selected Poems* by Gary Soto. Copyright © 1995 by Gary Soto. Visit www.chroniclebooks.com. Used with permission of Chronicle Books LLC, San Francisco.

Clarion Books, a division of Houghton Mifflin "A Backwoods Boy" from *Lincoln: A Photobiography*. Copyright © 1987 by Russell Freedman. Used by permission of Clarion Books/Houghton Mifflin Company. All rights reserved.

Ruth Cohen Literary Agency, Inc. "The All-American Slurp" by Lensey Namioka, copyright © 1987, from *Visions*, ed. by Donald R. Gallo. Used by permission of Lensey Namioka. All rights reserved by the Author.

Don Congdon Associates, Inc. "The Sound of Summer Running" by Ray Bradbury from *The Saturday Evening Post, 2/18/56*. Copyright © 1956 by the Curtis Publishing Company, copyright © renewed 1984 by Ray Bradbury. "Hard As Nails" from *The Good Times* by Russell Baker. Copyright © 1989 by Russell Baker. Used by permission of Don Congdon Associates, Inc.

Gary N. DaSilva Excerpt from *Brighton Beach Memoirs* by Neil Simon from *McGraw Hill Glencoe*, copyright © 1984 by Neil Simon.

Information Please "The Seven Wonders of the World" *www.infoplease.com./ipa/A0001327.html*, Info Please Database © 2007 Pearson Education, Inc. Used by permission of Pearson Education, Inc. publishing as Info Please. All rights reserved.

Dr. Francisco Jiménez "The Circuit" by Francisco Jiménez from *America Street: A Muliculural Anthology Of Stories*. Copyright © 1993 by Anne Mazer. Used with permission of the author Francisco Jiménez.

Alfred A. Knopf Children's Books "Jackie Robinson: Justice at Last" from *25 Great Moments* by Geoffrey C. Ward and Ken Burns with S.A. Kramer, copyright © 1994 by Baseball Licensing International, Inc., "He Lion, Bruh Bear, and Bruh Rabbit" from *The People Could Fly: American Black Folktales* by Virginia Hamilton illustrated by Leo and Diane Dillon, copyright © 1985 by Virginia Hamilton. Illustrations copyright © 1985 by Leo and Diane Dillon. "April Rain Song" from *The Collected Poems of Langston Hughes* by Langston Hughes, edited by Arnold Rampersad with David Roessel, Associate Editor, copyright © 1994 by The Estate of Langston Hughes. From *James and the Giant Peach* by Roald Dahl. Text copyright © 1961 by Roald Dahl. Text copyright renewed 1989 by Roald Dahl. Illustrations copyright © 1996 by Lane Smith. Used by permission of Alfred A. Knopf, an imprint of Random House Children's Books, a division of Random House, Inc.

The Lazear Literary Agency "Turkeys" by Bailey White from *Mama Makes Up Her Mind*. Copyright © 1993 by Bailey White. Used by permission.

Lescher & Lescher, Ltd. "The Southpaw" by Judith Viorst. Copyright © 1974 by Judith Viorst. From *Free To Be...You And Me*. This usage granted by permission of Lescher & Lescher, Ltd. All rights reserved.

Nelson Mandela Foundation "Nelson Mandela's Address to Rally in Cape Town on His Release from Prison" by Nelson Mandela from *db.nelsonmandela.org*. Used by permission.

The Marine Mammal Center "California Sea Lion" from *www.tmmc.org*. Copyright © 2007 The Marine Mammal Center. *www.marinemammalcenter.org*. All rights reserved. Used by permission.

Eve Merriam c/o Marian Reiner "Simile: Willow and Ginkgo" by Eve Merriam from *A Sky Full of Poems*. Copyright © 1964, 1970, 1973, 1986 by Eve Merriam. All rights reserved. Used by permission of Marian Reiner, Literary Agent, for the author.

MLB Advanced Media, L.P. "Why We Love Baseball - Players, management and fans chime in on Valentine's Day" by Mark Newman. Copyright © 2007 by Major League Baseball. Major League Baseball trademarks and copyrights are used with permission of MLB Advanced Media, L.P. All rights reserved.

Minnesota Public Radio "Angela Duckworth and the Research on 'Grit'" by Emily Hanford, from American Public Media's American Radio Works(r) Copyright © 2013. Minnesota Public Radio. Used with permission. All rights reserved.

Lillian Morrison c/o Marian Reiner "The Sidewalk Racer or On the Skateboard" by Lillian Morrison from *The Sidewalk Racer and Other Poems of Sports and Motion*. Copyright © 1965, 1967, 1968, 1977 by Lillian Morrison. Used by permission of Marian Reiner, for the author.

William Morrow & Company, Inc., a division of HarperCollins "The World is Not a Pleasant Place To Be" from *My House* by Nikki Giovanni. Copyright © 1972 by Nikki Giovanni. Used by permission of William Morrow & Company, Inc., a division of HarperCollins Publishers, Inc.

NASA Jet Propulsion Laboratory "Satellites and Sea Lions: Working Together to Improve Ocean Models" by Rosemary Sullivant from *http://www.nasa.gov/vision/earth/lookingatearth/sealion-20070206.html*. Used by permission of NASA/JPL-Caltech.

National Geographic World From *Race to the End of the Earth* by William G. Scheller from *National Geographic World, Number 294, February 2000*. Copyright © 2000 by National Geographic Society. Reproduction of the whole or any part of the contents of National Geographic World without permission is prohibited. Used by permission. All rights reserved.

New Directions Publishing Corporation "Wind and Water and Stone" by Octavio Paz, translated by Eliot Weinberger, from *Collected Poems 1957-1987*. Copyright © 1984 by Octavio Paz and Eliot Weinberger. Used by permission of New Directions Publishing Corp.

Orchard Books, an imprint of Scholastic Inc. "Becky and the Wheels-and-Brake Boys" from *A Thief In The Village And Other Stories* by James Berry. Published by Orchard Books, an imprint of Scholastic, Inc. Copyright © 1987 by James Berry. Used by permission.

PARS International Corporation From *The Sacramento Bee*, May 11th, 1998. "Birds Struggle to Recover from Egg Thefts of 1800s" by Edie Lau. Copyright © 1998. The McClatchy Company. All rights reserved. Used by permission and protected by the Copyright Laws of the United States.

Carmen Pauls "Memories of an All-American Girl" by Carmen Pauls Orthner. © 2005–2012. Used by permission.

Pearson Education "Gilgamesh" from *Scott Foresman Social Studies: The World*. Pg. 44 Copyright © 2003. Pearson Education, Inc., or its affiliates. Used by permission. All rights reserved. *The Prince and the Pauper*. Adapted from a book by Mark Twain, in Short Dramas and Teleplays. Copyright © 2000. Pearson Education, Inc., or its affiliates. Used by permission. All rights reserved.

Pearson Prentice Hall "Egyptian Pyramids" from *California Social Studies Ancient Civilizations (Grade 6/Section 5 - Pp. 118-121)*. Copyright © 2006 by Pearson Education, Inc. or its affiliates. Used by permission.

Penguin Group (USA) Inc. "Roll of Thunder, Hear My Cry" by Mildred D. Taylor from *Puffin Books*. Copyright © Mildred D. Taylor, 1976. "This Land Was Made for You and Me: Life & Songs of Woodie Guthrie" by Elizabeth Partridge from *Viking*. Copyright © Elizabeth Partridge, 2002. All rights reserved.

Pensacola News Journal "Jake Wood Baseball League is the Start of Something Special" by Reginald T. Dogan from *www.pensacolanewsjournal.com*. Copyright © 2007 Pensacola News Journal. Used by permission. All rights reserved.

Random House, Inc. From *You're a Good Man, Charlie Brown* by Clark Gesner. Copyright © 1967 by Clark Gesner. Coypright © 1965, 1966, 1967 by Jeremy Music, Inc. "Life Doesn't Frighten Me" copyright © 1978 by Maya Angelou, from *And Still I Rise* by Maya Angelou. Used by permission of Random House, Inc.

Reed Publishing (NZ) Ltd. "Prologue from The Whale Rider" by Witi Ihimaera from *The Whale Rider*. Copyright © 1987 Witi Ihimaera. All rights reserved. Used by permission of Reed Publishing (NZ) Ltd.

Marian Reiner, Literary Agent "Haiku ("An old silent pond...")" by Matsuo Bashō, translated by Harry Behn from *Cricket Songs: Japanese Haiku*. Copyright © 1964 by Harry Behn; Copyright © renewed 1992 Prescott Behn, Pamela Behn Adam and Peter Behn. "Haiku ("Over the wintry")" by Muso Soseki, translated by Harry Behn from *Cricket Songs: Japanese Haiku*. Copyright © 1964 Harry Behn. Copyright renewed © 1992 by Prescott Behn, Pamela Behn Adam, and Peter Behn. Used by permission of Marian Reiner.

Reuters From reuters.com, Red Sox get ready to celebrate 100 years at Fenway Park, Thursday April 19, 2012 © 2012 reuters.com. All rights reserved. Used by permission and protected by the Copyright Laws of the United States. The printing, copying, redistribution, or retransmission of this Content without express written permission is prohibited.

The Sacramento Bee "The Journey by Land" from *The Great American Gold Rush* by Rhoda Blumberg, *The Gold Rush* by Liza Ketchum, *The California Gold Rush*, published by American Heritage, *The California Gold Rush* by Elizabeth Van Steenwyk, *Hunting for Gold* by William Downie, *Sea Routes to the Gold Fields* by Oscar Lewis, *If You Traveled West in a Covered Wagon* by Ellen Levine, *The East Indiamen* by Russell Miller, Steve and Eric Chrissman of the National Nautical Heritage Society.

San Francisco Chronicle "O'Neil Belongs Inside this Hall" by Scott Ostler from *http://sfgate.com/*. Copyright © 2006 by San Francisco Chronicle. Used by permission of San Francisco Chronicle via Copyright Clearance Center.

San Francisco Public Library "San Francisco Public Library Card Policies and Application" from *http://sfpl.lib.ca.us/services/librarycard.htm*. Copyright © 2002-2006 by San Francisco Public Library. Used by permission.

Sarasota County Library "Sarasota County Library Card Services, Policies, and Application" from *http://suncat.co.sarasota.fl.us/services/librarycard.aspx*. Copyright © 2007 Sarasota County Library. Used by permission.

Scholastic Inc. "The Shutout" from *Black Diamond: The Story Of The Negro Baseball Leagues* by Patricia C. McKissack and Fredrick McKissack, Jr. Copyright © 1994 by Patricia C. McKissack and Fredrick McKissack, Jr. "Why Monkeys Live in Trees" from *How Many Spots Does A Leopard Have? And Other Tales* by Julius Lester. Copyright © 1989 by Julius Lester. Reproduced by permission of Scholastic Inc.

Scovil Chichak Galen Literary Agency, Inc. "Feathered Friend" from *The Other Side Of the Sky* by Arthur C. Clarke. Copyright © 1958 by Arthur C. Clarke. Used by permission of the author and the author's agents, Scovil Chichak Galen Literary Agency, Inc.

Scribner, a division of Simon & Schuster "Letter to Scottie" by F. Scott Fitzgerald, from *F. Scott Fitzgerald: A Life in Letters*, edited by Matthey J. Bruccoli. Used by permission of Scribner, an imprint of Simon & Schuster Adult Publishing Group. Copyright © 1994 by The Trustees under Agreement dated July 3, 1975. Created by Frances Scott Fitzgerald Smith.

Simon & Schuster Books for Young Readers "Parade" used by the permission of Simon & Schuster Books for Young Readers, an imprint of Simon & Schuster Children's Publishing Division from *Branches Green* by Rachel Field. Copyright © 1934 Macmillan Publishing Company; copyright © renewed 1962 by Arthur S. Pederson.

St. Martin's Press "The Market Square Dog" from *James Herriot's Treasury for Children* by James Herriot. Copyright © 1989 James Herriot. Used by permission of St. Martin's Press, LLC.

William Strauss, Director, The Cappies "You're a Good Man, Charlie Brown at Robert E. Lee (High School)" by Brianna Sonnefeld from *www.cappies.com/nca/news/reviews/06-07/le.htm*. Copyright © 2005 The Cappies, Inc., All Rights Reserved. Used by permission.

Talkin' Broadway "Happiness is a Charming Charlie Brown at Orlando Rep "by Matthew MacDermid from *www.talkinbroadway.com*. Copyright © TalkinBroadway.com, a project of www.TalkinBroadway.org, Inc. Used by permission.

Thorgate, LLC "Metric Metric: It's so nice, we say it twice!™" from *www.metricmetric.com*. Copyright © 2007 Metric Metric. Used by permission.

Dr. My-Van Tran "A Crippled Boy" from *Folk Tales from Indochina* by Dr. My-Van Tran. First published in 1987. Copyright © Vietnamese Language and Culture Publications and Tran My-Van. Used by permission.

University of Nebraska Press "The Old Woman Who Lived With the Wolves" reprinted from *Stories Of The Sioux* by Luther Standing Bear. Used by permission of the University of Nebraska Press. Copyright © 1934 by Luther Standing Bear. Copyright © renewed 1961 by May M. Jones.

University Press of New England "The Drive-In Movies" from *A Summer Life* copyright © 1990 by University Press of New England, Hanover, NH. Used by permission.

Viking Penguin, Inc. "La Lena Buena," (retitled) pages 113-144 from *Places Left Unfinished At The Time Of Creation* by John Phillip Santos, copyright © 1999 by John Phillip Santos. From *Zlata's Diary* by Zlata Filipovic from *Zlata's Life: A Child's Life in Sarajevo*. Translated by Christina Pribichevich-zoric. Copyright © 1994 Editions Robert Laffont/Fixot. Used by permission of Viking Penguin, a division of Penguin Group (USA) Inc.

Villard Books, a division of Random House, Inc. "The Lady and the Spider" from *All I Really Need to Know I Learned In Kindergarten* by Robert L. Fulghum. Copyright © 1986, 1988 by Robert L. Fulghum. Used by permission of Villard Books, a division of Random House, Inc.

World Book, Inc. From "Tornado" by Howard B. Bluestein from *World Book Reference Center*. Copyright © 2007. World Book, Inc. Used by permission of publisher. *www.worldbookonline.com*.

World of Escher "World of Escher Tessallation Contest" from *www.worldofescher.com/contest*. Copyright © 1995-2007 WorldofEscher.com. All rights reserved. Used by permission.

Jane Yolen "My Heart Is in the Highlands" by Jane Yolen from *My Heart Is In The Highlands*. Copyright © Jane Yolen.

Credits

Staff Credits